Exam 70-685: Pro: Windows 7, Enterprise Desktop Support Technician

OBJECTIVE	LOCATION IN BOOK
IDENTIFYING CAUSE OF AND RESOLVING DESKTOP APPLICATION ISSUES	
Identify and resolve new software installation issues.	Chapter 9, Lesson 1
Identify and resolve software configuration issues.	Chapter 9, Lesson 2
Identify cause of and resolve software failure issues.	Chapter 9, Lesson 1
IDENTIFYING CAUSE OF AND RESOLVING NETWORKING ISSUES	
Identify and resolve logon issues.	Chapter 4, Lesson 1
Identify and resolve network connectivity issues.	Chapter 2, Lesson 1
Identify and resolve names resolution issues.	Chapter 2, Lesson 2
Identify and resolve network printer issues.	Chapter 3, Lesson 1
MANAGING AND MAINTAINING SYSTEMS THAT RUN WINDOWS 7 CLIENT	
Identify and resolve performance issues.	Chapter 8, Lessons 1 and 2
Identify and resolve hardware failure issues.	Chapter 1, Lessons 1 and 2
SUPPORTING MOBILE USERS	
Identify and resolve wireless connectivity issues.	Chapter 2, Lesson 3
Identify and resolve remote access issues.	Chapter 6, Lessons 1 and 2
IDENTIFYING CAUSE OF AND RESOLVING SECURITY ISSUES	
Identify and resolve Windows Internet Explorer security issues.	Chapter 4, Lesson 2
Identify and resolve issues due to malicious software.	Chapter 5, Lesson 1
Identify and resolve encryption issues.	Chapter 4, Lesson 3
Identify and resolve software update issues.	Chapter 7, Lesson 1

Exam Objectives   The exam objectives listed here are current as of this book's publication date. Exam objectives are subject to change at any time without prior notice and at Microsoft's sole discretion. Please visit the Microsoft Learning Web site for the most current listing of exam objectives: *http://www.microsoft.com/learning/en/us/Exam.aspx?ID=70-685.*

MCITP Self-Paced Training Kit (Exam 70-685): Windows® 7 Enterprise Desktop Support Technician

Tony Northrup
J.C. Mackin

PUBLISHED BY
Microsoft Press
A Division of Microsoft Corporation
One Microsoft Way
Redmond, Washington 98052-6399

Library of Congress Control Number: 2010921440

Printed and bound in the United States of America.

2 3 4 5 6 7 8 9 WCT 2 1 0

Distributed in Canada by H.B. Fenn and Company Ltd.

A CIP catalogue record for this book is available from the British Library.

Microsoft Press books are available through booksellers and distributors worldwide. For further information about international editions, contact your local Microsoft Corporation office or contact Microsoft Press International directly at fax (425) 936-7329. Visit our Web site at www.microsoft.com/mspress. Send comments to tkinput@microsoft.com.

Acquisitions Editors: Ken Jones and Martin DelRe
Developmental Editor: Maria Gargiulo
Project Editors: Denise Bankaitis and Carol Vu
Editorial Production: Christian Holdener, S4Carlisle Publishing Services
Technical Reviewer: Bob Dean; Technical Review services provided by Content Master, a member of CM Group, Ltd.
Cover: Tom Draper Design

Body Part No. X16-75082

For my Gramma June.
　　—TONY NORTHRUP

To my nieces Cassidy and Mckenna, and to my nephew Ralph.
　　—J.C. MACKIN

Contents

What do you think of this book? We want to hear from you!

Microsoft is interested in hearing your feedback so we can continually improve our
books and learning resources for you. To participate in a brief online survey, please visit:

www.microsoft.com/learning/booksurvey/

What do you think of this book? We want to hear from you!

Microsoft is interested in hearing your feedback so we can continually improve our books and learning resources for you. To participate in a brief online survey, please visit:

www.microsoft.com/learning/booksurvey/

Acknowledgments

This book was put together by a team of respected professionals, and we, the authors, would like to thank them all for the great job they did. At Microsoft, Ken Jones and Martin DelRe worked out our contracts, and Maria Gargiulo was our developmental editor. Denise Bankaitis, Carol Vu, and Christian Holdener were the project editors, coordinating the many other people who worked on the book. Among those, Susan McClung was our copy editor, who was responsible for making sure the book is readable and consistent, and Lindsey Valich, Paul Connelly, and Nicole Schlutt provided additional editorial proofreading.

Bob Dean and Bob Hogan provided a technical review to help make the book as accurate as possible.

Tony Northrup would also like to thank his friends for helping him relax after long days of writing, especially Eddie and Christine Mercado (for the dinners), Jose and Lucy Mercado (*por el arroz y los frijoles*), Brian and Melissa Rheaume (for the drinks), Diane Glenn (for the cake), Jose Gonzalez (for the laughs), and Madelyn Knowles (for the patience).

J.C. Mackin would like to thank all his friends and family for their support and encouragement.

It makes a huge difference when you consider the people you work with to be friends. Having a great team not only improves the quality of the book, it makes it a more enjoyable experience. Writing this book was our most enjoyable project yet, and we hope we get the chance to work with everyone again in the future.

Introduction

This training kit is designed for IT support personnel who support Windows 7 at the Tier 1 or Tier 2 level in a wide range of environments and who plan to take the Microsoft Certified Information Technology Professional (MCITP) exam 70-685. We assume that before you begin using this kit you have a solid foundation-level understanding of Microsoft Windows client operating systems and common Internet technologies. The Preparation Guide for Exam 70-685 is available at *http://www.microsoft.com/learning/en/us/exam.aspx?ID=70-685*.

By using this training kit, you will learn how to do the following:

- Identify cause of and resolve desktop application issues
- Identify cause of and resolve networking issues
- Manage and maintain systems that run Windows 7 client
- Support mobile users
- Identify cause of and resolve security issues

Refer to the objective mapping page in the front of this book to see where in the book each exam objective is covered.

Hardware Requirements

You can complete almost all the practice exercises in this book, other than those in Lesson 3 of Chapter 2 (which requires a wireless network adapter), using virtual machines rather than server hardware. The minimum and recommended hardware requirements for Windows 7 are listed in Table I-1.

TABLE I-1 Windows 7 Minimum Hardware Requirements

HARDWARE COMPONENT	MINIMUM REQUIREMENTS	RECOMMENDED
Processor	1 GHz (x86), 1.4 GHz (x64)	2 GHz or faster
RAM	1 GB	2 GB or greater
Disk Space	16 GB	40 GB or greater

You also need to be able to install Windows Server 2008 R2, which is 64-bit. Therefore, you must use hardware or virtual machine software that supports 64-bit operating systems. As of the time of this writing, Microsoft Windows Virtual PC and Microsoft Virtual Server 2005 do not support 64-bit guests. Sun VirtualBox does support 64-bit guests and can be downloaded for free from *http://www.virtualbox.org*. Alternatively, you can use the Hyper-V feature of Windows Server 2008 R2, as described at *http://www.microsoft.com/windowsserver2008/en/us/hyperv-main.aspx*.

If you intend to implement several virtual machines on the same computer (recommended), a higher specification will enhance your user experience. In particular, a computer with 4 GB RAM and 60 GB free disk space can host all the virtual machines specified for all the practices in this book.

Practice Setup Instructions

The practice exercises in this training kit require a minimum of three computers or virtual machines, as follows:

- One server running Windows Server 2008 R2 Standard and configured as a domain controller. Name the server DC1. Name the domain nwtraders.msft.
- Two computers running Windows 7 and configured as domain members. Name the computers CLIENT1 and CLIENT2.

When installing the operating systems, accept all default settings except for the computer names listed above.

Using the Companion CD

The companion CD included with this training kit contains the following:

- **Practice tests**   You can reinforce your understanding of how to support Windows 7 by using electronic practice tests that you customize to meet your needs from the pool of Lesson Review questions in this book, or you can practice for the 70-685 certification exam by using tests created from a pool of about 200 realistic exam questions, which give you many practice exams to ensure that you are prepared.
- **Practice exercises**   Some chapters in this book include scripts that configure your test computers for the practice exercises at the end of every lesson. To install the scripts on your hard disk, run Setup.exe in the Practice Exercises folder on the companion CD. The default installation folder is \My Documents\Microsoft Press\MCITP Self-Paced Training Kit Exam 70-685.
- **An eBook**   An electronic version (eBook) of this book is included for times when you do not want to carry the printed book with you. The eBook is in Portable Document Format (PDF), and you can view it by using Adobe Acrobat or Adobe Reader.

> **Digital Content for Digital Book Readers:** If you bought a digital-only edition of this book, you can enjoy select content from the print edition's companion CD.
> Visit **http://go.microsoft.com/fwlink/?LinkId=183642** to get your downloadable content. This content is always up-to-date and available to all readers.

System Requirements for the Companion CD

To use the companion CD-ROM, you need a computer running Windows 7, Windows Server 2008, Windows Vista, Windows Server 2003, or Windows XP. The computer must meet the following minimum requirements:

- 1 GHz 32-bit (x86) or 64-bit (x64) processor
- 1 GB of system memory
- A hard disk partition with at least 1 GB of available space
- A monitor capable of at least 800 × 600 display resolution
- A keyboard
- A mouse or other pointing device
- An optical drive capable of reading CD-ROMs

The computer must also have the following software:

- A Web browser such as Microsoft Internet Explorer version 6 or later
- An application that can display PDF files, such as Adobe Acrobat Reader, which can be downloaded at *http://www.adobe.com/reader*

These requirements support use of the companion CD-ROM. To perform the practice exercises in this training kit, you will require additional hardware or software, as detailed previously.

How to Install the Practice Tests

To install the practice test software from the companion CD to your hard disk, perform the following steps:

1. Insert the companion CD into your CD drive and accept the license agreement. A CD menu appears.

    NOTE IF THE CD MENU DOES NOT APPEAR

    If the CD menu or the license agreement does not appear, AutoRun might be disabled on your computer. Refer to the Readme.txt file on the CD for alternate installation instructions.

2. Click Practice Tests and follow the instructions on the screen.

How to Use the Practice Tests

To start the practice test software, perform these steps:

1. Click Start, click All Programs, and then select Microsoft Press Training Kit Exam Prep.

   A window appears that shows all the Microsoft Press training kit exam prep suites installed on your computer.

2. Double-click the lesson review or practice test you want to use.

> **NOTE** **LESSON REVIEWS VERSUS PRACTICE TESTS**
>
> Select (70-685) Windows 7, Enterprise Desktop Support Technician Lesson Review to use the questions from the "Lesson Review" sections of this book. Select Windows 7, Enterprise Desktop Support Technician Practice Test to use a pool of more than 200 questions (per exam), similar to those that appear on the 70-685 certification exam.

Lesson Review Options

When you start a lesson review, the Custom Mode dialog box appears so that you can configure your test. You can click OK to accept the defaults, or you can customize the number of questions you want, how the practice test software works, which exam objectives you want the questions to relate to, and whether you want your lesson review to be timed. If you are retaking a test, you can select whether you want to see all the questions again or only the questions you missed or did not answer.

After you click OK, your lesson review starts as follows:

- To take the test, answer the questions and use the Next and Previous buttons to move from question to question.

- After you answer a question, if you want to see which answers are correct—along with an explanation of each correct answer—click Explanation.

- If you prefer to wait until the end of the test to see how you did, answer all the questions and then click Score Test. You will see a summary of the exam objectives you chose and the percentage of questions you got right, both overall and per objective. You can print a copy of your test, review your answers, or retake the test.

Practice Test Options

When you start a practice test, you choose whether to take the test in Certification Mode, Study Mode, or Custom Mode:

- **Certification Mode** Closely resembles the experience of taking a certification exam. The test has a set number of questions. It is timed, and you cannot pause and restart the timer.

- **Study Mode** Creates an untimed test, during which you can review the correct answers and the explanations after you answer each question.
- **Custom Mode** Gives you full control over the test options so that you can customize them as you like.

In all modes, the user interface when you are taking the test is basically the same but with different options enabled or disabled depending on the mode. The main options are discussed in the previous section, "Lesson Review Options."

When you review your answer to a practice test question, a "References" section is provided that lists where in the training kit you can find the information that relates to that question and provides links to other sources of information. After you click Test Results to score your entire practice test, you can click the Learning Plan tab to see a list of references for every objective.

How to Uninstall the Practice Tests

To uninstall the practice test software for a training kit, use the Uninstall A Program option in Windows Control Panel.

Microsoft Certified Professional Program

Microsoft certifications provide the best method for proving your command of current Microsoft products and technologies. The exams and corresponding certifications are developed to validate your mastery of critical competencies as you design and develop, or implement and support, solutions with Microsoft products and technologies. Computer professionals who become Microsoft certified are recognized as experts and are sought after industry-wide. Certification brings a variety of benefits to the individual and to employers and organizations.

> **MORE INFO** **ALL THE MICROSOFT CERTIFICATIONS**
>
> For a full list of Microsoft certifications, go to *http://www.microsoft.com/learning/mcp/default.asp*.

Support for This Book

Every effort has been made to ensure the accuracy of this book and the contents of the companion CD. As corrections or changes are discovered, they will be added to a Microsoft Knowledge Base article accessible via the Microsoft Help and Support site. Microsoft Press provides support for books, including instructions for finding Knowledge Base articles, at the following Web site:

http://www.microsoft.com/learning/support/books/

If you have questions regarding the book that are not answered by visiting the site above or viewing a Knowledge Base article, send them to Microsoft Press via e-mail to *tkinput@microsoft.com*.

Please note that Microsoft software product support is not offered through these addresses.

We Want to Hear from You

We welcome your feedback about this book. Please share your comments and ideas via the following short survey:

http://www.microsoft.com/learning/booksurvey

Your participation will help Microsoft Press create books that better meet your needs and your standards.

> **NOTE   CONNECT WITH MICROSOFT PRESS**
>
> We hope that you will give us detailed feedback via our survey. If you have questions about our publishing program, upcoming titles, or Microsoft Press in general, we encourage you to interact with us via Twitter at *http://twitter.com/MicrosoftPress*. For support issues, use only the e-mail address shown above.

CHAPTER 1

Troubleshooting Hardware Failures

Windows 7 is the newest addition to the family of Windows client operating systems, a family that includes Windows XP and Windows Vista. If you are an enterprise support technician in a company that has deployed Windows 7, you are likely to be responsible for supporting not only this operating system, but also any client applications that run on Windows 7 and the physical computers that support this software.

As part of this job, therefore, you need to know which tools you can use to diagnose faulty hardware and how to use them. Windows 7 includes many such tools, such as built-in troubleshooters, memory diagnostic software, disk diagnostic software, and other utilities.

This chapter introduces you to these tools, along with strategies for troubleshooting particular hardware components.

Exam objective in this chapter:
- Identify and resolve hardware failure issues.

Lessons in this chapter:

Before You Begin

To complete the exercises in the chapter, you must have the following:

- A computer running Windows 7 Professional, Enterprise, or Ultimate
- Basic knowledge of Microsoft Windows

Lesson 1: Using Windows 7 Hardware Troubleshooting Tools

In this lesson, you learn about tools available in Windows 7 (such as the Action Center, Windows 7 troubleshooters, Reliability Monitor, Event Viewer, and Device Manager) that you can use to start troubleshooting computer failures. The lesson then introduces other tools (such as Startup Repair, Windows Memory Diagnostic, Chkdsk, and Disk Defragmenter) that you can use to troubleshoot, diagnose, and repair failures related to a specific hardware component.

After this lesson, you will be able to:

- Use several tools in Windows 7 to troubleshoot hardware failures.

Estimated lesson time: 60 minutes

Troubleshooting with the Windows 7 Action Center

When you are troubleshooting a computer problem of an unknown origin, the first and easiest place to check for information about that problem is the Action Center. The *Action Center* is an expanded version of the tool that was called the Security Center in Windows Vista. In Windows 7, the newly expanded Action Center displays more than security warnings. Now it displays all types of important alerts that require user action. Although these alerts often indicate software problems related to security (such as faulty firewall or antivirus settings) or maintenance (such as failed backups), they can also indicate certain types of hardware problems, such as those related to missing or incompatible device drivers. The Action Center is shown in Figure 1-1.

FIGURE 1-1 The Windows 7 Action Center

You can access the Action Center by clicking the flag icon in the notification area of the taskbar. When you click this icon, a menu appears (as shown in Figure 1-2) and displays links to view any alert messages, to initiate recommended actions, and to open the Action Center itself.

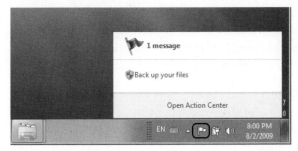

FIGURE 1-2 The Action Center displays a flag in the Notification Area.

Note that even if you don't see any alert messages in the Action Center that are related to the problem you are trying to solve, you can still use the Action Center to connect to other important troubleshooting tools. For example, from within the Action Center, you can open Control Panel troubleshooters and Reliability Monitor, both of which are described later in this chapter.

Enabling Alerts in the Action Center

You can configure the Action Center to limit the type of alert messages that it displays. For this reason, if you are troubleshooting a hardware failure and no related alerts are displayed in the Action Center, you should verify that Windows Troubleshooting messages have not been turned off. To do so, in the Action Center, first select the Change Action Center Settings option, as shown in Figure 1-3.

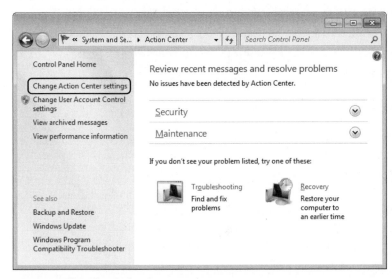

FIGURE 1-3 Changing Action Center settings

Then, under Turn Messages On Or Off, verify that the Windows Troubleshooting check box is selected, as shown in Figure 1-4.

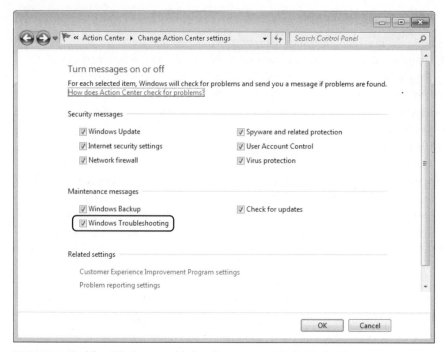

FIGURE 1-4 Disabling Windows troubleshooting messages in the Action Center

Troubleshooting with Windows 7 Troubleshooters

Another new tool you can use to diagnose hardware failures in Windows 7 is a troubleshooter. Troubleshooters are wizards that automatically attempt to diagnose and repair common computer problems. Windows 7 includes many built-in troubleshooters, but many more are likely to appear through third-party vendors by means of the new Windows Troubleshooting Platform. The Windows Troubleshooting Platform exposes detailed troubleshooting information about the Windows environment through a scripting interface and then provides a simple framework for creating new troubleshooting wizards. As a result, software vendors, equipment manufacturers, and even administrators can create new troubleshooters that help diagnose and fix a particular device, application, or configuration area.

For example, an external hard drive manufacturer can easily create a troubleshooter that helps customers diagnose and fix errors related to this hard drive before the customers call tech support. Also, an administrator can create a troubleshooter that detects and fixes the most commonly observed problems on the local business network, and then she can instruct users to run this troubleshooter before calling the help desk.

How useful are troubleshooters, really? The troubleshooters built into Windows 7 are not designed to provide Tier 2 support, so they are most useful in helping ordinary users check for basic problems. However, there is a reason to be optimistic about the future of this new technology because the power of the Windows Troubleshooting Platform is impressive. Troubleshooters have the potential to dig deep and investigate many low-level configuration settings in a way that will make these tools suitable for Tier 2 support. This potential is best exploited by vendors who know their specific product well and can make targeted troubleshooters that investigate these low-level settings. Troubleshooters will therefore be most useful to Tier 2 desktop support technicians if third-party vendors take advantage of the Windows Troubleshooting Platform to help support their products. Whether that actually happens in a significant way, however, remains to be seen.

At the time of this writing, Windows includes 23 built-in troubleshooters, all of which are shown in Table 1-1. A few of these built-in troubleshooters, such as Hardware And Devices, Playing Audio, and Network Adapter, are designed to help diagnose hardware problems specifically. In addition, the System Maintenance troubleshooter includes a routine to check locally attached hard disks for bad sectors, lost clusters, cross-linked files, and directory errors.

Of the 23 troubleshooters listed, all but Devices And Printers are available in Control Panel. The Devices And Printers troubleshooter is discussed later in this lesson in the section "Running the Devices And Printers Troubleshooter."

NOTE **TROUBLESHOOTING PACKS**

The features of each troubleshooter are defined in a set of scripts called a *troubleshooting pack.* Troubleshooting packs are created by using Windows PowerShell, a scripting language and execution environment used for Windows administration. Windows PowerShell is relatively easy to learn, so you do not have to be a seasoned programmer to create a troubleshooting pack. You can view the troubleshooting packs installed on your system by navigating to C:\Windows\Diagnostics\System.

TABLE 1-1 Built-in Windows 7 Troubleshooters

TROUBLESHOOTER	TROUBLESHOOTING GOAL	CATEGORY
Aero	Display Aero effects such as transparency.	Desktop Experience
Connection To A Workplace Using DirectAccess	Connect to your workplace network over the Internet.	Network
Devices And Printers	Establish functionality for a device or printer.	Device, Printing
Hardware And Devices	Use hardware and access devices connected to your computer.	Device
HomeGroup	View computers or shared files in a homegroup.	Network
Incoming Connections	Allow other computers to communicate with your computer through Windows Firewall.	Network
Internet Connections	Connect to the Internet or to a particular Web site.	Network
Internet Explorer Performance	Help prevent add-on problems, and optimize temporary files and connections.	Web Browser
Internet Explorer Safety	Help prevent malware, pop-ups, and online attacks.	Web Browser
Network Adapter	Establish functionality for Ethernet, wireless, or other network adapters.	Network
Performance	Help improve overall speed and performance of system.	Performance
Playing Audio	Play sounds and other audio such as music files.	Sound
Power	Help improve battery life and reduce power usage.	Power
Printer	Establish functionality for a printer.	Printing
Program Compatibility	Make older programs run in this version of Windows.	Programs
Recording Audio	Record audio input from a microphone or other source.	Sound
Search And Indexing	Find items on your computer using Windows Search.	Windows

TROUBLESHOOTER	TROUBLESHOOTING GOAL	CATEGORY
Shared Folders	Access shared files and folders on other computers.	Network
System Maintenance	Clean up unused files and shortcuts, check hard disk volumes for errors, and perform other maintenance tasks.	System
Windows Media Player DVD	Play a DVD by using Windows Media Player.	Media Player
Windows Media Player Library	Make media files show up in the Windows Media Player library.	Media Player
Windows Media Player Settings	Reset Windows Media player to default settings.	Media Player
Windows Update	Establish proper functionality for Windows Update.	Windows

Running Control Panel Troubleshooters

Most troubleshooters built into Windows 7 are available through the Troubleshooting item in Control Panel. You should become familiar with these Control Panel troubleshooters before you need them so that you know which ones can help you when a problem arises. For example, if in your job you are called upon to troubleshoot an audio device, it is helpful for you to know that a built-in Playing Audio troubleshooter is available through Control Panel. To access Control Panel troubleshooters, first open the Action Center and click Troubleshooting, as shown in Figure 1-5.

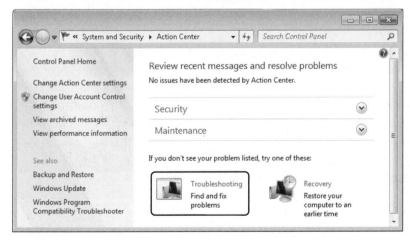

FIGURE 1-5 Opening Windows 7 troubleshooters in the Action Center

This step opens the main window of the Troubleshooting item in Control Panel, shown in Figure 1-6.

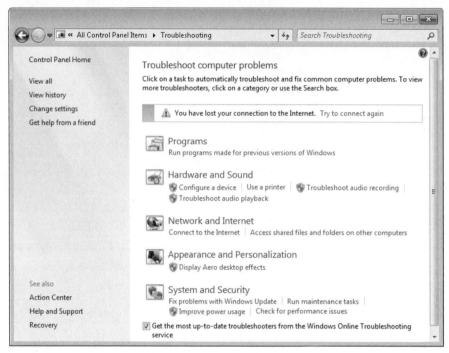

FIGURE 1-6 Troubleshooting in Control Panel

If you already see in this window a link to a particular troubleshooter (such as Configure A Device) that you want to run, you can select that link at this point. If you want to review a complete list of all available troubleshooters without categories, click View All on the left side of the window.

Otherwise, choose a troubleshooting category. For example, if you want to troubleshoot a device, click the Hardware And Sound category to open the Troubleshoot Problems - Hardware And Sound page, shown in Figure 1-7. Within the Hardware And Sound category, the Windows 7 troubleshooters that are available at the time of this writing are Playing Audio, Recording Audio, Hardware And Devices, Network Adapter, Printer, and Windows Media Player DVD.

From the list of available troubleshooters, select the troubleshooter that you want to run. For example, if you are having trouble with a network adapter, click Network Adapter. The first page of the Network Adapter troubleshooter is shown in Figure 1-8.

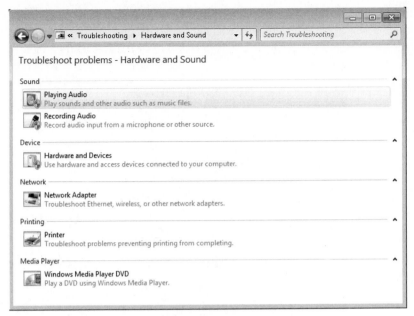

FIGURE 1-7 Hardware and sound troubleshooters in Windows 7

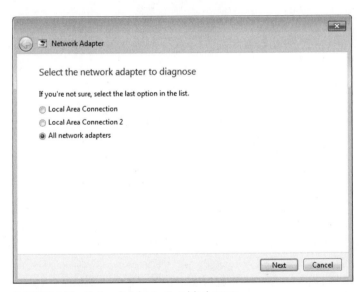

FIGURE 1-8 The Network Adapter troubleshooter

Running the Devices And Printers Troubleshooter

The Devices And Printers troubleshooter is a special, easy-to-access hardware troubleshooter that can quickly fix problems related to printers and peripheral devices.

Also known as the Troubleshoot command, this troubleshooter is available only through Devices And Printers, a new feature in Windows 7 that helps you manage peripheral devices and printers on the local machine. To open Devices And Printers, select Devices And Printers from the Start menu, as shown in Figure 1-9.

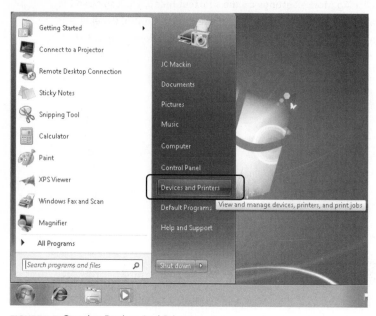

FIGURE 1-9 Opening Devices And Printers

Devices And Printers is shown in Figure 1-10.

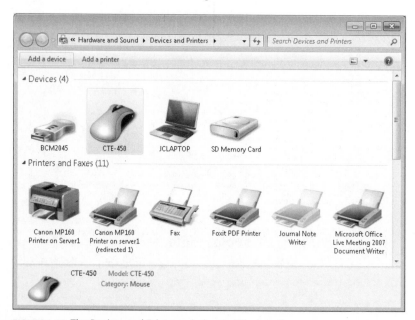

FIGURE 1-10 The Devices and Printers window in Windows 7

To start the Devices And Printers troubleshooter, simply right-click the device you want to troubleshoot and then select Troubleshoot from the shortcut menu, as shown in Figure 1-11.

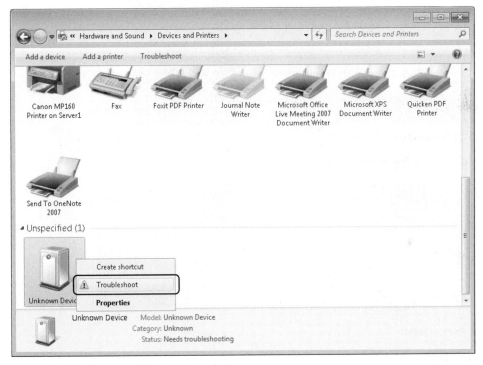

FIGURE 1-11 Starting a troubleshooter on a device

After you perform this step, the Devices And Printers troubleshooter starts running immediately, as shown in Figure 1-12.

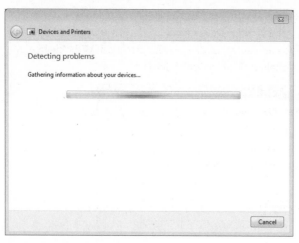

FIGURE 1-12 The Devices And Printers troubleshooter starts running immediately by default.

Using Hardware Troubleshooters

Troubleshooters typically scan for errors and then give you an opportunity to fix any errors that are detected. The last page of the wizard provides a summary of the results found in the error scan.

Although troubleshooters typically detect configuration errors as opposed to hardware failures, you can still use the troubleshooter to help you determine whether a problem with a device is caused by problems with the physical hardware.

For example, if you are troubleshooting a Bluetooth device, the Hardware And Devices troubleshooter might reveal that the device needs to be enabled, as shown in Figure 1-13. This outcome would suggest that the problems you are experiencing with the device are related to software configuration, not to the hardware itself.

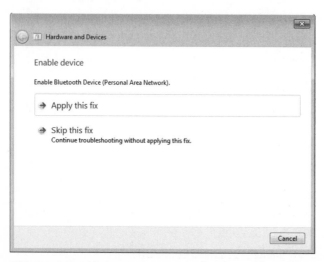

FIGURE 1-13 Troubleshooters can suggest fixes for problems discovered.

However, if a troubleshooter detects a problem but cannot provide any information about this problem (as shown in Figure 1-14), this outcome could suggest that the device itself is malfunctioning. In this case, you can use other diagnostics provided by the device manufacturer to further test the functionality of the physical device.

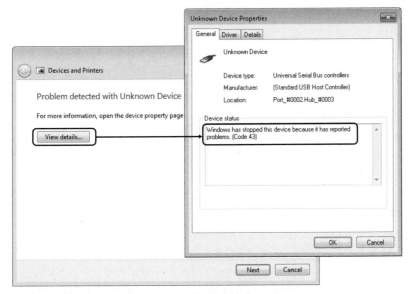

FIGURE 1-14 Unspecified errors require further troubleshooting.

Configuring Settings for Troubleshooters

Clicking the Change Settings option on the main window of the Troubleshooting item in Control Panel, as shown in Figure 1-15, opens the Change Troubleshooting Settings page.

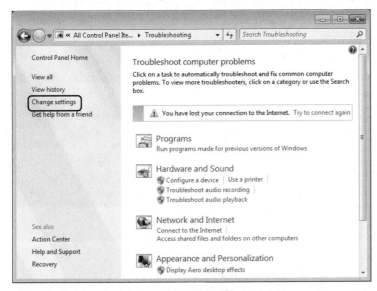

FIGURE 1-15 Changing settings for troubleshooters

This Change Troubleshooting Settings page is shown in Figure 1-16.

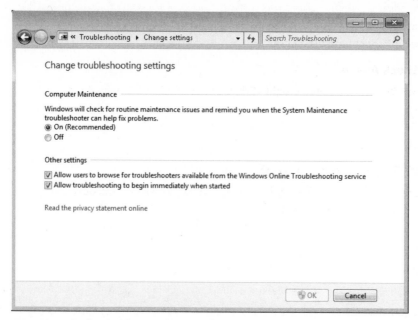

FIGURE 1-16 Configuring features for troubleshooters

The Change Troubleshooting Settings page allows you to modify three settings related to Troubleshooters.

- Windows Will Check For Routine Maintenance Issues And Remind You When The System Maintenance Troubleshooter Can Help Fix Problems

  By default, the routine checks are enabled (set to On). This setting is relevant for diagnosing hardware problems—specifically hard disk problems—because the System Maintenance troubleshooter can alert you to some problems detected with the physical disk.

- Allow Users To Browse For Troubleshooters Available From The Windows Online Troubleshooting Service

  By default, this setting is enabled. If your users do not see the list of available troubleshooters expanding over time, be sure to verify that this setting is enabled.

- Allow Troubleshooting To Begin Immediately When Started

  This setting affects only the Troubleshooting option in Devices And Printers; it simply determines whether this troubleshooter should skip the opening page of the wizard when this option is selected. By default, this setting is enabled.

Quick Check

- A mouse device doesn't seem to be working. What's the quickest way to run a troubleshooter on the mouse?

Quick Check Answer

- Open Devices And Printers, right-click the mouse, and click Troubleshoot from the shortcut menu.

Troubleshooting with Device Manager

If a troubleshooter does not automatically fix a problem related to hardware, open Device Manager for more information. Device Manager is a basic tool that you can use to determine whether there are any malfunctioning devices connected to the system.

To view failed hardware in Device Manager, follow these steps:

1. Click Start, right-click Computer, and then click Manage.

2. Under System Tools, click Device Manager.

3. Device Manager displays all locally attached devices. Problem devices (including any devices with which Windows 7 has failed to communicate) are displayed with a warning sign, as shown in Figure 1-17. If no categories are expanded and no devices are visible, then Windows has not detected a problem with any device.

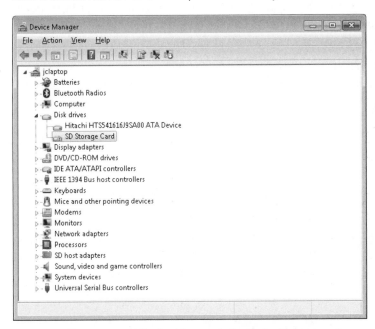

FIGURE 1-17 You can access Device Manager in Computer Management.

If Device Manager detects a problem with a device, right-click the device and open its Properties dialog box. The Properties dialog box for the problem device shown in Figure 1-17 is shown in Figure 1-18.

FIGURE 1-18 Open the Properties dialog box for problem devices in Device Manager.

A common cause of hardware failure is a faulty driver. If the General tab of the Properties dialog box reports a problem with a device driver, click the Driver tab, as shown in Figure 1-19. From this tab, you can choose to update the driver or roll it back to the previously installed version.

FIGURE 1-19 Use the Driver tab of a device to update or roll back its driver.

You should choose to roll back the driver if it was working before you last updated it. If the previously installed driver did not function, or if no previous driver was ever installed, you should update the driver. Note, however, that the normal way to update a driver is to download and run the most recent driver installation program from the device manufacturer's Web site. You should use the Update Driver option only if no installation program is available for a functioning driver.

Note also that if Device Manager indicates a problem with a device but can provide no specific information about this problem, you should begin to suspect a hardware malfunction.

Troubleshooting with Reliability Monitor

Reliability Monitor is a tool whose purpose is to measure the stability of a system over time. In Windows 7, you can access Reliability Monitor through the Action Center by expanding the Maintenance Area and then clicking View Reliability History, as shown in Figure 1-20.

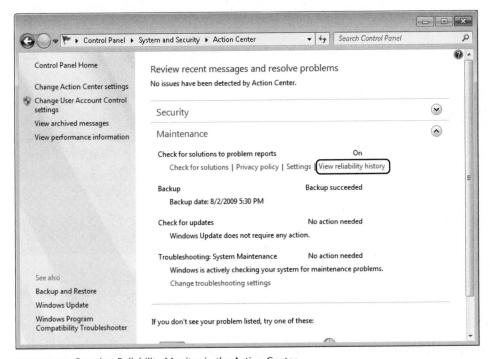

FIGURE 1-20 Opening Reliability Monitor in the Action Center

Reliability Monitor itself is shown in Figure 1-21.

Reliability Monitor presents a graphical view of the local computer's reliability over the past 20 days or 20 weeks. As it rates the stability of the system over that period on a scale from 1 (low) to 10 (high), it traces a continuous blue line.

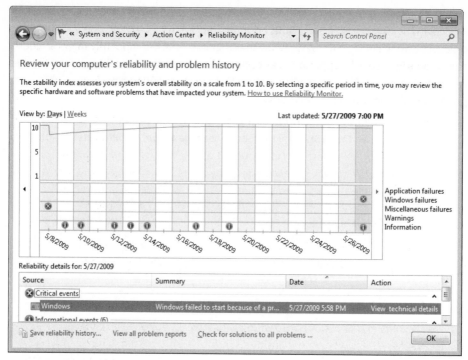

FIGURE 1-21 Reliability Monitor

To assess a system's stability, Reliability Monitor tracks the following five categories of events:

- Application failures
- Windows failures
- Miscellaneous failures
- Warnings
- Information

The Reliability Details area of Reliability Monitor provides more information about the tracked events. Note that any critical events that occur in the tracked categories lower the rating of the system during a given time period (day or week).

Using Reliability Monitor to Diagnose Hardware Failures

Reliability Monitor collects data about the *software* failures that have occurred in the recent history of the system. Because hardware failures lead to software failures, however, this information is important even when you are troubleshooting system failures that you ultimately determine to be caused by faulty hardware.

When troubleshooting a failure of any sort, therefore, check Reliability Monitor to see if Windows has recorded any relevant information about the problem over time. Look specifically for any critical events in the Windows Failures category. If a user complains about Windows crashing, for example, you might find that this problem originated on a date after there was a known change to the system. Crashes that occur very infrequently might suggest an association with a specific application, as opposed to a hardware-specific problem. Crashes that occur during periods of high read or write activity (such as during a backup) might suggest an association with a hard disk drive.

Though Reliability Monitor can provide useful information for troubleshooting, it is also worth noting the limitations of Reliability Monitor as a diagnostic tool. Reliability Monitor can indeed be used to diagnose hardware errors, but it is useful only for those hardware failures that can be recorded by Windows. For example, Reliability Monitor can help you trace the nature of a memory failure that repeatedly causes stop errors. However, hardware failures that occur before Windows even starts naturally cannot be diagnosed by using Reliability Monitor.

In general, consider Reliability Monitor one useful option among the Windows diagnostic tools at your disposal when you are trying to determine the cause of a system failure.

Troubleshooting with Event Viewer

Event Viewer records events that are written to event logs in Windows and other applications. On most computers, Event Viewer contains thousands of events, most of which can be safely ignored. However, when troubleshooting, you should examine the Event Log to find events that might help you uncover the source of the problem that you are trying to diagnose. Remember, however, that not all problems generate an event. For this reason, it is possible that you will not see any events related to the issue you are troubleshooting.

To open Event Viewer and view hardware-related events, follow these steps:

1. Click Start, right-click Computer, and then click Manage.
2. Under System Tools, expand Event Viewer.
3. Under Event Viewer, expand Windows Logs, and then click System.
4. In the Actions pane, click Filter Current Log.
5. In the Filter Current Log dialog box, select the Critical and Error check boxes, and click OK.

Once you perform these steps, Event Viewer appears with only critical events and errors displayed, as shown in Figure 1-22.

For more information on troubleshooting with Event Viewer, see Chapter 8, "Performance," and Chapter 9, "Troubleshooting Software Issues."

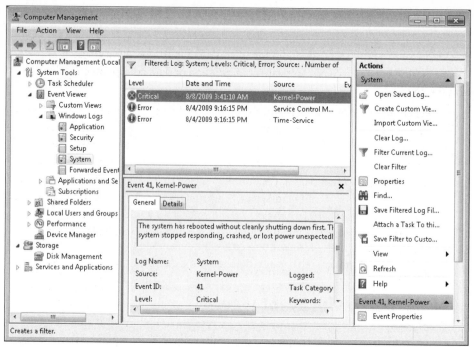

FIGURE 1-22 Event Viewer

Browse through this filtered list of events. In particular, pay close attention to events with a source related to the hardware component that is experiencing problems. For example, if you are experiencing disk errors, look for errors related to the system disk. If any such events are written, they could be crucial in helping you diagnose the issue in question.

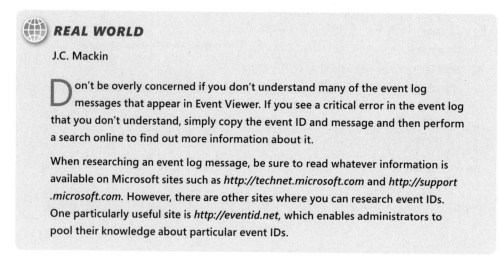

REAL WORLD

J.C. Mackin

Don't be overly concerned if you don't understand many of the event log messages that appear in Event Viewer. If you see a critical error in the event log that you don't understand, simply copy the event ID and message and then perform a search online to find out more information about it.

When researching an event log message, be sure to read whatever information is available on Microsoft sites such as *http://technet.microsoft.com* and *http://support* *.microsoft.com*. However, there are other sites where you can research event IDs. One particularly useful site is *http://eventid.net,* which enables administrators to pool their knowledge about particular event IDs.

Troubleshooting Startup Failures with Startup Repair

A physically malfunctioning disk, motherboard, or RAM module can prevent a system from starting, but so can a faulty disk configuration. If you need to troubleshoot a system that does not start, you first need to rule out software configuration or data corruption errors on the disks as the cause.

Startup Repair automatically detects and fixes many hard disk errors that prevent Windows from starting. Startup Repair begins by analyzing boot sectors, the boot manager, disk configuration, disk integrity, boot configuration data (BCD) registry file integrity, system file integrity, boot logs, and event logs. Then, it attempts to solve any problems it has found. This repair process can involve repairing configuration files, solving simple disk problems, replacing missing system files, or running System Restore to return the computer to an earlier state. Because Startup Repair performs these tasks automatically, you can solve startup problems much faster by using this tool than you would otherwise if you had to perform this analysis and repair manually.

Startup Repair helps you diagnose hardware failures precisely because it repairs common software configuration errors found on boot disks (typically hard disks). If Startup Repair fails to fix a Windows startup problem, you can normally remove disk configuration from the list of potential sources of the error you want to resolve. You can then turn your attention to other possible causes, such as a third-party disk partitioning utilities, physical disk problems, physical drive problems, an incorrectly configured basic input/output system (BIOS), faulty memory, or a faulty motherboard.

Launching the Startup Repair Tool

You access Startup Repair through the *Windows Recovery Environment* and its associated *System Recovery Options,* which are installed automatically on the boot disk by the Windows 7 Setup program. The Windows Recovery Environment is a light operating system that you can use to fix Windows problems offline. To open the Windows Recovery Environment, press F8 as your computer starts to open the Advanced Boot Options menu. Then, choose the Repair Your Computer option, as shown in Figure 1-23.

If the startup problem that you are diagnosing prevents you from accessing the Advanced Boot Options menu, you can access the Windows Recovery Environment and System Recovery Options by booting from the Windows 7 DVD. With this latter method, the Install Windows wizard opens. Then, select your language, click Next, and choose the Repair Your Computer option on the second page of the Install Windows wizard, as shown in Figure 1-24.

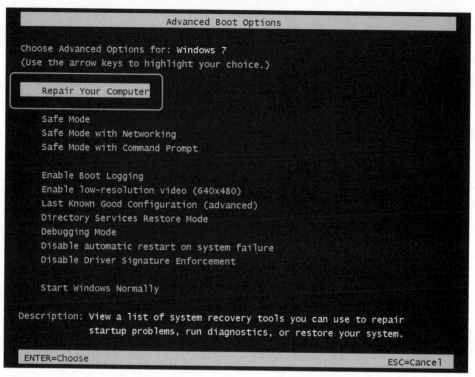

FIGURE 1-23 Opening the Windows Recovery Environment from the Advanced Boot Options menu

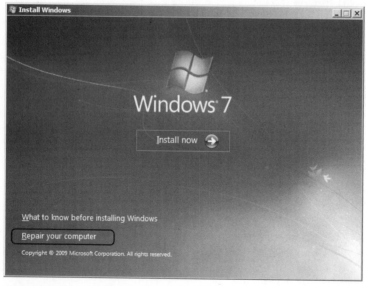

FIGURE 1-24 Opening the Windows Recovery Environment through the Windows 7 DVD

Either method of starting the Windows Recovery Environment opens the first page of the System Recovery Options wizard, one version of which is shown in Figure 1-25. This particular version of the first page appears when you boot from the Windows 7 DVD. If instead you have chosen Repair Your Computer through the Advanced Boot Options menu, you are asked to specify a language, and then, on a second page, you are prompted to provide local user credentials.

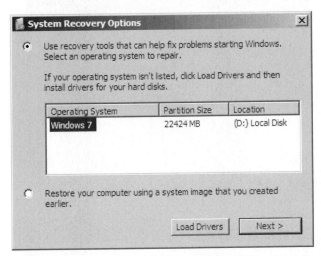

FIGURE 1-25 Opening System Recovery Options

The last page of the System Recovery Options wizard is the main page and is common to all versions: the Choose A Recovery Tool page. To launch the Startup Repair tool, choose that option on the page, as shown in Figure 1-26.

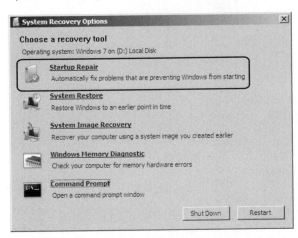

FIGURE 1-26 Choosing the Startup Repair recovery tool

Figure 1-27 shows the Startup Repair tool running. During this period, it runs the following tests:

- Check for updates
- System disk test
- Disk failure diagnosis
- Disk metadata test
- Target OS test
- Volume content check
- Boot manager diagnosis
- System boot log diagnosis
- Event log diagnosis
- Internal state check
- Boot status test

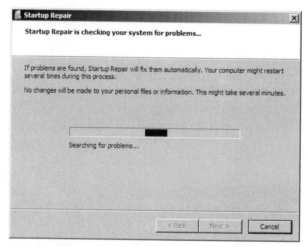

FIGURE 1-27 The Startup Repair tool

After it runs the tests and repairs the disk, Startup Repair displays a diagnosis of the startup error.

If Startup Repair finds no errors, you can turn to troubleshoot other system components, such as the physical memory or the physical disk.

Troubleshooting RAM with Windows Memory Diagnostic

Damage to RAM installed in a computer is a common source of system failures. Memory problems can prevent Windows from starting or can cause unpredictable stop errors when Windows is already running. Memory-related problems typically cause intermittent failures, and they are difficult to diagnose without a special diagnostic utility. If you suspect memory errors might be the cause of a computer problem, the special diagnostic utility that you can use in Windows 7 to test your computer's memory is *Windows Memory Diagnostic*.

You must run Windows Memory Diagnostic offline, but you can start the tool in a number of ways on a system running Windows 7. From within the Windows interface, you can schedule the tool to run the next time the system starts. You can also start the tool through the Windows Boot Manager menu or through System Recovery Options. Each of these three methods is described in the following section.

Scheduling Windows Memory Diagnostic to Start

Although you cannot run the Windows Memory Diagnostic tool while Windows is also running, you can use Windows to schedule the utility to run automatically the next time the system starts. To do so, click Windows Memory Diagnostic from the Administrative Tools menu. Alternatively, you can click Start, type **mdsched,** select Mdsched from the Programs list, and then press Enter. Either method opens the Windows Memory Diagnostic window, shown in Figure 1-28.

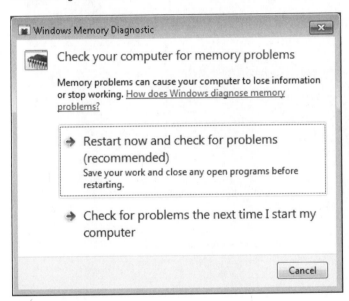

FIGURE 1-28 Scheduling Windows Memory Diagnostic to run

In this window, you can choose either to restart the computer immediately and check for memory errors, or to check automatically for memory errors whenever you start the computer next.

Starting Windows Memory Diagnostic in Windows Boot Manager

If you want to perform memory diagnostics and Windows is not running, you can start the Windows Memory Diagnostic tool by selecting it in Windows Boot Manager.

Windows Boot Manager is a feature that enables you to choose an operating system to start when multiple operating systems are installed on the local machine. Typically, Windows Boot Manager does not appear when you have only one operating system installed. However, you can force Windows Boot Manager to appear by repeatedly pressing the spacebar as your system starts.

When Windows Boot Manager does appear, press Tab to change the selection from Windows 7 to Windows Memory Diagnostic, as shown in Figure 1-29. Then, press Enter to start the diagnostic tool.

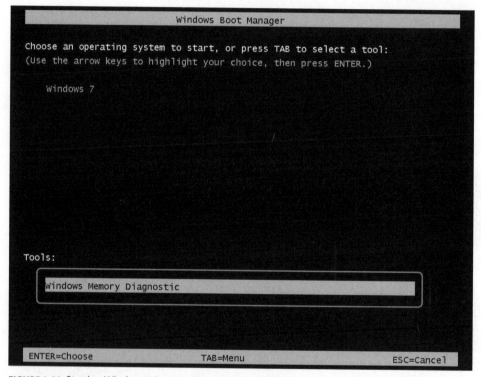

FIGURE 1-29 Starting Windows Memory Diagnostic from Windows Boot Manager

Starting Windows Memory Diagnostic from System Recovery Options

The third way you can start the Windows Memory Diagnostic tool is through System Recovery Options. Like the Startup Repair tool, Windows Memory Diagnostic is available as an option on the Choose A Recovery Tool page, as shown in Figure 1-30.

Running Windows Memory Diagnostic

Whichever of the methods you use to start Windows Memory Diagnostic, the tool begins testing memory immediately when the program starts, as shown in Figure 1-31.

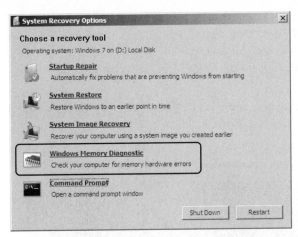

FIGURE 1-30 Selecting the Windows Memory Diagnostic recovery tool

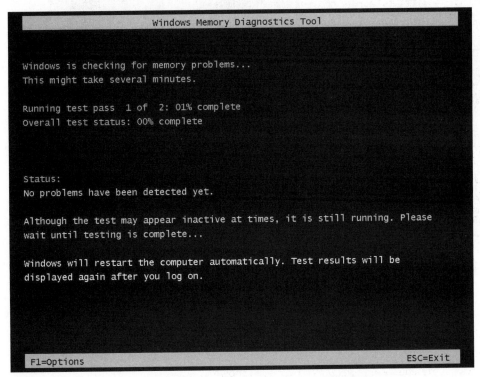

FIGURE 1-31 Windows Memory Diagnostic performs two test passes by default.

Pressing F1 reveals the Windows Memory Diagnostic - Options page, as shown in Figure 1-32.

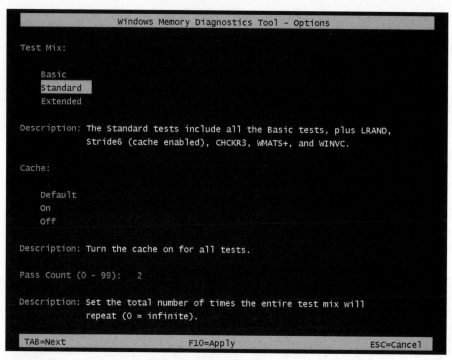

```
┌──────────────────────────────────────────────────────────────────────────┐
│             Windows Memory Diagnostics Tool - Options                      │
├──────────────────────────────────────────────────────────────────────────┤
│ Test Mix:                                                                  │
│                                                                            │
│    Basic                                                                   │
│    Standard                                                                │
│    Extended                                                                │
│                                                                            │
│ Description: The Standard tests include all the Basic tests, plus LRAND,   │
│              Stride6 (cache enabled), CHCKR3, WMATS+, and WINVC.            │
│                                                                            │
│ Cache:                                                                     │
│                                                                            │
│    Default                                                                 │
│    On                                                                      │
│    Off                                                                     │
│                                                                            │
│ Description: Turn the cache on for all tests.                              │
│                                                                            │
│ Pass Count (0 - 99):   2                                                   │
│                                                                            │
│ Description: Set the total number of times the entire test mix will        │
│              repeat (0 = infinite).                                        │
│                                                                            │
├──────────────────────────────────────────────────────────────────────────┤
│ TAB=Next                      F10=Apply                        ESC=Cancel  │
└──────────────────────────────────────────────────────────────────────────┘
```

FIGURE 1-32 Options for Windows Memory Diagnostic

As shown on the Options page, you can perform three levels of testing: Basic, Standard, and Extended. Standard is the default level; it performs eight types of tests. Basic performs only three types of memory tests, and Advanced performs 17. Whichever level you choose, the tests are performed twice by default. You can choose any number of test passes between 1 and 99.

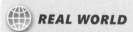 **REAL WORLD**

J.C. Mackin

I t is tempting to believe that you can simply run Windows Memory Diagnostic at the default settings to find out whether you need to replace a memory module. In truth, though, an individual circuit used to store data in memory can malfunction a relatively small percentage of the time. Infrequent errors in physical memory can cause occasional stop errors but still pass undetected by diagnostic tests that are not performed thoroughly.

Plan to use the default settings in Windows Memory Diagnostic for routine maintenance checks. But when a computer experiences stop errors for an unknown reason, you should plan to perform much more thorough checks and let them run for many hours. Also, remember that the less frequently the errors appear, the more thorough the testing needs to be.

After Windows Memory Diagnostic completes testing, Windows starts. On the desktop, Windows displays a notification bubble with the test results, as shown in Figure 1-33. You can view related events in the System Event Log with the source MemoryDiagnosticsResults (event ID 1201).

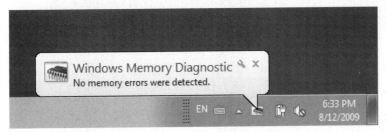

FIGURE 1-33 A notification bubble for Windows Memory Diagnostic

If you do identify a memory failure, be sure to replace the faulty RAM module. If the computer has multiple memory modules and you are unsure which module or modules are causing the problem, remove all modules except the first. Then, rerun Windows Memory Diagnostics to determine whether a fault is detected. Next, remove the first module, insert the second, and run Windows Memory Diagnostic again. Repeat the process for each module that your system includes until you find the source of the problem.

If problems persist even after replacing the memory, the problem is likely to be caused by an outside source. For example, high temperatures (often found in mobile PCs) can cause memory to be unreliable. Although computer manufacturers typically choose memory specifically designed to withstand high temperatures, adding third-party memory that does not meet the same specifications can cause failure. Besides heat, other devices inside the computer can cause electrical interference. Finally, remember that motherboard or processor problems may occasionally cause memory communication errors that resemble failing memory.

Troubleshooting Hard Disk Problems with Chkdsk

Chkdsk is a tool that automatically finds and repairs disk volume problems related to bad sectors, lost clusters, cross-linked files, and directory errors. You can run Chkdsk either in Windows or offline, but if you want to scan the system volume itself, you must run the tool outside of Windows. In this case, as with Windows Memory Diagnostic, you can schedule the tool to run the next time Windows starts.

> **NOTE TROUBLESHOOTING WITH Chkdsk**
> Disk errors are a common source of problems that appear in software. Bad sectors on a hard disk, for example, can result in stop errors, system freezes, or other errors. When you are troubleshooting problems that do not appear to be the result of a recent system change, you should always remember to use Chkdsk to scan your disks for errors.

The name *Chkdsk* refers to the spelling of the command-line version of the tool, but you can also start Chkdsk through the graphical user interface. To do so, open the properties of the volume you want to check and click the Tools tab. Then, click Check Now, as shown in Figure 1-34.

FIGURE 1-34 Running Chkdsk from Windows

This step opens the Check Disk dialog box, as shown in Figure 1-35. In this dialog box, you choose whether to fix both file system errors and bad sectors, or just file system errors. Once you have made the selection, click Start.

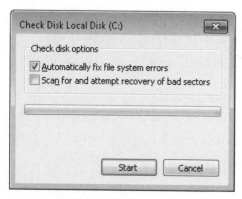

FIGURE 1-35 Chkdsk options

If you have selected the system volume to check, you see the message shown in Figure 1-36. This message indicates that the hard disk will be checked for errors the next time you start your computer.

FIGURE 1-36 Scheduling Chkdsk to run

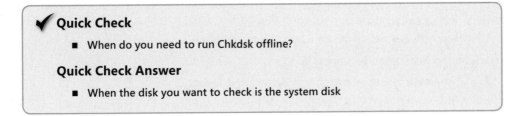

✓ **Quick Check**

- When do you need to run Chkdsk offline?

Quick Check Answer

- When the disk you want to check is the system disk

Troubleshooting Hard Disk Problems with Disk Defragmenter

Disk fragmentation refers to the gradual dispersion of data on a disk over time. Because disk fragmentation slows down your computer, your disks need to be defragmented regularly. *Disk Defragmenter* rearranges fragmented data so your disks and drives can work more efficiently. Disk Defragmenter runs automatically on a schedule in Windows 7 (every Wednesday at 1 A.M.), but you can also analyze and defragment your disks and drives manually.

To run Disk Defragmenter manually, follow these steps:

1. Click Start. Type Disk Defragmenter, and then press Enter when Disk Defragmenter appears highlighted in the Programs list.

   The Disk Defragmenter window opens.

2. Under Current Status, select the disk you want to defragment.

3. To determine if the disk needs to be defragmented or not, click Analyze Disk.

4. Once Windows is finished analyzing the disk, you can check the percentage of fragmentation on the disk in the Last Run column. If the number is above 10%, you should defragment the disk.

5. To defragment the disk, click Defragment Disk.

   Disk Defragmenter might take from several minutes to a few hours to finish, depending on the size and degree of fragmentation of your hard disk. You can still use your computer during the defragmentation process.

PRACTICE Troubleshooting in Windows 7

In this practice, you run a troubleshooter in Windows 7 and view the script contents that make up the troubleshooter. Then, you run the Startup Repair tool and observe the results.

EXERCISE 1 Running a Windows 7 Troubleshooter

In this exercise, you run the Playing Audio troubleshooter. You then browse to C:\Windows\ Diagnostics\System and view the contents of the Windows PowerShell scripts that make up the troubleshooting pack associated with this troubleshooter.

1. Log on to a computer running Windows 7 as an administrator.

2. Open Control Panel, and then click System And Security.

3. Within the Action Center category, click Troubleshoot Common Computer Problems.

4. On the Troubleshoot Computer Problems page, click Hardware And Sound.

5. On the Troubleshoot Problems - Hardware And Sound page, click Playing Audio.

    The first page of the Playing Audio troubleshooter opens.

6. Click Advanced.

    The Apply Repairs Automatically check box is selected by default.

7. Click Next.

8. The Playing Audio wizard scans for problems and attempts to repair any problems that it finds.

9. When the wizard completes, click View Detailed Information.

10. Spend a few moments to review the contents of the troubleshooting report.

11. Click Next, and then click Close.

12. In Windows Explorer, browse to C:\Windows\Diagnostics\System.

    This folder contains the locally installed troubleshooting packs that support troubleshooters available on the system.

13. Open the Audio folder.

    This folder contains the Windows PowerShell scripts that run when you run the Playing Audio troubleshooter.

14. Spend a few minutes viewing the Windows PowerShell scripts in this folder.

    The scripts are used to query the local system for very detailed configuration and status information.

15. Close all open windows.

EXERCISE 2   Running Startup Repair

In this exercise, you start the computer and open the Advanced Boot Options menu by pressing F8. From this menu, you choose the Repair Your Computer option. In the Windows Recovery Environment that opens, you complete the System Recovery Options wizard and select the Startup Repair tool.

1. If your computer running Windows 7 is running, restart it. If it is not running, start it now.

2. As soon as the computer starts, press the F8 key and hold it down.

   The Advanced Boot Options menu appears.

3. Verify that Repair Your Computer is selected, and then press Enter.

   The first page of the System Recovery Options wizard appears.

4. In the Select A Keyboard Input Method drop-down list, verify that your desired keyboard input method is selected, and then click Next.

5. On the second page of the System Recovery Options wizard, enter local administrator credentials, and then click OK.

   The Choose A Recovery Tool page opens.

6. Click Startup Repair.

   Startup Repair opens and checks for errors.

7. When Startup Repair has finished the check, click View Diagnostic And Repair Details.

8. Review the Startup Repair diagnosis and repair log.

9. Click Close.

10. Click Finish.

11. Click Shut Down.

Lesson Summary

- The Action Center is a good place to begin troubleshooting.
- Windows 7 includes many built-in troubleshooters that are part of the new extensible Windows Troubleshooting Platform.
- Reliability Monitor enables you to learn about the relative stability of a system in recent history.
- To fix common startup problems, use the Startup Repair tool, which is available in the list of System Recovery Options in the Windows Recovery Environment.
- To check physical memory for errors, use Windows Memory Diagnostic.
- To check a physical disk for errors, use Chkdsk.
- To check a physical disk for fragmentation, use Disk Defragmenter.

Lesson Review

You can use the following questions to test your knowledge of the information in Lesson 1, "Using Windows 7 Hardware Troubleshooting Tools." The questions are also available on the companion CD if you prefer to review them in electronic form.

> **NOTE** **ANSWERS**
>
> Answers to these questions and explanations of why each answer choice is correct or incorrect are located in the "Answers" section at the end of the book.

1. You are an enterprise support technician for a large company. The help desk asks for your assistance in resolving a computer problem. The computer in question is running Windows 7 and has been experiencing system freezes with increasing frequency. The help desk staff informs you that except for critical Windows Updates, no software changes have been made to the system since the problem first appeared. In addition, a thorough virus scan has revealed no malware on the system.

   Which of the following tools is most likely to reveal a problem on the system that is consistent with the issue reported?

   A. Chkdsk

   B. Disk Defragmenter

   C. Startup Repair

   D. Device Manager

2. You are troubleshooting a system failure. When you turn the computer on, a message appears indicating that the partition table is invalid. You have verified that the system includes only a single volume, and that Windows 7 is installed on the volume.

   Which of the following tools should you first use to troubleshoot the problem reported?

   A. Chkdsk

   B. Reliability Monitor

   C. Windows Memory Diagnostic

   D. Startup Repair

Lesson 2: Troubleshooting Hardware Components

Whereas Lesson 1 introduced many tools in Windows 7 that you can use to troubleshoot hardware problems, this lesson introduces a targeted set of strategies for troubleshooting particular components.

When troubleshooting computer failures in general, your plan should be to narrow down the scope of the problem to determine first whether the failure is hardware- or software-related. Once you suspect that faulty hardware is responsible for the computer failure, you can focus your troubleshooting efforts on a particular hardware component (such as the motherboard or hard disk) to determine whether that component is the cause of the failure. Knowing which component to troubleshoot first requires a basic understanding of the computer boot process. It also requires you to know the typical behaviors associated with the failure of each component.

In this lesson, you learn basic procedures for troubleshooting the four hardware components that are most often responsible for computer failures: the power supply unit, the motherboard, RAM, and hard disks. In the process, you learn the behaviors associated with the failure of these component types.

> **After this lesson, you will be able to:**
> - Use several tools in Windows 7 to diagnose hardware failures.
>
> **Estimated lesson time: 30 minutes**

Distinguishing Hardware Failures from Software Failures

When a computer system fails, you should first try to determine whether the failure is a result of software or hardware errors. This determination isn't always easy. Though some hardware-related failures are simple to distinguish from software-related ones, others (for example, those resulting from a damaged memory module) exhibit behaviors remarkably similar to software-related failures.

In general, however, the following rule applies to failures caused by faulty hardware.

A system failure is caused by a hardware problem when one of the following occurs:

- The failure occurs before the operating system loads.
- The failure occurs randomly, in a way that suggests no relation to any particular software activity.

If you suspect that a system failure is caused by a hardware problem, you can use the information in this lesson along with the tools described in Lesson 1 to diagnose the particular nature of the problem.

Understanding the Boot Process

If a hardware device is not functioning, this problem often reveals itself before the operating system loads. For this reason, when you are troubleshooting hardware issues, it is important to understand in a computer boot sequence the steps that precede the start of the operating system. If you can observe at what point the failure occurs, familiarity with this sequence can help you pinpoint the particular component that is failing.

The following steps summarize the boot sequence, up to and including the load of the operating system:

1. Power on.

   During this phase, the power supply feeds power to the motherboard and the CPU (chip).

2. Perform instructions contained in the BIOS.

   Once the CPU has power, it immediately starts executing the instructions that are written in the BIOS. The BIOS is an example of firmware, or low-level software that works closely with hardware. A computer's *BIOS* contains the processor-dependent code that is responsible for testing basic hardware functionality of the computer and for passing control to the boot device.

   The BIOS also contains software interfaces to hardware that enable the operating system to use features such as power management, virtualization, hot swapping, and booting from universal serial bus (USB) devices.

> **NOTE   EXTENSIBLE FIRMWARE INTERFACE (EFI)**
>
> EFI is an advanced replacement for BIOS that is beginning to appear in some new computers. Whether a computer uses BIOS or EFI for its firmware, the essential role of this firmware in the computer's boot process is the same.

   During the boot phase, the instructions in the BIOS consist of two steps:

   a. Perform the power on self test (POST)

      The POST is the hardware check that is performed by the BIOS as soon as the computer is turned on. When the POST detects a hardware error such as a failed video device, it signals the error with a beep code indicating the type of failure detected.

   b. Read instructions on the boot device

      The second function performed by the BIOS is to pass control to the boot device and read the instructions on that boot device. The boot device should be the device on which the operating system is stored. Typically, this boot device is an internal hard disk, but in the BIOS Setup program, you can specify the order of devices that you want the BIOS to investigate for boot code.

3. Operating system loads from boot device.

If the boot sequence fails to reach this point, the problem can be the result of an incorrectly configured selection of boot device in the BIOS Setup program, of a faulty Master Boot Record (MBR) on the hard disk, of a failed driver (typically for a SCSI hard drive), or of a hardware failure.

It is worth mentioning that if a computer crashes after the operating system begins to load from the boot device, the failure is somewhat more likely to be the result of a software problem than a hardware problem. But this is not a rule; hardware-related crashes can occur at any time.

EXAM TIP

You might need to upgrade your BIOS to enable certain features such as booting from a USB or network device.

> **NOTE BASIC TROUBLESHOOTING STRATEGY**
>
> When troubleshooting, always begin by taking the overall least risky, costly, and difficult action that can help you narrow down or identify the source of the problem. Then, if you need more information to identify the problem, take the overall next-least risky, costly, and difficult action, and so on.

Troubleshooting the Power Supply Unit

The power supply unit converts AC current from the wall outlet into DC current at the proper voltages needed by various computer components such as the motherboard.

The following section provides a set of basic strategies for troubleshooting power supply problems.

> **CAUTION UNPLUG YOUR COMPUTER BEFORE OPENING THE CASE!**
>
> Do not touch internal components when a computer is plugged in. You can electrocute yourself or seriously damage the computer. Note also that computer circuits are extremely sensitive to static electricity, even at levels that we can't feel. Before you touch any components, always ground yourself by first touching the metal structure of the computer case.

The computer appears dead. (There are no fans, lights, sounds, or signs of movement when you attempt to start it.)

1. Verify that the wall outlet is working.
2. Verify that the power cords are properly attached to the wall outlet, to the computer, and to the motherboard. (Remember that most modern motherboards require two power connectors.)

3. Verify that any internal power switch is turned on. If such a switch exists and is turned on, and if the power supply works in another computer, replace the switch.

4. If your power supply has a voltage switch, verify that the switch is set to the proper AC voltage for your country.

5. If the previous steps do not uncover the source of the problem, replace the power supply.

The computer freezes before the operating system starts.

1. Compare the power requirements of your devices with the power capacity of the power supply unit. Verify that the power supply unit provides the wattage necessary to power all the computer devices in your computer. If not, replace the power supply with a more powerful unit.

2. Test with a multimeter to determine whether the power supply unit is supplying correct and consistent voltage to the machine. If not, replace the power supply.

The computer suddenly shuts off at unpredictable moments.

1. Verify that the power supply unit fan is working. If not, you can replace just the power supply fan.

2. Verify that the motherboard fan is working. Replace this fan if necessary.

3. Run Windows Memory Diagnostic to check your RAM for hardware faults, as described in Lesson 1 of this chapter.

4. Run motherboard diagnostic software to check the functionality of the motherboard. To obtain this software, consult the motherboard manufacturer.

5. If the previous steps do not uncover the source of the problem, replace the entire power supply unit.

The power supply unit is making a loud, continuous noise.

Replace the power supply unit.

Troubleshooting the Motherboard

The motherboard is the main component of the computer. It includes the CPU or CPUs, slots for memory modules; expansion slots for other devices; and (typically with modern motherboards) built-in components and related ports for Ethernet, sound, video, and USB.

Figure 1-37 shows a modern motherboard with built-in components for video, USB, Ethernet, and audio.

The following section provides a set of basic strategies for troubleshooting motherboard problems.

When you attempt to start the computer, you see no video and hear no beep codes.

1. Disconnect all external accessories, such as external drives and PC cards, and then attempt to restart the computer. If you can start the computer, attempt to isolate the problem device by attaching one more device and restarting and until the failure reappears. Once you determine the external device that is causing the problem, contact the device manufacturer for further troubleshooting instructions.

FIGURE 1-37 Modern motherboards usually include built-in components for video, USB, Ethernet, and audio.

2. Verify that the monitor is in fact receiving power and is plugged into the computer.

3. Verify that the power supply fan is running. If it is not running, troubleshoot the power supply.

4. Verify that all required power connectors are plugged into the motherboard and into other computer devices. (Remember that most modern motherboards require two power connectors.)

5. Verify that any internal power switch is turned on.

6. If your power supply has a voltage switch, verify that the switch is set to the proper AC voltage for your country.

7. Verify that the motherboard is seated properly and that the CPU is fitted properly in its slot.

8. Verify that your RAM modules are seated properly and in the correct slots according to the motherboard manufacturer's specifications.

9. Run Windows Memory Diagnostic and replace any RAM modules if necessary.

10. Reset the BIOS to default settings. (To learn how to do this, consult the manual for the motherboard. Note that you can also reset the BIOS by removing the battery on the motherboard for 30 minutes.)

11. Use the manual for the motherboard to verify that any jumpers on the motherboard are properly set.

12. If your computer has no internal speaker (which would allow you to hear beep codes), replace the video card.

13. Replace the power supply unit.

14. Replace the motherboard.

When you turn on the computer, you hear beep codes, but the computer fails to start.

1. Disconnect all external accessories such as external drives and PC cards, and then attempt to restart the computer. If you can start the computer, attempt to isolate the problem device by attaching one more device and restarting until the failure reappears.

2. Consult the motherboard manual or manufacturer Web site to determine the meaning of the beep code you hear.

3. Try to fix the faulty component denoted by the beep code. This step might include attaching power connectors, reseating components such as RAM or the CPU, resetting the BIOS, or resetting motherboard jumpers.

4. If necessary, replace the faulty component denoted by the beep code.

The computer repeatedly loses power whenever it runs for a number of minutes.

1. Verify that the CPU fan on the motherboard is working. If not, replace the CPU fan.

2. Adjust the environment around the computer so that hot air cannot build up in its vicinity. (Laptops are especially sensitive to this.)

The computer shuts down randomly at unpredictable intervals.

1. Run Windows Memory Diagnostic to check your RAM for hardware faults, as described in Lesson 1 of this chapter.

2. Run motherboard diagnostic software to check the functionality of the motherboard. To obtain this software, consult the motherboard manufacturer.

3. Adjust the environment around the computer so that hot air cannot build up in its vicinity. (Laptops are especially sensitive to this.)

The operating system cannot use power management, virtualization, USB or network boot, hot swapping, or other features that are supported by your hardware.

Enable the desired feature in the BIOS Setup program.

Troubleshooting RAM

In the context of personal computers, the term *RAM* refers specifically to the volatile, dynamic random access memory supplied by modules such as dual inline memory modules (DIMMs). This type of memory is used to store relatively large amounts of data in a location that the processor can access quickly. An important limitation of computer RAM is that it can store data only when power is supplied to it.

The most typical symptom of a memory problem is a system crash or stop error in Windows. When these errors occur, you might see a message explicitly indicating a memory problem. However, memory problems can also prevent Windows from starting in the first place. If you see an error message directly related to memory, or if you need to rule out faulty memory as the cause of computer crashes or startup failures, perform the following steps:

1. Run Windows Memory Diagnostic software, as described in Lesson 1 of this chapter.
2. If no errors are found, or if some of the installed RAM is not recognized, do the following:
    a. Verify that the memory modules are seated properly.
    b. Verify that the memory modules are seated in the proper slots according to the motherboard manufacturer's specifications.
    c. Verify that the memory used is the type required according to the motherboard manufacturer's specifications.
    d. If the problem persists, remove all modules, clean the memory slots, insert one module in the first slot, and then restart the computer. Use this method to test all your memory modules.

Troubleshooting Hard Disks

Described technically, a hard disk drive represents a type of non-volatile memory storage device that encodes data on a spinning magnetic platter. Though the technology is decades old, it is still the most common type of computer storage today. However, hard disk drives are starting to be replaced by alternative forms of non-volatile storage, such as solid-state drives.

The following section provides a set of basic strategies for troubleshooting hard disk problems.

You hear a loud whirring, screeching, or clicking.

1. Back up your data. The hard drive could be about to fail.
2. Replace the drive.

The operating system fails to start, and you receive an error message similar to any of the following:

```
Hard disk error.
Invalid partition table.
A disk-read error occurred.
Couldn't find loader.
```

1. Verify that the BIOS Setup program is configured to boot from the hard drive.
2. Verify that the hard drive contains an operating system.
3. Run the Startup Repair tool, as described in Lesson 1 of this chapter.
4. Verify that the power connectors are attached to the hard drive.
5. Verify that any jumpers on your hard drives are configured properly according to manufacturer specifications.
6. Attempt to recover the disk by using the System Image Recovery option.
7. Replace the hard drive.

The operating system loads, but performance gradually decreases over time.

Run Disk Defragmenter, as described in Lesson 1 of this chapter.

The operating system loads, but you find evidence of data corruption.

OR

The system occasionally freezes and remains unresponsive.

1. Run Chkdsk, as described in Lesson 1 of this chapter.

2. Run software diagnostics from the hard disk drive manufacturer to test the physical functionality of the hard disk drive.

 Quick Check

- Is a system freeze more likely to be the result of damage to the hard disk or the RAM?

Quick Check Answer

- A system freeze is more likely to be the result of damage to the hard disk.

MORE INFO **TROUBLESHOOTING HARDWARE COMPONENTS**

For more detailed guidance about troubleshooting hardware components, see *Computer Repair with Diagnostic Flowcharts: Troubleshooting PC Hardware Problems from Boot Failure to Poor Performance, Revised Edition* (Foner Books, 2008), by Morris Rosenthal. You can find substantial excerpts from this book at *http://www.fonerbooks.com/pcrepair.htm*.

PRACTICE **Testing Specific Hardware Components**

In this practice, you run diagnostics to test the integrity of your computer memory and hard disk.

EXERCISE 1 Testing your RAM with Windows Memory Diagnostic

In this exercise, you restart your computer, open the Windows Boot Manager menu, choose Windows Memory Diagnostic, and perform a memory test.

1. Remove all CD or DVD discs from the local drives on a computer that is running Windows 7.

2. Start or restart the computer.

3. As the computer is starting, press the spacebar repeatedly (once per second is sufficiently fast).

   The Windows Boot Manager menu appears.

4. Press the Tab key to select Windows Memory Diagnostic on the Windows Boot Manager menu, and then press Enter.

   The Windows Memory Diagnostic tool opens.

5. Review the contents of the screen, and then press F1 to open the Options screen.

6. In the Options screen, use the Tab key, arrow keys, and number keys to set the test mix to Basic and the pass count to 1.

7. Press F10 to apply the new settings.

8. A quick memory test begins. After the memory test is complete, Windows restarts automatically. Soon after you next log on, a notification bubble will appear indicating whether any errors were found.

EXERCISE 2 Testing Your Hard Disk with Chkdsk

In this exercise, you log on to Windows 7, open an elevated command prompt, and run the Chkdsk command from the command line.

1. Log on to Windows 7 and open an elevated command prompt. You can do this by selecting Start\All Programs\Accessories\, right-clicking Command Prompt, selecting Run As Administrator from the shortcut menu, and then clicking Yes on the User Account Control message prompt that appears.

2. At the command prompt, type **chkdsk /?**.

3. Read the output and review the options available with the Chkdsk command.

4. At the command prompt, type **chkdsk c: /f /v /i /c**.

   (If your system drive is assigned a letter other than C:, then replace the **c:** in this command with the drive letter to which you have assigned the system drive. For example, if your system drive is assigned E:, then you should type **chkdsk e: /f /v /i /c**.)

   This set of options automatically fixes errors (*/f*) that are found and displays cleanup messages (*/v*). However, Chkdsk performs a faster test that skips certain types of checks (*/i* and */c*).

5. A message output appears, indicating that Chkdsk cannot run because it is in use by another process and asks if you would like to schedule the volume to be checked the next time the system restarts.

   This message appears because the volume you have chosen to test is currently being used to run Windows. You can run Chkdsk only on a volume that is not otherwise in use.

6. Type **Y**, and then restart the system.

7. When Windows restarts, a message appears while Chkdsk is being run and indicates that because the */i* and */c* options were specified, the disk could still be corrupt even if no errors are found.

   When Chkdsk finishes, Windows starts automatically.

Lesson Summary

- Begin troubleshooting a computer failure by trying to determine whether the problem is related to hardware or software.

- Once you determine that a failure is hardware-related, choose a particular component to troubleshoot. Use your familiarity with the computer boot sequence and with hardware failure behavior in general to determine which hardware component to troubleshoot first.

- The steps for troubleshooting hardware components are specific to each component.

Lesson Review

You can use the following questions to test your knowledge of the information in Lesson 2, "Troubleshooting Hardware Components." The questions are also available on the companion CD if you prefer to review them in electronic form.

NOTE ANSWERS

Answers to these questions and explanations of why each answer choice is correct or incorrect are located in the "Answers" section at the end of the book.

1. You are troubleshooting a problem on a computer running Windows 7. The computer is configured with an external hot-swappable Serial Advanced Technology Attachments (SATA) drive. However, whenever you turn off the drive and remove a disk, the removal generates errors.

   Which of the following steps is most likely to enable you to hot-swap the disk in the drive without generating errors?

   A. Enable the High Performance power plan in Control Panel.

   B. Run Chkdsk on the disks.

   C. Ensure that the jumpers on internal Integrated Development Environment (IDE) drives are configured properly.

   D. Upgrade the BIOS and ensure that it is configured properly.

2. You are troubleshooting a computer that is running Windows 7. The computer is shared by an administrator at night and a non-administrator during the day. The non-administrator is complaining that the performance seems to be sluggish. Thorough virus testing has detected no malware on the system. The Action Center, Reliability Monitor, Event Viewer, and Device Manager reveal nothing out of the ordinary.

   Which of the following troubleshooting steps should you perform next?

   A. Run Chkdsk.

   B. Use Disk Defragmenter to analyze the disk for fragmentation.

   C. Run Startup Repair.

   D. Run Windows Memory Diagnostic.

Chapter Review

To further practice and reinforce the skills you learned in this chapter, you can perform the following tasks:

- Review the chapter summary.
- Review the list of key terms introduced in this chapter.
- Complete the case scenarios. These scenarios set up real-world situations involving the topics of this chapter and ask you to create a solution.
- Complete the suggested practices.
- Take a practice test.

Chapter Summary

- Windows 7 includes several tools that you can use to diagnose problems related to hardware.
- When troubleshooting hardware, it is very useful to learn the various troubleshooting strategies that are particular to each type of component.

Key Terms

Do you know what these key terms mean? You can check your answers by looking up the terms in the glossary at the end of the book.

- **Action Center**
- **basic input/output system (BIOS)**
- **Chkdsk**
- **Disk Defragmenter**
- **Reliability Monitor**
- **Startup Repair**
- **System Recovery Options**
- **troubleshooting pack**
- **Windows Boot Manager**
- **Windows Memory Diagnostic**
- **Windows Recovery Environment**

Case Scenarios

In the following case scenarios, you apply what you've learned about subjects covered in this chapter. You can find answers to these questions in the "Answers" section at the end of this book.

Case Scenario 1: Troubleshooting Stop Errors

You work as an enterprise support technician in a large firm. Your manager asks you to troubleshoot a computer that has been removed from a user's desk. The user has reported a number of stop errors in the past week, and these errors appeared while he was reading Web pages. The computer is running Windows 7.

After you log on to the computer, you find that the Action Center and Event Viewer contain no information that is pertinent to the issue you are investigating.

With the following facts in mind, answer the following questions:

1. Which tool could you use to determine how long the problem has been occurring?
2. If you learn that the problem started occurring soon after a memory upgrade, what troubleshooting tool should you use next?
3. If you find errors with the new memory module, what action should you recommend to fix the problem?

Case Scenario 2: Troubleshooting System Crashes

You work as an enterprise support technician for Humongous Insurance, an Atlanta-based automobile insurance company with 250 employees. The main office branch includes 200 client computers running Windows 7 and 10 servers running Windows Server 2008.

You receive a call from the help desk informing you about a problem that the help desk support technician was unable to resolve. An insurance agent's computer has crashed without warning several times today. You interview both the insurance agent and the help desk Support Technician.

Interviews

The following is a list of company personnel interviewed and their statements:

- **The insurance agent** "It's happened three times today already, and I keep losing my work. Each time I was working for about a number of minutes, and then it just loses power without warning. When the problem happened, once I was writing an e-mail, and the other two times, I was filling out forms."

- **The help desk support technician** "There were no errors in the Action Center. I ran a few troubleshooters, and no problems were found. I didn't see anything strange in Device Manager, and Windows has been updating properly. There are some errors in Event Viewer from the past few weeks, but I can't decipher them. The user says that there is no stop error when the computer restarts."

Questions

1. Why is this problem more likely to be hardware-related than software-related?

2. You confirm that the problem seems to occur about 15 minutes after booting. What should you check next?

Suggested Practices

To help you master the exam objectives presented in this chapter, complete the following tasks.

Identify and Resolve Hardware Failure Issues

Perform the following activities to develop your skills in troubleshooting hardware:

- **Practice 1**   Consult the manual for your motherboard. Memorize the beep codes associated with various types of hardware failures.

- **Practice 2**   From your motherboard manufacturer's Web site, download and run any utilities that test the functionality of your motherboard and associated chipsets.

- **Practice 3**   Run Windows Memory Diagnostic overnight, with the extended option and the pass count set to 20.

- **Practice 4**   From your hard disk drive manufacturer's Web site, download and run any utilities that test the functionality of your hard disk drive.

- **Practice 5**   As your computer is starting, press the key associated with the BIOS Setup program. In the BIOS Setup, read every option available, and then choose to exit the program without saving.

- **Practice 6**   From your motherboard manufacturer's Web site, determine whether a more recent version of your BIOS is available. If a more recent version is available, download and run this BIOS update.

Take a Practice Test

The practice tests on this book's companion CD offer many options. For example, you can test yourself on just one exam objective, or you can test yourself on all the 70-685 certification exam content. You can set up the test so that it closely simulates the experience of taking a certification exam, or you can set it up in study mode so that you can look at the correct answers and explanations after you answer each question.

> **MORE INFO   PRACTICE TESTS**
>
> For details about all the practice test options available, see the section entitled "How to Use the Practice Tests," in the Introduction to this book.

CHAPTER 2

Networking

Because users depend on network resources to use critical applications such as e-mail, you must be able to diagnose common network problems quickly. Windows 7 can diagnose many common problems automatically and includes tools that you can use to test other conditions manually. This chapter teaches you how to configure network settings on computers running Windows 7 and how to troubleshoot problems when they arise.

Wireless networks are becoming increasingly common, and most mobile computers regularly connect to one or more wireless networks. Many traveling users connect to dozens of wireless networks—some at the office, some in their homes, and some at public wireless hotspots in coffee shops or airports.

To ensure that users can stay connected, you must understand how to configure and troubleshoot both wired and wireless networks. This chapter teaches you how to use network troubleshooting tools to diagnose and resolve connectivity problems, including name resolution problems.

Exam objectives in this chapter:

- Identify and resolve network connectivity issues.
- Identify and resolve names resolution issues.
- Identify and resolve wireless connectivity issues.

Lessons in this chapter:

Before You Begin

To complete the lessons in this chapter, you should be familiar with Windows 7 and be comfortable with the following tasks:

- Installing Windows 7
- Physically connecting a computer to a network
- Configuring a wireless access point
- Performing basic administration tasks on a Windows Server 2008 R2–based domain controller

To complete the practices in Lesson 3, "Troubleshooting Wireless Networks," you must have a wireless access point and a computer that is running Windows 7 and has a wireless network adapter.

 REAL WORLD

Tony Northrup

This chapter teaches you to use a variety of different network troubleshooting tools, including Ping, PathPing, Nslookup, and Ipconfig. The most important troubleshooting tool, however, is the one that requires almost no training: Windows Network Diagnostics. Windows Network Diagnostics automates the process of diagnosing network problems, and it can even automatically resolve many problems related to network configuration.

Automating diagnosis eliminates many aspects of human error. When I used to troubleshoot network problems manually, I often started with a hunch. For example, if the router had failed in the past, I might assume that the problem was the router and attempt to ping it. If the ping failed, I'd assume that that confirmed my hunch—however, the failed ping could also have been caused by a failed network adapter, an IP misconfiguration, or a firewall setting. I might have even mistyped the router's IP address.

Sometimes, starting with a hunch can save you time. If your hunch is wrong, however, you can waste hours trying to fix a problem that doesn't exist. Windows Network Diagnostics never starts with a hunch, but it's not wasting time, because it performs complex diagnostics in just a few seconds. It never skips steps, forgets to check something, or makes a typo.

In the real world, Windows Network Diagnostics should always be the first place you start troubleshooting. You can then use the other troubleshooting tools to confirm the problem or perform additional diagnosis if Windows Network Diagnostics doesn't give you a useful answer.

Lesson 1: Troubleshooting Network Connectivity

If a network adapter, network cable, switch, router, Internet connection, or server fails, it appears to a user that he can't connect to a network. Often, this means that he can't do his job, making it critical that you identify and solve the problem quickly. Because network failures can be caused by many different components, it is important that you understand how each component works and the tools that you can use to identify whether any given component has failed. This lesson describes how to identify the source of network connectivity problems and, when possible, resolve the problem.

After this lesson, you will be able to:

- Use Windows Network Diagnostics to troubleshoot common network problems automatically.
- Use Ping, PathPing, PortQry, and Nslookup to troubleshoot network problems manually.
- Troubleshoot problems connecting to shared folders.
- Troubleshoot an Automatic Private IP Addressing (APIPA) address.
- Troubleshoot a name resolution problem.
- Troubleshoot a network or application connectivity problem.

Estimated lesson time: 45 minutes

How to Use Windows Network Diagnostics

Windows 7 includes diagnostic tools that automate the process of testing for common network problems. Windows 7 can also automatically fix many network problems that are configuration-related or that simply require the network adapter to be reset.

There are several ways to start Windows Network Diagnostics:

- In the system tray, right-click the network icon and click Troubleshoot Problems, as shown in Figure 2-1.

FIGURE 2-1 You can start Windows Network Diagnostics from the networking icon in the system tray.

- Open Network And Sharing Center (for example, by right-clicking the networking icon in the system tray and then clicking Open Network And Sharing Center). On the Network Map, click the link with an X over it (as shown in Figure 2-2).

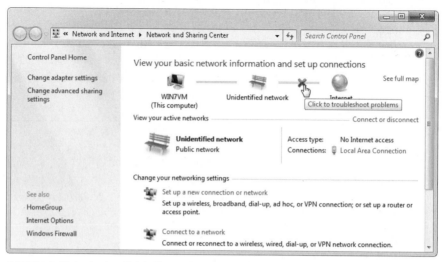

FIGURE 2-2 Click a broken link in Network And Sharing Center to diagnose a problem.

- Open Network And Sharing Center. Near the bottom of the right pane, click the Troubleshoot Problems link.

- From the Network Connections page in Control Panel, right-click a network adapter and then click Diagnose.

- When Windows Internet Explorer is unable to access a Web site, click the Diagnose Connection Problems link.

- Hold down the Windows logo key and press R to open the Run dialog box. Type **rundll32.exe ndfapi,NdfRunDllDiagnoseIncident** (a case-sensitive command), and then press Enter.

After Windows Network Diagnostics completes diagnostics, it displays a list of detected problems. For example, Figure 2-3 shows that the computer was connected to the network properly but that the Domain Name System (DNS) server was unavailable. An unavailable DNS server resembles a complete connectivity failure because no computers identified by a host name are available; however, solving the problem requires either configuring a different DNS server IP address or bringing the DNS server back online.

Figure 2-4 shows a problem that Windows Network Diagnostics solved: a disabled network adapter. In this scenario, the user simply followed the wizard prompts to reenable the network adapter.

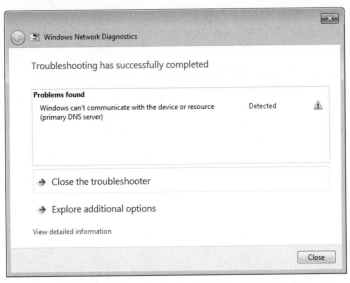

FIGURE 2-3 Use Windows Network Diagnostics to quickly identify problems that would be time-consuming for a person to isolate.

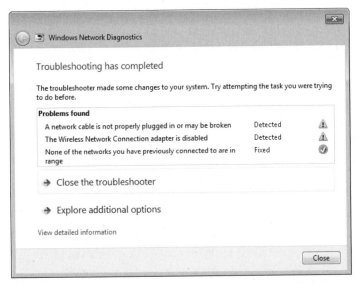

FIGURE 2-4 Windows Network Diagnostics can solve some configuration problems automatically.

Windows Network Diagnostics records detailed information about the troubleshooting process that you can use to further isolate the problem, if necessary. To view detailed Windows Network Diagnostics information after running Windows Network Diagnostics, follow these steps:

1. Click Start, right-click Computer, and then click Manage.

2. Select Computer Management, System Tools, Event Viewer, Windows Logs, and finally System.

3. In the Actions pane, click Filter Current Log.

4. In the Filter Current Log dialog box, click the Event Sources list, and then select Diagnostics-Networking. Click OK.

5. The Event Viewer snap-in displays a list of events generated by Windows Network Diagnostics with detailed information about every troubleshooting session.

Network Troubleshooting Tools

If Windows Network Diagnostics does not isolate the source of the problem, Windows 7 provides many tools you can use to perform manual troubleshooting. The sections that follow describe the most important tools. Later, this chapter will describe how to use each tool to troubleshoot specific network problems.

Ipconfig

The network troubleshooting tool that most administrators use to begin diagnosing a problem is the command-line tool Ipconfig. Ipconfig can be used in many different ways, which are discussed throughout this chapter.

To view the computer's current IP configuration quickly, run the following command:

```
C:\ipconfig /all
Windows IP Configuration

    Host Name . . . . . . . . . . . . : WIN7
    Primary Dns Suffix  . . . . . . . :
    Node Type . . . . . . . . . . . . : Mixed
    IP Routing Enabled. . . . . . . . : No
    WINS Proxy Enabled. . . . . . . . : No


Ethernet adapter Local Area Connection:

    Media State . . . . . . . . . . . : Media disconnected
    Connection-specific DNS Suffix  . :
    Description . . . . . . . . . . . : Broadcom NetXtreme 57xx Gigabit Controller
    Physical Address. . . . . . . . . : 00-15-C5-07-BF-34
    DHCP Enabled. . . . . . . . . . . : Yes
    Autoconfiguration Enabled . . . . : Yes


Wireless LAN adapter Wireless Network Connection:

    Connection-specific DNS Suffix  . :
    Description . . . . . . . . . . . : Intel(R) PRO/Wireless 3945ABG Network Connection
    Physical Address. . . . . . . . . : 00-13-02-1E-E6-59
    DHCP Enabled. . . . . . . . . . . : Yes
    Autoconfiguration Enabled . . . . : Yes
    IPv4 Address. . . . . . . . . . . : 192.168.1.130(Preferred)
    Subnet Mask . . . . . . . . . . . : 255.255.255.0
```

```
Lease Obtained. . . . . . . . . . : Wednesday, August 05, 2009 12:48:35 PM
Lease Expires . . . . . . . . . . : Thursday, August 06, 2009 12:48:34 PM
Default Gateway . . . . . . . . . : 192.168.1.1
DHCP Server . . . . . . . . . . . : 192.168.1.1
DNS Servers . . . . . . . . . . . : 192.168.0.1
NetBIOS over Tcpip. . . . . . . . : Enabled
```

If you examine the sample output, you'll notice that the Gigabit wired Ethernet controller is disconnected. The computer is connected to a wireless network, however, and a Dynamic Host Configuration Protocol (DHCP) server has assigned it the Internet Protocol (IP) address 192.168.1.130. The default gateway is at IP address 192.168.1.1, and the DNS server is at IP address 192.168.0.1.

You can also use Ipconfig to update a computer's IP configuration. If a computer has been assigned an IP address automatically by a DHCP server (as most clients are), you can acquire a new IPv4 address by running the following two commands:

```
ipconfig /release
ipconfig /renew
```

To acquire a new IPv6 address, run the following two commands:

```
ipconfig /release6
ipconfig /renew6
```

Ipconfig also has DNS troubleshooting capabilities, as described in Lesson 2, "Troubleshooting Name Resolution."

Ping

Ping is the best-known network diagnostic tool. Unfortunately, as more and more computers and routers block Internet Control Message Protocol (ICMP) requests (ICMP is the network protocol Ping uses), it has become less useful over time. Ping still works on most local area networks (LANs), however.

To use Ping, open a command prompt and run the command Ping *host name*. For example:

```
C:\>ping www.contoso.com
Pinging contoso.com [207.46.197.32] with 32 bytes of data:

Reply from 207.46.197.32: bytes=32 time=95ms TTL=105
Reply from 207.46.197.32: bytes=32 time=210ms TTL=105
Reply from 207.46.197.32: bytes=32 time=234ms TTL=105
Reply from 207.46.197.32: bytes=32 time=258ms TTL=105

Ping statistics for 207.46.197.32:
    Packets: Sent = 4, Received = 4, Lost = 0 (0% loss),
Approximate round trip times in milli-seconds:
    Minimum = 95ms, Maximum = 258ms, Average = 199ms
```

Ping tells you several useful things. If you receive replies, you know that the network host is turned on and connected to the network. The time, measured in milliseconds (ms), indicates the round-trip latency between you and the remote host. *Latency* is the delay between sending a packet and receiving a response, and it is caused by the time that it takes routers to forward packets between networks and the time that signals take to traverse electrical or fiber optic links. If the latency is greater than a second, all network communications probably seem very slow.

Many hosts do not respond to Ping requests even though they are online. For example, the Microsoft.com Web servers drop ICMP requests even though they are online and will respond to Web requests, as the following sample demonstrates:

```
C:\>ping www.microsoft.com
Pinging lb1.www.microsoft.com [10.46.20.60] with 32 bytes of data:

Request timed out.
Request timed out.
Request timed out.
Request timed out.

Ping statistics for 10.46.20.60:
    Packets: Sent = 4, Received = 0, Lost = 4 (100% loss),
```

You can use Ping as a very simplistic network monitoring tool if you are waiting for a remote computer to turn off or on. To ping a host continually, use the –t parameter, as the following example demonstrates. Ping sends requests until you press Ctrl+C to cancel the command or you close the command prompt:

```
C:\>ping www.contoso.com –t
```

PathPing

Although Ping uses ICMP to test connectivity to a specific host, PathPing uses ICMP to test connectivity to a remote host and all routers between you and the remote host. This can help you identify problems in the way your network is routing traffic, such as routing loops (where traffic crosses the same router more than once), a failed router (which might make it seem like the entire network has failed), or poor network performance. Figure 2-5 demonstrates how PathPing functions.

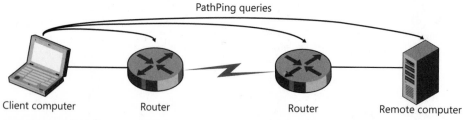

FIGURE 2-5 PathPing sends requests to every host between the client and a destination.

Use PathPing in the exact same way as Ping. PathPing attempts to list every router between you and the destination (just as Tracert would). Then, PathPing spends a few minutes calculating statistics for the entire route:

```
C:\>pathping www.contoso.com
Tracing route to contoso.com [10.46.196.103]over a maximum of 30 hops:  0  contoso-test
[192.168.1.207]   1   10.211.240.1    2   10.128.191.245    3   10.128.191.73
4  10.125.39.213    5  gbr1-p70.cb1ma.ip.contoso.com [10.123.40.98]
6  tbr2-p013501.cb1ma.ip.contoso.com [10.122.11.201]    7  tbr2-p012101.cgcil.ip.contoso
.com [10.122.10.106]   8  gbr4-p50.st6wa.ip.contoso.com [10.122.2.54]
9  gar1-p370.stwwa.ip.contoso.com [10.123.203.177]  10  10.127.70.6  11  10.46.33.225
12  10.46.36.210  13  10.46.155.17  14  10.46.129.51  15  10.46.196.103
```

```
Computing statistics for 625 seconds...            Source to Here    This Node/LinkHop
RTT     Lost/Sent = Pct  Lost/Sent = Pct  Address   0
contoso-test [192.168.1.207]                              0/ 100 =  0%   |  1    50ms
1/ 100 =  1%     1/ 100 =  1%  10.211.24.1                        0/ 100 =  0%
|  2    50ms      0/ 100 =  0%     0/ 100 =  0%  10.128.19.245
0/ 100 =  0%   |  3    50ms     2/ 100 =  2%     2/ 100 =  2%  10.128.19.73
0/ 100 =  0%   |  4    44ms     0/ 100 =  0%     0/ 100 =  0%  10.12.39.213
0/ 100 =  0%   |  5    46ms     0/ 100 =  0%     0/ 100 =  0%  gbr1-p70.cb1ma.ip.contoso
.com [10.12.40.98]
0/ 100 =  0%   |  6    40ms     2/ 100 =  2%     2/ 100 =  2%
tbr2-p013501.cb1ma.ip.contoso.com [10.12.11.201]
0/ 100 =  0%   |  7    62ms     1/ 100 =  1%     1/ 100 =  1%
tbr2-p012101.cgcil.ip.contoso.com [10.12.10.106]
0/ 100 =  0%   |  8   107ms     2/ 100 =  2%     2/ 100 =  2%  gbr4-p50.st6wa.ip.contoso
.com [10.12.2.54]
0/ 100 =  0%   |  9   111ms     0/ 100 =  0%     0/ 100 =  0%  gar1-p370.stwwa.
ip.contoso.com [10.12.203.177]
0/ 100 =  0%   | 10   118ms     0/ 100 =  0%     0/ 100 =  0%  10.12.70.6
0/ 100 =  0%   | 11   ---     100/ 100 =100%   100/ 100 =100%  10.46.33.225
0/ 100 =  0%   | 12   ---     100/ 100 =100%   100/ 100 =100%  10.46.36.210
0/ 100 =  0%   | 13   123ms     0/ 100 =  0%     0/ 100 =  0%  10.46.155.17
0/ 100 =  0%   | 14   127ms     0/ 100 =  0%     0/ 100 =  0%  10.46.129.51
1/ 100 =  1%   | 15   125ms     1/ 100 =  1%     0/ 100 =  0%  10.46.196.103 Trace
complete.
```

NOTE NETWORK LINGO

The term *hop* is another name for a router or gateway. *Node* or *link* are other names for a computer or router. RTT stands for "Round Trip Time," which is the time it takes a packet to get from the client to the destination, plus the time for the response to be returned to the client.

If the statistics show a single router with an extremely high latency, that node might be causing network problems. Typically, a router with high latency increases the latency for every router listed afterward. However, only the first router is experiencing the problem. If one router has high latency but the routers listed afterward have low latency, the latency probably isn't a sign of a problem. Routers handle ICMP requests at a lower priority than other traffic, so PathPing showing high latency isn't always indicative of overall latency.

You can often determine from the name of the router whether it is on your internal network, the network of your Internet service provider (ISP), or elsewhere on the Internet. If it is on your internal network or your ISP's network, contact your network administrator for troubleshooting assistance. If it is somewhere else on the network, there is probably nothing you can do but wait for the administrators of the router to solve the problem. However, if you contact your ISP, they might be able to contact the remote ISP to ensure that they are aware of the problem and to receive an estimate for when the problem will be solved.

To speed up the display of PathPing, use the *-d* command option to keep PathPing from attempting to resolve the name of each intermediate router address.

PortQry

Ping uses ICMP packets to test whether a remote computer is connected to the network. However, even if a computer responds to ICMP packets, it doesn't tell you whether the computer is running the network service that you need. For example, if you're having a problem downloading your e-mail, you need to test whether the mail service itself is responding, not whether the mail server is responding to ICMP requests.

PortQry tests whether a specific network service is running on a server. To use PortQry, open a command prompt and run the following command:

```
portqry -n destination -e portnumber
```

For example, the Hypertext Transfer Protocol (HTTP) uses TCP port 80. To test HTTP connectivity to *www.microsoft.com*, type the following command at the command line:

```
portqry -n www.microsoft.com -e 80
```

This command produces output that is similar to the following example:

```
Querying target system called:
 www.microsoft.com
Attempting to resolve name to IP address...
Name resolved to 10.209.68.190
TCP port 80 (http service): LISTENING
```

For a list of common port numbers, refer to the section entitled "How to Troubleshoot Application Connectivity Problems," later in this lesson.

Unfortunately, PortQry is not included with any version of Microsoft Windows, including Windows 7. Instead, you must download it from Microsoft.com at *http://www.microsoft.com/ downloads/details.aspx?FamilyID=89811747-C74B-4638-A2D5-AC828BDC6983*. When deploying Windows 7, consider adding PortQry to the %Windir%\System32\ folder so that it is readily available for troubleshooting.

If you are using a computer that does not have PortQry installed, you can use the Telnet client to test a remote service. For more information, read the section entitled "How to Troubleshoot Application Connectivity Problems," later in this lesson.

Nslookup

Use Nslookup to test whether your DNS server can properly resolve a host name to an IP address. For example:

```
C:\>nslookup contoso.com
Server:  dns.fabrikam.com
Address:  192.168.1.1:53

Non-authoritative answer:
Name:    contoso.com
Addresses:  207.46.232.182, 207.46.197.32
```

In the previous example, the client contacted the default DNS server (192.168.1.1) and successfully received a response indicating that contoso.com has two IP addresses: 207.46.232.182 and 207.46.197.32. This indicates that the DNS server is working correctly.

> **NOTE ROUND-ROBIN DNS ADDRESSING**
>
> Some host names, including contoso.com and microsoft.com, resolve to multiple IP addresses. Your Web browser is smart enough to connect to a different address if the first address isn't working properly, allowing multiple Web servers with different IP addresses to respond to requests for the same host name. This provides both scalability (the ability to handle more simultaneous requests) and redundancy (the ability for a website to stay online if one server fails).

The following response to the same query would indicate that the DNS server could not find an IP address for the contoso.com host name:

```
*** dns.fabrikam.com can't find contoso.com: Non-existent domain
```

The following response indicates that no DNS server is responding:

```
Server:  dns.fabrikam.com
Address:  192.168.1.1:53

DNS request timed out.
    timeout was 2 seconds.
```

```
DNS request timed out.
    timeout was 2 seconds.
*** Request to dns.fabrikam.com timed-out
```

Use Nslookup any time you think that a network problem might be caused by a failed DNS server or invalid name resolution. For more information about Nslookup, refer to Lesson 2.

 **Quick Check**

- Which tool would you use to determine whether a computer can communicate with the default gateway?

Quick Check Answer

- Ping is the quickest way. You could also run PathPing to check an Internet address, and it checks the default gateway along with every other gateway between you and the destination.

How to Troubleshoot an APIPA Address

Windows 7 assigns an *Automatic Private IP Addressing (APIPA)* address in the range 169.254.0.0 through 169.254.255.255 when the computer is configured to use automatic IP addressing but is unable to contact a DHCP server. APIPA addresses allow computers connected to a LAN without a DHCP server to communicate; however, they do not allow the computers to connect to non-APIPA computers.

An APIPA address can be caused by several problems:

- The DHCP server was temporarily unavailable.
- The computer was not connected to the network properly.
- The computer was not authorized to connect to the network.

As with most connectivity issues, you should use Windows Network Diagnostics as your first troubleshooting step. If that does not solve the problem, verify that the computer is connected to the local network and that the network hardware is functioning properly. Then, follow these steps to attempt to retrieve an IP address from a DHCP server:

1. Click Start. Type **cmd**, right-click Cmd in the Start menu, and then click Run As Administrator. This opens an administrative command prompt, which is required to renew the IP address.

2. At the command prompt, run the following two commands:

```
ipconfig /release
ipconfig /renew
```

The first command causes Windows 7 to drop the current IP configuration (if it has one), and the second command attempts to contact a DHCP server to retrieve an new configuration.

If the network adapter still has an APIPA address after running these commands and you are connected to the network, the DHCP server is either offline or has determined that your computer is not authorized to connect to the network. Bring a DHCP server online and then restart the computer. If the network does not use a DHCP server, configure a static or alternate IPv4 address provided by your network administrator.

 Quick Check

- How can you recognize an APIPA address?

Quick Check Answer

- It begins with 169.254.

 REAL WORLD

Tony Northrup

If you can't get an address from the DHCP server but you do seem to be connected to the network, try manually configuring an IP address on the computer. First, log on to a computer that is working properly on the network and make note of its IP address, subnet mask, default gateway, and DNS server addresses. Then, disconnect the computer from the network or shut it down completely. Now, configure the computer that can't connect to the network using the working computer's IP configuration. If everything works properly with the new configuration, you know the problem is just the DHCP server and not the network infrastructure.

After using this technique to determine whether the DHCP server is the cause of the problem, you should immediately reconfigure the computer to act as a DHCP client. Two computers on the same network cannot simultaneously have the same IP address.

How to Troubleshoot Connectivity Problems

Network connectivity problems prevent any application from accessing a network resource, whereas application connectivity problems prevent only specific applications from accessing resources. Most network connectivity problems result from one of the following issues (starting with the most likely):

- Misconfigured network adapter
- Misconfigured network hardware

- Failed network connection
- Faulty network cables
- Failed network adapter
- Failed network hardware

Application connectivity problems, however, tend to result from one of the following issues (starting with the most likely):

- The remote service is not running. For example, if you're trying to control a computer remotely, Remote Desktop might not be enabled on the remote computer.
- The remote server has a firewall configured that is blocking that application's communications from the client computer.
- A firewall between the client and server computer is blocking that application's communications.
- Windows Firewall on the local computer might be configured to block the application's traffic.
- The remote service has been configured to use a nondefault port number. For example, Web servers typically use TCP port 80, but some administrators might configure TCP port 81 or a different port.

The sections that follow describe how to troubleshoot network and application connectivity problems.

How to Troubleshoot Network Connectivity Problems Manually

To identify the source of a connectivity problem without using Windows Network Diagnostics, follow these steps and answer the questions until you are directed to a different section:

1. Click the networking notification icon in the system tray, and then click Open Network And Sharing Center.

   - If a red X is displayed over a network link, click the link to start Windows Network Diagnostics and follow the prompts that appear. If the red X is between the network and the Internet, the problem is with the Internet connection and not the local computer. Contact the network administrator for assistance.

   - If no network adapters appear, either a network adapter isn't present, network adapters are disabled, the hardware has failed, or the driver is not functioning. Re-enable any disabled network adapters. If the problem persists, restart the computer. If the network adapter is still not available, use Device Manager (Devmgmt.msc) to diagnose the problem. If possible, update the driver by using Microsoft Update or by checking the network adapter vendor's Web site.

2. Can other computers connect to the same network? If not, the problem is with the network and not the computer you're troubleshooting. Contact the network administrator for assistance.

3. Can you connect to other network resources? For example, if you can browse the Web but you can't connect to a shared folder, you are probably experiencing an application connectivity problem. For more information, read the section entitled "How to Troubleshoot Application Connectivity Problems," later in this lesson.

4. Open a command prompt and run **ipconfig /all.** Examine the output:

   ■ If the computer has an IP address in the range 169.254.0.0 through 169.254.255.255, the computer is configured to use DHCP addressing but a DHCP server was not available. Follow the instructions in the section entitled "How to Troubleshoot an APIPA Address," earlier in this chapter.

   ■ If you have a valid IP address but do not have a default gateway or a DNS server, the problem is caused by an invalid IP configuration. If the computer has a DHCP-assigned IP address, run **ipconfig /release** and **ipconfig /renew** from an administrative command prompt. If the computer has a manually configured IP address, obtain the correct configuration from a network administrator.

   ■ If no network adapters are listed, the computer either lacks a network adapter or (more likely) it does not have a valid driver installed. Use Device Manager to identify the network adapter and then install an updated driver. If the hardware has failed, replace the network adapter (or add a new network adapter if the network adapter is built in).

   ■ If all network adapters show a Media State of Media Disconnected, the computer is not physically connected to a network. Connect the computer to a wired or wireless network. If you are connected to a wired network and you still see this error, disconnect and reconnect both ends of the network cable. If the problem continues, replace the network cable. Attempt to connect a different computer to the same network cable; if the new computer can connect successfully, the original computer has a failed network adapter. If neither computer can connect successfully, the problem is with the network wiring, the network switch, or the network hub. Replace the network hardware as necessary.

   ■ If all network adapters show DHCP Enabled: No in the display of the *Ipconfig /all* command, the network adapter might be misconfigured. If DHCP is disabled, the computer has a static IPv4 address, which is an unusual configuration for client computers. Update the network adapter IPv4 configuration to Obtain An IP Address Automatically and Obtain DNS Server Address Automatically. Then, configure the Alternate Configuration tab of the IP Properties dialog box with the current static IP configuration.

5. If you have a valid IP address and you can ping your default gateway, open a command prompt and run the command "Nslookup <*servername*>." If Nslookup cannot resolve a valid name and does not display an answer similar to the following, you have a name resolution problem. See the section entitled "How to Troubleshoot Name Resolution Problems," in Lesson 2.

```
C:\>nslookup contoso.com
Non-authoritative answer:
Name:    contoso.com
Addresses:  10.46.232.182, 10.46.130.117
```

Those troubleshooting steps should allow you to identify the cause of most network problems.

 Quick Check

- Which two commands would you run to get a new IP address from the DHCP server?

Quick Check Answer

- *Ipconfig /release and Ipconfig /renew.*

How to Troubleshoot Application Connectivity Problems

If one application (or network protocol) works correctly but others don't, you are experiencing an application connectivity issue. To troubleshoot this type of problem, follow these steps:

1. Make sure that you do not have a name resolution problem by using Nslookup to query the server name you are trying to contact. If Nslookup cannot resolve the name, refer to Lesson 2.

2. Often, a firewall might block your application's communications. Before you can test whether this is the case, you must identify the network protocol and port number used by the application. Table 2-1 lists port numbers for common applications. If you are not sure which port numbers your application uses, consult the application's manual or contact the technical support team. Often, searching the Internet for the phrase "*<application_name>* port number" identifies the required port numbers. Sometimes, administrators change port numbers to nonstandard values. If that is the case, you will need to ask the administrator for the new port number.

TABLE 2-1 Default Port Assignments for Common Services and Tasks

SERVICE NAME OR TASK	USER DATAGRAM PROTOCOL (UDP)	TRANSMISSION CONTROL PROTOCOL (TCP)
Web servers, HTTP, and Internet Information Services (IIS)	—	80
Web servers that use Hypertext Transfer Protocol Secure (HTTPS)	—	443
File Transfer Protocol (FTP) servers		20, 21
DNS queries	53	53

SERVICE NAME OR TASK	USER DATAGRAM PROTOCOL (UDP)	TRANSMISSION CONTROL PROTOCOL (TCP)
DHCP client		67
File and printer sharing	137	139, 445
Internet Relay Chat (IRC)		6667
Incoming e-mail: Internet Mail Access Protocol (IMAP)		143
Incoming e-mail: IMAP (Secure Sockets Layer [SSL])		993
Incoming e-mail: Post Office Protocol 3 (POP3)		110
Incoming e-mail: POP3 (SSL)		995
Outgoing e-mail: Simple Mail Transfer Protocol (SMTP)		25
Connecting to an Active Directory Domain Services (AD DS) domain controller	389, 53, 88	135, 389, 636, 3268, 3269, 53, 88, 445
Network Management: Simple Network Management Protocol (SNMP)	161, 162	
SQL Server		1433
Telnet		23
Terminal Server, Remote Desktop, and Remote Assistance		3389
Virtual Machine Remote Control (VMRC) client for Microsoft Virtual Server 2005 R2		5900

3. After you identify the port numbers required by your application, test whether you can connect manually to that port on the server. If it is a TCP port, you can use either PortQry or Telnet. To test a TCP port with Telnet (which is available if you turn on the Telnet Client feature by using the Turn Windows Features On Or Off tool in Control Panel), run the following command:

```
Telnet <hostname_or_address> <TCP_port>
```

For example, to determine whether you can connect to the Web server at *www.microsoft.com* (which uses port 80), you would run the following command:

```
Telnet www.microsoft.com 80
```

If the command prompt clears or if you receive text from the remote service, you successfully established a connection, which means you do not have an application connectivity problem. Instead, you might have an authentication problem or there might be a problem with the client or server software.

If Telnet displays "Could not open connection to the host," this verifies that you do indeed have an application connectivity issue. Either the server is offline or a misconfigured firewall is blocking the application's network traffic. Follow these steps to continue troubleshooting the problem:

1. Verify that the server is online by connecting to a different service running on the same server. For example, if you are attempting to connect to a Web server and you know that the server has File Sharing enabled, attempt to connect to a shared folder. If you can connect to a different service, the problem is almost certainly a firewall configuration problem on the server. If you don't know that another service is running on the server, contact the server administrator to verify that it's running.

2. Attempt to connect from different computers on the same and different subnets. If you can connect from a computer on the same subnet, the problem is caused by a firewall or application configuration problem on your computer. Verify that a firewall exception is created either for your application or for the port numbers it uses. (For more information, see Chapter 5, "Protecting Client Systems.") If you can connect from a client computer on a different subnet but not from the same subnet, a firewall on the network or on the server is probably filtering traffic from your client network. Contact a network administrator for assistance.

PRACTICE   Troubleshoot a Connectivity Problem

In this practice, you troubleshoot two common network problems.

EXERCISE 1   Solve a Network Problem Automatically

In this exercise, you run a batch file to generate a networking problem, and then you troubleshoot it using Windows Network Diagnostics. This practice simulates a network problem on your computer. Before you run it, verify that you are connected to the network and can access network resources and be prepared to be disconnected from the network. Do not perform this exercise on a server or other computer that would affect users if it went offline.

1. After installing the practice files from the companion CD, browse to the installation folder on your computer. Then, right-click that file on your desktop and click Run As Administrator.

2. You can ignore the command window that appears; the batch file just simulates a networking failure. Now, you will troubleshoot the problem.

3. Open Internet Explorer and attempt to view a Web site. Notice that the Internet is not available.

4. Right-click the networking icon in the system tray (which should now have a red X over it) and then click Open Network And Sharing Center.

5. Network And Sharing Center appears and displays the Network Map.

6. Click the red X on the network map, which indicates that you are not connected to the LAN.

7. Follow the troubleshooting instructions that appear and try the repairs as an administrator when prompted. When Windows Network Diagnostics identifies the problem, click the solution that is presented to solve it.

   Windows Network Diagnostics fixes the network problem. Notice that the steps were simple enough that a user could have followed them. Although this exercise demonstrated the use of Network And Sharing Center to start Windows Network Diagnostics, you also could have clicked Diagnose Connection Problems from Internet Explorer or right-clicked the networking icon and then clicked Troubleshoot Problems.

EXERCISE 2   Solve a Network Problem Manually

In this exercise, you run a batch file to generate a networking problem, and then you troubleshoot it using manual network troubleshooting tools. This practice simulates a network problem on your computer. Before you run it, verify that you are connected to the network and can access network resources and be prepared to be disconnected from the network. Do not perform this exercise on a server or other computer that would affect users if it went offline.

1. On the companion CD, browse to the folder for this chapter. Copy the Chapter2-Lesson1-Exercise2.bat file to your desktop. Right-click that file on your desktop and click Run As Administrator.

   You can ignore the command window that appears; the batch file just simulates a networking failure. Now, you troubleshoot the problem.

2. Open a command prompt and run the command **ipconfig /all**.

3. Examine the output.

   Notice that no network adapters appear. To investigate the problem further, you should view the network adapter configuration.

4. Click the networking notification icon in the system tray (which should now have a red X over it), and then click Open Network And Sharing Center.

5. In the left pane, click Change Adapter Settings.

6. Notice that the network adapters are disabled. To re-enable each network adapter, right-click it, and then click Enable.

   Wait a few moments for the network adapter to retrieve a new IP address. Then, verify that you can connect to the network.

Lesson Summary

- Windows Network Diagnostics can identify many common network problems automatically. Windows Network Diagnostics can be started from many places, and it often prompts the user to run it when a network problem is detected.

- Use Ping to test connectivity to a remote host. PathPing functions similarly but also lists the routers between you and the remote host. Use PortQry or Telnet to determine whether a remote server is listening for connections on a specific port. Use Nslookup to troubleshoot DNS name resolution problems.

- You can troubleshoot problems connecting to shared folders from either the client or the server. Most often the problem is related to insufficient privileges. However, the server might be offline, Windows Firewall might be blocking the connection, or a network firewall might be filtering the network traffic.

- APIPA addresses are in the range 169.254.0.0 through 169.254.255.255. If a computer is assigned one of these addresses, it means that the computer is configured to receive a DHCP address but a DHCP server was not available. You can resolve this problem by verifying that a DHCP server is online and then refreshing the DHCP configuration by running **ipconfig /release** and then **ipconfig /renew**.

- Connectivity problems can be caused by either the network or the application. Network connectivity problems prevent any traffic from being sent. Application connectivity problems block just the application's specific traffic. Typically, application connectivity problems occur because a Windows Firewall exception was not created on the server or a network firewall is blocking the application's communications.

Lesson Review

You can use the following questions to test your knowledge of the information in Lesson 1, "Troubleshooting Network Connectivity." The questions are also available on the companion CD if you prefer to review them in electronic form.

> **NOTE** **ANSWERS**
>
> Answers to these questions and explanations of why each answer choice is correct or incorrect are located in the "Answers" section at the end of the book.

1. Microsoft Office Outlook gives you an error message when you attempt to download your mail. You verify that you can connect to other computers on the network. Which tools could you use to determine whether the mail server is responding to incoming e-mail requests? (Choose all that apply.)

   A. Ping

   B. Telnet

   C. PortQry

   D. PathPing

2. Which of the following IP addresses would indicate that a client computer could not retrieve an IP address from a DHCP server and did not have an alternate configuration?

    A. 10.24.68.20

    B. 127.0.0.1

    C. 192.168.22.93

    D. 169.254.43.98

3. You are unable to connect to a server on the Internet. However, you can still reach servers on the intranet. You need to determine whether your local router has failed, if your ISP is experiencing problems, or if the problem is with a different ISP. Which tools should you use to troubleshoot the problem most efficiently? (Choose all that apply.)

    A. Nslookup

    B. Tracert

    C. Ipconfig

    D. PathPing

Lesson 2: Troubleshooting Name Resolution

Computers use IP addresses to identify computers on the network. People, however, typically use host names. For example, if a person types the host name *www.contoso.com* into the Internet Explorer address bar, Internet Explorer must translate that host name into an IP address such as 10.32.93.124.

Problems with name resolution can be narrow or widespread. For example, if an invalid IP address is stored in the DNS cache, it could cause one client to be unable to access a single server. If the DNS server is offline, the results would resemble a total loss of network connectivity for all clients, because they would be unable to connect to network servers. This lesson describes how to identify name resolution problems, and when possible, how to resolve the problem.

After this lesson, you will be able to:

- Use Nslookup to troubleshoot name resolution problems.
- View and clear the DNS cache.

Estimated lesson time: 20 minutes

How to Troubleshoot Name Resolution Problems

Before two computers can communicate, the client must translate the server's host name (such as *www.contoso.com*) to an IP address (such as 192.168.10.233 or the IPv6 address 2001:db8::1). This translation is called *name resolution*. Most of the time, a DNS server performs name resolution and returns the IP address to the client computer.

As with most network problems, you should use Windows Network Diagnostics as your first troubleshooting step. If that does not solve the problem, verify that the computer is connected to the local network and then perform these steps:

1. Verify that you can connect to other computers using IP addresses. If you cannot connect to a server by using its IP address, the source of your problems is network connectivity rather than name resolution. To test this, open a command prompt and run the command **ipconfig**. Make note of the default gateway. Then, attempt to ping the default gateway. For example, if the default gateway is 192.168.1.1, you could run the following command from a command prompt:

    ```
    ping 192.168.1.1
    ```

    If you receive replies, you are definitely connected to the network and your problem is probably related to name resolution. If you don't receive a reply, you might not be connected to the network. Before troubleshooting the problem as a name resolution problem, verify that the computer is connected properly to the local network.

2. Open a command prompt and use Nslookup (a tool for testing name resolution) to look up the host name you are attempting to contact, as the following example shows:

```
nslookup www.microsoft.com
```

Examine the output by using the following criteria:

1. If Nslookup resolves the name, name resolution isn't the problem. However, the server might be offline, a firewall might be blocking your traffic, the program you're using might be misconfigured, or the DNS server database is incorrect and returning an invalid IP address.

2. If Nslookup displays only "DNS request timed out" (and doesn't later resolve the name), your DNS servers are not responding. First, run Nslookup again to make sure it's not an intermittent problem. Then, verify that your computer has the correct IP addresses listed for the DNS servers. If the DNS server IP addresses are correct, the DNS servers or the network they are connected to is offline.

> **TIP FINDING THE CORRECT DNS SERVER CONFIGURATION**
>
> If you're not sure what the DNS servers are supposed to be, check the configuration of a working computer on the same network.

3. If Nslookup displays the message, "Default servers are not available," the computer does not have a DNS server configured. Update the client network configuration with DNS server IP addresses or configure the computer to acquire an address automatically. DHCP almost always assigns DNS servers to clients.

 REAL WORLD

Tony Northrup

Here's a tip you can use to work around name resolution problems: If the DNS server isn't working correctly or a DNS update hasn't yet taken effect and you need to reach a particular server by name, you can add the name and IP address to the computer's Hosts text file. The Hosts file (it doesn't have a file extension) is located at %Windir%\System32\Drivers\Etc\Hosts.

First, use the Nslookup command on a working computer to look up the server's IP address. Then add it to the Hosts file.

To open the Hosts file, run Microsoft Notepad using administrative permissions. Then, open the Notepad %Windir%\System32\Drivers\Etc\Hosts file (it does not have a file extension). To add an entry to the Hosts file to enable name resolution without using DNS, add lines to the bottom of the Hosts file, as demonstrated here for IPv4 and IPv6 addresses:

```
192.168.1.10       www.contoso.com
2001:db8::1    mail.fabrikam.com
```

Save the hosts file and restart the Web browser (if necessary), and Windows contacts the IP address that you specified instead of trying to query the DNS server. Don't forget to remove the line from the Hosts file when the DNS is working correctly—otherwise, the user won't be able to reach the server when its IP address changes.

How to Manage the DNS Cache

Applications regularly make multiple network requests to a single server. For example, when downloading files to a Web server, Internet Explorer 8 might open six simultaneous connections to a single server. Rather than sending six consecutive DNS requests for the same address, Windows caches the first request, and uses the cached DNS result to determine the destination server's IP address for subsequent requests. DNS requests are cached among multiple users. In fact, you can view the DNS cache to identify some of the computers other users on the same computer have recently connected to.

Typically, you don't need to manage the DNS cache. However, the sections that follow describe how to view, clear, and disable the DNS cache.

How to View the DNS Cache

To view the DNS cache, open a command prompt and run the following command:

```
ipconfig /displaydns
```

The output shows every record in the DNS cache, the type of record, the time to live (TTL), and the address or CNAME record that the record resolves to. The TTL is the number of seconds that the record remains valid. The TTL is defined by the primary DNS server for the queried DNS record.

The following sample shows output from the *ipconfig /displaydns* command:

```
Windows IP Configuration
    www.contoso.com
    ----------------------------------------
    Record Name . . . . . : www.contoso.com
    Record Type . . . . . : 1
    Time To Live  . . . . : 40724
    Data Length . . . . . : 4
    Section . . . . . . . : Answer
    A (Host) Record . . . : 10.32.98.220
```

```
www.fabrikam.com
---------------------------------------
Record Name . . . . . : www.fabrikam.com
Record Type . . . . . : 5
Time To Live  . . . . : 11229
Data Length . . . . . : 4
Section . . . . . . . : Answer
CNAME Record  . . . . : fabrikam.com
```

How to Clear the DNS Cache

To clear the DNS cache, run the following command at a command prompt:

```
ipconfig /flushdns
```

Afterwards, you can run *ipconfig /displaydns* to verify that the DNS cache is empty. If it is empty, Windows 7 displays the message, "Could not display the DNS Resolver Cache."

How to Disable the DNS Cache

To disable the DNS cache, stop the DNS Client service from the Services And Applications\ Services node within the Computer Management console or by running the following command from an administrative command prompt:

```
net stop dnscache
```

Stopping and restarting the DNS Client service also clears the DNS cache.

 **Quick Check**

- ■ What command would you run to flush the DNS cache?

Quick Check Answer

- ■ *Ipconfig /flushdns*

PRACTICE   **Solving a Name Resolution Problem**

In this practice, you troubleshoot a common name resolution problem.

EXERCISE   Troubleshoot a Name Resolution Problem

In this exercise, you run a batch file to generate a networking problem and then you troubleshoot it using multiple tools. This exercise simulates a network problem on your computer. Before you run it, verify that you are connected to the network and can access network resources, and be prepared to be disconnected from the network.

1. On the companion CD, browse to the folder for this chapter. Copy the Chapter2-Lesson2-Exercise1.bat file to your desktop. Right-click the Chapter2-Lesson2-Exercise1.bat file on your desktop and then click Run As Administrator.

   You can ignore the command window that appears; the batch file just simulates a networking failure. Now, you troubleshoot the problem.

2. Open Internet Explorer and attempt to view a Web site. Notice that the Internet is not available.

3. On the Internet Explorer error page that appears, click Diagnose Connection Problems. Windows Network Diagnostics attempts to identify the problem.

4. Make note of the problem that Windows Network Diagnostics displays. Then, click Close. Notice that the problem is still not resolved.

5. Open a command prompt by clicking Start, typing **Cmd**, and then pressing Enter.

6. Type **Ipconfig /all** and press Enter to view the current network configuration.

7. Attempt to ping the default gateway. The default gateway should respond, indicating that you are successfully connected to your LAN.

8. Run the command **Nslookup www.microsoft.com**. Notice that the DNS server does not respond, indicating one of several possible problems:

   - The DNS server is offline.
   - A network connecting your computer to the DNS server is offline.
   - Your computer has the wrong DNS server address configured.

9. Verify that the IP address of the DNS server is correct. You can find the correct DNS server address in the file %Windir%\System32\Previous_ip_configuration.txt. Double-click this file and note the correct DNS server address. Normally, you would get this from your network administrator, but the batch file that you ran saved this copy of your previous network configuration automatically.

10. Because the IP address of the DNS server is different, you need to update it. Right-click the networking icon in the system tray and then click Open Network And Sharing Center.

11. In Network And Sharing Center, beside the Connections label in the View Your Active Networks group, click your network adapter.

12. Click Properties.

13. Click Internet Protocol Version 4 (TCP/IPv4) and then click Properties.

14. Configure the network settings to match those in the %Windir%\System32\Previous_ip_configuration.txt file. If you use DHCP, click Obtain DNS Server Address Automatically to return the interface to using the DNS server configuration provided by the DHCP server.

15. Click OK, and then click Close twice.

16. Return to Internet Explorer and verify that you can connect to the Internet.

Lesson Summary

- Name resolution problems occur when both the client and server are online but the client cannot determine the server's IP address. Typically, name resolution problems are caused by an incorrect DNS server configuration on the client, a DNS server that is offline, or a DNS server that has an incorrect IP address listed for the server.

- Use the Ipconfig command to view and clear the DNS cache. To view the DNS cache, run **Ipconfig /displaydns**. To clear the DNS cache, run **Ipconfig /flushdns**. You might need to clear the DNS cache if a DNS record is updated on the server, but the client requested the DNS record prior to the update.

Lesson Review

You can use the following questions to test your knowledge of the information in Lesson 2, "Troubleshooting Name Resolution." The questions are also available on the companion CD if you prefer to review them in electronic form.

> **NOTE ANSWERS**
>
> Answers to these questions and explanations of why each answer choice is correct or incorrect are located in the "Answers" section at the end of the book.

1. Which tool would you use to determine whether a connectivity problem you are currently experiencing is related to name resolution?

    A. Nslookup

    B. Ipconfig

    C. Ping

    D. Netstat

2. You are attempting to access an Internet Web server, but you receive the error message, "Internet Explorer cannot display the webpage." You look up the IP address of the server on a computer that is connected to a different network, and then type that address in the Internet Explorer address bar. The Web page displays correctly. What could be the possible cause of the problem? (Choose all that apply.)

    A. The DNS server is offline.

    B. The HOSTS file does not exist.

    C. The client has an incorrect DNS server configured.

    D. The client has an APIPA address.

3. A user calls you because she is unable to connect to an internal database server. After some troubleshooting, you determine that the database server is offline. You contact the database support team, who start a backup server with the same host name but a different IP address. You attempt to connect to the database server, but the connection attempt fails. Other users are able to connect to the database server. How can you resolve the problem?

   A. Run the command **nslookup <*database_server*>**.

   B. Run the commands **ipconfig /release** and **ipconfig /renew**.

   C. Run the command **ipconfig /flushdns**.

   D. Run the command **ipconfig /all**.

Lesson 3: Troubleshooting Wireless Networks

Because the user interface of Windows 7 is so intuitive, and because wireless network connections can be configured using Group Policy settings in AD DS, most users will have no problem connecting to wireless networks. However, problems can still occur when users have weak signals, malfunctioning hardware, or incorrect network credentials. For that reason, troubleshooting wireless network problems is extremely important.

This lesson describes how to troubleshoot common wireless networking problems.

After this lesson, you will be able to:

- Describe the purpose of wireless networks.
- Connect to wireless networks.
- Configure wireless network profiles.
- Change the wireless network profile type from all-user to per-user.
- Troubleshoot common wireless network problems.
- Use Event Viewer to analyze wireless connection problems.

Estimated lesson time: 45 minutes

Wireless Networking Overview

For most users, mobile computers are much more useful when they're connected to a network. Even if traveling users can connect only briefly to a network between flights, the network access gives them the opportunity to send and receive e-mail, check for important news, and synchronize files.

Though many airports and hotels offer wired network connections that mobile users can access, wired networks don't scale well because you need a separate network port for every user. Additionally, wired network ports are difficult to maintain in public places because the wires can be broken, or the ports can be physically jammed with something (it doesn't take long for someone to stick some gum in a network port).

Wireless networks, on the other hand, are much more efficient. A single wireless access point can service a radius of several hundred feet, and potentially grant network access to hundreds of individuals. The wireless access point can be secured physically in a closet, protecting it from damage. Additionally, users don't need to carry an Ethernet cable to connect to the network.

For these reasons, and the fact that services can charge money for access to wireless networks, public wireless networks have become very common (and now completely cover many metropolitan areas). Wireless networks have also become very popular in home environments, allowing users to network an entire home instantly without running Ethernet cable through their walls—a very expensive proposition. Additionally, wireless networks have become popular for business networking, too, because they allow users to bring mobile computers to meeting rooms, cafeterias, and other locations where a wired connection is not available.

The primary benefit of wireless networks is that users don't need to connect a network cable physically. Unfortunately, this is also the primary drawback. Wireless networks are much more vulnerable to attacks than wired networks because attackers don't need physical access to the inside of a building to connect to a network. An attacker can connect to a wireless network from the parking lot, the street, or a nearby building. Fortunately, Windows 7 supports wireless network security technologies that provide protection to meet most organizations' security requirements.

Connecting to Wireless Networks

There are several different ways to connect to wireless networks: manually, using Group Policy, and using scripts. The sections that follow describe each of these techniques.

Connecting Manually to a Wireless Network in Range

To connect to a wireless network that is currently in range, follow these steps:

1. Click the networking notification icon in the system tray, and then click the name of the network you want to connect to, as shown in Figure 2-6. If you have never connected to the network previously and you want to connect to it automatically, select the Connect Automatically check box, and then click Connect.

FIGURE 2-6 You can connect to a wireless network with just two or three clicks.

NOTE **CONFIGURING SERVICES FOR WIRELESS NETWORKING**

The WLAN AutoConfig service must be started for wireless networks to be available. This service is set by default to start automatically.

2. If the Type The Network Security Key dialog box appears, as shown in Figure 2-7, type the network security key, and then click OK.

FIGURE 2-7 If the wireless network is protected, you must type the security key.

Windows 7 connects to the network. If you want to disconnect from the wireless network, you can follow these steps to connect to a different wireless network. To disconnect from all wireless networks, click the networking notification icon in the system tray, click the name of the current network, and then click Disconnect.

Creating a New Wireless Network Profile Manually

The easiest way to connect to a wireless network is to click the networking notification icon in the system tray, click the network, and follow the prompts that appear. However, that works only if the wireless network is currently in range and broadcasting a *Service Set Identifier (SSID)*, which identifies the network by name. If you want to preconfigure a wireless network so that Windows 7 can connect to it automatically later when the network is in range, perform these steps:

1. Click the networking notification icon in the system tray, and then click Open Network And Sharing Center.

2. In the Network And Sharing Center, click Manage Wireless Networks.

3. Click Add.

4. The Manually Connect To A Wireless Network wizard appears. Click Manually Create A Network Profile.

5. On the Enter Information For The Wireless Network You Want To Add page, as shown in Figure 2-8, type the required information. Then, click Next.

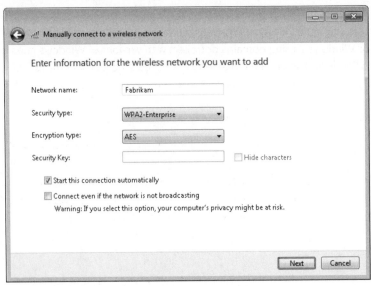

FIGURE 2-8 Configure a wireless network manually if it is not currently visible.

6. On the Successfully Added page, click Close.

You can also preconfigure wireless networks using Group Policy settings or scripts.

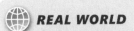 **REAL WORLD**

Tony Northrup

When wireless networks were new, some security experts told administrators that they should turn off SSID broadcasting to reduce security risks. It seemed like a good idea because if a wireless access point does not broadcast a SSID, client computers won't detect it automatically.

The problem is, turning off SSID broadcasting makes it more difficult for legitimate users to connect to the wireless network. It doesn't make it any more difficult for an attacker, however. Although it's not built into the operating system, there are free tools available on the Internet that immediately detect wireless networks that aren't broadcasting a SSID.

Connecting to Wireless Networks Using Group Policy Settings

Connecting to a wireless network manually works well when configuring a small number of computers. In AD DS environments, you should use Group Policy settings to configure client computers instead. For best results, you should have Windows Server 2003 with SP1 or later installed on your domain controllers because Microsoft extended support for wireless Group Policy settings when they released Service Pack 1.

Before you can configure wireless networks for client computers running Windows XP, Windows Vista, or Windows 7 using domain controllers with versions of Windows released prior to Windows Server 2008, you need to extend the AD DS schema using the 802.11Schema. ldf file from *http://www.microsoft.com/technet/network/wifi/vista_ad_ext.mspx*. To extend the schema, follow these steps:

1. Copy the 802.11Schema.ldf file to a folder on a domain controller.

2. Log on to the domain controller with Domain Admin privileges and open a command prompt.

3. Select the folder containing the 802.11Schema.ldf file, and run the following command (where Dist_Name_of_AD_Domain is the distinguished name of the AD DS domain, such as "DC=contoso,DC=com" for the contoso.com AD DS domain):

```
ldifde -i -v -k -f 802.11Schema.ldf -c DC=X Dist_Name_of_AD_Domain
```

4. Restart the domain controller.

If you have domain controllers running Windows Server 2008 or later or you have an earlier version of Windows, and you have extended the schema, you can configure a wireless network policy from a domain controller by following these steps:

1. Open the AD DS Group Policy Object (GPO) in the Group Policy Object Editor.

2. Expand Computer Configuration, Policies, Windows Settings, Security Settings, and then click Wireless Network (IEEE 802.11) Policies.

3. Right-click Wireless Network (IEEE 802.11) Policies, and then click Create A New Wireless Network Policy For Windows Vista And Later Releases (if the server is running Windows Server 2008 R2) or Create A New Windows Vista Policy (if the server is running an earlier version of Windows).

4. The New Wireless Network Policy Properties dialog box appears, as shown in Figure 2-9.

5. To add an infrastructure network, click Add, and then click Infrastructure to open the Connection tab of the New Profile Properties dialog box. In the Network Names list, type a valid internal SSID in the Network Names box, and then click Add. Repeat this to configure multiple SSIDs for a single profile. If the network is hidden, select the Connect Even If The Network Is Not Broadcasting check box.

6. In the New Profile Properties dialog box, click the Security tab. Use this tab to configure the wireless network authentication and encryption settings. Click OK.

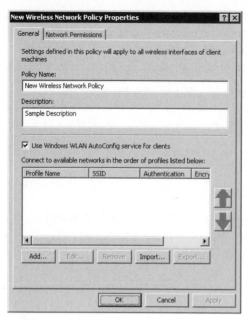

FIGURE 2-9 You can use Group Policy settings to configure wireless network clients running Windows 7.

These settings configure client computers to connect automatically to your internal wireless networks and keep them from connecting to other wireless networks.

Connecting to Wireless Networks Using Scripts

You can also configure wireless settings using commands in the **netsh wlan** context of the Netsh command-line tool, which enables you to create scripts that connect to different wireless networks (whether encrypted or not). To list available wireless networks, run the following command:

```
netsh wlan show networks
Interface Name : Wireless Network Connection
There are 2 networks currently visible

SSID 1 : Nwtraders1
    Network Type            : Infrastructure
    Authentication          : Open
    Encryption              : None

SSID 1 : Nwtraders2
    Network Type            : Infrastructure
    Authentication          : Open
    Encryption              : WEP
```

Before you can connect to a wireless network using Netsh, you must have a profile saved for that network. Profiles contain the SSID and security information required to connect to a network. If you have connected to a network previously, the computer has a profile for that network saved. If a computer has never connected to a wireless network, you need to save a profile before you can use Netsh to connect to it. You can save a profile from one computer to an Extensible Markup Language (XML) file, and then distribute the XML file to other computers in your network. To save a profile, run the following command after manually connecting to a network:

```
netsh wlan export profile name="<SSID>"
```

Before you can connect to a new wireless network, you can load a profile from a file. The following example demonstrates how to create a wireless profile (which is saved as an XML file) from a script or the command line:

```
netsh wlan add profile filename="C:\profiles\nwtraders1.xml"
```

To connect quickly to a wireless network, use the *netsh wlan connect* command and specify a wireless profile name (which must be configured or added previously). The following examples demonstrate different but equivalent syntaxes for connecting to a wireless network with the Nwtraders1 SSID:

```
netsh wlan connect Nwtraders1
netsh wlan connect Nwtraders1 interface="Wireless Network Connection"
```

Note that you need only to specify the interface name if you have multiple wireless network adapters, which is very rare. You can use the following command to disconnect from all wireless networks:

```
netsh wlan disconnect
```

You can use scripts and profiles to simplify the process of connecting to private wireless networks for your users. Ideally, you should use scripts and profiles to keep users from ever needing to type wireless security keys.

You can also use Netsh to allow or block access to wireless networks based on their SSIDs. For example, the following command allows access to a wireless network with the Nwtraders1 SSID:

```
netsh wlan add filter permission=allow ssid=Nwtraders1
networktype=infrastructure
```

Similarly, the following command blocks access to the Contoso wireless network:

```
Netsh wlan add filter permission=block ssid=Contoso networktype=adhoc
```

To block all ad hoc networks, use the Denyall permission, as the following example demonstrates:

```
netsh wlan add filter permission=denyall networktype=adhoc
```

To prevent Windows 7 from automatically connecting to wireless networks, run the following command:

```
netsh wlan set autoconfig enabled=no interface="Wireless Network Connection"
```

Netsh has many other commands for configuring wireless networking. For more information, run the following at a command prompt:

```
netsh wlan help
```

Reconfiguring a Wireless Network

After you first connect to the network, Windows 7 stores those settings for future connections. If the configuration of the wireless access point changes, you might not be able to connect to it in the future.

To change the configuration of a wireless network after the original configuration, perform these steps:

1. Click the networking notification icon in the system tray, and then click Open Network And Sharing Center.

2. In the Network And Sharing Center, click Manage Wireless Networks.

3. Right-click the network you want to reconfigure, and then click Properties.

   The Wireless Network Properties dialog box appears.

4. As shown in Figure 2-10, you can use the Connection tab to specify whether Windows 7 will connect automatically to the network when it is in range (assuming no other wireless connection already exists).

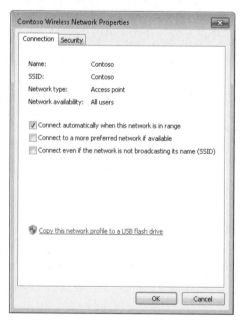

FIGURE 2-10 The Connection tab of the Wireless Network Properties dialog box allows you to change automatic connection settings.

5. As shown in Figure 2-11, you can use the Security tab to specify the security and encryption types. Depending on the security type, Windows 7 shows other options in the dialog box.

FIGURE 2-11 Use the Wireless Network Properties dialog box to change security settings.

6. Click OK.

After reconfiguring the network connection, attempt to reconnect to the network to verify your settings. As an alternative, you can right-click a wireless network from the Manage Wireless Networks tool and then click Remove Network. After removing the network, you can reconnect to the network as if it were a new network.

Changing the Priorities of Wireless Networks

Many locations have multiple wireless networks available at the same time. For example, if your office is located over a coffee shop, you might be able to connect to either your office wireless network or the coffee shop's public wireless network. To complicate matters more, you might specifically want to use the coffee shop wireless network when you're not in the office and use your office wireless network at all other times.

To ensure that you connect to the correct network when multiple networks are available, you can prioritize wireless networks. To set the priority of wireless networks, perform these steps:

1. Click the networking notification icon in the system tray, and then click Open Network And Sharing Center.

2. In the Network And Sharing Center, click Manage Wireless Networks.

3. In the Manage Wireless Networks window, click a wireless network profile, and then click Move Up or Move Down.

When multiple networks are available, Windows 7 always connects to the network listed first.

Wireless Networking Security

Many wireless networks are unencrypted and unauthenticated—they completely lack any security features. Wired networks are typically unencrypted, too (at least at Layer 2), but it's not a significant problem because an attacker would need to connect an Ethernet cable physically to the network to gain access, and most organizations stop unauthorized people from walking into their buildings. With a wireless network, however, an attacker can connect physically to the network from the organization's lobby, parking lot, or even a nearby building.

 REAL WORLD

Tony Northrup

If someone commits a crime using the Internet, often, the primary evidence that law enforcement officials have about the perpetrator's identity is the IP address. Knowing the IP address, the law enforcement officials contact the ISP and issue a subpoena to force the ISP to reveal the subscriber that was assigned that IP address at the time of the crime.

Many would-be criminals are aware of this, and avoid using a personal Internet connection to commit crimes. Often, they'll find an unprotected wireless network that offers Internet access and abuse that connection. Then, law enforcement officials trace the origin back to the owner of the wireless network rather than the criminal. So, by leaving a wireless network unprotected, you might be helping a criminal avoid authorities.

To provide even a minimal level of protection, wireless networks need both authentication (to allow only authorized computers to connect) and encryption (to prevent attackers from viewing network traffic). All wireless security standards provide both authentication and encryption; however, some are much more secure than others.

Windows 7 supports the following wireless security standards:

- **No security**   Many consumer wireless access points are configured with wireless networking that is enabled without security by default. As a result, unprotected wireless networks are common. Not requiring security makes it extremely convenient to connect to a network because the user does not need to provide a passphrase or key. However, the security risks are significant. Anyone within several hundred feet of the wireless access point can connect to it and possibly abuse it. Additionally, attackers can view any traffic sent to or from the wireless access point, including e-mails, instant messages, and any other unencrypted traffic. Today, most wireless networks that lack wireless security require the user to authenticate to the wireless access point after he has connected to the wireless network.

- **Wired Equivalent Protection (WEP)**   Available using either 64-bit or 128-bit encryption, WEP was the original wireless security standard. It's still commonly used today because it's almost universally supported—almost every operating system, wireless access point, wireless bridge, or other wireless network device (such as printers and home media extenders) supports WEP. Although WEP offers better protection than using no wireless security at all, it is easily cracked by a knowledgeable attacker. A 128-bit WEP offers significantly better protection than 64-bit WEP, but either typically can be cracked within just a few minutes. Regardless, using WEP is still safer than not using any wireless security because WEP prevents casual users from abusing your network.

- **Wi-Fi Protected Access (WPA)**   WPA is the successor to WEP, offering significantly better protection. WPA is not as universally supported as WEP, however, so if you have non-Windows wireless clients or wireless devices that do not support WEP, you might need to upgrade them to support WPA. Windows 7 supports both WPA-Personal and WPA-Enterprise, as follows:

  - WPA-PSK (for pre-shared key), also known as WPA-Personal, is intended for home environments. WPA-PSK requires a user to enter an 8- to 63-character passphrase into every wireless client. WPA converts the passphrase to a 256-bit key.

  - WPA-EAP (Extensible Authentication Protocol), also known as WPA-Enterprise, relies on a back-end server running Remote Authentication Dial-In User Service (RADIUS) for authentication. The RADIUS server can then authenticate the user to the AD DS or by verifying a certificate. WPA-EAP enables very flexible authentication, and Windows 7 enables users to use a smart card to connect to a WPA-Enterprise protected network.

- **WPA2**   WPA2 (also known as IEEE 802.11i) is an updated version of WPA, offering improved security and better protection from attacks. Like WPA, WPA2 is available as both WPA2-PSK and WPA2-EAP.

- **Open with 802.1X**   802.1X is a network authentication method traditionally used for wired networks. When network administrators require 802.1X authentication for a wired network, the network switch communicates with an authentication server when a new user connects an Ethernet cable to the network. If the user is authenticated, the switch grants them access to the network. With Open With 802.1X wireless security, the wireless access point does not require any encryption. However, once a wireless client has connected to the network, the computer must authenticate using 802.1X before they will be granted network access. This security type provides authentication, but not encryption.

Windows 7 and Windows Vista include built-in support for WEP, WPA, and WPA2. Windows XP can support both WPA and WPA2 by installing updates available from Microsoft.com. Recent versions of Linux and Mac OS, as well as many wireless mobile devices, are capable of supporting WEP, WPA, and WPA2.

Configuring WPA-EAP Security

The static keys used by WEP and WPA-PSK aren't manageable in enterprise environments. If an employee ever left, you'd need to change the key on the wireless access point to prevent the employee from connecting to the network in the future. Then, you would need to update every wireless client computer in your organization.

Remember that the EAP in WPA-EAP stands for Extensible Authentication Protocol. Because it is extensible, you can authenticate using several different methods:

- PEAP-MS-CHAPv2 to enable users to connect to a wireless network using their domain credentials
- Certificates stored on the user's computers
- Certificates stored on smart cards

Whichever authentication method you choose, Windows uses the same authentication process. As shown in Figure 2-12, the wireless client computer passes the credentials to the wireless access point, which forwards them to a RADIUS server, which then authenticates the user against AD DS. Though Figure 2-12 shows the RADIUS server and the domain controller as separate servers, you can install both services on the same physical computer.

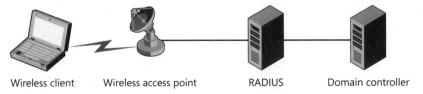

Wireless client   Wireless access point   RADIUS   Domain controller

FIGURE 2-12 WPA uses a RADIUS server for authentication.

Windows Server 2008 includes the Network Policy Server (NPS), which acts as a RADIUS server that is integrated tightly with AD DS. When configuring NPS, you can specify a domain security group that will be granted access to the wireless network. For this reason, you should create a group specifically for users with the right to access the wireless network.

> **MORE INFO** **MORE ABOUT NPS**
>
> Because this certification exam focuses on Windows 7, it will not cover how to configure the RADIUS server. For more information about configuring NPS with Windows Server 2008, read Chapters 14 through 19 of *Windows Server 2008 Networking and Network Access Protection* by Joseph Davies and Tony Northrup (Microsoft Press, 2008).

By default, when you connect to a new WPA-EAP or WPA2-EAP network, Windows 7 is configured to use the Secured Password (EAP-MSCHAP v2) authentication method to allow users to authenticate with their domain credentials. If users should authenticate using a certificate (whether stored on the local computer or a smart card), create a wireless network profile for the network using the default settings, and then follow these steps to configure the wireless network security:

1. Click the networking notification icon in the system tray, and then click Open Network And Sharing Center.

2. In the Network And Sharing Center, click Manage Wireless Networks.

3. Right-click the network and then click Properties. Then, click the Security tab.

4. Click the Choose A Network Authentication Method list, and then click Microsoft: Smart Card Or Other Certificate, as shown in Figure 2-13.

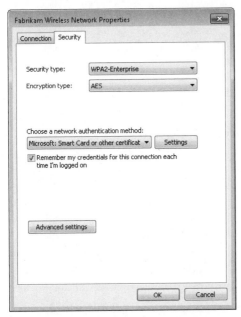

FIGURE 2-13 You must edit a wireless network profile's properties manually to authenticate using a certificate.

NOTE REQUIRING SMART CARDS

Notice that the Remember My Credentials For This Connection Each Time I'm Logged On check box is selected by default. If you want the user to insert her smart card every time she connects to the network, clear this check box.

5. Click Settings. If the certificate is stored on the local computer, click Use A Certificate On This Computer in the When Connecting group, as shown in Figure 2-14. If you are using a smart card, click Use My Smart Card.

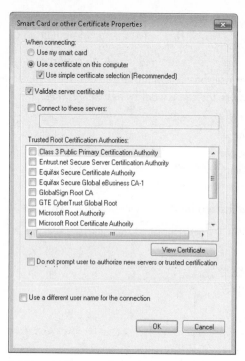

FIGURE 2-14 You can choose between storing a certificate on the local computer or a smart card.

> **NOTE VALIDATING SERVERS**
>
> Notice that the Validate Server Certificate check box is selected by default. This verifies that the RADIUS server has a certificate from a trusted certification authority (CA) before sending the credentials. That's important because you wouldn't want to send your credentials to a malicious server that could then misuse them. However, it causes the client to reject the RADIUS server if the RADIUS server has a certificate from an Enterprise CA (or any CA that isn't trusted by default) and the client computer hasn't connected to the domain because the Enterprise CA was added to the domain. To work around this the first time you connect to a domain (after which the client computer trusts the enterprise CA), clear the Validate Server Certificate check box, connect to the wireless network and to the domain, and then select the Validate Server Certificate check box again.

6. Click OK twice.

The next time the user connects using the profile, Windows 7 automatically attempts to find a suitable certificate. If it cannot find one, or if the user needs to insert a smart card, Windows 7 prompts the user to select a certificate.

Configuring Wireless Network Profile Types

Most mobile computers are used by only a single user. However, if mobile computers in your organization are shared between multiple users, you might want to configure wireless networks to use per-user profiles. With per-user profiles, one user can connect to a wireless network without other users being able to use the same wireless network connection.

Per-user wireless profiles are important if, for example, a user configures a shared mobile computer to connect to a home wireless network. The default configuration of all-user profiles would allow any other user of that computer to visit the original user's home and connect to the wireless network without being prompted for a security key—even if the wireless network uses security.

To change a wireless profile to per-user instead of all-user, follow these steps:

1. Click the networking notification icon in the system tray, and then click Open Network And Sharing Center.

   The Network And Sharing Center appears.

2. In the left pane, click Manage Wireless Networks.

   a. Click Profile Types.

   b. In the Wireless Network Profile Types dialog box, click Use All-User And Per-User Profiles, as shown in Figure 2-15.

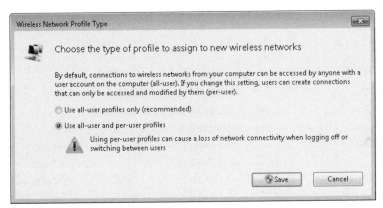

FIGURE 2-15 Per-user wireless profiles prevent users from sharing wireless connection configurations.

   c. Click Save.

After enabling per-user profiles, all existing wireless profiles are still available to all users. However, the next time you connect to a new wireless network, Windows 7 prompts you to choose how you want to store the wireless network profile. If you want to convert an existing wireless network profile from all-users to per-user, delete it and re-create it. One of the negative side effects of per-user wireless profiles is that the computer is disconnected from the wireless network when a user logs off.

Troubleshooting Common Wireless Network Problems

Once you are successfully connected to a wireless network, you can use the same troubleshooting techniques that you would use while connected to a wired network. However, wireless networks require very different troubleshooting techniques during the connection process. Some of the most common problems you might encounter include the following:

- **Network adapter cannot see any wireless networks** If your network adapter cannot see any wireless networks even though wireless networks are available, the network adapter might be turned off at the hardware level. Most mobile computers include either a dedicated hardware switch or a key combination that turns the wireless radio on or off. As shown in Figure 2-16, Windows Network Diagnostics correctly detects this condition.

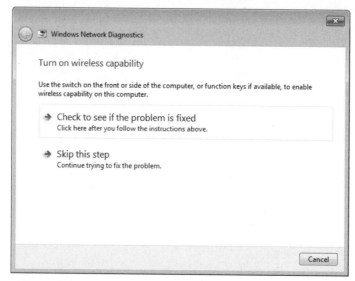

FIGURE 2-16 One of the most common wireless problems: a radio that has been turned off at the hardware level

You should also use Device Manager to verify that your wireless network adapter was detected and has a valid driver. To start Device Manager, click Start, type **devmgmt.msc**, and press Enter. Then, expand Network Adapters. If the wireless radio is off, Windows still detects the network adapter—it just won't be able to use it.

- **Weak wireless signal** The farther you move from the wireless access point, the weaker the signal is going to be. The weaker the signal, the slower the network performance. You can, however, do several things to improve the range of a wireless signal:

  - Move the wireless access point away from metal cabinets, computers, or other objects that might block the wireless signals.

  - If attempting to connect from outdoors, remove screens from windows. Screens do not block a wireless signal, but they introduce a significant amount of noise.

- Adjust the antenna on the wireless access point. For greatest efficiency, have someone slowly move the wireless access point antenna while a second person monitors the signal strength from a computer at the target location.

- Use a high-gain antenna, also known as a *directional antenna*. A low-gain antenna (also known as an *omnidirectional antenna*) broadcasts in all directions relatively equally. High-gain antennas are very directional. If you need to cover a specific area, point a high-gain antenna at the location. Some wireless network adapters also support high-gain antennas. For best efficiency, use a high-gain antenna on both the wireless access point and the computer.

> **NOTE   USING A HIGH-GAIN ANTENNA**
>
> Many people incorrectly believe that high-gain antennas are more powerful. The antenna itself can't increase power—that's controlled by the transmitter within the wireless access point. The antenna does, however, control the direction of the signal. High-gain antennas just focus the transmitting power in a specific direction, offering a stronger signal in some areas while decreasing the signal in other locations.

- Increase the power at the transmitter. Many wireless access points allow you to configure the transmitter power. Although the default setting is typically the maximum, another administrator might have reduced the transmitter power.

- Increase the power at the client computer. All network connections are two-way. Therefore, for a connection to be established, the signals transmitted by the computer must be strong enough to reach the wireless access point. Many wireless network adapters allow you to configure the transmitter power from the wireless network adapter Properties dialog box, as shown in Figure 2-17. This is different for every wireless network adapter. Increasing the transmitter power can also increase battery usage.

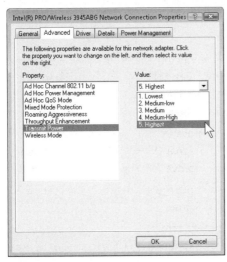

FIGURE 2-17 Some wireless network adapters allow you to configure the transmitter strength.

- **Windows cannot reconnect to a wireless network**   Typically, if you cannot connect to a wireless network that you have connected to previously, it is because security settings on the network have changed. For example, if the wireless network uses WEP, an administrator might have changed the key. To change the security key, follow the steps in the section entitled "Reconfiguring a Wireless Network," earlier in this lesson. Alternatively, you could simply remove the wireless network profile and connect to the network as if it were a new network.

- **Poor performance**   Several factors can cause poor network performance:

  - **A weak wireless signal, as discussed previously.**

  - **Interference.**   802.11b, 802.11g, and 802.11n use the 2.4 gigahertz (GHz) radio frequency, whereas 802.11a uses the 5.8-GHz frequency. Cordless phones and other wireless devices on the same frequency can introduce performance problems.

  - **Overlapping wireless access points.**   Wireless access points can broadcast on 1 of 11 channels (from 1 to 11). If two wireless access points broadcast on the same channel or on a channel within five channels of another wireless access point, the performance of both can be reduced. For best results, use channels 1, 6, and 11 when wireless access points overlap.

  - **Multiple wireless frequencies.**   802.11n and 802.11g are backward-compatible with 802.11b. However, supporting 802.11b clients on either 802.11n or 802.11g networks can reduce performance significantly. If possible, upgrade all wireless clients to the fastest wireless network standard supported by your wireless access points. Then, configure your wireless access point to use "802.11g Only" or "802.11n Only" mode.

  - **Significant network traffic.**   All wireless clients compete for a limited amount of bandwidth. If one client is downloading a large file, that can affect the performance of all clients.

- **Intermittent or otherwise unexplained problems**   Wireless network protocols have changed a great deal in a short time. Unfortunately, it's common that wireless network hardware from different vendors have difficulty interoperating. For example, many vendors released wireless access points based on the 802.11n standard before the standard was finalized. If you're using a wireless network adapter that fully implements 802.11n and you're attempting to connect to a wireless access point based on pre-802.11n standards, you might not be able to connect, you might experience intermittent failures, or performance might be reduced. For best results, upgrade all wireless access point firmware and network adapter drivers to the latest versions. Then, work with the hardware vendor's technical support to continue troubleshooting the problem.

MORE INFO **TROUBLESHOOTING WIRELESS SERVICES**

For detailed information about wireless services, visit the Microsoft TechNet networking page at *http://technet.microsoft.com/en-us/library/dd393010.aspx*. For more information about troubleshooting networking problems, read Chapter 31 of *Windows 7 Resource Kit* by Mitch Tulloch, Tony Northrup, and Jerry Honeycutt (Microsoft Press, 2009).

Using Event Viewer to Analyze Wireless Connection Problems

If a user calls you to discuss a problem connecting to a wireless network, that user might not have all the critical technical details that you need to know. Although the user might remember the SSID, the user probably doesn't know the security type required by the network, or whether the network was 802.11b, 802.11g, or something different. Fortunately, Windows 7 records these technical details every time a user connects to a network.

To view the details of wireless networks a user has connected to, perform these steps:

1. Click Start. Right-click Computer, and then click Manage.

2. Under Computer Management, expand System Tools, Event Viewer, Applications And Services Logs, Microsoft, Windows, and WLAN-AutoConfig. Then, select Operational.

3. In the middle pane, select an event log entry.

This event log shows the details of attempted and successful connections to a wireless network. Figure 2-18 shows an example of Event ID 8001, which provides the details of a successful wireless network connection. As you can see, it shows the wireless network's SSID (Contoso), the wireless network type (802.11g), and the authentication type (WPA2-Enterprise).

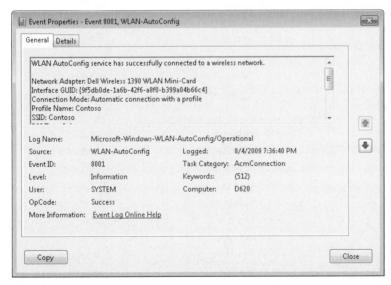

FIGURE 2-18 Windows 7 creates an event when it successfully connects to a wireless network.

Figure 2-19 shows an example of Event ID 11006, which indicates a wireless authentication failure. As you can see, this event shows the wireless network's SSID (Contoso) and the reason for the failure (Explicit EAP Failure Received). Using the time of the event, you could correlate the authentication failure with an event on the RADIUS server or the domain controller. Other events that can indicate a wireless authentication failure include Event IDs 8002 and 12013.

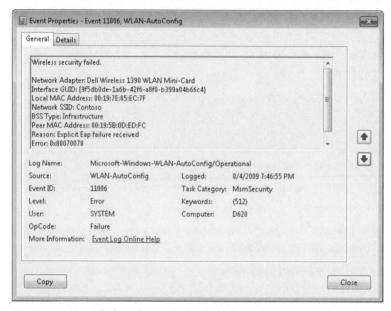

FIGURE 2-19 How Windows 7 records detailed information about wireless network problems

Windows 7 adds several events for any successful or unsuccessful connection. Additionally, if the user started Windows Network Diagnostics for troubleshooting assistance, you might find useful information in the System event log and the Applications And Services Logs\Microsoft\Windows\Diagnostics-Networking\Operational event log.

PRACTICE Working with Wireless Networks

In this practice, you configure and troubleshoot wireless networks.

EXERCISE 1   Configure a WPA-PSK Encrypted Wireless Access Point

In this exercise, you connect to a wireless network protected by WPA-PSK. To complete this exercise, you must have a wireless access point and a computer running Windows 7 with a wireless network adapter.

1. Access your wireless access point's configuration page. Typically, you can manage wireless access points using a Web browser. Specify a SSID of Contoso with WPA2-PSK security if available, or WPA-PSK (also known as WPA-Personal) security. Provide a complex passphrase between 8 and 63 characters—the longer, the more secure—and note that key.

2. On your computer running Windows 7, click the networking icon in the system tray, click Contoso, and then click Connect.

   The Connect To A Network dialog box appears.

3. Type the security key, and then click OK.

4. If the Select A Location For The Contoso Network dialog box appears, click Public.

Note that WPA-PSK encryption requires exactly the same process as WEP. Both WEP and WPA-PSK use a static key, which provides a management challenge because every client computer uses the same key. If you ever need to change the network key, you need to reconfigure every client computer.

EXERCISE 2   Troubleshoot a Wireless Network

In this exercise, you attempt to connect to a wireless network that has been previously configured with incorrect settings. To complete this exercise, you must have completed Exercise 1 in this lesson.

1. Access your wireless access point's configuration page. Change the network passphrase to something different.

2. On your computer running Windows 7, notice that the network icon shows that the computer is no longer connected. Click the network icon, and then click Contoso (or Contoso 2). Click Connect.

   The Connect To A Network Wizard appears.

3. The Connect To A Network dialog box displays an error message. Click Troubleshoot Problems.

   Windows Network Diagnostics attempts to identify the problem.

4. Follow the instructions provided by Windows Network Diagnostics. When prompted, click Detailed Information to view the Troubleshooting Report. Examine the detailed information.

5. Because Windows Network Diagnostics were unable to resolve the problem, you must delete and re-create the wireless profile manually. Click the network icon in the system tray, and then click Open Network And Sharing Center.

6. In the left pane, click Manage Wireless Networks.

7. In the Manage Wireless Networks tool, right-click Contoso, click Remove Network, and then click Yes. Note that you could also edit the network properties and manually update the passphrase using the Security tab.

8. On your computer running Windows 7, click the networking icon in the system tray, click Contoso, and then click Connect.

   The Connect To A Network dialog box appears.

9. Type the security key, and then click OK.

Now, open Internet Explorer to verify that you can connect to the Internet across your wireless link.

Lesson Summary

- Wireless networks allow computers to be connected using radio signals rather than an Ethernet cable. Wireless networks are more complex than wired networks because there are multiple security standards and wireless signal strength can vary.

- Windows 7 includes a new user interface for connecting to wireless networks. With Windows 7, users simply click the networking icon in the system tray and then click an available network.

- If network settings change, you can use the Manage Wireless Networks tool in Control Panel to update them.

- You can also use the Manage Wireless Networks tool in Control Panel to change the priority of wireless networks. When multiple wireless networks are available, Windows 7 connects to the highest-priority network.

- Windows 7 supports several different types of network security: open (which uses no security); WEP, WPA-PSK, and WPA2-PSK (which use a static key for authentication and encryption); and WPA-EAP and WPA2-EAP (which use a RADIUS server for authentication). Additionally, you can configure wireless clients running Windows 7 to use open security with 802.1X network authentication.

- The most common wireless network problem is turning off a mobile computer's wireless radio; this is solved by turning the wireless radio back on. Other common problems include weak signal strength, poor network performance, incompatibilities, and wireless network settings that have changed since the network was first configured.

- You can use the Applications And Services Logs\Microsoft\Windows\WLAN-AutoConfig\Operational to determine which networks a user has connected to and view any problems that occurred.

Lesson Review

You can use the following questions to test your knowledge of the information in Lesson 3, "Troubleshooting Wireless Networks." The questions are also available on the companion CD if you prefer to review them in electronic form.

> **NOTE ANSWERS**
>
> Answers to these questions and explanations of why each answer choice is correct or incorrect are located in the "Answers" section at the end of the book.

1. A user complains that she attempted to connect to a wireless network but the connection failed. She didn't write down any details of the connection. In which log would you look to find the details of her connection attempt?

    A. Applications And Services Logs\Microsoft\Windows\Diagnostics-Networking\Operational

    B. System

C. Applications And Services Logs\Microsoft\Windows\Wired-AutoConfig\Operational

D. Applications And Services Logs\Microsoft\Windows\WLAN-AutoConfig\Operational

2. You attempt to connect to a wireless network by clicking the networking icon in the system tray. However, Windows 7 does not detect any wireless networks in the area. You look at the person next to you, and he is able to connect to a wireless network. You verify that Device Manager shows a wireless network adapter under the Network Adapters node. Which of the following might be the cause of your problem? (Choose all that apply.)

A. You do not have a wireless network adapter installed.

B. Your wireless radio has been turned off at the hardware level.

C. The wireless network is configured not to broadcast a SSID.

D. The wireless network is secured and you have not been granted access.

3. Which of the following wireless network security types requires additional infrastructure servers to authenticate users?

A. WEP

B. WPA-PSK

C. WPA-EAP

D. WPA2-PSK

Chapter Review

To further practice and reinforce the skills you learned in this chapter, you can perform the following tasks:

- Review the chapter summary.
- Review the list of key terms introduced in this chapter.
- Complete the case scenarios. These scenarios set up real-world situations involving the topics of this chapter and ask you to create a solution.
- Complete the suggested practices.
- Take a practice test.

Chapter Summary

- Windows 7 includes Windows Network Diagnostics, a tool that can automatically diagnose common network problems. Windows Network Diagnostics should always be your first troubleshooting step. If that does not allow you to identify the problem, you can use Ping, PathPing, PortQry, and Nslookup to determine whether the problem is a network connectivity problem, an application connectivity problem, or a name resolution problem.
- To troubleshoot name resolution problems, use Ipconfig to view the current configuration and use Nslookup to send DNS queries to the DNS server manually. If an administrator updates a DNS record that you have recently queried, you can run the command **Ipconfig /flushdns** to clear the DNS cache.
- Wireless network problems are often related to signal strength, security keys, and adapter settings. Windows 7 provides a convenient user interface for connecting to wireless networks. If a user experiences problems, Windows Network Diagnostics can often diagnose or fix the problem. In other circumstances, you might need to delete the wireless network profile so that Windows can automatically re-create it when you next connect to the wireless network.

Key Terms

Do you know what these key terms mean? You can check your answers by looking up the terms in the glossary at the end of the book.

- **Automatic Private IP Address (APIPA)**
- **hotspot**
- **latency**
- **name resolution**

- **Service Set Identifier (SSID)**
- **Wired Equivalent Protection (WEP)**
- **Wi-Fi Protected Access (WPA)**

Case Scenarios

In the following case scenarios, you apply what you've learned about troubleshooting network problems. You can find answers to these questions in the "Answers" section at the end of this book.

Case Scenario 1: Troubleshooting a Network Problem

You are a desktop support technician for Contoso Pharmaceuticals. Recently, you helped deploy 20 computers running Windows Vista to a new location in Tulsa, Oklahoma. One of the users, Gordon L. Hee, calls you for help with a networking problem: His network is down.

Questions

1. What is the first step you should have Gordon take?
2. How can you determine whether the problem is with the local network or the wide area network (WAN)?
3. How can you determine whether Gordon's problem is a name resolution problem?

Case Scenario 2: Troubleshooting Problems Connecting to a Wireless Network

You are a desktop support technician for City Power & Light. You receive a phone call from Parry Bedi, who is attempting to connect to the wireless network at the airport but is experiencing problems. Parry can connect to the network, but the connection doesn't seem stable—e-mail is downloading extremely slowly, and occasionally the connection disappears completely.

Questions

1. What is the most likely cause of Parry's problem, and how can Parry fix it?
2. What are some other possible causes of Parry's problem?

Suggested Practices

To help you master the exam objectives presented in this chapter, complete the following tasks.

Identify and Resolve Network Connectivity Issues

Troubleshooting is a skill that requires real-world experience. Although this chapter can discuss concepts and tools, only practicing gives you the skills that you need to troubleshoot network connectivity problems and pass the exam. Perform as many of these practices as possible to build your troubleshooting skills.

- **Practice 1:** Visit *http://answers.microsoft.com/windows/* and browse the Wireless And Networking newsgroup. Read the posts to determine how people solved their different network problems.

- **Practice 2:** Separately, connect to your home and work networks. Examine the network configuration for each. Does it use DHCP or manual IP addressing? Do you have more than one DNS server available? What is the IP address of your default gateway?

- **Practice 3:** Try pinging your default gateway, DNS servers, computers on your local network, and Web servers on the Internet. Which of those responds to ping requests and which ignore ping requests?

- **Practice 4:** Use Tracert for troubleshooting instead of PathPing. Although PathPing is more effective, knowing Tracert is a requirement for the exam.

- **Practice 5:** Use Ipconfig to determine the IP address of your DHCP server and make note of how long ago you received your IP address. Ping the DHCP server.

- **Practice 6:** Use Ipconfig to view your current IP address. Then, use Ipconfig to release and renew your IP address. Did you get the same IP address or a different IP address?

- **Practice 7:** Have a friend induce one of the following network problems. Then, use the tools built into Windows Vista to diagnose and repair the problem:

  - The computer is unplugged from the LAN.
  - The wireless network adapter is turned off (using the laptop's hardware switch).
  - The network adapter is disabled.
  - The router is disconnected from the Internet.
  - The DNS server is unavailable or misconfigured.
  - The default gateway is offline.

Identify and Resolve Names Resolution Issues

Name resolution is a vast topic. This chapter has focused on DNS name resolution issues that are most likely to be covered by the 70-685 exam. A broader understanding of name resolution helps you with both the exam and real-world troubleshooting. Complete as many of these practices as you have time for.

- **Practice 1:** Use Nslookup to query several host names: www.microsoft.com, www.conotoso.com, and not-valid.contoso.com.

- **Practice 2:** Use Nslookup to find a domain's mail server. Run the command **nslookup –type=mx microsoft.com** to identify Microsoft's default mail server. Use the Internet to research MX records and other types of DNS records.

- **Practice 3:** Learn to use Nslookup in interactive mode by running Nslookup at a command prompt without any parameters. Then, enter the command **help**.

- **Practice 4:** Search the Internet, particularly *http://technet.microsoft.com*, to research NetBIOS name resolution and WINS servers. Practice using Nbtstat to view the local cache of NetBIOS names.

Identify and Resolve Wireless Connectivity Issues

Complete at least the first two practices to get more experience troubleshooting wireless connectivity issues. If you have time and you want a better overall understanding of real-world wireless networking, complete practices 3 and 4 as well.

- **Practice 1:** Connect to a wireless network with a mobile computer. Open a command prompt and run the command *ping -t gateway* to ping your default gateway continuously. The ping loop enables you to monitor whether you are connected to the LAN. Now, begin walking away from the wireless access point. How far do you get before you start to lose your connection? How does Windows 7 behave?

- **Practice 2:** Visit *http://answers.microsoft.com/windows/* and browse the Wireless And Networking newsgroup. Read the posts to determine how people solved their different wireless network problems.

- **Practice 3:** Connect to a wireless public hotspot at a hotel, coffee shop, or airport. Browse the Web. Does it require you to authenticate or accept a usage agreement?

- **Practice 4:** Search the Internet for tools that facilitate cracking WEP or WPA-PSK. How easy are they to use? If you have compatible hardware (most hardware does not support cracking), attempt to crack your personal wireless network. How long does it take?

Take a Practice Test

The practice tests on this book's companion CD offer many options. For example, you can test yourself on just one exam objective, or you can test yourself on all the 70-685 certification exam content. You can set up the test so that it closely simulates the experience of taking a certification exam, or you can set it up in study mode so that you can look at the correct answers and explanations after you answer each question.

> *MORE INFO* **PRACTICE TESTS**
>
> **For details about all the practice test options available, see the section entitled "How to Use the Practice Tests," in the Introduction to this book.**

CHAPTER 3

Printers

Printers bridge the gap between the virtual world and the physical world, allowing people to touch what they have created with their computers. Most users only print the most important documents, and therefore, it is important that printers work when users expect them to. If a user needs to print handouts twenty minutes before an important meeting and they encounter an error, you must be able to quickly diagnose and resolve the problem.

To keep users productive, you must understand how to configure and troubleshoot shared printers. This chapter shows you how to troubleshoot common problems with printer drivers, sharing, and hardware.

Exam objective in this chapter:

- Identify and resolve network printer issues.

Lesson in this chapter:

Before You Begin

To complete the lessons in this chapter, you should be familiar with Windows 7 and be comfortable with the following tasks:

- Installing Windows 7
- Connecting a computer to a network physically
- Configuring and managing printers
- Performing basic administration tasks on a Windows Server 2008 R2–based domain controller

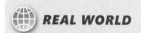

REAL WORLD

Tony Northrup

This book has entire chapters dedicated to troubleshooting hardware and network problems. So, why do network printers get their own chapter? After all, troubleshooting network printers should be a combination of network and hardware troubleshooting.

Though it doesn't necessarily make sense, Windows 7 treats printers very differently from other hardware components. First, you won't find a Printers node in Device Manager. Instead, you have to open the printer's properties dialog box to change drivers. Second, standard users can't install most driver types, but they can install printer drivers (if you let them). Printers are also the only hardware component that's commonly shared across a network.

Besides the unique way Windows 7 handles printers, printers deserve their own chapter because they cause so many more support calls than other hardware types. Many travelling users connect to different printers on a regular basis, depending on whether they are at home, at the office, or in a hotel. Each printer might require a new connection and drivers. Printers are also much higher-maintenance than other pieces of hardware because they run out of paper or ink regularly, and their complex inner workings can cause them to fail more often than other hardware components.

Lesson 1: Troubleshooting Network Printers

This lesson describes the processes and tools that you can use to troubleshoot complex problems with shared printers, including failed services, invalid drivers, firewall configuration problems, and network outages. For simpler problems, Windows 7 makes the troubleshooting so straightforward that no instruction is necessary. For example, if a printer runs out of paper, Windows 7 simply informs the user. Similarly, if a user lacks sufficient privileges to print, Windows 7 displays an error message describing the problem.

This lesson is written on the assumption that you are already familiar with configuring and managing printers in Windows 7 and Windows Server 2008 R2.

> **After this lesson, you will be able to:**
> - Use the Printer Troubleshooter built into Windows 7.
> - Examine printer-related events in the event log.
> - Configure Group Policy settings to facilitate printer troubleshooting.
> - Troubleshoot problems with a print server.
> - Troubleshoot printer driver problems.
> - Troubleshoot problems connecting to printers across a network.
>
> **Estimated lesson time: 25 minutes**

Using the Printer Troubleshooter

Windows provides a built-in troubleshooting feature for diagnosing problems related to printers. The troubleshooter is designed to be easy enough for users to utilize, but it is also the best first step for systems administrators to take when diagnosing a printer problem.

If you are having a problem connecting to a shared printer, follow these steps to open the Printer Troubleshooter:

1. Click Start and then click Control Panel.
2. Click System And Security.
3. Under Action Center, click Troubleshoot Common Computer Problems.
4. Under Hardware And Sound, click Use A Printer.
5. The Printer Troubleshooter appears and attempts to diagnose the problem. Follow the steps that appear.
6. On the Troubleshoot And Help Prevent Computer Problems page, click Next.
7. On the Which Printer Would You Like To Troubleshoot? page, click My Printer Is Not Listed. Click Next.

8. Respond to the prompts that appear to troubleshoot your problem.

If you are having a problem printing to an existing printer, follow these steps to run the Printer Troubleshooter:

1. Click Start and then click Devices And Printers.

2. Right-click the printer and then click Troubleshoot.

   The Printer Troubleshooter appears and attempts to diagnose the problem.

3. Respond to the prompts that appear.

The Printer Troubleshooter can detect the following problems:

- No physical printer is installed.
- A new printer hasn't yet been detected.
- The printer is not the default printer.
- The printer is not shared.
- The printer is out of paper.
- The printer is out of toner.
- The printer has a paper jam.
- The printer driver needs to be updated.
- The printer is turned off.
- A print job is preventing other print jobs from printing.
- The Print Spooler service is not running or has an error.

As shown in Figure 3-1, the Printer Troubleshooter can repair some configuration-related problems automatically (though Administrative privileges might be required).

Monitoring Printer Events

Windows 7 adds printer-related events to the Applications And Services Logs\Microsoft\ Windows\PrintService\Admin event log. Common events include:

- Changing the default printer
- Errors related to initializing a new printer or driver
- Errors occurring when attempting to connect to a network printer
- Errors occurring when attempting to share a printer

Windows 7 can add events to the Security event log when users initially connect to a printer. To add an event when users connect, use Group Policy to enable success or failure auditing for the Audit Logon Events policy in the Computer Configuration\Windows Settings\ Security Settings\Local Policies\Audit Policy node.

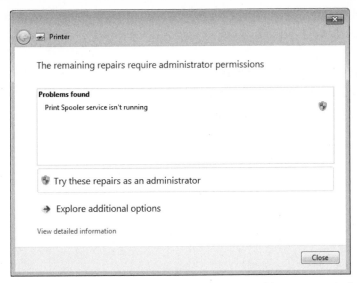

FIGURE 3-1 The Printer Troubleshooter can fix some problems automatically.

Windows 7 does not support auditing when users print or manage printers. However, Windows Server 2008 R2 does support object auditing for printers. First, enable success or failure auditing for the Audit Object Access policy in the Computer Configuration\Windows Settings\Security Settings\Local Policies\Audit Policy node. Then, follow these steps to enable auditing for the printer:

1. Click Start and then click Devices And Printers.

2. Right-click the printer and then click Printer Properties.

   The printer properties dialog box appears.

3. On the Security tab, click Advanced.

   The Advanced Security Settings dialog box appears.

4. On the Auditing tab, click Add.

   The Select User, Computer, Service Account, Or Group dialog box appears.

5. Type the name of the user or group that you want to audit, and then click OK.

   The Auditing Entry dialog box appears.

6. Select success or failure auditing for the different access types, as shown in Figure 3-2. Click OK three times.

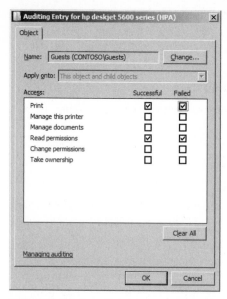

FIGURE 3-2 Windows 7 does not support printer auditing, but Windows Server 2008 R2 does.

Now, Windows Server 2008 R2 adds events to the Security event log when users in the group that you specified perform the types of access that you specified.

Group Policy Settings for Troubleshooting

Windows 7 provides many Group Policy settings that allow you to configure the behavior of printers and printer drivers in the Computer Configuration\Administrative Templates\Printers node. In addition, you can configure client computers to connect automatically to a shared printer by adding the printer to the Computer Configuration\Windows Settings\Deployed Printers or User Configuration\Windows Settings\Deployed Printers node.

Because the 70-685 exam focuses on troubleshooting, this book does not describe Group Policy settings related to deploying or managing printers. However, the following Group Policy settings can be useful for troubleshooting printers on computers running Windows 7:

- **Execute Print Drivers In Isolated Processes**   By default, the print spooler keeps print drivers in a separate process. This enables the print spooler to continue to function even if a print driver fails. The default setting is best for troubleshooting, but if you find that the print spooler is failing, you should verify that this setting has not been disabled.

- **Override Print Driver Execution Compatibility Setting Reported By Print Driver**   Print Drivers provide a driver isolation compatibility flag that indicates whether the print driver should be run in a separate process from the print spooler. If you enable this setting (which is disabled by default), the print spooler runs all print drivers in a separate process, regardless of their driver isolation compatibility flag. If you find that the print spooler is failing, you should enable this setting.

- **Allow Print Spooler To Accept Client Connections**   This setting prevents a computer from acting as a print server. If you experience problems sharing a printer, verify that this setting is enabled (the default).

Troubleshooting Server Problems

In home environments, users typically connect their computers to their printers using a universal serial bus (USB) cable. In business environments, printers are often shared between many users. To connect many different users to a printer, printers must be accessible from the network.

There are two common methods for sharing a printer on a network:

- **Connecting the printer directly to the network**   Printers must have networking capabilities, which require them to have an Ethernet port or wireless network capabilities.

- **Connecting the printer to a computer and sharing it on the network**   In this scenario, the computer that is connected directly to the printer becomes the print server. All recent client and server versions of Microsoft Windows are capable of acting as print servers.

Choosing Whether to Use a Print Server

Connecting a printer directly to the network can reduce your upfront costs by not requiring you to purchase or configure a server. In addition, a printer that is shared directly from the network does not go offline if a server fails. Depending on the management capabilities of the networked printer, a direct network connection might be the best choice for your environment. However, configuring a computer to act as the print server offers several advantages:

- **Integration with Windows security**   When you share a printer from Windows, you can configure which Active Directory Domain Services (AD DS) accounts have access to print or perform different management functions.

- **Integration with AD DS browsing**   You can publish printers to your AD DS and allow users to browse to find the closest printer.

- **Automatic installation of printer drivers**   Windows print servers can provide print drivers to client computers the first time they connect, simplifying management.

- **Integration with enterprise management tools**   Problems with printers generate events in the event log, which you can manage using standard enterprise management tools, including Microsoft Systems Center Operations Manager.

Requirements for a Print Server

For a computer to share printers, it must have two services running:

- **Server**   This service is required for sharing either files or printers across the network.
- **Print Spooler**   This service is required for printing.

Client computers connecting to the shared printer require the Workstation service and the Print Spooler service. If a required service does not start, verify that all the service's prerequisite services are started. Then, review events in the System event log and the Applications And Services Logs\Microsoft\Windows\PrintService\Admin event log.

How to Share a Printer

In Windows Server 2008 R2 or Windows 7, follow these steps to manage a shared printer:

1. Click Start, and then click Devices And Printers.

2. Right-click the printer and then click Printer Properties. Do not click Properties; Printer Properties is in the middle of the shortcut list.

3. On the Sharing tab, select the Share This Printer check box. You then have three additional options:

   - Select the Render Print Jobs On Client Computers setting to reduce the processor performance impact on the server by forcing the client to do more of the print rendering. If your print server has more processing power than client computers and print performance does not suffer, clear this check box.

   - If you are part of an AD DS environment, you can select the List In Directory check box. This publishes the printer to AD DS, so that users can browse to find printers near their location.

   - Click Additional Drivers to select other processor types to store drivers for. Clients can download a driver automatically from the server if the driver type is available. When you click OK, you might be prompted to select a path where the driver is located. Click OK.

How to Manage Print Jobs on a Printer

In Windows Server 2008 R2 or Windows 7, follow these steps to manage a shared printer:

1. Click Start, and then click Devices And Printers.

2. Double-click the printer you want to manage.

3. Click See What's Printing.

4. Windows displays the *print queue*, a first-in, first-out collection of documents waiting to be printed. You can right-click any document and then click Pause, Restart, or Cancel.

Troubleshooting the Print Queue

If you ever encounter a document that won't leave the print queue, you can clear it by restarting the Print Spooler service. You can use the Services node in the Computer Management tool, or you can run *net stop spooler* and *net start spooler* from an administrative command prompt. To restart the Print Spooler service in a single command, run *net stop spooler && net start spooler*.

If restarting the print spooler does not remove unwanted documents from the print queue, you can remove them manually by following these steps:

1. First, stop the Print Spooler service, as described earlier in this section.

2. Next, use Windows Explorer to delete all files in the %WinDir%\System32\Spool\ Printers folder. This folder has two files for every document in the print queue: one .SHD file, and one .SPL file.

3. Start the Print Spooler service.

EXAM TIP

You must understand the importance of the Print Spooler service for the exam. The service must be running on both the client and the server to be able to print or manage printers. Restarting the Print Spooler service clears the print queue, which can resolve the problem of a document that won't print and prevents other documents from printing.

Troubleshooting Driver Problems

Drivers handle communications between Windows and any piece of hardware. For example, Windows has drivers for video adapters, keyboards, mice, and monitors, in addition to printer drivers. For most hardware components, you use Device Manager to manage printer drivers. For printers, however, you use the printer properties dialog box.

How to Update a Driver for the Print Server

When you connect a new printer, Windows 7 detects the new hardware and attempts to install a driver automatically. If the standard driver causes problems, follow these steps to install a different driver:

1. Click Start, and then click Devices And Printers.

2. Right-click the printer you want to manage and then click Printer Properties.

3. On the Advanced tab, click New Driver to add a driver.

4. The Add Printer Driver Wizard guides you through the process. You can select a driver built in to Windows, download a driver from Windows Update, or choose a driver that you have saved to the hard disk.

Occasionally, a driver installation fails, causing the printer to stop working. The quickest way to reinstall the driver is to reinstall the printer by following these steps:

1. Remove any documents from the print queue, as described in the section entitled "Troubleshooting the Print Queue," earlier in this lesson.

2. Remove the printer by right-clicking it and then clicking Remove Device.

3. Use the Uninstall A Program tool in Control Panel to uninstall any printer-related software.

4. Reinstall the printer with the latest version of the driver. In the Devices And Printers window, click Add A Printer and follow the prompts that appear.

If reinstalling the printer does not solve the problem, you might need to remove files related to the driver installation manually by following these steps:

1. First, stop the Print Spooler service.

2. Use Windows Explorer to browse to either the %WinDir%\System32\Spool\Drivers\ W32x86\3\ folder (or 32-bit versions of Windows) or the %WinDir%\System32\Spool\ Drivers\x64\3\ folder (or 64-bit versions of Windows).

3. Inside the selected folder, remove any numbered subfolders.

4. Finally, start the Print Spooler service.

For information about troubleshooting non-driver-related hardware problems, refer to Chapter 1, "Troubleshooting Hardware Failures."

How to Add Drivers for Shared Printer Clients

When connecting to a new printer, clients running Windows can install automatically drivers that are stored on the print server. By default, the print server has only the drivers required for the print server to print. For example, a 64-bit print server running Windows 7 has 64-bit printer drivers but not 32-bit printer drivers. Therefore, 64-bit clients running Windows 7 automatically install the driver from the print server, but 32-bit clients running Windows 7 need to download a driver from Windows Update or prompt users to provide their own drivers.

While managing the print server, you can store drivers for different processor architectures for a specific printer, or you can store drivers for any model of printer you specify. For example, you can add a 32-bit printer driver to a 64-bit print server and allow 32-bit Windows 7 clients to automatically download the driver.

To store drivers for different processor architectures, follow these steps:

1. Click Start, and then click Devices And Printers.

2. Right-click the printer and then click Printer Properties.

3. On the Sharing tab, click Additional Drivers.

4. In the Additional Drivers dialog box, select the processor architectures for which you want to store drivers. By default, only the driver for the server's processor architecture is available. Click OK.

5. In the Install Print Drivers dialog box, select a path with the driver. For example, if you have installed the 32-bit version of Windows 7 and you want to provide the printer driver automatically to clients running the 64-bit version of Windows 7, you should download the 64-bit version of the driver and select it now. Click OK twice.

To store drivers for any printer, follow these steps:

1. Click Start, and then click Devices And Printers.
2. Click any printer, and then click Print Server Properties on the toolbar.
3. On the Drivers tab of the Print Server Properties dialog box, click Add.

   The Add Printer Driver Wizard appears.
4. On the Welcome To The Add Printer Driver Wizard page, click Next.
5. On the Processor And Operating System Selection page, select the processor architectures for which you want to install drivers. Click Next.
6. On the Printer Driver Selection page, select the driver that you want to install from the list of drivers included with Windows 7. If the driver that you want to install is not available, you can download the driver and click Have Disk to select the driver. Click Next.
7. Click Finish.
8. If prompted, provide a path for printer drivers.

If updating the driver does not solve the problem, or only one version of the driver is available, you should determine whether disabling advanced printing features resolves the problem. To disable advanced printing features for a printer, follow these steps:

1. Click Start, and then click Devices And Printers.
2. Right-click the printer and then click Printer Properties.
3. On the Advanced tab of the printer properties dialog box, clear the Enable Advanced Printing Features check box and click OK.

Troubleshooting Point And Print

By default, Windows 7 allows standard users to install only trustworthy drivers. Windows 7 considers drivers provided with Windows or drivers provided in digitally signed printer-driver packages trustworthy. By limiting users to install only trustworthy drivers, you reduce the risk that a non-trustworthy driver will decrease system stability (because the driver is unreliable) or perform malicious acts (because the driver is malware). Windows 7 includes a large number of printer drivers, so most users can connect to printers while they travel and install drivers on demand.

In Windows Vista and Windows 7, the ability to install printer drivers automatically is called *Point And Print*. You can use the Point And Print Restrictions Group Policy setting and the Package Point And Print – Approved Servers Group Policy setting to restrict Point And Print to specific servers. If you find that Point And Print fails, verify that the Point And Print Restrictions setting is not enabled, or add the print server to the list of approved Point And Print print servers.

If users receive unwanted User Account Control (UAC) prompts, enable the Point And Print Restrictions policy, and adjust the Security Prompts settings, as shown in Figure 3-3.

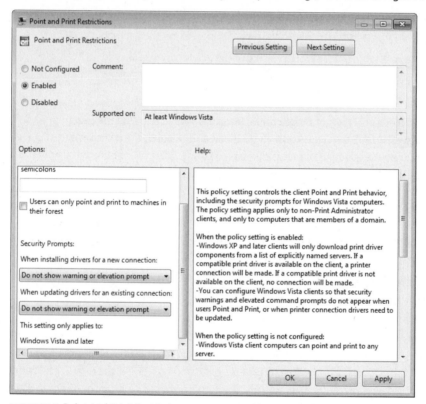

FIGURE 3-3 Point And Print Restrictions can cause problems printing to new printers.

Troubleshooting Network Problems

Problems connecting to shared printers can be caused by several different factors:

- The client can't find the server because of a name resolution problem.
- A firewall is preventing the client from connecting to the server.
- The server is rejecting the user's credentials.

In most cases, printer troubleshooting begins when a user calls to complain. Therefore, you typically begin troubleshooting from the client computer. Depending on the nature of the problem, you might also have to log on to the print server. The following sections describe the troubleshooting process, assuming that the client and server are domain members.

For more information about troubleshooting network problems, read Chapter 2, "Networking." Also, refer to Chapter 31, "Troubleshooting Network Issues," in the *Windows 7 Resource Kit* by Mitch Tulloch, Tony Northrup, and Jerry Honeycutt (Microsoft Press, 2009).

How to Troubleshoot Printer Sharing from the Client

Perform these steps to troubleshoot problems connecting to shared printers:

1. Stop the Offline Files service if it is started. If the Offline Files service is running, Windows might report that it can connect to a remote server even though the server is not available. You can stop the Offline Files service from the Services console or by running the command *net stop cscservice* from an administrative command prompt.

2. If you are connecting using File And Printer Sharing, instead of using Internet Printing Protocol (IPP) or Line Printer Daemon/Line Printer Remote (LPD/LPR), attempt to establish a NetBIOS connection manually. Open a command prompt and issue the command *net view \\server*. If the connection succeeds, it tells you the exact name of the shared printer, and you know there is not a network or firewall connectivity problem. If you receive an "Access is denied" message when attempting to connect to the printer, the user account lacks sufficient permissions to access the shared printer. Depending on the server configuration, you might be able to identify authentication problems by viewing the Security event log on the server. For more information about security auditing, see the section entitled "Monitoring Printer Events," earlier in this lesson. For more information about adjusting privileges, see the section entitled "How to Troubleshoot Printer Sharing from the Server," later in this lesson.

3. If you stopped the Offline Files service in step 1, restart it now using the Services console or by running the command *net start cscservice* from an administrative command prompt.

4. Verify that you can resolve the server's name, as described in Lesson 2, "Troubleshooting Name Resolution," of Chapter 2. If you cannot resolve the server's name because the Domain Name System (DNS) server is offline, you can work around the name resolution problem by connecting using the server's Internet Protocol (IP) address rather than the server's host name. For example, instead of connecting to \\servername\printer, you might connect to \\10.1.42.22\printer.

5. If you are connecting using File And Printer Sharing, use PortQry to test whether the client can connect to TCP port 445 or TCP port 139 on the server. If you are connecting with IPP, test whether the client can connect to TCP port 80 on the server.

If you are still unable to connect, continue troubleshooting from the server, as described in the next section.

Quick Check

- Which tools can you use to verify that a firewall is not preventing you from connecting across the network to a shared printer?

Quick Check Answer

- You can use the *net use* command to connect to the print server, or you can use the *PortQry* command to verify that the server is listening for incoming network connections on the ports used by printer sharing (primarily TCP 445 or TCP 139).

How to Troubleshoot Printer Sharing from the Server

If you are sharing a printer from a computer running Windows 7, you can troubleshoot it by performing these steps:

1. Verify that you can print from the print server. If you cannot print, the problem is not related to printer sharing. Instead, you should troubleshoot the problem as a local printer problem. Start by using the Printer Troubleshooter, as described in the section entitled "Using the Printer Troubleshooter," earlier in this lesson. Clear the print queue, as described in the section entitled "Troubleshooting the Print Queue," earlier in this lesson, and then attempt to print again. If you are still unable to print, reinstall the printer with the latest driver, as described in the section entitled "How to Update a Driver for the Print Server," earlier in this lesson.

2. Verify that the folder or printer is shared. To do this, right-click the printer and then click Printer Properties. Then, click the Sharing tab, and verify that Share This Printer is selected.

3. Though the Printer Troubleshooter already should have verified this, you can verify manually that the Server and Print Spooler services are running. To do this, click Start, right-click Computer, and then click Manage. Under Services And Applications, select the Services node. Verify that the Server and Print Spooler services are started and the Startup Type is set to Automatic.

4. Verify that users have the necessary permission to access the resources. To do this, right-click the printer and then click Printer Properties. In the printer properties dialog box, click the Security tab. Verify that the user account is a member of a group that appears on the list and that the Print Allow check box is selected. If the account is not on the list, add it to the list and grant the Print Allow permission.

5. Check the Windows Firewall exceptions to verify that they are configured properly by performing the following steps:

   a. Click Start and then click Control Panel.

   b. Click System And Security and then click Windows Firewall.

c. In the Windows Firewall dialog box, note the Network Location. Click Allow A Program Or Feature Through Windows Firewall.

d. On the Allowed Programs window, determine whether the File And Printer Sharing check box is selected. If it is not selected, click Change Settings and select it for the current network location. If it is selected, verify that no other firewall rule is blocking File And Printer Sharing. Click OK.

Firewall Configuration

Firewalls, including Windows Firewall, selectively block network traffic that has not been allowed explicitly. Most firewalls block incoming connections (connections sent from a client to a server) by default, and allow all outgoing connections (connections sent from a server to a client). Therefore, if printer sharing has not been allowed explicitly on a print server, clients are unable to connect. If clients are unable to connect to a print server, you should check the firewall configuration on the print server. If the client and server are not on the same local area network (LAN), you must also check the configuration of any firewalls that might block traffic between the client and server.

How you configure the firewall depends on the network protocol used to connect to the print server:

- **File And Printer Sharing**   This type of printer connection uses a Universal Naming Convention (UNC) path such as *servername*\printer or \\192.168.1.10\printer. If the File And Printer Sharing exception is enabled on the print server, as shown in Figure 3-4, Windows Firewall allows connections to the shared printer. This firewall exception is enabled automatically when you share a printer; however, administrators might have removed the exception either manually or by using Group Policy.

- **Internet Printing Protocol (IPP)**   This type of printer connection uses a Universal Resource Locator (URL) path such as *http://server/printers/printer/.printer*. Windows Vista and Windows 7 can only act as an IPP client; they cannot share a printer using IPP. However, Windows XP, Windows Server 2003, and Windows Server 2008 can share printers using IPP. For HTTP connections, the server must allow incoming connections using TCP port 80. For HTTPS connections, the server must allow incoming connections using TCP port 443.

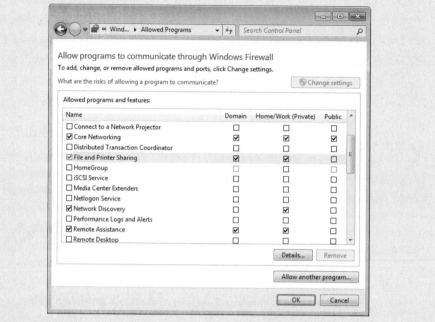

FIGURE 3-4 Verify that the File And Printer Sharing firewall exception is enabled.

Troubleshooting Printer Problems

In this practice, you troubleshoot two different printer problems.

EXERCISE 1   Troubleshooting Printer Sharing

In this exercise, you troubleshoot a client computer that cannot print to a print server.

1. Connect a printer to your domain controller, DC1. Alternatively, you can connect a printer to any computer running Windows 7 or Windows Server 2008 R2 in your test environment. The computer should not be part of a production environment, however. If you do not have a printer, you can install a printer driver manually for a printer that is not connected.

2. Share the printer from DC1 by following these steps:

    a. On DC1, click Start and then click Devices And Printers.

    b. Right-click the printer and then click Printer Properties.

    c. On the Sharing tab, select the Share This Printer check box and the List In The Directory check box. Click OK.

3. Connect to the printer from CLIENT1 by following these steps:

    a. On CLIENT1, click Start and then click Devices And Printers.

    b. Click Add A Printer.

The Add Printer wizard appears.

   a. On the What Type Of Printer Do You Want To Install? page, click Add A Network, Wireless, Or Bluetooth Printer.

   b. On the next page, click the printer you shared from DC1, and then click Next.

   c. On the You've Successfully Added page, click Next.

   d. Click Print A Test Page to verify that the printer is installed successfully. Then, click Finish.

4. On DC1, verify that the page prints successfully. If you do not have a physical printer, double-click the printer from the Devices And Printers page and verify that a document is in the queue.

5. Right-click the script Ch3-lesson1-ex1-script1.cmd and then click Run As Administrator to introduce a printer problem that you will solve in the steps that follow.

6. From CLIENT1, attempt to print again. You can print by double-clicking the printer from the Devices And Printers page, clicking Customize Your Printer, and then clicking Print Test Page from the General tab of the Printer Properties dialog box. Notice that the document is added to the print queue on CLIENT1, but it does not appear on the print queue in DC1. This indicates that the connection between the client and server is unavailable.

7. From CLIENT1, troubleshoot the network connectivity problem by performing the following steps:

   a. Open an administrative command prompt and attempt to ping DC1 from CLIENT1. You should be able to ping DC1 successfully, indicating that CLIENT1 and DC1 can communicate.

   b. While still at the command prompt on CLIENT1, attempt to stop the Offline Files service by running the command *net stop cscservice*. Make note of whether the service was already stopped or whether Windows 7 had to stop it.

   c. While still at the command prompt on CLIENT1, attempt to establish a NetBIOS connection by running the command *net view \\dc1*. Notice that the connection attempt fails with the message "The network name cannot be found." This indicates that CLIENT1 cannot connect to the Server service on DC1. You know the computer must be online and connected to the network because the previous ping attempt succeeded; therefore, you can conclude that the Server service is unavailable.

   d. If you had to stop the Offline Files service in step b, restart it by running the command *net start cscservice* at the administrative command prompt on CLIENT1.

   e. Verify that the Server service is running. To do this, on DC1, click Start, right-click Computer, and then click Manage. In the Computer Management console, select the Services And Applications\Services node. Scroll to the Server service and verify that it is running and that the Startup Type is set to Automatic.

f. Verify that File And Printer Sharing is allowed in Windows Firewall. Click Start and then click Control Panel. Click System And Security, and then click Allow A Program Through Windows Firewall. Verify that File And Printer Sharing is selected.

   g. While still in the Windows Firewall Allowed Programs window, examine other firewall rules, and notice the rule named Block File And Printer Sharing. As indicated by the name, this firewall rule might be blocking the connection attempt. Click Change Settings, and then clear the Block File And Printer Sharing check box. Click OK.

8. On DC1, switch to the printer window. Notice that the document you printed earlier is now in the queue or is already printing, indicating that you solved the problem.

9. Finally, right-click the script Ch3-lesson1-ex1-script2.cmd and then click Run As Administrator to remove the firewall rule that the first script added. Then, remove the printer that you added in step 1 of this exercise.

EXERCISE 2   **Troubleshooting a Local Printer**

In this exercise, you install a printer and troubleshoot problems printing locally.

1. Connect a printer to your computer running Windows 7, CLIENT1. Alternatively, you can connect a printer to any computer running Windows 7 or Windows Server 2008 R2 in your test environment. The computer should not be part of a production environment, however. If you do not have a printer, you can install a printer driver manually for a printer that is not connected. When you install the printer, choose to print a test page and verify that the printer functions correctly.

2. Right-click the script Ch3-lesson1-ex2-script1.cmd and then click Run As Administrator to introduce a printer problem that you will solve in the steps that follow.

3. From CLIENT1, open Windows Internet Explorer. Then, press Ctrl+P to print the current Web page. Notice that you receive an error indicating that you do not have a printer installed. Click OK, and then click Cancel.

4. From CLIENT1, troubleshoot the local printer problem by performing the following steps:

   a. Verify that your printer is still installed. Click Start, and then click Devices And Printers. Notice that no printers are listed. This can happen if either all printers were deleted or if the Print Spooler service is not running.

   b. Verify that the Print Spooler service is running. Click Start, right-click Computer, and then click Manage. In the Computer Management console, select the Services And Applications\Services node. Scroll to the Print Spooler service and notice that it does not have a Status of Started. Right-click the service and then click Start.

5. Return to Internet Explorer and press Ctrl+P again to print the current Web page. Click Print to verify that you can print successfully.

6. Finally, remove the printer that you added in step 1 of this exercise.

Lesson Summary

- Use the Printer Troubleshooter built into Windows 7 to diagnose and solve common problems quickly.

- Use the Applications And Services Logs\Microsoft\Windows\PrintService\Admin event log to determine whether Windows 7 has added any printer-related events. If the print server is running Windows Server 2008 R2, you can enable object access auditing to add events to the Security event log when users access printers.

- You can configure several Group Policy settings to facilitate printer troubleshooting, especially for driver-related problems.

- Print servers must have both the Print Spooler and the Server services running to share a printer. The most common print server-related problem is a print queue that stops processing print jobs. To resolve that issue, restart the Print Spooler service.

- Both the print server and the client must have a printer driver installed. You can update drivers from the printer properties dialog box. If a driver update fails to install correctly, remove the printer and then reinstall it.

- Troubleshoot problems connecting across the network to a shared printer by verifying that the client can resolve the name of the server, that no firewall is blocking file and printer sharing communications, and that the client can establish a file and printer sharing connection to the server.

Lesson Review

You can use the following questions to test your knowledge of the information in Lesson 1, "Troubleshooting Network Printers." The questions are also available on the companion CD if you prefer to review them in electronic form.

> **NOTE   ANSWERS**
>
> Answers to these questions and explanations of why each answer choice is correct or incorrect are located in the "Answers" section at the end of the book.

1. A user is attempting to connect to a network printer using the UNC name *servername*\printer. The user receives the error message "Windows couldn't connect to the printer." Which of the following might be the cause of the problem?

    A. The Server service is not started on the client.

    B. The Workstation service is not started on the server.

    C. The File And Printer Sharing firewall exception is not enabled on the server.

    D. The File And Printer Sharing firewall exception is not enabled on the client.

2. A user previously has been able to print to a network printer, but the printer appears to be unavailable. You want to verify that all the required services are running. Which of the following services are required on the print server? (Choose all that apply.)

   A. Workstation

   B. Print Spooler

   C. Server

   D. Peer Name Resolution Protocol

3. A user calls to complain that she is experiencing a problem with her printer. When she prints a large print job, the printer adds a blank page between each printed page. You research the problem and discover that it is driver-related. The hardware manufacturer recommends using a driver for a different printer to resolve the problem. Which tool should you use to change the driver?

   A. Services

   B. Device Manager

   C. Event Viewer

   D. Printer Properties dialog box

Chapter Review

To further practice and reinforce the skills you learned in this chapter, you can perform the following tasks:

- Review the chapter summary.
- Review the list of key terms introduced in this chapter.
- Complete the case scenarios. These scenarios set up real-world situations involving the topics of this chapter and ask you to create a solution.
- Complete the suggested practices.
- Take a practice test.

Chapter Summary

- Problems with network printers can have several different sources: client or server print drivers, the print queue, printer permissions, and network connectivity.
- To solve driver problems, add the latest driver version to the print server, or replace the driver by reinstalling the printer. In addition, you can store printer drivers on the print server so new clients can install the printer driver automatically.
- To solve print queue problems, restart the Print Spooler service.
- To diagnose problems related to printer permissions, enable security and examine the Security event log. To resolve the security problems, adjust the printer permissions.
- You can use standard network troubleshooting tools to troubleshoot network connectivity. To verify that you can establish a connection to a print server, use the *net use* command.

Key Terms

Do you know what these key terms mean? You can check your answers by looking up the terms in the glossary at the end of the book.

- **print queue**
- **Point And Print**

Case Scenarios

In the following case scenarios, you apply what you've learned about subjects of this chapter. You can find answers to these questions in the "Answers" section at the end of this book.

Case Scenario 1: Troubleshooting Insufficient Privileges

Your manager calls you into his office because he is unable to connect to a network printer. The printer appears as an option in the Add Printer Wizard, but when he selects it, the wizard prompts him for a user name and password. When he provides his AD DS user name and password, he receives the message "The credentials supplied are not sufficient to access this printer."

Answer the following questions for your manager:

1. Why is he receiving the error message?
2. How can you solve the problem?

Case Scenario 2: Troubleshooting a Printer Problem

A user calls to complain that she is unable to print to a network printer. You are familiar with the printer, and you know that it is being shared from a computer running Windows Server 2008 R2. The user previously has printed to the printer successfully.

You log on to the print server and verify that you can print from the server itself. You also verify that the user has sufficient privileges.

Answer the following questions related to the troubleshooting process:

1. What questions should you ask the user?
2. How would you narrow down the cause of the problem?
3. What are some possible causes of the problem?

Suggested Practices

To help you master the exam objectives presented in this chapter, complete the following tasks.

Identify and Resolve Network Printer Issues

Troubleshooting is a skill that requires real-world experience. Although this chapter can discuss concepts and tools, only practice gives you the skills that you need to troubleshoot network printer problems and pass the exam. Perform as many of these practices as possible to build your troubleshooting skills.

- **Practice 1**   Visit *http://social.answers.microsoft.com/Forums/en-US/categories* and browse the questions related to printing. Read the posts to determine how people solved their printing problems.

- **Practice 2**   Connect to a shared printer and simulate different hardware problems to see how the client communicates the error to the user. First, disconnect the shared printer from the print server. Next, remove all paper from the printer. Finally, stop sharing the printer.

- **Practice 3**   Use the *net use* command-line command to establish a connection from a Windows 7 client to a server.

- **Practice 4**   Share a printer. Add printer drivers for a different processor architecture to allow clients with that processor architecture to install the printer driver automatically.

Take a Practice Test

The practice tests on this book's companion CD offer many options. For example, you can test yourself on just one exam objective, or you can test yourself on all the 70-685 certification exam content. You can set up the test so that it closely simulates the experience of taking a certification exam, or you can set it up in study mode so that you can look at the correct answers and explanations after you answer each question.

> **MORE INFO   PRACTICE TESTS**
>
> For details about all the practice test options available, see the section entitled "How to Use the Practice Tests," in the Introduction to this book.

CHAPTER 4

Security

F or some users, problems begin before they even log on. Authentication, the process of identifying users and validating their credentials, can be very complex in a Windows 7 environment. Although home users might never run into problems typing their user names and passwords, in Active Directory Directory Services (AD DS) environments, users authenticate to domain controllers and other servers on the network. In addition, authentication can use smart cards or biometrics as well as passwords. User Account Control (UAC) adds another layer of complexity because a user might use multiple sets of credentials within a single session.

In recent years, more and more security compromises are initiated when users visit a Web site. For example, Web sites might trick the user into providing confidential information, or they might exploit a vulnerability in the browser to run code without the user's explicit permission. In Windows 7, Windows Internet Explorer 8.0 includes several features to reduce this risk.

Though network attacks are the most widespread, the increase in mobile users has led to an increase in physical data theft. If someone steals a computer, he or she can bypass all your security controls except encryption. Windows 7 provides two ways to encrypt the files on your computer: Encrypting File System (EFS), which encrypts individual files and folders on a per-user basis, and BitLocker, which encrypts entire volumes.

This chapter describes how to configure and troubleshoot authentication, Internet Explorer, EFS, and BitLocker.

Exam objectives in this chapter:
- Identify and resolve logon issues.
- Identify and resolve Windows Internet Explorer security issues.
- Identify and resolve encryption issues.

Lessons in this chapter:

Before You Begin

To complete the lessons in this chapter, you should be familiar with Windows 7 and be comfortable with the following tasks:

- Installing Windows 7
- Connecting a computer physically to a network
- Performing basic administration tasks on a Windows Server 2008 R2–based domain controller

 REAL WORLD

Tony Northrup

To businesses, security is a math problem: if a countermeasure reduces risk by more than it costs, then they use it.

Unfortunately, calculating risk and cost is rarely straightforward. For example, consider the risk of an attacker stealing a mobile computer and misusing confidential files. I'm making very rough estimates, but a mobile computer might have a 2 percent chance of being stolen in a given year. Out of those laptops, perhaps 10 percent of thieves find and abuse confidential information. Therefore, there is a 0.2 percent chance of confidential data being abused annually per laptop.

However, the cost can be significant. To a big business, such a compromise could cost millions—so let's estimate that a single compromise would cost $10 million. If the business has 100 computers with confidential data on them, the total risk is $2 million annually.

If the risk is $2 million annually, you wouldn't want to spend more than that to mitigate it. Windows 7 includes BitLocker Drive Encryption to mitigate the risk of a stolen computer. However, it's not effective if a user is currently logged in, if the attacker also steals the universal serial bus (USB) flash drive, or if the attacker can guess the user's personal identification number (PIN). For the sake of this example, let's assume that properly training users, automatically locking computers that are not in use, and requiring BitLocker Drive Encryption with either a USB flash drive or a PIN as a startup key is 80 percent effective at mitigating the risk of stolen computers.

By reducing the $2 million dollar risk by 80 percent, you've just saved the fictional company $1.6 million annually. You've incurred some cost, though. IT needs to upgrade computers with confidential data to Windows 7, upgrade hardware where necessary, and spend time training users. Let's estimate that this will cost $3,000 per user up front. If the computer stays in service for three years, the cost is $1,000 per user annually, or $100,000 total—reducing the annual savings from $1.6 million to $1.5 million. BitLocker has ongoing costs, too, especially if you require a startup key, because some users will forget their USB flash drive or PIN and be locked out of their computers, losing productivity and incurring a call to IT. These costs get very difficult to estimate, but if 10 percent of the 100 users with confidential data have a problem in one year, and the lost productivity and support call cost $500 per user, then the cost is $5,000 per year.

Given those estimates of risk and cost, BitLocker is a very worthwhile to this fictional company. Not all security features are worthwhile, though. The next time you're troubleshooting a security problem, think about whether the time you're spending troubleshooting the problem and the productivity that users are losing are worth the benefits of the security feature. For more information, read the Security Risk Management Guide at *http://technet.microsoft.com/en-us/library/cc163143.aspx*.

Lesson 1: Authenticating Users

Before a user can log on to a computer running Windows 7, connect to a shared folder, or browse a protected Web site, the resource must validate the user's identity using a process known as *authentication*. Windows 7 supports a variety of authentication techniques, including the traditional user name and password, smart cards, and third-party authentication components. In addition, Windows 7 can authenticate users with the local user database or an AD DS domain.

This lesson provides a basic background in authentication technologies and then describes how to audit logons and troubleshoot authentication problems.

After this lesson, you will be able to:

- Describe authentication and list common authentication techniques.
- Add user names and passwords manually to Credential Manager to enable automatic authentication to network resources.
- Troubleshoot authentication issues.

Estimated lesson time: 25 minutes

What Is Authentication?

Authentication is the process of identifying a user. In home environments, authentication is often as simple as clicking a user name at the Windows 7 logon screen. However, in enterprise environments, almost all authentication requests require users to provide both a user name (to identify themselves) and a password (to prove that they really are the user they claim to be).

Windows 7 also supports authentication using a smart card. The smart card, which is about the size of a credit card, contains a chip with a certificate that uniquely identifies the user. So long as a user doesn't give the smart card to someone else, inserting the smart card into a computer sufficiently proves the user's identity. Typically, users also need to type a password or PIN to prove that they aren't using someone else's smart card. When you combine two forms of authentication (such as both typing a password and providing a smart card), it's called *multifactor authentication*. Multifactor authentication is much more secure than single-factor authentication.

Biometrics is another popular form of authentication. Although a password proves your identity by testing "something you know" and a smart card tests "something you have," biometrics test "something you are" by examining a unique feature of your physiology. Today the most common biometric authentication mechanisms are fingerprint readers (now built into many mobile computers) and retinal scanners.

How to Use Credential Manager

Credential Manager is a *single-sign on* feature, originally for Windows Server 2003 and Windows XP, that enables users to input user names and passwords for multiple network resources and applications. When different resources require authentication, Windows can then automatically provide the credentials without requiring the user to type them.

In Windows Vista and Windows 7, Credential Manager can roam stored user names and passwords between multiple Windows computers in an AD DS domain. Windows stores credentials in the user's AD DS user object. This enables users to store credentials once and use them from any logon session within the AD DS domain. For example, if you connect to a password-protected Web server and you select the Remember My Password check box, Internet Explorer will be able to retrieve your saved password later, even if you log on to a different computer running Windows Vista or Windows 7.

Users can take advantage of Credential Manager without even being aware of it. For example, each time a user connects to a shared folder or printer and selects the Reconnect At Logon check box, Windows automatically stores that user's credentials within Credential Manager. Similarly, if a user authenticates to a Web site that requires authentication and selects the Remember My Password check box in the Internet Explorer authentication dialog box, Internet Explorer stores the user name and password in Credential Manager.

Windows automatically adds credentials used to connect to shared folders to the Credential Manager. However, you might want to add a user name and password manually so that Windows can provide those credentials automatically for a group of computers in a different domain. To add a user name and password manually to Credential Manager, follow these steps:

1. Click Start, and then click Control Panel.
2. Click the User Accounts link twice.
3. In the left pane, click the Manage Your Credentials link.

The Credentials Manager window appears, as shown in Figure 4-1.

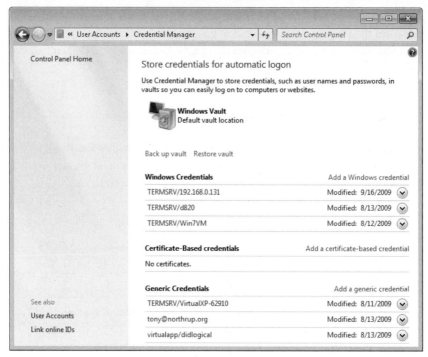

FIGURE 4-1 Using Credential Manager to authenticate automatically to resources that require credentials other than those you use to log on

4. Click Add A Windows Credential. Note that you can also add certificate-based credentials and generic credentials.

5. In the Internet Or Network Address box, type the server name. You can use an asterisk (*) as a wildcard. For example, to use the credential for all resources in the contoso.com domain, you could type *.contoso.com.

6. In the User Name and Password boxes, type your user credentials. Click OK.

> *NOTE* WEB SITES THAT CREDENTIAL MANAGER CAN AUTHENTICATE TO AUTOMATICALLY
>
> The only Web sites that Credential Manager can authenticate to automatically are those that use Hypertext Transfer Protocol (HTTP) authentication. When visiting the site, the Web browser opens a dialog box to prompt for credentials. Credential Manager cannot remember your user name and password for Web sites that use a Hypertext Markup Language (HTML) form of authentication (such as those that have a logon page), which is much more common. Credential Manager can also remember .NET Passport credentials.

You can also back up and restore credentials manually in Credential Manager.

How to Troubleshoot Authentication Issues

Sometimes, users might experience problems authenticating to resources that have more complex causes than mistyping a password or leaving the Caps Lock key on. The sections that follow describe troubleshooting techniques that can help you better isolate authentication problems.

UAC Compatibility Problems

Users often confuse authentication and authorization issues. This isn't a surprise because both types of problems can show the exact same error message: "Access is denied." Because UAC limits the user's privileges and many applications were not designed to work with UAC, security errors are bound to be even more frequent in Windows Vista and Windows 7 than they were in Windows XP.

Most UAC-related problems are authorization-related, not authentication-related. If the user doesn't receive a UAC prompt at all but still receives a security error, it's definitely an authorization problem. If the user receives a UAC prompt and the user's credentials are accepted (or if the user logs on as an administrator and only needs to click Continue), it's definitely an authorization problem. UAC problems are authentication-related only if UAC prompts a user for credentials and rejects the user's password.

Identifying Logon Restrictions

Often, authentication problems occur because administrators have configured logon restrictions to enforce the organization's security requirements. Logon restrictions include locking accounts after several incorrect attempts at typing a password, allowing users to log on only during specific hours, requiring users to change their passwords regularly, disabling accounts, and accounts that expire on a specific date. The sections that follow describe each of these types of logon restrictions.

> **NOTE DETERMINING LOGON CONTEXT**
>
> Users can authenticate to the local user database or an AD DS domain. Logon restrictions defined for the domain only apply to domain accounts, and vice versa. Therefore, when examining logon restrictions for users, you must determine their logon context.
>
> The quickest way to do this is to open a command prompt and run the command *set* to display all environment variables. Then, look for the USERDOMAIN line. If the user logged on with a local user account, this will be the computer name (shown on the COMPUTERNAME line). If the user logged on with an AD DS user account, this will be the name of the domain. You can also check the LOGONSERVER line to determine whether a domain controller or the local computer authenticated the user.

ACCOUNT LOCKOUT

If a user provides incorrect credentials several times in a row (for example, if an attacker is attempting to guess a user's password, or if a user repeatedly mistypes a password), Windows can block all authentication attempts for a specific amount of time.

Account lockout settings are defined by Group Policy settings in the Computer Configuration\Windows Settings\Security Settings\Account Policies\Account Lockout Policies\ node as follows:

- The number of incorrect attempts is defined by the Account Lockout Threshold setting.
- The time that the number of attempts must occur within is defined by the Reset Account Lockout Counter After policy.
- The time that the account is locked out is defined by the Account Lockout Duration policy.

Use the Resultant Set Of Policy tool (Rsop.msc) to identify a computer's effective Group Policy settings. To use the Resultant Set Of Policy tool, follow these steps:

1. Click Start, type **rsop.msc**, and press Enter.
2. In the Resultant Set Of Policy window, within the Computer Configuration\Windows Settings\Security Settings\Account Policies\Account Lockout Policies\ node.
3. The Details pane shows only the account lockout policy settings that have been defined, and which Group Policy object defined them.

If a user receives an error message indicating that her account is locked out, or she cannot log in even if she thinks she has typed her password correctly, you should validate the user's identity and then unlock the user's account. To unlock a user's account, view the user's Properties dialog box, and clear the Account Is Locked Out check box (for local Windows 7 user accounts) or the Unlock Account check box (for Windows Server 2008 R2 AD DS accounts), as shown in Figure 4-2. Then, click Apply.

You can identify locked out accounts by examining logon audit failures in the domain controller's Security event log with Event ID 4625.

LOGON HOUR RESTRICTIONS

Administrators can also use the Account tab of an AD DS user's properties to restrict logon hours. This is useful when administrators do not want a user to log on outside his normal working hours.

If a user attempts to log on outside his allowed hours, Windows 7 displays the error message "Your account has time restrictions that prevent you from logging on at this time. Please try again later." The only way to resolve this problem is to adjust the user's logon hours by clicking the Logon Hours button on the Account tab of the user's Properties dialog box. Figure 4-3 shows a user who is allowed to log on between the hours of 10 and 6, Monday through Friday.

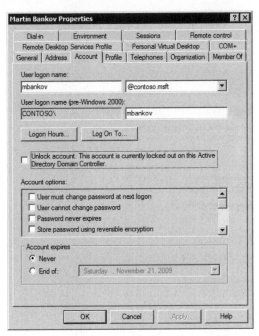

FIGURE 4-2 Windows Server 2008 R2 changes the label of the Unlock Account check box if an account is locked out.

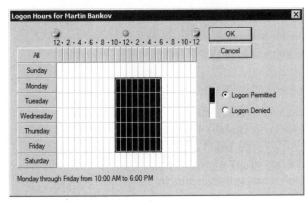

FIGURE 4-3 Logon hours restrict users from logging on during specific times of the day during the week.

PASSWORD EXPIRATION

Most security experts agree that users should be required to change their passwords regularly. Changing user passwords accomplishes two things:

- If attackers are attempting to guess a password, it forces them to restart their efforts. If users never change their passwords, attackers would be able to guess them eventually.

- If an attacker has guessed a user's password, changing the password prevents the attacker from using these credentials in the future.

Password expiration settings are defined by Group Policy settings in the Computer Configuration\Windows Settings\Security Settings\Account Policies\Password Policy node as follows:

- The time before a password expires is defined by the Maximum Password Age policy.

- The number of different passwords that users must have before they can reuse a password is defined by the Enforce Password History policy.

- The time before users can change their password again is defined by the Minimum Password Age policy. When combined with the Enforce Password History policy, this can prevent users from changing their password back to a previous password.

If users attempt to log on interactively to a computer and their password has expired, Windows prompts them to change their password automatically. If users attempt to access a shared folder, printer, Web site, or other resource using an expired password, they will simply be denied access. Therefore, if a user calls and complains that she cannot connect to a resource, you should verify that the user's password has not expired. You can prevent specific accounts from expiring by selecting the Password Never Expires check box on the Account tab of the user's Properties dialog box.

DISABLED ACCOUNT

Administrators can disable user accounts to prevent a user from logging on. This is useful if a user is going on vacation and you know she won't be logging on for a period of time, or if a user's account is compromised and IT needs the user to contact them before logging on.

To enable a user's disabled account, clear the Account Is Disabled check box in the user's Properties dialog box.

ACCOUNT EXPIRATION

In AD DS domains, accounts can be configured to expire. This is useful for users who will be working with an organization for only a limited amount of time. For example, if a contract employee has a two-week contract, domain administrators might set an account expiration date of two weeks in the future.

To resolve an expired account, edit the account's properties, select the Account tab, and set the Account Expires value to a date in the future. If the account should never expire, you can set the value to Never.

How to Use Auditing to Troubleshoot Authentication Problems

By default, Windows 7 does not add an event to the event log when a user provides incorrect credentials (such as when a user mistypes a password). Therefore, when troubleshooting authentication problems, your first step should be to enable auditing for logon events so that you can gather more information about the credentials the user provided and the resource being accessed.

Windows 7 (and earlier versions of Windows) provides two separate authentication auditing policies:

- **Audit Logon Events**   This policy audits authentication attempts for local resources, such as a user logging on locally, elevating privileges using a UAC prompt, or connecting over the network (including connecting using Remote Desktop or connecting to a shared folder). All authentication attempts will be audited, regardless of whether the authentication attempt uses a domain account or a local user account.

- **Audit Account Logon Events**   This policy audits domain authentications. No matter which computer the user authenticates to, these events appear only on the domain controller that handled the authentication request. Typically, you do not need to enable auditing of account logon events when troubleshooting authentication issues on computers running Windows 7. However, successful auditing of these events is enabled for domain controllers by default.

To log failed authentication attempts, you must enable auditing by following these steps:

1. Click Start and then click Control Panel. Click System And Security. Click Administrative Tools, and then double-click Local Security Policy.

2. In the Local Security Policy console, expand Local Policies, and then select Audit Policy.

3. In the right pane, double-click Audit Logon Events.

4. In the Audit Logon Events Properties dialog box, select the Failure check box to add an event to the Security event log each time a user provides invalid credentials. If you also want to log successful authentication attempts (which include authentication attempts from services and other nonuser entities), select the Success check box.

5. Click OK.

6. Restart your computer to apply the changes.

With auditing enabled, you can view audit events in Event Viewer by following these steps:

1. Click Start, right-click Computer, and then click Manage.

2. Expand System Tools, Event Viewer, Windows Logs, and then select Security.

   Event Viewer displays all security events. To view only successful logons, click the Filter Current Log link in the Actions pane and show only Event ID 4624. To view only unsuccessful logon attempts, click the Filter Current Log link and show only Event ID 4625.

Figure 4-4 shows an example of a logon audit failure that occurred when the user provided invalid credentials at a UAC prompt. Notice that the Caller Process Name (listed under Process Information) is Consent.exe, the UAC process.

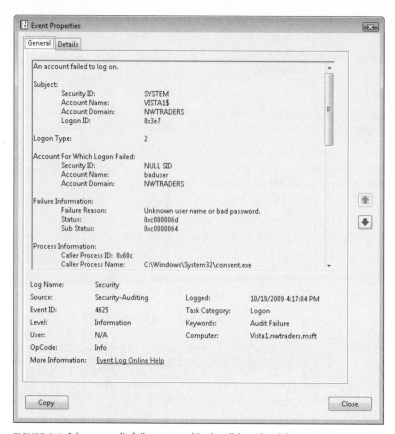

FIGURE 4-4 A logon audit failure caused by invalid credentials

Audits from failed authentication attempts from across the network resemble the following code. In particular, the Account Name, Account Domain, Workstation Name, and Source Network Address are useful for identifying the origin computer.

```
An account failed to log on.

Subject:
        Security ID:            NULL SID
        Account Name:           -
        Account Domain:         -
        Logon ID:               0x0

Logon Type:                     3

Account For Which Logon Failed:
        Security ID:            NULL SID
        Account Name:           baduser
        Account Domain:         NWTRADERS
```

```
Failure Information:
        Failure Reason:            Unknown user name or bad password.
        Status:                    0xc000006d
        Sub Status:                0xc0000064

Process Information:
        Caller Process ID:         0x0
        Caller Process Name:       -

Network Information:
        Workstation Name:          CONTOSO-DC
        Source Network Address:    192.168.1.212
        Source Port:               4953

Detailed Authentication Information:
        Logon Process:             NtLmSsp
        Authentication Package:    NTLM
        Transited Services:        -
        Package Name (NTLM only):  -
        Key Length:                0
```

When you are authenticating to network resources, authentication failures are always logged on the server, not on the client. For example, if you attempt to connect to a shared folder and you mistype the password, the event won't appear in your local event log—it appears instead in the event log of the computer sharing the folder.

> **NOTE DON'T TRUST THE REPORTED COMPUTER NAME**
>
> The computer sending the authentication attempt communicates its own workstation name. Therefore, if the attack is malicious, the workstation name might be intentionally invalid. The Internet Protocol (IP) address should always be correct, however.

 Quick Check

1. Which auditing type should you enable to audit local logon events?

2. Which event log should you examine to find audited events?

Quick Check Answers

1. Audit Logon Events

2. Security

How to Troubleshoot Network Authentication Issues

To improve network security, network administrators often require *802.1X authentication* before allowing client computers to connect to either wireless or wired networks. 802.1X authentication works at the network infrastructure layer to provide full network access only to computers that are able to authenticate. For example, on most wireless networks, client computers must be configured with a network security key or a certificate to connect to the wireless access point. On wired networks, network switches that support 802.1X allow a newly connected computer to access only a limited number of servers until the computer is authenticated.

Network authentication can be a problem if Group Policy settings are used to distribute the certificates required for network authentication because the client computer must first connect to the network to retrieve the certificate. To work around this requirement for 802.1X-protected wireless networks, connect client computers to a wired network long enough to update Group Policy settings.

If your organization requires authentication for wired networks (a less common requirement than requiring wireless authentication), work with the domain administrators to identify a procedure for temporarily connecting to the network when wired 802.1X authentication fails. This process might involve connecting the computer across a virtual private network (VPN), manually importing the client certificate on the client computer, or using a smart card to authenticate to the network.

How to Troubleshoot an Untrusted Certification Authority

Certificates, such as those issued by an enterprise certification authority (CA), are often used for authentication. Windows 7 can store certificates locally to authenticate a user or the computer itself, and users can carry certificates with them on smart cards. Typically, domain administrators should manage certificates and settings should be propagated to client computers using Group Policy settings. However, if you receive an error informing you that the CA that issued a certificate is not trusted, you can view existing CAs and then import the CA's certificate to configure Windows to trust any certificates issued by the CA.

To view trusted CAs, follow these steps:

1. Click Start, type **mmc**, and then press Enter to open a blank Microsoft Management Console (MMC). Respond to the UAC prompt if it appears.
2. Click File, and then click Add/Remove Snap-in.
3. Select Certificates and click Add.
4. If prompted, select My User Account, and then click Finish.
5. Click OK to close the Add Or Remove Snap-Ins dialog box.
6. Expand Certificates – Current User, expand Trusted Root Certification Authorities, and then select Certificates.

   The middle pane shows a list of trusted CAs. By default, this includes more than 10 default public CAs. In addition, it should include any internal CAs used by your organization. If your organization has an enterprise CA and it does not appear on this list, contact the domain administrator for assistance because the CA trust should be configured by using Group Policy.

Alternatively, you can trust a CA manually by following these steps from within the Certificates snap-in:

1. Below Trusted Root Certification Authorities, right-click Certificates, click All Tasks, and then click Import.

    The Certificate Import Wizard appears.

2. On the Welcome To The Certificate Import Wizard page, click Next.

3. On the File To Import page, click Browse. Select your CA certificate (which can be provided by the CA administrator or exported from a computer that trusts the CA), and then click Next.

4. On the Certificate Store page, accept the default certificate store (Trusted Root Certification Authorities) and then click Next.

5. On the Completing The Certificate Import Wizard page, click Finish.

6. If prompted with a security warning, click Yes.

7. Click OK to confirm that the import was successful.

    Now your user account will trust any certificates issued by the CA.

How to Troubleshoot Untrusted Computer Accounts

Computers have accounts in AD DS domains, just like users have accounts. Typically, computer accounts (also known as *machine accounts*) do not require ongoing management because Windows and the domain controller automatically create a password and authenticate the computer at startup.

However, computer accounts can become untrusted, which means the computer's security identifier (SID) or password are different from those stored in the AD DS. This occurs when either of the following occurs:

-   Multiple computers have the same SID. This can happen when a computer is deployed by copying the hard disk image and the Sysprep deployment tool is not used to reset the SID.

-   The computer account is corrupted in the AD DS.

You cannot reset the password on a computer account as you can the password of a user account. If a computer account becomes untrusted, the easiest way to solve the problem is to rejoin the computer to the domain by following these steps:

1. On the untrusted computer, click Start. Right-click Computer, and then click Properties. The System window appears.

2. In the Computer Name, Domain, And Workgroup Settings group, click Change Settings. The System Properties dialog box appears.

3. Click Change. The Computer Name/Domain Changes dialog box appears.

4. Click Workgroup, and then click OK. This removes the computer from the domain. Restart the computer when prompted.

5. In the Active Directory Users And Computers tool on a domain controller, right-click the computer account and then click Reset Account.

6. On the untrusted computer, repeat steps 2–4 to open the Computer Name/Domain Changes dialog box. Then, click Domain, and type the name of your domain. Provide domain administrator credentials to add the computer to the domain, and restart the computer when prompted.

Alternatively, you can use the Netdom command-line tool on a computer running Windows Server 2008 R2 to reset a computer account password. For earlier server versions of Windows, Netdom was included in the Support\Tools folder on the Windows DVD. For more information about Netdom, run *netdom /?* at a command prompt. Netdom is not included with Windows 7, however.

PRACTICE Save Credentials for Future Use

In this practice, you use Credential Manager to store credentials, enabling you to authenticate to a remote computer automatically.

EXERCISE Use Credential Manager

In this exercise, you use Credential Manager to save credentials for future use.

1. Log on to a computer running Windows 7. Create a new user account with the user name MyLocalUser and assign a password. This account will not exist on any network computers. Therefore, when connecting to remote computers, the user will always need to provide alternate credentials.

2. On a remote computer, create a shared folder. Make note of the server and share name.

3. Log on as MyLocalUser.

4. Click Start, and then click Computer. Then, click Map Network Drive.

5. In the Map Network Drive dialog box, type ***server**share*** to attempt to connect to the share you created in step 2. Click Finish.

6. When the Connect To *Server* dialog box appears, click Cancel twice.

   This dialog box appeared because your current account did not have privileges on the remote server and you had not entered credentials in Credential Manager.

> **NOTE** **CONFIGURE THE CREDENTIALS FOR THIS PRACTICE MANUALLY**
>
> For the purpose of this practice, you should configure the credentials manually using Credential Manager. However, a much easier way to accomplish the same thing is to complete the User Name and Password fields and then select the Remember My Password check box. This causes Windows Explorer to store the credentials automatically.

7. Click Start, and then click Control Panel.

8. Click the User Accounts link twice.

9. In the left pane, click the Manage Your Credentials link.

   Credential Manager appears.

10. Click Add A Windows Credential.

11. In the Internet Or Network Address, type the name of the server that you attempted to connect to in step 5.

12. In the User Name and Password boxes, type your administrative credentials to the remote server.

13. Click OK.

14. Click Start, and then click Computer. Then, click Map Network Drive.

15. In the Map Network Drive dialog box, type **\\server\share** to attempt to connect to the same share you specified in step 5. Clear the Reconnect At Logon check box, and then click Finish.

    Windows Explorer automatically connects to the shared folder without prompting you for credentials. Instead of requiring you to type the user name and password, it retrieved them from Credential Manager.

Lesson Summary

- Authentication is the process of identifying a user and proving the user's identity.

- Credential Manager stores user credentials to provide automatic authentication during future attempts to access a resource. You can add credentials manually using the Stored User Names And Passwords tool in Control Panel.

- When troubleshooting user authentication issues, you should enable failure logon auditing, reproduce the authentication problem, and then examine the Security event log for details of the authentication failure. When troubleshooting network authentication issues, verify that Group Policy settings have been updated and work with network administrators to resolve the problem. When troubleshooting a problem with an untrusted CA, import the CA's certificate into the list of trusted root CAs.

Lesson Review

You can use the following questions to test your knowledge of the information in Lesson 1, "Authenticating Users." The questions are also available on the companion CD if you prefer to review them in electronic form.

NOTE **ANSWERS**

Answers to these questions and explanations of why each answer choice is right or wrong are located in the "Answers" section at the end of the book.

1. Which of the following might support automatic authentication using Credential Manager? (Choose all that apply.)

    A. Connecting to a shared folder

    B. Connecting to a shared printer

    C. Authenticating to a Web site that uses an HTML form

    D. Authenticating to a Web site that prompts for user credentials using a dialog box

2. Which of the following types of auditing would you enable to track when a user mistypes his user name and password when logging on to a domain member computer running Windows 7 using a local user account?

    A. Audit Logon Events, Success

    B. Audit Logon Events, Failure

    C. Audit Account Logon Events, Success

    D. Audit Account Logon Events, Failure

3. Which of the following events would be logged in the local event log if you enabled auditing for successful and failed logon attempts? (Choose all that apply.)

    A. Logging on locally to a computer running Windows 7

    B. Typing a user name and password at a remote Web site

    C. Connecting to a remote shared folder

    D. Elevating privileges at a UAC prompt

Lesson 2: Configuring and Troubleshooting Internet Explorer Security

In recent years, more and more security compromises are initiated when users visit a Web site. For example, Web sites might trick the user into providing confidential information, or they might exploit a vulnerability in the browser to run code without the user's explicit permission.

In Windows 7, Windows Internet Explorer 8.0 is configured by default to minimize security risks. As a result, many add-ons will not run by default and Internet Explorer runs with minimal privileges. As an administrator, you must understand these restrictions and know how to work around them to enable Web applications to run correctly when they require the restricted features. In addition, you must understand how to troubleshoot common problems with Web browsing, including using certificates and identifying Group Policy restrictions.

After this lesson, you will be able to:

- Configure add-ons in Internet Explorer (including ActiveX controls) and troubleshoot problems related to add-ons.
- Add sites to the Trusted Sites list.
- Describe and configure Protected Mode.
- Resolve problems related to Secure Sockets Layer (SSL) certificates.
- Identify Group Policy restrictions.

Estimated lesson time: 40 minutes

Internet Explorer Add-Ons

Add-ons extend Internet Explorer capabilities to enable Web sites to provide much richer, more interactive content. For example, the following are commonly used add-ons:

- **Shockwave Flash** An add-on that enables complex animations, games, and other interactive capabilities
- **Windows Media Player** An add-on that enables Web pages to integrate audio and video
- **Microsoft Virtual Server VMRC Control** An add-on that enables users to remotely control a remote virtual machine from within Internet Explorer

The sections that follow describe how to configure add-ons and troubleshoot problems related to add-ons.

How to Enable and Disable Add-Ons

After starting Internet Explorer, you can disable or delete add-ons by following these steps:

1. Click the Tools button on the toolbar, and then click Manage Add-Ons.

   The Manage Add-Ons dialog box appears, as shown in Figure 4-5.

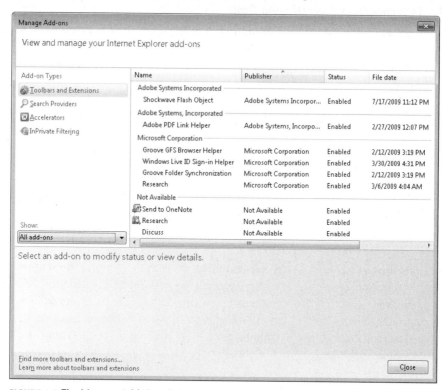

FIGURE 4-5 The Manage Add-Ons dialog box

2. In the Manage Add-Ons dialog box, select an add-on, and then click Disable to prevent the add-on from automatically loading. If the add-on is an ActiveX control, you can click Delete to permanently remove it.

If an add-on is causing serious enough problems that you can't start Internet Explorer, you can disable the add-on without opening Internet Explorer by following these steps:

1. Click Start, and then click Control Panel.

2. Click the Network And Internet link.

3. Under Internet Options, click the Manage Browser Add-Ons link.

   The Internet Properties dialog box appears.

4. Click Manage Add-Ons.

5. In the Manage Add-Ons dialog box, select an add-on, and then click Disable to prevent the add-on from automatically loading.

How to Start Internet Explorer without Add-Ons

A buggy or malicious add-on can cause problems with starting Internet Explorer. To work around this problem and launch Internet Explorer without add-ons, follow these steps:

1. Click Start. Then, click All Programs, Accessories, and System Tools.

2. Click Internet Explorer (No Add-Ons).

   Internet Explorer starts with all add-ons disabled. If a Web page opens a new window when you click a link, that new window also has add-ons disabled. Add-ons will be enabled automatically the next time you start Internet Explorer using the standard shortcut.

Alternatively, you can start Internet Explorer manually using the *-extoff* parameter by clicking Start, typing **iexplore -extoff**, and pressing Enter.

How to Configure Add-Ons in AD DS Domain Environments

As with earlier versions of Internet Explorer, you can use the Group Policy settings in User Configuration\Policies\Administrative Templates\Windows Components\Internet Explorer\ Security Features\Add-on Management to enable or disable specific add-ons throughout your organization. Typically, you need to use two settings in this group to block all unapproved add-ons in your organization:

- **Add-On List**   Enable this setting, and then specify the approved add-ons in your organization. To specify an add-on, provide the class identifier (CLSID) for the add-on you need to add as the Value Name in the Add-On List. The CLSID should be in brackets, such as "{BDB57FF2-79B9-4205-9444-F5FE85F37312}." You can find the CLSID for an add-on by reading the *<object>* tag from the HTML of a Web page that references the add-on. To specify that the add-on should be denied, specify a value of 0. To allow an add-on, specify a value of 1. To both allow an add-on and permit users to manage the add-on, specify a value of 2.

- **Deny All Add-Ons Unless Specifically Allowed In The Add-On List**   After specifying the add-ons you want to allow in the Add-On List setting, enable this policy to block all other add-ons automatically. You can use the combination of these two settings to block all unapproved add-ons.

Two other Group Policy settings related to add-on management are located within both User Configuration and Computer Configuration at Administrative Templates\Windows Components\Internet Explorer. The settings that relate to managing add-ons are:

- **Turn Off Crash Detection**   By default, Internet Explorer detects an add-on that crashes and disables it the next time you start Internet Explorer. If you have a problematic add-on that is required for a critical Web application, you can enable this policy to ensure that even a failing add-on continues to run.

- **Do Not Allow Users To Enable Or Disable Add-Ons**   By default, users can open the Manage Add-Ons dialog box and enable or disable add-ons. If you enable this policy, they won't be able to configure add-ons.

How to Configure ActiveX Add-Ons

ActiveX is a technology that enables powerful applications with rich user interfaces to run within a Web browser. For that reason, many organizations have developed ActiveX components as part of a Web application, and many attackers have created ActiveX components to abuse the platform's capabilities. Some examples of ActiveX controls include the following:

- A component that enables you to manage virtual computers from a Microsoft Virtual Server Web page
- A Microsoft Update component that scans your computer for missing updates
- Shockwave Flash, which many Web sites use to publish complex animations and games
- A component that attempts to install malware or change user settings without the user's knowledge

Earlier versions of Internet Explorer installed ActiveX controls without prompting the users. This provided an excellent experience for Web sites that used ActiveX controls because the user was able to enjoy the control's features without manually choosing to install it. However, malware developers soon abused this capability by creating malicious ActiveX controls that installed software on the user's computer or changed other settings, such as the user's home page.

To enable you to use critical ActiveX controls while blocking potentially dangerous ActiveX controls, Microsoft built strong ActiveX management capabilities into Internet Explorer. The sections that follow describe how to configure ActiveX on a single computer and within an enterprise.

HOW TO CONFIGURE ActiveX OPT-IN

In Internet Explorer 8, ActiveX controls are not installed by default. Instead, when users visit a Web page that includes an ActiveX control, they see an information bar that informs them that an ActiveX control is required. Users then have to click the information bar and click Install ActiveX Control. If the users do nothing, Internet Explorer does not install the ActiveX control. Figure 4-6 shows the Genuine Microsoft Software Web page, which requires users to install an ActiveX control before their copy of Windows can be validated as genuine.

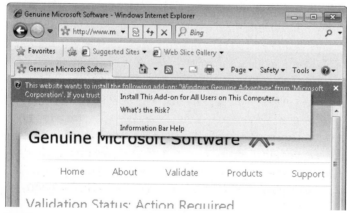

FIGURE 4-6 The Genuine Microsoft Software page

After the user clicks Install This Add-on, the user needs to respond to a UAC prompt for administrative credentials. Then the user receives a second security warning from Internet Explorer. If the user confirms this security warning, Internet Explorer installs and runs the ActiveX control.

ActiveX Opt-in is enabled by default for the Internet and Restricted Sites zones but disabled by default for the Local Intranet and Trusted Sites zones. Therefore, any Web sites on your local intranet should be able to install ActiveX controls without prompting the user. To change the setting default for a zone, perform these steps:

1. Open Internet Explorer. Click the Tools button on the toolbar, and then click Internet Options.

2. In the Internet Options dialog box, click the Security tab. Select the zone you want to edit, and then click the Custom Level button.

3. Scroll down in the Settings list. Under ActiveX Controls And Plug-Ins, change the setting for the first option, which is Allow Previously Unused ActiveX Controls To Run Without Prompt. If this is disabled, ActiveX Opt-in is enabled. Click OK twice.

EXAM TIP

The name "ActiveX Opt-in" can be confusing. Enabling ActiveX Opt-in causes Internet Explorer *not* to install ActiveX controls by default, instead requiring the user to explicitly choose to configure the add-on.

ActiveX Opt-in applies to most ActiveX controls. However, it does not apply for ActiveX controls on the preapproved list. The preapproved list is maintained in the registry at HKEY_LOCAL_MACHINE\SOFTWARE\Microsoft\Windows\CurrentVersion\Ext\PreApproved. Within this key, there are several subkeys, each with a Class ID (CLSID) of a preapproved ActiveX control. You can identify an ActiveX control's CLSID by viewing the source of a Web page and searching for the *<object>* tag. For best results, try searching for "<object" in the source of a Web page.

HOW TO CONFIGURE ActiveX ON A SINGLE COMPUTER

The previous section described how to configure ActiveX Opt-in on a single computer. In addition to that setting, you can configure several other per-zone settings related to ActiveX from the Security Settings dialog box:

- **Automatic Prompting For ActiveX Controls** This setting is disabled by default for all zones. If you choose to enable this setting, it bypasses the information bar and instead actively prompts the user to install the ActiveX control.

- **Download Signed ActiveX Controls** The developer can sign ActiveX controls. Typically, signed ActiveX controls are more trustworthy than unsigned controls, but you shouldn't trust all signed ActiveX controls. By default, this setting is set to prompt the user. You can reduce the number of prompts the user receives by changing this setting to Enable.

- **Download Unsigned ActiveX Controls** By default, unsigned ActiveX controls are disabled. If you must distribute an unsigned ActiveX control, add the site that requires the control to your Trusted Sites list and change this setting for the Trusted Sites zone to Prompt.

- **Initialize And Script ActiveX Controls Not Marked As Safe For Scripting** This setting is disabled by default for all zones. You should enable it only if you experience a problem with a specific ActiveX control and the developer informs you that this setting is required. In that case, you should add the site to the Trusted Sites list and enable this control only for that zone.

- **Run ActiveX Controls And Plug-Ins** This setting controls whether ActiveX controls will run, regardless of how other settings are defined. In other words, if this setting is disabled, users cannot run ActiveX controls, even using ActiveX Opt-in. This setting is enabled for all zones except for the Restricted Sites zone.

- **Script ActiveX Controls Marked Safe For Scripting** Some ActiveX controls are marked safe for scripting by the developer. This setting is enabled for all zones except for the Restricted Sites zone. Typically, you should leave this at the default setting. Because the developer chooses whether the control is marked safe for scripting, this marking does not indicate that the ActiveX control is more trustworthy than any other control.

HOW TO MANAGE ActiveX ADD-ONS ON A SINGLE COMPUTER

To configure ActiveX on a single computer, follow these steps:

1. Open Internet Explorer.

2. Click the Tools button on the toolbar, click Manage Add-Ons, and then click Enable Or Disable Add-Ons.

   The Manage Add-Ons dialog box appears.

3. Click the Show list, and then click Downloaded ActiveX Controls.

4. Select the ActiveX control you want to manage, and then select either of the following. Click OK.

   - Disable to disable the ActiveX control.

   - Delete to remove the ActiveX control.

How to Configure ActiveX Installer Service

Some critical Web applications might require ActiveX controls to run. This can be a challenge if your users lack administrative credentials because UAC requires administrative credentials to install ActiveX controls (although any user can access an ActiveX control after it is installed).

Fortunately, you can use the ActiveX Installer Service to enable standard users to install specific ActiveX controls. To configure the list of sites approved to install ActiveX controls, perform these steps:

1. Open the Group Policy Object (GPO) in the Group Policy Object Editor.

2. Browse to Computer Configuration\Administrative Templates\Windows Components\ ActiveX Installer Service.

3. Double-click the Approved Installation Sites For ActiveX Controls setting. Enable it.

4. Click Show to specify host Uniform Resource Locators (URLs) that are allowed to distribute ActiveX controls. In the Show Contents dialog box, click Add and configure the host URLs as follows:

   - Configure each item name as the host name of the Web site from which clients will download the updated ActiveX controls, such as *http://activex.microsoft.com*.

   - Configure each value name using four numbers separated by commas (such as "2,1,0,0"). These values are described later in this section.

5. Click OK to save the setting for the new policy.

When you configure the list of approved installation sites for ActiveX Controls, you configure a name and value pair for each site. The name will always be the URL of the site hosting the ActiveX control, such as *http://activex.microsoft.com*. The value consists of four numbers:

- **Trusted ActiveX Controls**   Define the first number as 0 to block trusted ActiveX controls from being installed, as 1 to prompt the user to install trusted ActiveX controls, or as 2 to install trusted ActiveX controls automatically, without prompting the user.

- **Signed ActiveX Controls**   Define the second number as 0 to block signed ActiveX controls from being installed, as 1 to prompt the user to install signed ActiveX controls, or as 2 to install signed ActiveX controls automatically, without prompting the user.

- **Unsigned ActiveX Controls**   Define the third number as 0 to block unsigned ActiveX controls from being installed or define this number as 1 to prompt the user to install unsigned ActiveX controls. You cannot configure unsigned ActiveX controls to be installed automatically.

- **Server Certificate Policy**   Set this value to 0 to cause the ActiveX Installer Service to abort installation if there are any certificate errors. Alternatively, you can set it to 256 to ignore an unknown CA, 512 to ignore invalid certificate usage, 4096 to ignore an unknown common name in the certificate, or 8192 to ignore an expired certificate. Add these numbers to ignore multiple types of certificate errors.

For example, the numbers 2,1,0,0 would cause the ActiveX Installer Service to silently install trusted ActiveX controls, prompt the user for signed controls, never install unsigned controls, and abort installation if any Hypertext Transfer Protocol Secure (HTTPS) certificate error occurs.

When a user attempts to install an ActiveX control that has not been approved, the ActiveX Installer Service creates an event in the Application Log with an Event ID of 4097 and a source of AxInstallService.

How Internet Explorer Works in 64-bit Versions of Windows 7

Because it provides a wider data bus, allowing many times greater scalability, 64-bit computing is the future. Right now, however, most users run 32-bit versions of Windows.

Unfortunately, although 64-bit versions of Windows are fundamentally superior, they do have some compatibility problems in the real world. In particular, 64-bit versions of Internet Explorer can't use 32-bit components (such as ActiveX controls, which might provide critical functionality for many Web sites). Although 64-bit components are becoming more common, some critical components still aren't available for 64-bit.

For that reason, the 32-bit version of Internet Explorer is the default even in 64-bit versions of Windows. If a user instead chooses to use the 64-bit version of Internet Explorer (there's a shortcut for it on the Start menu), test any problematic Web pages in the 32-bit version of Internet Explorer before doing any troubleshooting.

Adding Sites to the Trusted Sites List

Internet Explorer is configured by default to prevent Internet Web sites from performing many actions that might compromise the computer's security or the user's privacy. However, some legitimate Web sites might need to perform those actions to allow Web applications to run properly.

Administrators can add sites to the Trusted Sites list to grant them additional privileges. To add a site to the Trusted Sites list, follow these steps:

1. In Internet Explorer, click the Tools menu on the toolbar, and then click Internet Options.

2. In the Internet Options dialog box, click the Security tab. Click Trusted Sites, and then click Sites.

3. In the Trusted Sites dialog box, clear the Require Server Verification check box if you access the server using HTTP rather than HTTPS.

4. In the Add This Website To The Zone box, type the URL of the Web site, such as **http://www.contoso.com,** and then click Add.

5. Click Close.

The next time you visit the site, Internet Explorer grants it all the privileges assigned to the Trusted Sites list.

Protected Mode

Before Windows Vista, many computers were compromised when Web sites containing malicious code succeeded in abusing the Web browsers of visitors to run code on the client computer. Because any new process spawned by an existing process inherits the privileges of the parent process and the Web browser ran with the user's full privileges, maliciously spawned processes received the same privilege as the user. With the user's elevated privileges, the malicious process could install software and transfer confidential documents.

In Windows Vista and Windows 7, Internet Explorer hopes to reduce this type of risk using a feature called *Protected Mode*. With Protected Mode (originally introduced with Internet Explorer 7), Internet Explorer 8 runs with very limited privileges on the local computer—even fewer privileges than those that the standard user has in Windows 7. Therefore, even if malicious code on a Web site were to abuse Internet Explorer successfully to spawn a process, that malicious process would have privileges only to access the Temporary Internet Files folder and a few other locations—it would not be able to install software, reconfigure the computer, or read the user's documents.

For example, most users log on to computers running Windows XP with administrative privileges. If a Web site exploits a vulnerability in Windows XP that hasn't been fixed with an update and successfully starts a process to install spyware, the spyware installation process would have full administrator privileges to the local computer. On a computer running Windows 7 the spyware install process would have minimal privileges—even less than those of a standard user—regardless of whether the user was logged on as an administrator.

Protected Mode is a form of defense-in-depth. Protected Mode is a factor only if malicious code successfully compromises the Web browser and runs. In these cases, Protected Mode limits the damage the process can do without the user's permission. Protected Mode is not available when Internet Explorer is installed on Windows XP because it requires several security features unique to Windows Vista and Windows 7.

The sections that follow provide more information about Protected Mode.

How Protected Mode Works

One of the features of Windows 7 that enables Protected Mode is *Mandatory Integrity Control (MIC)*. MIC labels processes, folders, files, and registry keys using one of four integrity access levels (ILs), as shown in Table 4-1. Internet Explorer runs with a low IL, which means it can access only other low IL resources without the user's permission.

TABLE 4-1 Mandatory Integrity Control Levels

IL	SYSTEM PRIVILEGES
System	System; processes have unlimited access to the computer.
High	Administrative; processes can install files to the Program Files folder and write to sensitive registry areas like HKEY_LOCAL_MACHINE.
Medium	User; processes can create and modify files in the user's Documents folder and write to user-specific areas of the registry, such as HKEY_CURRENT_USER. Most files and folders on a computer have a medium integrity level because any object without a mandatory label has an implied default integrity level of Medium.
Low	Untrusted; processes can write only to low-integrity locations, such as the Temporary Internet Files\Low folder or the HKEY_CURRENT_USER\Software\LowRegistry key.

Low IL resources that Internet Explorer in Protected Mode can access include:

- The History folder
- The Cookies folder
- The Favorites folder
- The %Userprofile%\AppData\Local\Microsoft\Windows\Temporary Internet Files\Low\ folder
- The Temporary Files folders
- The HKEY_CURRENT_USER\Software\Microsoft\Internet Explorer\LowRegistry key

How the Protected Mode Compatibility Layer Works

To minimize both the number of privilege elevation requests and the number of compatibility problems, Protected Mode provides a compatibility layer. The *Protected Mode Compatibility Layer* redirects requests for protected resources to safer locations. For example, any requests for the Documents library are redirected automatically to subfolders contained within the hidden %Userprofile%\AppData\Local\Microsoft\Windows\Temporary Internet Files\ Virtualized folder. The first time that an add-on attempts to write to a protected object, the Protected Mode Compatibility Layer copies the object to a safe location and accesses the copy. All future requests for the same protected file access the copy.

The Protected Mode Compatibility Layer applies only to Internet Explorer add-ons written for versions of Windows prior to Windows Vista because anything written for Windows Vista or Windows 7 would access files natively in the preferred locations.

How to Enable Compatibility Logging

Some Web applications and Internet Explorer add-ons developed for earlier versions of Internet Explorer have compatibility problems when you run them with Internet Explorer 8 and Windows 7. One way to identify the exact compatibility problem is to enable compatibility logging using Group Policy. To enable compatibility logging on your local computer, perform these steps:

1. Click Start, type **gpedit.msc**, and then press Enter.

2. In the Group Policy Object Editor, browse to User Configuration\Administrative Templates\Windows Components\Internet Explorer. If you need to enable compatibility logging for all users on the computer, browse to Computer Configuration\Administrative Templates\Windows Components\Internet Explorer.

3. Double-click the Turn On Compatibility Logging setting. Select Enabled, and then click OK.

4. Restart Internet Explorer if it is currently open; otherwise, start it.

With compatibility logging enabled, you should reproduce the problem you are experiencing. You can then view events in the Event Viewer snap-in under Applications And Service Logs\Internet Explorer. Some events, such as Event ID 1037, will not have a description unless you also install the Application Compatibility Toolkit.

> **NOTE   COMPATIBILITY LOGGING**
>
> For more information about compatibility logging, read "Finding Security Compatibility Issues in Internet Explorer 7," at *http://msdn.microsoft.com/en-us/library/bb250493.aspx*. It applies equally well to Internet Explorer 8.

How to Disable Protected Mode

If you are concerned that Protected Mode is causing problems with a Web application, you can disable it temporarily to test the application. Protected Mode is enabled on a zone-by-zone basis and is disabled by default for Trusted Sites.

To disable Protected Mode, perform these steps:

1. Open Internet Explorer.

2. Click the Tools button on the toolbar, and then click Internet Options.

3. Click the Security tab.

4. Select the zone for which you want to disable Protected Mode. Then, clear the Enable Protected Mode check box.

5. Click OK twice.

6. Restart Internet Explorer.

If the application works when Protected Mode is disabled, the problem is probably related to Protected Mode. In that case, you should re-enable Protected Mode and work with the application developer to solve the problems in the Web application. Alternatively, you could add the site to the Trusted Sites zone, thus permanently disabling Protected Mode for that site.

How to Troubleshoot Certificate Problems

Certificates are used for several security-related tasks in Internet Explorer:

- **Encrypting traffic** The most common use for certificates in Internet Explorer. Many Web sites, especially e-commerce Web sites that accept credit card numbers, have an SSL certificate installed. This SSL certificate enables HTTPS communications, which behave similar to HTTP, but with encryption and authentication. With standard, unencrypted HTTP, if an attacker has access to the network, the attacker can read all data transferred to and from the server. With encrypted HTTPS, an attacker can capture the traffic, but it will be encrypted and cannot be decrypted without the server's private certificate.

- **Authenticating the server** SSL certificates authenticate the server by allowing the client to verify that the certificate was issued by a trusted CA and that one of the names in the certificate matches the host name used to access the site. This helps to prevent man-in-the-middle attacks, whereby an attacker tricks a client computer into visiting a malicious server that impersonates the legitimate server. Web sites on the public Internet typically have SSL certificates issued by a third-party CA that is trusted by default in Internet Explorer. Intranet Web sites can use certificates issued by an internal CA as long as client computers are configured to trust the internal CA.

- **Authenticating the client** Intranet Web sites can issue certificates to clients on their network and use the client certificates to authenticate internal Web sites. When using AD DS Group Policy, it is very easy to distribute client certificates throughout your enterprise.

If Internet Explorer detects a problem with a certificate, it displays the message, "There is a problem with this website's security certificate," as shown in Figure 4-7.

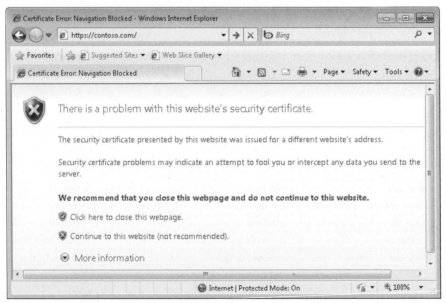

FIGURE 4-7 How Internet Explorer detects mismatched SSL certificates

The following list describes common problems that can occur when using certificates in Internet Explorer and how to troubleshoot them.

- **The security certificate presented by this Web site was issued for a different Web site's address** In this case, there are several possible causes:

  - The host name you are using to access the Web site is not the Web site's primary address. For example, you might be attempting to access the Web site by Internet Protocol (IP) address. Alternatively, you might be accessing an alternative host name, such as "constoso.com" instead of "www.contoso.com."

    > **NOTE   SUBJECT ALTERNATIVE NAMES**
    >
    > Historically, SSL certificates have specified the host name for which they are valid by using the Common Name field. For example, you might specify www.contoso.com as the Common Name for your Web site certificate. However, if a user accessed the same site using the host name contoso.com, the browser would return an error.
    >
    > Since about 2003, most popular browsers have supported SSL certificates with Subject Alternative Names (SANs). SANs are host names for which an SSL certificate is valid. For example, you could create an SSL certificate with a SAN list and allow users to access a single Web server using either contoso.com or www.contoso.com.
    >
    > You can view a certificate's SAN list by visiting the site using HTTPS and clicking the padlock icon in the address bar of Internet Explorer. Click View Certificates, and then click the Details tab. Select the Subject Alternative Name field to view every host name for which the certificate is valid.

  - The server administrator made a mistake. For example, the administrator might have mistyped the server's host name when requesting the certificate or the administrator might have installed the wrong certificate on the server.

  - The server is impersonating a server with a different host name. For example, an attacker might have set up a Web site to impersonate www.fabrikam.com. However, the attacker is using a different SSL certificate on the Web site. Earlier versions of Internet Explorer show a less intimidating error message, so many users might have bypassed the error and continued to the malicious site.

- **The certificate has expired** Certificates have a limited lifespan—usually one to five years. If the certificate has expired, the server administrator should request an updated certificate and apply it to the server.

- **Internet Explorer is not configured to trust the certificate authority** Anyone, including attackers, can create a CA and issue certificates. Therefore, Internet Explorer does not trust all CAs by default. Instead, Internet Explorer trusts only a handful of public CAs. If the certificate was issued by an untrusted CA and the Web site is on the public Internet, the server administrator should acquire a certificate from a trusted CA. If the Web site is on your intranet, a client administrator should configure Internet Explorer to trust the issuing CA. In AD DS domains, member computers automatically trust enterprise CAs. For more information, complete the exercises at the end of this lesson.

How to Identify Group Policy Restrictions

Businesses need complete control over their users' Web browsing abilities, and Internet Explorer provides an extreme amount of flexibility. For example, administrators can use Group Policy settings to turn off tabbed browsing, allow pop-ups, turn off suggestions, restrict search providers, or turn off the Favorites bar.

If a user complains that an Internet Explorer feature is not working correctly, you should determine whether Group Policy restrictions might be responsible. You can use the Resultant Set Of Policy tool to determine which settings have been defined for a user or computer, and which Group Policy objects are responsible. To use the Resultant Set Of Policy tool, perform these steps:

1. Click Start, type **rsop.msc**, and press Enter.

2. In the Resultant Set Of Policy window, within both the Computer Configuration or User Configuration, select the Administrative Templates\Windows Components\Internet Explorer node.

3. As shown in Figure 4-8, the Details pane shows Internet Explorer settings that have been defined, and which GPO defined them.

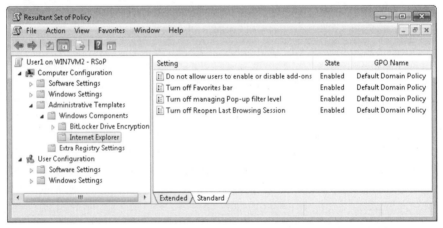

FIGURE 4-8 Resultant Set Of Policy shows which Group Policy settings have been applied and the Group Policy object responsible

Troubleshoot Certificate Problems

In this practice, you configure the ActiveX Installer Service to trust ActiveX controls from MSN. Then, you troubleshoot certificate-related problems by generating an untrusted certificate, viewing how Internet Explorer responds to that certificate, and then configuring Internet Explorer to trust the certificate.

EXERCISE 1 Simulate an Invalid Certificate

In this exercise, you open a Web page using a host name other than the common name specified in the SSL certificate and view how Internet Explorer handles it.

1. Open Internet Explorer. In the Address bar, type **https://www.microsoft.com**. Press Enter.

   Internet Explorer opens the *www.microsoft.com* home page using encrypted HTTPS. Note the gold lock in the Address bar, as shown in Figure 4-9.

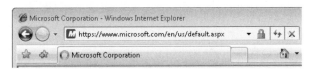

   FIGURE 4-9 The gold lock in the address bar, which signifies that communications with the site are encrypted and the certificate is valid

2. Click the gold lock in the address bar to display the Web site identification. Notice that the identification page displays "www.microsoft.com," which exactly matches the host name you typed in the address bar.

3. In the Address bar, type **https://microsoft.com**. Notice that this time the host name does not begin with "www." Press Enter.

   Internet Explorer displays the There Is A Problem With This Website's Security Certificate Web page. This happens because the host name in the certificate, www.microsoft.com, does not exactly match the host name you typed in the address bar, microsoft.com. Users would see this same error message if they attempted to visit a site that was impersonating another site.

EXERCISE 2 Issue an Untrusted Certificate

In this exercise, you must issue an internal certificate to a Web server and determine how Windows 7 handles it both as a member of the domain and from outside the domain.

1. Connect to a Windows Server 2008 R2 AD DS domain controller in a test environment, and log on as an administrator.

2. Click Start, click Administrative Tools, and then click Server Manager.

3. In Server Manager, click the Roles node, and then click Add Roles.

4. On the Before You Begin page, click Next.

5. On the Select Server Roles page, select Active Directory Certificate Services, and then click Next.

6. On the Introduction To Active Directory Certificate Services page, click Next.

7. On the Select Role Services page, select Certification Authority, Certification Authority Web Enrollment, and Online Responder. When prompted to add other services, click Add Required Role Services. Click Next.

8. On the Specify Setup Type page, click Enterprise. Click Next.

9. On the Specify CA Type page, leave Root CA selected, and then click Next.

10. On the Set Up Private Key page, leave Create A New Private Key selected. Click Next.

11. On the Configure Cryptography For CA page, click Next.

12. On the Configure CA Name page, type the host name for your CA (such as DCSRV1.nwtraders.msft) and then click Next.

13. On the Set Validity Period page, click Next.

14. On the Configure Certificate Database page, click Next.

15. On the Web Server page, click Next.

16. On the Role Services page, click Next.

17. On the Confirmation page, click Install.

18. Click Close, and click Yes to restart the computer.

19. After the computer restarts, log on again. Allow Server Manager to finish completing the installation of the server roles, and then click Close.

20. Click Start, click Administrative Tools, and then click Internet Information Services (IIS) Manager.

21. In the Internet Information Services (IIS) Manager, click your computer.

22. Double-click Server Certificates.

23. In the Actions pane, click Create Domain Certificate.

24. On the Distinguished Name Properties page, type the full host name in the Common Name box, such as **dc1.nwtraders.msft.** Type **Northwind Traders** in the Organization box and type **IT** in the Organizational Unit box. In the City, State, and Country boxes, provide your local information. Then, click Next.

25. On the Online Certification Authority page, click Select. Select the domain controller, and then click OK. In the Friendly Name box, type DC1. Click Finish.

26. In the Internet Information Services (IIS) Manager, expand Sites and then click Default Web Site. Right-click Default Web Site and then click Edit Bindings.

27. In the Site Bindings dialog box, click Add.

28. In the Add Site Binding dialog box, click the Type list and then select HTTPS. In the SSL Certificate list, select dc1.nwtraders.msft. Click OK, and then click Close.

29. Now you have configured your domain controller as a Web server with an SSL certificate. Open Internet Explorer. In the address bar, enter **https://common_name,** where *common_name* is the name you entered in the certificate, such as dc1.nwtraders.msft. Press Enter.

    Internet Explorer opens the page. Notice that the gold lock icon appears in the address bar, signifying that the SSL certificate is valid.

30. On a second computer running Windows 7 that is not a member of your domain, open Internet Explorer. Alternatively, if you do not have a second computer, you can remove your computer running Windows 7 from the domain temporarily. In Internet Explorer, enter **https://*common_name*** and press Enter.

Internet Explorer displays a warning message indicating that the certificate was not issued by a trusted CA, as shown in Figure 4-10.

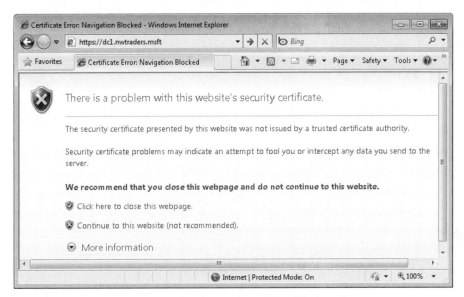

FIGURE 4-10 The warning message given by Internet Explorer if it doesn't trust the certificate authority

Now, continue to Exercise 3 to resolve this problem.

EXERCISE 3   Trust a Certificate Authority

In this exercise, you must export your CA's root certificate and trust that certificate on your nondomain computer running Windows 7 so that you can open the SSL-encrypted Web site without a warning. To complete this exercise, you must have completed Exercise 2.

1. On your domain controller, in the Certification Authority console, right-click your server and then click Properties.

2. Click the General tab. Click Certificate #0, and then click View Certificate.

3. In the Certificate dialog box, click the Details tab. Then, click Copy To File.

4. The Certificate Export Wizard appears. Click Next.

5. On the Export File Format page, accept the default export format, and then click Next.

6. On the File To Export tab, type **C:\root.cer** and then click Next.

7. Click Finish, and then click OK three times.

8. On your client computer running Windows 7 that is not a member of your test domain, open Internet Explorer. In Internet Explorer, click the Tools button on the toolbar, and then click Internet Options.

9. In the Internet Options dialog box, click the Content tab and then click Certificates.

10. In the Certificates dialog box, click the Trusted Root Certification Authorities tab and then click Import.

11. The Certificate Import Wizard appears. On the Welcome To The Certificate Import Wizard page, click Next.

12. On the File To Import page, click Browse. In the Open dialog box, type ***server_name*\ c$\root.cer.** Then click Open and click Next.

13. On the Certificate Store page, notice that the Certificate Import Wizard imports the certificate into the Trusted Root Certification Authorities store by default. This is the correct place. Click Next.

14. On the Completing The Certificate Import Wizard page, click Finish.

15. A Security Warning dialog box appears. Click Yes to install the certificate and then click OK.

16. Click Close and then click OK.

17. In Internet Explorer, enter **https://*common_name*** and press Enter.

    Internet Explorer opens the page. Notice that the gold lock icon appears in the address bar, signifying that the SSL certificate is valid. Because this computer is not a member of the AD DS domain, you had to trust the root certificate manually. Then, all certificates issued by that CA will be trusted. If the computer had been a member of the AD DS domain, Group Policy would have caused the computer to trust the enterprise CA automatically.

Lesson Summary

- Web application developers often use Internet Explorer add-ons to extend the Web browser's capabilities. However, some add-ons can cause reliability problems, and others might compromise your organization's security. Fortunately, Internet Explorer provides tools to disable add-ons and delete ActiveX controls. If an add-on is preventing Internet Explorer from starting, you can start Internet Explorer with all add-ons disabled.

- Internet Explorer restricts what Web sites on the public Internet can do to help protect the user's security. However, these restrictions can prevent some legitimate Web applications from working correctly. If you encounter a Web application that does not work correctly and you trust the Web site, you can add the Web site to the Trusted Sites list. Sites on the Trusted Sites list receive more privileges than sites on the public Internet, and thus are more likely to be compatible.

- Protected Mode is one of the most important security features of Windows Internet Explorer 8.0, and it's available only when using Windows Vista or Windows 7. By default, Protected Mode causes Internet Explorer to run with low privileges, which prevents Internet Explorer (or any process started by Internet Explorer) from accessing most resources on the computer. The user must confirm permissions if Internet Explorer or an add-on requires elevated privileges.

- Many Web sites use certificates to authenticate the Web server and to provide encrypted communications. Certificates are extremely important for Web sites that provide access to confidential information or that collect private information from users (such as credit card numbers). The most common certificate problem is a nonmatching server host name, which typically can be resolved by providing the host name listed in the certificate. For servers on your intranet, users might experience certificate problems if the computer hasn't been correctly configured to trust the CA.

- Group Policy gives administrators detailed control over Internet Explorer features. If a user has a problem because a feature does not seem to be working correctly, it might be the result of a deliberate configuration setting by administrators. To check which Internet Explorer Group Policy restrictions are applied to a computer, run the Resultant Set Of Policy tool (Rsop.msc). Then, browse to the Computer Configuration\Administrative Templates\Windows Components\Internet Explorer and User Configuration\Administrative Templates\Windows Components\Internet Explorer nodes. The Resultant Set Of Policy tool shows all settings that have been defined and the GPOs that define them.

Lesson Review

You can use the following questions to test your knowledge of the information in Lesson 2, "Configuring and Troubleshooting Internet Explorer Security." The questions are also available on the companion CD if you prefer to review them in electronic form.

> **NOTE ANSWERS**
>
> Answers to these questions and explanations of why each answer choice is right or wrong are located in the "Answers" section at the end of the book.

1. A user is attempting to visit one of the many internal Web sites run by your IT department. The user's shortcut is set up to use SSL by default. Today, when the user attempted to open the page, Internet Explorer showed the user the following message:

   There is a problem with this Web site's security certificate.

   The security certificate presented by this Web site was issued for a different Web site's address.

Which of the following might cause this message? (Choose all that apply.)

A. The certificate is expired.

B. An attacker is redirecting traffic to a malicious Web server.

C. Internet Explorer no longer trusts the CA that issued the certificate.

D. The Web site certificate was issued for a different host name than that stored in the user's shortcut.

2. Which of the following would Internet Explorer block by default (until confirmed by a user)? (Choose all that apply.)

A. Animated GIFs

B. Background music in a Web page

C. Video embedded in a Web page

D. Viewing the source code of a Web page

3. Which of the following types of requests would the Internet Explorer Protected Mode Compatibility Layer redirect to a virtualized location?

A. Storing a cookie

B. Storing a file in the Documents folder

C. Prompting the user to choose a file to upload to a Web site

D. Storing a file in the Temporary Internet Files folder

4. You receive a support call from a user attempting to access a Web page. The user recently upgraded to Windows 7; previously, the user had been using Windows XP and Internet Explorer 6.0. The Web page contains an ActiveX control, but it isn't appearing on the Web page for the user. Which of the following are valid ways for the user to resolve the problem? (Choose all that apply.)

A. Right-click the page, and then click Run ActiveX Control.

B. Click the Information Bar, and then click Run ActiveX Control.

C. Add the site to the Trusted Sites list.

D. Clear the Enable Protected Mode check box in the Internet Security dialog box.

Lesson 3: Using Encryption to Control Access to Data

If an attacker has physical access to data, that person can easily circumvent operating system security features such as NTFS file permissions. However, with encryption, you can protect data even if it falls into the wrong hands.

Encryption makes data completely unreadable without a valid decryption key. With encryption, attackers need access to both the data and the decryption key before they can access your private files. Windows 7 provides two file encryption technologies: EFS (for encrypting individual files and folders) and BitLocker (for encrypting the entire system drive). In many environments you will need to use both together.

This lesson describes how to configure and troubleshoot EFS and BitLocker.

> **After this lesson, you will be able to:**
> - Configure EFS, grant multiple users access to EFS-encrypted files, and back up and recover EFS certificates.
> - Describe how BitLocker encryption differs from EFS, enable BitLocker, and recover data on a BitLocker-encrypted volume.
>
> **Estimated lesson time: 40 minutes**

Encrypting File System (EFS)

EFS is a file encryption technology (supported only on NTFS volumes) that protects files from offline attacks such as hard disk theft. Because EFS works at the file system level, EFS is entirely transparent to users and applications. In fact, the encryption is apparent only when a user who doesn't have a decryption key attempts to access an encrypted file. In that case, the file is completely inaccessible.

EFS is designed to protect sensitive data on mobile or shared computers, which are more susceptible to attack by techniques that circumvent the restrictions of access control lists (ACLs) such as file permissions. An attacker can steal a computer, remove the hard disk drives, place the drives in another system, and gain access to the stored files (even if they're protected by file permissions). When the attacker does not have the decryption key, however, files encrypted by EFS appear as unintelligible characters.

In most ways, EFS in Windows 7 is exactly the same as it was in Windows XP and Windows Vista.

> **NOTE** **VERSIONS OF WINDOWS 7 THAT DO NOT FULLY SUPPORT EFS**
> Windows 7 Starter, Windows 7 Home Basic, and Windows 7 Home Premium do not support EFS.

How to Encrypt a Folder with EFS

With EFS, you can encrypt specific files and folders. To enable EFS for a folder, perform these steps:

1. Click Start, and then click Computer.

   A Windows Explorer window opens.

2. Right-click the folder you want to encrypt and then click Properties. For example, if you want to encrypt the user's profile, expand C:\Users\, right-click the user's profile folder, and then click Properties.

3. On the General tab, click Advanced.

4. In the Advanced Attributes dialog box, select the Encrypt Contents To Secure Data check box.

5. Click OK twice.

6. In the Confirm Attribute Changes dialog box, accept the default setting to encrypt subfolders by clicking OK.

> **NOTE** **RECOGNIZING EFS-ENCRYPTED FILES AND FOLDERS IN WINDOWS EXPLORER**
> In Windows Explorer, EFS-encrypted files and folders are colored green. Other users can still browse EFS-encrypted folders, but they cannot access EFS-encrypted files.

During the encryption process, you might receive error messages saying that a file (such as NTUSER.dat, the user registry hive) is currently in use. In addition, to prevent users from encrypting a file that might stop the computer from starting, you cannot encrypt any file that is marked with the System attribute. Encrypted files cannot be compressed with NTFS compression.

> **NOTE** **EFS ENCRYPTED FILES CANNOT BE INDEXED**
> By default, EFS encrypted files are not indexed and will not be returned with search results. You can enable indexing of encrypted files by opening the Indexing Options tool in Control Panel, clicking Advanced, and then selecting the Index Encrypted Files check box. Alternatively, you can enable the Allow Indexing Of Encrypted File Group Policy setting at Computer Configuration\Administrative Templates\Windows Components\Search\.

How to Create and Back Up EFS Certificates

EFS uses certificates to encrypt and decrypt data. If you lose an EFS certificate, you will be unable to decrypt your files. Therefore, it is extremely important to back up EFS certificates.

The backup tools built into Windows automatically back up your certificates. In addition, Windows 7 provides a wizard interface for manually creating and backing up EFS certificates. To use the interface, perform these steps:

1. Click Start, and then click Control Panel.

2. Click the User Accounts link. Then, click the User Accounts link again.

3. In the left pane, click the Manage Your File Encryption Certificates link.

   The Encrypting File System Wizard appears.

4. On the Manage Your File Encryption Certificates page, click Next.

5. On the Select Or Create A File Encryption Certificate page, as shown in Figure 4-11, select Use This Certificate if an EFS certificate already exists (Windows 7 automatically generates a certificate the first time a user encrypts a file) and you want to back it up. To select a different certificate than the default, click Select Certificate. If you want to generate a certificate manually, select Create A New Certificate.

FIGURE 4-11 Using the Encrypting File System Wizard to back up EFS certificates

6. If you are creating a new certificate, the Which Type Of Certificate Do You Want To Create? page appears. If you want to use a smart card to store the certificate, insert your smart card and select A Self-Signed Certificate Stored On My Smart Card. If your domain has an enterprise CA available, select A Certificate Issued By My Domain's Certification Authority. Otherwise, leave the default setting and click Next.

7. On the Back Up The Certificate And Key page, click Browse to select an unencrypted folder in which to save the certificate. For best results, you should save it to removable media that will be stored securely. Then, type your password into the Password and Confirm Password boxes. Click Next.

8. If the Update Your Previously Encrypted Files page appears, it means some files were encrypted with a different key than you selected. To avoid problems decrypting files in the future, you should always update encrypted files. Select the All Logical Drives check box, and then click Next. The Encrypting File System Wizard updates the keys associated with all encrypted files. This might take a few minutes, or it might take several hours, depending on how many files need to be updated.

   The Encrypting File System Wizard backs up your key and saves it to the specified file. Keep this file safe.

9. On the last page, click Close.

To restore an EFS certificate, simply double-click the certificate, and then follow the steps in the Certificate Import Wizard. For step-by-step instructions, read Exercise 3 at the end of this lesson.

As an alternative to using Control Panel, you can back up EFS certificates in Windows Explorer by performing these steps:

1. Open Windows Explorer and select a file that you have encrypted. You must select a file, not a folder.

2. Right-click the file and then select Properties.

3. On the General tab, click Advanced.

4. In the Advanced Attributes dialog box, click Details to open the User Access dialog box.

5. Select your user name and then click Back Up Keys to open the Certificate Export Wizard.

6. Click Next to select the file format to use.

7. Click Next and enter a password to protect the key. Repeat the entry and then click Next.

8. Enter a path and file name to save the file to or browse for a path. Click Next.

9. Click Finish to export the certificate, and then click OK to confirm that it was saved successfully.

Anyone with access to an EFS certificate can decrypt that user's files. Therefore, it is extremely important to keep the backup secure.

How to Grant an Additional User Access to an EFS-encrypted File

By default, only the user who encrypted a file is able to access it. However, Windows 7 (as well as Windows Vista, Windows XP, and Windows Server 2003, but not Microsoft Windows 2000) allows you to grant more than one user access to an EFS-encrypted file. This is possible because EFS doesn't encrypt files using the user's personal EFS key; instead, EFS encrypts files with a File Encryption Key (FEK) and then encrypts the FEK with the user's personal EFS key. Therefore, decryption requires two separate keys. However, the FEK key can be encrypted multiple times for different users, and each user can access his or her own encrypted copy of the FEK key to decrypt files.

To allow encrypted files to be shared between users on a computer, perform these steps:

1. In Windows Explorer, right-click the file, and then click Properties.

2. On the General tab, click Advanced.

3. In the Advanced Attributes dialog box, click Details.

    The User Access dialog box appears, showing the users who have access to the file and the users who can act as recovery agents.

4. Click Add.

    The Encrypting File System dialog box appears and displays a list of users who have logged on to the local computer and who have an EFS certificate. A domain administrator can generate EFS certificates, or Windows 7 will generate one automatically the first time a user encrypts a file.

5. To add a domain user who is not on the list but who has a valid encryption certificate, click the Find User button. If EFS informs you that no appropriate certificates correspond to the selected user, the user has not been granted an EFS certificate. The user can generate by encrypting a file, or a domain administrator can distribute an EFS certificate to the user.

NOTE IMPORTING A CERTIFICATE MANUALLY

If a user has a certificate but you can't find it, you can manually import it. First, have the user export the certificate as described in the previous section. Then, import the certificate as described in the next section.

6. Select the user that you want to add, and then click OK.

7. Repeat steps 3–5 to add more users, and then click OK three times.

You cannot share encrypted folders with multiple users, only individual files. In fact, you cannot even share multiple encrypted files in a single action—you must share each individual file. However, you can use the Cipher.exe command-line tool to automate the process of sharing files.

Granting a user EFS access to a file does not override NTFS permissions. Therefore, if a user still lacks the file permissions to access a file, Windows will still prevent that user from accessing a file.

Any users who have access to an EFS-encrypted file can, in turn, grant other users access to the file.

How to Import Personal Certificates

You can share encrypted files with other users if you have the certificate for the other user. To allow another user to use a file that you have encrypted, you need to import the user's certificate onto your computer and add the user's name to the list of users who are permitted access to the file, as described in the previous section.

To import a user certificate, perform these steps:

1. Click Start, type **mmc**, and then press Enter to open a blank MMC.
2. Click File, and then click Add/Remove Snap-in.
3. Select Certificates and click Add. Select My User Account and click Finish. Click OK to close the Add Or Remove Snap-ins dialog box.
4. Select Certificates, and then select Trusted People.
5. Right-click Trusted People. On the All Tasks menu, click Import to open the Certificate Import Wizard.
6. Click Next and then browse to the location of the certificate you want to import.
7. Select the certificate and then click Next.
8. Type the password for the certificate and then click Next.
9. Click Next to place the certificate in the Trusted People store.
10. Click Finish to complete the import.
11. Click OK to acknowledge the successful import, and then exit the MMC.

Now you can grant that user access to EFS-encrypted files.

How to Recover to an EFS-encrypted File Using a Data Recovery Agent

EFS grants data recovery agents (DRAs) permission to decrypt files so that an administrator can restore an encrypted file if the user loses his or her EFS key. By default, workgroup computers configure the local Administrator account as the DRA. In domain environments, domain administrators configure one or more user accounts as DRAs for the entire domain.

Because DRA certificates are not copied automatically when an administrator logs onto a computer, the process of copying the DRA certificate and recovering an EFS-encrypted file is somewhat lengthy (but straightforward). To recover an EFS-encrypted file, perform these steps:

1. First, you need to obtain a copy of the DRA certificate. By default, this is stored in the Administrator user account on the first domain controller in the domain. To do this, using the DRA account, log on to the administrator account on the first domain controller in the domain.

2. Click Start, and then click Run. Type **mmc**, and then press Enter. Respond to the UAC prompt that appears.

3. Click File, and then click Add/Remove Snap-In.

4. Click Add.

   A list of all the registered snap-ins on the current computer appears.

5. Double-click the Certificates snap-in.

6. If the Certificates Snap-In Wizard appears, select My User Account, and then click Finish. Click OK.

   The MMC console now shows the Certificates snap-in.

7. Browse to Certificates - Current User\Personal\Certificates. In the details pane, right-click the domain DRA certificate, click All Tasks, and then click Export (as shown in Figure 4-12). By default, this is the Administrator certificate that is also signed by the Administrator, and it has the Intended Purpose shown as File Recovery.

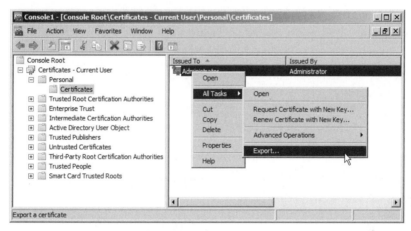

FIGURE 4-12 Exporting a certificate for EFS recovery

8. In the Certificate Export Wizard, click Next.

9. On the Export Private Key page, select Yes, Export The Private Key, and then click Next.

10. On the Export File Format page, accept the default settings shown in Figure 4-13, and then click Next. For security reasons, you might want to select the Delete The Private Key If The Export Is Successful check box and then store the private key on removable media in a safe location. Then, use the removable media when you need to recover an EFS-encrypted file.

11. On the Password page, type a recovery password twice. Click Next.

12. On the File To Export page, type a file name to store the recovery password on removable media. Click Next.

13. On the Completing The Certificate Export Wizard page, click Finish. Then, click OK.

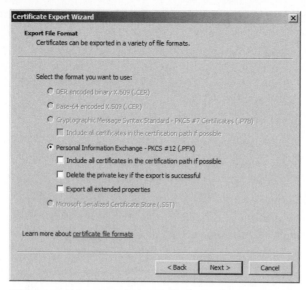

FIGURE 4-13 Using the default .PFX file format for the DRA recovery key

Now you are ready to import the DRA key on the client computer that requires recovery. Log on to the client computer and perform these steps:

1. Click Start, and then click Run. Type **mmc**, and then press Enter.

2. Click File, and then click Add/Remove Snap-In. Respond to the UAC prompt that appears.

3. Click Add.

    A list of all the registered snap-ins on the current computer appears.

4. Double-click the Certificates snap-in.

5. In the Certificates Snap-In Wizard, select My User Account, and then click Finish. Click OK.

    The MMC console now shows the Certificates snap-in.

6. Right-click Certificates - Current User\Personal\Certificates, click All Tasks, and then click Import.

7. In the Certificate Import Wizard, click Next.

8. On the File To Import page, click Browse. In the Open dialog box, click the file types list (above the Open button) and select Personal Information Exchange. Then, select the DRA key file and click Open. Click Next.

9. On the Password page, type the password you used to protect the DRA key. Click Next.

10. On the Certificate Store page, leave the default selection to store the certificate in the Personal store. Click Next.

11. Click Finish, and then click OK.

Now you can open or decrypt the files just as if you had been added as an authorized user. To decrypt the files, view the properties for the file or folder and clear the Encrypt Contents To Secure Data check box. After you click OK twice, Windows uses the DRA key to decrypt the files. Now that the files are unencrypted, the user who owns the files should immediately re-encrypt them.

> **TIP DECRYPTING RECOVERED FILES**
>
> If you use Windows Backup, files recovered from backup media will still be encrypted with EFS. Simply recover the files to a computer and have the DRA log on to that computer to decrypt them.

After recovering files, remove any copies of your DRA. Because the DRA can be used to decrypt any file in your domain, it's critical that you not leave a copy of it on a user's computer.

BitLocker

NTFS file permissions provide access control when the operating system is online. EFS supplements NTFS file permissions by using encryption to provide access control that is in effect even if an attacker bypasses the operating system (for example, by starting the computer from a bootable DVD). *BitLocker Drive Encryption,* like EFS, uses encryption. However, BitLocker has several key differences from EFS:

- BitLocker encrypts entire volumes, including the system volume and all user and system files. EFS cannot encrypt system files.

- BitLocker protects the computer at startup before the operating system starts. After the operating system starts, BitLocker is completely transparent.

- BitLocker provides computer-specific encryption, not user-specific encryption. Therefore, you still need to use EFS to protect private files from other valid users.

- BitLocker can protect the integrity of the operating system, helping to prevent *rootkits* and offline attacks that modify system files.

> **NOTE EDITIONS OF WINDOWS 7 CONTAINING BitLocker**
>
> BitLocker is a feature of Windows 7 Enterprise and Windows 7 Ultimate. It is not supported on other editions of Windows 7.

Previous versions of Windows required administrators to configure BitLocker partitions manually. Windows 7 setup automatically configures partitions compatible with BitLocker.

How to Use BitLocker with TPM Hardware

If available, BitLocker seals the symmetric encryption key in a Trusted Platform Module (TPM) 1.2 chip (available in some newer computers). If the computer does not have a TPM chip, BitLocker stores the encryption key on a USB flash drive that must be provided every time the computer starts or resumes from hibernation.

Many TPM-equipped computers have the TPM chip disabled in the basic input/output system (BIOS). Before you can use it, you must enter the computer's BIOS settings and enable it. After you enable the TPM chip, BitLocker performs the TPM initialization automatically. To allow you to initialize TPM chips manually and turn them on or off at the operating system level, Windows 7 includes the TPM Management snap-in, as shown in Figure 4-14. To use it, open a blank MMC console and add the snap-in.

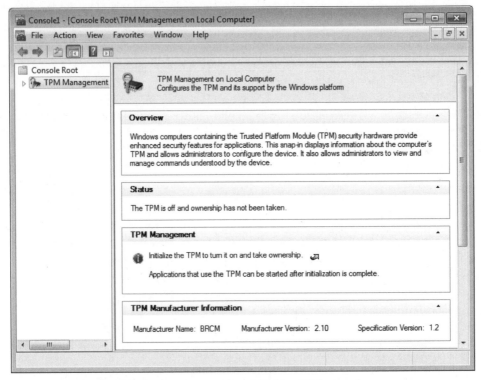

FIGURE 4-14 Using the TPM Management snap-in to initialize a TPM manually

> **NOTE BitLocker INITIALIZES A TPM BY ITSELF**
>
> Because BitLocker handles the TPM initialization for you, the TPM Management snap-in is not discussed further in this book.

BitLocker has several modes available on computers with TPM hardware:

- **TPM only**   This mode is transparent to the user, and the user logon experience is exactly the same as it was before BitLocker was enabled. During startup, BitLocker communicates with the TPM hardware to validate the integrity of the computer and operating system. However, if the TPM is missing or changed, if the hard disk is moved to a different computer, or if critical startup files have changed, BitLocker enters recovery mode. In recovery mode, the user needs to enter a 40-digit recovery key or insert a USB flash drive with a recovery key stored on it to regain access to the data. TPM-only mode provides protection from hard-disk theft with no user training necessary.

- **TPM with external key**   In this mode, BitLocker performs the same integrity checks as TPM-only mode but also requires the user to provide an external key (usually a USB flash drive with a certificate stored on it) to start Windows. This provides protection from both hard-disk theft and stolen computers (assuming the computer was shut down or locked); however, it requires some effort from the user.

- **TPM with PIN**   In this mode, BitLocker requires the user to type a PIN to start Windows.

- **TPM with PIN and external key**   In this mode, BitLocker requires the user to provide an external key and to type a PIN.

When TPM hardware is available, BitLocker validates the integrity of the computer and operating system by storing "measurements" of various parts of the computer and operating system in the TPM chip. In its default configuration, BitLocker instructs the TPM to measure the master boot record, the active boot partition, the boot sector, the Windows Boot Manager, and the BitLocker storage root key. Each time the computer is booted, the TPM computes the SHA-1 hash of the measured code and compares this to the hash stored in the TPM from the previous boot. If the hashes match, the boot process continues; if the hashes do not match, the boot process halts. At the conclusion of a successful boot process, the TPM releases the storage root key to BitLocker; BitLocker decrypts data as Windows reads it from the protected volume. Because no other operating system can do this (even an alternate instance of Windows 7), the TPM never releases the key and therefore the volume remains a useless encrypted blob. Any attempts to modify the protected volume will render it unbootable.

How to Enable the Use of BitLocker on Computers without TPM

If TPM hardware is not available, BitLocker can store decryption keys on a USB flash drive instead of using a built-in TPM module. Using BitLocker in this configuration can be risky, however, because if the user loses the USB flash drive, the encrypted volume is no longer accessible and the computer cannot start without the recovery key. Windows 7 does not make this option available by default.

To use BitLocker encryption on a computer without a compatible TPM, you need to change a computer Group Policy setting by performing these steps:

1. Open the Group Policy Object Editor by clicking Start, typing **gpedit.msc**, and pressing Enter. Respond to the UAC prompt that appears.

2. Navigate to Computer Configuration\Administrative Templates\Windows Components\ BitLocker Drive Encryption\Operating System Drives.

3. Enable the Require Additional Authentication At Startup setting. Then select the Allow BitLocker Without A Compatible TPM check box. Click OK.

If you plan to deploy BitLocker in an enterprise using USB flash drives instead of TPM, you should deploy this setting with domain-based Group Policy settings.

How to Enable BitLocker Encryption

Individual users can enable BitLocker from Control Panel, but most enterprises should use AD DS to manage keys.

> **MORE INFO   CONFIGURING AD DS TO BACK UP BitLocker**
>
> For detailed instructions on how to configure AD DS to back up BitLocker and TPM recovery information, read "Configuring Active Directory to Back up Windows BitLocker Drive Encryption and Trusted Platform Module Recovery Information" at *http://go.microsoft.com/fwlink/?LinkId=78953*.

To enable BitLocker from Control Panel, perform these steps:

1. Perform a full backup of the computer, and then run a check of the integrity of the BitLocker partition using ChkDsk.

2. Open Control Panel. Click the System And Security link. Under BitLocker Drive Encryption, click the Protect Your Computer By Encrypting Data On Your Disk link.

3. On the BitLocker Drive Encryption page, click Turn On BitLocker.

4. On the BitLocker Drive Encryption Setup page, click Next.

5. If the Preparing Your Drive For BitLocker page appears, click Next. If you are required to restart your computer, do so.

6. If the Turn On The TPM Security Hardware page appears, click Next, and then click Restart.

7. If the volume is the system volume and the choice has not been blocked by a Group Policy setting, in the Set BitLocker Startup Preferences dialog box (shown in Figure 4-15), select your authentication choice. The choices vary depending on whether the computer has a built-in TPM chip.

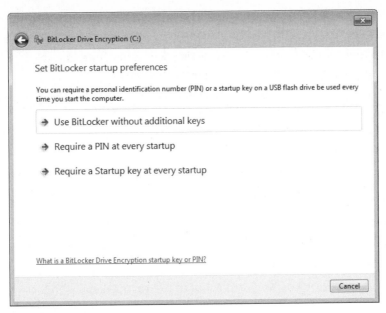

FIGURE 4-15 Startup options in BitLocker

The choices include the following:

- **Use BitLocker Without Additional Keys**   Uses the TPM to verify the integrity of the operating system at every startup. This option does not prompt the user during startup, providing completely transparent protection.

- **Require PIN At Every Startup**   Uses the TPM to verify the integrity of the operating system at startup and requires the user to type a PIN to verify the user's identity. This option provides additional protection but can inconvenience the user. If you choose to use a PIN, the Enter A Startup Pin page appears. Type your PIN and then click Set PIN.

- **Require Startup USB Key At Every Startup**   Does not require TPM hardware. This option requires the user to insert a USB key containing the decryption key at startup. Alternatively, users can type a recovery key to gain access to the encrypted system partition. If you choose to use a USB key, the Save Your Startup Key page appears. Select the startup key and then click Save.

> *NOTE*   **REQUIRING BOTH A STARTUP USB KEY AND A PIN**
>
> The BitLocker wizard allows you to choose either a PIN or a startup USB key. If you want to use both, use the Manage-bde command-line tool. For example, to protect the C:\ drive with both using a startup key located on the E:\ drive, you would run the command *manage-bde –protectors –add C: -TPMAndPINAndStartupKey –tsk E:*.

8. On the Save The Recovery Password page, choose the destination (a USB drive, a local or remote folder, or a printer) to save your recovery password. The recovery password is a small text file containing brief instructions, a drive label and password ID, and the 48-digit recovery password. Save the password and the recovery key on separate devices and store them in different locations. Click Next.

9. On the Encrypt The Volume page, select the Run BitLocker System Check check box and click Continue if you are ready to begin encryption. Click Restart Now. Upon rebooting, BitLocker ensures that the computer is fully compatible and ready to be encrypted.

10. BitLocker displays a special screen confirming that the key material was loaded. Now that this has been confirmed, BitLocker begins encrypting the C:\ drive after Windows 7 starts, and BitLocker is enabled.

BitLocker encrypts the drive in the background so that you can continue using the computer.

How to Manage BitLocker Keys on a Local Computer

To manage keys on the local computer, follow these steps:

1. Open Control Panel and click the System And Security link. Under BitLocker Drive Encryption, click the Manage BitLocker link.

2. In the BitLocker Drive Encryption window, click Manage BitLocker.

Using this tool, you can perform the following actions (which vary depending on the authentication type chosen):

- **Save Or Print Recovery Key Again**   Provides the following options:
  - Save The Recovery Key To A USB Flash Drive
  - Save The Recovery Key To A File
  - Print The Recovery Key

- **Duplicate The Startup Key**   When you use a USB startup key for authentication, this allows you to create a second USB startup key with an identical key.

- **Reset The PIN**   When you use a PIN for authentication, this allows you to change the PIN.

To manage BitLocker from an elevated command prompt or from a remote computer, use the Manage-bde tool, which replaces the Manage-bde.wsf script in Windows Vista. For example, to view the current BitLocker configuration, run *manage-bde –status*. The following example demonstrates the configuration of a computer with one decrypted data drive and one encrypted system drive:

```
manage-bde -status
BitLocker Drive Encryption: Configuration Tool version 6.1.7600
Copyright (C) Microsoft Corporation. All rights reserved.
```

```
Disk volumes that can be protected with
BitLocker Drive Encryption:
Volume E: [Flash]
[Data Volume]

    Size:                   0.12 GB
    BitLocker Version:      None
    Conversion Status:      Fully Decrypted
    Percentage Encrypted:   0%
    Encryption Method:      None
    Protection Status:      Protection Off
    Lock Status:            Unlocked
    Identification Field:   None
    Automatic Unlock:       Disabled
    Key Protectors:         None Found

Volume C: []
[OS Volume]

    Size:                   126.90 GB
    BitLocker Version:      Windows 7
    Conversion Status:      Fully Encrypted
    Percentage Encrypted:   100%
    Encryption Method:      AES 128 with Diffuser
    Protection Status:      Protection On
    Lock Status:            Unlocked
    Identification Field:   None
    Key Protectors:
        External Key
        Numerical Password
```

For detailed information about how to use Manage-bde, run *manage-bde -?* at a command prompt.

How to Recover Data Protected by BitLocker

When you use BitLocker to protect the system partition, the partition will be locked if the encryption key is not available, causing BitLocker to enter recovery mode. Likely causes of the encryption key not being available include:

- One of the boot files is modified.

- BIOS is modified and the TPM disabled.

- The TPM is cleared.

- An attempt is made to boot without the TPM, PIN, or USB key being available.

- The BitLocker-encrypted disk is moved to a new computer.

After the drive is locked, you can boot only to recovery mode, as shown in Figure 4-16. On most keyboards, you can use the standard number keys from 0–9. However, on some non-English keyboards, you need to use the function keys by pressing F1 for the digit 1, F2 for the digit 2, and so on, with F10 being the digit 0.

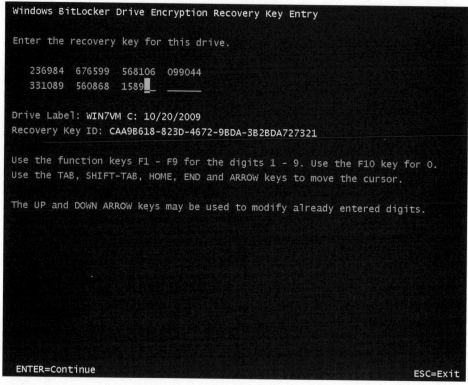

```
Windows BitLocker Drive Encryption Recovery Key Entry

Enter the recovery key for this drive.

    236984   676599   568106   099044
    331089   560868   1589_    _____

Drive Label: WIN7VM C: 10/20/2009
Recovery Key ID: CAA9B618-823D-4672-9BDA-3B2BDA727321

Use the function keys F1 - F9 for the digits 1 - 9. Use the F10 key for 0.
Use the TAB, SHIFT-TAB, HOME, END and ARROW keys to move the cursor.

The UP and DOWN ARROW keys may be used to modify already entered digits.




ENTER=Continue                                                    ESC=Exit
```

FIGURE 4-16 Gaining access to a BitLocker-encrypted drive by typing a 48-character recovery password

If you have the recovery key on a USB flash drive, you can insert the recovery key and press the Esc key to restart the computer. BitLocker reads the recovery key automatically during startup.

If you cancel out of recovery, the Windows Boot Manager might provide instructions for using Startup Repair to fix a startup problem automatically. Do not follow these instructions; Startup Repair cannot access the encrypted volume. Instead, restart the computer and enter the recovery key.

As a last resort, you can use the BitLocker Repair Tool (Repair-bde) to help recover data from an encrypted volume. The BitLocker Repair Tool was a separate download for earlier versions of Windows, but it is included in Windows 7 and Windows Server 2008 R2.

You can use the BitLocker Repair Tool to copy the decrypted contents of an encrypted volume to a different volume. For example, if you have used BitLocker to protect the D:\ data volume and the volume has become corrupted, you might be able to use the BitLocker Repair

Tool to decrypt the contents and copy them to the E:\ volume, if you can provide a recovery key or password. The following command would attempt this:

```
repair-bde D: E: -RecoveryPassword 111111-222222-333333-444444-5555555-6666666-7777777-
888888
```

You can also attempt to repair a volume without copying the data by using the *–NoOutputVolume* parameter, as the following command demonstrates:

```
repair-bde C: -NoOutputVolume -RecoveryKey D:\RecoveryKey.bek
```

If the system volume becomes corrupted, you can start Windows 7 Setup from the Windows 7 DVD, start the repair tools, and open a command prompt to run the BitLocker Repair Tool. Alternatively, you could attempt to mount the volume to a different computer and run the BitLocker Repair Tool.

> **NOTE** **BACKING UP ENCRYPTED DRIVES**
>
> Because it can be difficult or impossible to recover a corrupted BitLocker-protected drive, it's especially important to back up BitLocker-protected drives regularly. Note, however, that your backups might not be encrypted by default. This applies to system image backups, as well. Although system image backups make a copy of your entire disk, BitLocker functions at a lower level than system image backups. Therefore, when system image backup reads the disk, it reads the BitLocker-decrypted version of the disk.

How to Disable or Remove BitLocker Drive Encryption

Because BitLocker intercepts the boot process and looks for changes to any of the early boot files, it can cause problems in the following nonattack scenarios:

- Upgrading or replacing the motherboard or TPM
- Installing a new operating system that changes the master boot record or the boot manager
- Moving a BitLocker-encrypted disk to another TPM-enabled computer
- Repartitioning the hard disk
- Updating the BIOS
- Third-party updates that occur outside the operating system (such as hardware firmware updates)

To avoid entering BitLocker recovery mode, you can disable BitLocker temporarily, which allows you to change the TPM and upgrade the operating system. When you re-enable BitLocker, the same encryption keys will be used. You can also choose to decrypt the BitLocker-protected volume, which will completely remove BitLocker protection. You can re-enable BitLocker only by repeating the process to create new keys and reencrypt the volume.

To disable BitLocker temporarily or decrypt the BitLocker-protected volume permanently, perform these steps:

1. Log on to the computer as Administrator.

2. From Control Panel, open BitLocker Drive Encryption.

3. Click Suspend Protection for the volume that has BitLocker enabled to use a clear key. To remove BitLocker completely, click Turn Off BitLocker.

Troubleshooting BitLocker Problems

Several common BitLocker problems are actually "features." The problems occur because BitLocker is designed to provide protection from specific types of attacks. Often these legitimate uses resemble attacks and cause BitLocker to refuse to allow the computer to start or the BitLocker encryption to prevent you from accessing files:

- **The operating system fails to start in a dual-boot configuration** You can dual-boot a computer after enabling BitLocker. However, the second operating system instance must be configured on a different partition. You cannot dual-boot to a second operating system installed on the same partition.

- **The operating system fails to start if you move the hard disk to a different computer** BitLocker is designed to protect data from offline attacks, such as attacks that bypass operating system security by connecting the hard disk to a different computer. The new computer will be unable to decrypt the data (even if it has a TPM chip in it). Before moving a BitLocker-encrypted disk to a different computer, disable BitLocker. Re-enable BitLocker after transferring the disk. Alternatively, you can use the recovery key to start Windows after moving the hard disk to the new computer.

- **The data on the hard disk is unreadable using standard disk recovery tools** For the same reasons stated in the previous bullet point, BitLocker files are unreadable using standard disk recovery tools. Some day recovery tools that support decrypting BitLocker files using a recovery key might be available. As of the time of this writing, your only opportunity for recovering BitLocker encrypted files is to start Windows 7 using the BitLocker recovery key. For this reason it is very important to regularly back up BitLocker-encrypted volumes.

PRACTICE **Encrypt and Recover Encrypted Data**

In this practice, you simulate the recovery of a lost EFS encryption certificate.

EXERCISE 1   Encrypt Data

In this exercise, you encrypt a file. Windows 7 automatically generates an EFS key if you don't already have one.

1. Log on to a computer running Windows 7 as a standard user.

2. Create a file named Encrypted.txt in your Documents folder.

3. Right-click the Encrypted.txt file, and then click Properties.

4. On the General tab of the Properties dialog box, click Advanced.

5. Select the Encrypt Contents To Secure Data check box, and then click OK twice.

6. In the Encryption Warning dialog box, select Encrypt The File Only, and then click OK. Notice that Windows Explorer displays the Encrypted.txt file in green.

7. Double-click the Encrypted.txt file to open it in Microsoft Notepad. Then add the text "This file is encrypted." Save the file and close Notepad.

8. Double-click the file to verify that you can open it, and then close Notepad again.

Now you have encrypted a file, and no user can access it without your EFS key.

EXERCISE 2 Back Up an EFS Key

In Exercise 1, you encrypted a file. In this exercise, you back up the EFS key that was generated automatically when you encrypted the file. Then you delete the original key and determine whether you can access the EFS-encrypted file. To complete this practice, you must have completed Exercise 1.

1. Click Start, and then click Control Panel.

2. Click the User Accounts link twice.

3. In the left pane, click the Manage Your File Encryption Certificates link.

   The Encrypting File System Wizard appears.

4. On the Manage Your File Encryption Certificates page, click Next.

5. On the Select Or Create A File Encryption Certificate page, leave the default certificate (your EFS certificate) selected, and then click Next.

6. On the Back Up The Certificate And Key page, click Browse and select the Documents folder. For the file name, type **EFS-cert-backup.pfx**. Click Save, and then type a complex password in the Password and Confirm Password fields. Click Next.

7. If the Update Your Previously Encrypted Files page appears, leave all check boxes cleared and then click Next.

8. On the Encrypting File System page, click Close.

9. In Windows Explorer, open your Documents folder and verify that the EFS certificate was exported correctly.

   Now that you have backed up your EFS key, you can lose it safely. Simulate a corrupted or lost key by following these steps to delete it:

10. Click Start, type **mmc**, and then press Enter to open a blank MMC.

11. Click File, and then click Add/Remove Snap-in.

12. Select Certificates and click Add.

13. Select My User Account, and then click Finish.

14. Click OK.

15. Expand Certificates – Current User, expand Personal, and then select Certificates.

16. In the middle pane, right-click your EFS certificate, and then click Delete.

17. In the Certificates dialog box, click Yes to confirm that you want to delete the certificate.

18. Log off the current desktop session and then log back on. Windows 7 caches the user's EFS certificate. Thus, if you remained logged on, you would still be able to open your encrypted file.

19. Open the Documents folder and double-click the Encrypted.txt file. Notepad should appear and display an "Access is denied" error message. This indicates that the file is encrypted but you don't have a valid EFS certificate.

EXERCISE 3   Recover Encrypted Data

In this exercise, you recover a lost EFS key and use it to access encrypted data. To complete this exercise, you must have completed Exercises 1 and 2.

1. In the Documents folder, double-click the EFS-cert-backup.pfx file that you created in Exercise 2.

   The Certificate Import Wizard appears.

2. On the Welcome To The Certificate Import Wizard page, click Next.

3. On the File To Import page, click Next.

4. On the Password page, type the password you assigned to the certificate. Then click Next.

5. On the Certificate Store page, click Next.

6. On the Completing The Certificate Import Wizard page, click Finish.

7. Click OK to confirm that the import was successful.

8. Open the Documents folder and double-click the Encrypted.txt file. Notepad should appear and display the contents of the file, indicating that you successfully recovered the EFS key and can now access encrypted files.

Lesson Summary

- Use EFS to encrypt individual files and folders. Because encrypted files are unavailable if the user loses his or her EFS certificate, it's important to have a backup EFS certificate and a recovery key. In environments where multiple users log on to a single computer, you can grant multiple users access to EFS-encrypted files.

- Use BitLocker to encrypt the entire system volume. If available, BitLocker makes use of TPM hardware to seal the encryption key. BitLocker then works with the TPM hardware during computer startup to verify the integrity of the computer and operating system. If TPM hardware is available, you can optionally require the user to insert a USB flash drive with a special key or type a password to gain access to the BitLocker-encrypted volume. BitLocker is disabled by default on computers without TPM hardware, but you can enable BitLocker without TPM hardware by using Group Policy settings. If TPM hardware is not available, users are required to insert a USB flash drive or a recovery key to start Windows 7.

Lesson Review

You can use the following questions to test your knowledge of the information in Lesson 3, "Using Encryption to Control Access to Data." The questions are also available on the companion CD if you prefer to review them in electronic form.

> **NOTE ANSWERS**
>
> Answers to these questions and explanations of why each answer choice is right or wrong are located in the "Answers" section at the end of the book.

1. Which tool would you use to back up an EFS certificate?
   A. BitLocker Drive Encryption
   B. Computer Management
   C. Certificates
   D. Services

2. In the Certificates console, which node would you access to back up the DRA certificate?
   A. Certificates – Current User\Personal\Certificates
   B. Certificates – Current User\Active Directory User Object
   C. Certificates (Local Computer)\Personal\Certificates
   D. Certificates (Local Computer)\Active Directory User Object

3. Which of the following configurations does BitLocker support? (Choose all that apply.)
   A. Use BitLocker with a TPM but without additional keys
   B. Use BitLocker with a TPM and require a PIN at every startup
   C. Use BitLocker without a TPM and require a PIN at every startup
   D. Use BitLocker without a TPM and require a USB key at every startup

Chapter Review

To further practice and reinforce the skills you learned in this chapter, you can perform the following tasks:

- Review the chapter summary.
- Review the list of key terms introduced in this chapter.
- Complete the case scenarios. These scenarios set up real-world situations involving the topics of this chapter and ask you to create a solution.
- Complete the suggested practices.
- Take a practice test.

Chapter Summary

- Authentication is the process of identifying a user and validating the user's identity. To troubleshoot authentication problems, first verify that the user does not have a logon restriction, such as a locked-out account, an expired password, or a disabled account. If you need to monitor authentication errors, enable failure auditing for Account Logon Events and then examine the Security event log. If a computer account becomes untrusted, you can either leave and rejoin the domain or reestablish the trust with the Netdom tool.

- Internet Explorer is one of the most important tools in Windows because it provides users access to Web applications and the Internet. Therefore, it's vital that you know how to configure Internet Explorer and troubleshoot common problems. Historically, many users have experienced problems with add-ons, which extend Internet Explorer's capabilities but also have the potential to behave unreliably or maliciously. Fortunately, Internet Explorer gives administrators complete control over which add-ons can be installed, as well as the capability to quickly start Internet Explorer without any add-ons. To reduce security risks when using Internet Explorer, Protected Mode runs Internet Explorer with minimal privileges. If a Web page, Internet Explorer, an add-on, or any process launched from within Internet Explorer requires elevated privileges, the elevation must be approved before Internet Explorer can take action. To provide privacy and authentication, many Web sites use SSL certificates. Therefore, it's vital that you understand the causes of common certificate problems and how to fix these problems.

- Encryption provides data protection even if an attacker bypasses operating system security. Windows Vista includes two encryption technologies: EFS and BitLocker. EFS encrypts individual files and folders, while BitLocker encrypts the entire system volume. If a user loses their key, they will be unable to access encrypted files. Therefore, it is important to maintain EFS data recovery agents and BitLocker recovery keys, as well as data backups. To manage BitLocker from a command prompt, use the Manage-bde tool. To repair BitLocker from a command prompt, use the Repair-bde tool.

Key Terms

Do you know what these key terms mean? You can check your answers by looking up the terms in the glossary at the end of the book.

- **ActiveX**
- **BitLocker Drive Encryption**
- **Encrypting File System (EFS)**
- **Mandatory Integrity Control (MIC)**
- **Multifactor Authentication**
- **Protected Mode**
- **Protected Mode Compatibility Layer**
- **Rootkit**

Case Scenarios

In the following case scenarios, you apply what you've learned about subjects of this chapter. You can find answers to these questions in the "Answers" section at the end of this book.

Case Scenario 1: Recommend Data Protection Technologies

You are a desktop support technician at Wingtip Toys. Recently, Adina Hagege, your organization's CEO, stopped you in the hallway to ask a couple of quick questions.

Questions

Answer the following questions for your CEO:

1. "Can you give me a quick second opinion about something? I travel almost constantly, and I keep the company financials and all the plans for our new toys on my laptop. The IT department says they have file permissions set up so that only I can view these files. Is that good enough to protect me if someone steals my laptop?"

2. "Is there some way I can protect my data even if my laptop is stolen? What are my options?"

3. "Sometimes I share files with people across the network. Which of those technologies will allow me to share files this way?"

Case Scenario 2: Unwanted Internet Explorer Add-On

You are a systems administrator for Humongous Insurance. Recently, one of your brokers called the support desk because he was experiencing odd problems when using Internet Explorer. Specifically, his home page had changed and the pop-up blocker no longer seemed to be working.

Your manager is concerned that this will be more than an isolated incident and asks you to interview key people and then come to his office to make recommendations about how to deal with this type of problem in the future.

Interviews

Following is a list of company personnel interviewed and their statements:

- **David Barber, Broker**   "I had installed an add-on because it said it would make browsing the Web faster. I didn't notice any improvement. After that, though, my Internet Explorer home page changed and I began to get a lot of advertisements popping up on my screen."

- **Julian Price, Internet Development Project Manager**   "We recently converted all of our internal software to the ASP.NET Web application platform. To do some of the more complicated stuff, we install custom client-side add-ons in Internet Explorer. So, whatever you do, don't block all add-ons. We use add-ons internally, and we update them regularly, so we really need users to be able to install the add-ons automatically."

Questions

Answer the following questions for your manager:

1. If this comes up again, what's the best way to remove the unwanted add-on?
2. Are there any features enabled by default in Windows 7 that protect users from unwanted add-ons? What are they?
3. What's the best way to prevent unwanted add-ons in the future?

Suggested Practices

To help you master the exam objectives presented in this chapter, complete the following tasks.

Identify and Resolve Logon Issues

For this task, you should complete both practices.

- **Practice 1**   Visit *http://social.answers.microsoft.com/Forums/en-US/categories* and browse the Security, Privacy, And User Accounts newsgroup. Read the posts to determine how administrators solved authentication problems.

- **Practice 2** On your production computer, enable success and failure auditing for the Audit Logon Events policy. Leave this enabled for several days, and then analyze the audit events in the Security event log to identify the types of events that are added during normal computer usage.

Identify and Resolve Encryption Issues

For this task, you should complete Practice 1. If you want a better understanding of BitLocker, complete Practices 2 and 3.

- **Practice 1** In a domain environment, use EFS to encrypt a file. Then, copy the domain DRA key to that computer and use a different account to recover the encrypted file.

- **Practice 2** Enable BitLocker Drive Encryption on a computer running Windows 7. Then, search the Internet for a free .ISO file for a bootable operating system and burn the .ISO file to a CD or DVD. Restart the computer from the bootable media and attempt to view files on the BitLocker-protected volume.

- **Practice 3** Enable BitLocker Drive Encryption on a computer running Windows 7. Then, connect the hard disk to a different computer and attempt to load Windows. When prompted, provide the recovery key.

Identify and Resolve Windows Internet Explorer Security Issues

For this task, you should complete at least Practices 1 through 3. If you want in-depth knowledge of how Internet Explorer handles both legitimate and malicious changes, complete Practice 4 as well.

- **Practice 1** On your day-to-day computer, open Internet Explorer and view the Manage Add-Ons dialog box. Examine the different add-ons that are already installed.

- **Practice 2** Start Internet Explorer with add-ons disabled. Browse to your favorite Web sites and notice any differences caused by the missing add-ons.

- **Practice 3** On your day-to-day computer, use Explorer to browse \%userprofile%\ AppData\Local\Microsoft\Windows\Temporary Internet Files\Virtualized\ and its subfolders. The folder is hidden, so you will need to type the full path. Make note of the applications that the Internet Explorer compatibility layer has virtualized and the types of files that were virtualized.

- **Practice 4** Perform a fresh installation of Windows 7 on a computer used only for testing. Browse to your favorite Web sites and notice how the Information Bar, Protected Mode, and UAC work together to protect the user from potentially unwanted add-ons. Next, use Internet Explorer to browse to potentially dangerous Web sites that might try to install malicious software and view how Internet Explorer responds (Hint: search for combinations of words such as "crack," "hack," "warez," and "serials").

Take a Practice Test

The practice tests on this book's companion CD offer many options. For example, you can test yourself on just one exam objective, or you can test yourself on all the 70-685 certification exam content. You can set up the test so that it closely simulates the experience of taking a certification exam, or you can set it up in study mode so that you can look at the correct answers and explanations after you answer each question.

> **MORE INFO** **PRACTICE TESTS**
>
> For details about all the practice test options available, see the section entitled "How to Use the Practice Tests," in the Introduction to this book.

CHAPTER 5

Protecting Client Systems

Any computer that is connected to the Internet faces a barrage of network-based threats in the form of malicious software attacks. These threats are growing in number and sophistication every year, and as an enterprise support technician, you are responsible for protecting client systems from these evolving dangers.

As part of your company's broad defense strategy, you need to know how to configure in Windows 7 the features whose purpose is to protect your clients. Specifically, you need to know how to minimize the risk of damage from malware by implementing User Account Control (UAC) at an appropriate level, by using Windows Defender, and by removing unwanted software if it is discovered.

Exam objective in this chapter:

- Identify and resolve issues due to malicious software.

Lesson in this chapter:

- Lesson 1: Resolving Malware Issues **195**

Before You Begin

To perform the exercises in this chapter, you need:

- A domain controller running Windows Server 2008 R2
- A client computer running Windows 7 that is a member of the same domain

 REAL WORLD

J.C. Mackin

I often hear people repeating a number of misconceptions about viruses and other malware, and I'm convinced that these misconceptions have lulled users and administrators into a false sense of security about the dangers their systems face. Often these misconceptions are based on an accurate understanding of what *was* the state of malware threats about 10 years ago. But the nature of these threats has evolved significantly, and it continues to evolve. So in the interest of learning how best to defend ourselves today, let's deal with the most common of these misconceptions.

- "As long as you keep Windows updated, you're fine."

  It's certainly true that you need to keep Microsoft Windows updated, but you need to keep *all* your software updated. Security holes can be found in applications as easily as they can be found in operating systems, and the security holes in many of these can be exploited to completely compromise a system. Microsoft Office applications in particular are often targeted. Remember that your systems are not safe from exploits if you are keeping only Windows updated.

- "As long as you aren't tricked into opening anything, you're fine."

  A long time ago, it was true that malicious software needed user assistance to be installed on a system. Now, the situation is completely different. Merely browsing to the wrong site, for example, can lead to a secret drive-by download of malicious software. Even worse, some of the most harmful attacks come from Internet worms, which need no user involvement whatsoever. It is still essential for users to avoid opening unknown software, but this preventative measure alone is not enough to keep your systems safe from infection.

- "As long as you keep your antivirus software up to date and scan daily, you're fine."

  This might be the most common of all misconceptions regarding malware. While it's true that a robust anti-malware solution is one of the essential pillars of a sound client protection strategy, the sad truth is that such software has its limitations. Malware developers who are serious about exploiting computers naturally design their programs in a way that avoids detection by antivirus solutions. For example, a rootkit is a relatively new type of malware that—so far—few anti-malware applications have had good success in detecting. But even more familiar types of malware can be designed to evade detection. As a result, when your antivirus software fails to detect malware on a system, you should know that the system still could very easily be infected.

These three misconceptions all have a common thread running through them: the belief that you can protect your systems by adopting a small number of well-known defenses against malware. In truth, adequately protecting client systems requires your company to adopt a wide array of strategies that include effective software updates, antivirus software, user education, firewalls, and most important of all, effective management of these and other security features.

Lesson 1: Resolving Malware Issues

The number of new malware applications being released today actually exceeds that of new legitimate applications. As an enterprise support technician, you need to adequately protect your clients from these mounting threats and know how to handle malware infections once they are discovered.

Windows 7 includes two features that assist you in this fight against malware. User Account Control (UAC) helps prevent programs from secretly altering protected areas of the operating system, and Windows Defender scans your system for spyware and offers to remove any unwanted software that is detected.

Though you will need to use additional applications such as Microsoft Forefront and a managed anti-malware solution to protect your network, understanding how to use and configure these built-in features of Windows 7 represents part of the essential skill set you need on your job.

After this lesson, you will be able to:

- Configure User Account Control (UAC) to display notifications in a way that suits the needs of your organization.
- Configure Windows Defender settings.
- Detect and remove some malware manually in case your anti-malware applications fail.

Estimated lesson time: 30 minutes

Understanding Malware

Malware is an umbrella term for many different types of unwanted software. It's important to understand the nature of these different threats, but it's also important to recognize that many malware applications blend features from more than one of these malware types. The following list discusses the most common types of malware:

- **Virus**   A *virus* is a self-replicating program that can install itself on a target computer. Viruses do not propagate over networks automatically; they need to be spread through e-mail or another means. Once installed, viruses usually alter, damage, or compromise a system in some way.

- **Worm**   A *worm* is a self-replicating program that can spread automatically over a network without any help from a user or a program such as an e-mail client or Web browser. Worms vary greatly in the potential damage they can cause. Some worms simply replicate and do little other than consume network bandwidth. Others can be used to compromise a system completely.

- **Trojan horse**   A Trojan horse is a program that is presented to users as a desirable application but that is intentionally written to harm a system. Unlike viruses and worms, Trojan horses do not copy themselves automatically or install themselves automatically; they rely on users to install them.

- **Spyware**   *Spyware* is a type of privacy-invasive software that secretly records information about user behavior, often for the purposes of market research. Typically spyware is injected into a system when a user installs a free tool or visits a Web site with browser security settings set to a low level. The most common function of such spyware is to record the Web sites that a user visits. More rarely, some spyware, such as keyloggers (which record every keystroke), can be installed deliberately by a third party and be used to gather personal information. The biggest threat posed by most spyware is system performance degradation. All types of spyware reduce system performance by hijacking the resources of the computer for their own purposes. Unlike viruses and worms, spyware does not self-replicate.

- **Adware**   Adware is similar to spyware and is often installed alongside it. The purpose of adware is to display unsolicited advertisements to the user in the form of pop-up windows or Web browser alterations. Adware can also download and install spyware.

> **NOTE   SPYWARE AND ADWARE**
>
> The term *spyware* is often used as a general term for all unwanted software that runs in the background and that gathers market research information, displays advertisements, or alters the behavior of applications such as Web browsers. Microsoft uses the phrase "spyware and potentially unwanted software" to refer to the type of software that is unwanted but is not unambiguously harmful.

- **Backdoor**   A backdoor is a program that gives a remote, unauthorized party complete control over a system by bypassing the normal authentication mechanism of that system. Backdoors have been known to be installed by worms that exploit a weakness in a well-known program. To protect your system against backdoors, it is essential to keep your applications (not just your operating system) updated.

- **Rootkit**   A rootkit is a persistent type of malware that injects itself beneath the application level and that as a result, tends to be much harder to detect from within the operating system. A rootkit can alter the core functionality of the operating system, or it can install itself as its own operating system invisible to the user and to most anti-malware software. Other rootkits can operate at the firmware (BIOS) level. Typically, a rootkit is used to provide a backdoor to a system.

Although malware has been proliferating in type and number, the defenses against these threats have improved as well. When UAC is enabled in Windows 7, for example, a malware application cannot install itself easily without the user's knowledge. This next section provides an overview of UAC, which was introduced in Windows Vista and has been refined in Windows 7.

Understanding UAC

UAC is a set of security features designed to minimize the danger of running Windows as an administrator and to maximize the convenience of running Windows as a standard user. In versions of Windows before Windows Vista, the risks of logging on as an administrator were significant, yet the practice of doing so was widespread. Meanwhile, running as a standard user was generally safe, but the inconveniences prevented many from adopting the practice.

In versions of Windows before Windows Vista, malware could use the credentials of a locally logged-on administrator to damage a system. For example, if you were logged on to Windows XP as an administrator and unknowingly downloaded a Trojan horse from a network source, this malware could use your administrative privileges to reformat your hard disk drive, delete all your files, or create a hidden administrator account on the local system.

The main reason that users in previous versions of Windows often ran as administrators despite these dangers is that many common tasks, such as installing an application or adding a printer, required a user to have administrator privileges on the local machine. Because in previous versions of Windows there was no easy way to log on as a standard user and "elevate" to an administrator only when necessary, organizations whose users occasionally needed administrator privileges simply tended to configure their users as administrators on their local machines.

> **NOTE WHAT IS ELEVATION?**
>
> The term *elevation* is used when a user adopts administrator privileges to perform a task.

How Does UAC Address the Problem of Administrator Privileges?

UAC is the result of a new Windows security design in which both standard users and administrators use the limited privileges of a standard user to perform most actions. When users are logged on, UAC prompts them in different ways to confirm actions that make important changes to the computer. If an administrator is logged on, the action is performed only if he or she confirms it. If a standard user is logged on, the action is performed only if he or she can provide administrator credentials. In both cases, the elevation to administrator-level privileges is temporary and used to perform only the action required. Through this new system, UAC inhibits malware from secretly using a logged-on administrator's privileges.

Understanding UAC Notifications for Administrators

By default, UAC is configured to notify administrators only when programs request elevation. For example, administrators see UAC notification when they attempt to run a program (such as Cmd.exe) at elevated administrator privileges, as shown in Figure 5-1. According to this default setting, administrators in Windows 7 do not see a UAC notification when they adjust Windows settings that require administrator privileges.

FIGURE 5-1 Opening an elevated command prompt

The UAC notification that normally appears for administrators is called a *consent prompt* and is shown in Figure 5-2. Note that by default, the entire screen darkens when the notification appears and freezes until the user responds to the prompt. This feature is called the *Secure Desktop* and can be disabled.

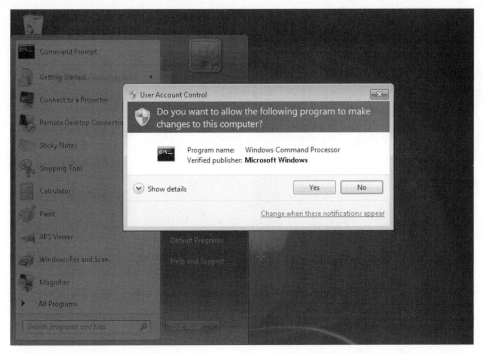

FIGURE 5-2 By default, UAC displays a consent prompt on a Secure Desktop to administrators who request to run a program with elevation.

Understanding UAC Notifications for Standard Users

The UAC notifications shown to standard users are distinct from those shown to administrators in that the notifications for standard users prompt these users to provide administrator credentials. As with administrators, standard users by default receive UAC notifications when they attempt to run a program such as a command prompt at elevated privileges, or when a program independently requests elevation. In addition, standard users by default receive UAC notifications when they attempt to make changes on the system that require administrator privileges. For example, if standard users open the System page in Control Panel and click Remote Settings, they see the credential prompt shown in Figure 5-3.

> **NOTE THE DEFAULT BEHAVIOR OF UAC IS THE SAME FOR STANDARD USERS IN WINDOWS 7**
>
> Although UAC in Windows 7 offers many notification levels that did not exist in Windows Vista or Windows Server 2008, the default behavior for standard users is the same. Whenever standard users attempt to make a change that requires administrator privileges, a credential prompt appears on a Secure Desktop.

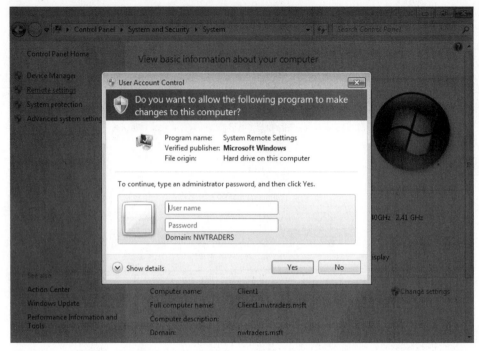

FIGURE 5-3 By default, UAC displays a credential prompt on a Secure Desktop to standard users who request elevation.

Configuring UAC in Control Panel

In a domain environment, it is recommended that UAC be controlled centrally by Group Policy instead of by configuration settings on each local machine. However, in workgroup environments or in domain environments in which Group Policy allows local UAC configuration, you can configure UAC through Control Panel.

To configure UAC in Control Panel, perform the following steps:

1. In Control Panel, click System and Security.

2. Under Action Center, click Change User Account Control Settings, as shown in Figure 5-4.

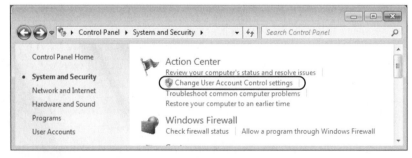

FIGURE 5-4 You can access UAC settings through the Action Center.

This step opens the User Account Settings window, one version of which is shown in Figure 5-5. Note that the set of options that appears is different for administrators and standard users, and that each user type has a different default setting.

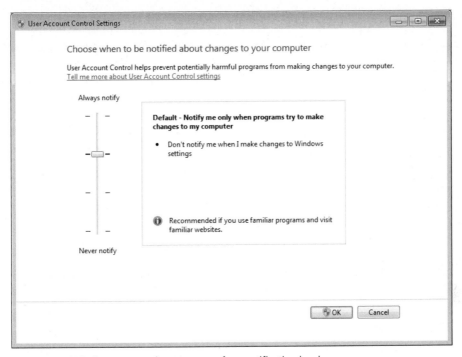

FIGURE 5-5 UAC allows you to choose among four notification levels.

3. Choose one of the following notification levels:

- **Always Notify**   This level is the default for standard users, and it configures UAC to act as it does in Windows Vista. At this level, users are notified whenever any changes that require administrator privileges are attempted on the system.

- **Notify Me Only When Programs Try To Make Changes To My Computer**   This level is the default for administrators and is not available for standard users. At this level, administrators are not notified when they make changes that require administrator privileges. However, users are notified through a consent prompt when a program requests elevation.

- **Always Notify Me (And Do Not Dim My Desktop)**   This level is not available for administrators. It is similar to the default setting for standard users, except that at this particular level, the Secure Desktop is never displayed. Disabling the Secure Desktop tends to reduce protection against malware, but it improves the user experience. This setting might be suitable for standard users who very frequently need to request elevation.

- **Notify Me Only When Programs Try To Make Changes To My Computer (Do Not Dim The Desktop)** This level is available for both standard users and administrators. At this level, the behavior is the same as with the default administrator level ("Notify me only when programs try to make changes to my computer"), but with this option the Secure Desktop is not displayed.

- **Never Notify** This level disables notifications in UAC. Users are not notified of any changes made to Windows settings or when software is installed. This option is appropriate only when you need to use programs that are incompatible with UAC.

4. Click OK.

Configuring UAC Through Group Policy

You can configure UAC through Local Security Policy or Group Policy settings. To find UAC-related policy settings in a GPO, navigate to the following node:

Computer Configuration\Policies\Windows Settings\Security Settings\Local Policies \Security Options

This location is shown in Figure 5-6.

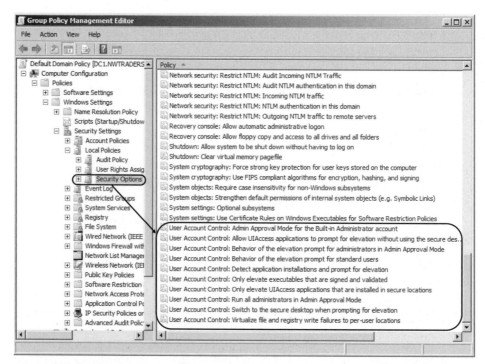

FIGURE 5-6 You can find UAC settings in Security Options in a GPO or in Local Security Policy

The following 10 UAC-related policy settings are available. The next section describes each of these configurable settings.

- **User Account Control: Admin Approval Mode For The Built-in Administrator Account** This policy applies only to the built-in Administrator account, and not to other accounts that are members of the local Administrators group. When you enable this policy setting, the built-in Administrator account sees UAC notifications just as other administrative accounts do. When you disable the setting, the built-in Administrator account behaves just like it does in Windows XP, and all processes run using Administrator privileges. This setting is disabled in Local Security Policy by default.

- **User Account Control: Allow UIAccess Applications to Prompt For Elevation Without Using The Secure Desktop** This setting controls whether user Interface Accessibility (UIAccess) programs can disable the Secure Desktop automatically. When enabled, UIAccess applications (such as Remote Assistance) automatically disable the Secure Desktop for elevation prompts. Disabling the Secure Desktop causes elevation prompts to appear on the standard desktop. By default, this setting is disabled in Local Security Policy.

- **User Account Control: Behavior Of The Elevation Prompt For Administrators In Admin Approval Mode** This policy setting controls the behavior of the elevation prompt for administrators. Six options are available:

  - **Elevate Without Prompting** With this option, administrators never see elevation prompts.

  - **Prompt For Credentials On The Secure Desktop** When this option is chosen, administrators see credential prompts on a Secure Desktop when elevation is requested.

  - **Prompt For Consent On The Secure Desktop** With this option, administrators see a consent prompt on a Secure Desktop when elevation is requested.

  - **Prompt For Credentials** When this option is selected, administrators see a credential prompt on a normal desktop when elevation is requested.

  - **Prompt For Consent** When this option is selected, administrators see a consent prompt on a normal desktop when elevation is requested.

  - **Prompt For Consent For Non-Windows Binaries** This option is the default setting in Local Security Policy. It causes a consent prompt to appear any time an application requests elevation.

- **User Account Control: Behavior Of The Elevation Prompt For Standard Users** This policy setting controls the behavior of the elevation prompt for standard users. Three options are available:

  - **Automatically Deny Elevation Requests** When this option is enforced, standard users are not able to perform tasks that require elevation.

  - **Prompt For Credentials On The Secure Desktop** With this option (the default setting in Local Security Policy), standards users see a credential prompt on the Secure Desktop when elevation is requested.

  - **Prompt For Credentials** When this option is chosen, standard users see a credential prompt on the normal desktop whenever elevation is requested.

- **User Account Control: Detect Application Installations And Prompt For Elevation**   When enabled, this policy setting configures UAC to prompt for administrative credentials when the user attempts to install an application that makes changes to protected aspects of the system. When disabled, the prompt won't appear. Domain environments that use delegated installation technologies such as Group Policy Software Install (GPSI) or Microsoft Systems Management Server (SMS) can disable this feature safely because installation processes can escalate privileges automatically without user intervention. By default, this setting is enabled in Local Security Policy.

- **User Account Control: Only Elevate Executables That Are Signed And Validated**   When this policy setting is enabled, Windows 7 refuses to run any executable that isn't signed with a trusted certificate, such as a certificate generated by an internal Public Key Infrastructure (PKI). When disabled, this policy setting allows users to run any executable, potentially including malware. If your environment requires all applications to be signed and validated with a trusted certificate, including internally developed applications, you can enable this policy to increase security greatly in your organization. This setting is disabled in Local Security Policy by default.

- **User Account Control: Only Elevate UIAccess Applications That Are Installed In Secure Locations**   When enabled, this policy setting causes Windows 7 to grant user interface access only to those applications that are started from Program Files or subfolders, from Program Files (x86) or subfolders, or from \Windows\System32\. When disabled, the policy setting grants user interface access to applications regardless of where they are started in the file structure. This policy setting is enabled by default in Local Security Policy.

- **User Account Control: Run All Administrators In Admin Approval Mode**   This policy setting, enabled by default in Local Security Policy, causes all accounts with administrator privileges *except* for the local Administrator account to see consent prompts when elevation is requested. If you disable this setting, administrators never see consent prompts and the Security Center displays a warning message.

- **User Account Control: Switch To The Secure Desktop When Prompting For Elevation**   The Secure Desktop is a feature that darkens the screen and freezes all activity except for the UAC prompt. It reduces the possibility that malware can function, but some users might find that the feature slows down their work too much. When enabled, this policy setting causes the Secure Desktop to appear with a UAC prompt. When disabled, this policy setting allows UAC prompts to appear on a normal desktop. This policy setting is enabled by default in Local Security Policy.

- **User Account Control: Virtualize File And Registry Write Failures To Per-User Locations**   This policy setting, enabled by default in Local Security Policy, improves compatibility with applications not developed for UAC by redirecting requests for protected resources. When disabled, this policy setting allows applications not developed for UAC to fail.

Disabling UAC Through Local or Group Policy

To force UAC to a disabled state, you can use Local Security Policy or Group Policy. First, set the User Account Control: Behavior Of The Elevation Prompt For Administrator In Admin Approval Mode setting to Elevate Without Prompting. Then, disable the User Account Control: Detect Application Installations And Prompt For Elevation and User Account Control: Run All Administrators In Admin Approval Mode settings. Finally, set User Account Control: Behavior Of The Elevation Prompt For Standard Users setting to Automatically Deny Elevation Requests. Then, restart the computers on which you want to apply the new settings.

Best Practices for Using UAC

To receive the security benefits of UAC while minimizing the costs, follow these best practices:

- Leave UAC enabled for client computers in your organization.

- Have all users—especially IT staff—log on with standard user privileges.

- Each user should have a single account with only standard user privileges. Do not give standard domain users accounts with administrator privileges to their local computers.

- Domain administrators should have two accounts: a standard user account that they use to log on to their computers, and a second administrator account that they can use to elevate privileges.

- Train users *not* to approve a UAC prompt if it appears unexpectedly. UAC prompts should appear only when the user is installing an application or starting a tool that requires elevated privileges. A UAC prompt that appears at any other time might have been initiated by malware. Rejecting the prompt helps prevent malware from making permanent changes to the computer.

> ✔ **Quick Check**
>   - Which Group Policy setting could you enable to prevent executables from running if they aren't signed with a trusted certificate?
>
> **Quick Check Answer**
>   - User Account Control: Only Elevate Executables That Are Signed And Validated

Whereas UAC is a set of features that broadly aims to protect core areas of the operating system, another Windows 7 tool—Windows Defender—has a much narrower goal of detecting and removing unwanted software.

Protecting Clients from Spyware with Windows Defender

Windows Defender is a tool in Windows 7 whose purpose is to detect and remove spyware on a client system. By default, Windows Defender is configured to download new spyware definitions regularly through Windows Update and then use these definitions to scan for spyware on the local system. Often, you do not need to change this default configuration, though in large networks you might want to disable some Windows Defender features through Group Policy.

> **NOTE USE WINDOWS DEFENDER IN SMALL NETWORKS**
>
> Windows Defender is a basic anti-malware program that is suitable for use in small networks or as a temporary solution before an advanced anti-malware solution is purchased. In large networks, you should use a centrally managed anti-malware solution such as Microsoft Forefront Client Security.

To view Windows Defender, open Control Panel, select View By Large Icons, and then scroll down to click Windows Defender, as shown in Figure 5-7. (Alternatively, you can click Start, type **windows defender**, and select Windows Defender in the Start menu.)

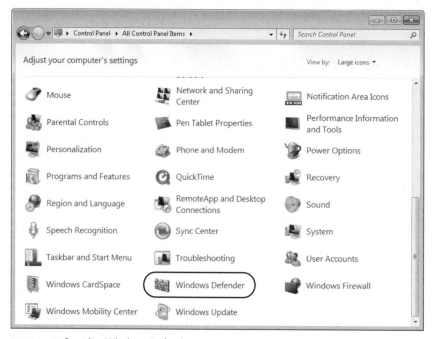

FIGURE 5-7 Opening Windows Defender

Windows Defender is shown in Figure 5-8.

By default, Windows Defender provides two types of protection:

- **Automatic scanning** Windows Defender is configured by default to download new definitions and then perform a quick scan for spyware at 2 A.M. daily.

- **Real-time protection** With this feature, Windows Defender constantly monitors computer usage in areas such as the Startup folder, the Run keys in the registry, and Windows add-ons. If an application attempts to make a change to one of these areas, Windows Defender prompts the user either to Permit (allow) or Deny (block) the change.

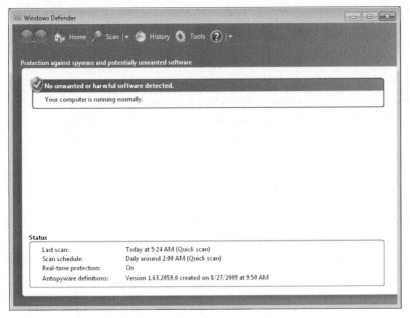

FIGURE 5-8 Windows Defender automatically checking for spyware

Besides providing this automatic functionality, Windows Defender also lets you perform a manual scan of the system. You can start a manual scan by selecting Quick Scan, Full Scan, or Custom Scan from the Scan menu, as shown in Figure 5-9.

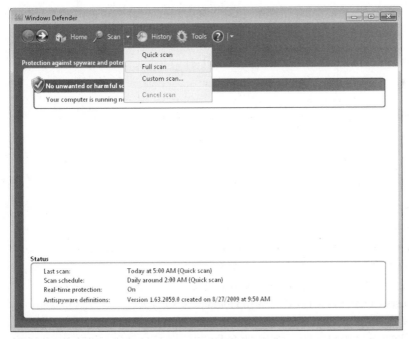

FIGURE 5-9 Performing a manual scan in Windows Defender

These three scan types are described in the following list:

- **Quick Scan**   This type of scan scans only the areas of a computer most likely to be infected by spyware or other potentially unwanted software. These areas include the computer's memory and portions of the registry that link to startup applications. A quick scan is sufficient to detect most spyware.

- **Full Scan**   This type of scan scans every file on the computer, including common types of file archives and applications already loaded in the computer's memory. A full scan typically takes several hours and can even take more than a day. You need to run a full scan only if you suspect that a user's computer is infected with unwanted software after the quick scan is run.

- **Custom Scan**   Custom scans begin with a quick scan and then perform a detailed scan on the specific portions of a computer that you choose.

> **NOTE   YOU CAN WORK ON A COMPUTER WHILE A SCAN IS IN PROGRESS**
>
> Although scans slow the computer down, a user can continue to work on the computer while a scan is in progress. Note also that scans consume battery power on mobile computers very quickly.

Handling Detected Spyware

If Windows Defender finds spyware or potentially unwanted software as a result of a scan, it displays a warning and provides you with four options for each item detected:

- **Ignore**   This option allows the detected software to remain untouched on your computer and stay detectable by Windows Defender whenever the next scan is performed. This option might be appropriate when you need to research the software that Windows Defender has found before you decide to remove it.

- **Quarantine**   This option isolates the detected software. When Windows Defender quarantines software, it moves it to another location on your computer and then prevents the software from running until you choose to restore it or remove it from your computer. This option is used most often when the detected software cannot be removed successfully.

- **Remove**   This option deletes the detected software from your computer. You should choose this option unless you have a compelling reason not to.

- **Always Allow**   The option adds the software to the Windows Defender Allowed list and allows it to run on your computer. Windows Defender stops alerting you to actions taken by the program. You should choose this option only if you trust the software and the software publisher.

Configuring Windows Defender Through Group Policy

In an AD DS environment, it is recommended that you configure clients by using Group Policy instead of individually on each machine. To find the Group Policy settings for Windows Defender, open a GPO and navigate to Computer Configuration\Policies\Administrative Templates\Windows Components\Windows Defender, as shown in Figure 5-10.

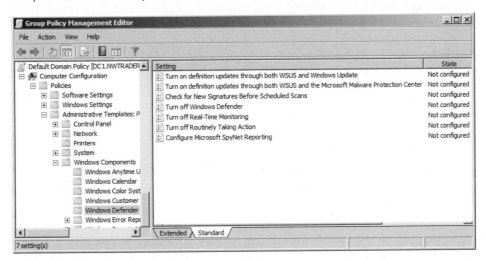

FIGURE 5-10 Group Policy settings for Windows Defender

The following seven policy settings for Windows Defender are available:

- **Turn On Definition Updates Through Both WSUS And Windows Update**   If you enable or do not configure this policy setting and the Automatic Updates client is configured to point to a WSUS server, Windows Defender obtains definition updates from Windows Update if connections to that WSUS server fail. If you disable this setting, Windows Defender checks for updates only according to the setting defined for the Automatic Updates client—either by using an internal WSUS server or Windows Update.

- **Turn On Definition Updates Through Both WSUS And The Microsoft Malware Protection Center**   If you enable or do not configure this policy setting and the Automatic Updates client is configured to point to a WSUS server, Windows Defender checks for definition updates from both WSUS and the Microsoft Malware Protection Center if connections to that WSUS server fail. If you disable this setting, Windows Defender checks for updates only according to the setting defined for the Automatic Updates client—either by using an internal WSUS server or Windows Update.

- **Check For New Signatures Before Scheduled Scans**   If you enable this policy setting, Windows Defender always checks for new definitions before it begins a scheduled scan of the computer. When you disable or do not configure this setting, Windows Defender does not check for new definitions immediately before beginning scheduled scans.

- **Turn Off Windows Defender**   If you enable this policy setting, Windows Defender no longer performs any real-time or scheduled scans. (However, users can still perform manual scans.) You should enable this setting if you have implemented a more advanced anti-spyware solution such as Microsoft Forefront Client Security. If you disable or do not configure this policy setting, Windows Defender performs both real-time scans and any scheduled scans.

- **Turn Off Real-Time Monitoring**   If you enable this policy setting, Windows Defender does not automatically prompt users to allow or block activity in protected areas of the operating system. If you disable or do not configure this policy setting, by default Windows Defender prompts users to allow or block potential spyware activity on their computers.

- **Turn Off Routinely Taking Action**   If you enable this policy setting, Windows Defender only prompts the user to choose how to respond to a threat but not to take any automatic action. If you disable or do not configure this policy setting, Windows Defender automatically takes action on detected threats after approximately 10 minutes.

- **Configure Microsoft SpyNet Reporting**   SpyNet is an online community that pools information about threats experienced by its members. SpyNet learns from the user responses to these threats to determine which threats are benign and which are malicious.

  If you enable this policy setting and choose the "No Membership" option, SpyNet membership is disabled, and no information is sent to Microsoft. If you enable this policy setting and choose the "Advanced" option, SpyNet membership is set to Advanced, and information about detected threats and the responses to those threats is sent to Microsoft.

  If you disable or do not configure this policy setting, SpyNet membership is disabled by default, but local users can change the membership setting.

> **NOTE   USING A BOOTABLE ANTIVIRUS CD**
>
> When a computer has become severely infected with malware, the computer might run so slowly that it's difficult to perform an anti-malware scan. In this case, it's a good idea to perform an offline scan from a bootable CD if you have one available. By performing the scan outside of Windows, you avoid running the malware programs that consume resources and slow down the system.

Best Practices for Using Windows Defender

To receive the security benefits of Windows Defender while minimizing the costs, follow these best practices:

- Before deploying Windows 7, test all applications with Windows Defender enabled to ensure that Windows Defender does not alert users to normal changes that the application might make. If a legitimate application does cause warnings, add the application to the Windows Defender Allowed list.

- Change the scheduled scan time to meet the needs of your business. By default, Windows Defender scans at 2 A.M. If third-shift staff uses computers overnight, you might want to find a better time to perform the scan. If users turn off their computers when they are not in the office, you should schedule the scan to occur during the day.

- Use WSUS to manage and distribute signature updates.

- Use antivirus software with Windows Defender. Alternatively, you might disable Windows Defender completely and use client-security software that provides both anti-spyware and antivirus functionality.

- Do not deploy Windows Defender in large enterprises. Instead, use Forefront or a third-party client-security suite that can be managed more easily in enterprise environments.

MORE INFO **WINDOWS DEFENDER**

For more information about Windows Defender, visit the Windows Defender Virtual Lab Express at *http://www.microsoftvirtuallabs.com/express/registration.aspx?LabId=92e04589-cdd9-4e69-8b1b-2d131d9037af.*

Determining When Your System Is Infected with Malware

As a enterprise support technician, you need to know how to recognize the symptoms of a malware infection on your client computers. Then, if your antivirus and anti-spyware are not functioning or not detecting any malware, you need to know how to remove malware manually.

Here are a few common signs of a computer being infected by a virus, worm, or Trojan horse:

- Sluggish computer performance
- Unusual error messages
- Distorted menus and dialog boxes
- Antivirus software repeatedly turning itself off
- Screen freezing
- Computer crashing
- Computer restarting
- Applications not functioning correctly
- Inaccessible disk drives, or a CD-ROM drive that automatically opens and closes
- Notification messages that an application has attempted to contact you from the Internet
- Unusual audio sounds
- Printing problems

Note that, although these are common signs of infection, these symptoms might also indicate other types of hardware or software problems that are unrelated to malware.

Signs of a spyware infection tend to be slightly different from those of other types of malware. If you see any of the following symptoms, suspect spyware:

- A new, unexpected application appears.
- Unexpected icons appear in the system tray.
- Unexpected notifications appear near the system tray.
- The Web browser home page, default search engine, or favorites change.
- New toolbars appear, especially in Web browsers.
- The mouse pointer changes.
- The Web browser displays additional advertisements when visiting a Web page, or pop-up advertisements appear when the user is not using the Web.
- When the user attempts to visit a Web page, she is redirected to a completely different Web page.
- The computer runs more slowly than usual.

Some spyware might not have any noticeable symptoms, but it still might compromise private information.

How to Resolve Malware Infections

The most important way to resolve malware infections is to prevent them in the first place by running antivirus and anti-spyware programs daily with the latest virus and spyware definitions. If malware is discovered on a system, use the application to remove the malware if possible and quarantine it if not. If it is a new malware program, you might need to run a removal tool or perform a series of steps to remove it manually.

These steps naturally apply to malware that is detected. However, as important as it is to remember to use antivirus and anti-spyware daily, it is just as important to remember that no anti-malware application is foolproof. Many malware programs are in fact written around anti-malware software so that they cannot be detected. And if even a single malicious feature remains after a scan, that remaining malware program can install other malware programs.

If you suspect a problem related to malware after running antivirus and anti-spyware applications with the latest definitions, take the following steps:

1. If you notice changes to Windows Internet Explorer, such as unwanted add-ons or a new home page, use Control Panel to look for and uninstall any unnecessary programs.

2. Use the Startup tab of the System Configuration utility (Msconfig.exe) to clear any unnecessary startup programs. Note the Registry entry associated with any of these programs. (You can use this Registry information to delete the associated Registry keys if necessary.) Use the Services tab to disable any unnecessary services.

3. Open Task Manager. Note any unusual services listed on the Services tab or unusual processes listed on the Processes tab. (Be sure to click Show Processes From All Users so you can see all running processes.) Use the Go To Process option on the Services tab and the Go To Service(s) option on the Processes tab to help learn the connection between services and processes that are unknown to you. Then, perform Web searches on services and processes that lack descriptions or that otherwise seem suspicious. If you can determine from your research that any services or processes are associated with malware, right-click them to stop them. Then, in the Services console, disable the associated service so that it cannot run again.

4. Open the Registry Editor (Regedit.exe). Navigate to HKLM\Software\Microsoft\ Windows\CurrentVersion\Run. In the details pane, note any Registry values associated with unwanted started programs. Write the path names provided to the target files in the Data column, as shown in Figure 5-11, and then delete the Registry values. Then, navigate to HKCU\Software\Microsoft\Windows\CurrentVersion\Run and do the same.

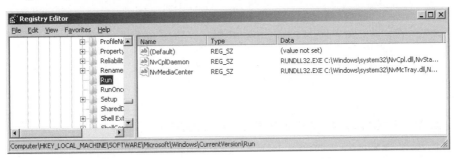

FIGURE 5-11 Copy down the path names to files associated with unwanted startup programs, and then delete the Registry values.

5. Using the path name information that you copied in step 4, visit these locations in the Windows file structure and delete the target files.

6. If you still see signs of malware, install an additional anti-spyware and antivirus application from a known and trusted vendor. Your chances of removing all traces of malware increase by using multiple applications, but you should not configure multiple applications to provide real-time protection.

7. If problems persist, shut down the computer and use the Startup Repair tool to perform a System Restore. Restore the computer to a date prior to the malware infection. System Restore typically removes any startup settings that cause malware applications to run, but it does not remove the executable files themselves. Do this only as a last resort: Although System Restore does not remove a user's personal files, it can cause problems with recently installed or configured applications.

Performing this series of steps resolves a great majority of malware problems. However, once malware has run on a computer, you can never be certain that the software is removed completely. In particular, rootkits are difficult to detect and remove. In these circumstances, if you suspect a rootkit and cannot remove it, you might be forced to reformat the hard disk, reinstall Windows, and then restore user files using a backup created prior to the infection.

Enforcing an Anti-Malware Policy Through Group Policy

In this practice, you use Group Policy to enforce specific settings for UAC and Windows Defender. These exercises require a domain controller running Windows Server 2008 R2 and a client running Windows 7 that is a member of the same domain.

EXERCISE 1   Enforcing UAC Settings Through Group Policy

In this exercise, you enforce new UAC default settings on computers running Windows 7 in the domain.

1. Log on to the domain controller.

2. Open Group Policy Management by clicking Start\All Programs\Administrative Tools\ Group Policy Management.

3. In the Group Policy Management console tree, navigate to Group Policy Management\ Forest: *Forest Name*\Domains*Domain Name*\Default Domain Policy.

4. Right-click Default Domain Policy, and then click Edit from the shortcut menu. The Group Policy Management Editor opens.

5. In the Group Policy Management Editor, navigate to Default Domain Policy\ Computer Configuration\Policies\Windows Settings\Security Settings\Local Policies\ Security Options.

6. In the details pane, double-click to open User Account Control: Switch To The Secure Desktop When Prompting For Elevation.

7. On the Security Settings tab, click Define This Policy Setting, select Disabled, and then Click OK.

8. In the details pane, double-click to open User Account Control: Behavior Of The Elevation Prompt For Standard Users.

9. On the Security Settings tab, click Define This Policy Setting, select Prompt For Credentials from the drop-down list, and then Click OK.

   These settings remove the Secure Desktop from all UAC prompts.

10. Click OK.

11. Switch to the client running Windows 7. Restart the client, and then log on to the domain from the client as a domain administrator.

12. Open an elevated command prompt by clicking Start\All Programs\Accessories, then right-clicking Command Prompt and clicking Run As Administrator from the shortcut menu.

13. A consent prompt appears without a Secure Desktop.

14. Log off the client, and then log on again to the domain from the client as a standard user without administrative privileges.

15. In Control Panel, beneath User Accounts, click Change Account Type. A credential prompt appears without a Secure Desktop.

16. Log off the client.

EXERCISE 2   Disabling Real-Time Monitoring for Windows Defender

A large corporate network should use a managed anti-spyware solution, which Windows Defender is not. Using Windows Defender to provide a secondary daily scan for malware on clients is a good idea, but you should not have two applications performing real-time monitoring. If your managed anti-spyware solution provides real-time monitoring, you should disable the same feature on Windows Defender by using Group Policy.

In this exercise, you use Group Policy to disable real-time monitoring for Windows Defender.

1. Log on to the domain controller.

2. Using the steps described in Exercise 1, open Group Policy Management and then choose to edit the Default Domain Policy.

3. In the Group Policy Management Editor, navigate to Default Domain Policy\Computer Configuration\Policies\Administrative Templates\Windows Components\Windows Defender.

4. In the details pane, double-click to open Turn Off Real-Time Monitoring.

5. In the Turn Off Real-Time Monitoring dialog box, select Enabled, and then click OK.

6. Switch to Client1. Log on to the domain from Client1 as a domain administrator.

7. Open a command prompt and type **gpupdate**. You might see a notification bubble appear indicating that Windows Defender is turned off.

8. After the command finishes executing, click Start, type **windows defender**, and then click Windows Defender in the Start menu.

9. In Windows Defender, click Tools, and then click Options.

10. Select Real-Time Protection from the list of options.

11. The settings are dimmed. Real-time monitoring is disabled.

12. Return to the domain controller and the Default Domain Policy. Revert the Turn Off Real-Time Monitoring policy setting to Not Configured, and then click OK.

13. Rerun **gpupdate** on Client1, and then close all open windows on both computers.

Lesson Summary

- UAC helps prevent malware from secretly installing itself on Windows systems by notifying the user whenever a request is made to write to protected areas of the operating system. Users must be educated to dismiss these notifications if they have not initiated them.

- You can configure the behavior of UAC notifications. By default, administrators see consent prompts on a Secure Desktop when a program requests elevation. Standard users by default see credential prompts on a Secure Desktop whenever they or a program requests elevation.

- Windows Defender is a built-in feature of Windows 7 that provides basic spyware filtering and detection. Often Windows Defender needs no configuration, but you might want to disable it in larger networks that require a managed anti-spyware solution.

- You should how to check for and remove malware manually in case your anti-malware solution isn't functioning as desired. To do so, investigate unknown processes and services to stop and disable them if necessary, and look in the Registry for programs that are set to run automatically. Delete associated files.

Lesson Review

You can use the following questions to test your knowledge of the information in Lesson 2, "Resolving Malware Issues." The questions are also available on the companion CD if you prefer to review them in electronic form.

1. You work as an enterprise support technician in a large company. Your manager reports that some network administrators are using the built-in Administrator account for the domain and that, when logged on with this account, they are not seeing UAC notifications. She asks you to change configuration settings so that users logged on to the domain with the built-in Administrator account see UAC consent prompts. What should you do?

    A. Configure Local Security Policy to set the User Account Control: Admin Approval Mode For The Built-in Administrator Account option to Enabled.

    B. Configure Group Policy to set the User Account Control: Admin Approval Mode For The Built-in Administrator Account option to Enabled.

    C. Configure Local Security Policy to set the User Account Control: Run All Administrators In Admin Approval Mode option to Enabled.

    D. Configure Group Policy to set the User Account Control: Run All Administrators In Admin Approval Mode option to Enabled.

2. You work as an enterprise support technician in a company whose AD DS domain consists of 20 servers running Windows Server 2008 R2 and 500 client computers running Windows 7, 10 of which are portable and are used by employees who travel globally for work. These users have complained that Windows Defender tends to start a scan when the computer is operating on the battery source, and the scan quickly

consumes battery power. You want to prevent Windows Defender from consuming needed battery power without reducing the protection that it provides. What should you do?

A. Instruct the users to perform a manual scan when their computers are connected to a power source.

B. Choose the option to run a scan only when idle.

C. Instruct the users to adjust the schedule for automatic scanning.

D. Disable automatic scanning on all 10 computers.

Chapter Review

To further practice and reinforce the skills you learned in this chapter, you can perform the following tasks:

- Review the chapter summary.
- Review the list of key terms introduced in this chapter.
- Complete the case scenario. The scenario sets up a real-world situation involving the topics of this chapter and asks you to create a solution.
- Complete the suggested practices.
- Take a practice test.

Chapter Summary

- Windows Firewall blocks all incoming connection requests by default. To allow a network program to initiate a connection with a computer running Windows 7, you need to create a firewall exception for that program.
- To combat malware, you need to educate yourself and users continually about the evolving nature of threats. You also need to manage antivirus software, anti-spyware software such as Windows Defender, and UAC effectively. Finally, you need to know how to recognize classic symptoms of an infection and how to remove an infection manually if needed.

Key Terms

Do you know what these key terms mean? You can check your answers by looking up the terms in the glossary at the end of the book.

- **Exception**
- **Malware**
- **Spyware**
- **Virus**
- **Worm**

Case Scenario

In the following case scenario, you apply what you've learned about protecting client systems. You can find answers to these questions in the "Answers" section at the end of this book.

Case Scenario 1: Resolving Malware Infections

You work as an enterprise support technician for Contoso, Ltd., a marketing research firm with 500 employees. You receive a call from the help desk to investigate a research assistant's notebook computer that is apparently running very slowly. A help desk support technician was unable to resolve the issue.

You perform some basic testing on the computer, and you discover that several toolbars associated with spyware are installed in Internet Explorer. Your company uses a combined antivirus/anti-spyware solution, and Windows Defender is disabled on the network.

You conduct interviews with the Research Assistant and the Help Desk Support Technician.

Interviews

The following is a list of company personnel interviewed and their statements:

- **Research Assistant** "The problem has been getting progressively worse for about six months. It's gotten to the point that everything takes forever. I used to take this computer home with me, but now I don't even bother."

- **Help Desk Support Technician** "I tried to run an anti-malware scan, but nothing seemed to happen."

Questions

1. You want to immediately stop any malware that might be running. How should you achieve this?

2. Your testing reveals that the anti-malware client software installed on the computer does not run when it is opened. What can you do to perform an anti-malware scan on the computer?

Suggested Practices

To help you master the exam objectives presented in this chapter, complete the following tasks.

Identify and Resolve Issues Due to Malicious Software

Perform these practices to learn about tools that help detect and remove malware.

- **Practice 1** Perform a Web search for the term "Sysinternals Suite" or visit *http://technet.microsoft.com/en-us/sysinternals/bb842062.aspx*. Download the Sysinternals Suite and unzip the file. Within the suite, locate Autoruns. Run Autoruns to discover the programs that are configured to start up automatically on your computer. Then, locate and run Rootkitrevealer to discover any rootkits on your system.

- **Practice 2** Perform a Web search for the term "bootable anti-malware CD" and research the various bootable anti-malware CDs that are available online. Create or download a bootable anti-malware CD and then use it to perform a malware scan on your system.

Take a Practice Test

The practice tests on this book's companion CD offer many options. For example, you can test yourself on just one exam objective, or you can test yourself on all the 70-685 certification exam content. You can set up the test so that it closely simulates the experience of taking a certification exam, or you can set it up in study mode so that you can look at the correct answers and explanations after you answer each question.

> *MORE INFO* **PRACTICE TESTS**
>
> For details about all the practice test options available, see the section entitled "How to Use the Practice Tests," in the Introduction to this book.

CHAPTER 6

Understanding and Troubleshooting Remote Access Connections

As an enterprise support technician, you might be called on to help remote users who have trouble connecting to the corporate network. The most common way that users access a corporate network remotely is through a virtual private network (VPN), but with Windows Server 2008 R2 and Windows 7, Microsoft has introduced DirectAccess, a much-improved alternative to VPNs. To resolve remote access issues, you need to understand the components that make up a VPN and DirectAccess infrastructure and how these components work together when a user initiates a remote access connection.

Exam objective in this chapter:
- Identify and resolve remote access issues.

Lessons in this chapter:

Before You Begin

To perform the exercises in this chapter, you need:
- A domain controller running Windows Server 2008 R2
- A client running Windows 7 Enterprise that is a member of the domain
- A basic understanding of IPv6

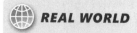
REAL WORLD

J.C. Mackin

DirectAccess, introduced with Windows 7 and Windows Server 2008 R2, is the first major feature of Windows built exclusively on IPv6 and that lacks any failback to IPv4. You should view the arrival of this feature as something of a wake-up call. To this point, many IT professionals have considered IPv6 a topic they can worry about tomorrow, and many even have been disabling IPv6 in the mistaken belief that it somehow degrades network performance (it doesn't). That many have been living in IPv6 denial is perhaps not surprising: IPv6 has always been a technology of the future.

However, that future is now rapidly approaching. The Internet Assigned Numbers Authority (IANA), the body that governs the distribution of IP addresses, has predicted that new IPv4 addresses will be depleted as soon as 2011. Starting very soon, then, IPv6 will become and remain a key cornerstone networking technology. I recommend that you take this topic seriously and become familiar with the IPv6 addressing as soon as possible.

For a good introduction to IPv6 in Windows networks, I recommend *Understanding IPv6,* Second Edition (Microsoft Press, 2008), by Joseph Davies.

Lesson 1: Understanding VPN Client Connections

The most common way for remote users to access a corporate network is through a VPN, so troubleshooting remote access typically requires you to understand how VPNs work. However, achieving this familiarity is not easy. The successful negotiation of a VPN depends on many factors, including the proper configuration of the VPN infrastructure, the user and/or computer authentication, and user authorization. Besides the complexity of the VPN connection process in general, Windows 7 and Windows Server 2008 R2 also offer different VPN types, each with particular requirements, advantages, and disadvantages.

This lesson begins with an overview of VPNs and then describes the components that make up a VPN connection. Next, it provides a summary of the various VPN types and explains the steps in establishing a remote access VPN connection. Finally, it concludes with a general checklist for troubleshooting remote access VPNs.

> **After this lesson, you will be able to:**
> - Describe the elements of a VPN infrastructure
> - Describe the advantages and disadvantages of the VPN types offered in Windows networks
> - Describe the VPN connection process
> - Troubleshoot VPN connectivity
>
> **Estimated lesson time: 120 minutes**

Understanding VPNs

A VPN is a private, encrypted network connection that crosses the public Internet. Typically, a VPN is used either to connect two office sites or to enable remote computers to access a single office network. In the case of a site-to-site VPN (shown in Figure 6-1), no special configuration is required for the clients. The negotiation of the private connection for these VPNs is performed by the VPN servers at each office, and clients in opposite branches communicate with each other as they would communicate with clients in their own branch.

In a remote access VPN, however, the client running Windows 7 must be configured to negotiate a connection to the VPN server. For this reason, it is only the remote access VPN that is covered on the 70-685 exam. A remote access VPN is shown in Figure 6-2.

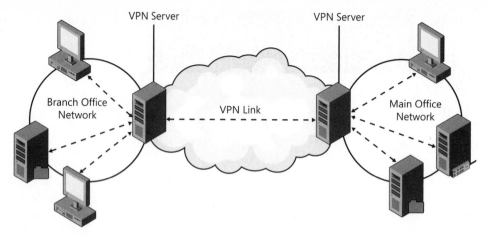

FIGURE 6-1 A site-to-site VPN

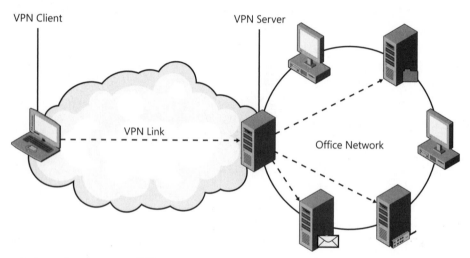

FIGURE 6-2 A remote access VPN

Understanding VPN Encapsulation and Tunneling

A VPN works by taking the communication exchanges that computers would use if they were located on the same network, encrypting these exchanges, and then encapsulating the information with the additional networking data needed to cross the Internet.

As a result of this encapsulation, the physical network through which private data is sent becomes transparent to the two endpoints of communication, as shown in Figure 6-3. In the illustration, two computers, Computer1 and Computer2, are connected physically only through the Internet, but the transparency of the physical link is revealed in the results of the Tracert command run at each computer. Although many hops separate the two computers, each appears to the other as only one hop away through the VPN connection. Communication occurs between the two private IP addresses, each within the 192.168.10.0/24 subnet, as if the computers were both located on the same network segment.

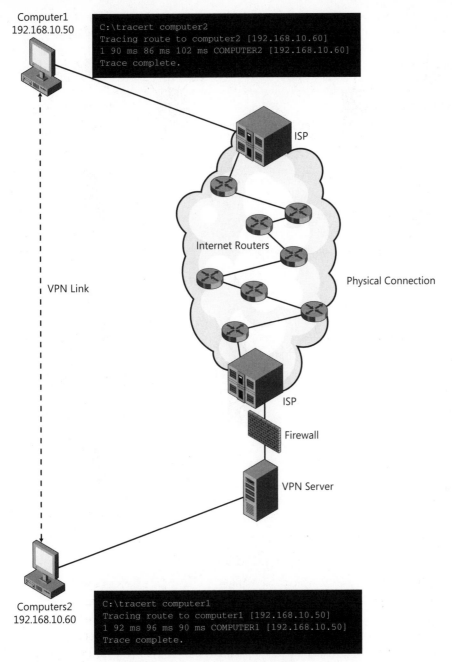

Computer1
192.168.10.50

```
C:\tracert computer2
Tracing route to computer2 [192.168.10.60]
1 90 ms 86 ms 102 ms COMPUTER2 [192.168.10.60]
Trace complete.
```

ISP

Internet Routers

Physical Connection

VPN Link

ISP

Firewall

VPN Server

Computers2
192.168.10.60

```
C:\tracert computer1
Tracing route to computer1 [192.168.10.50]
1 92 ms 96 ms 90 ms COMPUTER1 [192.168.10.50]
Trace complete.
```

FIGURE 6-3 A VPN connection makes remote computers appear local.

The term used to describe this process of encapsulating private data within public data is *tunneling*. A VPN tunneling protocol creates a secure channel between two VPN servers or between a VPN server and a VPN client. Within a VPN tunnel, encryption is used to protect data as it crosses the public network. Private data is encrypted before the data is sent out onto the tunnel and then decrypted when it reaches the end of the tunnel.

Data authentication is also performed by most VPN tunneling protocols to validate the data in two ways. First, tunneling protocols can perform data integrity checking, which ensures that the data remains untouched from its original version. Second, they can perform data origin authentication, which ensures that the data is truly sent from the party that claims to be sending it.

Understanding Remote Access VPN Infrastructure

To provide remote access to VPN clients, a Windows-based network must include a number of features, as shown in Figure 6-4. At a minimum, these features include the VPN client and client software (or network connection in Windows), a VPN server running Routing and Remote Access Services (RRAS), and an internal DNS server. Typically, however, a VPN infrastructure will also include a domain controller, a certificate server, and a DHCP server. Finally, a Network Policy Server (NPS) might also be used. The role of these VPN infrastructure components is described in the following section.

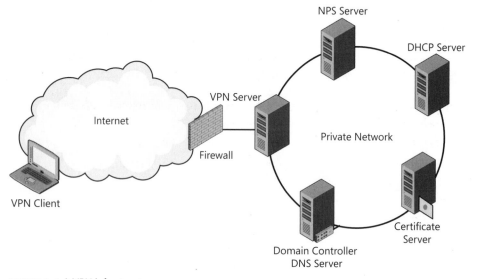

FIGURE 6-4 A VPN infrastructure

VPN CLIENT AND CLIENT SOFTWARE

For a computer running Windows 7 to act as a VPN client, Windows needs to be configured with a VPN client. Generally speaking, VPN clients can be any of three types: a Windows 7 VPN connection, a Connection Manager (CM) client, or a third-party client.

First, in Windows 7, you can configure a VPN connection in the Network and Sharing Center by first clicking Set Up A New Connection Or Network, as shown in Figure 6-5.

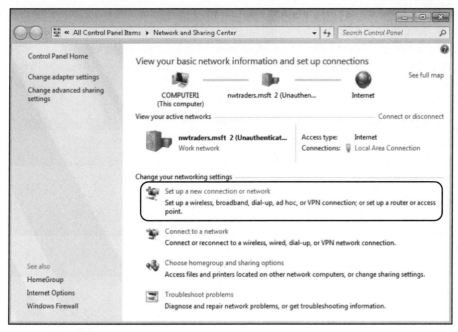

FIGURE 6-5 Creating a VPN connection in Windows 7

This step opens the Set Up A Connection Or Network wizard. To create a VPN connection, select Connect To A Workplace, as shown in Figure 6-6, and then follow the prompts to complete the wizard.

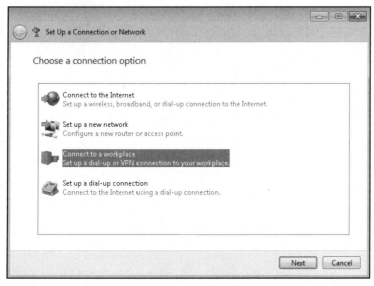

FIGURE 6-6 Using the Set Up A Connection Or Network wizard

Once you have completed the wizard, Windows 7 displays the new VPN connection in Network Connections, which you can open by clicking Change Adapter Settings in the Network And Sharing Center. A Windows 7 VPN connection is shown in Figure 6-7.

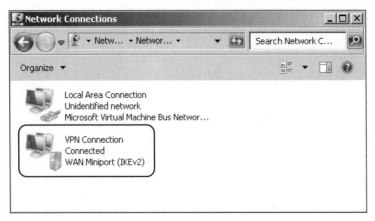

FIGURE 6-7 A VPN connection

Although this first type of VPN client is easy to create and configure on a single machine, no method built into Windows allows you to create many such VPN clients in a large network. As an alternative, many administrators use the *Connection Manager Administration Toolkit* (CMAK) to create client connection profiles that can be distributed and installed as CM clients. The advantage of this method is that users can create and install VPN clients from the profile without needing any technical knowledge. As a third option, third-party VPN client software can also be deployed to client desktops through Group Policy or another means.

> *NOTE* **WHAT ARE CM AND THE CMAK?**
>
> CM is a client network connection tool that allows a user to connect to a remote network, such as a corporate network protected by a VPN server.
>
> The CMAK is a feature in Windows Server 2008 that you can install by using the Add Feature Wizard. It allows you to automate for remote users the creation of predefined connections to remote servers and networks.
>
> To create and customize a CM client for your users, you use the CMAK wizard. The CMAK wizard allows you to automate many aspects of a connection (such as the IP address of the VPN server) so that users do not need to handle any technical details manually.

VPN SERVER

The VPN server in a Windows VPN infrastructure runs RRAS, which in Windows Server 2008 is a role service of the Network Policy and Access Service server role. Servers configured with RRAS can receive requests from remote access users located on the Internet, authenticate these users, authorize the connection requests, and finally either block the requests or route the connections to private internal network segments.

> **NOTE REMOTE ACCESS AUTHENTICATION VS. AUTHORIZATION**
>
> Authentication is the process of validating—through verification of a password or of alternative credentials such as a certificate or smart card—that the user is in fact the person he or she claims to be.
>
> Whereas authentication refers to the process of validating user credentials, authorization refers to the process of allowing users access to resources. After remote access authentication occurs, the remote access connection is authorized only if the proper permissions are configured both on the Dial-in tab of the user account Properties dialog box (discussed in the section entitled "Domain Controller" later in this lesson) and in the network policy that applies to the connection.

For authentication, RRAS can be configured to forward the authentication request to a RADIUS (NPS) server or to use Windows authentication. When configured to use Windows authentication and the local VPN server is *not* a member of a domain, RRAS authenticates users by checking the received credentials against those stored in its local security account manager (SAM) database. When configured to use Windows authentication and the local VPN server *is* a member of a domain, RRAS passes user credentials to an available domain controller.

> **NOTE REMOTE ACCESS AUTHENTICATION IS SEPARATE FROM DOMAIN LOGON AUTHENTICATION**
>
> Remote access authentication precedes domain logon authentication; if a VPN user is attempting to log on to a domain remotely, the VPN connection must be authenticated, authorized, and established before normal domain logon occurs.

After the credentials submitted with the remote access connection are authenticated, the connection must be authorized. Remote access authorization consists of two steps: first, verification of the dial-in properties of the user account submitted by the VPN connection, and second, application of the first matching network policy defined on the VPN server (or NPS server if RRAS is configured for RADIUS authentication).

> **NOTE** **WHAT ARE NETWORK POLICIES?**
>
> Network policies define various connection types by specific conditions such as Windows group membership, health policies, or operating system, and then either allow or deny requests that match those conditions. Network policies can be defined in RRAS or in NPS. Network policies are shown in Figure 6-8.

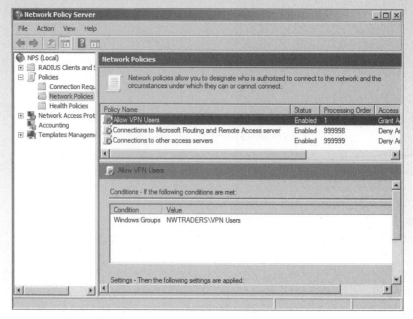

FIGURE 6-8 Network policies are used to authorize connection requests.

DNS SERVER

VPN clients that connect to a private network must be configured with the address of an internal DNS server that can resolve the names of resources on that private network. Usually, the domain controller that authenticates the remote access user also acts as the DNS server.

DOMAIN CONTROLLER

In a VPN infrastructure, a domain controller is most often used to authenticate and authorize users who attempt to connect to the corporate network through the VPN. Besides authenticating the user credentials, a domain controller is also used to authorize the user account for remote access. For a user account to be authorized for remote access, the account must be configured with either the Allow Access or the Control Access Through NPS Network Policy network access permission.

You can configure the network access permission for an individual user on the Dial-in tab of that user's Properties dialog box in the Active Directory Users And Computers console, as shown in Figure 6-9. By default, domain user accounts are configured with the Control Access Through NPS Network Policy setting.

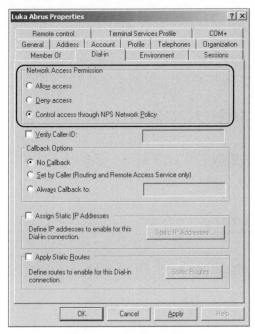

FIGURE 6-9 The Network Access Permission setting of a user account

CERTIFICATE SERVER

Many VPNs use a form of encryption that relies on public key cryptography and a public key infrastructure (PKI). In a PKI, certificates are used both to validate the certificate holder's identity and to encrypt or decrypt data. Each certificate is associated with a *key pair*, made up of a *public key* (which is attached to the public certificate and presented freely to the world) and a *private key* (which is generated locally and never sent over the network). If the private key is used to encrypt data, the associated public key is used to decrypt that data. If the public key is used to encrypt data, the associated private key is used to decrypt that data. In a typical scenario, a sender uses the receiver's public key to encrypt a message sent to that receiver. Only the receiver then has access to the private key needed to decrypt the message.

In a PKI, certificates are created and issued by a certification authority (CA), such as a computer running Windows Server 2008 and configured with the Active Directory Certificate Services server role.

DHCP SERVER

An internal DHCP server normally is used to provide VPN clients with an IP address. When such a DHCP server is used for this purpose, the external adapter of the VPN server must be configured with a DHCP Relay Agent that can respond to the DHCP requests from external VPN clients. Alternatively, the VPN server itself can be configured to assign addresses to VPN clients without the help of the DHCP server on the corporate network.

NPS SERVER

NPS is the Microsoft implementation of a RADIUS server and proxy. You can use NPS to manage authentication, authorization, and health policy centrally for VPN connections, dial-up connections, 802.11 wireless connections, and 802.1x connections. NPS can also act as a health evaluation server for Network Access Protection (NAP). Like RRAS, NPS is a role service of the Network Policy and Access Service server role in Windows Server 2008.

Figure 6-10 shows an example of how NPS can be used as a central authentication and authorization point for network access. In the illustration, NPS acts as a RADIUS server for a variety of access clients. For user credential authentication, NPS uses a domain controller.

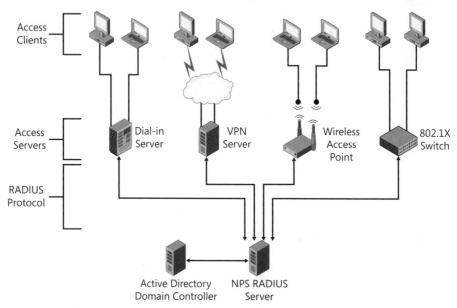

FIGURE 6-10 An NPS server can be used to manage authentication and authorization centrally.

> **NOTE** **NPS AND INTERNET AUTHENTICATION SERVICE (IAS)**
>
> NPS is the replacement for Internet Authentication Service (IAS) in Windows Server 2003.

Understanding Windows 7 VPN Tunneling Protocols

Windows 7 supports four tunneling protocols for remote access VPN connections to corporate networks. Each of these is used in different remote access scenarios, and each has different requirements for the operating system, configuration, and infrastructure. The following section introduces these four VPN protocols in more detail.

Understanding IKEv2

New in Windows 7 and Windows Server 2008 R2, Internet Key Exchange version 2 (IKEv2) is a tunneling protocol that uses Internet Protocol Security (IPSec) for encryption. An important performance advantage of an IKEv2-based VPN is its support of *VPN Reconnect* (also called Mobility). VPN Reconnect is a feature that enables VPN connections to be maintained when a VPN client moves between wireless hotspots or switches from a wireless to a wired connection. Another important advantage of IKEv2 is that, like Secure Socket Tunneling Protocol (SSTP) and Point-to-Point Tunneling Protocol (PPTP) VPNs (and unlike those based on the Layer 2 Tunneling Protocol [L2TP]), client computers do not need to provide authentication through a machine certificate or a preshared key. Finally, compared to the other VPN type that is based on IPSec encryption (L2TP), IKEv2 offers improved performance in that the connectivity is established more quickly.

EXAM TIP

For the 70-685 exam, you have to know what VPN Reconnect is, and that only IKEv2 VPNs support this feature.

IKEv2 VPNs require a PKI. In an IKEv2 VPN, the server must present a server authentication certificate to the client, and the client needs to be able to validate this certificate. To perform this validation, the root certificate for the CA that has issued the server authentication certificate must be installed on the client computer in the Trusted Root Certification Authorities certificate store.

From the standpoint of performance and security, IKEv2 is the preferred VPN type and should be deployed when operating system requirements for such a VPN are met. Those requirements are Windows 7 for the VPN client and Windows Server 2008 R2 on the VPN server.

Understanding SSTP

SSTP VPNs were introduced in Windows Server 2008 and can be used by clients running Windows Vista SP1 or later. This type of VPN is based on the same HTTP-over-SSL protocol used for secure Web sites. The most important feature of an SSTP-type VPN is that it uses only TCP port 443 for communication, a port left open on most firewalls for secure Web traffic. The fact that most firewalls do not need to be reconfigured for SSTP communication enables SSTP VPN clients to connect through most Network Address Translation (NAT) devices, firewalls, and Web proxies. Other VPN types often cannot traverse these network features. An SSTP VPN is therefore an unusually flexible type of remote access VPN that can be implemented in more network scenarios than other VPNs can.

Like IKEv2 and PPTP VPNs, and unlike L2TP-based VPNs, SSTP VPNs do not require client computer authentication by default (though they can be configured to require it). However, as with a secure Web server, the SSTP VPN server must present a computer certificate to the requesting client at the beginning of the communication session. The VPN client must then be able to validate the server's computer certificate. For this to occur, the root certificate of the CA that has issued the VPN server's computer certificate must be installed in the Trusted Root Certification Authorities certificate store on the VPN client computer.

Understanding L2TP

L2TP is an industry-standard tunneling protocol designed to run natively over IP networks. Security for L2TP VPN connections is provided by IPSec, which performs the data authentication and encryption needed to ensure that L2TP tunnels are protected. The combination of L2TP with IPSec for tunneling purposes is usually referred to as L2TP over IPSec or L2TP/IPSec.

L2TP/IPSec VPNs have certain drawbacks compared to IKEv2 and SSTP VPNs. First, besides requiring user authentication as all VPN protocols do, L2TP/IPSec requires client computer authentication. Because of this requirement, all VPN client computers from which a user might connect must be configured either with a computer certificate or a preshared key specific to the VPN server. Therefore, L2TP/IPSec prevents a user from establishing a VPN connection from public terminals or from any computer that has not been specially configured for the VPN.

To configure a VPN client connection running Windows 7 to use either a computer certificate or a preshared key for L2TP/IPSec authentication, open the Properties dialog box of the VPN connection, click the Security tab, and then click Advanced Settings. This step opens the Advanced Properties dialog box, as shown in Figure 6-11. By default, certificate authentication is selected. To obtain a client authentication certificate to use with this setting, you typically need to submit a request to the CA on the corporate network and then install the certificate after the request is approved. If you change the setting to Use Preshared Key For Authentication, you need to supply the key in the area provided.

Besides the requirement of client computer authentication, another limitation of L2TP/IPSec VPNs is that they do not natively support the traversal of NAT devices. However, you can enable L2TP/IPSec to cross a NAT device if you change a particular registry value on both the VPN client computer and the VPN server.

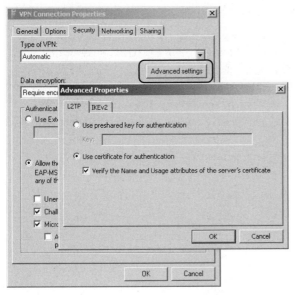

FIGURE 6-11 Configuring VPN client authentication for L2TP/IPSec

MORE INFO   **CONFIGURING L2TP/IPSEC FOR NAT TRAVERSAL**

For instructions on performing the registry edit to enable NAT traversal in L2TP/IPSec, visit *http://support.microsoft.com/kb/926179*.

Understanding PPTP

PPTP is the easiest VPN protocol to implement in Windows networks. Unlike other tunneling protocols, PPTP does not require any certificates or preshared keys on either the VPN client or server. Another important feature of PPTP is that it can be used with older Windows operating systems: It is the only native Windows VPN protocol that can run on Microsoft Windows NT 4.0, and it is compatible with all versions of Windows since Microsoft Windows 2000.

PPTP, however, includes significant disadvantages, the biggest of which is that it is not as secure as other VPN protocols. Although PPTP does encrypt data, it does not ensure data integrity or data origin authentication. Another important limitation to PPTP is that it can traverse NAT devices only through PPTP-enabled NAT routers.

Table 6-1 compares important features of the four VPN protocols available in Windows networks.

TABLE 6-1 VPN Protocols in Windows Networks

VPN PROTOCOL	OS SUPPORT	SCENARIO	TRAVERSAL	VPN RECONNECT/ MOBILITY	AUTHENTICATION
IKEv2	Windows 7, Windows Server 2008 R2	Remote Access	NAT	Yes	Machine or user authentication via IKEv2; VPN server requires a server certificate
SSTP	Windows Vista SP1, Windows Server 2008, Windows 7, Windows Server 2008 R2	Remote Access	NAT, Firewalls, Web Proxy	No	User authentication via Point-to-Point Protocol (PPP); VPN server requires server certificate
L2TP/ IPSec	Windows 2000 and later	Remote Access, Site-to-Site	NAT, only with a special registry fix	No	Machine authentication via IPSec followed by user authentication via PPP; VPN client requires a computer certificate or a preshared key
PPTP	Windows NT 4.0, Windows 2000, and later.	Remote Access, Site-to-Site	NAT, only through PPTP-enabled NAT routers	No	User authentication via PPP

Understanding the Remote Access VPN Connectivity Process

When a VPN client requests access to a corporate network running Windows, a number of steps need to occur before the client is able to connect to that network successfully. If an error occurs at any stage of the process, no connectivity will be established. Knowing the steps in the VPN connection process is a prerequisite for troubleshooting because it enables you to understand how particular connection failures might relate to particular errors in your VPN configuration.

Remote access VPN connectivity occurs in the following steps:

1. **The VPN client contacts the VPN server.**

   In the first stage of a VPN connection attempt, the VPN client attempts to contact the VPN server. Successful completion of this stage requires the client to be properly configured with the IP address of the VPN server. The VPN server also needs to be publicly available. If the VPN server is located behind a firewall, the firewall needs to be configured to allow the VPN client access.

2. **The VPN tunnel is negotiated.**

   After the VPN client contacts the VPN server, it submits a request for a tunnel type. A VPN network connection can be set to any of five settings: Automatic, PPTP, L2TP/IPSec, SSTP, and IKEv2, as shown in Figure 6-12.

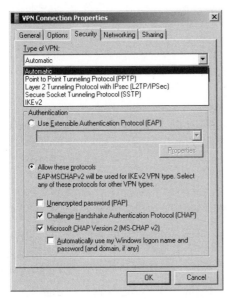

FIGURE 6-12 Configuring the VPN type

The default setting is Automatic. According to this setting, the VPN connection makes VPN protocol requests prioritized in the following order: IKEv2, SSTP, L2TP/IPSec, and PPTP. The VPN type that is negotiated eventually is the first for which the VPN server can answer the request.

During this phase, the authentication protocol is also negotiated. For IKEv2 VPNs, the EAP-MSCHAPv2 authentication protocol is used. For other VPN types, MS-CHAPv2 is preferred if it is also available on the VPN server. Otherwise, CHAP is requested.

Finally, encryption is negotiated during this phase. Like authentication settings, encryption settings are defined on the Security tab in a VPN connection Properties dialog box in Windows 7, as shown in Figure 6-13. For encryption to be negotiated properly, the client settings defined here must be compatible with those defined on the VPN server. For example, if Maximum Strength Encryption is defined on the client, the server must be able to provide maximum strength encryption or the VPN connection fails.

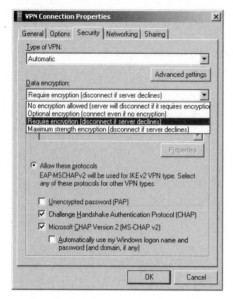

FIGURE 6-13 Configuring data encryption in the VPN connection

3. The VPN tunnel is created.

If the VPN tunnel type, authentication protocol, and encryption strength can be agreed upon, the VPN tunnel is created between the VPN client and VPN server. After this point, all exchanges are encrypted.

In the case of IKEv2 and SSTP VPNs, the tunnel creation is performed with the help of the VPN server's computer certificate. The VPN client must therefore be able to validate the certificate; to do so, the certificate of the issuing root CA must be installed in the Trusted Root Certification Authorities store on the VPN client computer.

In the case of L2TP/IPSec VPNs, preshared keys or computer certificates are used to create the encryption terms for the tunnel. These elements must therefore be configured properly for the negotiation to work. (PPTP VPNs use Microsoft Point-to-Point Encryption to create the secure tunnel and do not require a PKI.)

A final requirement for a VPN tunnel to be negotiated is that the VPN client-server communication must be able to traverse the network elements that lie between them. For example, if a firewall is located between the VPN client and server, the ports used by the VPN protocol must be left open. If a NAT device is located between the VPN client and server, the VPN protocol must be able to traverse that NAT device.

4. Remote access authentication is performed.

During this phase, the user credentials submitted with the VPN connection request are sent to the VPN server by using the previously agreed upon authentication protocol. The VPN server then either performs the authentication locally, or forwards the authentication request to an available domain controller, or forwards the authentication request to a RADIUS server. For this step to occur, the VPN user must submit proper credentials, and the VPN server must be configured to forward the authentication to the appropriate location.

5. **Remote access authorization is performed.**

   In this phase, the user account properties are checked to verify that the user is authorized for remote access. Then, the list of network policies configured on the VPN server or NPS server is checked. The first policy whose conditions match the connection request is applied to that request and then either allows or denies the request. Note that constraints (such as time of day) that affect the authorization of the connection request might also be defined in the policy.

6. **The VPN connection is established.**

   If the remote access connection request is authorized, the VPN server allows the VPN user to log on to the domain. After domain logon occurs, the VPN user has access to the corporate network.

Troubleshooting VPN Client Connectivity

Use the following list to help you troubleshoot VPN client connectivity:

- Verify that the VPN client connection is configured properly with the VPN server name or IP address.
- Verify that the VPN client computer has an active Internet connection. The VPN connection can be established only when the client is connected to the Internet.
- Verify that the proper user credentials are defined in the VPN connection.
- Verify that the user is authorized for remote access.
- Verify that certificates are configured properly for the VPN connection. For instance, verify that the certificate of the root CA that has issued the VPN server's computer certificate is installed in the Trusted Root Certification Authorities store on the VPN client computer. In the case of an L2TP/IPSec VPN, verify that the VPN client computer has installed a computer certificate that can be validated by the VPN server.
- If an error message with code 741 appears and indicates that the local computer does not support encryption, verify that that encryption settings defined in the VPN connection are compatible with those defined on the server.

PRACTICE   **Creating an IKEv2 VPN Connection**

In this practice, you create a simulated IKEv2 VPN connection between a client running Windows 7 and a server running Windows Server 2008 R2.

Note that the two-computer network used in this practice does not approximate the environment in which such a connection would be used in the real world. In a real-world scenario, a VPN connection would link a client on the Internet through a firewall to a VPN server, which would be a member server of the local Active Directory Domain Services (AD DS) domain. A separate server acting as a domain controller would be used to authenticate the user. Yet another server would act as the certificate server used to generate the certificates for the connection. Instead of that scenario, this practice has a single server running Windows Server 2008 R2 acting as the VPN server, domain controller, and certificate server.

In this practice, you perform the following steps:

1. On the domain controller, you create a domain user account and assign that user account the Allow Access dial-up permission. (Exercise 1)

2. You install Active Directory Certificate Services on the server. Using Certificate Services, you generate both a server authentication certificate to be installed on the server and a root CA certificate to be installed on the client. (Exercises 2–8)

3. You install and configure the Network Policy and Access Services server role on the server; this step enables the server to receive and route VPN connections. (Exercises 9–11)

4. You create and test the VPN connection on the client. (Exercises 12–13)

To prepare for this practice, name the server DC1.nwtraders.msft and the client Client1.nwtraders.msft. Configure both computers with a single network adapter and connect them to the same network. DC1 should be a domain controller in the Nwtraders.msft domain and Client1 should be a member of the same domain.

DC1 should be configured only with the following roles:

- AD DS
- DHCP Server
- DNS Server

> **NOTE   REMOVE ANY OTHER ROLES**
>
> If any other roles have been installed on DC1, remove them before beginning this practice. (You can make an exception for the Active Directory Certificate Services server role. If you installed this role when the server was named DC1.nwtraders.msft, you can leave the role installed.) Note also that if you have installed the Routing and Remote Access Services role service of the Network Policy and Access Services server role, you should first disable the Routing and Remote Access service before removing this associated server role.

Finally, when removing the server roles, use the same domain administrator account that you will use during the practice exercises.

EXERCISE 1   Creating a Domain User with Network Access Permissions

In this exercise, you create a domain user account in Active Directory Users And Computers and then grant that user account the Allow Access network access permission.

1. Log on Nwtraders from DC1 as a domain administrator.

2. Open the Active Directory Users And Computers console by clicking Start, clicking Administrative Tools, and then clicking Active Directory Users And Computers.

3. In the Active Directory Users And Computers console tree, expand nwtraders.msft, right-click Users, click New, and then click User.

4. On the first page of the New Object-User wizard, enter into the corresponding fields a first name, last name, and user logon name that you want to give a VPN user, and then click Next.

5. On the second page of the New Object-User wizard, enter a password into the Password and Confirm Password text boxes.

6. Clear the check box next to User Must Change Password At Next Logon, and then click Next.

7. On the Final page of the New Object-User wizard, click Finish.

8. In the Active Directory Users And Computers console, locate and then open the properties for the user account you just created.

9. In the Properties dialog box, on the Dial-in tab, click Allow Access in the Network Access Permission area.

10. Click OK to close the user Properties dialog box.

EXERCISE 2 Installing Active Directory Certificate Services and Web Server (IIS) Server Roles

> **NOTE HAVE YOU ALREADY INSTALLED THESE SERVER ROLES?**
>
> You can skip this exercise if you have performed "Exercise 2: Issue an Untrusted Certificate," in Lesson 2 of Chapter 4, "Security." In this case, you have already installed the Certification Authority and Certification Authority Web Enrollment role services of the Active Directory Certificate Services server role on the domain controller. If these role services are installed on your domain controller, skip this exercise and move to Exercise 3.

In this exercise, you install the Certification Authority and Certification Authority Web Enrollment role services of the Active Directory Certificate Services server role. Choosing the second of these role services initiates the additional installation of the Web Server (IIS) role. Together, these features are needed to create the infrastructure needed to support IKEv2-enabled VPN connections.

Perform the steps in this exercise while you are still logged on to DC1 as a domain administrator.

1. In Server Manager, select the Roles node and then click Add Roles in the Roles Summary area of the details pane.

    The Add Roles Wizard opens.

2. On the Before You Begin page, click Next.

3. On the Select Server Roles page, select Active Directory Certificate Services, and then click Next.

4. On the Introduction To Active Directory Certificate Services page, read all the text on the page, and then click Next.

5. On the Select Role Services page, select both Certification Authority and Certification Authority Web Enrollment.

6. In the Add Role Services And Features Required For Certification Authority Web Enrollment? dialog box, click Add Required Role Services.

7. Click Next.

8. On the Specify Setup Type, verify that Enterprise is selected, and then click Next.

9. On the Specify CA Type page, verify that Root CA is selected, and then click Next.

10. On the Set Up Private Key page, verify that Create A New Private Key is selected, and then click Next.

11. On the Configure Cryptography For CA page, click Next to accept the default cryptographic settings.

12. On the Configure CA Name page, click Next to accept the default CA common name and suffix.

13. On the Set Validity Period page, click Next to accept the default validity period.

14. On the Configure Certificate Database page, click Next to accept the default locations.

15. On the Web Server (IIS) page, click Next.

16. On the Select Role Services page, click Next to accept the default choices.

17. In the Confirm Installation Selections dialog box, click Install.

    The installation might take several minutes. When the installation completes, the Installation Results page appears.

18. On the Installation Results page, click Close.

EXERCISE 3 Creating and Issuing a Certificate Template

After you install Active Directory Certificate Services, you must use the new CA on DC1 to generate a server certificate. This server certificate will be used later to authenticate the VPN server.

No certificate template exists by default for the kind of server certificate needed to authenticate a VPN server for an IKEv2 connection. Before you can submit a request to the CA for such a certificate, then, you need to create a certificate template that includes the proper extended key usage (EKU) options: Server Authentication and IP Security IKE Intermediate.

In this exercise, you create a certificate template that will enable you to request a server certificate with the required EKU options applied. Perform the steps in this exercise while you are still logged on to DC1 as a domain administrator.

1. Open the Certification Authority console by clicking Start, clicking Administrative Tools, and then clicking Certification Authority.

2. In the Certification Authority console tree, expand the nwtraders-DC1-CA node.

3. Right-click Certificate Templates, and then click Manage.

   The Certificate Templates Console appears.

4. In the details pane, locate and right-click the IPSec template in the list, and then click Duplicate Template.

5. In the Duplicate Template dialog box, verify that Windows Server 2003 Enterprise is selected, and then click OK. The Properties Of New Template dialog box opens.

6. On the General tab, change the Template Display Name to IKEv2 VPN.

7. On the Request Handling tab, select Allow Private Key To Be Exported.

8. On the Subject Name tab, select Supply In The Request. If a message box appears, click OK to dismiss the message.

9. On the Extensions tab, verify that Application Policies is selected, and then click Edit. The IP Security IKE Intermediate policy is already present in the list of application policies.

10. Click Add, select Server Authentication, and then click OK.

11. Click OK to return to the Extensions tab.

12. Click OK to save your completed template.

13. Close the Certificate Templates Console window.

14. In the Certification Authority console tree, right-click Certificate Templates, select New, and then click Certificate Template To Issue.

15. In the Enable Certificate Templates dialog box, select IKEv2 VPN, and then click OK.

16. Restart DC1.

EXERCISE 4 Configuring Windows Internet Explorer to Allow Certificate Publishing

The new certificate template is now ready to be used for certificate requests. Before you can request one, however, you must configure Windows Internet Explorer security settings to work with the certificate publishing web page.

1. Log on to DC1 as a domain administrator.

2. Click Start, right-click Internet Explorer, and then click Run As Administrator.

3. Click Tools, and then click Internet Options.

4. On the Security tab, under Select A Zone To View Or Change Security Settings, click Local Intranet.

5. In the Security Level For This Zone area, change the security level for Local Intranet from Medium-low to Low, and then click OK.

> **NOTE CUSTOM LEVEL IS PREFERABLE**
>
> In a real-world scenario, it is preferable to adjust the individual ActiveX control settings by using Custom Level than to lower the overall security level.

EXERCISE 5 Requesting a Server Authentication Certificate by Using Internet Explorer

After you have adjusted its security settings, Internet Explorer is now ready to be used to request and install certificates on the local computer. In this exercise, you perform this action. You do this while still logged on to DC1 as a domain administrator.

1. In the Internet Explorer address bar, type **http://localhost/certsrv**, and then press Enter.

2. Under Select A Task, click Request A Certificate.

3. Under Request A Certificate, click Advanced Certificate Request.

4. Under Advanced Certificate Request, click Create And Submit A Request To This CA.

5. On the first confirmation dialog box, click Yes to allow the ActiveX control.

6. On the second confirmation dialog box, click Yes to allow the certificate operation.

7. In the Certificate Template list, select IKEv2 VPN.

8. Under Identifying Information, in the Name field, type **DC1.nwtraders.msft**.

> *NOTE* **USE THIS SAME NAME IN THE CONNECTION SETTINGS**
>
> The name is the certificate subject name and must be the same as the Internet address used in the IKEv2 connection settings configured in Exercise 12 in this practice.

9. Under Key Options, verify that Mark Keys As Exportable is selected, and then click Submit.

10. Click Yes in each of the confirmation dialog boxes.

11. Click Install This Certificate. A message appears indicating that the certificate has been installed.

EXERCISE 6 Moving the New Certificate to the Machine Store

By default, the server authentication certificate you have just requested and installed is created in the user personal store. However, the certificate must be moved to the machine store to be used. In this exercise, you perform this step. You do this while you are still logged on to DC1 as a domain administrator.

1. Click Start, type **mmc**, and then press Enter. A Microsoft Management Console (MMC) window named Console1 appears.

2. In Console1, click File, and then click Add/Remove Snap-in.

3. In the Add Or Remove Snap-ins window, under Available Snap-ins, click Certificates, and then click Add.

4. In the Certificates snap-in window, click Finish to accept the default setting of My User Account.

5. In the Add Or Remove Snap-ins window, click Add a second time, click Computer Account, and then click Next.

6. In the Select Computer dialog box, click Finish to accept the default setting of Local Computer.

7. Click OK to close the Add Or Remove Snap-ins dialog box.

8. In the Console1 console tree, expand Certificates – Current User, expand Personal, and then click Certificates.

9. In the details pane, right-click the DC1.nwtraders.msft certificate, click All Tasks, and then click Export. The Certificate Export Wizard opens.

10. On the Welcome page, click Next.

11. On the Export Private Key page, click Yes, Export The Private Key, and then click Next.

12. On the Export File Format page, click Next to accept the default file format.

13. On the Password page, type a password in both text boxes, and then click Next.

14. On the File To Export page, click Browse.

15. Under Favorites, click Desktop.

16. In the File Name text box, type **DC1cert**, and then click Save to save the certificate to the desktop.

17. Back on the File To Export page, click Next.

18. On the Completing The Certificate Export Wizard page, click Finish to close the wizard, and then click OK in the confirmation dialog box.

19. In the Console1 console tree, expand Certificates (Local Computer), and then expand Personal.

20. Right-click Certificates, point to All Tasks, and then click Import. The Certificate Import Wizard opens.

21. On the Welcome page, click Next.

22. On the File To Import page, click Browse.

23. Under Favorites, click Desktop.

24. In the file type drop-down list, select Personal Information Exchange (*.pfx, *.p12).

25. In the list of files, double-click DC1cert.

26. On the File To Import page, click Next.

27. On the Password page, type the password you assigned to the certificate in step 13, and then click Next.

28. On the Certificate Store page, click Next to accept the Personal store location.

29. Click Finish to close the wizard, and then click OK in the confirmation dialog box.

EXERCISE 7 Generating a Root Certificate

In this exercise, you use Internet Explorer to generate a root certificate for the local CA. This root certificate is later imported on Client1. You do this while still logged on to DC1 as a domain administrator.

1. In the Internet Explorer address bar, type **http://localhost/certsrv**, and then press Enter.

2. Under Select A Task, click Download A CA Certificate, Certificate Chain, Or CRL.

3. Click Yes to allow the ActiveX control, and Yes again to allow the certificate operation.

4. Click Download CA Certificate.

5. Save the certificate to the Desktop with the name RootCACert.

EXERCISE 8   Configuring the VPN Client with the Root Certificate

This exercise is performed on Client1. In the exercise, you install the root certificate for the CA that issued the server authentication certificate. This step is required for the client computer to trust the server authentication certificate and complete the VPN connection.

1. Log on to Nwtraders from Client1 as a domain administrator.

2. Click Start, type **mmc**, and then press Enter. A Microsoft Management Console (MMC) window named Console1 appears.

3. In the Console1 window, click File, and then click Add/Remove Snap-in.

4. Under Available Snap-ins, select Certificates, and then click Add.

5. In the Certificates Snap-in dialog box, select Computer Account, and then click Next.

6. In the Select Computer dialog box, click Finish to accept the default selection of Local Computer.

7. Click OK to close the Add/Remove Snap-ins dialog box.

8. In the Console1 console tree, expand Certificates (Local Computer), expand Trusted Root Certification Authorities, right-click Certificates, click All Tasks, and then click Import. The Certificate Import Wizard opens.

9. On the Welcome page, click Next.

10. On the File To Import page, click Browse.

11. In the Open window, in the address text box, type **\\dc1.nwtraders.msft\c$\users**, and then press Enter.

12. In the list of folders, double-click to open the folder whose name corresponds to the name of the domain administrator account with which you have performed the previous exercises in this practice. The folders associated with the user account appear.

13. Double-click the Desktop folder to open it.

14. Select RootCACert from the file list, and then Click Open.

15. With the path to the certificate now complete on the File To Import page, click Next.

16. On the Certificate Store page, click Next to select the default value of placing the certificate in the Trusted Root Certification Authorities store.

17. On the Completing The Certificate Import Wizard page, click Finish, and then click OK to close the message box indicating that the import was successful.

EXERCISE 9   Installing the Network Policy and Access Services Server Role

You perform this exercise on DC1 logged on as a domain administrator. In the exercise, you use the Add Roles Wizard to add the Network Policy Server and Routing And Remote Access Services roles services. These two role services are features of the Network Policy and Access Services server role.

1. Open Server Manager.

2. In the Server Manager console tree, select the Roles node, and then click Add Roles in the Roles Summary area of the details pane. The Add Roles Wizard opens.

3. On the Before You Begin page, click Next.

4. On the Select Server Roles page, click Network Policy And Access Services, and then click Next.

5. On the Network Policy And Access Services page, click Next.

6. On the Select Role Services page, select both Network Policy Server and Routing And Remote Access Services, and then click Next.

7. On the Confirm Installation Selections page, click Install.

8. On the Installation Results page, click Close.

EXERCISE 10 **Configuring DC1 as a VPN Server**

In this exercise, you enable and configure the Routing and Remote Access service so that DC1 can receive and establish connections from VPN clients. You do this while still logged on to DC1 as a domain administrator.

1. Open the Routing and Remote Access console by clicking Start, pointing to Administrative Tools, and then clicking Routing And Remote Access.

2. In the Routing And Remote Access console tree, right-click DC1 (Local), and then click Configure And Enable Routing And Remote Access.

3. On the Welcome To The Routing And Remote Access Server Setup Wizard page, click Next.

4. On the Configuration page, click Next to accept the default setting of Remote Access (Dial-up Or VPN).

5. On the Remote Access page, select VPN, and then click Next.

6. On the VPN Connection page, under Network Interfaces, verify that the connection that is associated with the network shared by DC1 and Client1 is selected.

7. Clear the option Enable Security On The Selected Interface By Setting Up Static Packet Filters, and then click Next.

> **NOTE** **ENABLING SECURITY ON A PUBLIC INTERFACE**
>
> In a production environment, you should leave security enabled on the public interface. For the purposes of testing connectivity in a lab environment, however, you can disable it.

8. On the IP Address Assignment page, click Next to accept the default setting of Automatically.

9. On the Managing Multiple Remote Access Servers page, click Next to accept the default setting of using Routing and Remote Access to authenticate connection requests.

10. On the Completing The Routing And Remote Access Server Setup Wizard page, click Finish.

11. On the warning about possible NPS policy conflicts, click OK.

EXERCISE 11 Configuring Network Policy Services (NPS)

In this exercise, you enable and configure the remote access policies required for an IKEv2-based VPN connection. Perform this exercise while you are still logged on to DC1 as a domain administrator.

1. Open the Routing and Remote Access console if it is not already open.

2. In the Routing and Remote Access console tree, expand DC1 (Local).

3. Select and right-click Remote Access Logging & Policies, and then select Launch NPS. The Network Policy Server console opens.

4. In the details pane, in the Network Access Policies section, click the Network Access Policies link.

5. In the details pane, in the Network Policies area, double-click Connections To Microsoft Routing And Remote Access Server. The Connections To Microsoft Routing And Remote Access Server Properties dialog box opens.

6. On the Overview tab, in the Access Permission section, select Grant Access. Grant Access If The Connection Request Matches This Policy.

7. Select the Constraints tab. In the Constraints list, Authentication Methods is selected by default. In the right pane, two EAP types are listed: Microsoft: Secured Password (EAP-MSCHAP v2) and Microsoft: Smart Card Or Other Certificate. In this exercise, only the first authentication method is needed.

8. Select Microsoft: Smart Card Or Other Certificate and click Remove to remove this EAP type.

9. Click OK to save your changes.

10. Close all open windows.

EXERCISE 12 Creating the VPN Connection on the VPN Client

In this exercise, you create a VPN connection on Client1 that you will use later to connect to DC1.

1. If you have not already done so, log on the Nwtraders from Client1 as a domain administrator.

2. Click Start, type **Network and Sharing Center**, and then press Enter. The Networking And Sharing Center opens.

3. Click Set Up A New Connection Or Network.

4. Click Connect To A Workplace, and then click Next.

5. Click Use My Internet Connection (VPN).

6. Click I'll Set Up An Internet Connection Later.

7. In the Internet Address text box, type **DC1.nwtraders.msft**. Leave VPN Connection as the destination name, and then click Next.

8. In the User Name and Password text boxes, type the name and password of the VPN user account you created in Exercise 1.

9. Select the Remember This Password check box.

10. In the Domain (Optional) text box, type **nwtraders.msft**.

11. Click Create, and then click Close.

EXERCISE 13 Configuring and Testing the VPN Connection

In this exercise, you verify that you can establish a VPN connection between Client1 and DC1. You do this while still logged on to Client1 as a domain administrator.

1. In the Network and Sharing Center, click Change Adapter Settings.

2. Double-click VPN Connection, and then click Properties.

3. On the Security tab, in the Type Of VPN drop-down list, select IKEv2, and then click OK.

4. In the Connect VPN Connection dialog box, click Connect. The user is authenticated, and the VPN connection is established successfully.

Lesson Summary

- In a Windows network, a VPN infrastructure includes at least a VPN client, a VPN server running RRAS, and a DNS server. However, additional elements are typically used, such as a domain controller, a certificate server/PKI, a DHCP server, and an NPS server.

- Four VPN tunneling protocols are available in Windows 7, and a Windows 7 VPN client attempts to negotiate tunneling protocols in this order: IKEv2, SSTP, L2TP/IPSec, and PPTP.

- IKEv2 is a new tunneling protocol that requires Windows 7 and Windows Server 2008 R2. An advantage of IKEv2 is its support of VPN Reconnect, a feature that allows client mobility between wireless access points without losing the VPN connection.

- To attempt a VPN connection, a VPN client first contacts the VPN server with a request for a tunneling protocol. The terms of the VPN tunnel are then negotiated, after which the VPN tunnel is created. Remote access authentication of the user (and sometimes the computer) follows. Finally, if the user and connection request is determined to be authorized for remote access, the VPN connection is established.

Lesson Review

You can use the following questions to test your knowledge of the information in Lesson 1, "Understanding VPN Client Connections." The questions are also available on the companion CD if you prefer to review them in electronic form.

> **NOTE ANSWERS**
> Answers to these questions and explanations of why each answer choice is correct or incorrect are located in the "Answers" section at the end of the book.

1. You work as a desktop support technician in a large enterprise. The company has recently upgraded all client computers to Windows 7 Enterprise. All servers are running Windows Server 2008.

   Your company supports many mobile users who access the corporate network through a VPN. Your VPN users have complained that when they are connecting to the Internet wirelessly, they lose their VPN connection when they switch between wireless access points. You want VPN users to be able to move between wireless access points without losing a connection. Which of the following steps must you take to achieve this?

   A. Instruct VPN users to select SSTP as the Type Of VPN in the adapter settings of the VPN connection.

   B. Instruct VPN users to configure the maximum encryption strength in the adapter settings of the VPN connection.

   C. Configure the server running Windows acting as the VPN server to forward authentication to an NPS server.

   D. Upgrade the server running Windows acting as the VPN server to Windows Server 2008 R2.

2. Which of the following actions do you need to perform to enable a client running Windows 7 to access a corporate network through an IKEv2 VPN?

   A. Install the VPN server certificate on the client running Windows 7.

   B. Ensure that the root certificate of the CA that has issued the VPN server's server certificate has been installed in the Trusted Root Certification Authorities certificate store on the client running Windows 7.

   C. In the VPN connection properties on the client running Windows 7, configure the Type Of VPN setting as IKEv2.

   D. Obtain a computer certificate for the client running Windows 7.

Lesson 2: Understanding DirectAccess Client Connections

DirectAccess is a new feature of Windows 7 and Windows Server 2008 R2 that automatically and transparently connects a remote user to a private corporate network from any location on the Internet. DirectAccess was developed to eventually replace traditional VPNs, which require users to initiate a VPN connect once their computer is connected to the Internet. This lesson provides an overview of the benefits of Direct Access, how it works, and how to troubleshoot settings on the DirectAccess client.

> **After this lesson, you will be able to:**
> - Understand the benefits of DirectAccess
> - Understand the prerequisites and features of a DirectAccess infrastructure
> - Understand the steps performed in a DirectAccess connection
> - Perform basic troubleshooting of DirectAccess client connections
>
> **Estimated lesson time: 45 minutes**

Overview of DirectAccess

DirectAccess is a new technology that automatically establishes bidirectional connectivity between a remote user's computer and that user's company intranet. The remote user does not have to initiate the connection to the intranet manually, and administrators can manage this and other remote computers outside the office through the same DirectAccess connection. DirectAccess is supported on Windows 7 Enterprise, Windows 7 Ultimate, and Windows Server 2008 R2.

Understanding the Limitations of VPNs

Traditionally, users connect to intranet resources with a VPN. However, using a VPN has a number of disadvantages, including the following:

- Connecting to a VPN takes several steps, and the user needs to wait for authentication. For organizations that check the health of a computer before allowing the connection, establishing a VPN connection can take several minutes.
- Anytime users lose their Internet connection, they need to reestablish the VPN connection.
- VPN client machines typically are not subject to Group Policy.
- Internet performance is slowed if both intranet and Internet traffic goes through the VPN connection.

Because of these inconveniences, many users avoid connecting to a VPN. Instead, they use application gateways, such as Microsoft Outlook Web Access (OWA), to connect to intranet resources. With OWA, users can retrieve internal e-mail without establishing a VPN connection. However, users still need to connect to a VPN to open documents that are located on intranet file shares, such as those that are linked to in an e-mail message.

Understanding the Benefits of DirectAccess

DirectAccess overcomes the limitations of VPNs by providing the following benefits to enterprises and their users:

- **Always-on connectivity** Unlike with a VPN, a DirectAccess connection is always on, even before the user logs on to his or her computer.

- **Seamless connectivity** To the user, the DirectAccess connection to the corporate network is completely transparent. Aside from any delay that could be caused by a slow Internet connection, the user experience is the same as if the user's computer were connected directly to the corporate network.

- **Bidirectional access** With DirectAccess, the user's remote computer not only has access to the corporate intranet, but the intranet can also see the user's computer. This means that the remote computer can be managed using Group Policy and other management tools in exactly the same way that computers located on the internal network are managed.

- **Enhanced security** DirectAccess provides administrators with flexibility in how they control access to internal resources for remote users and their computers. For example, DirectAccess can be configured to provide user access only to selected resources. In addition, Direct Access fully integrates with Server and Domain Isolation solutions and the NAP infrastructure to help ensure compliance with security, access, and health policies for both local and remote computers.

  In addition, DirectAccess includes the following security features:

  - DirectAccess is built on a foundation of standards-based technologies: IPSec and IPv6.

  - DirectAccess uses IPSec to authenticate both the computer and user. If you want, you can require a smart card for user authentication.

  - DirectAccess also uses IPSec to provide encryption for communications across the Internet.

Understanding DirectAccess and IPv6 Transition Technologies

DirectAccess clients must have globally routable IPv6 addresses. For organizations that are already using a native IPv6 infrastructure, DirectAccess can easily extend this existing infrastructure to DirectAccess client computers. These client computers can also still access Internet resources by using IPv4.

For organizations that have not yet begun deploying IPv6, a number of IPv6 transition technologies are available to begin IPv6 deployment without requiring an infrastructure upgrade.

These technologies are described in the next sections.

ISATAP

Intra-site Automatic Tunnel Addressing Protocol (ISATAP) is a tunneling protocol that allows an IPv6 network to communicate with an IPv4 network through an ISATAP router, as shown in Figure 6-14.

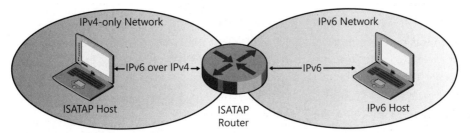

FIGURE 6-14 ISATAP routers allow IPv4-only and IPv6-only hosts to communicate with each other.

ISATAP allows IPv4 and IPv6 hosts to communicate by performing a type of address translation between IPv4 and IPv6. In this process, all ISATAP clients receive an address for an ISATAP interface. This address is composed of an IPv4 address encapsulated inside an IPv6 address.

ISATAP is intended for use within a private network.

6to4

6to4 is a protocol that tunnels IPv6 traffic over IPv4 traffic through 6to4 routers. 6to4 clients have their router's IPv4 address embedded in their IPv6 address and do not require an IPv4 address. Whereas ISATAP is intended primarily for intranets, 6to4 is intended to be used on the Internet. You can use 6to4 to connect to IPv6 portions of the Internet through a 6to4 relay even if your intranet or your ISP supports only IPv4.

A sample 6to4 network is shown in Figure 6-15.

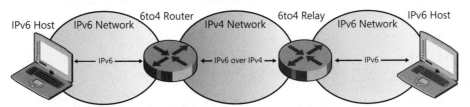

FIGURE 6-15 6to4 allows IPv6-only hosts to communicate over the Internet.

Teredo

Teredo is a tunneling protocol that allows clients located behind an IPv4 NAT device to use IPv6 over the Internet. Teredo is used only when no other IPv6 transition technology (such as 6to4) is available.

Teredo relies on an infrastructure, illustrated in Figure 6-16, that includes Teredo clients, Teredo servers, Teredo relays, and Teredo host-specific relays.

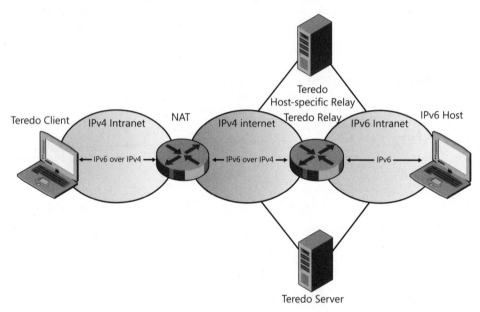

FIGURE 6-16 Teredo allows hosts located behind a router performing IPv4 NAT to use IPv6 over the Internet to communicate with each other or with IPv6-only hosts.

- **Teredo client**   A Teredo client is a computer that is enabled with both IPv6 and IPv4 and that is located behind a router performing IPv4 NAT. The Teredo client creates a Teredo tunneling interface and configures a routable IPv6 address with the help of a Teredo server. Through this interface, Teredo clients communicate with other Teredo clients or with hosts on the IPv6 Internet (through a Teredo relay).

- **Teredo server**   A Teredo server is a public server connected both to the IPv4 Internet and to the IPv6 Internet. The Teredo server helps perform the address configuration of the Teredo client and facilitates initial communication either between two Teredo clients or between a Teredo client and an IPv6 host.

    To facilitate communication among Windows-based Teredo client computers, Microsoft has deployed Teredo servers on the IPv4 Internet.

- **Teredo relay**   A Teredo relay is a Teredo tunnel endpoint. It is an IPv6/IPv4 router that can forward packets between Teredo clients on the IPv4 Internet and IPv6-only hosts.

- **Teredo host-specific relay** A Teredo host-specific relay is a host that is enabled with both IPv4 and IPv6 and that acts as its own Teredo relay. A Teredo host-specific relay essentially enables a Teredo client that has a global IPv6 address to tunnel through the IPv4 Internet and communicate directly with hosts connected to the IPv6 Internet.

IP-HTTPS

IP-HTTPS is a new protocol developed by Microsoft for Windows 7 and Windows Server 2008 R2. It enables hosts located behind a Web proxy server or firewall to establish connectivity by tunneling IPv6 packets inside an IPv4-based Hypertext Transfer Protocol Secure (HTTPS) session. HTTPS is used instead of HTTP so that Web proxy servers do not attempt to examine the data stream and terminate the connection. IP-HTTPS is used as the fallback technology for DirectAccess clients when neither 6to4 nor Teredo is available.

IPv6/IPv4 NAT

Some NAT routers are able to provide connectivity between global IPv6 addresses and private IPv4 addresses. To perform this function, these devices typically conform to the Network Address Translation/Protocol Translation (NAT-PT) standard or the Network Address Port Translation + Protocol Translation (NAPT-PT) standard, as defined in RFC 2766. Although these two technologies are still available on some networks, they have been deprecated by the Internet Engineering Task Force (IETF) because of technical problems. NAT64 is the name of another mechanism to perform this same function in the future.

> *NOTE* **CONFIGURING IPv6 SETTINGS IN GROUP POLICY**
>
> You can configure client settings for IPv6 transition technologies in Local Computer Policy or Group Policy. You can find these settings in a GPO by navigating to Computer Configuration\Policies\Administrative Templates\Network\TCPIPSettings\IPv6 Transition Technologies.

Understanding DirectAccess Infrastructure Features

Figure 6-17 shows the primary features of a DirectAccess infrastructure. These features include general network infrastructure requirements such as a PKI (including a certification authority and CRL distribution points), domain controllers, IPv6 transition technologies, and DNS servers. A DirectAccess infrastructure also has the elements that form the core of the DirectAccess solution, including DirectAccess clients, DirectAccess servers, and a network location server.

These elements of a DirectAccess infrastructure are described in more detail in the following section.

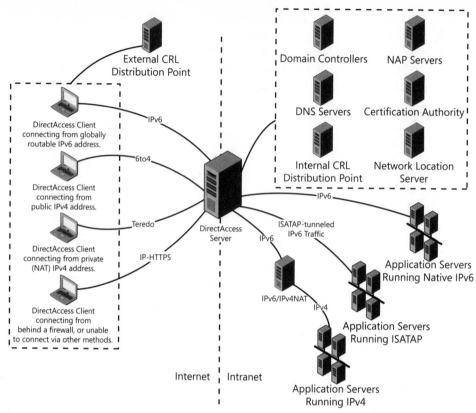

FIGURE 6-17 A DirectAccess infrastructure

DirectAccess Server

At least one domain-joined server must be running Windows Server 2008 R2 so it can act as the DirectAccess server. This server typically resides on your perimeter network and acts as both a relay for IPv6 traffic and an IPSec gateway. The server can accept connections from DirectAccess clients and (like a VPN server) facilitate communication with intranet resources. The DirectAccess server needs to be configured with two physical network adapters and at least two consecutive, publicly-addressable IPv4 addresses that can be externally resolved through the Internet DNS.

To create a DirectAccess server, use Server Manager to add the DirectAccess Management Console feature in Windows Server 2008 R2. Then use the DirectAccess Setup Wizard in this console to configure the server.

DirectAccess Client

Client computers must be domain-joined and running Windows 7 Enterprise or Ultimate to use DirectAccess. To perform the initial configuration of computers as DirectAccess clients, add them to a Windows group, and then specify this group when you run the DirectAccess Setup Wizard on the DirectAccess server.

To allow DirectAccess clients to separate Internet traffic from intranet traffic, Windows 7 and Windows Server 2008 R2 include the Name Resolution Poilcy Table (NRPT). The NRPT is applied to clients only through Local Computer Policy or Group Policy—it cannot be configured locally on the client. To locate NRPT settings in a GPO, navigate to Computer Configuration\Policies\Windows Settings\Name Resolution Policy.

> *NOTE* **WHAT IS THE NRPT?**
>
> The NRPT is a new feature that allows a client to assign a DNS server address to particular namespaces rather than to particular interfaces. The NRPT essentially stores a list of name resolution rules that are applied to clients through Group Policy. Each rule defines a DNS namespace and DNS client behavior for that namespace. When a DirectAccess client is on the Internet, each name query request is compared against the namespace rules stored in the NRPT. If a match is found, the request is processed according to the settings in the NRPT rule. The settings determine the DNS servers to which each request will be sent.
>
> If a name query request does not match a namespace listed in the NRPT, it is sent to the DNS servers configured in the TCP/IP settings for the specified network interface.

Network Location Server

A network location server is a Web server accessed by a DirectAccess client to determine whether the client is located on the intranet or Internet. The DirectAccess server can act as the network location server, but it is preferable to use a separate, high-availability Web server for the network location server instead. This separate Web server does not have to be dedicated as a network location server. You can configure network location server settings in Local Computer Policy or Group Policy. To find the settings in a GPO, navigate to Computer Configuration\Policies\Administrative Templates\Network\Network Connectivity Status Indicator.

Domain Controllers

An AD DS infrastructure is required for DirectAccess. At least one domain controller in the domain needs to be running Windows Server 2008 or later.

IPv6-capable Network

DirectAccess uses IPv6 to enable remote client computers to maintain connectivity with intranet resources over an Internet connection. Because most of the public Internet currently uses IPv4, however, DirectAccess clients use IPv6 transition technologies when no IPv6 connectivity is available. The order of connection methods attempted by DirectAccess clients is as follows:

1. **Native IPv6**   This method is used if the DirectAccess client is assigned a globally routable IPv6 address.
2. **6to4**   This method is used if the DirectAccess client is assigned a public IPv4 address.
3. **Teredo**   This method is used if the DirectAccess client is assigned a private IPv4 address.
4. **IP-HTTPS**   This method is attempted if the other methods fail.

For remote client computers to reach computers on the internal corporate network through DirectAccess, the internal computers must be fully IPv6-compatible.

Computers on your IPv4 network are fully IPv6-compatible if any of the following is true:

- The computers are running Windows 7, Windows Vista, Windows Server 2008, or Windows Server 2008 R2.

- You have deployed ISATAP on your intranet to enable internal servers and applications to be reachable by tunneling IPv6 traffic over your IPv4-only intranet.

- You are using a NAT-PT device to translate traffic between your DirectAccess clients and your intranet computers that support only IPv4.

IPSec

DirectAccess uses IPSec to provide end-to-end security for remote client computers accessing resources on the internal corporate network. IPSec policies are used for authentication and encryption of all DirectAccess connections. These policies can be configured and applied to client computers using Group Policy.

PKI

A PKI is required to issue computer certificates for client and server authentication and also for issuing health certificates when NAP has been implemented. These certificates can be issued by a CA on the internal network—they do not need to be issued by a public CA.

CRL Distribution Points (CDPs)

In a DirectAccess infrastructure, CDPs are the servers that provide access to the CRL that is published by the CA issuing certificates for DirectAccess. Separate CDPs should be published for clients internal to the corporate network and for external clients on the Internet.

Perimeter Firewall Exceptions

On your corporate network perimeter firewall, the following ports must be opened to support DirectAccess:

- UDP port 3544 to enable inbound Teredo traffic

- IPv4 protocol 41 to enable inbound 6to4 traffic

- TCP port 443 to enable inbound IP-HTTPS traffic

If you need to support client computers that have native IPv6 addresses, the following exceptions will also need to be opened:

- ICMPv6

- IPv4 protocol 50

Configuring DirectAccess Client Settings for IPv6 Manually

Although DirectAccess clients normally are configured automatically when you run the DirectAccess Setup wizard on the DirectAccess server, you can configure client IPv6 settings manually to help resolve connectivity problems. Use the information in Table 6-2 to configure remote clients with the proper IPv6 transition technology: Teredo, 6to4, or IP-HTTPS.

TABLE 6-2 Manual IPv6 Configuration for DirectAccess Clients

PURPOSE	COMMAND	GROUP POLICY SETTING
Configure the Teredo client as an enterprise client and configure the IPv4 address of the Teredo server (the DirectAccess server).	*netsh interface teredo set state type=enterpriseclient servername*=FirstPublicIPv4 AddressOfDirectAccessServer	Computer Configuration\Policies\ Administrative Templates\ Network\TCPIP Settings\IPv6 Transition Technologies\Teredo State=Enterprise Client and Computer Configuration\Policies\ Administrative Templates\Network\ TCPIP Settings\Ipv6 transition Technologies\Teredo Server Name= *FirstPublicIPv4AddressOfDirect AccessServer*
Configure the public IPv4 address of the 6to4 relay (the DirectAccess server).	*netsh interface 6to4 set relay name*=FirstPublicIPv4 AddressOfDirect AccessServer	Computer Configuration\Policies\ Administrative Templates\Network\ TCPIP Settings\Ipv6 transition Technologies\6to4 Relay Name= *FirstPublicIPv4AddressOf DirectAccessServer*
Enable the IP-HTTPS client and configure the IP-HTTPS Uniform Resource Locator (URL).	*netsh interface httpstunnel add interface client https://*FQDNofDirectAccess Server/*IPHTTPS*	Computer Configuration\Policies\ Administrative Templates\Network\ TCPIP Settings\Ipv6 transition Technologies\IP-HTTPS State set to Enabled and the IP-HTTPS URL of *https://*SubjectOfIP-HPPTSCertificate: *443/IPHTTPS*

Configuring IPv6 Internet Features on the DirectAccess Server Manually

For troubleshooting purposes, you can configure your DirectAccess server manually for Teredo, 6to4, and IP-HTTPS. Use the features listed in Table 6-3 to help you perform these steps.

TABLE 6-3 Configuring DirectAccess Internet Features

FEATURE	PURPOSE	COMMAND
Teredo server	Configure Teredo with the name or IPv4 address of the Teredo server	netsh interface ipv6 set teredo server FirstIPv4AddressOfDirectAccessServer
IPv6 interfaces	Configure the IPv6 interfaces for the correct forwarding and advertising behavior	Run the following command for the 6to4 and Teredo interfaces: *netsh interface ipv6 set interface* InterfaceIndex *forwarding=enabled* If a LAN interface is present with a native IPv6 address, run the following command: *netsh interface ipv6 set interface* InterfaceIndex *forwarding=enabled* For the IP-HTTPS interface, run the following command: *netsh interface ipv6 set interface IPHTTPSInterface forwarding=enabled advertise=enabled*
6to4	Enable 6to4	*netsh interface 6to4 set state enabled*
SSL certificates for IP-HTTPS connections	Configure the certificate binding	Install the Secure Sockets Layer (SSL) certificate using manual enrollment. Use the *netsh http add sslcert* command to configure the certificate binding.
IP-HTTPS interface	Configure the IP-HTTPS interface	*netsh interface httpstunnel add interface server https://PublicIPv4AddressOrFQDN:443/iphttps enabled certificates*
IP-HTTPS routing	Configure IPv6 routing for the IP-HTTPS interface	*netsh interface ipv6 add route IP-HTTPSPrefix ::/64 IPHTTPSInterface publish=yes* where *IP-HTTPSPrefix* is one of the following: ■ *6to4-basedPrefix :2* if you are using a 6to4-based prefix based on the first public IPv4 address assigned to the Internet interface of the DirectAccess server. ■ *NativePrefix :5555* if you are using a 48-bit native IPv6 prefix. 5555 is the Subnet ID value chosen by the DirectAccess Setup Wizard.

Understanding the DirectAccess Connection Process

A DirectAccess connection to a target intranet resource is initiated when the DirectAccess client connects to the DirectAccess server through IPv6. IPSec is then negotiated between the client and server. Finally, the connection is established between the DirectAccess client and the target resource.

This general process can be broken down into the following specific steps:

1. The DirectAccess client computer running Windows 7 detects that it is connected to a network.

2. The DirectAccess client computer attempts to connect to the network location server. If the network location server is available, the DirectAccess client determines that it is already connected to the intranet, and the DirectAccess connection process stops. If the network location server is not available, the DirectAccess client determines that it is connected to the Internet and the DirectAccess connection process continues.

3. The DirectAccess client computer connects to the DirectAccess server using IPv6 and IPSec. If a native IPv6 network isn't available, the client establishes an IPv6-over-IPv4 tunnel using 6to4 or Teredo. The user does not have to be logged in for this step to complete.

4. If a firewall or proxy server prevents the client computer using 6to4 or Teredo from connecting to the DirectAccess server, the client automatically attempts to connect using the IP-HTTPS protocol, which uses a SSL connection to ensure connectivity.

5. As part of establishing the IPSec session, the DirectAccess client and server authenticate each other using computer certificates for authentication.

6. By validating AD DS group memberships, the DirectAccess server verifies that the computer and user are authorized to connect using DirectAccess.

7. If NAP is enabled and configured for health validation, the DirectAccess client obtains a health certificate from a Health Registration Authority (HRA) located on the Internet prior to connecting to the DirectAccess server. The HRA forwards the DirectAccess client's health status information to a NAP health policy server. The NAP health policy server processes the policies defined within the NPS and determines whether the client is compliant with system health requirements. If so, the HRA obtains a health certificate for the DirectAccess client. When the DirectAccess client connects to the DirectAccess server, it submits its health certificate for authentication.

8. The DirectAccess server begins forwarding traffic from the DirectAccess client to the intranet resources to which the user has been granted access.

Troubleshooting DirectAccess Connections

The following list describes a number of areas in which a DirectAccess connection must be properly configured. You can use this list as a set of principles and procedures to help troubleshoot DirectAccess clients.

- The DirectAccess client must have a global IPv6 address. (Global IPv6 addresses start with a 2 or 3.)

  Use the *Ipconfig /all* command on the DirectAccess client.

  If the DirectAccess client is assigned public IPv4 address, you should see an interface named Tunnel Adapter 6TO4 Adapter listed in the Ipconfig output. This interface should be configured with an address that starts with 2002. The Tunnel Adapter 6TO4 Adapter should also be assigned a default gateway.

  If the DirectAccess client is assigned a private IPv4 address, you should see a listing for a Teredo interface, and this interface should be configured with an address that starts with 2001.

  For IP-HTTPS, look for an interface named Tunnel Adapter Iphttpsinterface. Unless you had a native IPv6 infrastructure in place prior to running the DirectAccess Setup Wizard, the Tunnel Adapter Iphttpsinterface should be configured with an address that starts with 2002. The Tunnel Adapter Iphttpsinterface should also be assigned a default gateway.

- The DirectAccess client must be able to reach the IPv6 addresses of the DirectAccess server.

  Use the *Ipconfig /all* command on the DirectAccess server. Note the global IPv6 addresses of the DirectAccess server. From the DirectAccess client, you should be able to ping any of the global IPv6 addresses of the DirectAccess server.

  If this attempt is not successful, troubleshoot the connection by looking for the break in IPv6 connectivity between the DirectAccess client and server.

  Use the following methods to help fix IPv6 connectivity breaks:

  If your DirectAccess client is assigned a private IPv4 address, ensure that the local Teredo client is configured as an enterprise client and that the IPv4 address of the DirectAccess server is configured as the Teredo server. To do so, type the following command:

  netsh interface teredo set state type=enterpriseclient servername=*FirstPublicIP v4AddressOfDirectAccessServer*

  If your DirectAccess client is assigned a public IPv4 address, ensure that the DirectAccess server IPv4 address is assigned as the 6to4 relay by typing the following command:

  netsh interface 6to4 set relay name=*FirstPublicIPv4AddressOfDirectAccessServer*

  If these methods fail, you can attempt to use IP-HTTPS to establish IPv6 connectivity to the DirectAccess server. To do so, type the following command:

  netsh interface httpstunnel add interface client https://*FQDNofDirectAccessServer*/ IPHTTPS

> **NOTE** **USING PING OVER IPSec**
>
> To use Ping as a troubleshooting tool, ensure that Internet Control Message Protocol (ICMP) is exempt from IPSec protection between the DirectAccess client and the remote endpoint of the IPSec connection.

- The intranet servers must have global IPv6 addresses.

  Use the *Ipconfig /all* command on any intranet server that cannot be contacted. The output of the command should list a global IPv6 address.

  If not, troubleshoot the IPv6 infrastructure on your intranet. For ISATAP networks, ensure that your DNS servers running Windows Server 2008 or later have the name *ISATAP* removed from their global query block lists. In addition, verify that the DirectAccess server has registered an ISATAP A record in the intranet DNS.

  > **NOTE USING IPV6/IPV4 NAT DEVICES**
  >
  > If you are using a NAT-PT or NAT64 device to reach the intranet server, the intranet server will not have a global IPv6 address. In this case, ensure that the NAT-PT or NAT64 device has a global IPv6 address.

- The DirectAccess client on the Internet must correctly determine that it is not on the intranet.

  Type **netsh namespace show effectivepolicy** to display the NRPT on the DirectAccess client. You should see NRPT rules for the intranet namespace and an exemption for the fully qualified domain name (FQDN) of the network location server.

  If not, determine the network location server URL by typing the following command:

  ```
  reg query
  HKLM\software\policies\microsoft\windows\NetworkConnectivityStatusIndicator\
  CorporateConnectivity /v DomainLocationDeterminationUrl
  ```

  Ensure that the FQDN of this URL either matches an exemption entry or does not match the DNS suffix for your intranet namespace in the NRPT.

- The DirectAccess client must not be assigned the domain firewall profile.

  Type **netsh advfirewall monitor show currentprofile** to display the attached networks and their determined firewall profiles. If you have not yet established a DirectAccess connection, none of your networks should be in the Domain profile.

  If any of your networks has been assigned the domain profile, determine if you have an active remote access VPN connection or a domain controller that is available on the Internet, and disable that connection.

- The DirectAccess client must be able to contact its intranet DNS servers through IPv6.

  Type **netsh namespace show effectivepolicy** on the client to obtain the IPv6 addresses of your intranet DNS servers. Ping these IPv6 addresses from the DirectAccess client.

  If not successful, locate the break in IPv6 connectivity between the DirectAccess client and the intranet DNS servers. Ensure that your DirectAccess server has only a single IPv4 default gateway that is configured on the Internet interface. Also ensure that your DirectAccess server has been configured with the set of IPv4 routes on the intranet interface that allow it to access all of the IPv4 destinations of your intranet.

- The DirectAccess client must be able to use intranet DNS servers to resolve intranet FQDNs.

  Type **nslookup *IntranetFQDN IntranetDNSServerIPv6Address*** to resolve the names of intranet servers (for example: **nslookup dc1.corp.contoso.com 2002:836b:2:1::5efe:10.0.0.1**). The output should display the IPv6 addresses of the specified intranet server.

  If the intranet DNS server cannot be contacted, troubleshoot connectivity to that DNS server. If the server can be contacted but the server name specified is not found, troubleshoot the intranet DNS. (Determine why a AAAA record for the intranet server is not available.)

- The DirectAccess client must be able to reach intranet servers.

  Use Ping to attempt to reach the IPv6 addresses of intranet servers.

  If this attempt does not succeed, attempt to find the break in IPv6 connectivity between the DirectAccess client and the intranet servers.

- The DirectAccess client must be able to communicate with intranet servers using application layer protocols.

  Use the application in question to access the appropriate intranet server. If File And Printer Sharing is enabled on the intranet server, test application layer protocol access by typing **net view *IntranetFQDN***.

PRACTICE **Demonstrating DirectAccess in a Test Lab (Optional)**

The requirements for a DirectAccess infrastructure far surpass the two-computer network that is used in this book. However, if you have a computer with sufficient RAM to run six virtual machines, it is recommended that you download *Step By Step Guide: Demonstrate DirectAccess in a Test Lab*, available at *http://www.microsoft.com/downloads/details.aspx?familyid=8D47ED5F-D217-4D84-B698-F39360D82FAC*, and use the instructions in the guide to set up a test network for DirectAccess. You will need at least four hours to complete the project.

Lesson Summary

- DirectAccess is a new technology that replaces a traditional VPN. When configured, it enables remote clients running Windows 7 Enterprise or Windows 7 Ultimate to establish an always-available, bidirectional connection with the corporate network automatically, even before the user logs on.

- DirectAccess runs on IPv6 only. To use DirectAccess in an IPv4 network, computers rely on IPv6 transition technologies such as Teredo, 6to4, ISATAP, and IP-HTTPS.

- A DirectAccess infrastructure includes a DirectAccess client, a DirectAccess server at the edge of the corporate network, domain controllers, a network location server, and a PKI.

- To establish a DirectAccess connection, a client first determines its location by attempting to contact the network location server. If the client determines it is on the Internet, it attempts to contact the DirectAccess server over IPv6 (using a transition technology if necessary). It then creates an IPSec tunnel with the DirectAccess server. Finally, the server validates that the client is authorized for remote access, and the DirectAccess connection is established.

Lesson Review

You can use the following questions to test your knowledge of the information in Lesson 2, "Understanding DirectAccess Client Connections." The questions are also available on the companion CD if you prefer to review them in electronic form.

> **NOTE ANSWERS**
>
> Answers to these questions and explanations of why each answer choice is correct or incorrect are located in the "Answers" section at the end of the book.

1. Which of the following operating systems CANNOT act as a DirectAccess client?
   A. Windows 7 Enterprise
   B. Windows 7 Professional
   C. Windows 7 Ultimate
   D. Windows Server 2008 R2

2. Which of the following is NOT required to establish a DirectAccess connection successfully to a remote client?
   A. A server certificate on the DirectAccess server
   B. A computer certificate on the DirectAccess client
   C. A global IPv6 address on the DirectAccess client
   D. A global IPv4 address on the DirectAccess client

Chapter Review

To further practice and reinforce the skills you learned in this chapter, you can perform the following tasks:

- Review the chapter summary.
- Review the list of key terms introduced in this chapter.
- Complete the case scenarios. These scenarios set up real-world situations involving the topics of this chapter and ask you to create a solution.
- Complete the suggested practices.
- Take a practice test.

Chapter Summary

- To troubleshoot a remote access VPN connection, you need to understand the requirements of a VPN infrastructure and the many steps to establish such a connection. Those steps include the VPN client contacting the VPN server, the negotiation of the terms of the VPN tunnel, the creation of the VPN tunnel, remote access authentication, and remote access authorization.
- To troubleshoot a DirectAccess connection, you need to understand the requirements of a DirectAccess infrastructure and the many steps of establishing such a connection. Those steps include the DirectAccess client contacting the network location server, the client contacting the DirectAccess server over IPv6, the client establishing an IPSec tunnel with the DirectAccess server, and the server authorizing the client for remote access.

Key Terms

Do you know what these key terms mean? You can check your answers by looking up the terms in the glossary at the end of the book.

- **tunneling**
- **data authentication**
- **VPN Reconnect**

Case Scenarios

In the following case scenarios, you will apply what you've learned about troubleshooting remote access connections. You can find answers to these questions in the "Answers" section at the end of this book.

Case Scenario 1: Troubleshooting a Remote Access VPN

You work as a desktop support technician for a company whose network includes 600 clients running Windows 7 and 30 servers running Windows Server 2008 R2. Your network infrastructure includes an L2TP/IPSec VPN that employees use to access the corporate intranet remotely. The VPN server is running RRAS, and authentication is performed by using a preshared key. The company network does not include its own PKI, and no computer certificates are installed on either the VPN clients or the VPN server.

The help desk receives many complaints about VPN access. Remote users complain that the VPN connection takes too long to be established, and that connectivity is frequently disrupted when they move among wireless access points. Users also complain that they have trouble connecting to the network from behind remote NAT devices or firewalls. Your manager asks you to review the situation and to answer the following questions:

1. What technical actions can be taken to resolve the problems of VPN performance? Assume that the VPN connections on all clients running Windows 7 have the Type Of VPN security setting configured as Automatic (the default).

2. What technical actions can be taken to allow users to connect to the VPN from behind remote NAT devices or firewalls?

Case Scenario 2: Troubleshooting DirectAccess

You work as an enterprise support technician for Contoso.com, a large pharmaceutical company with over 2,000 employees. Many company employees travel with laptops, and your IT department has implemented DirectAccess as a means to connect users' computers automatically to the corporate network when they are removed from the company premises. The company no longer has any alternate VPN access.

Over the course of a day, you receive the following calls from the help desk about problems related to DirectAccess connections.

1. The help desk informs you that a user cannot connect to the corporate intranet from a public wireless hotspot. Help desk support staff have already determined that the user's only assigned IPv4 address is 192.168.0.110, and the only IPv6 address on his computer begins with "fe80::".

    You want to enable the user's remote computer to connect to the DirectAccess server. Which IPv6 interface or transition technology on the client should you first attempt to configure by specifying the DirectAccess server's first public IPv4 address, and why?

2. You later receive a call from the help desk about another remote user who cannot establish a DirectAccess connection to the corporate network successfully. In this case, the help desk has established that the user's only assigned IPv4 address is 207.46.197.32, and that the only IPv6 address begins with "fe80::".

    Which IPv6 interface or transition technology on the client should you first attempt to configure by specifying the DirectAccess server's first public IPv4 address, and why?

Suggested Practices

To help you master the exam objectives presented in this chapter, complete the following tasks.

Identify and Resolve Remote Access Issues

Perform both practices to increase your experience with remote access in Windows 7.

- **Practice 1** Create an IKEv2 or SSTP remote access VPN. Set up a VPN server running Windows Server 2008 R2. Create a VPN connection on a computer running Windows 7, and then attempt to connect to the VPN server over the Internet.

- **Practice 2** Deploy a DirectAccess server. Add the DirectAccess feature to a server running Windows Server 2008 R2, and then follow the instructions to deploy all of the DirectAccess prerequisites, such as a PKI. When the prerequisites are met, run the DirectAccess Setup Wizard.

Take a Practice Test

The practice tests on this book's companion CD offer many options. For example, you can test yourself on just one exam objective, or you can test yourself on all the 70-685 certification exam content. You can set up the test so that it closely simulates the experience of taking a certification exam, or you can set it up in study mode so that you can look at the correct answers and explanations after you answer each question.

> **MORE INFO** **PRACTICE TESTS**
>
> For details about all the practice test options available, see the section entitled "How to Use the Practice Tests," in the Introduction to this book.

CHAPTER 7

Updates

Although Windows 7 is designed to minimize security risks out of the box, attackers are constantly developing new security vulnerabilities. To adapt to changing security risks, improve the reliability of Windows, and add support for new hardware, you must deploy updates to your client computers.

In homes and small offices, Windows automatically downloads the newest critical updates from Microsoft, allowing computers to stay up to date without any administrative effort. This approach does not scale to enterprises, which must manage thousands of computers. In enterprises, IT departments need to test updates to ensure that they do not cause widespread compatibility problems. In addition, having each computer download the same update across the Internet would waste your bandwidth, potentially affecting your network performance when Microsoft releases large updates.

This chapter discusses managing, testing, and troubleshooting updates for client computers running Windows 7.

Exam objective in this chapter:
- Identify and resolve software update issues.

Lesson in this chapter:

Before You Begin

To complete the lessons in this chapter, you should be familiar with Windows 7 and be comfortable with the following tasks:

- Installing Windows 7
- Connecting a computer to a network physically
- Performing basic administration tasks on a Windows Server 2008 R2–based domain controller

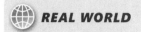 **REAL WORLD**

Tony Northrup

In July 2001, the Code Red worm spread quickly across Microsoft Internet Information Server (IIS)–based Web servers on the Internet. At the time, I was part of a team that managed hundreds of IIS Web servers.

The Code Red worm exploited a buffer overflow vulnerability in IIS on Microsoft Windows 2000 Server and Microsoft Windows NT 4.0. About a month prior, Microsoft released an update that fixed the vulnerability and would prevent the Code Red worm from compromising Web servers.

So, my servers should have been safe, right? Unfortunately, no. At the time, deploying updates was very difficult. Automatic Updates was not an option, and Windows Server Update Services (WSUS) did not yet exist. We had a third-party infrastructure for automatically installing updates, but it frequently caused errors. Because updates almost always required servers to be restarted (causing downtime), we had to schedule every update with the customer. Because of the time required to install updates and the frequency with which Microsoft was releasing updates, we were several months behind on our update deployments.

The Code Red worm infected hundreds of thousands of IIS Web servers, including dozens of servers that my organization managed. The patching team had to work long hours for weeks at a time to repair damage that could have been prevented easily by installing the update promptly. The cost to our reputation was immeasurable.

Nowadays, Microsoft has made update management far more efficient. The importance of installing updates has only increased, however. Malware authors have become more sophisticated, and when an exploit is found, it can be difficult or impossible to remove. For that reason, this chapter is the most important chapter in the book to master for the real world.

Lesson 1: Updating Software

Because security threats are evolving constantly, Microsoft must release updates to Windows 7 and other Microsoft software regularly. Deploying and managing these updates are some of the most important security tasks an IT department can perform.

This lesson describes the different techniques for deploying updates to computers running Windows 7 and explains how to install and manage updates and how to troubleshoot update problems.

After this lesson, you will be able to:

- Choose a deployment technique for distributing updates within your organization.
- Install updates automatically, manually, and to new computers.
- Troubleshoot problems installing updates.
- Uninstall updates.

Estimated lesson time: 45 minutes

Methods for Deploying Updates

Microsoft provides several techniques for applying updates:

- **Directly from Microsoft**   For home users and small businesses, Windows 7 is configured to retrieve updates directly from Microsoft automatically. This method is suitable only for smaller networks with fewer than 50 computers.

- **Windows Server Update Services (WSUS)**   WSUS enables administrators to approve updates before distributing them to computers on an intranet. If you want, updates can be stored and retrieved from a central location on the local network, reducing Internet usage when downloading updates. This approach requires at least one infrastructure server.

- **Microsoft Systems Center Configuration Manager 2007 (Configuration Manager 2007)**   The preferred method for distributing software and updates in large, enterprise networks, Configuration Manager 2007 provides highly customizable, centralized control over update deployment, with the ability to audit and inventory client systems. Configuration Manager 2007 typically requires several infrastructure servers.

The sections that follow describe the Windows Update client, WSUS, and Configuration Manager 2007.

Windows Update Client

Whether you download updates from Microsoft or use WSUS, the Windows Update client is responsible for downloading and installing updates on computers running Windows 7 and Windows Vista. The Windows Update client replaces the Automatic Updates client available in earlier versions of Windows. Both Windows Update in Windows 7 and Automatic Updates in earlier versions of Windows operate the same way: they download and install updates from Microsoft or an internal WSUS server. Both clients install updates at a scheduled time and automatically restart the computer if necessary. If the computer is turned off at that time, the updates can be installed as soon as the computer is turned on. Alternatively, Windows Update can wake a computer from sleep and install the updates at the specified time if the computer hardware supports it.

The Windows Update client provides for a great deal of control over its behavior. You can configure individual computers by using the Control Panel\System And Security\Windows Update\Change Settings page, as described in the section entitled "How to Configure Windows Update Using Graphical Tools" later in this chapter. Networks that use Active Directory Domain Services (AD DS) can specify the configuration of each Windows Update client by using Group Policy, as described in the section entitled "How to Configure Windows Update Using Group Policy Settings," later in this chapter.

After the Windows Update client downloads updates, the client checks the digital signature and the Secure Hash Algorithm (SHA1) hash on the updates to verify that they have not been modified after they were signed by Microsoft. This helps mitigate the risk of an attacker either creating malware that impersonates an update or modifying an update to add malicious code.

Windows Server Update Services

WSUS is a version of the Microsoft Update service that you can host on your private network. WSUS connects to the Microsoft Update site, downloads information about available updates, and adds them to a list of updates that require administrative approval.

After an administrator approves and prioritizes these updates, WSUS automatically makes them available to any computer running Windows Update (or the Automatic Updates client on earlier versions of Windows). Windows Update (when properly configured) then checks the WSUS server and automatically downloads and installs updates as configured by the administrators. As shown in Figure 7-1, you can distribute WSUS across multiple servers and locations to scale to enterprise needs. WSUS meets the needs of medium-size organizations and many enterprises.

You must install WSUS on at least one infrastructure server, such as a computer running Windows Server 2003, Windows Server 2008, or Windows Server 2008 R2. To deploy updates to computers running Windows 7, you must have WSUS 3.0 SP2 or later installed on your server.

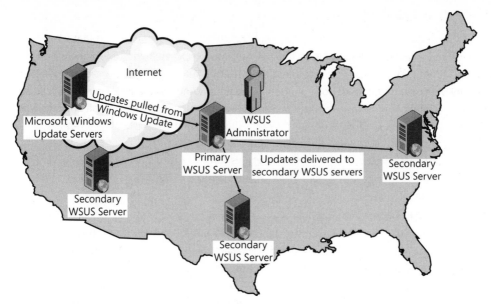

Internet

Updates pulled from Windows Update

Microsoft Windows Update Servers

WSUS Administrator

Primary WSUS Server

Updates delivered to secondary WSUS servers

Secondary WSUS Server

Secondary WSUS Server

Secondary WSUS Server

FIGURE 7-1 WSUS can scale to support thousands of computers.

MORE INFO WSUS

For more information about update management with WSUS, visit *http://www.microsoft .com/wsus/*.

Configuration Manager 2007

Configuration Manager 2007 is a tool for efficiently managing, distributing, and inventorying software in enterprise environments. Although WSUS is sufficient to meet the needs of medium-size organizations, Configuration Manager 2007 can supplement WSUS in enterprise organizations that manage hundreds or thousands of computers.

EXAM TIP

You definitely won't need to know how to use Configuration Manager 2007 for the exam, but it wouldn't hurt to be familiar with what it can do. For more information about Configuration Manager 2007, visit the Configuration Manager 2007 Web site at *http://www.microsoft.com/sccm*.

How to Check Update Compatibility

Microsoft performs some level of compatibility testing for all updates. *Critical updates* (small updates that fix a single problem) receive the least amount of testing because they occur in large numbers and they must be deployed quickly. *Service packs* (large updates that fix many problems previously fixed by different critical updates) receive much more testing because they are released infrequently.

Whether you are planning to deploy critical updates or a service pack, you can reduce the chance of application incompatibility by testing the updates in a lab environment. Most enterprises have a *Quality Assurance (QA)* department that maintains test computers in a lab environment with standard configurations and applications. Before approving an update for deployment in the organization, QA installs the update on the test computers and verifies that critical applications function with the update installed.

Whether you have the resources to test updates before deploying them, you should install updates on pilot groups of computers before installing the updates throughout your organization. A *pilot group* is a small subset of the computers in your organization that receive an update before wider deployment. Ideally, pilot groups are located in an office with strong IT support and have technology-savvy users. If an update causes an application compatibility problem, the pilot group is likely to discover the incompatibility before it affects more users.

If you are using WSUS to deploy updates, you can configure a pilot group by creating a computer group named Pilot and adding computers to the Pilot group. Then, approve updates for the Pilot group before you approve them for the rest of your organization.

EXAM TIP

This exam focuses on Windows 7, and WSUS runs only on server versions of Windows. Therefore, the exam will probably not require you to know exactly how to deploy updates with WSUS. For that reason, this lesson discusses WSUS only at a high level.

Practice 2, at the end of this lesson, walks you through the process of installing WSUS on a computer running Windows Server 2008 R2, synchronizing updates from Microsoft, and then approving updates. Practice 2 should give you sufficient experience with WSUS to pass this exam; however, after completing the practice, you should add to your real-world experience with WSUS by examining every aspect of the software, including creating a pilot group of computers.

If users experience problems that you think might be related to an update, you can use Reliability Monitor to help identify updates that might be related to the cause of the problem. For information about how to use Reliability Monitor, refer to Chapter 1, "Troubleshooting Hardware Failures."

How to Install Updates

Ideally, you would deploy new computers with all current updates already installed. After deployment, you can install updates manually, but you'll be much more efficient if you choose an automatic deployment technique. For situations that require complete control over update installation but still must be automated, you can script update installations.

The sections that follow describe how to apply updates to new computers, how to install updates manually, how to install updates automatically, and how to script update installations.

How to Apply Updates to New Computers

When you deploy new computers, you should deploy them with as many recent updates as possible. Even though Windows 7 immediately checks for updates the first time it starts (rather than waiting for the scheduled automatic update time), it might take hours for Windows to download and install all updates. Applying updates to new computers provides improved security for the computer the first time it starts, reducing the risk that a patched vulnerability will be exploited before updates can be applied.

You can use the following techniques, in order of most secure to least secure, to apply updates to new computers:

- **Integrate updates into Windows 7 setup files**   If you use an automatic deployment technology such as the Microsoft Deployment Toolkit (MDT) 2010, you can ensure that updates are present during setup by installing Windows 7 and all updates on a lab computer and then using Windows PE and the XImage tool to create an operating system image (a .wim file) that you can deploy to new computers.

> **MORE INFO**   **MDT 2010**
>
> For more information about MDT, visit *http://www.microsoft.com/mdt*.

- **Install updates automatically during setup**   Using scripting, you can install updates automatically during setup. Ideally, you would distribute the update files with your Windows 7 installation media or on the distribution server. You can use MDT to configure updates for installation during setup, or you can configure updates manually using one of the following techniques:

  - Use the Windows System Image Manager to add a RunSynchronous command to an answer file in your Windows 7 image. RunSynchronous commands are available in the *<platform>*-Microsoft-Windows-Setup, *<platform>*-Microsoft-Windows-Deployment, and the *<platform>*-Microsoft-Windows-Shell-Setup features. For detailed instructions, read "Add a Custom Command to an Answer File," at *http://technet.microsoft.com/library/dd799295.aspx*. For information about how to install updates from a script, read "How to Script Updates" later in this lesson.

  - Edit the %windir%\Setup\Scripts\SetupComplete.cmd file in your Windows 7 image. Windows 7 runs any commands in this file after Windows Setup completes. Commands in the SetupComplete.cmd file are executed with local system privilege and actions are logged to the SetupAct.log file. You cannot reboot the system and resume running SetupComplete.cmd; therefore, you must install all updates in a single pass.

- Add the update package to the distribution share or answer file. For more information, read "Add Applications, Drivers, Packages, Files, and Folders," at *http://technet.microsoft.com/library/dd744568.aspx*.

- **Install updates manually using removable media** One of the best ways to minimize the risk of a new computer being attacked before it installs updates is to deploy computers while disconnected from the network, using removable media. If you choose this approach, you should also use removable media to install updates before connecting the computer to unprotected networks.

- **Use WSUS to apply updates to new computers** After Windows 7 starts the first time, it immediately attempts to download updates (rather than waiting for the scheduled Windows Update time). Therefore, even with the default settings, the time new computers spend without updates is minimized. To further minimize this, ask your WSUS administrators to configure the most critical updates with a deadline. The deadline forces new computers downloading the updates to install the critical updates and then immediately restart to apply them.

How to Install Updates Manually

With previous versions of Microsoft Windows, you could apply updates manually by visiting the *http://windowsupdate.com* Web site. In Windows 7, you must follow these steps:

1. Click Start, click All Programs, and then click Windows Update.

2. The Windows Update window appears. Click the Check For Updates link.

3. If any updates are available, click Install Updates, as shown in Figure 7-2. To install optional updates, click View Available Updates.

FIGURE 7-2 Using the Windows Update tool to check for updates

If an update does not appear on the list, it might have been hidden. To fix this, click the Restore Hidden Updates link in the Windows Update window.

4. Windows Updates downloads and installs the available updates.

5. If required, restart the computer by clicking Restart Now.

If you choose not to restart the computer immediately, Windows Update regularly prompts the user to restart. The user can postpone the update prompt for up to four hours. Administrative credentials are not required to install updates.

How to Install Updates Automatically

You can configure automatic updates by using either graphical, interactive tools or by using Group Policy. The sections that follow describe each of these techniques.

HOW TO CONFIGURE WINDOWS UPDATE USING GRAPHICAL TOOLS

During an interactive setup, Windows 7 prompts users to choose update settings. Setup recommends enabling automatic updates. To configure automatic updates on a computer manually, follow these steps (which require administrative privileges):

1. Click Start, and then click Control Panel.

2. Click the System And Security link.

3. Under Windows Update, click the Turn Automatic Updating On Or Off link.

4. Adjust the settings, including whether updates are installed automatically and the time they are installed, and then click OK.

HOW TO CONFIGURE WINDOWS UPDATE USING GROUP POLICY SETTINGS

You can configure Windows Update client settings using local or domain Group Policy settings. This is useful for the following tasks:

- Configuring computers to use a local WSUS server
- Configuring automatic installation of updates at a specific time of day
- Configuring how often to check for updates
- Configuring update notifications, including whether non-administrators receive update notifications
- Configure client computers as part of a WSUS target group, which you can use to deploy different updates to different groups of computers

Windows Update settings are located at Computer Configuration\Administrative Templates\Windows Components\Windows Update. The most useful Windows Update Group Policy settings are as follows:

- **Configure Automatic Updates** Specifies whether client computers will receive security updates and other important downloads through the Windows Update service. You also use this setting to configure whether the updates are installed automatically and what time of day the installation occurs.

- **Specify Intranet Microsoft Update Service Location** Specifies the location of your WSUS server.

- **Automatic Updates Detection Frequency** Specifies how frequently the Windows Update client checks for new updates. By default, this is a random time between 17 and 22 hours.

- **Allow Non-Administrators To Receive Update Notifications** Determines whether all users or only administrators will receive update notifications, as shown in Figure 7-3. Non-administrators can install updates using the Windows Update client.

FIGURE 7-3 Users are notified of available updates with a notification bubble.

- **Allow Automatic Updates Immediate Installation** Specifies whether Windows Update will install updates immediately that don't require the computer to be restarted.

- **Turn On Recommended Updates Via Automatic Updates** Determines whether client computers install both critical and recommended updates, which might include updated drivers.

- **No Auto-Restart With Logged On Users For Scheduled Automatic Updates Installations** Specifies that to complete a scheduled installation, Windows Update will wait for the computer to be restarted by any user who is logged on instead of causing the computer to restart automatically.

- **Re-Prompt For Restart With Scheduled Installations** Specifies how often the Windows Update client prompts the user to restart. Depending on other configuration settings, users might have the option of delaying a scheduled restart. However, the Windows Update client will remind them automatically to restart based on the frequency configured in this setting.

- **Delay Restart For Scheduled Installations** Specifies how long the Windows Update client waits before automatically restarting.

- **Reschedule Automatic Updates Scheduled Installations** Specifies the amount of time for Windows Update to wait, following system startup, before continuing with a scheduled installation that was missed previously. If you don't specify this amount of time, a missed scheduled installation will occur one minute after the computer is next started.

- **Enable Client-Side Targeting** Specifies which group the computer is a member of.

- **Enabling Windows Update Power Management To Automatically Wake Up The System To Install Scheduled Updates** If people in your organization tend to shut down their computers when they leave the office, enable this setting to configure computers with supported hardware to start up automatically and install an update at the scheduled time. Computers will not wake up unless there is an update to be installed. If the computer is on battery power, the computer will return to Sleep automatically after two minutes.

In addition, the following two settings are available at the same location under User Configuration (which you can use to specify per-user settings) in addition to Computer Configuration:

- **Do Not Display 'Install Updates And Shut Down' Option In Shut Down Windows Dialog Box**   Specifies whether Windows shows the Install Updates And Shut Down option.

- **Do Not Adjust Default Option To 'Install Updates And Shut Down' In Shut Down Windows Dialog Box**   Specifies whether Windows automatically changes the default shutdown option to Install Updates And Shut Down when Windows Update is waiting to install an update.

Finally, one user setting is available only at User Configuration\Administrative Templates\ Windows Components\Windows Update:

- **Remove Access To Use All Windows Update Features**   When enabled, this setting prevents the user from accessing the Windows Update interface.

How to Script Updates

Windows 7 opens MSU files with the Windows Update Standalone Installer (Wusa.exe). To install an update from a script, run the script with administrative privileges, call Wusa and provide the path to the MSU file. For example, you can install an update named Windows6.0-KB929761-x86.msu in the current directory by running the following command:

```
wusa Windows6.0-KB929761-x86.msu
```

In addition, Wusa supports the following standard command-line options:

- **/?, /h, or /help**   Displays the command-line options.

- **/uninstall**   Removes the specified package. Add the */kb* option to specify the package to be removed using the Knowledge Base (KB) number.

- **/quiet**   Quiet mode. This is the same as unattended mode, but no status or error messages are displayed. Use quiet mode when installing an update as part of a script.

- **/norestart**   When combined with */quiet*, does not restart when installation has completed. Use this parameter when installing multiple updates simultaneously. All but the last update installed should have the */norestart* parameter.

- **/warnrestart**   When combined with */quiet*, the installer warns the user before restarting the computer.

- **/promptrestart**   When combined with */quiet*, the installer prompts the user to confirm that the computer can be restarted.

- **/forcerestart**   When combined with */quiet*, the installer closes all applications and restarts the computer.

Scripting is not usually the best way to install updates on an ongoing basis. Instead, you should use Windows Update, WSUS, or Systems Management Server (SMS). However, you might create a script to install updates on new computers or to install updates on computers that cannot participate in your standard update distribution method.

How to Verify Updates

Microsoft typically releases updates once per month. If a computer does not receive updates, or the updates fail to install correctly, the computer might be vulnerable to security exploits that it would be protected from if the updates were installed. Therefore, it's critical to the security of your client computers that you verify updates are regularly installed.

You can view the update history to verify that an individual computer has updates installed. To view the update history, follow these steps:

1. Click Start, click All Programs, and then click Windows Update.

2. The Windows Update window appears. Click the View Update History link.

3. The View Update History window appears, as shown in Figure 7-4. To view the details of an update, double-click it.

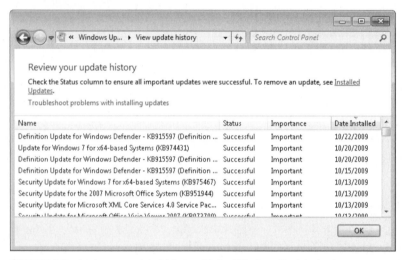

FIGURE 7-4 Reviewing an update history with the Windows Update tool

You can use WSUS or Configuration Manager 2007 to monitor update installation throughout the computers that you manage in your organization. To audit computers on a network-by-network basis (including computers that are not members of your AD DS, but that you do have administrative credentials to), you can use the Microsoft Baseline Security Analyzer (MBSA). As shown in Figure 7-5, MBSA scans a network to find computers running Windows, connects to them, and checks the current update level.

> **MORE INFO**   **MBSA**
>
> For more information about MBSA and to download the free tool, visit *http://www.microsoft .com/mbsa/*.

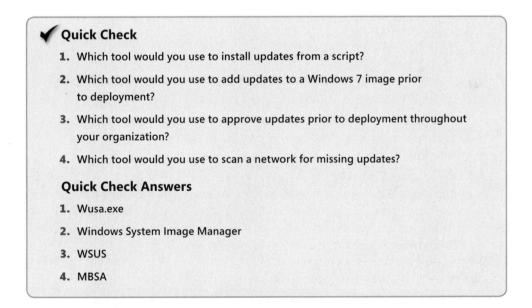

FIGURE 7-5 Preparing to scan a network with MBSA

✔ **Quick Check**

1. Which tool would you use to install updates from a script?

2. Which tool would you use to add updates to a Windows 7 image prior
   to deployment?

3. Which tool would you use to approve updates prior to deployment throughout
   your organization?

4. Which tool would you use to scan a network for missing updates?

Quick Check Answers

1. Wusa.exe

2. Windows System Image Manager

3. WSUS

4. MBSA

How to Troubleshoot Problems Installing Updates

Occasionally, you might experience a problem installing an update. Fortunately, Windows 7 provides detailed information about update installations. The sections that follow describe how to troubleshoot problems with Windows Update and Restart Manager.

How to Troubleshoot Windows Update

To identify the source of the problem causing an update to fail, follow these steps:

1. Examine recent entries in the %Windir%\WindowsUpdate.log file to verify that the client is contacting the correct update server and to identify any error messages. The following example shows a portion of the log file in which Windows Update downloaded Windows Defender information directly from Microsoft:

```
===========  Logging initialized (build: 7.3.7600.16385, tz: -0400)  ===========
Process: c:\program files\windows defender\MpCmdRun.exe
Module: C:\Windows\system32\wuapi.dll
-------------
-- START --  COMAPI: Search [ClientId = Windows Defender]
---------
<<-- SUBMITTED -- COMAPI: Search [ClientId = Windows Defender]
*************
** START **  Agent: Finding updates [CallerId = Windows Defender]
*********
  * Online = Yes; Ignore download priority = No
  * Criteria = "(IsInstalled = 0 and IsHidden = 0 and CategoryIDs contains
'8c3fcc84-7410-4a95-8b89-a166a0190486' and CategoryIDs contains 'e0789628-ce08-
4437-be74-2495b842f43b')"
  * ServiceID = {00000000-0000-0000-0000-000000000000} Third party service
  * Search Scope = {Machine}
Validating signature for C:\Windows\SoftwareDistribution\WuRedir\\muv4wuredir.cab:
Microsoft signed: Yes
```

   The WindowsUpdate.log file will also detail update errors that occur. For detailed information about how to read the WindowsUpdate.log file, refer to Microsoft Knowledge Base article 902093 at *http://support.microsoft.com/kb/902093/*.

2. If your organization uses WSUS, verify that the client can connect to the WSUS server by opening a Web browser and visiting *http://<WSUSServerName>/iuident.cab*. If you are prompted to download the file, this means that the client can reach the WSUS server and it is not a connectivity issue. Otherwise, you could have a name resolution or connectivity issue or WSUS is not configured correctly.

> **MORE INFO**   **TROUBLESHOOTING WSUS**
>
> For more information about troubleshooting WSUS from the WSUS client, read "Automatic Updates Must be Updated," at *http://technet.microsoft.com/library/cc708554.aspx*.

3. If you use Group Policy to configure the Windows Update client, use the Resultant Set of Policy (RSOP) tool (Rsop.msc) to verify the configuration. Within RSOP, browse to the Computer Configuration\Administrative Templates\Windows Components\Windows Update node and verify the configuration settings.

If you have identified a problem and made a configuration change that you hope will resolve it, restart the Windows Update service on the client computer to make the change take effect and begin another update cycle. You can do this using the Services console or by running the following command with administrative credentials:

```
net stop wuauserv | net start wuauserv
```

Within 6 to 10 minutes, Windows Update will attempt to contact your update server.

How to Troubleshoot Restart Manager

The need to update a file that is already in use is one of the most common reasons a user is required to restart a computer. *Restart Manager,* a feature of Windows Installer, strives to reduce this requirement by closing and restarting programs and services that have files in use. To diagnose a problem with Restart Manager, open Event Viewer and view the following event logs:

- Windows Logs\Application
- Applications and Services Logs\Microsoft\Windows\RestartManager\Operational

Search for Warning or Error events with a source of RestartManager. The following is an example of a Warning event with Event ID 10010:

```
Application 'C:\Program Files\Microsoft Office\OFFICE11\OUTLOOK.EXE' (pid 5592) cannot
be restarted - Application SID does not match Conductor SID.
```

You can also view general Windows Update events in the Application log by searching for events with a source of MsiInstaller.

How to Remove Updates

Occasionally, an update might cause compatibility problems. If you experience problems with an application or Windows feature after installing updates and one of the updates was directly related to the problem you are experiencing, you can uninstall the update manually to determine whether it is related to the problem.

To remove an update manually, follow these steps:

1. Click Start and then click Control Panel.
2. Under Programs, click the Uninstall A Program link.
3. Click the View Installed Updates link.
4. Select the update you want to remove. Then, click Uninstall, as shown in Figure 7-6.

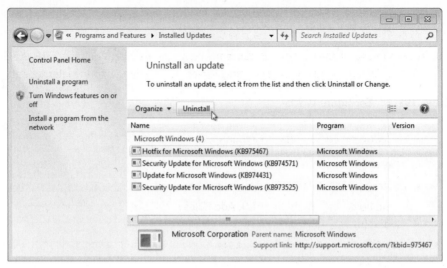

FIGURE 7-6 Uninstalling an update to determine whether it is the source of a problem

5. Follow the prompts that appear and restart the computer if required.

You can also remove an update using the Wusa.exe tool, as described in the section entitled "How to Script Updates," earlier in this chapter. If removing the update does not resolve the problem, you should reapply the update. If removing the update does solve the problem, inform the application developer (in the case of a program incompatibility) or your Microsoft support representative of the incompatibility. The update probably fixes a different problem, so you should make every effort to fix the compatibility problem and install the update.

PRACTICE Distribute Updates

In this practice, you configure a client running Windows 7 to download updates from a WSUS server.

EXERCISE 1 Check Current Update Level

In this exercise, you check the update level on your computer running Windows 7. If you have not installed any updates on the computer running Windows 7, skip to Exercise 2.

1. Log on to a computer running Windows 7 as an administrator.
2. Click Start and then click Control Panel.
3. Under Programs, click Uninstall A Program.
4. On the Programs And Features page, click View Installed Updates.
5. Right-click one of the updates and then click Uninstall. Click Yes when prompted. If prompted, restart the computer.

   Uninstalling this update allows you to reinstall it later using WSUS.

6. Click System And Security and then click Windows Update.

7. Click Check For Updates. At least one update should be available.

8. Click View Available Updates. Because the computer running Windows 7 has the default setting, Windows Update is contacting Microsoft directly to find the latest updates.

EXERCISE 2   Configure WSUS

In this exercise, you install WSUS on a server, approve updates, and then configure a client running Windows 7 to retrieve updates from that server.

1. Log on to a computer running Windows Server 2008 R2 as an administrator.

2. Click Start, click Administrative Tools, and then click Server Manager.

3. Click the Roles node, and then click Add Roles in the Details pane. The Add Roles Wizard appears.

4. On the Before You Begin page, click Next.

5. On the Select Server Roles page, select the Windows Server Update Services role. When prompted, add any required role services. Click Next four times, and then click Install.

6. When the Windows Server Update Services Setup Wizard appears (it might be behind the Add Roles Wizard), click Next.

> **NOTE   WSUS VERSION**
>
> When you add the WSUS server role, Windows Server 2008 R2 downloads the latest version directly from Microsoft. As of the time of this writing, the current version of WSUS is WSUS version 3.0 with Service Pack 2. If Microsoft has updated WSUS to a newer version, the steps required to install WSUS will vary. You probably can accept the default settings, but you should choose not to store updates locally.

7. On the License Agreement page, read the license agreement. Then, click I Accept The Terms Of The License Agreement, and click Next.

8. On the Required Components To Use Administration UI page, click Next.

9. On the Select Update Source page, clear the Store Updates Locally check box to prevent the WSUS server from copying updates locally. In a production environment, you would leave this check box selected so that clients could download updates from your WSUS (across your local area network) instead of directly from Microsoft (using your Internet connection). Click Next.

10. On the Database Options page, click Next.

11. If the Connecting To SQL Server Instance page appears, click Next.

12. On the Web Site Selection page, click Next to use the default IIS Web site. In a production environment, you would create a new WSUS Web site if the WSUS server hosted other Web sites.

13. On the Ready To Install page, click Next.

14. On the Completing The WSUS Setup Wizard page, click Finish.

15. On the Installation Results page, click Close. Restart your computer if prompted.

Next, you configure WSUS to install updates only after you approve them. To do so, perform these steps:

1. The Windows Server Update Services Configuration Wizard might have opened automatically. If it did not, click Start, click Administrative Tools, and then click Windows Server Update Services.

2. On the Before You Begin page, click Next.

3. On the Join The Microsoft Update Improvement Program page, click Next.

4. On the Choose Upstream Server page, click Next.

5. On the Specify Proxy Server page, click Next.

6. On the Connect To Upstream Server page, click Start Connecting. Wait while the WSUS Configuration Wizard downloads information from Microsoft Update. When the Next button is available, click it.

7. On the Choose Products page, notice that only Office and Windows updates are downloaded by default. Browse through the other update types that are available so that you become familiar with them, and then accept these default settings by clicking Next.

8. On the Choose Classifications page, select the All Classifications check box. Click Next.

9. On the Set Sync Schedule page, click Next.

10. On the Finish page, click Next.

11. On the What's Next page, make note of other WSUS configuration steps. Click Finish.

> **NOTE** **WSUS CONFIGURATION IN THE REAL WORLD**
>
> Because this exam focuses on the client running Windows 7 and not the WSUS server, this exercise does not go through all these configuration steps. However, in a production environment, WSUS would require additional configuration.

12. Next, you need to configure AD DS Group Policy settings so that domain members synchronize with the WSUS server. On the computer running Windows Server 2008 R2, click Start, click Administrative Tools, and then click Group Policy Management.

13. In the Group Policy Management console, select the Group Policy Management\ Forest\Domains\nwtraders.msft\Default Domain Policy node. Right-click Default Domain Policy, and then click Edit.

14. In the Group Policy Management Editor, select the Computer Configuration\Policies\ Administrative Templates\Windows Components\Windows Update node.

15. Double-click the Specify Intranet Microsoft Update Service Location setting. Click Enabled. In the Set The Intranet Update Service For Detecting updates box, type **http://** and the name of your computer running Windows Server 2008 R2 (such as **http://DC1**). This configures clients to which the Group Policy Object (GPO) is applied to contact the WSUS server instead of Microsoft Update. Click OK.

16. In the Group Policy Management Editor, double-click the Configure Automatic Updates policy. Click Enabled. In the Configure Automatic Updating list, examine the different possible settings. Select 3 – Auto Download And Notify For Install. Accept the default settings by clicking OK.

17. Double-click the Turn On Recommended Updates Via Automatic Updates policy. Click Enabled. This enables Windows Update to install both recommended updates, which include driver updates and new Windows features, and important updates. Click OK.

18. Open the Windows Server Update Services console from the Administrative Tools folder on the Start menu.

19. In the Update Services console, if your server does not appear in the Update Services list, click the Connect To Server link in the Actions pane, type the server name, and then click Connect.

20. Select the Update Services\<*server_name*>\Computers\Synchronizations node. If a synchronization is currently running, select it. Wait until the synchronization completes.

21. Select the Update Services\<*server_name*>\Updates\All Updates node. In the Approval, select Unapproved. In the Status list, select Failed Or Needed. Then, click Refresh, and wait several minutes for the Update Services console to display the list of unapproved updates.

22. Right-click any updates that appear, and then click Approve. To select all updates, press Ctrl+A. If no updates appear, verify that your computer running Windows 7 appears when you select the Computers\All Computers node. If you still see no updates, verify that the WSUS server has downloaded available updates from Microsoft. If updates have been synchronized, you might need to wait until Windows Update on the client notifies the WSUS server of its current status.

23. In the Approve Updates dialog box, select the All Computers list and then click Approved For Install, as shown in Figure 7-7. Then, click OK.

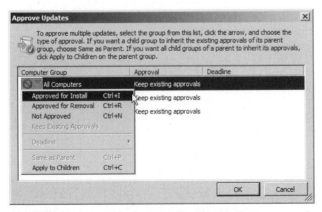

FIGURE 7-7 You can approve updates for all computers

24. If prompted, review the license terms and click I Accept as many times as necessary.

25. In the Approval Progress dialog box, click Close.

EXERCISE 3   Retrieve Updates from Windows Server Update Services

In this exercise, you check for updates on your client computer running Windows 7.

1. Log on to your computer running Windows 7.

2. Wait a few minutes for Windows 7 to display a notification bubble informing the user of the presence of updates. Click the bubble.

3. In the Windows Update window, click Install Updates. Follow the prompts that appear to complete the update installation, and restart the computer if required.

EXERCISE 4   Remove an Update

In this exercise, you remove an update from your client computer running Windows 7. In the real world, you might do this if an update caused application compatibility problems.

1. Log on to your computer running Windows 7.

2. Click Start and then click Control Panel.

3. Under Programs, click Uninstall A Program.

4. Click View Installed Updates.

5. Click one of the updates you installed in Exercise 3. Then, click Uninstall.

Lesson Summary

- Microsoft provides three techniques for distributing updates: the Windows Update client (built into Windows 7), WSUS (a free tool that can be installed on a computer running Windows Server 2008 R2), and Configuration Manager 2007 (an enterprise software distribution tool). These tools are designed for small, medium-size, and large organizations, respectively.

- You should test updates with critical applications before deploying them to large numbers of computers. To minimize the risk of application incompatibility further, deploy updates to a pilot group first. Members of the pilot group are likely to notice compatibility problems and notify IT before the update is distributed to the entire organization.

- You can verify that an update is installed on a single computer by viewing the update history. If you use WSUS in your organization, you can view the reports that WSUS provides to identify which computers have installed an update. If you need to audit computers on a network (regardless of whether they use WSUS), you can use the free MBSA tool.

- You can install updates interactively using the Windows Update tool in Control Panel. This would be very time-consuming, however. Instead, you should configure Windows Update either using graphical tools or by using Group Policy settings. If you need to install updates immediately (for example, as soon as a user logs on), you can create scripts that install updates.

- If you have a problem installing an update, you can diagnose the problem by viewing the Windows Update history, by analyzing the %Windir%\WindowsUpdate.log file, or by examining WSUS logs. You often can resolve simple problems by restarting the Windows Update service.

- If you discover a compatibility problem after deploying an update, you can remove it manually or use WSUS to uninstall it.

Lesson Review

You can use the following questions to test your knowledge of the information in Lesson 1, "Updating Software." The questions are also available on the companion CD if you prefer to review them in electronic form.

> **NOTE ANSWERS**
>
> Answers to these questions and explanations of why each answer choice is correct or incorrect are located in the "Answers" section at the end of the book.

1. Which of the following actions would you recommend for distributing updates to a small business with five client computers running Windows 7?

   A. Instructing employees to start Windows Update manually when they experience problems

   B. Configuring Windows Update on each computer to download updates directly from Microsoft

   C. Installing WSUS and configuring Windows Update to download updates from the WSUS server

   D. Deploying updates using SMS and WSUS

2. You are working for a medium-size organization that manages about 100 client computers. The IT department insists on testing all updates before they are applied to computers. Which of the following actions would you recommend for distributing updates within this organization?

   A. Instructing employees to start Windows Update manually when they experience problems

   B. Configuring Windows Update on each computer to download updates directly from Microsoft

   C. Installing WSUS and configuring Windows Update to download updates from the WSUS server

   D. Deploying updates using SMS and WSUS

3. You are creating a batch file that installs updates when a computer running Windows 7 starts for the first time. How should you do this?

   A. Call Update.exe and provide the path to the update file.

   B. Call Msiexec.exe and provide the path to the update file.

   C. Run the executable file included with the update.

   D. Call Wusa.exe and provide the path to the update file.

Chapter Review

To further practice and reinforce the skills you learned in this chapter, you can perform the following tasks:

- Review the chapter summary.
- Review the list of key terms introduced in this chapter.
- Complete the case scenarios. These scenarios set up real-world situations involving the topics of this chapter and ask you to create a solution.
- Complete the suggested practices.
- Take a practice test.

Chapter Summary

- Small offices that do not need to test updates prior to deployment can configure Windows Update to download and install updates from Microsoft automatically as they become available. If an update causes problems, administrators can then remove the update manually. Larger organizations can use WSUS to test and approve updates prior to deployment. Enterprises that require additional management capabilities can use Configuration Manager 2007 to completely control update management.

- When deploying new computers, you should plan to install updates immediately to prevent the computer from being compromised by a network attack. Fortunately, Microsoft provides a variety of approaches. If computers are on an isolated network and protected from attack, they can download and install updates the conventional way, using Microsoft Update. To reduce deployment time, you can add update packages to a Windows 7 image or script the installation of updates after setup completes.

- Occasionally, Windows might encounter problems installing updates. To give administrators the information they need to identify the cause of the problem, Windows Update records detailed information in the %Windir%\WindowsUpdate.log text log file and in the event log.

Key Terms

Do you know what these key terms mean? You can check your answers by looking up the terms in the glossary at the end of the book.

- **critical update**
- **Microsoft Systems Center Configuration Manager 2007 (Configuration Manager 2007)**

- pilot group
- Quality Assurance (QA)
- Restart Manager
- service pack
- Windows Server Update Services (WSUS)

Case Scenarios

In the following case scenarios, you apply what you've learned about subjects covered in this chapter. You can find answers to these questions in the "Answers" section at the end of this book.

Case Scenario 1: Distribute Updates

You are a systems administrator working at the administrative offices of Fourth Coffee, a small shop with three computers running Windows XP, three computers running Windows 7, and a domain controller running Windows Server 2008 R2. Recently, an update caused a compatibility problem with Fourth Coffee's internal accounting program. Currently, all computers are configured to download updates from Microsoft and automatically install them overnight.

Your manager has asked you to find a way to test updates before they're deployed to the computers in your organization.

Questions

Answer the following questions for your manager:

1. How can you test updates before they're deployed?
2. Would your recommended deployment technology require any infrastructure?
3. Will your recommended deployment technology work with both the computers running Windows XP and the computers running Windows 7?
4. How can you configure the client computers to use your new deployment technology?

Case Scenario 2: Audit Updates

You are a systems administrator for Fabrikam, Inc. Last month, Microsoft released a security update that fixes a vulnerability in Windows 7. Yesterday, an attacker released an exploit for the vulnerability on the Internet. The exploit has already infected tens of thousands of unpatched computers on the Internet.

You deployed the update last week from your WSUS server; however, your manager needs additional assurance that all the computers in your organization are protected.

Questions

Answer the following questions for your manager:

1. What's the quickest way to identify any computers that failed to install the update?

2. Is there a tool we can use to scan the network for computers that might not have the update installed, even if they are configured to download updates directly from Microsoft? What is the tool?

3. If users call and ask, I'd like to tell them how to check their own computer to make sure the update is installed. How can users determine if the update is installed?

Suggested Practices

To help you master the exam objectives presented in this chapter, complete the first four practices. Practice 5 gives you experience with MBSA, which might not be covered on the exam but is a valuable tool for managing computers in the real world. To gain more experience deploying updates with WSUS, complete the last two practices.

Identify and Resolve Software Update Issues

For this task, you should complete all seven practices to gain experience analyzing update installations.

- **Practice 1** Uninstall a recent update and then reinstall it.

- **Practice 2** Examine the System event log and identify any updates that have been installed recently.

- **Practice 3** Examine the %Windir%\WindowsUpdate.log file and identify any updates that have been recently installed.

- **Practice 4** Read the Windows Update Team Blog at *http://blogs.technet.com/mu/* and the WSUS Product Team Blog at *http://blogs.technet.com/wsus/*.

- **Practice 5** Use MBSA to scan the computers in your network for missing updates or other potential security vulnerabilities.

- **Practice 6** Configure all the computers in your lab environment to download updates from your WSUS server. Use Group Policy settings to configure computers to install updates automatically and restart the computer forcibly. Approve several new updates and wait for the updates to install.

- **Practice 7** Configure a second WSUS server to download updates directly from your first WSUS server.

Take a Practice Test

The practice tests on this book's companion CD offer many options. For example, you can test yourself on just one exam objective, or you can test yourself on all the 70-685 certification exam content. You can set up the test so that it closely simulates the experience of taking a certification exam, or you can set it up in study mode so that you can look at the correct answers and explanations after you answer each question.

> **MORE INFO**   **PRACTICE TESTS**
>
> For details about all the practice test options available, see the section entitled "How to Use the Practice Tests," in the Introduction to this book.

CHAPTER 8

Performance

Windows 7 should be the best performing version of Windows ever. However, all computers have limited processor, memory, and disk resources, and any computer will respond slowly under the right circumstances. Because you can't create a completely problem-free IT environment, you must plan to identify and resolve performance problems quickly when they do occur. Windows 7 includes several features that enable administrators to monitor and respond to performance problems.

First, Windows 7 can forward events between computers, enabling you to collect significant events centrally from across your network. With Task Manager, you can monitor performance in real time, adjust priorities and affinities of different processes to control how much processor time they consume, and end processes that are not responding to user input. Performance Monitor provides even more in-depth information about system performance, enabling you to monitor minute details of the operating system, applications, and hardware.

For performance problems that are short-lived, you can create a snapshot of system performance information using a data collector set and then analyze the performance information at your leisure. If you identify the hard disk as a source of your performance problems, you might need to free up some disk space using the Disk Cleanup tool so that Windows 7 can defragment the disk automatically.

Performance for mobile computers is more complex than desktop computers, because they typically have performance settings to optimize battery usage. To troubleshoot performance issues with mobile computers properly, you must understand how to configure the different performance settings. Finally, if a performance problem seems to be caused by a startup service or application, you can use the System Configuration tool to disable different startup services and applications temporarily to allow you to identify the source of the problem.

Exam objective in this chapter:
- Identify and resolve performance issues.

Lessons in this chapter:

Before You Begin

To complete the lessons in this chapter, you should be familiar with Windows 7 and be comfortable with the following tasks:

- Installing Windows 7
- Physically connecting a computer to a network
- Performing basic administration tasks on a Windows Server 2008 R2–based domain controller

 REAL WORLD

Tony Northrup

Recently, I was troubleshooting intermittent performance problems with a Web server. At seemingly random times, the Web server would slow down to the point that users couldn't browse the site. By the time I received a complaint from a user, however, the site would already be back online.

To identify the problem, I ran Performance Monitor in logging mode. This allowed me to discover that, during the 10-minute period when users had problems, total processor utilization increased to 100 percent (when it was normally about 10 percent), and the time required to respond to Web requests went above 30 seconds (when it was normally about 0.02 seconds). While I monitored the performance of each individual process, none of the processes were consuming the extra processor time—meaning that the process wasn't running at the time I configured Performance Monitor. Performance Monitor had helped me identify more symptoms of the problem, but I still hadn't found the specific problem.

I made note of the time at which the problem occurred and checked that time range in Event Viewer. I found Web server errors messages indicating that Web requests had taken too long to process. That wasn't the source of the problem, though; it was just a secondary condition caused by the high processor utilization.

That event was the key to troubleshooting the problem further, however, because it occurred consistently when the problem began. I set up an event trigger to send a message to my phone whenever the event occurred. The next time it occurred, I ran to the Web server console, opened Task Manager, and identified the process that was consuming all the processor time.

The process was a script that cleaned up the database. The way the script was written, it would use 100 percent of the processor time, slowing down the entire server. The Web server automatically started the script after a specific number of database transactions, which explained why it seemed to occur randomly.

To resolve the problem, I changed the way the script was started. Instead of starting the script directly, I called the Start.exe tool, used the */low* parameter to specify that the script run with a lower priority, and used the */affinity* parameter to specify that the script use only one of the four processor cores on the Web server. The script took longer to run, but it no longer interfered with normal Web server activity.

Lesson 1: Forwarding Events

In Microsoft Windows, both the operating system and applications add events to event logs. Most of these events are informational (such as an event indicating that the computer is starting up) and can be safely ignored. However, very important events are often buried within thousands of insignificant events. These important events might indicate an impending hard disk failure, a security compromise, or a user who cannot access critical network resources.

Every computer running Windows has a local event log. Because enterprises often have thousands of computers, each with its own local event log, monitoring significant events was very difficult with earlier versions of Windows. *Event forwarding* in Windows Vista and Windows 7 makes it much easier for enterprises to manage local event logs. With event forwarding, you can configure computers running Windows to forward important events to a central location. You can then more easily monitor and respond to these centralized events.

This lesson describes how to configure and manage event forwarding.

After this lesson, you will be able to:

- Describe how event forwarding works.
- Configure event forwarding in Active Directory Domain Services (AD DS) environments.
- Configure event forwarding in workgroup environments.
- Troubleshoot event forwarding.

Estimated lesson time: 30 minutes

How Event Forwarding Works

Event forwarding uses Hypertext Transfer Protocol (HTTP) or HTTPS (Hypertext Transfer Protocol Secure), the same protocols used to browse Web sites, to send events from a *forwarding computer* (the computer that is generating the events) to a *collecting computer* (the computer that is configured to collect events). With event forwarding, you can send important events from any computer in your organization to your workstation, so that you can monitor the events from a central location.

Even though HTTP is normally unencrypted, event forwarding sends communications encrypted with the Microsoft Negotiate security support provider (SSP) in workgroup environments or the Microsoft Kerberos SSP in domain environments. HTTPS uses a Secure Sockets Layer (SSL) certificate (which you will need to generate) to provide an additional layer of encryption. This additional layer of encryption is unnecessary in most environments.

EXAM TIP

For the exam, remember that event forwarding uses encryption even if you choose the HTTP protocol. That's counterintuitive because when you use HTTP to browse the Web, it's always unencrypted.

How to Configure Event Forwarding in AD DS Domains

To forward events, you must configure both the forwarding and collecting computers. The forwarding computer is the computer that generates the events, and the collecting computer is the management workstation that administrators use to monitor events. The configuration you create for forwarding and collecting events is called an *event subscription*.

Event forwarding is not enabled by default on Windows 7. Before you can use event forwarding, both the forwarding and collecting computer must have two services running:

- Windows Remote Management
- Windows Event Collector

In addition, the forwarding computer must have a Windows Firewall exception for the HTTP protocol. Depending on the event delivery optimization technique you choose, you might also have to configure a Windows Firewall exception for the collecting computer. Fortunately, Windows 7 provides tools that automate the configuration of forwarding and collecting computers.

The sections that follow describe step by step how to configure computers for event forwarding.

How to Configure the Forwarding Computer

To configure a computer running Windows 7 to forward events, follow these steps on the forwarding computer:

1. Open a command prompt with administrative privileges by clicking Start, typing **cmd**, and pressing Ctrl+Shift+Enter.

TIP   **OPENING AN ADMINISTRATIVE COMMAND PROMPT**

You can also open an administrative command prompt by right-clicking the command prompt in the Start menu and clicking Run As Administrator. Pressing Ctrl+Shift+Enter is just a shortcut to make the process quicker (especially for those who prefer to use the keyboard over the mouse).

2. At the command prompt, run the following command (shown in bold) to configure the Windows Remote Management service:

```
C:\>winrm quickconfig
WinRM is not set up to receive requests on this machine.
The following changes must be made:

Set the WinRM service type to delayed auto start.
Start the WinRM service.

Make these changes [y/n]?
```

3. Type **Y**, and then press Enter. The Windows Remote Management service prompts you again:

```
WinRM has been updated to receive requests.

WinRM service type changed successfully.
WinRM service started.
WinRM is not set up to allow remote access to this machine for management.
The following changes must be made:

Create a WinRM listener on HTTP://* to accept WS-Man requests to any IP on this machine.
Enable the WinRM firewall exception.

Make these changes [y/n]?
```

4. Type **Y**, and then press Enter. The Windows Remote Management service prompts you again.

   WinRm (the Windows Remote Management command-line tool) configures the computer to accept WS-Management requests from other computers. This involves making the following changes:

   - Sets the Windows Remote Management (WS-Management) service to Automatic (Delayed Start) and starts the service.
   - Configures a Windows Remote Management HTTP listener. A *listener* is a configuration setting that forwards specific incoming network communications to an application.
   - Creates a Windows Firewall exception to allow incoming connections to the Windows Remote Management service using HTTP on Transmission Control Protocol (TCP) port 80. This exception applies only to the Domain and Private profiles; traffic will still be blocked while the computer is connected to Public networks.

Next, you must add the computer account of the collector computer to the local Event Log Readers group on each of the forwarding computers by following these steps on the forwarding computer:

1. Click Start, right-click Computer, and then click Manage.

2. Under System Tools, expand Local Users And Groups, and then select Groups. Double-click Event Log Readers.

3. In the Event Log Readers Properties dialog box, click Add.

4. In the Select Users, Computers, Service Accounts, Or Groups dialog box, click Object Types. By default, it searches only users, service accounts, and groups. However, we need to add the collecting computer account. Select the Computers check box and clear the Groups, Users, and Service Accounts check boxes. Click OK.

5. In the Select Users, Computers, Or Groups dialog box, type the name of the collecting computer. Then, click OK.

6. Click OK again to close the Event Log Readers Properties dialog box.

Alternatively, you could perform this step from an elevated command prompt or a batch file by running the following command: *net localgroup "Event Log Readers" <computer_name>$@<domain_name> /add*.

For example, to add the computer WIN7 in the nwtraders.msft domain, you would run the following command: *net localgroup "Event Log Readers" win7$@nwtraders.msft /add*.

How to Configure the Collecting Computer

Windows 7 supports two types of event forwarding, which you specify when you create an event subscription:

- **Collector-initiated**   In collector-initiated subscriptions, the collecting computer establishes a connection to the forwarding computer.

- **Source computer–initiated**   In source computer–initiated subscriptions, the forwarding computer establishes a connection to the forwarding computer. Source computer–initiated subscriptions are the only subscription type available in workgroup environments.

If you plan to use collector-initiated subscriptions, Windows 7 prompts you to configure the collecting computer when you create a subscription, as described in the next section. Alternatively, you can preconfigure a collecting computer by performing these steps:

1. Open an elevated command prompt by clicking Start, typing **cmd**, and pressing Ctrl+Shift+Enter.

2. At the command prompt, run the following command to configure the Windows Event Collector service:

   ```
   wecutil qc
   ```

3. When prompted, press Y.

   Windows configures the Windows Event Collector service.

If you plan to use source computer–initiated subscriptions, you need to run *winrm quickconfig* on the collecting computer, as described in the section entitled "How to Configure the Forwarding Computer," earlier in this chapter.

Windows Server 2008 also includes the ability to collect forwarded events. However, versions of Windows released prior to Windows Vista do not support acting as a collecting computer or as a forwarding computer.

How to Create an Event Subscription

Subscriptions, as shown in Figure 8-1, are configured on a collecting computer and retrieve events from forwarding computers.

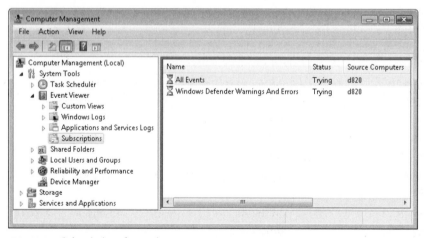

FIGURE 8-1 Subscriptions forward events to a management computer.

To create a subscription on a collecting computer, perform these steps:

1. In the Computer Management console, right-click Event Viewer\Subscriptions, and then click Create Subscription.

2. If prompted, click Yes to configure the Windows Event Collector service, as shown in Figure 8-2.

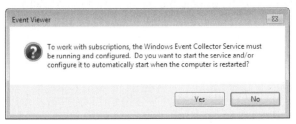

FIGURE 8-2 Pushing events from the forwarding computer to the collecting computer

The Subscription Properties dialog box appears.

3. In the Subscription Name box, type a name for the subscription, and if you want, type a description.

4. If you want, click the Destination Log list and select the log in which you want to store the forwarded events. By default, events are stored in the Forwarded Events log.

5. Select the subscription type, which is either Collector Initiated or Source Computer Initiated. Selecting Collector Initiated causes the collecting computer to contact the forwarding computers, whereas selecting Source Computer Initiated causes the forwarding computers to contact the collecting computer. Then, specify the computers to use as follows:

   - If you selected Collector Initiated, click Select Computers. Click Add Domain Computers. In the Select Computer dialog box, type the name of the computer that will be forwarding events, and then click OK. In the Computers dialog box, click Test. Click OK when Event Viewer verifies connectivity.

   - If you selected Source Computer Initiated, click Select Computer Groups. Click Add Domain Computers or Add Non-Domain Computers. Type the name of the computer that will be forwarding events and click OK. If you added a non-domain computer, click Add Certificates and select a certification authority (CA) to be used to authenticate the source computers. Click OK.

6. Click Select Events and create the query filter. You must specify either a log or a source. Click OK.

7. If you want, click Advanced to open the Advanced Subscription Settings dialog box. You can configure three types of subscriptions:

   - **Normal** This option ensures reliable delivery of events and does not attempt to conserve bandwidth. It is the appropriate choice unless you need tighter control over bandwidth usage or need forwarded events delivered as quickly as possible. It uses *pull delivery mode* (where the collecting computer contacts the forwarding computer) and downloads five events at a time unless 15 minutes pass, in which case it downloads any events that are available.

- **Minimize Bandwidth**   This option reduces the network bandwidth consumed by event delivery and is a good choice if you are using event forwarding across a wide area network or on a large number of computers on a local area network. It uses *push delivery mode* (where the forwarding computer contacts the collecting computer) to forward events every six hours.

- **Minimize Latency**   This option ensures that events are delivered with minimal delay. It is an appropriate choice if you are collecting alerts or critical events. It uses push delivery mode and sets a batch timeout of 30 seconds.

  In addition, you can use this dialog box to specify whether the subscription uses HTTP or HTTPS as the protocol. If you create a collector-initiated subscription, you can use this dialog box to configure the user account that the subscription uses. Whether you use the default Machine Account setting or you specify a user, you need to ensure that the account is a member of the forwarding computer's Event Log Readers group.

8. Click OK to close the Advanced Subscription Settings dialog box.

9. In the Subscription Properties dialog box, click OK.

By default, normal event subscriptions check for new events every 15 minutes. You can decrease this interval to reduce the delay in retrieving events. However, there is no graphical interface for configuring the delay; you must use the command-line Windows Event Collector (Wecutil) tool that you initially used to configure the collecting computer.

To adjust the event subscription delay, first create your subscription using Event Viewer. Then, run the following two commands at an elevated command prompt:

wecutil ss <subscription_name> /cm:custom

wecutil ss <subscription_name> /hi:<milliseconds_delay>

For example, if you created a subscription named Critical Events and you wanted the delay to be 1 minute, you would run the following commands:

wecutil ss "Critical Events" /cm:custom

wecutil ss "Critical Events" /hi:6000

Now, if you open the Subscription Properties dialog box and click Advanced, the Advanced Subscription Settings dialog box shows the Event Delivery Optimization setting as Custom, as shown in Figure 8-3. This option is not selectable using the graphical interface.

If you need to check the interval, run the following command:

wecutil gs <subscription_name>

For example, to verify that the interval for the Critical Events subscription is 1 minute, you run the following command and look for the HeartbeatInterval value:

wecutil gs "Critical Events"

FIGURE 8-3 Configuring a custom Event Delivery Optimization with the Wecutil command-line tool

The Minimize Bandwidth and Minimize Latency options both batch a default number of items at a time. You can determine the value of this default by typing the following command at a command prompt:

winrm get winrm/config

How to Configure Event Forwarding to Use HTTPS

To configure event forwarding to use the encrypted HTTPS protocol, you must perform the following additional tasks on the forwarding computer in addition to those described in the section entitled "How to Configure the Forwarding Computer," earlier in this chapter:

1. Configure the computer with a computer certificate. You can do this automatically in AD DS environments by using an enterprise CA.

2. Create a Windows Firewall exception for TCP port 443.

3. Run the following command at an elevated command prompt: _winrm quickconfig –transport:https_

On the collecting computer, you must modify the subscription properties to use HTTPS rather than HTTP. In addition, the collecting computer must trust the CA that issued the computer certificate—this will happen automatically if the certificate was issued by an enterprise CA and both the forwarding computer and the collecting computer are part of the same AD DS domain.

If you have configured Minimize Bandwidth or Minimize Latency Event Delivery Optimization for the subscription, you must also configure a computer certificate and an HTTPS Windows Firewall exception on the collecting computer.

How to Configure Event Forwarding in Workgroup Environments

Typically, event forwarding is required only in large environments that use AD DS domains. However, you can also configure event forwarding in workgroup environments. The process is very similar to that used in AD DS environments, with the following exceptions:

- You must add a Windows Firewall exception for Remote Event Log Management on each forwarding computer.

- You must add an account with administrator privileges to the Event Log Readers local group on each forwarding computer. You must specify this account in the Configure Advanced Subscription Settings dialog box when creating a subscription on the collector computer.

- On each collecting computer, run the following command to allow the forwarding computers to use NTLM authentication: *winrm set winrm/config/client @{TrustedHosts="<forwarding_computers>"}.*

  Provide a comma-separated list of forwarding computers for the *<forwarding computers>* value in the previous example. Alternatively, you can provide a wildcard, such as msft*.

EXAM TIP

For the exam, remember that you must configure the *TrustedHosts* parameter on the collecting computer, not the forwarding computer. This is counterintuitive and might be hard to remember.

 Quick Check

1. What command would you run to enable a collecting computer to use source computer–initiated subscriptions?

2. What protocols can event forwarding use?

3. Which group on the forwarding computer must the collecting computer be a member of?

How to Troubleshoot Event Forwarding

If event forwarding doesn't seem to function properly, follow these steps to troubleshoot the problem:

1. Verify that you have waited long enough for the event to be forwarded. Forwarding events using the Normal setting can take up to 15 minutes. The delay might be longer if either the forwarding or the collection computer has restarted recently because the Windows Remote Management service is set to start automatically, but with a delay so that it doesn't affect startup performance. The 15-minute counter doesn't start until after the Windows Remote Management service has started.

2. Check the Applications And Services Logs\Microsoft\Windows\Eventlog-ForwardPlugin\ Operational event log and verify that the subscription was created successfully. Event ID 100 indicates a new subscription, whereas Event ID 103 indicates a subscription has been unsubscribed.

3. Check the Security event log to verify that the forwarding and collecting computers are authenticating correctly. If necessary, enable success and failure auditing as described in Chapter 4, "Security."

4. Verify that the subscription is Active. On the collecting computer, browse to Event Viewer\Subscriptions. The subscription status should be Active. If it is not, right-click the subscription and then click Runtime Status. Event Viewer displays the Subscription Runtime Status dialog box with an error code.

5. Verify that the forwarding computer has the Windows Remote Management listener properly configured. From an elevated command prompt, run the following command: *winrm enumerate winrm/config/Listener*.

   If the Windows Remote Management listener isn't configured, there is no output. If the Windows Remote Management listener is configured properly for HTTP, the output resembles the following:

```
Listener
    Address = *
    Transport = HTTP
    Port = 80
    Hostname
    Enabled = true
    URLPrefix = wsman
    CertificateThumbprint
    ListeningOn = 127.0.0.1, 192.168.1.214, ::1, fe80::100:7f:ffe%9,
                  fe80::5efe:192.168.1.214%10
```

If the Windows Remote Management listener is configured properly for HTTPS, the output resembles the following (note that the host name must match the name the event collector uses to identify the computer):

```
Listener
    Address = *
    Transport = HTTPS
    Port = 443
    Hostname = win7.nwtraders.msft
    Enabled = true
    URLPrefix = wsman
    CertificateThumbprint = 52 31 db a8 45 50 1f 29 d9 3e 16 f0 da 82 ae
                            94 18 8f 61 5e
    ListeningOn = 127.0.0.1, 192.168.1.214, ::1, fe80::100:7f:ffe%9,
                  fe80::5efe:192.168.1.214%10
```

6. Verify that the collecting computer can connect to Windows Remote Management on the forwarding computer. From an elevated command prompt on the collecting computer, run the following command: *winrm id –remote:<computer_name>.<domain_name>*.

    For example, if the forwarding computer is named win7.nwtraders.msft, you would run the following command: *winrm id –remote:win7.nwtraders.msft*.

    The result would be as follows:

```
IdentifyResponse
    ProtocolVersion = http://schemas.dmtf.org/wbem/wsman/1/wsman.xsd
    ProductVender = Microsoft Corporation
    ProductVersion = OS: 6.0.6000 SP: 0.0 Stack: 1.0
```

    If you receive the message "WS-Management could not connect to the specified destination," verify that the Windows Remote Management service is started on the forwarding computer and that no firewall is blocking connections between the two computers.

7. Verify that the user account you configured the subscription to use has privileges on the forwarding computer. If necessary, enable failure security auditing on the remote computer as described in Chapter 4, wait for events to be forwarded, and then examine the Security event log for logon failures. In addition, you can configure the subscription temporarily to use a Domain Admin account—if the subscription works with the Domain Admin account, the source of your problem is definitely related to authentication. Troubleshoot the authentication problem and reconfigure the subscription to use the original user account.

8. If the subscription is configured to use Machine Account authentication, verify that the collecting computer's account is a member of the forwarding computer's Event Log Readers local group. If the subscription is configured to use a different user account, that account must be in the forwarding computer's Event Log Readers local group.

9. Verify that the following services are started on the forwarding computer:
   - Windows Remote Management (WS-Management)
   - Windows Event Collector

10. Verify that the Windows Event Collector service is started on the collecting computer.

11. Verify Windows Firewall settings on the forwarding computer as follows:
   - Verify that the Windows Remote Management (HTTP-In) firewall exception is enabled.
   - If you are using HTTPS instead of HTTP, verify that you have created and enabled a custom firewall exception for TCP port 443.
   - Verify that the forwarding computer and the collecting computer are both connected to Private or Domain networks, rather than to Public networks. To verify the network profile, right-click the network icon in the system tray and then click Open Network And Sharing Center. In the Network And Sharing Center, the profile type appears after the network name. If it shows Public Network, click Customize and change the profile type to Work Network, which uses the private network profile.

12. In addition to the forwarding computer, verify that the Windows Remote Management (HTTP-In) firewall exception is enabled on the collecting computer.

13. Verify that a network firewall is not blocking traffic by testing connectivity. Because the forwarding computer must have HTTP (and possibly HTTPS) available, you can attempt to connect to it from the collecting computer by using Windows Internet Explorer—simply type **http://computername** (or **https://computername** if you are using HTTPS) in the Address bar. If the firewall on the forwarding computer is configured correctly, you receive an HTTP 404 error and Internet Explorer displays the message, "The webpage cannot be found." If Internet Explorer displays the message, "Internet Explorer cannot display the webpage," the firewall exception on the forwarding computer has not been enabled.

14. Verify that the event query is valid by performing these steps:
   a. View the subscription properties, and click Select Events.
   b. Select the XML tab, select the contents of the query, and press Ctrl+C to copy it to the Clipboard.
   c. Open a second instance of Event Viewer. Right-click Event Viewer, and then click Connect To Another Computer. Select the forwarding computer, and then click OK.
   d. Right-click Custom Views, and then click Create Custom View.
   e. In the Create Custom View dialog box, select the XML tab. Select the Edit Query Manually check box, and click Yes when prompted.
   f. Click the query box and press Ctrl+V to paste the query. Then click OK.
   g. The new custom view appears and shows the matching events. If any events have appeared since you created the event forwarder, they should have been forwarded. If there are no new events, the problem is with your forwarding criteria. Try creating a custom view that matches the events that you want to forward and then importing that into a new subscription.

In this practice, you configure event forwarding between two computers using the default settings.

EXERCISE 1 Configuring a Computer to Collect Events

In this exercise, you configure a computer to collect events.

1. Log on to the computer running Windows 7 that you want to use to collect events using a domain account with administrative privileges.

2. Open an elevated command prompt by clicking Start, typing **cmd**, and pressing Ctrl+Shift+Enter.

3. At the command prompt, run the following command to configure the Windows Event Collector service:

   `wecutil qc`

4. When prompted to change the service startup mode to Delay-Start, type **Y**, and then press Enter.

EXERCISE 2 Configuring a Computer to Forward Events

In this exercise, you configure a computer running Windows 7 to forward events to the collecting computer. To complete this exercise, you must have completed Exercise 1.

1. Log on to the computer running Windows 7 that you want to use to forward events using a domain account with administrative privileges.

2. Open an elevated command prompt by clicking Start, typing **cmd**, and pressing Ctrl+Shift+Enter.

3. At the command prompt, run the following command to configure the Windows Remote Management service: *winrm quickconfig*.

4. When prompted to change the service startup mode, type **Y**, and then press Enter.

5. When prompted to create the WinRM listener and enable the firewall exception, type **Y** and then press Enter.

6. Verify that you have updated the Windows Firewall configuration by following these steps:

   a. Click Start and then click Control Panel.

   b. Click the System And Security link.

   c. Click the Windows Firewall link.

   d. Click the Advanced Settings link.

   e. Select the Inbound Rules node.

   f. In the Details pane, verify that the Windows Remote Management (HTTP-In) exception is enabled for the Domain and Private profiles.

7. Verify that the Windows Remote Management service is configured to start automatically by following these steps:

   a. Click Start, type **services.msc**, and then press Enter.

   b. In the Services console, select the Windows Remote Management (WS-Management) service. Verify that it is started and that the Startup Type is set to Automatic (Delayed Start).

8. Now you need to grant the collecting computer permission to read this computer's event log. If you skipped this step, you would need to configure the subscription to use an administrative user account. To grant access to the collecting computer account, perform these steps:

   a. Click Start, right-click Computer, and then click Manage.

   b. Under System Tools, expand Local Users And Groups. Then, select Groups.

   c. Double-click Event Log Readers.

   d. In the Event Log Readers Properties dialog box, click Add.

   e. In the Select Users, Computers, Service Accounts, Or Groups dialog box, click Object Types. By default, it searches only Users and Groups. However, we need to add the collecting computer account. Select the Computers check box and clear the Groups, Users, and Service Accounts check boxes. Click OK.

   f. In the Select Users, Computers, Or Groups dialog box, type the name of the collecting computer. Then, click OK.

   g. Click OK again to close the Event Log Readers Properties dialog box.

EXERCISE 3   Configuring an Event Subscription

In this exercise, you create an event subscription to gather events from the forwarding computer. To complete this exercise, you must have completed Exercises 1 and 2.

1. Log on to the computer running Windows 7 that you want to use to collect events using a domain account with administrative privileges.

2. Click Start, right-click Computer, and then click Manage.

3. In the Computer Management console, expand System Tools, expand Event Viewer, right-click Subscriptions, and then click Create Subscription.

4. In the Event Viewer dialog box, click Yes to configure the Windows Event Collector service (if prompted).

   The Subscription Properties dialog box appears.

5. In the Subscription Name box, type **Windows Defender Warnings And Errors**.

6. Click Select Computers. In the Computers dialog box, click Add Domain Computers. Type the name of the computer that will be forwarding events, and then click OK. In the Computers dialog box, click Test to verify that you can connect to the forwarding computer. Click OK twice.

7. Click Select Events. In the Query Filter dialog box, select the Error, Critical, Warning, and Information check boxes. Click By Source. Then, click the Event Sources list and select Windows Defender (as shown in Figure 8-4). Click OK.

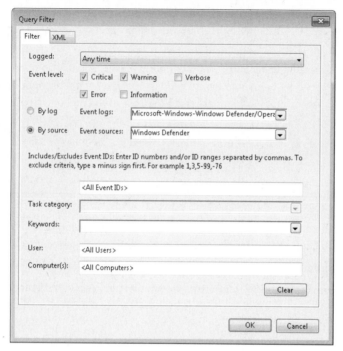

FIGURE 8-4 Configuring the Query Filter to forward important Windows Defender events

8. Click Advanced to open the Advanced Subscription Settings dialog box. Note that it is configured to use the Machine Account by default. This works because we have added this computer's domain account to the forwarding computer's Event Log Readers local group. Also, note that the subscription is configured by default to use Normal Event Delivery Optimization using the HTTP protocol. Click OK.

9. In the Subscription Properties dialog box, click OK.

10. Next, generate a Windows Defender event on the forwarding computer by following these steps:

    a. Log on to the forwarding computer.

    b. Click Start and type **Defender**. On the Start menu, click Scan For Spyware And Other Potentially Unwanted Software.

    Windows Defender scans the computer and adds an event to the event log.

11. While still using the forwarding computer, open Event Viewer and check the Applications And Services Logs\Microsoft\Windows\Windows Defender\Operational log. You should see several Informational events with a source of Windows Defender.

12. Using the collecting computer, select the Forwarded Events event log. If you don't see the Windows Defender event immediately, wait a few minutes—it might take up to 15 minutes for the event to appear.

Lesson Summary

- Event forwarding uses HTTP by default, allowing it to pass easily through most firewalls. You can also configure event forwarding to use HTTPS. However, communications are encrypted with standard HTTP.

- To configure event forwarding in a domain, run the *winrm quickconfig* command at the forwarding computer and run the *wecutil qc* command on the collecting computer. Then, add the collecting computer's account to the forwarding computer's Event Log Readers group.

- To configure event forwarding in a workgroup, follow the same steps that you would in a domain. In addition, you need to add a Windows Firewall exception for the Remote Event Log Management service on each forwarding computer, add a user account with administrator privileges to the forwarding computer's Event Log Readers group, and run the *winrm set* command to configure the collecting computer to trust the forwarding computers.

- To troubleshoot event forwarding, verify that you have waited long enough and that subscriptions are active, check the Windows Remote Management configuration on both the forwarding and collecting computers, and verify that the user account you specified for the subscription is a member of the forwarding computer's Event Log Readers group.

Lesson Review

You can use the following questions to test your knowledge of the information in Lesson 1, "Forwarding Events." The questions are also available on the companion CD if you prefer to review them in electronic form.

NOTE ANSWERS

Answers to these questions and explanations of why each answer choice is correct or incorrect are located in the "Answers" section at the end of the book.

1. When starting with the default configuration of a computer, which of the following steps are required to enable event forwarding? (Choose all that apply.)

   A. Start the Windows Remote Management service on the forwarding computer.

   B. Start the Windows Remote Management service on the collecting computer.

   C. Configure Microsoft Internet Information Services (IIS) on the forwarding computer.

   D. Enable a Windows Firewall exception on the forwarding computer.

   E. Nothing is required; event forwarding is enabled by default.

2. Which tool would you use to configure a subscription to use a 10-minute interval?

   A. Event Viewer

   B. Winrm

   C. Wecutil

   D. Wevutil

3. What is the standard interval for a subscription with a bandwidth optimization setting of Minimize Latency?

   A. 30 seconds

   B. 15 minutes

   C. 30 minutes

   D. 6 hours

4. Which of the following tasks do you need to perform in an AD DS domain environment to enable a computer to collect events from another computer?

   A. Run the following command on the collecting computer: *winrm set winrm/config/client @{TrustedHosts="<forwarding_computers>"}*.

   B. Run the following command on the forwarding computer: *winrm set winrm/config/client @{TrustedHosts="<collecting_computers>"}*.

   C. Add the forwarding computer's machine account to the Event Log Readers local group.

   D. Add the collecting computer's machine account to the Event Log Readers local group.

Lesson 2: Troubleshooting Performance Problems

When a user experiences a performance problem, you need to know how to identify the source of the problem quickly and, if necessary, resolve it. Fortunately, Windows 7 provides Task Manager to give you an overview of system performance. Task Manager also allows you to change the priority and affinity of a process to limit the processing resources it can consume. With Performance Monitor, you can examine thousands of details about system and application performance in real time, or log the data for later analysis.

Data collector sets create a snapshot of a system's state, storing detailed information about a computer's configuration for later analysis. If you identify disk input/output time as the source of a performance problem, you might be able to resolve it by freeing up disk space and defragmenting the disk. For mobile computers, you must consider settings that compromise system performance in favor of extended battery life. If a problem seems to be related to a startup service or application, you can use the System Configuration tool to selectively disable startup processes until you identify the process causing the problem.

> **After this lesson, you will be able to:**
> - Use Task Manager to examine system performance and control individual processes.
> - Use Performance Monitor to examine real-time statistics and compare logged data to a performance baseline.
> - Use data collector sets to generate reports that provide detailed information about a computer's configuration and the problems it's experiencing.
> - Troubleshoot disk performance problems by freeing wasted disk space.
> - Adjust how mobile computers optimize performance and battery life to meet users' needs.
> - Use the System Configuration tool to disable startup services and applications selectively.
>
> **Estimated lesson time: 45 minutes**

Task Manager

Task Manager is the quickest way to identify common performance problems. Windows 7 makes it easy to open Task Manager even if the user interface isn't responding correctly. You can open Task Manager in the following ways:

- Right-click the taskbar or the system clock and then click Start Task Manager.
- Press Ctrl+Alt+Del, and then click Start Task Manager. You can do this even if the user interface is completely non-responsive.

Task Manager has six tabs:

- **Applications**   A list of applications open by the current user. You can close an application by clicking it and then clicking End Task. If the Start menu is not working, you can start a new application by clicking New Task. If the Windows Explorer interface is not open, you can click New Task and then run Windows Explorer to open it.

- **Processes**   A list of processes open by the current user. You can view processes open by all users by clicking Show Processes From All Users. You can quickly identify the process that is using the most processor time by clicking the CPU column header to sort the processes by processor utilization. To end a process, select the process and then click End Process. Ending a process is particularly useful when a non-responsive application is consuming all the processor time and slowing the computer down.

- **Services**   Lists all the services on the computer, running or stopped. You can start and stop services by right-clicking the service. This tab provides similar functionality to the Services console, but with the convenience of Task Manager.

- **Performance**   Shows current processor and memory utilization. If a computer seems slow, open the Performance tab to determine whether processor or memory utilization is causing the problem. If processor utilization is causing the problem, one or more of the processors in the CPU Usage History chart will be at 100%, as the first processor is in Figure 8-5. If memory utilization is causing the problem, the value shown in the Memory chart will be close to the Total value shown in the Physical Memory group.

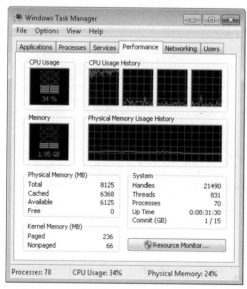

FIGURE 8-5 Task Manager shows processor and memory utilization.

- **Networking**   Charts the network utilization of each network interface. Use this tab to determine whether a slow network might be caused by an application using all the available bandwidth. Wired network connections typically do not support more than 70% utilization; therefore, a wired network at 65% utilization can be considered completely saturated. Available bandwidth for wireless network connections varies, but is typically around 35% as shown by the charts on the Networking tab.

- **Users** Lists the users currently logged on to the computer.

The sections that follow discuss how to perform different tasks with Task Manager.

How Windows Shares Processor Time Between Applications

To understand how to troubleshoot performance, you must know how applications, processes, and threads relate. An application or service typically has a single process associated with it, though some applications or services might start multiple processes. Processes run within threads. Every application has at least one thread, and it might start multiple threads. Some applications might use hundreds of threads.

A processor (or processor core) can only run one thread at a time. A computer with one processor can still run multiple applications, however, because Windows switches the processor between different processes and threads. Higher-priority threads receive more processor time than lower-priority threads.

Today, most new computers have processors with multiple cores. Each processor core functions like a separate processor. If you view the Performance tab of Task Manager, the CPU Usage graph shows the total utilization across all processors, and the CPU Usage History graph shows a separate graph for each processor core. If you see only one graph in the CPU Usage History box, click the View menu, click CPU History, and then click One Graph Per CPU.

One of the most important tasks Windows performs is distributing processor time. With multiple applications running, many having multiple threads, and multiple processor cores, the task of distributing processor time can be very complicated. Fortunately, as Figure 8-6 illustrates, Windows handles it automatically, and you rarely need to adjust the default settings.

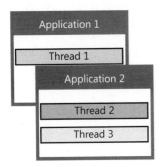
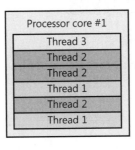

FIGURE 8-6 Windows assigns threads processor time.

There are some circumstances that might require you to control processes manually:

- A single process is using too much processor time, slowing down other processes.
- Applications are utilizing the processor fully, and you want one application to receive more or less processor time than other applications.
- An application is not responding, and you want to end the application's processes forcibly.

The sections that follow show you how to accomplish each of these.

How to Identify Which Program Is Using the Most Processor Time

You can use Task Manager to identify a process that is using excessive processor time. Optionally, you can end the process forcibly by performing these steps:

1. Start Task Manager.

2. On the Processes tab, click the CPU column heading.

3. The process consuming the most processor time is shown at the top of the list.

4. With the busiest process identified, you can change the priority of the process (which might improve the performance of other applications), end the process, or limit the process to specific processor cores by performing either of the following:

   - To change the priority of the process, right-click the process, select Set Priority, and then click the desired priority. Lower-priority processes receive less processor time, whereas higher-priority processes receive more processor time. Most processes run with Normal priority. Task Manager is a notable exception; it runs at High priority by default so that you can use it if another application is consuming significant amounts of processor time. Avoid giving any process Realtime priority, because it might slow the user interface.

   - By default, Windows can assign a process to run on any processor core. To limit the process to specific processor cores on a computer with multiple cores, right-click the process and then click Set Affinity. Figure 8-7 shows the Processor Affinity dialog box, which allows you to select which processor cores a process can use. Figure 8-7 shows Iexplore.exe (the Internet Explorer process) limited to two out of four processor cores, ensuring Internet Explorer never uses more than half the total processor time. Closing and restarting a process resets the processor affinity.

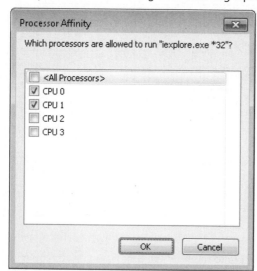

FIGURE 8-7 The Processor Affinity dialog box allows you to limit the processor cores on which a process can run.

- To end the process, right-click the process and then click End Process. Alternatively, you can click End Process Tree to end any processes that process started.

How to Stop a Program

Occasionally, a program might not respond. Typically, you can right-click the application on the task bar and then click Close Window. In a few seconds, Windows prompts you to terminate the nonresponsive application.

If that approach does not work, you can use Task Manager to close an application as follows:

1. In Task Manager, on the Applications tab, select the application.

2. Click End Task.

3. If Task Manager cannot end the application, the End Program dialog box appears. Click End Now.

If you want to identify which process is associated with an application, right-click the application on the Applications tab, and then click Go To Process.

Performance Monitor

Like earlier versions of Windows, the Performance Monitor snap-in graphically displays real-time data, as shown in Figure 8-8.

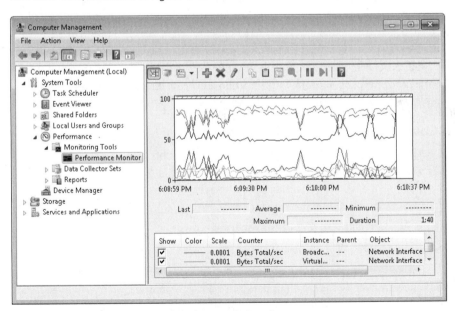

FIGURE 8-8 How Performance Monitor shows real-time data

The sections that follow describe how to monitor real-time data, how to configure the Performance Monitor chart, and how to compare multiple graphs.

How to Monitor Real-Time Performance Data

To open Performance Monitor, follow these steps:

1. Click Start, right-click Computer, and then click Manage.

2. Expand System Tools, expand Performance, and then expand Monitoring Tools. Select Performance Monitor.

3. Add counters to the real-time graph by clicking the green plus button on the toolbar. You can also display data from other computers on the network.

Each line on the graph appears in a different color. To make it easier to view a specific graph, select a counter and press Ctrl+H. The selected counter appears bold and in black on the graph.

Performance Monitor automatically assigns line colors and styles to the counters you select. To configure line colors and styles manually, follow these steps:

1. Click the Action menu, and then click Properties.

   The Performance Monitor Properties dialog box appears.

2. Click the Data tab.

3. In the Counters list, select the counter you want to configure. Then, adjust the Color, Width, and Style settings.

4. To increase the height of the graph for a counter, click the Scale list and click a higher number. To decrease the height of a graph, click the Scale list and click a lower number.

5. You can also adjust the scale for all counters by clicking the Graph tab and changing the Maximum and Minimum values in the Vertical Scale group. Click OK.

If you keep multiple Performance Monitor windows open simultaneously, you can make it easier to quickly distinguish between the windows by changing the background color on the chart using the Appearance tab in the Performance Monitor Properties dialog box.

How to Control How Much Data Appears in the Graph

By default, Performance Monitor updates the graphs once per second and displays 100 seconds of data. To display data over a longer period of time, you can increase the sampling interval or increase the amount of data displayed on the graph at once. To adjust these settings, follow these steps in Performance Monitor:

1. Click the Action menu, and then click Properties.

   The Performance Monitor Properties dialog box appears.

2. In the General tab, in the Graph Elements group, adjust the Sample Every box to change how frequently the graph updates. Use a longer interval (such as five seconds) to show a smoother, less jagged graph that is updated less frequently. If you are connecting to a computer across a network, longer intervals reduce bandwidth usage.

3. Adjust the Duration box to change how much data is displayed in the graph before Performance Monitor begins overwriting the graph on the left portion of the chart. To display one full hour of data in the graph, set the duration to 3,600. To display one full day of data in the graph, set the duration to 86,400. If you increase the Duration box, you should also increase the Sample Every box. Click OK.

By default, Performance Monitor begins overwriting graphed data on the left portion of the chart after the specified duration has been reached. When graphing data over a long period of time, it's typically easier to see the chart scroll from right to left, similar to the way Task Manager shows data. To configure the Performance Monitor graph to scroll data, perform these steps:

1. Click the Action menu, and then click Properties.

   The Performance Monitor Properties dialog box appears.

2. Click the Graph tab. In the Scroll Style group, select Scroll. Click OK.

Although the line chart shows the most information, you can select from the following chart types by clicking the Change Graph Type button on the toolbar or by pressing Ctrl+G:

- **Line**   The default setting, this shows values over time as lines on the chart.
- **Histogram bar**   This shows a bar graph with the most recent values for each counter displayed. If you have a large number of values and you're primarily interested in the current value (rather than the value of each counter over time), this will be easier to read than the line chart.
- **Report**   This text report lists each current value.

Data Collector Sets and Reports

Previous versions of Windows enabled you to log performance counter data and view it later. Windows Vista and Windows 7 greatly expand this capability. Now you can create a data collector set to log the following types of information:

- Performance counters and alerts (just like in previous versions of Windows)
- Event trace data showing detailed debugging information
- Registry settings showing system and application configuration

After running a data collector set, you can view the performance counters in Performance Monitor and you can view a summary of the other collected information in a report. The sections that follow describe how to create data collector sets and how to use reports.

Built-in Data Collector Sets

Windows 7 includes several built-in data collector sets located at Performance\Data Collector Sets\System:

- **System Performance**   Logs processor, disk, memory, and network performance counters and kernel tracing. Use this data collector set when troubleshooting a slow computer or intermittent performance problems.

- **System Diagnostics**   Logs all the information included in the System Performance data collector set, plus detailed system information. Use this data collector set when troubleshooting reliability problems such as problematic hardware, driver failures, or Stop errors. As shown in Figure 8-9, the report generated by the data collector set provides a summary of error conditions on the system without requiring you to browse Event Viewer and Device Manager manually.

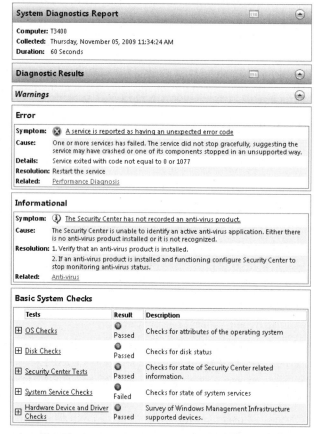

FIGURE 8-9 The System Diagnostics Report

To use a data collector set, right-click it, and then click Start. The System Performance data collector set stops automatically after a minute, and the System Diagnostics data collector set stops automatically after 10 minutes. To stop a data collector set manually, right-click it, and then click Stop.

After running a data collector set, you can view a summary of the data gathered in the Performance\Reports node. To view the most recent report for a data collector set, right-click the data collector set, and then click Latest Report. Reports are named automatically using the format *<Computer_Name>_yyyymmdd-######*.

To minimize the performance impact of data logging, log the least amount of information required. For example, you should use System Performance instead of System Diagnostics whenever possible because System Performance includes fewer counters.

When a problem is difficult to reproduce and is not performance-related, you should err on the side of logging too much data to minimize the chance that you will miss important information.

How to Create a Data Collector Set Using a Standard Template

You can save performance data to a log and then view and analyze the data in Performance Monitor at any time. It's important to create a *baseline* by logging performance data before making changes that you think might have a performance impact. After making the changes, you can compare new performance data to the original performance data to determine whether your changes were beneficial. If you don't have a baseline available when a problem appears, you can create one using a different computer with a similar configuration that does not have the problem.

To save performance data, follow these steps:

1. Under Performance, expand Data Collector Sets.

2. Right-click User Defined, click New, and then click Data Collector Set.

   The Create New Data Collector Set Wizard appears.

3. On the How Would You Like To Create This New Data Collector Set? page, type a name for the set. Make sure Create From A Template is selected. Then, click Next.

4. On the Which Template Would You Like To Use? page, choose from one of the three standard templates (or Browse to select a custom template) and click Next:

   - **Basic**   Logs all Processor performance counters, stores a copy of the HKLM\ Software\Microsoft\Windows NT\CurrentVersion registry key, and performs a Windows Kernel Trace.

   - **System Diagnostics**   Logs 13 useful performance counters (including processor, disk, memory, and network counters), stores a copy of dozens of important configuration settings, and performs a Windows Kernel Trace. By default, System Diagnostics logs data for one minute, giving you a snapshot of the computer's status.

   - **System Performance**   Logs 14 useful performance counters (including the same counters logged by the System Diagnostics template) and performs a Windows Kernel Trace. System Performance logs data for one minute.

5. On the Where Would You Like The Data To Be Saved? page, click Next to accept the default location for the data (%Systemdrive%\Perflogs\Admin).

6. On the Create The Data Collector Set page, leave Run As set to <Default> to run it using the current user's credentials, or click Change to specify other administrative credentials. Select one of three options before clicking Finish:

- **Open Properties For This Data Collector Set**   Immediately customize the Data Collector Set.

- **Start This Data Collector Set Now**   Immediately begin logging data without customizing the Data Collector Set.

- **Save And Close**   Close the Data Collector Set without starting it. You can edit the properties and start it at any time after saving it.

Custom data collector sets are always available under the User Defined node within Data Collector Sets.

How to Create a Custom Data Collector Set

After creating a new data collector set, you can modify it to log additional data sources by right-clicking the data collector set, clicking New, and then clicking Data Collector to open the Create New Data Collector wizard. On the What Type Of Data Collector Would You Like To Create? page, type a name for the data collector, select the type, and then click Next.

You can choose from the following types of data collectors (each of which provides different options in the Create New Data Collector wizard):

- **Performance Counter Data Collector**   Logs data for any performance counter available when using the Performance Monitor console. You can add as many counters as you like to a data collector. You can assign a sample interval (15 seconds, by default) to the data collector.

- **Event Trace Data Collector**   Stores events from an event trace provider that match a particular filter. Windows 7 provides dozens of event trace providers that are capable of logging even the most minute aspects of the computer's behavior. For best results, simply add all event trace providers that might relate to the problem you are troubleshooting. If the data collector logs a large amount of unnecessary data, you can use the provider properties to filter which trace events are stored.

- **Configuration Data Collector**   Stores a copy of specific registry keys, management paths, files, or the system state. If you are troubleshooting application problems or if you need to be aware of application settings, add the registry keys using a configuration data collector. To add a management path, file, or system state, create the data collector without specifying a registry key using the wizard. Then, view the new data collector properties, and select the Management Paths, File Capture, or State Capture tab.

- **Performance Counter Alert**   Generates an alert when a performance counter is above or below a specified threshold.

You can add as many data collectors to a data collector set as required.

How to Save Performance Data

After creating a data collector set, you can gather the data specified in the Data Collector Set by right-clicking it and clicking Start. Depending on the settings configured in the Stop Condition tab of the data collector set's Properties dialog box, the logging might stop after a set amount of time or it might continue indefinitely. If it does not stop automatically, you can manually stop it by right-clicking it and clicking Stop.

How to View Saved Performance Data in a Report

After using a data collector set to gather information and then stopping the data collector set, you can view the gathered information. To view a summary of the data saved using a data collector set, right-click the data collector set and then click Latest Report. The console expands the Reports node and selects the report generated when the data collector set ran. You can expand each section to find more detailed information.

If the data collector set included performance counters, you can also view them using the Performance Monitor snap-in by following these steps:

1. Under Performance, expand Monitoring Tools, and then select Performance Monitor.

2. Click the Action menu, and then click Properties. In the Performance Monitor Properties dialog box, click the Source tab. You can also click the View Log Data button on the toolbar or press Ctrl+L.

3. Under Data Source, select Log Files. Then, click Add. By default, Windows 7 stores data collector set data in the C:\Perflogs\ folder. Browse to select the data collector set data (the folder corresponds to the report name), and then click Open.

4. If you want, click Time Range and narrow the range of data you want to analyze.

5. Click OK.

6. In Performance Monitor, click the green Add button on the toolbar and add counters to the chart. Because you specified a data source, you can add only counters that were logged.

7. Performance Monitor shows the logged data instead of real-time data. To narrow the time range shown, click and drag your cursor over the graph to select a time range. Then, right-click the graph and click Zoom To, as shown in Figure 8-10.

8. The horizontal bar beneath the graph illustrates the currently selected time range. Drag the left and right sides of the bar to expand the selected time range. Then, right-click the graph and click Zoom To again to change the selection.

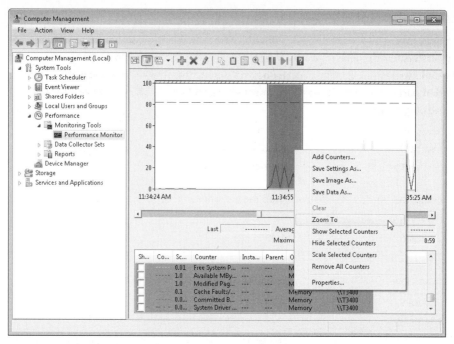

FIGURE 8-10 Using the Zoom To feature to analyze a narrow time span

Troubleshooting Disk Performance Problems

For many common tasks on a computer, the hard disk limits overall performance. Opening and saving files requires reading from and writing to the hard disk, which is much slower than accessing system RAM. In addition, if Windows needs to allocate more memory than it has physical RAM available, Windows uses the hard disk as virtual memory, reducing performance for any task that requires the memory stored on the hard disk.

Fortunately, there are several things you can do to improve performance without upgrading to a faster hard disk. The sections that follow discuss fragmentation and virtual memory.

Fragmentation and Free Space

To reduce fragmentation, increase the amount of free disk space. When a disk begins to run out of space, Windows needs to divide files into several different fragments, a process known as *fragmentation*. Because hard disks perform best when a file is not fragmented, fragmentation slows disk performance. As a general rule, you should keep at least 15 percent of a disk's space free, but having more free disk space can further improve performance.

You can use the Windows 7 Disk Cleanup tool to free up disk space automatically by following these steps:

1. Click Start, and then click Computer.

2. Right-click the drive you want to clean, and then click Properties.

3. On the General tab, click Disk Cleanup.

4. To remove system files (a task that requires administrative privileges), click Clean Up System Files.

5. Select the files that you want to delete. You can click each file type for a description of the files that will be removed. Click OK.

   The Disk Cleanup tool removes the files you specified.

Windows 7 automatically defragments your files, so you should never need to defragment manually. If you would like to defragment files manually, perform these steps:

1. Click Start, and then click Computer.

2. Right-click the drive you want to defragment, and then click Properties.

3. On the Tools tab, click Defragment Now.

4. To configure the defragmentation schedule, click Configure Schedule.

5. In the Disk Defragmenter tool, select the disk you want to defragment, and then click Defragment Disk.

   The Disk Defragmenter begins defragmenting the drive. You don't have to wait for it to complete before closing the window, however.

6. Click Close, and then click OK.

Virtual Memory

Depending on the disk configuration, you can maximize the performance of virtual memory by storing virtual memory on a different physical hard disk from other files. For example, if a computer has a separate C: and D: drive, Windows by default uses the C: drive for virtual memory. By moving the virtual memory to the D: drive, Windows might be able to read and write files stored on the C: drive at the same time it accesses virtual memory.

To configure which disk Windows stores virtual memory on, perform these steps:

1. Click Start, right-click Computer, and then click Properties.

2. Click Advanced System Settings.

3. On the Advanced tab of the System Properties dialog box, click Settings in the Performance group.

4. On the Advanced tab of the Performance Options dialog box, click Change.

5. Clear the Automatically Manage Paging File Size For All Drives check box.

6. Select the drive that you want to use to store virtual memory (also known as a *paging file*). Click System Managed Size, and then click OK.

7. Select the system drive which currently has the paging file assigned to it. Click No Paging File, and then click Set. Figure 8-11 shows a computer that has had virtual memory assigned to the G: drive and removed from the default C: drive. Click Yes when prompted.

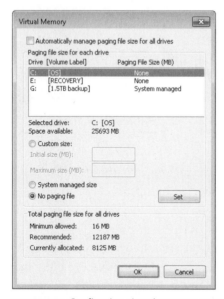

FIGURE 8-11 Configuring virtual memory storage

8. Click OK four times, and then click Restart Now to restart your computer.

Configuring Power Settings

Some aspects of a computer are a compromise between performance and power usage. For mobile computers running on battery power, the greater the power usage, the shorter the battery life. To maximize battery life, Windows 7 provides different power plans and switches between them automatically when a computer is plugged in or running on battery.

However, the default battery power plan can reduce performance. To set the power plan manually, perform these steps:

1. Click the power icon in the system tray, and then click More Power Options.

2. Click Change Plan Settings.

3. Click Change Settings That Are Currently Unavailable.

4. Change the display and sleep settings for times when the computer is plugged in or running on battery.

5. To change other settings, click Change Advanced Power Settings. Adjust the settings, and then click OK. Some of the more useful performance-related settings include:

   - **Turn Off Hard Disk After**   Windows can turn the hard disk off to save power if it is not used for a specific amount of time. Realistically, though, applications continue to use the hard disk even if the user is not actively working with the computer.

   - **Wireless Adapter Settings**   Wireless adapters can use a significant amount of battery power because they must transmit and receive radio signals. By default, Windows 7 enables power saving for wireless connections when running on battery power. If wireless performance significantly decreases while on battery power, you can change the power saving mode to Maximum Performance while on battery power.

   - **Sleep**   In Windows Vista and Windows 7, Sleep is a power-saving mode that combines both *Standby* (a low-power state that allows the computer to recover in a few seconds) and *Hibernation* (a zero-power state that stores the computer's memory to disk, but takes longer to recover). By default, Sleep in Windows 7 initially enters Standby mode and then enters Hibernation 20 minutes later. Adjust this setting to change that default.

   - **USB Settings**   USB devices draw power from a computer. With USB selective suspend, Windows 7 can reduce the power usage of some USB devices. By default, USB selective suspend is enabled while Windows 7 is on battery power.

   - **Power Buttons And Lid**   By default, Windows 7 automatically enters sleep mode when the lid of a mobile computer is closed. You can change this setting and configure how the power button functions.

   - **PCI Express**   Some mobile computers have a PCI Express interface. This setting configures the power savings mode used for the PCI Express interface when on battery power or plugged in.

   - **Processor Power Management**   Most modern processors can run at different speeds depending on the current processing requirements. When less processor time is needed, the processor runs slower, requiring less power. You can use these settings to change the minimum and maximum speed of the processor.

- **Multimedia Settings** You can use this setting to adjust video quality when on battery power. Enabling a higher video quality increases battery usage.

- **Battery** Adjust how Windows responds when a battery begins to run out of power.

6. Click Save Changes.

System Configuration

Troubleshooting often involves experimentation. For example, when troubleshooting a performance problem, you might stop a program or service from starting automatically and then test the computer to determine if the performance problem has been resolved. The challenge with this, however, is that you might disable useful applications and services not related to the problem.

The System Configuration Utility (Msconfig.exe) allows you to disable startup programs and system services individually or several at a time. Once you identify the source of the problem, you can easily re-enable the startup programs and services. To disable a startup program or service by using the System Configuration Utility, use these steps:

1. Click Start, type **msconfig**, and then press Enter.

2. To disable a service at startup, select the Services tab and clear the check box for the service.

3. To disable a startup program, select the Startup tab and clear the check box for the application.

4. Click OK. When prompted, click Restart.

   When Windows restarts, the changes you have made take effect.

5. When the computer restarts, determine whether your changes improved the computer's performance. If disabling the startup program or service did solve the problem, you can investigate it further. If there was no benefit, use the System Configuration utility to re-enable the startup program or service.

You can remove a startup program permanently using Control Panel. To prevent a service from starting automatically, use the Services console.

 Quick Check

1. Which tool would you use to adjust the processor affinity of a process, and why would you adjust it?

2. On which volume does Windows 7 store virtual memory by default?

Quick Check Answers

1. Task Manager. You would adjust processor affinity to limit the processor cores a process can run on.

2. On the system volume.

PRACTICE **Collect and Analyze Performance Data**

In this practice, you collect performance data using a data collector set and then analyze it using a report and Performance Monitor.

EXERCISE 1 Perform System Diagnostics

In this exercise, you collect performance data by using a built-in data collector set.

1. Click Start, right-click Computer, and then click Manage.

2. In the Computer Management console, expand System Tools, Performance, Data Collector Sets, and then System.

3. Right-click System Diagnostics, and then click Start. Notice that a green arrow appears on the System Diagnostics icon.

4. While the System Diagnostics data collector set is running, click System Diagnostics. Browse through the various data collectors. In particular, view the properties of the following data collectors:

   - Performance Counter
   - NT Kernel
   - Operating System
   - UAC Settings
   - Windows Update Settings

5. The green arrow disappears from the System Diagnostics icon after the data collector set has finished running in one minute. Now, right-click System Diagnostics, and click Latest Report.

6. Examine the Diagnostic Results section and investigate any error or warning conditions. Then, investigate each of the other sections of the report to identify the following pieces of information:

   - Processor utilization
   - The number of processors and whether the processors are hyperthreaded or not
   - Memory utilization
   - Total physical memory
   - Whether the operating system architecture is 32-bit or 64-bit
   - The name of the workgroup or domain the computer is a member of
   - The name of the anti-spyware, antivirus, and firewall software installed, if any
   - Whether User Access Control (UAC) is enabled
   - Whether the Computer Browser, Server, Workstation, and Windows Update services are running
   - Which service is using the most processor time

- Whether IRQ 3 is in use
- The Windows Experience Index rating for the processor, memory, and hard disk
- Basic input/output system (BIOS) type and version
- The Internet Protocol (IP) address that is sending the most bytes to the local computer
- The number of IPv4 and IPv6 connections
- The file causing the most disk input/output (I/O)
- The application with the largest working set

EXERCISE 2   **Create a Performance Graph**

In this exercise, you use Performance Monitor to analyze graphically the data you gathered in Exercise 1.

1. In the Computer Management console, select the System Tools\Performance\ Monitoring Tools\Performance Monitor node.
2. Click the View Log Data button on the toolbar to open the Source tab of the Performance Monitor Properties dialog box.
3. Select Log Files. Then, click Add. Select the C:\Perflogs\System\Diagnostics\ <Computer_Name>_yyyymmdd-######\Performance Counter.blg file to open the performance counter log created when you ran the System Diagnostics data collector set. Click Open.
4. Click OK to return to Performance Monitor.

   Now you are viewing the logged performance data. However, because you have not added any counters to the chart, nothing is visible.
5. Click the Add button on the toolbar. Add the following counters to the chart, and then click OK:
   - IPv4\Datagrams/sec
   - IPv6\Datagrams/sec
   - Memory\% Committed Bytes In Use
   - PhysicalDisk\Disk Bytes/sec
   - Processor\% Processor Time
   - System\Processes
6. Press Ctrl+H to highlight the selected counter. Browse through the available counters and examine their performance during the one minute log period.
7. Drag your mouse horizontally across the middle of the chart to select about 30 seconds of the chart. Then, right-click the chart and click Zoom To. Notice that the chart displays a smaller period of time.
8. Use the slider below the chart to select the entire chart time period. Then, right-click the chart and click Zoom To.

EXERCISE 3 Disable a Service Temporarily with the System Configuration Utility

In this exercise, you temporarily disable a service with the System Configuration utility.

1. Click Start, type **msconfig**, and then press Enter.

2. In the System Configuration Utility dialog box, on the Services tab, clear the check box next to the Computer Browser service.

3. Click OK.

4. In the System Configuration dialog box, click Restart. Windows restarts.

5. Log back on to Windows. Click Start, type **msconfig**, and then press Enter.

6. On the Services tab, is the Computer Browser service stopped or started?

   Stopped.

7. Select the check box next to the Computer Browser service, and then click OK.

8. In the System Configuration dialog box, click Restart.

Lesson Summary

- Task Manager provides a quick way to examine a computer's performance and solve some performance problems. With Task Manager, you can identify which processes are consuming the most resources and either lower the priority of those processes or end them.

- You can use Performance Monitor to analyze system statistics in real time or you can use it to analyze data logged using a data collector set.

- Data collector sets and reports gather performance and configuration data about a computer and enable you to analyze that information easily using reports or Performance Monitor.

- Disk performance problems are most often caused by low disk space and fragmentation. Windows 7 automatically defragments disks that need it, but if disk space is too low, some fragmentation occurs anyway. To free up wasted disk space, you can use the Disk Cleanup tool.

- If a startup program is causing performance problems, you can use the System Configuration (Msconfig.exe) tool to prevent it from starting. The System Configuration tool provides a convenient way to re-enable applications if you later determine that they are not the source of the problem.

Lesson Review

You can use the following questions to test your knowledge of the information in Lesson 2, "Troubleshooting Performance Problems." The questions are also available on the companion CD if you prefer to review them in electronic form.

1. You are a systems administrator for an enterprise company. A user calls to complain that his computer is responding very slowly, and that Microsoft Office Word is not responding. He has attempted to close Word, but it has not stopped. What can you do?

    A. Press Ctrl+Alt+Del, and then click Start Task Manager. On the Applications tab, click Word, and then click End Task.

    B. Press Ctrl+Alt+Del, and then click Start System Configuration Utility. On the Startup tab, click Microsoft Word, and then click OK.

    C. Press Alt+Tab, and then click Start Task Manager. On the Applications tab, click Word, and then click End Task.

    D. Press Alt+Tab, and then click Start System Configuration Utility. On the Startup tab, click Microsoft Word, and then click OK.

2. Which of the following factors most increases disk fragmentation?

    A. Running from battery power

    B. A large paging file

    C. Low free disk space

    D. Using a flash drive

3. Which of the following performance problems might occur on a mobile computer using battery power? (Choose all that apply.)

    A. Increased use of virtual memory

    B. Slower memory access

    C. Slower wireless networking

    D. Lower-quality video

Chapter Review

To further practice and reinforce the skills you learned in this chapter, you can perform the following tasks:

- Review the chapter summary.
- Review the list of key terms introduced in this chapter.
- Complete the case scenarios. These scenarios set up real-world situations involving the topics of this chapter and ask you to create a solution.
- Complete the suggested practices.
- Take a practice test.

Chapter Summary

- The Windows 7 event log contains a great deal of valuable information, including events that describe problems that have already occurred or might occur soon. By monitoring these events using event forwarding, you can respond to problems more quickly or prevent them from becoming critical.
- Using Task Manager, Performance Monitor, and data collector sets, you can identify the cause of performance problems quickly. Task Manager can even solve some performance problems by changing the priority of a running process or closing an application. If a startup program or service seems to be causing the performance problem, use the System Configuration tool to disable different programs temporarily during troubleshooting.

Key Terms

Do you know what these key terms mean? You can check your answers by looking up the terms in the glossary at the end of the book.

- **Collecting computer**
- **Event forwarding**
- **Forwarding computer**
- **Hibernation**
- **Listener**
- **Pull delivery mode**
- **Push delivery mode**
- **Standby**

Case Scenarios

In the following case scenarios, you apply what you've learned about subjects of this chapter. You can find answers to these questions in the "Answers" section at the end of this book.

Case Scenario 1: Monitoring Kiosk Computers

You are a systems administrator at the Baldwin Museum of Science. In addition to managing computers used by internal staff, you manage several computers running Windows Vista that are configured as kiosks in the museum's front lobby. Visitors to the museum can use these computers to browse a limited number of Web sites with science-related content. Desktop security restrictions limit the applications that users can run and the Web sites they can visit.

The museum attracts a large audience of intelligent, computer-savvy visitors. Unfortunately, some of them have taken it as a challenge to break into the kiosk computers. For example, you recently happened upon an attacker using an internal wireless connection to attack a kiosk computer across the network. You noticed the attack because you happened to discover an event in the event log, as shown in Figure 8-12.

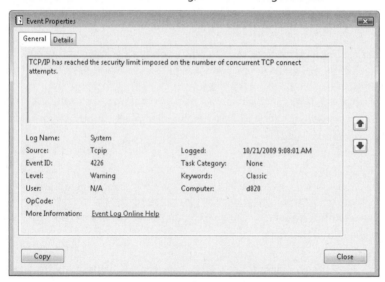

FIGURE 8-12 An event indicating an active attack in your organization

Questions

Answer the following questions for your manager:

1. You manage several kiosk computers. How can you monitor all their event logs easily to check for this particular event?

2. Which bandwidth optimization technique should you use for event forwarding?

3. If this event appears, you need to know about it immediately. How can you be actively notified of an attack?

Case Scenario 2: Troubleshooting a Performance Problem

You are the lead systems administrator at Woodgrove Bank. Several times a day your organization's IT support staff receives support requests from users who are experiencing a slow computer. However, the support staff has been unable to identify the cause of the performance problem, and resolves the problem by having the users restart their computer.

Interviews

Following is a list of company personnel interviewed and their statements:

- **Stuart Railson, Desktop Support Technician** "These users are so hard to help. This guy complained that his computer was slow, and he has this attitude like it's my fault. I think the cause of the problem is that the computer is too old. We should upgrade the processor or memory or something. I just have the users restart the computer. I think more users experience the slowdowns than actually call us, but they've figured out that they should just restart the computer to fix it."

- **Angela Barbariol, IT Manager** "As you know, all our computers are running Windows 7 with modern, dual-core processors and at least 3 GB of RAM. For the types of applications these users run, that should be plenty. Proof of this is that the computers perform fine when they're initially restarted. Frankly, I'm embarrassed that we've been solving the problem by restarting the computers because that interrupts user productivity. Let's find the source of the performance problems so we can fix them."

Questions

Answer the following questions for your manager:

1. Which tools would you use to identify the source of the problem? How would you use those tools?

2. What do you think the problem might be? Why would restarting the computer fix it temporarily?

Suggested Practices

To help you master the exam objectives presented in this chapter, complete the following tasks.

Identify and Resolve Performance Issues

For this task, you should complete at least Practices 1 and 2 to gain more experience with event forwarding. If you want a better understanding of how to configure event forwarding in an enterprise, complete Practice 3 as well. Completing these configuration tasks also helps you with your troubleshooting skills because problems are bound to arise when configuring non-default event forwarding.

Next, complete Practices 4 through 7 to get more experience monitoring computer performance. Finally, complete Practice 8 to get a better understanding of how much real-world disk space is wasted.

- **Practice 1** Configure a workgroup computer to forward events to another workgroup computer.

- **Practice 2** Configure a forwarding computer to send events to a collecting computer using each of the three standard bandwidth optimization techniques. Then, customize the event forwarding configuration by reducing the time required to forward events by half.

- **Practice 3** Use Group Policy to configure multiple client computers to forward events to a collecting computer. For the greatest scalability, use logon scripts to configure the forwarding computers—it would be too time-consuming to configure forwarding computers manually in an enterprise.

- **Practice 4** Run both standard data collector sets on several production computers. Analyze the report generated by each.

- **Practice 5** Leave the Performance of Task Manager open while you do other work on your computer. If you see utilization increase, use the Processes tab to identify the process causing the extra utilization. Repeat this practice with the Networking tab.

- **Practice 6** Start an application, such as Notepad, and then end the process using the Processes tab of Task Manager.

- **Practice 7** In Performance Monitor, add the Network Interface\Bytes Total/sec counter for your primary network interface. Then, copy a file across the network. Make note of the maximum bytes per second. Multiply that value times eight to determine the maximum bandwidth used in bits per second. What percentage of the total network bandwidth did the file transfer use?

- **Practice 8** Run the Disk Cleanup tool on several production computers. How much space are you able to free, on average?

Take a Practice Test

The practice tests on this book's companion CD offer many options. For example, you can test yourself on just one exam objective, or you can test yourself on all the 70-685 certification exam content. You can set up the test so that it closely simulates the experience of taking a certification exam, or you can set it up in study mode so that you can look at the correct answers and explanations after you answer each question.

> **MORE INFO** **PRACTICE TESTS**
>
> For details about all the practice test options available, see the section entitled "How to Use the Practice Tests," in the Introduction of this book.

CHAPTER 9

Troubleshooting Software Issues

Software errors can appear during the installation process, immediately after installation, or long afterwards. Those that appear during installation tend to result from policy or permission constraints, availability issues, or installation settings. Those that appear immediately after installation tend to be associated with policy restrictions or compatibility problems. Those that appear long after installation tend to result from configuration changes.

In this chapter, we look at the various causes of software errors and provide strategies for how to resolve them.

Exam objectives in this chapter:

- Identify and resolve new software installation issues.
- Identify and resolve software configuration issues.
- Identify cause of and resolve software failure issues.

Lessons in this chapter:

Before You Begin

To perform the exercises in this chapter, you need:

- A domain controller running Windows Server 2008 R2
- A client running Windows 7 Enterprise that is a member of the domain

Lesson 1: Understanding and Resolving Installation Failures

To troubleshoot installation failures, you need to understand the requirements of a successful installation. These requirements include—among other factors—administrator privileges, compatibility with Windows 7, availability of installation code and data, and the status of application dependencies. You also need to understand how administrative features such as Software Restriction Policies (SRP) and AppLocker can block an installation even when these requirements are met. This lesson provides an overview of issues such as these that are related both to successful and unsuccessful installations.

After this lesson, you will be able to:

- Troubleshoot software installation failures by verifying a number of well-known installation requirements.
- Understand how AppLocker can prevent software installations.
- Understand many of the feature improvements of AppLocker over Software Restriction Policies.
- Use AppLocker to block a Windows Installer program from running.

Estimated lesson time: 30 minutes

Verifying Software Installation Requirements

You can install new software on clients running Windows 7 in two general ways. First, you can push applications to clients by means of a software deployment technology such as Group Policy, Microsoft System Center Configuration Manager, or a third-party solution. The second option is to install a program manually.

Although some of the requirements for successful software installation are particular to the way in which the software is deployed, most requirements apply to all software installation methods. To begin troubleshooting a failed installation, therefore, you can verify the general requirements described in the following section.

Verifying Administrator Rights

One of the most basic requirements for a successful software installation is that the user account running the installer program needs local administrator privileges, and to have these local administrator privileges on a particular computer, the account needs to be a member of the Administrators group on that computer.

If you are not able to get past the User Account Control prompt when you attempt to install a program, therefore, you should verify that the account used for installation is granted local administrator privileges on the computer in question. Typically, having domain administrator privileges is sufficient because by default, domain administrators are members of the local

Administrators group on every computer that is a member of the same domain. However, you should perform this verification even if you are already a domain administrator because the Domain Admins group might have been removed from the local Administrators group.

To determine whether you are a member of the local Administrators group on a particular computer, you can use the Local Users And Groups console. To open this console in Windows 7, you can click Start, type **edit local users and groups**, and then press Enter. (Note that you can perform this step even if you are not already a local administrator.) Then, in the console tree of the Local Users And Groups console, select Groups, and then double-click the Administrators group in the details pane. This procedure opens the Administrators Properties dialog box, which is shown in Figure 9-1. This dialog box lists all the local administrators for that machine.

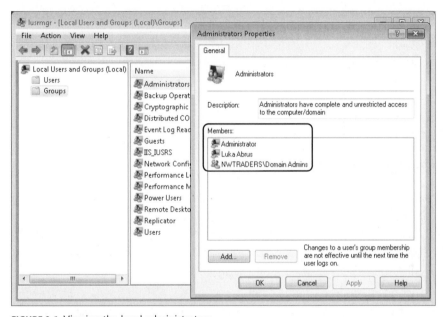

FIGURE 9-1 Viewing the local administrators

If you are a local administrator, you can then use the Add button in the Administrators Properties dialog box to add other local administrators if desired. Note, however, that in an enterprise network, it is preferable to control local group membership by using the Restricted Groups feature in Group Policy.

RUNNING AN INSTALLATION PROGRAM AS AN ADMINISTRATOR

If you can verify that you are a local administrator but you still see a message indicating that administrator rights are required to perform the installation, you should choose the option to run the installer program as an administrator. To do this, right-click the installation icon for the program, and then click Run As Administrator, as shown in Figure 9-2. If a User Account Control consent or credential prompt appears, provide confirmation or administrator credentials as needed.

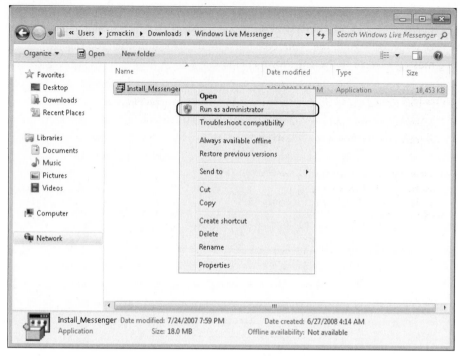

FIGURE 9-2 Running an installation with administrator privileges

Verifying Windows 7 Compatibility

If an application is known to be incompatible with Windows 7, you might receive a message informing you of this fact when you attempt to install the program. If no updated version of the software is available, you can try altering the compatibility settings on the installer program or hosting the application in a virtual environment. Handling software compatibility issues such as these is discussed in detail in Lesson 2 of this chapter, "Resolving Software Configuration and Compatibility Issues."

Verifying Trusted Publishers

When you install a new program, Windows 7 checks for a certificate and a digital signature to authenticate the publisher of the program. To verify this digital signature properly, the local computer must trust the root certification authority (CA) for the publisher certificate. Stated another way, the local computer must have installed in its Trusted Root Certification Authorities certificate store the root certificate in the certificate chain of the publisher certificate. An administrator can install this root certificate manually on a local computer or the certificate can be deployed to the Trusted Root Certification Authority certificate store on many clients through Group Policy.

If the certificate in the installer program is from a trusted publisher and the digital signature is verified, the installation proceeds normally. However, if no digital signature is present, or if the local computer is not configured to trust the publisher, you will see a warning message similar to the one shown in Figure 9-3.

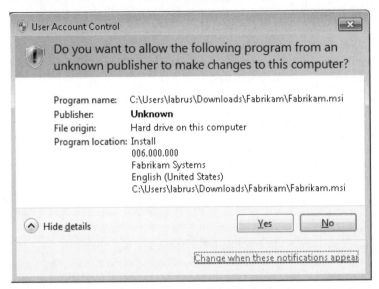

FIGURE 9-3 Avoid installing programs from untrusted publishers.

In general, you should avoid installing programs from unsigned publishers in an enterprise environment. Such programs might fail during installation, and even if they do install successfully, they could present stability problems or introduce malware into your network.

Verifying Software Logo Testing on a Client Running Windows 7

Occasionally, when you attempt to install an application, you will receive a warning that the application has not passed Windows 7 logo testing. In this case, you should avoid installing the software.

For an application to pass Windows 7 logo testing, it must meet a number of requirements, including compliance with specific anti-spyware guidelines, isolation from protected resources in Windows, a reversible installation, and a digital signature on all files.

Verifying the Installation Media Location

Before you attempt to install an application, ensure that all the files needed for installation are available in the required locations. For example, if you have copied an installer program from a network source to a local computer, be sure that you also copy all the associated secondary files that are called by the installer program when it runs. (These secondary files can include .cab files or .ini files.) If you are installing an application from over the network, verify that any secondary files are also accessible from the local computer and that you have Read and Execute permissions on these files.

Verifying Installation Settings

When you attempt to install an application, ensure that the settings that you have chosen for the installation are configured properly; otherwise, the installation might fail. For example, if you choose to install a program on a read-only disk, the installation fails.

Verifying External Connections

Certain applications require connectivity to external sources of data. For example, the application might require a connection to a database, mainframe, Web site, license server, or other application server. In this case, verify that the installation program can reach these external connections.

Verifying Licensing and Other Application Constraints

An application might include constraints that will prevent it from installing successfully. For example, a license or product key might be required to install the application, or the application might need to be installed with a specific user account. Verify also that the application architecture is compatible with the local processor. For example, you cannot install a 64-bit application on a computer with a 32-bit CPU.

Verifying Application Dependencies

Some applications can be installed only after you first install other updates, features, service packs, or other applications. Be sure to prepare the client running Windows 7 for application installation by first installing all the necessary software dependencies.

> **MORE INFO**   **DEPLOYING APPLICATIONS**
>
> The following Web sites are good resources for automating the installation of applications, as well as other deployment topics:
>
> - AppDeploy.com at *http://www.appdeploy.com*
>
>   This Web site provides information about deploying applications that are packaged using a variety of technologies.
>
> - SourceForge at *http://unattended.sourceforge.net*
>
>   This Web site describes how to automate the installation of many older installers.

Understanding Installation Restrictions with AppLocker

Occasionally, when you are attempting to install an application, you might receive an error such as the one shown in Figures 9-4 or 9-5.

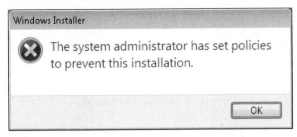

FIGURE 9-4 An installation prevented by AppLocker

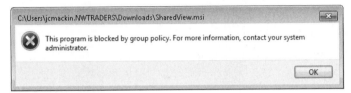

FIGURE 9-5 An installation prevented by SRP

If you see such a message, the AppLocker or SRP feature has been used to prevent the application from being installed. Both technologies are available in Windows 7 and Windows Server 2008 R2. AppLocker is essentially a new and improved version of SRP, but SRP is still included in these newer operating systems for compatibility with networks running older versions of Windows.

As with SRP, you configure AppLocker through Group Policy. To locate AppLocker, open a Group Policy Object (GPO) and navigate to Computer Configuration\Policies\Windows Settings\Security Settings\Application Control Policies\AppLocker, as shown in Figure 9-6. (In Local Security Policy, the path is simply Security Settings\Application Control Policies.)

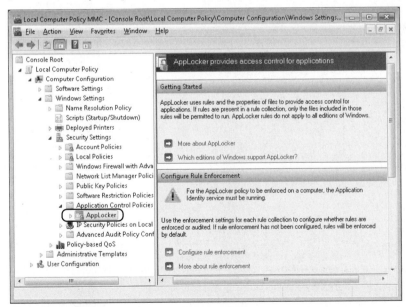

FIGURE 9-6 AppLocker is configured in a GPO.

You can see that the container for AppLocker (Application Control Policies) is found immediately below SRP.

The next section introduces AppLocker and describes the differences between it and SRP.

OVERVIEW OF APPLOCKER

AppLocker is a new feature in Windows 7 and Windows Server 2008 R2. It allows administrators to restrict the programs that users can run or install in your organization.

AppLocker resembles SRP in a number of ways. First, you configure both AppLocker and SRP in a GPO. Also like SRP, AppLocker allows you to create rules specifying an application to which you want to allow or deny access. Finally, as in SRP, in AppLocker you can define a program by specifying—among other methods—a hash of or a path to its file.

AppLocker, however, provides the following important improvements over SRP:

- Publisher rule condition

  In AppLocker, you can specify a program by extracting information from its digital signature, as shown in Figure 9-7. You can then use part of or all of this publisher information to define the programs you want to allow or deny. This publisher condition essentially replaces Certificate Rules in SRP.

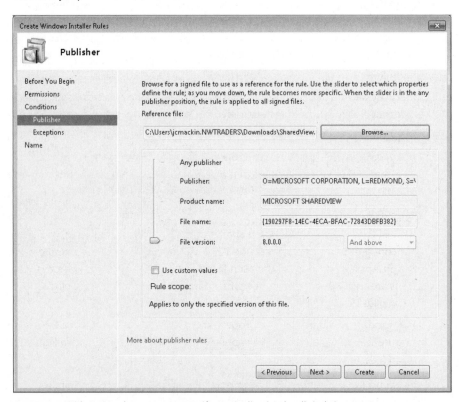

FIGURE 9-7 With AppLocker, you can specify an application by digital signature.

Using publisher information from a digital signature is by far the best way to specify an application in AppLocker. First, you can use this publisher information to create rules at various levels of specificity: You can make the rule apply to the publisher in general, to any version of the particular application, or to specific versions of the application (including all previous or future versions). Second, the publisher condition solves a key problem with SRP: In SRP, there is no comparable way to restrict access to an application through multiple updates. If you specify a path to an application that you want to restrict, users can simply move the program to a new path to avoid the restriction. If you specify a hash for the application, you have to create a new rule every time the application is updated.

- AppLocker blocks all programs that are not specifically allowed

  In SRP, rules by default are used to block access to chosen applications. However, within any company network, the number of applications that you want to block typically far exceeds the number that you want to allow. AppLocker accounts for this disparity by locking all applications that are not allowed. More specifically, AppLocker rules are enabled for one of four file type (executables, Windows Installer programs, scripts, or DLL files) when you first create a rule for that file type. Then, when AppLocker is enabled, all applications of that file type are locked if they are not allowed by a rule. To prevent system lockouts, AppLocker provides the Create Default Rules and Automatically Create Rules options. These options create allow-type rules for most applications. You can then create additional rules to change this default configuration.

- Assign Rules to Specific Users and Groups

  In AppLocker, you can create rules that apply to everyone or only to specific users and groups. In SRP, you can create only rules that apply to everyone.

- Exceptions

  AppLocker enables you to create a rule with an exception. For example, you can create a rule that allows any application to run except a specific .exe file. This feature is not available in SRP.

- Audit-only mode

  Unlike SRP, AppLocker includes an audit-only mode. Through auditing, you can test your configuration without enforcing AppLocker rules. When you configure AppLocker to audit AppLocker rules for a chosen file type (such Windows Installer programs), events are written to the event log when AppLocker would normally block access to that application.

  Audit mode is configured in the properties of the AppLocker node in a GPO, as shown in Figure 9-8. Audit events as they appear in Event Viewer are shown in Figure 9-9.

- Import and export rules

  In AppLocker, you can export and import rules to and from other computers, which allows administrators to copy and edit rules easily.

FIGURE 9-8 Configuring AppLocker rules for audit only

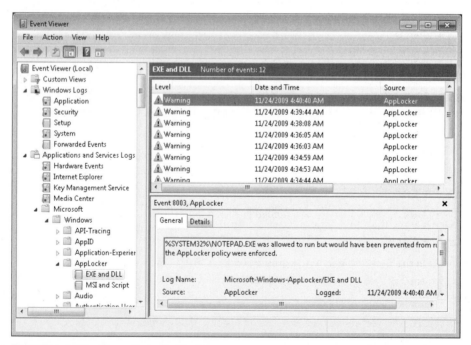

FIGURE 9-9 Audit-only events for AppLocker

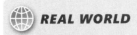 **REAL WORLD**

J.C. Mackin

AppLocker is a great feature in many ways, but I don't believe it sufficiently warns administrators about the dangers of configuring it incorrectly. If you create a new rule without also creating the default rules, for example, you can easily lock yourself and everyone else out of your computer.

I actually experienced this problem firsthand when I originally saw AppLocker in a Windows 7 beta. I simply made a rule in Local Security Policy denying access to Notepad.exe, and I ignored the messages prompting me to create the default rules. Immediately afterwards, I was dismayed to see that Windows could not start. What I didn't know at the time was that AppLocker is enabled when you create the first rule. After you create that first rule, all programs of the same type—executables, in this case—are denied if you have not allowed them.

Luckily for me, this was only a virtual environment, and I had made a data snapshot of the computer before making any changes. It was easy for me to return the computer to the previous state. But I thought—what if this were a real environment? It's not unusual for administrators to explore new features on their own machines. Few people would suspect that the punishment for incorrectly configuring such a feature would be locking themselves out of their computer indefinitely. Worse yet, what if someone actually applied such a policy to the entire domain, and the domain controllers themselves were rendered unusable? It could be a disastrous situation.

What you should remember is always to create the default rules first in AppLocker and then create additional rules to modify the behavior of those default rules. When creating new rules, always test your results first in audit-only mode or use a virtual machine environment so that you can easily revert to a previous state if necessary.

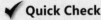 **Quick Check**

- How do you find messages related to AppLocker in Event Viewer?

Quick Check Answer

- In the Event Viewer console tree, navigate to Event Viewer (Local)\Applications and Services Logs\Microsoft\Windows\AppLocker.

APPLOCKER AVAILABILITY AND COMPATIBILITY

AppLocker rules are enforced on computers running only Windows Server 2008 R2, Windows 7 Ultimate, and Windows 7 Enterprise. AppLocker rules are not enforced on computers running other versions of Windows, such as Windows Server 2008, Windows 7 Professional, or Windows Vista.

In a GPO containing only SRP rules, the rules are enforced on all computers running Windows, including those running Windows Server 2008 R2, Windows 7 Ultimate, and Windows 7 Professional. However, if a GPO contains both SRP rules and AppLocker rules, these same three operating systems read only the AppLocker rules. The SRP rules are applied to computers running other Windows operating systems.

APPLOCKER RELIES ON THE APPLICATION IDENTITY SERVICE

AppLocker rules are enforced on eligible clients only when those clients are running the Application Identity Service. By default, this service is not configured to start automatically on computers running Windows 7. If you want to enforce AppLocker rules, therefore, you should use Group Policy to set the Startup Type parameter to Automatic for the Application Identity Service.

PRACTICE   **Preventing Software Installation with AppLocker**

In this practice, you download an .msi file from the Microsoft Web site and then prevent installation of that .msi file through AppLocker.

EXERCISE 1   Obtaining an .msi File

In this exercise, you download the file SharedView.msi from the Microsoft Download Center. You then begin a new installation to test its functionality.

1. Log on to the domain from the client running Windows 7 (Computer1) as a domain administrator.

2. In Windows Internet Explorer, visit the Microsoft Download Center at *http://download .microsoft.com*. Search for the file "SharedView.msi," and save it to your Downloads folder on Computer1. (If you do not have Internet access from Computer1, you can download the file from another computer and copy it to Computer1.)

> **NOTE**   **YOU CAN USE ANY .MSI FILE**
>
> Although we will use the file SharedView.msi in this exercise, you can replace this file with any other that you can locate and copy to the Downloads folder on Computer1.

3. Share the Downloads folder by granting Read access to Everyone. To perform this step, right-click the Downloads folder, choose Share With on the shortcut menu, and then click Specific People. In the File Sharing window, type **Everyone**, click Share, and then click Done.

4. Open the Downloads folder and double-click SharedView.msi to begin the installation.

5. If an Open File-Security Warning message box appears and asks if you want to run the file, click Run.

6. The first page of the Microsoft SharedView Setup wizard appears. The fact that the wizard has started indicates that the .msi file is not blocked.

7. Click Cancel and then Yes to close the Microsoft SharedView Setup wizard.

EXERCISE 2   Configuring AppLocker to Block an .msi

In this exercise, you create a GPO, and then, in the new GPO, you create the default rules for AppLocker in the Windows Installer rule collection. Finally, you create a new Windows Installer rule that denies SharedView.msi.

1. Switch to the domain controller (DC1), and log on as a domain administrator.

2. Open Group Policy Management, which is available through the Start menu in the Administrative Tools folder.

3. In the Group Policy Management console tree, locate and expand the Domains container, and then select the domain (Nwtraders.msft) node.

4. Right-click the Nwtraders.msft node, and then click Create A GPO In This Domain, And Link It Here in the shortcut menu.

5. In the New GPO dialog box, type **AppLocker Block SharedView.msi**, and then click OK.

6. In the Group Policy Management console, in the details pane, right-click the AppLocker Block SharedView.msi GPO, and then click Edit. The Group Policy Management Editor opens.

7. In the Group Policy Management Editor console tree, navigate to Computer Configuration\Policies\Windows Settings\Security Settings\Application Control Policies\AppLocker\Windows Installer Rules.

8. Select and then right-click the Windows Installer Rules node, and then click Create Default Rules from the shortcut menu.

   In the details pane, three new rules appear. These rules allow everyone to run all digitally signed Windows Installer files, everyone to run all Windows Installer files (signed or not) in the %Systemdrive%\Windows\Installer directory, and administrators to run all Windows Installer files without exception.

9. Right-click the Windows Installer Rules node, and then click Create New Rule on the shortcut menu. The Before You Begin page of the Create Windows Installer Rules wizard opens.

10. Read all of the text on the page, and then click Next.

11. On the Permissions page, click Deny, and then click Next.

12. On the Conditions page, leave the default selection of Publisher, and then click Next.

13. On the Publisher page, click Browse.

14. In the Open window, in the File Name field, type **\\computer1\users*username***
    Downloads\SharedView.msi, and then click Open. For the variable *username*, specify
    the name of the account that you used in Exercise 1 to copy SharedView.msi to the
    Downloads folder. On the Publisher page, the information from the digital signature in
    the .msi file has populated the gray fields next to the slider.

15. Raise the slider two notches so that it is positioned next to Product Name. Next to the
    slider, MICROSOFT SHAREDVIEW still appears in the associated field, but the two fields
    beneath contain only an asterisk ("*").

16. Click Next.

17. On the Exceptions page, click Next.

18. On the Name And Description page, type **Block SharedView.msi** in the Name text
    box, and then click Create. The new Deny rule now appears in the details pane.

19. In the Group Policy Management Editor console tree, navigate to Computer
    Configuration\Policies\Windows Settings\Security Settings\System Services.

20. In the details pane, double-click to open the Application Identity service.
    The Application Identity Properties dialog box opens.

21. In the Application Identity Properties dialog box, check Define This Policy Setting, click
    Automatic, and then click OK. Clients need to run this service for AppLocker to work.

22. Close the Group Policy Management Editor console and the Group Policy
    Management console.

23. Switch to Computer1, and then restart Computer1.

EXERCISE 3   **Testing the Configuration**

In this exercise, you test the results of implementing the new GPO that you created in the last
exercise.

1. After Computer1 has finished restarting, log on to the domain from Computer1 as
   a domain administrator.

2. Open your Downloads folder, and then double-click SharedView.msi.

3. If an Open File-Security Warning message box appears and asks if you want to run the
   file, click Run.

4. A Windows Installer warning message appears, indicating that the system
   administrator has set policies to prevent this installation.

5. Click OK to close the message.

6. Return to DC1. In the Group Policy Management console tree, locate the GPO named
   AppLocker Block SharedView.msi.

7. Right-click the AppLocker Block SharedView.msi GPO, and clear Link Enabled on the
   shortcut menu. This step effectively disables the policy.

8. Log off both computers.

Lesson Summary

- The successful installation of software depends on many requirements. These requirements include local administrator privileges, Windows 7 compatibility, proper installation settings, and other factors. To troubleshoot problems with an installation, you should verify that all of these requirements are met.
- A Windows Installer program can also be blocked by SRP or AppLocker.
- AppLocker is an improved version of SRP that is new to Windows 7 and Windows Server 2008 R2. Improvements in AppLocker include the publisher rule condition, the ability to assign rules to specific users and groups, and audit-only mode.

Lesson Review

You can use the following questions to test your knowledge of the information in Lesson 1, "Understanding and Resolving Installation Failures." The questions are also available on the companion CD if you prefer to review them in electronic form.

NOTE ANSWERS

Answers to these questions and explanations of why each answer choice is correct or incorrect are located in the "Answers" section at the end of the book.

1. You work for Fabrikam, Inc., a firm whose network consists of a single Active Directory Domain Services (AD DS) domain.

   Fabrikam's development team periodically tests new software tools for various departments. Recently the team has been testing a tool created by another company, a new partner named Contoso.com. Whenever authorized users attempt to install the program, however, they receive a warning informing them that the program is from an unknown publisher.

   You want to allow authorized users to install applications made by Contoso without receiving a warning. What should you do?

   A. Ensure that all authorized users are administrators of the computers on which they are installing the software.

   B. Provide authorized users with the credentials of a domain administrator and instruct them to provide these credentials at the User Account Control prompt when they attempt to install the software.

   C. Use Group Policy to deploy the public certificate provided with the software to the Trusted Publishers certificate store on all required computers.

   D. Use Group Policy to deploy the root certificate for Contoso.com to the Trusted Root Certification Authorities certificate store on all required computers.

2. You want to use AppLocker to prevent users from running a file named NewApp.msi for versions 7.0 and earlier. You have already created the default rules. How can you achieve this objective?

   A. Create a new Executable rule with the Publisher rule condition.

   B. Create a new Executable rule with the File Hash rule condition.

   C. Create a new Windows Installer rule with the Publisher rule condition.

   D. Create a new Windows Installer rule with the File Hash rule condition.

Lesson 2: Resolving Software Configuration and Compatibility Issues

If a program that fails is known to be compatible with Windows 7, the failure is typically the result of a faulty configuration. In this case, resolving the issue requires you to review the program settings to pinpoint the configuration error causing the problems experienced. If on the other hand a program that fails is not fully compatible with Windows 7, you can often resolve the issue by adjusting compatibility settings or finding an alternate host for the application.

After this lesson, you will be able to:

- Understand strategies and features used to resolve software configuration errors.
- Understand the features in Windows 7 that are most likely to create an application compatibility problem.
- Configure an application to run with settings compatible with an older version of Windows.
- Understand Group Policy settings that can affect compatibility handling and reporting.

Estimated lesson time: 30 minutes

Resolving Software Configuration Issues

Installed applications that have been working properly sometimes malfunction or fail unexpectedly for an unknown reason. Application errors such as these often result from changes in configuration settings that are specific to the application, but there are some general guidelines that can help you in your efforts to resolve these issues.

The following list includes general strategies and features to use in troubleshooting software configuration problems.

- **Review application settings**   If an application suddenly fails, it is often the result of a configuration change. If you can open the application, proceed systematically through the available menus and configuration areas of the interface to see if any settings have been set improperly. If an application relies on a database or specific type of file (such as Microsoft Outlook, which relies on .pst files), then make sure that the database or file in question is accessible and not corrupted. If the application relies on a network resource, check network settings and ensure that the network resource is both accessible and available.

    During this phase of troubleshooting, you should also perform research on the Web about the issue experienced and contact the application manufacturer if necessary.

- **Using Event Viewer** As part of your troubleshooting process, you should use Event Viewer to find error messages related to the application you are troubleshooting. Event Viewer can help you determine when errors related to the application started appearing and ultimately help you determine the cause of failure. Pay special attention to the Application log and any logs that are specific to the application in question. Use the Filter Current Log function to locate only Critical, Warning, and Error messages. If you find errors that seem relevant, perform Web searches on these errors to learn more about them if necessary.

- **Using Event Forwarding** Troubleshooting a network-wide application issue might require you to review logs on multiple computers. To simplify this procedure, you can use *Event Forwarding*, a feature in which multiple computers are configured to forward a particular event to a collecting computer. Using the Event Forwarding feature requires that you configure both the forwarding computers, called the *source computers,* and the collecting computer, called the *collector.*

    To configure event forwarding, perform the following steps:

    1. On each source computer, type the following at an elevated command prompt:

        `winrm quickconfig`

    2. On the collector computer, type the following at an elevated command prompt:

        `wecutil qc`

    3. Add the computer account of the collector computer to the local Administrators group on each of the source computers.

    4. In Event Viewer on the collector computer, choose Create Subscription, and then follow the prompts to specify both the event you want to collect and the source computers on which you want to collect them.

> **NOTE   EVENT FORWARDING REQUIRES CERTAIN SERVICES TO BE RUNNING**
>
> Event forwarding depends on the Windows Remote Management (WinRM) service and the Windows Event Collector (Wecsvc) service. Both of these services must be running on computers participating in the forwarding and collecting process.

- **System Restore** An application can fail because of changes to the operating system. If an application stops functioning after you install an update or make a system change, consider using the System Restore feature to revert the computer's configuration to a time when the application functioned properly. Although this feature does not remove or change user files such as documents or e-mail, it will remove any applications, updates, or system changes that have occurred since the system restore point.

> **NOTE   OPENING SYSTEM RESTORE**
>
> To start the System Restore Wizard, click Start, type **system restore**, and then press Enter.

- **Repairing or reinstalling software** If software stops functioning but you cannot revert to an earlier state manually or automatically, you should attempt to repair the software in question. A repair option, if available, essentially reinstalls the application while preserving user files and settings for that application. If no such repair option is available, you can back up the user files and simply reinstall the software. To perform a fresh installation, you might need to uninstall the software first.

- **Restoring from backup** If a critical application fails but you cannot repair it by using any of the methods listed previously, you should restore the entire system from a backup of the last functioning version of the computer. Before doing so, be sure to perform a backup of the user's personal files and folders.

Understanding Application Compatibility

Each release of Windows includes new features and capabilities that affect how applications run. Before making adjustments to improve application compatibility, you should gain some understanding of the particular features in Windows 7 that are most likely to cause application compatibility problems. These particular features can generally be classified as security enhancements and operating system changes.

Security Enhancements Affecting Application Compatibility

Many organizations deploying Windows 7 will be replacing Windows XP on their clients, not Windows Vista. Compared to Windows XP, the Windows 7 environment offers a number of important security-related enhancements. The following security features are the ones most likely to lead to compatibility problems with third-party applications:

- **User Account Control** Introduced in Windows Vista, User Account Control (UAC) separates standard user privileges from administrator privileges in a way that helps reduce the effect of malware, unauthorized software installation, and unapproved system changes. If you are logged on as an administrator, UAC by default prompts you to confirm some tasks that you want to perform that require administrator privileges. If you are logged on as a standard user and attempt to perform a task that requires administrator privileges, UAC gives you an opportunity to enter administrator credentials instead of denying you the right to perform the task outright.

  UAC can introduce problems in applications that are not compliant with this technology enhancement. For this reason, it is important to test applications with UAC enabled before you deploy them.

- **Windows Resource Protection (also called File and Registry Virtualization)** *Windows Resource Protection* is a feature in Windows Vista and Windows 7 that intercepts any application requests to write to protected system files or registry locations and then redirects these requests to safe and temporary locations. Although most applications can handle this redirection without generating an error, some applications require full access to the protected areas and cannot handle the redirection process.

- **Internet Explorer Protected Mode** *Protected Mode* is a feature of Windows Internet Explorer 8 that protects computers from malware by restricting the browser's access within the registry and file system. Although Protected Mode helps maintain the integrity of client computers, it can affect the proper operation of older applications, ActiveX controls, and other script code.

- **Operating system and Internet Explorer versioning** Many applications check the version of the operating system and behave differently or fail to run when an unexpected version number is detected. You can resolve this issue by setting appropriate compatibility modes or applying versioning shims (application-compatibility fixes).

Operating System Changes Affecting Application Compatibility

Of the many operating system changes introduced by Windows 7, the following features are most likely to lead to application compatibility difficulties:

- **New system Application Programming Interfaces (APIs)** APIs expose layers of the Windows 7 operating system differently than they did in previous versions of Windows. Antivirus and firewall software are examples of applications that rely on these new APIs to monitor and protect Windows 7.

  Applications that relied on outdated APIs will need to be upgraded or replaced for Windows 7.

- **Windows 7 64-bit** Neither 16-bit applications nor 32-bit drivers are supported in the Windows 7 64-bit environment. The automatic registry and system file redirection that allows some older applications to function in the 32-bit version of Windows 7 are not available for the 64-bit environment. For these reasons, new 64-bit applications must comply fully with Windows 7 application standards.

- **Operating system version** Many older applications check for a specific version of Windows and stop responding when they fail to find this specific version. Features built into Windows 7 such as the Program Compatibility Assistant (discussed in the next section) can usually resolve this type of issue automatically.

- **New folder locations** User folders, My Documents folders, and folders with localization have changed since Windows XP. Applications with hard-coded paths may fail.

Using Windows 7 Built-in Compatibility Tools

Although you should perform extensive application compatibility testing before you deploy Windows 7, compatibility problems may unexpectedly appear or persist after deployment. To help you improve the compatibility of older programs after deployment, Windows 7 provides three tools: the Program Compatibility Assistant (PCA), the Program Compatibility Troubleshooter, and the Compatibility tab in a program's Properties dialog box.

- **PCA** The PCA is a tool that automatically appears when Windows 7 detects known compatibility issues in older programs. When it does appear, the PCA can offer to fix the problem. For example, the PCA can resolve conflicts with UAC, or it can run the program in a mode that simulates earlier versions of Windows. If you agree to the changes PCA proposes, these changes are then performed automatically. Alternatively, if the compatibility issue detected is serious, the PCA can warn you or block the program from running.

When the PCA recognizes a problem but cannot offer a fix, it will give you an option to check online for possible solutions, as shown in Figure 9-10.

FIGURE 9-10 The PCA triggers a message when a program incompatibility is found.

- **Program Compatibility Troubleshooter** The Program Compatibility Troubleshooter is a Control Panel program that you can use to configure the compatibility settings for an older program if you notice that the program is not running smoothly. For example, you can configure the program to run in a simulated environment of a previous version of Windows, to run with specific display settings, or to run with Administrator privileges.

To start the wizard, in Control Panel, first click Programs, and then, in the Programs and Features category, click Run Programs Made For Previous Versions Of Windows. You can also start the Program Compatibility Troubleshooter by right-clicking an application and selecting Troubleshoot Compatibility from the shortcut menu, as shown in Figure 9-11.

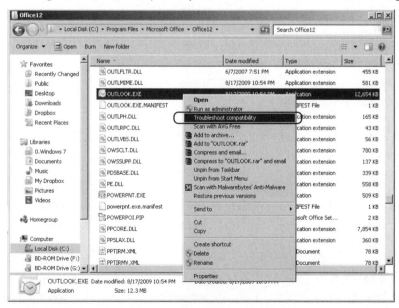

FIGURE 9-11 Launching the Program Compatibility Troubleshooter

A page of the Program Compatibility Troubleshooter is shown in Figure 9-12.

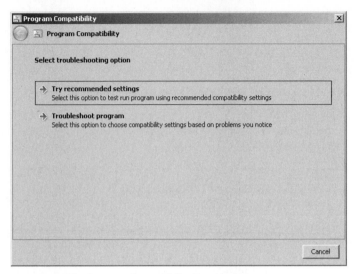

FIGURE 9-12 The Program Compatibility Troubleshooter

- **Compatibility Tab** As an alternative to running the Program Compatibility Troubleshooter, you can simply configure compatibility settings on the Compatibility tab within the Properties sheet of any given program. The options provided on this tab are the same as those you can configure through the Program Compatibility Troubleshooter. The Compatibility Tab is shown in Figure 9-13.

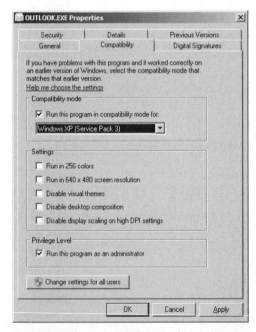

FIGURE 9-13 The Compatibility tab of an application

Note that adjusting the compatibility settings of a program does not always fix the problem. If issues persist, you should attempt alternate hosting or obtain an updated version of the program.

Alternate Hosting for Application Compatibility

In some cases, your organization will need to support an application whose compatibility issues with Windows 7 cannot be resolved immediately. For example, if you are running a 64-bit version of Windows 7, you cannot run 16-bit applications by merely adjusting the compatibility settings of the program. Until a newer, more compatible version of the application appears (or until your organization finds an alternate application), you must find a temporary fix for the application compatibility problem.

The most common temporary fix for unresolved application compatibility problems such as this is simply to run the program within the old operating system in a virtual machine, on a remote server that can be accessed through Remote Desktop, or both.

The following list describes various options of hosting an older application on an older operating system:

- **Microsoft Virtual PC 2007**   You can use Virtual PC to run applications that function properly only with older versions of Windows. For example, if your organization needs to support a 16-bit application within a 64-bit version of Windows 7, you can use Virtual PC 2007 to run the program within a virtual machine running a previous version of Windows. Although virtual machine software such as Virtual PC is required to run 16-bit applications in 64-bit versions of Windows 7, the use of Virtual PC need not be reserved only for this purpose. Virtual PC also lets users keep a previous version of Windows until upgraded versions of older applications are developed. Whenever you need to support an older application that does not run smoothly in Windows 7 and that cannot be upgraded, you should consider running the application inside a virtual machine.

- **Windows XP Mode**   *Windows XP Mode* is essentially a downloadable enhancement to Virtual PC that is available in Windows 7 Professional, Enterprise, and Ultimate. Windows XP Mode also requires special virtualization technology. Specifically, Windows XP Mode requires a CPU with Intel-VT or AMD-V technology, and this technology must be enabled in the BIOS.

  For eligible computers, Windows XP Mode enables you to access through the Start menu in Windows 7 any applications installed in a Windows XP guest virtual machine in Virtual PC. You then interact with these applications exactly as if they were installed natively in Windows 7. Windows XP Mode also provides an enormous performance advantage: It gives the Windows XP guest operating system direct access to the system hardware, so performance is much better than it is in Virtual PC alone.

  To install Windows XP Mode is easy: First download and install Virtual PC, and then download and install Windows XP Mode. You can perform both tasks from the Virtual PC Web site at *http://www.microsoft.com/windows/virtual-pc/download.aspx*. (Both Virtual PC and Windows XP Mode are free.)

MORE INFO   WINDOWS XP MODE

For step-by-step instructions on using Windows XP Mode, including installing and using applications, visit *http://www.microsoft.com/windows/virtual-pc/support/default.aspx*. You can also view a five-minute introduction to Windows XP Mode at *http://windows.microsoft.com/en-us/windows7/help/videos/using-windows-xp-mode*.

- **Hyper-V on Windows Server 2008**   Hyper-V is a high-performance virtualization environment available in Windows Server 2008. It allows you to create guest virtual machines with direct access to the hardware. On the virtual machines, you can install any version of Windows.

  If you choose to host an application on a virtual machine inside Hyper-V, clients running Windows 7 or other operating systems can then connect remotely to this application from over the network.

  Hyper-V requires a 64-bit processor with virtualization technology (Intel-VT or AMD-V).

- **Remote Desktop Services for Hosting Applications**   Hosting older applications on Remote Desktop Services lets you deliver Windows-based applications or the Windows desktop itself to virtually any computer device on your network. Clients running Windows 7 can connect to these application-hosting environments through Remote Desktop.

✔ **Quick Check**

- Which CPU technology must be available to use Windows XP Mode on a client running Windows 7?

Quick Check Answer

- Intel-VT or AMD-V

Understanding the Application Compatibility Toolkit (ACT)

The Application Compatibility Toolkit (ACT) is a tool you can use to identify application compatibility issues before Windows 7 deployment.

The following are some of the major components that make up the ACT solution:

- **Application Compatibility Manager**   A tool that enables you to collect and analyze your data so that you can identify any issues prior to deploying a new operating system or deploying a Windows update in your organization. You use this program heavily during the initial phases of an application migration project. Consider this tool as the primary user interface for ACT.

- **Application Compatibility Toolkit Data Collector** The Application Compatibility Toolkit Data Collector is distributed to each computer. It then performs scans by using compatibility evaluators. Data is collected and stored in the central compatibility database.

- **Setup Analysis Tool (SAT)** The SAT automates the running of application installations while monitoring the actions taken by each application's installer.

- **Standard User Analyzer (SUA)** The SUA determines the possible issues for applications running as a standard user in Windows 7.

ACT is an important tool for testing applications across a wide variety of computers and operating systems within your organization.

Configuring Application Compatibility Diagnostics Through Group Policy

Windows Server 2008 includes a set of policy options related to application compatibility diagnostics. To browse these settings in a GPO, browse to Computer Configuration\Policies\ Administrative Templates\System\Troubleshooting And Diagnostics\Application Compatibility Diagnostics.

The Application Compatibility Diagnostics container includes the following six policies:

- **Notify Blocked Drivers** This policy setting determines whether the PCA will notify the user if drivers are blocked because of compatibility issues. If you enable this policy setting, the PCA notifies the user of blocked driver issues and provides the user with an option to check the Microsoft Web site for solutions. (This behavior is also the default behavior in Windows 7.) If you disable this policy setting, the PCA does not notify the user of blocked driver issues. Note that if this policy setting is configured as disabled, the user is not presented with solutions to blocked drivers.

- **Detect Application Failures Caused By Deprecated Windows COM Objects** This policy setting determines whether the PCA will notify the user when a COM object creation failure is detected in an application. If you enable this policy setting, the PCA detects programs creating older COM objects that are removed in this version of Windows. (This behavior is also the default behavior in Windows 7.) When this failure is detected, after the program is terminated, PCA notifies the user about this problem and provides an option to check the Microsoft Web site for solutions. If you disable this policy setting, the PCA does not detect programs creating older COM objects.

- **Detect Application Failures Caused By Deprecated Windows DLLs** This policy setting determines whether the PCA will notify the user when a DLL load failure is detected in an application. If you enable this policy setting, the PCA detects programs trying to load older Microsoft Windows DLLs that are removed in this version of Windows. (This behavior is also the default behavior in Windows 7.) When this failure is detected, PCA notifies the user about this problem after the program is terminated and provides an option to check the Microsoft Web site for solutions. If you disable this policy setting, the PCA does not detect programs trying to load older Windows DLLs.

- **Detect Application Install Failures**   This policy setting configures the PCA to notify the user when an application installation has failed. If you enable this policy setting, the PCA detects application installation failures and provides the user with an option to restart the installer in Windows XP compatibility mode. (This behavior is also the default behavior in Windows 7.) If you disable this policy setting, the PCA does not detect program installation failures.

- **Detect Application Installers That Need To Be Run As Administrator**   This policy setting determines whether the PCA will notify the user when application installations have failed because they need to be run as an administrator. If you enable this policy setting, the PCA detects such installation failures and provides the user with an option to restart the installer programs as an administrator. (This behavior is also the default behavior in Windows 7.) If you disable this policy setting, the PCA does not notify users when installer program failures have occurred for this reason.

- **Detect Applications Unable To Launch Installers Under UAC**   This policy setting configures the PCA to notify the user when UAC is preventing an application from launching an installer (typically an updater program). If you enable this policy setting, the PCA detects programs that fail to start installers and grants administrator privileges that allow this task to be performed the next time the program is run. (This behavior is also the default behavior in Windows 7.) If you disable this policy setting, the PCA does not detect applications that fail to launch installers run under UAC.

EXAM TIP

You need to understand these application compatibility diagnostics Group Policy settings for the 70-685 exam.

PRACTICE   **Configuring Application Compatibility Diagnostics**

In this exercise, you configure application compatibility settings in Group Policy.

EXERCISE   Creating a Policy for Application Compatibility Settings

In this exercise, you create a new GPO named Application Compatibility Diagnostics Policy. In the GPO, you enable two settings that enable particular behaviors in the PCA.

1. Log on to the domain controller as a domain administrator.
2. Click Start, type **Group Policy Management**, and then click OK. The Group Policy Management console opens.
3. In the Group Policy Management console tree, expand Forest: nwtraders.msft and then Domains.
4. Beneath the Domains container, select and right-click the Nwtraders.msft icon, and then click the option to Create A GPO In This Domain, And Link It Here. The New GPO dialog box opens.

5. In the New GPO dialog box, type **Application Compatibility Diagnostics Policy**, and then click OK.

6. In the Details pane of the Group Policy Management console, ensure that the Linked Group Policy Objects tab is selected. Then, in the list of GPOs, right-click Application Compatibility Diagnostics Policy, and then click Edit. A Group Policy Management Editor window opens.

7. In the console tree of the Group Policy Management Editor, navigate to Computer Configuration\Policies\Administrative Templates\System\Troubleshooting and Diagnostics\Application Compatibility Diagnostics.

8. In the details pane of the Group Policy Management Editor, double-click the policy named Detect Application Failures Caused By Deprecated Windows DLLs. The associated policy setting Properties dialog box opens.

9. Read the description of the policy setting. Note that the Diagnostic Policy Service and the Program Compatibility Assistant Service must be running on Windows 7 for the Program Compatibility Assistant to execute. These services run by default on domain-joined computers running Windows 7.

10. Click Enabled.

11. In the Scenario Execution Level drop-down list box, ensure that Detection, Troubleshooting, And Resolution is selected.

12. Click OK. In the details pane of the Group Policy Management Editor, the policy setting should now appear as Enabled.

13. In the details pane of the Group Policy Management Editor, double-click the policy setting named Detect Application Install Failures. The associated policy setting Properties dialog box opens.

14. Read the description of the policy setting, and then click Enabled.

15. Click OK. In the details pane of the Group Policy Management Editor, the policy setting should now appear as Enabled.

16. Close all open windows.

Lesson Summary

- If an application malfunctions after it has been working correctly, the problem is usually a result of a configuration error or a system change. To discover or undo the error, you should use a variety of strategies, such as reviewing application settings, reviewing event logs, using System Restore, repairing or reinstalling the application, and restoring the system from backup.

- Each new release of Windows introduces features that affect the functionality of programs written for earlier operating systems. With Windows 7, the features most likely to affect application compatibility include UAC, Windows Resource Protection, and new system APIs.

- Windows 7 includes tools that help detect and mitigate compatibility problems for older applications. The PCA automatically appears when Windows 7 detects known compatibility issues. The Program Compatibility Troubleshooter is a wizard that enables you to run an older program with settings used in a previous version of Windows. You can configure these same compatibility settings on the Compatibility Tab of the program.

- If you need to support an application that is not compatible with Windows 7, you can run the program in a compatible operating system within a virtual machine. Alternatively, you can use a Remote Desktop connection to a computer running the application and a compatible operating system.

- Windows 7 includes several Group Policy settings that allow you to determine how the PCA will diagnose and troubleshoot application compatibility problems.

Lesson Review

You can use the following questions to test your knowledge of the information in Lesson 2, "Resolving Software Configuration and Compatibility Issues." The questions are also available on the companion CD if you prefer to review them in electronic form.

> **NOTE ANSWERS**
>
> Answers to these questions and explanations of why each answer choice is correct or incorrect are located in the "Answers" section at the end of the book.

1. You receive a call from the help desk about a user who is experiencing problems with an application on a computer running Windows 7. The application was functioning well until the user installed an optional update to Windows. She has made no other changes to the system since. Now, however, she is unable to start the application. Unfortunately, neither she nor the help desk staff has been able to return the application to its original functioning state.

   Which of the following steps should you take to solve the problem?

   A. Use the System Restore feature to return the computer to the point in time just before the user installed the optional update to Windows.

   B. Restore her user files from the latest backup.

   C. Configure Event Forwarding to forward messages in the application log to your computer.

   D. Uninstall and reinstall the application.

2. After upgrading the client computers in your organization from Windows XP to Windows Vista, you discover that a certain application installs without error but no longer runs properly in the new operating system. How can you ensure that users will receive any possible notifications telling them why the application has failed?

   A. In Group Policy, enable the Detect Application Failures Caused By Deprecated Windows DLLs Or COM Objects policy.

   B. In Group Policy, enable the Notify Blocked Drivers policy.

   C. In Group Policy, enable the Detect Application Install Failures policy.

   D. In Group Policy, enable the Detect Application Installers That Need To Be Run As Administrator policy.

3. Which of the following applications is least likely to run on the 32-bit version of Windows 7 without a software update?

   A. A 16-bit application written for Microsoft Windows 2000

   B. A 32-bit application written for Windows XP that requires administrative privileges to run properly

   C. An application written for Windows 2000 that writes to a protected area of the registry

   D. An application written for Windows XP that writes to protected system files

Chapter Review

To further practice and reinforce the skills you learned in this chapter, you can perform the following tasks:

- Review the chapter summary.
- Review the list of key terms introduced in this chapter.
- Complete the case scenarios. These scenarios set up real-world situations involving the topics of this chapter and ask you to create a solution.
- Complete the suggested practices.
- Take a practice test.

Chapter Summary

- To troubleshoot installation issues, verify administrator rights, Windows 7 compatibility, installation settings, application constraints and dependencies, resource availability, and any policy restrictions set in SRP or AppLocker.
- Applications can fail because of an improper configuration or because of a fundamental compatibility issue with Windows 7. For configuration issues, first attempt to identify and fix the problem manually, but if necessary, you can use System Restore, software repair, or system backups to resolve the issue. For compatibility issues, you can modify the program's compatibility settings, find a remote or virtual older host for the application, or simply upgrade your software to a newer version that is compatible with Windows 7.

Key Terms

Do you know what these key terms mean? You can check your answers by looking up the terms in the glossary at the end of the book.

- **Event Forwarding** A feature in which multiple source computers on a network are configured to forward particular events to a single collector computer.
- **Windows Resource Protection** A feature of Windows Vista and Windows 7 in which requests by programs to write to protected areas of the operating system are intercepted and redirected to safe areas.
- **Windows XP Mode** In Windows 7, a downloadable enhancement to Virtual PC in which you can access and interact with programs transparently in a guest Windows XP virtual machine. Windows XP Mode requires a CPU with Intel-VT or AMD-V technology.

Case Scenarios

In the following case scenarios, you apply what you've learned about protecting client systems. You can find answers to these questions in the "Answers" section at the end of this book.

Case Scenario 1: Restricting Software with AppLocker

You work as an enterprise support technician in a large company whose network consists of a single AD DS domain. All the clients in the company are running Windows 7, and all the domain controllers are running Windows Server 2008 R2.

You want to use AppLocker to allow users to run Windows Installer programs from Microsoft. You also want to prevent them from running Windows Installer programs from other companies. You begin by creating a new GPO and linking it to the domain.

With this scenario in mind, answer the following questions:

1. You are creating a Windows Installer rule in the new GPO. What kind of rule condition should you specify if you want to allow Windows Installer programs from Microsoft to be run?

2. You successfully create a Windows Installer rule that allows everyone to run .msi files from Microsoft. You have not created any default rules. If the GPO is enforced without making further changes, will users be able to run Windows Installer programs created by other companies? Why or why not?

Case Scenario 2: Configuring Application Compatibility Settings

You work as an enterprise support technician for Contoso, Inc. The Contoso network includes 20 computers running Windows Server 2008 R2, 150 client computers running Windows XP Professional, and 100 client computers on which Windows 7 Professional has been installed recently.

You currently are handling issues related to application compatibility on the clients running Windows 7.

With this scenario in mind, answer the following questions:

1. A certain application used infrequently by the Advertising department was written for Windows XP. Users report that the application is unstable in Windows 7. Assuming that no updates for the application are yet available, what is the first remedy that you should investigate?

2. Users report that sometimes applications fail to install, but that they receive no notification about the failure. What can you do to ensure that users receive notification when applications fail to install?

Suggested Practices

To help you master the exam objectives presented in this chapter, complete the following tasks.

Identify and Resolve New Software Installation Issues

Perform the following activities to learn to resolve common installation issues:

- **Practice 1**   Attempt to install on Windows 7 an older program that was written for Windows XP or Windows 2000. If the installation fails, run the installation as an administrator and see if it succeeds.
- **Practice 2**   In a test domain, obtain a certificate from a third-party software publisher. Use Group Policy to deploy that certificate to the Trusted Publishers certificate store on all clients in the domain.

Identify and Resolve Software Configuration Issues

Perform the following activity to learn to troubleshoot many computers on a network:

- **Practice 1**   In a test domain, enable Event Forwarding on multiple source computers. Enable Event Forwarding on the collector computer, and then specify a common error to collect in order to test the results.

Identify Cause of and Resolve Software Failure Issues

Perform the following activity to learn one way to resolve an application compatibility issue:

- **Practice 1**   On a computer whose CPU includes Intel-VT or AMD-V technology, enable that feature in the BIOS. Then, download and install Virtual PC, and then download and install Windows XP Mode. Use Windows XP Mode to access applications installed in a virtual machine from the Start menu of Windows 7.

Take a Practice Test

The practice tests on this book's companion CD offer many options. For example, you can test yourself on just one exam objective, or you can test yourself on all the 70-685 certification exam content. You can set up the test so that it closely simulates the experience of taking a certification exam, or you can set it up in study mode so that you can look at the correct answers and explanations after you answer each question.

> **MORE INFO   PRACTICE TESTS**
>
> For details about all the practice test options available, see the section entitled "How to Use the Practice Tests," in the Introduction to this book.

Configuring Windows Firewall

Every network needs a firewall to keep out external threats. In recent years, however, as the need for network security has increased, it has become just as important to protect each computer with its own individual (or "host") firewall. Windows 7 provides such a feature with Windows Firewall, and though Windows Firewall doesn't replace the need for a network firewall, it does provide an important level of defense for each client computer.

As an enterprise support technician, you need to be able to configure Windows Firewall in a way that both protects your clients and allows them to communicate with other trusted computers on the network.

Understanding Windows Firewall

Windows Firewall is a host firewall that is built into Windows 7. Unlike firewall devices that control traffic between networks, host firewalls define which traffic types are allowed to pass between the local computer and the rest of the network.

You can configure Windows Firewall by using two separate tools. If you want to control inbound traffic based on its associated application, use the Windows Firewall page in Control Panel. To open this tool, open Control Panel, click System and Security, and then click Windows Firewall, as shown in Figure A-1.

FIGURE A-1 Accessing Windows Firewall settings in Control Panel

The Windows Firewall page is shown in Figure A-2.

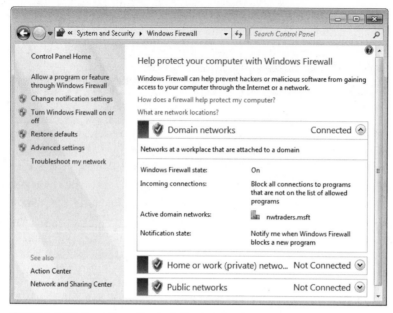

FIGURE A-2 Windows Firewall page in Control Panel

If you want to control outbound traffic, or if you want to control inbound traffic based on additional criteria such as source address or destination port, you need to use the Windows Firewall with Advanced Security (WFAS) console. To open this console, click Advanced Settings on the Windows Firewall page in Control Panel, as shown in Figure A-3.

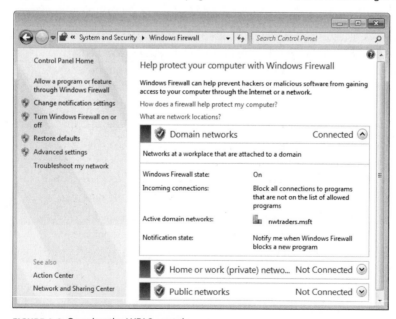

FIGURE A-3 Opening the WFAS console

The WFAS console is shown in Figure A-4.

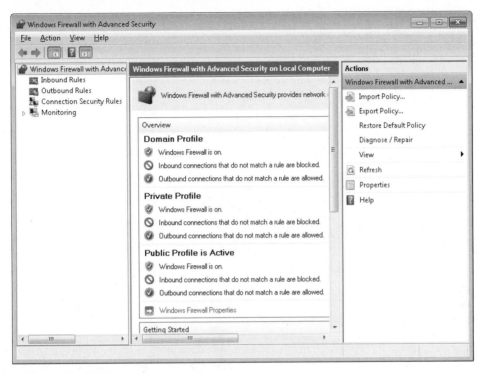

FIGURE A-4 The WFAS console

Allowing Inbound Traffic

By default, Windows Firewall blocks all incoming connections to the local computer that originate from an external source. *Exceptions* (also known as *allow rules*) are then made to allow any desired connections to the local computer, connections such as traffic to locally hosted network shares or traffic for approved network applications such as Windows Live Messenger.

After exceptions are defined, Windows Firewall inspects all incoming packets and compares them against this list of allowed traffic. If a packet matches an entry in the exception list, Windows Firewall passes the packet to the TCP/IP protocol stack for further processing. If the packet does not match an entry in the list, Windows Firewall discards the packet and, if logging is enabled, creates an entry in the Windows Firewall logging file.

This process is illustrated in Figure A-5, where exceptions are defined only for Windows Live Messenger and Windows File Sharing. These two programs are able to initiate connections that pass through the Windows Firewall, but the firewall blocks the connection attempt made by another network program.

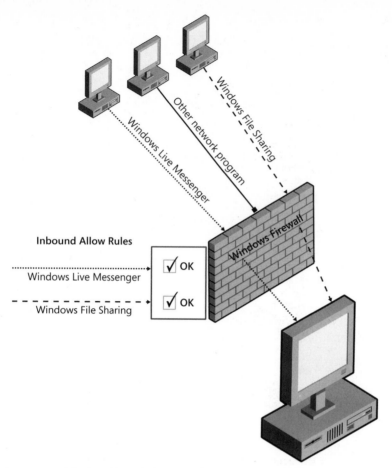

FIGURE A-5 Windows Firewall blocks inbound connections that are not allowed explicitly.

Denying Outbound Traffic

By default, Windows Firewall allows all outbound connections from the local computer. However, you can configure Windows Firewall to deny any outbound connections that you specify. For example, you might want to create a rule that denies outbound traffic to a specific address that you know is associated with a known malware application named "Z." Such a firewall rule would not affect traffic to other network addresses. This scenario is illustrated in Figure A-6.

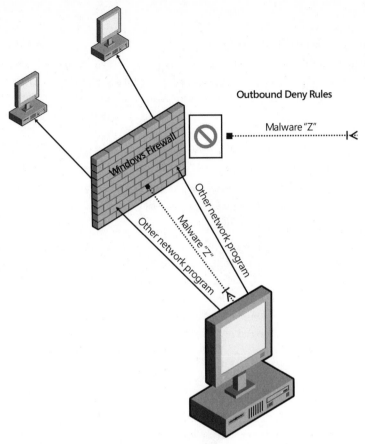

Outbound Deny Rules

Malware "Z"

Windows Firewall

Other network program

Malware "Z"

Other network program

FIGURE A-6 Windows Firewall allows all outbound connections that are not denied explicitly.

Defining Complex Traffic Types

In the previous examples, firewall rules allow or deny traffic that is defined by a single criterion: a specific network program or an IP address. However, by using the WFAS console, you can also allow or deny traffic based on any combination of criteria, such as source or destination IP address, source or destination port, or Internet Protocol Security (IPSec) encryption status. For example, such a rule would enable you to allow inbound connections from a specific network application that originates only from a specific address or range of addresses.

Understanding Network Locations

Network locations are essentially security categories applied to network connections. Four network locations are available: Home, Work, Public, and Domain. Every connection is assigned to one, and only one, of these four network locations.

Network locations restrict some network features for environments that require high security. For example, Network Discovery is a multicast protocol that enables a computer to discover neighboring computers and devices on the local area network (LAN). Because this feature is not usually desirable for environments that require high security, Network Discovery is disabled by default in the Public and Domain network locations. Similarly, a homegroup is a new feature of Windows 7 that helps you create a password-protected share of your local Libraries. This feature is available only in the Home network location; it cannot be enabled in any other network location.

Network locations can be set automatically or manually. When a client is a member of a domain, all its connections are assigned automatically to the Domain network location when the computer starts, and this network location cannot be changed. For connections outside domain networks, you choose the network location manually.

EXAM TIP

For all Microsoft certification exams such as 70-685 that cover Windows 7, you will be tested on your familiarity with supporting this operating system in an enterprise setting only. In such settings, virtually all connections in Windows 7 are assigned to the Domain network location. Remember that for any domain-joined computer such as a laptop, the network location remains set to Domain even when you physically remove the computer from the enterprise network.

Table A-1 provides a summary of the default security settings in the four network locations. Note that with the exception of the homegroups feature, you can change the default setting for any feature in any network location. You can find these configuration settings by searching for the term "Manage advanced sharing settings" from the Start menu or by navigating to the following page: Control Panel\Network and Internet\Network and Sharing Center\Change Advanced Sharing Settings.

TABLE A-1 Features by Network Location

	HOME NETWORK LOCATION	WORK NETWORK LOCATION	PUBLIC NETWORK LOCATION	DOMAIN NETWORK LOCATION
Network Discovery	Enabled by default	Enabled by default	Disabled by default	Disabled by default
File and Printer Sharing	Disabled by default	Disabled by default	Disabled by default	Disabled by default
Public Folder Sharing	Disabled by default	Disabled by default	Disabled by default	Disabled by default

	HOME NETWORK LOCATION	WORK NETWORK LOCATION	PUBLIC NETWORK LOCATION	DOMAIN NETWORK LOCATION
Media Streaming	Disabled by default	Disabled by default	Disabled by default	Disabled by default
File Sharing Connections	Uses 128-bit connections by default	Uses 128-bit connections by default	Uses 128-bit connections by default	Uses 128-bit connections by default
Homegroups	Available	Not available	Not available	Not available

> **MORE INFO** The Network Map feature, which creates a visual map of the LAN, is enabled by default only in the Home and Work network locations. To enable it in the Domain network location, you must use Group Policy. In a Group Policy Object (GPO), navigate to Computer Configuration\Policies\Administrative Templates\Network\Link-Layer Topology Discovery\, and configure both the Turn On Mapper I/O (LLTDIO) Driver and the Turn On Responder (RSPNDR) Driver settings to allow operation while in a domain.

Understanding Firewall Profiles

Network locations serve as the basis for firewall profiles, which are simply sets of firewall rules. The firewall profiles match network locations as follows:

- **Domain Networks firewall profile** Defines the firewall rules for connections assigned to the Domain network location

- **Home or Work (Private) Networks firewall profile** Defines the firewall rules for connections assigned to either the Home network location or the Work network location

- **Public Networks firewall profile** Defines the firewall rules for connections assigned to the Public network location

> **NOTE UNIDENTIFIED NETWORKS**
>
> If a network connection cannot be identified because of a network issue or lack of identifiable characteristics, the network location type is set to Unidentified and its firewall profile is set to Public Networks by default.

For computers outside a domain environment, firewall profiles enable you to set different levels of security for the different networks to which your computer can connect. For example, a laptop user in a small business might allow others to initiate instant messaging communication in the Home and Work network locations but not in a Public network location. You could achieve this by using the WFAS console to create an inbound allow rule for the program that applies only to the Private network profile.

For domain-joined computers, the Domain Networks firewall profile and firewall rules are applied to all network connections as the computer starts. If a certain number of employees in your company use portable computers, for example, the firewall settings that are defined in the Domain Networks profile are applied to network connections as the computer starts even after the computer is removed physically from the company premises.

Creating Inbound Exceptions

Although client computers generally need to be protected from undesired incoming connections, it is also true that in an enterprise setting, client computers often need to provide incoming access to specific network programs or features. For example, many office networks run backup software that is managed centrally. To allow the network backup software to connect to and back up a client computer, the client needs to allow access to that backup application. For network management software, the same is true: Clients often need to allow access to a remote server so that an application running on that server can read log files and record errors for administrators to see.

Firewall exceptions in Windows Firewall typically are created automatically whenever you install a client feature for that application or feature. However, there are a number of reasons why you might need to create firewall exceptions manually. First, some network applications do not have any installable client feature, so you might need to create an exception manually to allow access to that application. Another reason why you might need to create a firewall exception manually is if the original firewall exception for a network program has been deleted. Finally, you might want to modify an existing exception manually to improve security. For example, if a firewall exception for a network backup application has already been created, you might want to modify that exception manually so that the backup application is allowed only when the connection originates from the backup server.

To create a basic firewall exception for all inbound connections from a network program or feature, perform the following steps:

1. In Control Panel, browse to System and Security, Windows Firewall, and then click Allow A Program Or Feature Through Windows Firewall, as shown in Figure A-7.

   This step opens the Allowed Programs page, which is shown in Figure A-8.

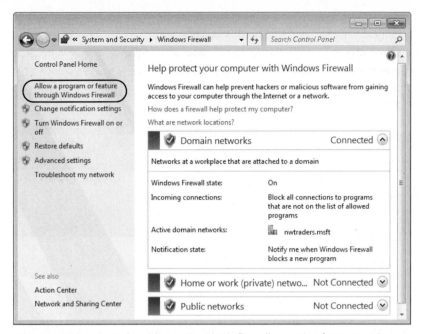

FIGURE A-7 Using Control Panel to create a basic firewall exception for a network program or feature

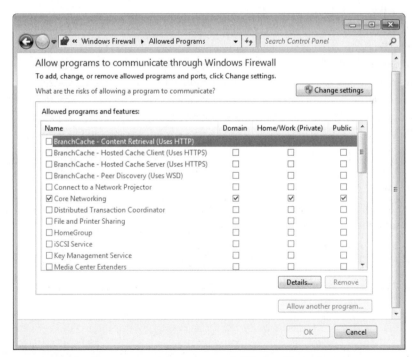

FIGURE A-8 Allowing programs inbound access in Windows Firewall

2. Click Change Settings.

3. If you can see the program to which you want to allow inbound access in the Allowed Programs And Features list, select the check box associated with that program. Verify that the check boxes are selected only for the profiles desired, and then click OK.

4. If the program is not listed, click Allow Another Program. The Add A Program window, which is shown in Figure A-9, opens.

FIGURE A-9 Adding a program exception

5. Select the desired program from the list, click Add, and then click OK.

This method enables you to create a basic inbound exception for a program in Windows Firewall. To configure any other type of firewall rule, such as one that creates an exception based on source address, you need to use the WFAS console.

To create an advanced firewall rule, perform the following steps.

1. In Control Panel, browse to System and Security, Windows Firewall, and then click Advanced Settings. The Windows Firewall With Advanced Security console opens.

2. In the console tree, right-click Inbound Rules, and then click New Rule. The New Inbound Rule Wizard opens.

3. On the Rule Type page, click Custom, and then click Next.

4. On the Program page, specify any program or service to which you want this rule to apply, and then click Next.

5. On the Protocol And Ports page, specify the combination of protocol type, protocol number, local ports, remote ports, and Internet Control Message Protocol (ICMP) type to which you want this rule to apply, and then click Next.

6. On the Scope page, specify the local and remote IP addresses to which you want this rule to apply, and then click Next.

7. On the Action page, specify whether you want the rule to allow the specified connection, block the specified connection, or allow the connection only if it is secured by using IPSec, and then click Next.

8. On the Profile page, specify the firewall profiles to which you want the rule to apply, and then click Next.

9. On the Name page, specify a name for the firewall rule, and then click Finish.

Creating Inbound Exceptions in Group Policy

You can create an inbound allow rule in a GPO that applies to every computer and that falls within the scope of that GPO. Such an allow rule would be enforced; it could not be deleted or disabled by local settings. To achieve this, you can open a GPO on a server running Windows Server 2008 and navigate to Computer Configuration\Policies\Windows Settings\Windows Firewall With Advanced Security\Windows Firewall With Advanced Security\Inbound Rules. Then, right-click the Inbound Rules node and click New Rule from the shortcut menu, as shown in Figure A-10. This step opens the same New Inbound Rule Wizard described in the last procedure. Note also that you can perform the same procedure in Local Security Policy, which you can use to enforce a firewall rule on a single client computer.

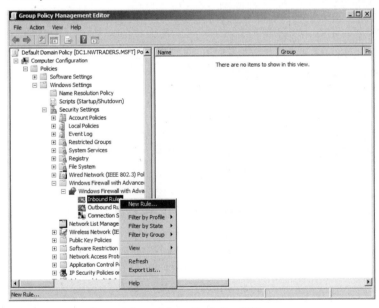

FIGURE A-10 Creating an inbound firewall rule in a GPO

Troubleshooting Windows Firewall

If Windows Firewall is not behaving as expected, you should review configuration settings in Control Panel, in the WFAS console, and in Group Policy. You should also review the Windows Firewall logs (which first need to be enabled) and the Windows event logs. The following sections provide a summary of these basic troubleshooting steps.

Troubleshooting Windows Firewall Settings in Control Panel

To begin troubleshooting Windows Firewall, first use Control Panel to verify that the firewall state is on, and then determine whether the firewall is configured to allow exceptions.

If the firewall is turned off, the Windows Firewall page in Control Panel displays a red shield, and the Window Firewall State is designated as Off, as shown in Figure A-11.

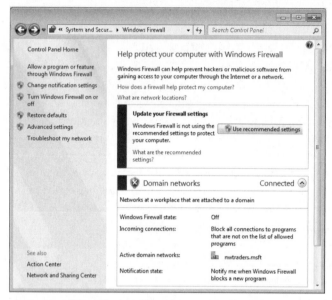

FIGURE A-11 When Windows Firewall is turned off, a red shield is displayed.

If Windows Firewall is turned on and configured to allow no exceptions, the Windows Firewall page displays a "No" icon (a red circle with a bar through it), as shown in Figure A-12.

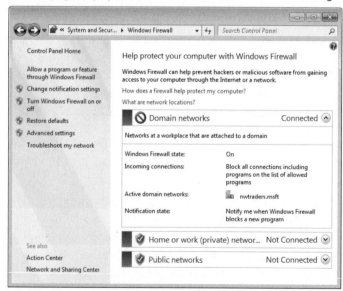

FIGURE A-12 If exceptions are not working, they could be disabled.

If you want to enable or disable either firewall exceptions or the firewall itself, click Turn Windows Firewall On Or Off. This step opens the Customize Settings page in the Windows Firewall feature of Control Panel, which is shown in Figure A-13.

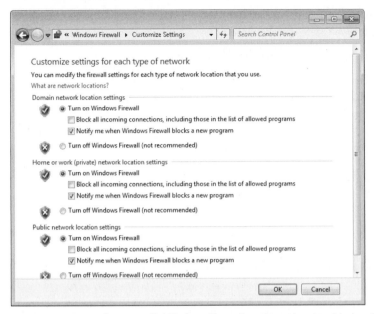

FIGURE A-13 Remember to verify Windows Firewall settings when troubleshooting.

This page allows you to configure three settings for Windows Firewall in each network location:

- Turn Windows Firewall On Or Off
- Block All Incoming Connections, Including Those In The List Of Allowed Programs
- Enable Or Disable Notification Messages That Appear When An Incoming Program Is Blocked

NOTE **TROUBLESHOOTING WINDOWS FIREWALL NOTIFICATION MESSAGES**

Start on the Customize Settings page of Control Panel if you want to troubleshoot notification messages for Windows Firewall.

Troubleshooting Allowed Programs

If reviewing these configuration settings for Windows Firewall does not solve the problem you are trying to troubleshoot, you should review the list of allowed programs (exceptions) that you have defined in Control Panel. Verify that the correct ones—and only the correct ones—are created and enabled.

One of the most common problems that administrators face in new installations of Windows is that by default, clients running Windows do not respond to ping (ICMP Echo Request) messages. Although you can solve this problem by creating an allow rule for ICMP Echo Requests in the WFAS console, you can also configure a client to respond to pings simply by creating an exception for File And Printer Sharing in Control Panel.

Troubleshooting Windows Firewall by Using the WFAS Console

Because the WFAS console is the main configuration tool for Windows Firewall, it is also its main troubleshooting tool. You can use the WFAS console to perform troubleshooting procedures such as reviewing the firewall configuration in the Monitoring node, reviewing settings configured in the firewall properties, verifying all locally defined firewall rules, and verifying Connection Security Rules.

> **NOTE CONNECTION SECURITY RULES**
>
> Connection Security Rules are used to apply IPSec security requirements to inbound and outbound connections.

REVIEWING THE FIREWALL CONFIGURATION IN THE MONITORING NODE

The Monitoring node in the WFAS console, shown in Figure A-14, can be used to review the firewall configuration. Specifically, through the Monitoring node, you can review the following:

- The active profile
- The firewall state
- General settings (including notification settings)
- Logging settings
- Active (enabled) firewall rules on the computer
- Active connection security rules on the computer and detailed information concerning their settings
- Active security associations for IPSec connections

> **MORE INFO USING THE WFAS CONSOLE**
>
> For additional information on monitoring by using the WFAS console, visit *http://technet .microsoft.com/en-us/library/dd421717(WS.10).aspx.*

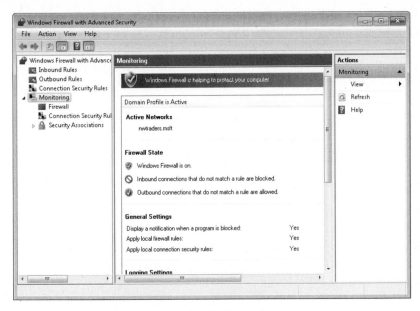

FIGURE A-14 The Monitoring node of the WFAS console

REVIEWING WINDOWS FIREWALL PROPERTIES

Windows Firewall properties are the settings configured in the properties of the root node of the WFAS console tree (that is, the node named Windows Firewall With Advanced Security). You can also access Windows Firewall properties by selecting the root node and then clicking Windows Firewall Properties in the center pane, as shown in Figure A-15.

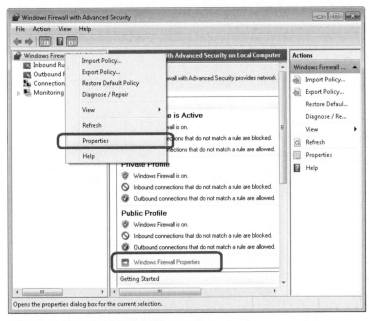

FIGURE A-15 Opening Windows Firewall Properties

These settings affect the following behaviors for the Domain, Private, and Public profiles:

- Whether incoming or outgoing connections as a whole are blocked
- Whether a notification occurs when an incoming network program is blocked
- Whether the local computer allows unicast responses to any broadcast or multicast messages that it sends on the network
- Whether logging is performed for successful connections
- Whether logging is performed for dropped packets

Be sure to review these settings when troubleshooting Windows Firewall.

VERIFYING FIREWALL RULES

When you are troubleshooting an issue with Windows Firewall, you often need to review all the firewall rules, both active and inactive, that are configured in the WFAS console. You can take this step by using the Inbound Rules and Outbound Rules nodes. Through these nodes, you can see all rules created on the system, even those you might have configured as an allowed program (exception) in Control Panel.

If, for example, you find that a network program cannot communicate with the local computer, you should verify the following by investigating firewall rules:

- Verify that an inbound allow rule defined for that program is configured for the active firewall profile.
- If the rule exists, verify that the rule itself is active. (Active rules are designated with a green check icon, and inactive rules are designated with a gray check icon.)
  - If the rule is inactive when you believe it should be active, check the properties of the rule to ensure that you have defined traffic for the rule correctly.
  - If the desired inbound allow rule is active, verify that no other rules such as inbound deny rules are preventing it from functioning as you expect. Deny rules override allow rules.

If no allow rule for the program exists, create a new rule for that program.

VERIFYING CONNECTION SECURITY RULES

Connection Security Rules enforce IPSec authentication on specified connections. If a Connection Security Rule requires security, it can block traffic from a program even if Firewall Rules allow it. For example, an active Connection Security Rule might require that all inbound traffic be authenticated. In this case, traffic from a network source that cannot be authenticated is dropped even if you have created an allow rule for the traffic in question.

For this reason, you need to review Connection Security Rules when you are troubleshooting Windows Firewall. If you need to allow traffic from a remote source that cannot be authenticated, be sure to configure an exemption for that remote source. Alternatively, you can modify Connection Security Rules so that they only request authentication but do not require it.

Troubleshooting Windows Firewall with Group Policy

When you are troubleshooting Windows Firewall, be sure to review Group Policy and Local Computer Policy settings (including those in Local Security Policy) because these settings affect the Windows Firewall configuration.

Group Policy provides two places to configure Windows Firewall in every GPO. As mentioned earlier in this chapter, every GPO contains a Windows Firewall With Advanced Security node in Computer Configuration\Policies\Windows Settings\Security Settings. This part of a GPO enables you to define firewall rules that are created automatically on every computer running Windows Vista and later that falls within the scope of the policy. The second location in a GPO where you can configure Windows Firewall settings is found in Computer Configuration\Policies\Administrative Templates\Network\Network Connections. This location is shown in Figure A-16.

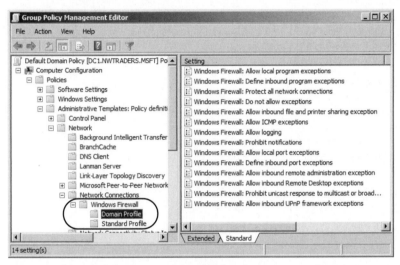

FIGURE A-16 Windows Firewall settings in Group Policy

Through this location in the Administrative Templates section of a GPO, you can configure the following Windows Firewall–related policy settings:

- **Windows Firewall: Allow Authenticated IPSec Bypass**   Unlike the other settings mentioned in this list, this policy setting appears at the root of the Windows Firewall folder in Administrative Templates. This setting allows the computers that you specify to bypass the local Windows Firewall if they can authenticate by using IPSec.

- **Windows Firewall: Allow Local Program Exceptions**   This policy setting allows administrators to use Control Panel to define a local program exceptions list. When set to Disabled, this policy setting prevents administrators from creating Windows Firewall exceptions in Control Panel. If an administrator is unable to create program exceptions, you should check this policy setting.

- **Windows Firewall: Define Inbound Program Exceptions**   This policy setting allows you to define firewall exceptions for a set list of programs. These programs are then defined as allowed programs in Windows Firewall on all computers that fall within the scope of the policy. When you disable this setting, the program exceptions list that you have defined in this policy setting is deleted.

- **Windows Firewall: Protect All Network Connections**   This setting allows you to force Windows Firewall into an "on" or "off" state.

- **Windows Firewall: Do Not Allow Exceptions**   If you enable this policy setting, any exceptions that you define in Control Panel are ignored.

- **Windows Firewall: Allow Inbound File And Printer Sharing Exception**   If you enable this policy setting, Windows Firewall opens these ports so that this computer can receive print jobs and requests for access to shared files. Note that allowing File And Printer Sharing also allows clients to receive and respond to ping (ICMP Echo Request) messages.

- **Windows Firewall: Allow ICMP Exceptions**   This policy setting allows you to define the specific type of ICMP message types that Windows Firewall allows.

- **Windows Firewall: Allow Logging**   This policy setting allows Windows Firewall to record information about the unsolicited incoming messages that it receives. If you enable this policy setting, Windows Firewall writes the information to a log file.

- **Windows Firewall: Prohibit Notifications**   This policy setting prevents Windows Firewall from displaying notifications to the user when a program requests that Windows Firewall add the program to the program exceptions list.

- **Windows Firewall: Allow Local Port Exceptions**   This policy setting allows administrators to enable or disable the port exceptions list. If you disable this policy setting, port exceptions are ignored.

- **Windows Firewall: Allow Inbound Remote Administration Exception**   This policy setting allows remote administration of the local computer by using administrative tools such as the Microsoft Management Console (MMC) and Windows Management Instrumentation (WMI).

- **Windows Firewall: Allow Inbound Remote Desktop Exceptions**   This policy setting allows the local computer to receive inbound Remote Desktop requests (through TCP port 3389). If you disable this policy setting, Windows Firewall blocks this port, which prevents this computer from receiving Remote Desktop requests.

- **Windows Firewall: Prohibit Unicast Response To Multicast Or Broadcast Requests**   This policy prevents the local computer from receiving unicast responses to its outgoing multicast or broadcast messages. This policy does not affect Dynamic Host Configuration Protocol (DHCP).

- **Windows Firewall: Allow Inbound UPnP Framework Exceptions**   This policy allows the local computer to receive unsolicited inbound Universal Plug and Play (UPnP) messages sent by network devices, such as routers with built-in firewalls.

Troubleshooting Windows Firewall by Using Firewall Logs

Windows Firewall logging is not enabled by default. If you are experiencing a firewall issue
that you cannot resolve, or if you want to have the option of troubleshooting by using firewall
logs in the future, you should enable logging.

To enable logging on Windows Firewall on client computers throughout the network,
you should use a GPO to enable the Allow Logging policy setting discussed in the previous
section. To enable Windows Firewall logging on a single computer, open Windows Firewall
properties and then in the Logging area, click Customize, as shown in Figure A-17.

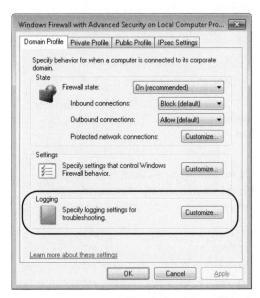

FIGURE A-17 You can enable Windows Firewall logging in the Properties dialog box
of the root node of the WFAS console.

This action opens the Customize Logging Settings dialog box shown in Figure A-18, which lets
you configure:

■ Where the log file is created and how big the file can grow

■ Whether you want the log file to record information about dropped packets, successful
connections, or both

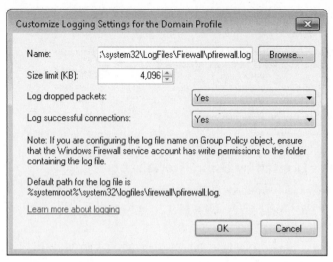

FIGURE A-18 Enabling logging for dropped packets and successful connections

Note that if you choose to log successful connections, make sure that you have plenty of storage space available. If you need to move the default location of the log to provide enough storage space, you need to assign the Windows Firewall service account write permissions to the folder containing the file.

Troubleshooting Windows Firewall by Using Event Logs

You can also use the Windows event logs to monitor Windows Firewall and to troubleshoot any issues that may arise. The event logs for Windows Firewall are found in the following location in Event Viewer:

Applications and Services Logs\Microsoft\Windows\Windows Firewall with Advanced Security

As shown in Figure A-19, there are four event logs you can use for monitoring and troubleshooting Windows Firewall activity:

- ConnectionSecurity
- ConnectionSecurityVerbose
- Firewall
- FirewallVerbose

The two verbose logs are disabled by default because of the large amounts of information they collect. To enable these logs, right-click them and select Enable Log.

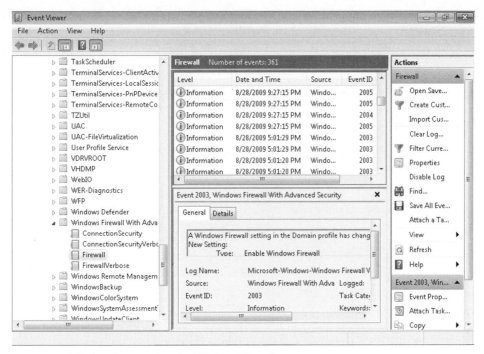

FIGURE A-19 Viewing the event logs for Windows Firewall

PRACTICE **Creating Exceptions for Windows Firewall**

In this practice, you compare and contrast creating Windows Firewall exceptions through two different methods: by using Control Panel and by using Local Security Policy. This practice requires a two-computer domain, with the domain controller running Windows Server 2008 R2 and the client running Windows 7.

EXERCISE 1 Creating a Program Exception for File And Printer Sharing

In this exercise, you attempt to ping the client computer from the server. Next, you create a firewall exception for File And Printer Sharing, test the ability to ping again, and finally revert to the original default configuration.

> **NOTE** **CREATE THIS EXCEPTION ONLY WHEN A CLIENT NEEDS FILE AND PRINTER SHARING**
>
> It is useful to know that making an exception for File And Printer Sharing also creates an exception for Ping. However, you shouldn't use this method to enable Ping if the client does not also need File And Printer Sharing. Doing so would expose the client system unnecessarily to potential attacks. If you want to be able to ping a client that does not need File And Printer Sharing, use the WFAS console to create an inbound allow rule for ICMP Echo Requests as described in Exercise 2.

1. Log on to the domain from the client computer with a domain administrator account.

2. Open Control Panel, browse to System And Security, and then, in the Windows Firewall category, click Allow A Program Through Windows Firewall.

3. On the Allowed Programs page, verify that File And Printer Sharing is not selected. If it is selected, click Change Settings, clear the Domain, Home/Work (Private), and Public check boxes associated with File And Printer Sharing, and then click OK. Leave Control Panel open.

4. Log on to the domain controller. Open a command prompt and attempt to ping the client by name.

   The ping attempt fails.

5. Return to the client. Again, click Allow A Program Through Windows Firewall.

6. On the Allowed Programs page, click Change Settings, and then click the check box to the left of File And Printer Sharing.

7. Verify that the Domain check box is now selected, and then click OK.

8. Return to the domain controller. Attempt to ping the client again.

   The ping now succeeds. The File And Printer Sharing exception creates an exception for ping as well as for file sharing.

9. Return to the client and open Control Panel. Remove the File And Printer Sharing exception that you just created, and then click OK.

EXERCISE 2   **Enforcing an Allow Rule Through Local Security Policy**

Although Exercise 1 demonstrates a simple way to allow ping requests through Windows Firewall, this method has two disadvantages. First, it creates a firewall exception for File And Printer Sharing, which is unnecessary if you want to allow only ping requests through the firewall. If a computer does not host any shared folders or printers, it is not optimal to allow network access to the computer in this way. Second, the Control Panel method does not enforce the allow rule that you created. The rule can be deleted or disabled easily by an administrator.

In this exercise, you open Local Security Policy and create a persistent allow rule to allow ICMP Echo requests through Windows Firewall. You then test the effects of this new rule.

1. Log on to the domain controller if you have not already done so, and verify that you cannot ping the client computer. If you can ping the client computer, remove any firewall exceptions that you have created that allow you to ping the client computer successfully.

2. If you have not already done so, log on to the domain from the client as a domain administrator.

3. On the client, click Start, type **Local Security Policy** in the Search Programs And Files text box, and then click Local Security Policy from the Start menu.

4. In Local Security Policy, navigate to Security Settings\Windows Firewall With Advanced Security\Windows Firewall With Advanced Security – Local Group Policy Object\ Inbound Rules.

5. Right-click the Inbound Rules node and then click New Rule from the shortcut menu. The New Inbound Rule Wizard appears.

6. On the Rule Type page, click Custom, and then click Next.

7. On the Program page, click Next.

8. On the Protocols And Ports page, from the Protocol Type drop-down list box, select ICMPv4.

9. In the Customize ICMP Settings window, select Specific ICMP types, select Echo Request, and then click OK.

10. On the Protocols And Ports page, click Next.

11. On the Scope Page, click Next.

12. On the Action page, ensure that the Allow The Connection check box is selected, and then click Next.

13. On the Profile page, click Next.

14. On the Name page, give the rule a name of Allow Ping, and then click Finish.

    The Allow Ping rule now appears in Local Security Policy.

15. Restart the client computer.

16. When the computer finishes restarting, attempt to ping the computer from the domain controller.

    The ping attempt is successful.

17. Log on to the domain from the client computer by using your domain administrator account.

18. Open the WFAS console by clicking Start, All Programs, Administrative Tools, and Windows Firewall With Advanced Security.

19. In the WFAS console tree, select the Inbound Rules node and wait for the list of rules to populate.

    The Allow Ping rule appears first in the list.

20. Right-click the rule and review the options on the associated shortcut menu.

    No options for Delete Rule or Disable Rule are available. Unlike the other rules visible in the WFAS console, this rule cannot be disabled or deleted because it is enforced through the Local Security Policy. Similarly, you could enforce this rule throughout the network by using Group Policy.

21. Close all open windows.

Summary

- Windows Firewall blocks all incoming connection requests unless they are allowed explicitly and allows all outgoing connection requests unless they are blocked explicitly.

- You can use Control Panel to allow specific programs through Windows Firewall. These allowances are called program exceptions. Common programs for which you might need to create exceptions include Remote Desktop, Windows Live Messenger, and File And Printer Sharing.

- You can use the WFAS console to define very specific traffic types to allow or deny through Windows Firewall. For example, you can create an allow rule to allow inbound connection requests that originate only from a specific range of addresses and that are destined only for a certain TCP port.

- You can enforce Windows Firewall settings through Local Computer Policy or Group Policy. When troubleshooting Windows Firewall, be sure to review the policy settings that have been enforced this way.

Managing User Files and Settings

As an enterprise support technician, one of your key responsibilities is to help users access the resources they need, when they need them. Certain features of Windows 7 can assist you in achieving this goal. Offline Files, for starters, enables users to work offline with files stored on a network share and then have these same files synchronize when the users return to the network. Roaming user profiles, meanwhile, allow users to connect to their centrally stored files and settings wherever they roam on the network. Yet another feature, Folder Redirection, enables an administrator to change the target of common folders transparently to a destination on a file server.

This appendix introduces you to these and other features that help you manage user files and settings in an enterprise environment.

Managing Offline Files

Users in enterprise environments typically store personal files on a file server because doing so provides many benefits, such as more opportunities to collaborate with other users, an improved ability to locate important files, and (when users don't save local copies) fewer file version conflicts. However, there are also some major drawbacks to using network storage. When a user stores a file on a network share, for example, she can normally access that file only when she is connected to the network. In addition, performance is much slower when users work with files stored on a remote drive, as opposed to ones stored on a locally attached disk. If users temporarily save local copies of files to improve performance, versioning problems can occur, especially for files that are edited by multiple users.

Offline Files is a feature that enables users to enjoy the benefits of shared file storage while avoiding its main disadvantages. It is enabled by default in Windows 7.

Understanding Offline Files

Offline Files is a Windows feature that allows you to keep local copies of files stored on a network share. When you disconnect from the network share, you can still access the local files you have made available offline. These local copies appear as if they were found in the same network location as before you disconnected: You access the files offline by specifying the same network path you normally use to access them online. Later, when you reconnect to the network share, the local copies are synchronized with the original source files automatically, and you are directed once again to the original network location.

For example, if you are connected to your corporate LAN by means of a portable computer, you might be working on a file named FileA that is stored on the network at the location \\ServerA\ShareA\FileA, as shown in Figure B-1. You might access this file by clicking a shortcut you have stored on your desktop, or you might specify the path directly by using Windows Explorer or the Search feature of the Start menu.

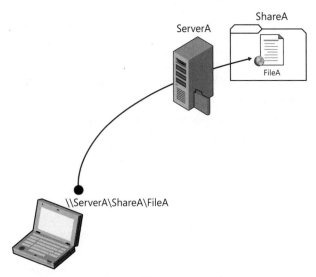

FIGURE B-1 Connecting to a file on a remote share

If you have chosen to make FileA available offline, you can work on the file even when you disconnect your computer from the corporate LAN. To open FileA, you still navigate to the address \\ServerA\ShareA\FileA by using the same desktop shortcut, by using Windows Explorer, or by using the Search feature of the Start menu. Offline Files recognizes the network location and automatically redirects the network request to the locally cached copy of the file, as shown in Figure B-2.

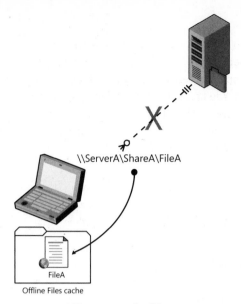

FIGURE B-2 When you work offline, requests are redirected to a local copy.

Later, when you reconnect to the network and specify the network path to the shared file, the request is again directed to the original source file on the network. At this point, the local copy of the file is synchronized automatically with the version stored on that network share, as illustrated in Figure B-3.

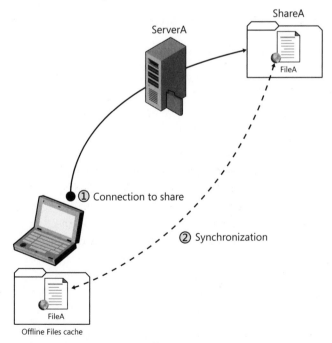

FIGURE B-3 The two versions are synchronized when you reconnect to the network share.

Why Use Offline Files?

The Offline Files feature improves the availability, reliability, and performance of network shares. Users who travel often, for example, can improve the availability of shared files by making these files available offline. Away from the network, they can edit the local copy of the files and then have the files synchronize automatically when they return. Offline Files also improves the reliability of network shares by providing a failover copy of network folders in case of network outages. If users become disconnected from a remote share for any reason, Offline Files allows them to keep working without interruption. Finally, Offline Files improves efficiency over a slow connection. In cases where the performance in viewing and editing a remote file seems slow, users can choose to work with the local copy of the file offline and then synchronize the file with the copy on the network share when they are done working with the file.

Working with Offline Files

To make a file available offline, navigate to the network share on which the file is stored, select and right-click the file, and finally choose Always Available Offline from the shortcut menu, as shown in Figure B-4.

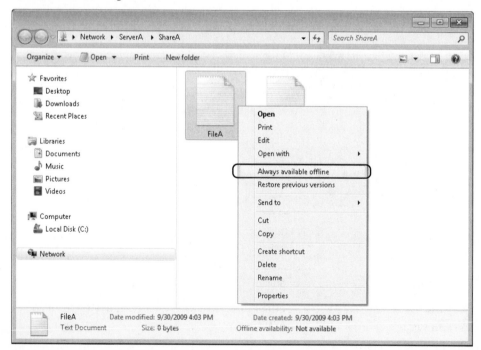

FIGURE B-4 Making a file available offline

After this step, the file you have made available offline will be designated with the green circle and clockwise arrows that form the symbol of Offline Files, as shown in Figure B-5.

To make all files on a network folder or share available offline, simply right-click the share in Windows Explorer and then select Always Available Offline, as shown in Figure B-6.

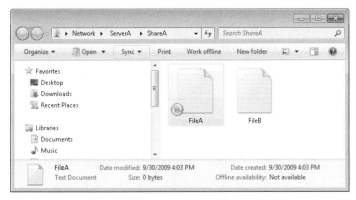

FIGURE B-5 A green circle designates files available offline

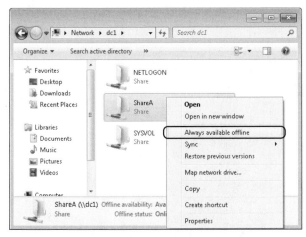

FIGURE B-6 Making an entire share available offline

If you make an entire share available offline, the share itself will be designated by the Offline Files symbol, as shown in Figure B-7.

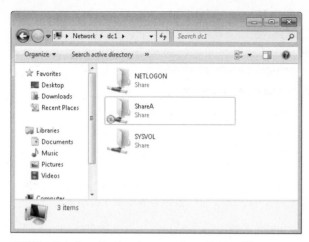

FIGURE B-7 A share that has been made available offline

Removing Offline Files

When you make a file or folder available offline, the Always Available Offline option on the shortcut menu will be checked. If you no longer want a network file or folder to be available offline, right-click the file or folder, and then clear the check next to the Always Available Offline option, as shown in Figure B-8.

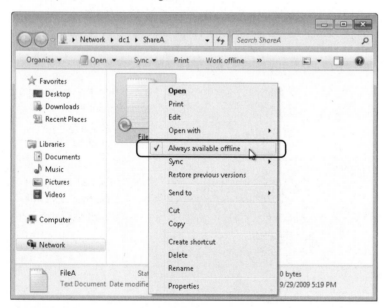

FIGURE B-8 Removing the offline copy of a file

When Does Automatic Synchronization Occur?

When you make a shared file or folder available offline, Windows automatically creates a copy of that file or folder on your computer. Windows 7 then automatically synchronizes the two versions of the file or folder in the following instances by default:

- If you are working online and save changes to the file.
- If you are working online and open the file.
- If you start the computer when you are disconnected from the network, edit the files, and later reconnect to the network folder containing those files.
- If, while connected to the network, you choose the option to work offline and later choose the option to work online again. (Note that synchronization in this case is not necessarily immediate.)
- If the Offline Files connection to the network share is broken abruptly and then reset. The Offline Files connection can be broken if you are disconnected suddenly from your network and attempt to connect to a network share. In this case, Windows eventually fails over to a locally stored copy if one is available. If the network connection is reestablished, Offline Files resets and synchronizes the files after several minutes. (You can also reset the Offline Files connection by restarting the computer and logging back on to the network.)

> **NOTE HANDLING FILE CONFLICTS**
>
> If both you and someone else have made changes to a file since you last connected to the source network folder, a conflict occurs when the files attempt to synchronize, and Windows asks you which version you want to keep.

Synchronizing Offline Files Manually

When other users save changes to a file that you have made available offline, these changes are not synchronized automatically with your local copy of the file. The latest version *number* of the file, however, is updated and propagated to all clients that have made the same file available offline. In this way, Offline Files can recognize when the locally stored copy of the file is not the most recent version available.

If you are working online, your local copy of the file synchronizes with the newest version when you open the file. However, if you go offline before synchronizing a file that is known to be outdated, you cannot open the file offline. Instead, you see the error shown in Figure B-9.

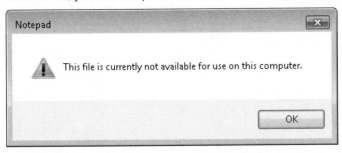

FIGURE B-9 You cannot open a file that is known to be outdated.

To prevent this error, you should synchronize your files manually before going offline if you plan to work with files that other people might have edited. To synchronize manually all files that you have made available offline, you can use the notification area of the taskbar. In the notification area, click the up arrow, right-click the Offline Files symbol, and then click Sync All, as shown in Figure B-10.

> **NOTE USING SYNC CENTER TO CUSTOMIZE SYNCHRONIZATION BEHAVIOR**
>
> To help prevent users from seeing the error shown in Figure B-9, you can use Sync Center to configure automatic synchronizations to occur at specific times. This option is discussed in the section entitled "Using Sync Center to Manage Synchronizations," later in this appendix.

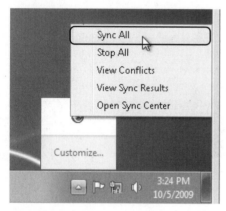

FIGURE B-10 Synchronizing offline files manually

Working Offline

If you want to work with a file offline, you can simply shut down your computer and then start your computer when you are disconnected from the network. However, if you want to start working with a file offline without shutting down your computer, you should choose the Work Offline option manually. Doing so helps application stability and performance because you can start working with the offline file immediately instead of waiting for a timeout to an unavailable network share. Choosing the Work Offline option also allows you to reconnect to the source network folder and synchronize your offline files as soon as you are ready.

To begin working offline, browse to the share and then click Work Offline on the Windows Explorer toolbar, as shown in Figure B-11.

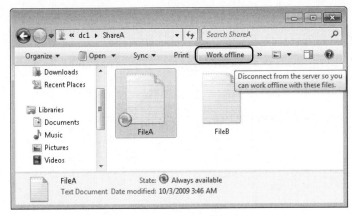

FIGURE B-11 Choosing the option to work offline

Then, when you are ready to reconnect to the network folder, click Work Online, as shown in Figure B-12. This step once again synchronizes your local copy with the version on the network share.

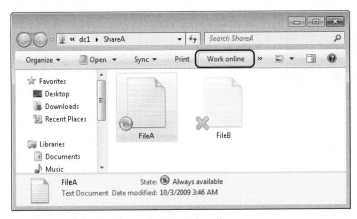

FIGURE B-12 Choosing the option to work online

Viewing Your Offline Files

If you work with offline files in different folders, you might want to view all of them without opening each folder individually. To view all of your offline files in one place, use the following procedure:

1. Click Start, type **manage offline files,** and then press Enter.

   The Offline Files dialog box opens.

2. On the General tab, click View Your Offline Files, as shown in Figure B-13.

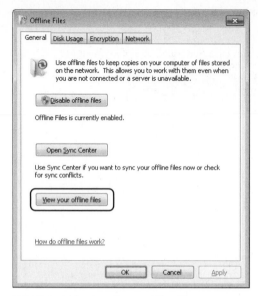

FIGURE B-13 Viewing all your offline files

Using Sync Center to Manage Synchronizations

Sync Center is a tool in Windows 7 that allows you to set up and manage synchronizations. To open Sync Center, click Start, type **sync center,** and then press Enter. Sync Center is shown in Figure B-14.

FIGURE B-14 Sync Center in Windows 7

To set up an automatic synchronization schedule for Offline Files, perform the following steps:

1. In Sync Center, select Offline Files, and then click Schedule, as shown in Figure B-15.

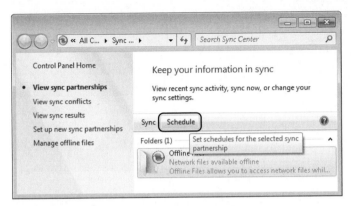

FIGURE B-15 Creating a synchronization schedule

This step opens the Offline Files Sync Schedule Wizard, as shown in Figure B-16.

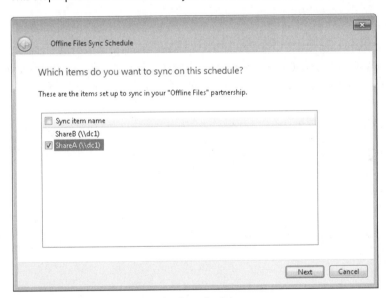

FIGURE B-16 Creating a synchronization schedule

2. Select the item in the list for which you want to set up a synchronization schedule, and then click Next.

   This step opens the When Do You Want This Sync To Begin? page, as shown in Figure B-17.

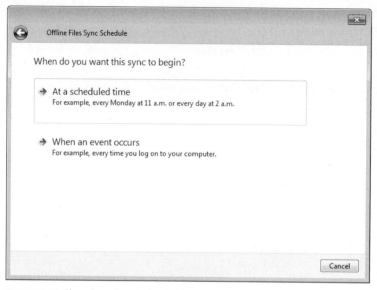

FIGURE B-17 Choosing when to begin the sync

3. Choose one of the following options:

- **At A Scheduled Time**   This option enables you to start a synchronization process at any time you specify, with a schedule to repeat at any frequency you choose.

- **When An Event Occurs**   This option enables you to start a synchronization process when any of four conditions are met: when you log on to your computer, when your computer is idle for a specified amount of time, when you lock Windows, or when you unlock Windows.

Both the At A Scheduled Time and the When An Event Occurs options provide a More Options button, which, when clicked, opens the More Scheduling Options dialog box shown in Figure B-18. This dialog box enables you to further restrict when to start a synchronization and to set conditions under which to stop a synchronization.

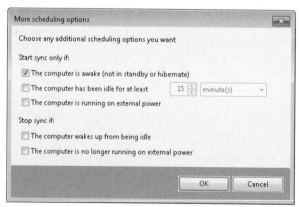

FIGURE B-18 Refining your synchronization schedule

✓ **Quick Check**

1. Can you configure Offline Files in Windows 7 to synchronize automatically when a user logs on?

2. Can you configure Offline Files in Windows 7 to synchronize automatically when a user logs off?

Quick Check Answers

1. Yes

2. No

VIEWING SYNCHRONIZATION RESULTS IN SYNC CENTER

You can use Sync Center to check the results of recent synchronization activity. To do so, you can click Start, type **view sync results,** and then press Enter. This step opens the window shown in Figure B-19.

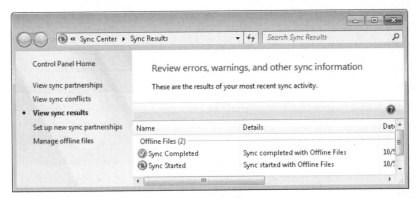

FIGURE B-19 Viewing synchronization results in Sync Center

This screen displays the most recent synchronization procedures are listed, along with the results.

Managing Disk Space for Offline Files

In a manner based on the amount of free space available and the size of your hard disk, Offline Files calculates a percentage of your hard disk to reserve for the Offline Files cache. This percentage effectively sets a limit on the storage space available to Offline Files. You can view and modify these limits through the Disk Usage tab of the Offline Properties dialog box.

To open this tab, click Start, type **manage disk space used by your offline files,** and then press Enter. The Disk Usage tab of the Offline Properties dialog box is shown in Figure B-20.

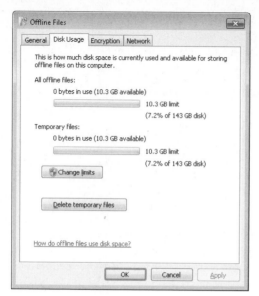

FIGURE B-20 Viewing the disk usage limits for Offline Files

This tab shows you the amount that is allocated for Offline Files and how much is currently in use. To adjust the limits available for Offline Files, click Change Limits. This step opens the Offline Files Disk Usage Limits dialog box, shown in Figure B-21.

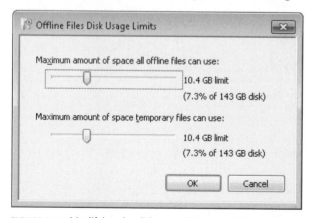

FIGURE B-21 Modifying the disk usage limits for Offline Files

Both in the Offline Files Disk Usage Limits dialog box and on the Disk Usage tab of the Offline Properties dialog box, two general measurements are displayed. The top value shows how much space is allocated to Offline Files in general, and the bottom value shows how much of this space is available just for the temporary files associated with Offline Files.

To adjust these values, use the slider in the Offline Files Disk Usage Limits dialog box. Typically you can leave these values at their defaults unless you need to conserve disk storage space or if the number or size of the files you need available offline is unusually large.

As a general principle, remember to keep more than 10 percent (and preferably more than 15 percent) of your hard disk free. You should lower these limits if the proportion of free space on your hard disk is approaching 10 percent.

REAL WORLD

J.C. Mackin

In certain situations, you might want to move the Offline Files cache from its default location in *%Systemdrive%*\CSC. For example, you might have Windows 7 installed on C:\, a relatively small volume of 30 gigabytes (GB), whereas your E:\ drive has 250 GB of free storage reserved just for work files. Unfortunately, Windows 7 does not provide a simple setting or dialog box that allows you to adjust this Offline Files cache location.

Instead, moving the Offline Files cache requires you to modify the registry directly, but it isn't difficult to do. If you want to move the Offline Files cache on a computer, perform the following steps:

1. Synchronize all your offline files. The contents of your current Offline Files cache are deleted in this procedure, so you first want the source files on the server to be updated with any changes you have made locally.

2. Create and then run a batch file called ResetCache.bat. Include just the following line in the batch file:

   ```
   REG ADD "HKLM\System\CurrentControlSet\Services\CSC\Parameters"/v
   FormatDatabase /t REG_DWORD /d 1 /f
   ```

   You can use this batch file in the future whenever you want to delete the contents of your Offline Files cache.

3. Restart your computer.

4. Open Regedit. Add the following key to HKEY_LOCAL_MACHINE\System\CurrentControlSet\Services\CSC\Parameters:

   ```
   Type: String (REG_SZ)

   Name: CacheLocation

   Value: \??\new cache location
   ```

   (Include the question marks in the string. For example, to move the cache to E:\CSC, type \??\E:\CSC.)

5. Using the name and location you specified in the previous step, create the new folder you will use for the Offline Files cache.

6. Restart your computer.

7. Synchronize your Offline Files. This step will populate your new cache with the files you have made available offline.

Configuring Offline Files Through Group Policy

You can use Group Policy to customize the behavior of Offline Files and to enforce this behavior throughout your organization. To find the Group Policy settings for Offline Files, open a Group Policy Object (GPO) and navigate to Computer Configuration\Policies\Administrative Templates\Network\Offline Files, as shown in Figure B-22. This Computer Configuration area of a GPO includes 28 settings for Offline Files. A subset of 15 of these settings can be found in the User Configuration section of a GPO at User Configuration\Policies\Administrative Templates\Network\Offline Files. However, the majority of these policy settings in both Computer Configuration and User Configuration are reserved for use with versions of Microsoft Windows before Windows Vista.

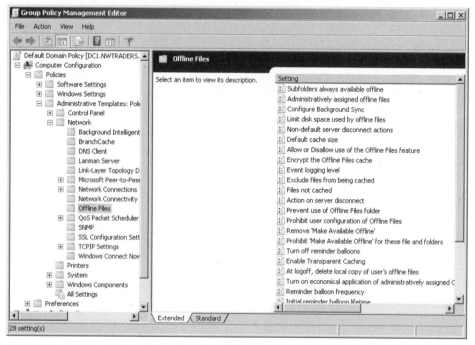

FIGURE B-22 Locating Offline Files settings in a GPO

The following is a list of the 10 Group Policy settings that affect Offline Files in Windows 7:

- **Administratively Assigned Offline Files** This policy setting allows you to enforce specific network shares or shared files to be available offline.

- **Configure Background Sync** This policy setting is new for Windows 7 and Windows Server 2008 R2. It allows you to customize a synchronization behavior for network folders over slow links.

  By default, network folders in Slow-Link mode are synchronized with the server every 360 minutes, with the start of the sync varying between 0 and 60 additional minutes.

However, when this policy setting is enabled, a sync for network folders in Slow-Link mode is performed instead with the frequency specified in the policy.

The Configure Background Sync policy setting is shown in Figure B-23.

- **Limit Disk Space Used By Offline Files**   This policy setting allows you to enforce a storage space limit (expressed in megabytes) to be allocated to Offline Files.

- **Allow Or Disallow Use Of The Offline Files Feature**   This policy setting allows you to force Offline Files to remain in an enabled or a disabled state.

- **Encrypt The Offline Files Cache**   This policy setting allows you to force offline files to remain encrypted in the client-side cache, a feature that might be required in some high-security environments.

- **Exclude Files From Being Cached**   This policy setting is new for Windows 7 and Windows Server 2008 R2. It enables you to specify file types (defined by file extension) that you do not want users to be able to make available offline.

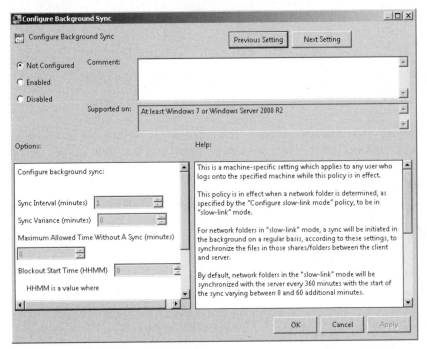

FIGURE B-23 The Configure Background Sync policy setting in Windows 7

The Exclude Files From Being Cached setting is shown in Figure B-24.

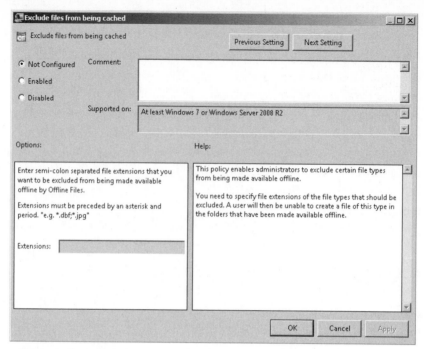

FIGURE B-24 The Exclude Files From Being Cached policy setting in Windows 7

- **Remove 'Make Available Offline'** This policy setting removes the Make Available Offline option from the shortcut menu on folders and files. However, this setting does not prevent the system from saving local copies of files that have been designated for automatic caching.

- **Enable Transparent Caching** This policy setting is new for Windows 7 and Windows Server 2008 R2. It is used to force clients to cache temporarily any network file opened over a slow link. Subsequent reads to the same file are then satisfied from the local cache after the integrity of the cached copy is verified. This policy improves user response times and decreases bandwidth consumption over the wide area network (WAN) links to the server. Note that the cached files are temporary and are not available to the user when offline. The cached files are also not kept in sync with the version on the server, and the most current version from the server is always available for subsequent reads.

  In this policy, you define the slow link in terms of milliseconds for the round-trip latency between the client and server. For example, if you define a network latency of 60, the client defaults to locally cached copies of offline files when the round-trip latency is greater than 60 milliseconds.

  The Enable Transparent Caching policy setting is shown in Figure B-25.

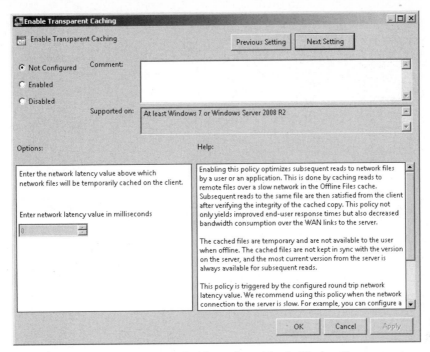

FIGURE B-25 The Enable Transparent Caching policy setting in Windows 7

- **Turn On Economical Application Of Administrative Assigned Offline Files**   This policy setting allows you to force only administratively assigned folders to be synchronized at logon.

- **Configure Slow-Link Mode**   This policy enables you to determine when clients use slow-link mode. (Slow link mode is enabled by default for computers running Windows 7 and Windows Server 2008 R2 when latencies exceed 80 milliseconds.) In slow-link mode, all network file requests are satisfied from the Offline Files cache, but manual synchronizations still occur online.

Restoring Previous Versions of Files or Folders

*P*revious Versions is another feature of Windows 7 that improves the experience of working with user files. With Previous Versions, Windows 7 allows you to restore versions of files or folders that have automatically been captured from system restore points or backups. To restore a previous version of a file or folder, select and right-click that file or folder, and then click Restore Previous Versions, as shown in Figure B-26.

This step opens the Previous Versions tab of the file's Properties dialog box, shown in Figure B-27. As shown in the figure, the tab lists the previous versions of the file that have been saved from backups and restore points.

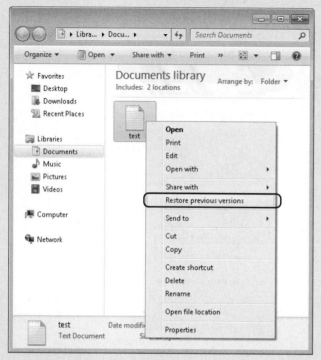

FIGURE B-26 Restoring a previous version of a file

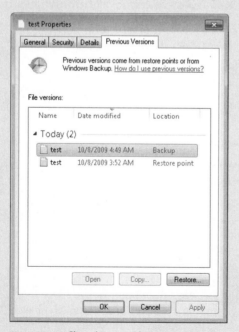

FIGURE B-27 Choosing a version to restore

To restore a previous version, select the copy that you wish to restore and then click Restore. If you choose to restore a previous version saved by a restore point, you see the dialog box shown in Figure B-28.

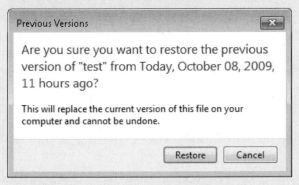

FIGURE B-28 Restoring a previous version saved by a restore point

If you choose to restore a previous version saved by a backup, Windows treats the procedure as a file copy, and you are prompted with the dialog box shown in Figure B-29.

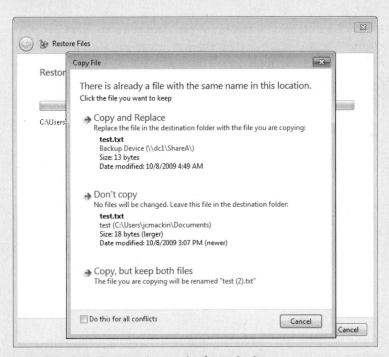

FIGURE B-29 Restoring a previous version from a backup

Note the following points about restoring previous versions of files and folders:

- Not all previous versions of files and folders are available to be restored. Windows makes available only files and folders saved from restore points and backups.
- If you change the name of a file, you must restore the entire folder to restore an old version of the file.
- Restore points are created by the System Protection feature, which is enabled only on the system volume by default. To enable System Protection on another volume, open System Control Panel, click System Protection, and click Configure. Then, in the System Protection dialog box, shown in Figure B-30, choose either Restore System Settings And Previous Versions Of Files or Only Restore Previous Versions Of Files. Finally, adjust the slider to assign a Max Usage for disk space, and press OK.
- Before you restore a previous version of a file, you can open previous versions of files that have been saved by restore points. You can do this to verify which version of the file is the best to restore. Note, however, that you cannot open previous versions of files that have been saved by backups.
- When you restore a previous version of a file or folder, the procedure cannot be undone.
- If the Restore button isn't available, you can't restore a previous version of the file or folder to its original location. However, you might be able to open it or save it to a different location.

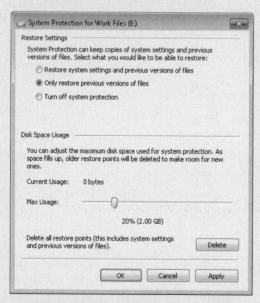

FIGURE B-30 Enabling System Protection on a disk

- If you want to save a version of a file or folder to be available as a previous version in the future, you can create a new restore point manually. To do so, open System Control Panel, click System Protection, and then click Create, as shown in Figure B-31.

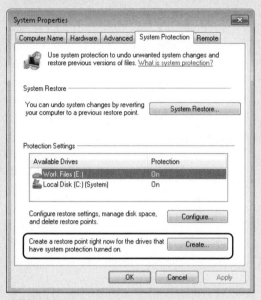

FIGURE B-31 Creating a restore point manually

PRACTICE **Exploring Offline Files**

In this practice, you test the basic functionality of Offline Files.

EXERCISE 1   Working with Offline Files

In this exercise, you create a network share and configure a file on that share to be always available offline. You then make changes to the file while both online and offline, and observe the effects. To perform this exercise, you will need:

- A domain controller running Windows Server 2008 R2.
- A client computer running Windows 7 that is a member of the same domain.

1. Log on to the domain controller with a domain administrator account.
2. Create a folder named Share1 in the root of the C:\ drive.
3. Right-click the Share1 folder, select Share With from the shortcut menu, and then click Specific People.

4. On the Choose People On Your Network To Share With page of the File Sharing wizard, type **Domain Users,** and then click Add.

5. Assign the Read/Write permission level to Domain Users, and then click Share.

6. On the Your Folder Is Shared page of the File Sharing wizard, click Done.

7. Log on to the client running Windows 7 with a domain user account.

8. Click Start, type ***domain controller name*\Share1,** and then press Enter. For example, if the name you have assigned to the domain controller is dc1, type **\\\\dc1\Share1,** and then press Enter.

9. In Share1, create a new text file named Test1.txt.

10. Select and right-click Test1.txt, and then select Always Available Offline from the shortcut menu.

11. Open Test1.txt, type **Version 1,** and then save and close the file.

12. Select Test1.txt. On the Windows Explorer menu bar, click Work Offline.

13. Open Test1.txt, type **Version 2,** and then save and close the file.

14. Return to the domain controller. Locate and open Test1.txt in Share1.

    Test1.txt still shows the text "Version 1."

15. Close Test1.txt.

16. Return to the client running Windows 7. On the Windows Explorer menu bar, click Work Online.

17. Right-click Test1.txt, select Sync, and then click Sync Selected Offline Files.

18. Return to the domain controller, and then open Test1.txt.

    Test1.txt now shows the text "Version 2."

19. Return to the client running Windows 7, and choose once again the option to work offline.

20. Open Test1.txt, type **Version 3,** and then save and close the file.

21. Return to the domain controller, open Test1.txt, type **Version 3.1,** and then save and close the file.

22. Return to the client running Windows 7, choose the option to work online, and then attempt to sync the file.

    A Resolve Conflict window appears and prompts you to save one of the two files, or to keep both.

23. Click Keep Both Versions.

    A second version of the file now appears in Share1.

24. Log off both computers.

Managing Data for Roaming Users

In a large network, you want to improve the availability of your users' files and settings. This goal includes making files available both online and offline, as discussed earlier in this appendix, but it also includes making users' files and settings available from any computer on the network.

This section introduces two complementary methods—roaming user profiles and Folder Redirection—that are used to make a user's data available throughout the network.

Understanding User Profiles in Windows 7

In general terms, a *user profile* simply refers to the collection of data that comprises a user's individual environment, including a user's individual files, application settings, and desktop configuration. More specifically, a user profile refers to the contents of the personal folder, automatically created by Windows, which bears the name of an individual user. By default, this personal folder is created in the C:\Users folder when a user logs on for the first time to a computer running Windows 7. It contains subfolders such as My Documents, Desktop, and Downloads, as well as a personal data file named Ntuser.dat. For example, by default, a user named StefanH stores the data that makes up his personal environment in a folder named C:\Users\StefanH, part of which is shown in Figure B-32.

Although each user profile is stored in C:\Users by default, this default location is often not suitable for corporate environments, especially when users tend to switch computers. Ideally, users' documents and settings should follow them from computer to computer and not be restricted to a single computer or be dispersed among several computers. To allow documents and settings to roam with users in an organization in this preferred way, network administrators traditionally have configured roaming user profiles in a domain environment. A *roaming user profile* is a profile that is stored on a network share and that is accessible to a user when he or she logs on to any computer in the network. To configure domain user accounts with roaming user profiles, you simply need to modify the properties of those accounts so that the profiles are stored on a central network share instead of on the local machine. When you do this, the same personal folder containing a user's documents and settings is downloaded from the network share to the local computer when the user logs on, regardless of which domain computer the user logs on to.

In all versions of Windows before Windows 7, any changes made to the user profile are copied back to the central network share only when the user logs off. However, in a network consisting of clients running Windows 7 and servers running Windows Server 2008 R2, changes to user settings can be synchronized periodically with a remote network share. This feature is discussed in the section entitled "Background Registry Roaming in Windows 7," later in this appendix.

FIGURE B-32 A user profile

A user account configured with a roaming user profile is shown in Figure B-33.

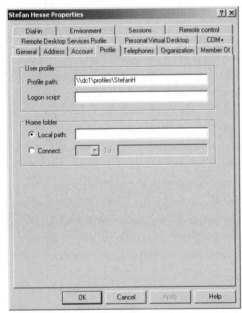

FIGURE B-33 A roaming user profile configured with the properties of a user account

Understanding User Profile Differences Since Windows Vista

Significant changes to the location, structure, and contents of user profiles were introduced with Windows Vista. Although the changes to user profiles introduced in Windows 7 are minor compared to those introduced in Windows Vista, many companies deploying Windows 7 include only pre–Windows Vista operating systems such as Windows XP and Windows Server 2003. For this reason, it is important to understand the differences in user profiles between pre–Windows Vista operating systems and post–Windows Vista operating systems. Beginning with Windows Vista, user profile data has been reorganized and stored in new locations in the Windows file structure.

The following list summarizes the changes that were introduced to Windows user profiles in Windows Vista and Windows 7:

- The root of the user profile namespace has been moved from %SystemDrive%\Documents And Settings to %SystemDrive%\Users. This means, for example, that the user profile folder for user Michael Allen (mallen@contoso.com) is now found at %SystemDrive%\Users\mallen instead of %SystemDrive%\Documents And Settings\mallen.

- The "My" prefix has been dropped from some folders to simplify their appearance. For example, documents are now stored in a folder named Documents instead of in a folder named My Documents. Note that in Windows Vista, these folders are displayed in the same way (that is, without the "My" prefix) in both the Windows Explorer shell and at the command prompt. Beginning with Windows 7, however, these folders display a "My" prefix when viewed within Windows Explorer but not when viewed at the command prompt. In other words, Windows Explorer in Windows 7 adds a "My" prefix to the displayed representation of these folders in the graphical user interface, but the actual folders in the underlying file system do not include this prefix in their names.

- My Music, My Pictures, and My Videos in Windows Vista and later are no longer subfolders of My Documents. Instead, these and similar user-managed data folders are now stored under the root profile folder and are peers of the My Documents folder. The user profile namespace has been flattened in this way to help provide better separation between user-managed data and application settings and to simplify how Folder Redirection works.

- New subfolders have been added under the root profile folder to help better organize user-managed data and settings and to help prevent "profile pollution," when users or applications save data files in the root profile folder or in subfolders not intended for that particular purpose. Specifically, the following new profile subfolders have been added in Windows Vista and later:
  - **Contacts**   The default location for storing the user's contacts
  - **Downloads**   The default location for saving all downloaded content
  - **Searches**   The default location for storing saved searches
  - **Links**   The default location for storing Explorer Favorite Links
  - **Saved Games**   The default location for storing saved games

- A new, hidden folder named AppData located under the profile root is used as a central location for storing all per-user application settings and binaries. In addition, the following three subfolders under AppData better separate state information and help applications roam:

  - **Local** This folder stores computer-specific application data and settings that cannot (or should not) roam, as well as user-managed data or settings too large to support roaming effectively. The AppData\Local folder within a Windows Vista or later user profile is essentially the same as the Local Settings\Application Data under the root folder of a Windows XP user profile.

  - **Roaming** This folder stores user-specific application data and settings that should (or must) roam along with the user when roaming user profiles are implemented. The AppData\Roaming folder within a user profile in Windows Vista or later is essentially the same as the Application Data folder under the root folder of a Windows XP user profile.

  - **LocalLow** This folder allows low-integrity processes to have Write access to it. Low-integrity processes perform tasks that could compromise the operating system. For example, applications started by the protected mode of Internet Explorer must use this profile folder for storing application data and settings. The LocalLow profile folder has no counterpart in Windows XP.

- The All Users profile has been renamed Public. The Public profile provides a way to add user data to all user profiles without editing each user profile individually. Adding a shortcut to the desktop of the Public profile, for example, would result in all users receiving the shortcut on their desktops when they log on.

- Users now can share individual files easily and securely from within their user profile folders and subfolders.

- The Default User profile has been renamed Default. As with Default User in Windows XP, the Default profile in Windows Vista and later is never loaded and is copied only when creating new profiles. The Default profile thus acts as a template for creating each user's profile when he or she logs on for the first time.

Table B-1 summarizes the many differences between pre–Windows Vista and post–Windows Vista user profiles. (Note that many of the folders mentioned in Table B-1 are hidden by default.)

TABLE B-1 Windows Profile Changes

WINDOWS VISTA, WINDOWS SERVER 2008, AND WINDOWS 7 USER PROFILE FOLDER LOCATION (BELOW C:\USERS*USERNAME*\...)	WINDOWS 2000, WINDOWS XP, AND WINDOWS SERVER 2003 USER PROFILE FOLDER LOCATION (BELOW C:\DOCUMENTS AND SETTINGS*USERNAME*\...)
...\AppData\Roaming	...\Application Data
...\AppData\Local	...\Local Settings\Application Data
...\AppData\Local\Microsoft\Windows\History	...\Local Settings\History
...\AppData\Local\Temp	...\Local Settings\Temp
...\AppData\Local\Microsoft\Windows\Temporary Internet Files	...\Local Settings\Temporary Internet Files
...\AppData\Roaming\Microsoft \Windows\Cookies	...\Cookies
...\AppData\Roaming\Microsoft \Windows\Libraries (Windows 7 and Windows Server 2008 R2 only)	Not applicable
...\AppData\Roaming\Microsoft\Windows\Network Shortcuts	...\Nethood
...\AppData\Roaming\Microsoft\Windows\Printer Shortcuts	...\PrintHood
...\AppData\Roaming\Microsoft\Windows\Recent Items	...\Recent
...\AppData\Roaming\Microsoft\Windows\Send To	...\SendTo
...\AppData\Roaming\Microsoft\Windows\Start Menu	...\Start Menu
...\AppData\Roaming\Microsoft\Windows\Templates	...\Templates
...\Contacts	Not applicable
...\Desktop	...\Desktop
...\My Documents (called simply Documents in Windows Vista and Windows Server 2008 R1)	...\My Documents
...\Downloads	Not applicable
...\Favorites	...\Favorites
...\My Music (called simply Music in Windows Vista and Windows Server 2008 R1)	...\My Music

WINDOWS VISTA, WINDOWS SERVER 2008, AND WINDOWS 7 USER PROFILE FOLDER LOCATION (BELOW C:\USERS*USERNAME*\...)	WINDOWS 2000, WINDOWS XP, AND WINDOWS SERVER 2003 USER PROFILE FOLDER LOCATION (BELOW C:\DOCUMENTS AND SETTINGS*USERNAME*\...)
...\My Videos (called simply Videos in Windows Vista and Windows Server 2008 R1)	...\My Videos
...\My Pictures (called simply Pictures in Windows Vista and Windows Server 2008 R1)	...\My Pictures
...\Searches	Not applicable
...\Links	Not applicable
...\Saved Games	Not applicable

BACKGROUND REGISTRY ROAMING IN WINDOWS 7

Another significant change in user profiles relates specifically to roaming user profiles. Beginning in Windows 7, users with roaming user profiles can have their current user settings (which are stored in the file Ntuser.dat) periodically synchronized back to the server while they are logged on to their computers. This is a change from roaming user profiles in Windows Vista and earlier, where roaming user profiles were synchronized back to the server only upon logoff.

Background Registry Roaming is disabled by default in Windows 7 and can be enabled on targeted computers by using Group Policy. The following Group Policy setting can be used to control this behavior:

Computer Configuration\Policies\Administrative Templates\System\User Profiles\Background Upload Of A Roaming User Profile's Registry File While User Is Logged On

When you enable this policy setting, you can configure Background Registry Roaming to synchronize on either of the following schedules:

- At a set time interval (the default is 12 hours and can range from 1 to 720 hours)
- At a specified time of day (the default is 3 A.M.)

UNDERSTANDING LIBRARIES IN WINDOWS 7

Perhaps the most significant addition to Windows 7 profiles is the new Libraries feature. Libraries is a feature that provides easy access to important files and folders on your hard disks and network shares. In Windows 7, the Start menu includes links to the Documents, Music, and Pictures libraries by default. You also see these four libraries whenever you open Windows Explorer, as shown in Figure B-34.

FIGURE B-34 The four default libraries created by Windows 7

Note that these libraries are not simply shortcuts to the folders with the same names. For example, the Documents library is not simply a shortcut to the Documents folder. It in fact includes all the files and folders stored in two locations by default:

- **My Documents** The C:\Users\Username\Documents folder within the user's profile
- **Public Documents** The C:\Users\Public\Documents folder that can be accessed by any user who is logged on to the computer interactively

In other words, when you open the Documents library, by default you see the combined contents of My Documents and Public Documents. The other default libraries work in a similar manner: The Pictures library by default includes the combined contents of the My Pictures folder and the Public Pictures folder, the Videos library by default includes the combined contents of the My Videos folder and the Public Videos folder, and so on.

You can create new libraries or modify the contents of an existing library by adding folders to it. When you do so, its contents are displayed within the library and are searchable from the library.

Understanding Roaming Profile Incompatibility

The fact that user profiles have changed so significantly is a very important consideration for Windows 7 deployment because Windows 7 (along with Windows Vista and Windows Server 2008) *cannot share profiles for roaming users with versions of Windows before Windows Vista.* This incompatibility can be a problem if you have just deployed Windows 7 on a network that previously included only Microsoft Windows 2000, Windows XP, and Windows Server 2003. In this scenario, whenever a user for whom you have configured a roaming user profile first logs on to a computer running Windows 7, a second user profile folder named *username*.V2 is created on the central network share for use just with Windows 7. The data stored in this new folder is not accessible to users when they log on to a computer running Windows 2000, Windows XP, or Windows Server 2003.

For instance, before Windows 7 deployment, if user CLee is configured with a roaming user profile, she is able to log on to any computer running Windows 2000, Windows XP, or Windows Server 2003 in her workplace and see—among other things—the same desktop and the same My Documents folder. On a central network share, all of CLee's documents and settings are stored in a profile named CLee. However, after you deploy Windows 7 in the organization, CLee logs on to a computer running Windows 7 but does not see any part of her familiar environment by default: Her desktop has changed, and none of her documents can be found. On the central network share, a new folder named CLee.V2 now appears alongside the CLee folder. Any changes that CLee makes to her new Windows 7 environment follow her to other computers running Windows 7, but these documents and settings are kept separate from those available to her in Windows 2000, Windows XP, and Windows Server 2003.

This side-by-side listing of roaming user profile folders for Windows 7 and Windows XP is shown in Figure B-35.

```
▲ 📁 Profiles
   ▷ 📁 ABarbariol
   ▷ 📁 ABarbariol.V2
   ▷ 📁 BKurmann
   ▷ 📁 BKurmann.V2
   ▷ 📁 CLee
   ▷ 📁 CLee.V2
   ▷ 📁 DSmith
   ▷ 📁 DSmith.V2
   ▷ 📁 EKulikov
   ▷ 📁 EKulikov.V2
   ▷ 📁 GSingh
   ▷ 📁 GSingh.V2
   ▷ 📁 HKupkova
   ▷ 📁 HKupkova.V2
   ▷ 📁 INeri
   ▷ 📁 INeri.V2
   ▷ 📁 JChen
   ▷ 📁 JChen.V2
```

FIGURE B-35 Roaming user profile folders for Windows XP and Windows 7

OTHER LIMITATIONS OF ROAMING USER PROFILES

Besides the lack of default compatibility between Windows 7 roaming user profiles and those used in versions of Windows before Windows Vista, there are other important limitations related to traditional roaming user profiles in general for all versions of Windows:

- **Slow logon and logoff**   As a user configured with a roaming user profile logs on to a domain, all of the data stored in the user profile on the network share is copied to the local computer. This process can result in a slow logon, especially when the size of the user profile grows beyond 20 MB. When a user logs off the system, the same profile must be copied back to the network share; this process results in a slow logoff.

- **Lack of real-time data synchronization with earlier versions of Windows**   For all versions of Windows before Windows 7 and Windows Server 2008 R2, the changes a user makes to his or her roaming profile are copied back to the central network share only when the user logs off. This lack of real-time data synchronization can complicate matters for users who frequently switch systems while performing their jobs.

- **Network problems can disperse profile data**   If a user configured with a roaming user profile experiences network problems during logon, the roaming user profile does not load. In this case, a new profile on the local system can be created automatically for that user. Any work saved during this logon session becomes unavailable to the user during future sessions if he or she is once again able to connect to the network share.

- **Lack of roaming user profile automation**   Although you can configure roaming user profiles on many existing accounts simultaneously, there is no method built into Windows that allows you to configure newly created users with a roaming user profile by default. This lack of automation results in increased administrative overhead and in increased opportunity for misconfiguration.

To address the limitations of roaming user profiles, you can use a feature called Folder Redirection, either in place of roaming user profiles or in addition to them.

Understanding Windows 7 Folder Redirection

Folder Redirection is a Windows feature that allows you to change the target location of user profile folders in a way that is transparent to the user. For example, if an administrator has redirected your C:\Users*User Name*\My Documents folder to a central network share, you still see the My Documents folder in the same location on your local computer. Whenever you open the My Documents folder, however, the window reveals contents stored at the redirected location on the central network share. In this way, Folder Redirection essentially turns chosen user profile folders into shortcuts that point to network shares. When the user logs on, only the shortcut is loaded, not the contents of the remote share.

You can configure and enforce Folder Redirection for domain users through Group Policy. The folders that you can redirect through Group Policy are shown in Figure B-36.

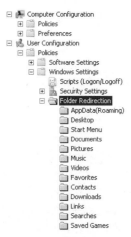

FIGURE B-36 Folder Redirection in Windows 7

When configured, Folder Redirection offers a number of important advantages over traditional roaming user profiles:

- **Compatibility between Windows 7 and earlier versions of Windows**   In Windows 7, you can configure Folder Redirection in such a way that most of the important elements of a user profile are accessible across all Windows versions since Windows 2000. For example, you can configure your Application Data, Desktop, Start Menu, and My Documents folders to be redirected to a specific set of folders on a network server regardless of whether you log on to a computer running Windows XP or Windows 7. Folder Redirection is therefore an essential method of providing data consistency for users who roam among computers running Windows 7 and computers running Windows 2000, XP, or Server 2003.

- **Faster logons**   When you redirect folders such as the My Documents folder, the redirected data is essentially separated from the user profile. This redirected data is never downloaded to the local computer at logon, even when you also configure roaming user profiles. Instead, the data is accessed only as needed, much as it would be accessed through a desktop shortcut to a network share. The desktop shortcut is part of the user profile, but the data behind the shortcut is not.

  The same factor that allows for faster logons also allows for equally fast logoffs.

- **Real-time data synchronization**   Folder Redirection enables Offline Files if it is not already enabled. The combination of Folder Redirection and Offline Files allows users to witness instantly any data changes they make to redirected data on other computers they simultaneously log on to.

- **Network problems do not disperse data**   If network problems prevent a user from connecting to a redirected folder, the user can access the local copies of the data made available from Offline Files. This data is then synchronized automatically when network connectivity is reestablished. If you turn off the Offline Files feature or if the data has never been synchronized, the user simply receives an error message and fails to connect to the source data. In either case, a faulty network connection does not lead to data being dispersed among separate user profiles for the redirected folders in question.

- **Folder Redirection can be automated through Group Policy**   By configuring Folder Redirection in a domain environment through Group Policy, you can ensure that the feature will apply both to the current users and to the new users who fall under the scope of the policy.

IMPROVEMENTS IN FOLDER REDIRECTION IN WINDOWS 7

Folder Redirection in Windows Vista and earlier had one large drawback: potentially poor logon performance when a user logs on to her computer for the first time after it has been enabled. This is because in Windows Vista and earlier, the user is blocked from logging on until all of her redirected data is migrated to the server. For a user with large amounts of data, this can result in long wait times during which she is prevented from doing useful work on her computer. The problem can be especially frustrating for a user who is logging on over a slow connection. In circumstances where the user has large amounts of data that needs to be redirected, it can take an hour or longer for the user's desktop to appear when she logs on for the first time after Folder Redirection has been enabled.

Beginning in Windows 7, however, if Offline Files is enabled on the user's computer, the performance of the first logon with Folder Redirection is improved significantly. Now, the user's redirected data is first copied into the local Offline Files cache on the user's computer, which is a much faster operation than copying across the network to the server. The user's desktop then appears, and the Offline Files cache handles uploading the user's redirected data to the server using Offline Files synchronization and continues copying the user's data to the server until all the data has been copied.

Additional enhancements in Windows 7 for improving first logon performance with Folder Redirection include the following:

- Before Windows attempts to copy the user's redirected data to the local Offline Files cache, it now checks to make sure there is enough room in the cache to hold the data. If the data won't fit in the cache, the data will be uploaded to the server during logon, resulting in similar behavior to what happens in Windows Vista and a possibly lengthy delay before the user's desktop appears.

- If the local Offline Files cache has been disabled on the user's computer, Windows now checks if the server has room for the user's data before attempting to upload the data to the server. If there is not enough room on the server, no data is uploaded, resulting in the user's desktop quickly becoming available. An event is logged in the event log to indicate that the logon occurred without redirecting any data.

Because Offline Files is enabled by default on Windows 7 computers, this improved first logon performance with Folder Redirection also occurs by default.

 Quick Check

1. Why does implementing Folder Redirection speed the logon times of users for whom roaming user profiles have been configured?

2. True or False: Folder Redirection can be used with or without roaming user profiles.

Quick Check Answers

1. Folder Redirection separates data from the roaming user profile so that less data needs to be downloaded to the local desktop.

2. True.

Configuring Folder Redirection

Windows Server 2008 includes a Folder Redirection node for the Group Policy Management Console (GPMC) that allows you to configure Folder Redirection for clients running any version of Windows since Windows 2000. You can choose the following settings for each folder listed in the Folder Redirection node:

- **Not Configured**   The Not Configured Folder Redirection setting is available to all folders listed in the snap-in. When you select this setting, you are returning the Folder Redirection policy for the named folder to its default state. Folders previously redirected with the policy stay redirected. User folders on clients without any previous knowledge of the folder redirection policy remain local unless acted on by another policy.

- **Basic**   The Basic setting allows you to redirect the selected folder to the same share for all users.

- **Advanced**   You use the Advanced setting when you want to redirect the selected folder to different locations for different security groups. For example, you would use advanced folder redirection when you want to redirect folders belonging to the Accounting group to the Finance server and folders belonging to the Sales group to the Marketing server.

Figure B-37 shows an example of a folder configured with advanced redirection. Note that the %Username% environmental variable is used to provide a unique path based on each user's name.

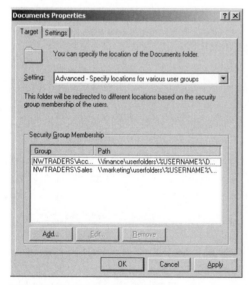

FIGURE B-37 Advanced Redirection

- **Follow The Documents Folder**   The Music, Pictures, and Videos folders support another Folder Redirection setting called Follow The Documents Folder. The Follow

The Documents Folder setting redirects the Music, Pictures, and Videos folders as subfolders of the My Documents folder. This folder redirection will make the selected folder inherit folder redirection options from the My Documents folder and disable the folder redirection options for the selected folder.

The Follow The Documents Folder setting is shown in Figure B-38.

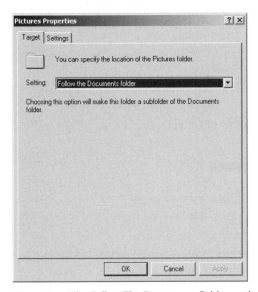

FIGURE B-38 The Follow The Documents Folder setting

Configuring a Target Folder Location

If you have not opted to configure a folder to follow the My Documents folder, you need to configure the folder with a target location. Windows 7 provides four options when selecting a target folder location:

- **Create A Folder For Each User Under The Root Path**   This option redirects the selected folder to the location that you specify in the Root Path text box. Also, this option adds a folder named after the user logon name. For example, if you redirect the My Documents folder to the root path of \\server\share, Folder Redirection creates the My Documents folder under the path \\Server\Share*Username*.

- **Redirect To The Following Location**   This option redirects the named folder to the exact path listed in the Root Path. This has the capacity to redirect multiple users using the same share path for the redirected folder. For example, you could use this option so that multiple users have the same Desktop or Start menu.

- **Redirect To The Local User Profile Location**   This option redirects the named folder to the local user profile. The local user profile for Windows Vista, Windows Server 2008, and Windows 7 is Users*Username*. The local user profile for Windows 2000, Windows XP, and Windows Server 2003 is Documents and Settings*Username*.

- **Redirect To The User's Home Directory**   This option, available only for the My Documents folder, redirects the My Documents folder to the home folder path configured in the properties of the user object. (A home folder is the default location some programs use to save files.)

These four target location settings are shown in Figure B-39.

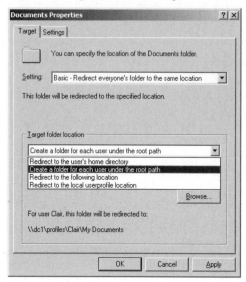

FIGURE B-39 Target Location settings

Configuring the Folder Redirection Settings Tab Options

The Folder Redirection Settings tab options, shown for the My Documents folder in Figure B-40, include both redirection settings and policy removal settings.

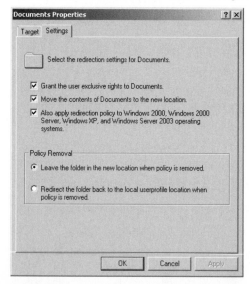

FIGURE B-40 Folder Redirection Settings tab options

The following redirection settings are available on the Settings tab for folders you choose to redirect:

- **Grant The User Exclusive Rights To <*Folder*>**   This option controls the NTFS permissions of the newly created *%Username%* folder, allowing the user and Local System to have Full Control of the newly created folder. This is the default behavior.

- **Move The Contents Of <*Folder*> To The New Location**   This option moves all the user data in the named folder to the redirected folder. This setting defaults to Enabled.

- **Also Apply Redirection Policy To Windows 2000, Windows 2000 Server, Windows XP, And Windows Server 2003 Operating Systems**   This option directs the Folder Redirection management tool to write the redirection policy in a format recognized by the previous operating systems listed. When this setting is cleared, Windows writes the redirection policy in a format exclusive to Windows Vista, Windows Server 2008, and Windows 7.

The Settings tab also allows you to configure policy removal settings. These settings allow you to choose the behavior that occurs for redirected folders and their contents after a folder redirection policy no longer applies to a given user. A Folder Redirection policy might stop applying to a user, for example, when an administrator unlinks or deletes the policy or when the user joins a security group for which the policy is blocked.

The following policy removal settings are available:

- **Leave Folder In New Location When Policy Is Removed**   When you enable this option, the data that a user has stored in the redirected location stays in that location once the policy no longer applies to that user.

- **Redirect The Folder Back To The Local User Profile Location When Policy Is Removed**   When you enable this option, the data that a user has stored in the redirected location is copied to the local user profile once the policy no longer applies to the user.

PRACTICE   Configuring Roaming User Profiles and Folder Redirection

In this practice, you create a new domain user account and configure a roaming user profile for that new user. Then, you configure a roaming profile for the user and observe the effects after the user logs on to computers running Windows XP, Windows 7, and Windows Server 2008. Finally, you will configure Folder Redirection and observe the difference in behavior between Folder Redirection and traditional roaming user profiles.

To perform these exercises, you will need:

- A domain controller running Windows Server 2008 R2.
- A client computer running Windows 7 that is a member of the same domain.
- A client computer running Windows XP that is a member of the same domain.

EXERCISE 1   Configuring a New User with a Roaming User Profile

In this exercise, you first create a share named Profiles on the domain controller, which should be running Windows Server 2008 R2. Then you create a new account named RoamingUser in the domain and configure the new user with a roaming user profile.

1. Log on to the domain controller as an administrator.

2. On the C: drive of the domain controller, create a new folder named Profiles.

3. Right-click the Profiles folder, select Share With, and then click Specific People.

4. On the File Sharing page of the File Sharing wizard, type **everyone**, and then press Enter.

5. Configure permissions so that Everyone is assigned the Read/Write permission level.

6. Click Share to confirm the changes and then click Done to close the File Sharing wizard.

7. Open Active Directory Users And Computers.

8. In the console tree, right-click the Users container, point to New, and then click User.

9. In the New Object – User dialog box, type the following information:

   ■ First Name: **Roaming**

   ■ Last Name: **User**

   ■ User Logon Name: **Roaminguser**

10. Click Next.

11. In the New Object – User dialog box, enter a password in the Password and Confirm Password text boxes.

12. Clear the User Must Change Password At Next Logon check box.

13. In the New Object – User dialog box, click Next, and then click Finish.

14. In the details pane of Active Directory Users And Computers, locate the new Roaming User domain user account you have just created.

   You need to add Roaming User to the Server Operators group so that you can log on to the domain controller with this new account.

15. Right-click the Roaming User user account, and click Add To A Group from the shortcut menu.

16. In the Select Groups dialog box, type **server operators**, and then press Enter.

   An Active Directory Domain Services message box appears, indicating that the Add To Group operation was successfully completed.

17. Click OK to close the message box.

18. Open the Properties dialog box for the Roaming User user account.

19. In the Roaming User Properties dialog box, click the Profile tab.

20. In the Profile Path text box, type the following:

    domain controller name\profiles\%username%. *For example, if the name of your domain controller is DC1, type* **\\dc1\profiles\%username%.**

21. In the Roaming User Properties dialog box, click OK.

EXERCISE 2   Testing the Roaming User Profile on Windows 7 Computers

In this exercise, you log on to the domain from a computer running Windows 7. You then make a change to your desktop, log off, and observe the results when you log on to the domain controller. Finally, you log on to a computer running Windows XP and observe any changes.

1. Log on to the domain from the Windows 7 client with the Roaminguser user account.

2. Create a text file on the desktop named Test1, and then log off the Windows 7 client.

3. Log on to the domain controller with the Roaminguser user account.

4. Verify that the file named Test1 appears on Roaminguser's desktop on the domain controller.

5. Answer the following question: Did the file move from one computer to another?

   Answer: No, it is stored centrally on the server.

6. On the domain controller, navigate to the C: drive, and open the Profiles folder.

7. Answer the following question: What is the name of the folder in which Roaminguser's data is being stored?

   Answer: Roaminguser.V2

8. Answer the following question: For which operating systems does this folder hold roaming user profile data?

   Answer: Windows Vista, Windows Server 2008, and Windows 7

9. Log on to the domain from the client running Windows XP with the Roaminguser user account.

10. Answer the following question: Why doesn't the Test1 file appear on the desktop on the client running Windows XP?

    Answer: Because roaming user profiles are not compatible between Windows XP and Windows 7

11. Log off or shut down the client running Windows XP.

12. Return to the domain controller and navigate once more to C:\Profiles.

13. Answer the following question: Which new folder has appeared in the Profiles folder since you logged on to the domain from the computer running Windows XP?

Answer: A folder named Roaminguser

14. Answer the following question: For which operating systems does this second folder hold roaming user profile data?

Answer: For computers running Windows 2000, Windows XP, and Windows Server 2003

EXERCISE 3   Configuring Folder Redirection for Use with Windows XP and Windows 7

In this exercise, you create a GPO that redirects common folders to a central location.

1. Log on to the domain controller with a domain administrator account.

2. Click Start, type **gpmc.msc,** and then press Enter.

3. The GPMC opens.

4. In the console tree, expand the Forest container and the Domains container.

5. Below the Domains container, right-click the icon corresponding to the name of the domain (such as nwtraders.msft), and then click Create A GPO In This Domain, And Link It Here.

6. In the New GPO window, type **Folder Redirection for all Windows Operating Systems,** and then press Enter.

7. In the details pane of the GPMC, locate and right-click the new GPO you have just created, and then click Edit.

   The Group Policy Management Editor opens.

8. In the console tree, below User Configuration, expand the Policies container, expand the Windows Settings container, and then expand the Folder Redirection container.

9. Take a minute to browse the various folders beneath the Folder Redirection container. These are the folders that you can redirect to any available location, such as a central server.

10. Open the Properties of the AppData(Roaming) folder.

11. On the Target tab, select the setting of Basic – Redirect Everyone's Folder To The Same Location.

12. In the Root Path text box, type **\\\domain controller name\profiles.** For example, if the name of your domain controller is DC1, type **\\dc1\profiles.**

13. On the Settings tab, select the check box next to Also Apply Redirection Policy To Windows 2000, Windows 2000 Server, Windows XP, And Windows Server 2003 Operating Systems.

    This option makes Folder Redirection compatible among all Windows operating systems since Windows 2000.

14. Click OK.

15. If a Warning box appears, read the Warning, and then click Yes to continue.

16. Perform steps 10 through 15 for the Desktop, Start Menu, and Documents folders.

17. Log off the clients running Windows XP and Windows 7.

EXERCISE 4   Testing Folder Redirection

In this exercise, you log on to both the client running Windows XP and the client running Windows 7 from a domain user account. You then make changes to the user environment and observe the effects.

1. Log on to the domain from the client running Windows XP as Roaminguser.

2. Create a text file on the desktop named Test2.

3. Log on to the domain from the client running Windows 7 as Roaminguser.

4. If you do not see the Test2 text file on the desktop, log off and then log back on again.

5. When the Test2 file appears on the desktop, create a new text file named Test3.

6. Switch to the client running Windows XP.

   You should see Test3 on the desktop of the client running Windows XP.

7. On the client running Windows 7, open the Documents folder, and then create a new text file named Test4 in that folder.

8. Switch to the client running Windows XP, and then answer the following question: Where does Test4 appear on the client running Windows XP?

   Answer: In the My Documents folder

9. Log off all machines.

Summary

- Offline Files allows you to store a local, automatically synchronized copy of files stored on network shares. To make a fi le or folder available offline, right-click the file, and then select Always Available Offline.

- Although files can synchronize automatically, you also need to synchronize files manually to ensure that they are up to date, especially if you plan to work offline. You can also create scheduled synchronizations to ensure that your files are updated with the latest revisions.

- You can adjust the amount of space available for Offline Files.

- Group Policy includes three new settings for Offline Files in Windows 7: Configure Background Sync, Exclude Files From Being Cached, and Enable Transparent Caching.

- Through the Previous Versions tab, you can easily restore older versions of files or folders that have been saved by a restore point or a Windows backup.

- A user profile is a collection of personal files and settings stored in a folder bearing a user's name.

- User profiles changed significantly in Windows Vista. This fact is relevant if you are deploying Windows 7 in a network whose clients are running pre–Windows Vista operating systems such as Windows XP.

- A roaming user profile is a profile that is stored centrally on a network share. It is configured in the properties of the user account in Active Directory Users And Computers.

- By default, roaming user profiles in pre–Windows Vista operating systems such as Windows XP are not compatible with roaming user profiles in post–Windows Vista operating systems such as Windows Vista and Windows 7.

- Folder Redirection is a feature of Windows that enables you to redirect to network shares the target of user folders such as Documents and Desktop. By implementing Folder Redirection, you can allow roaming users to see their data regardless of the Windows version they log on to.

Key Terms

Do you know what these key terms mean? You can check your answers by looking up the terms in the glossary at the end of the book.

- **Folder Redirection**
- **Offline Files**
- **Previous Versions**
- **Roaming user profile**
- **User profile**

Configuring Startup and Troubleshooting Startup Issues

> **NOTE** This material was originally published in a slightly different form in *Windows 7 Resource Kit* by Mitch Tulloch, Tony Northrup, Jerry Honeycutt, Ed Wilson, and the Windows 7 Team at Microsoft (Microsoft Press, 2010).

Diagnosing and correcting hardware and software problems that affect the startup process require different tools and techniques than troubleshooting problems that occur after the system starts because the person troubleshooting the startup problem does not have access to the full suite of the Windows 7 operating system troubleshooting tools. Resolving startup issues requires a clear understanding of the startup process, the core operating system features, and the tools used to isolate and resolve problems.

This appendix covers changes to the Windows 7 startup process, how to configure startup settings, and how to troubleshoot problems that stop Windows 7 from starting and allowing a user to complete the interactive logon process successfully.

What's New with Windows Startup

Windows 7 includes a few improvements to startup. Most significantly, setup now automatically installs Windows Recovery Environment (WinRE). WinRE, which includes the Startup Repair tool, was available for Windows Vista, but it was not automatically installed. IT professionals could configure the required partition and install the tools to the computer's hard disk, but this was not done by default. Therefore, most users started WinRE from the Windows Vista setup DVD. With Windows 7, users can start WinRE directly from the hard disk if Windows cannot start, and Windows startup will automatically open WinRE if Windows fails to start. If the hard disk is damaged, users can still start WinRE from the Windows 7 DVD.

Other than the automatic installation of WinRE, Windows 7 also reduces the time to start up, shut down, and resume from sleep. Because the changes to startup are minimal with Windows 7, most of this appendix focuses on changes introduced since Windows XP. These changes are all available in both Windows 7 and Windows Vista.

Several aspects of the Windows Vista and Windows 7 startup process have changed when compared to Windows XP. Most significantly, Ntldr (the feature of Windows XP that displayed the boot menu and loaded the Windows XP kernel) has been replaced by the Windows Boot Manager and the Windows Boot Loader. The Boot.ini file (a file that contains entries describing the available boot options) has been replaced by the boot configuration data (BCD) registry file. Ntdetect.com functionality has been merged into the kernel, and Windows Vista no longer supports hardware profiles. In fact, hardware profiles are no longer required: Windows will automatically detect different hardware configurations without requiring administrators to explicitly configure profiles. Finally, the command-line recovery console has been replaced by the graphical WinRE, which simplifies troubleshooting. This appendix discusses these changes in more detail.

Boot Configuration Data

The BCD registry file replaces the Boot.ini files used in Windows XP and earlier versions of Windows to track operating system locations, and it allows for a variety of new Windows Vista and Windows 7 features, including the Startup Repair tool and the Multi-User Install shortcuts. The BCD is stored in a data file that uses the same format as the registry and is located on either the Extensible Firmware Interface (EFI) system partition (for computers that support EFI) or on the system volume. On BIOS-based operating systems, the BCD registry file is located at \Boot\Bcd on the active partition. On EFI-based operating systems, the BCD registry file is located in the \EFI\Microsoft\Boot\ folder on the EFI system partition.

The BCD registry file can contain the following types of information:

- Entries that describe Windows Boot Manager (\Bootmgr) settings
- Entries to start the Windows Boot Loader (\Windows\System32\WinLoad.exe), which can then load Windows Vista
- Entries to start Windows Resume Application (\Windows\System32\WinResume.exe), which can then restore Windows Vista from hibernation
- Entries to start Windows Memory Diagnostic (\Boot\MemTest.exe)
- Entries to start Ntldr to load previous versions of Windows
- Entries to load and execute a Volume Boot Record, which typically starts a non-Microsoft boot loader

Additionally, you can add more entries to load custom applications, such as recovery tools.

You can modify the BCD registry file in several different ways:

- **Startup And Recovery** With the Startup And Recovery dialog box (available on the Advanced tab of the System Properties dialog box), you can select the default operating system to start if you have multiple operating systems installed on your computer. You can also change the time-out value. This dialog box has changed very little when compared to Windows XP; however, it now changes the BCD registry file instead of the Boot.ini file.

- **System Configuration utility (Msconfig.exe)** Msconfig.exe is a troubleshooting tool that you can use to configure startup options. The Boot tab in Windows 7 provides similar functionality to the Boot.ini tab in Windows XP, such as starting in safe mode, enabling a boot log, or disabling the graphical user interface (GUI).

- **BCD Windows Management Instrumentation provider** The BCD Windows Management Instrumentation (WMI) provider is a management interface that youcan use to script utilities that modify BCD. This is the only programmatic interface available for BCD; you should always use this interface rather than attempting to access the BCD registry file directly. For more information, see "BCD WMI Provider Classes" at *http://msdn2.microsoft.com/en-us/library/aa362675.aspx*.

- **BCDEdit.exe** BCDEdit.exe is a command-line utility that replaces Bootcfg.exe in Windows XP. BCDEdit can be run from within Windows 7 at an administrative command prompt, from within Windows RE or even from within earlier versions of Windows (if the BCDEdit.exe file is available). BCDEdit provides more configuration options than the Startup And Recovery dialog box.

- **Non-Microsoft tools** Third-party software vendors have released tools to simplify editing the BCD registry file, including:
  - BootPRO, available at *http://www.vistabootpro.org*
  - EasyBCD, available at *http://neosmart.net*

You cannot use Bootcfg.exe to modify BCD. However, Bootcfg.exe will remain in the operating system to support configuring older operating systems that might be installed on the same computer.

For EFI computers, BCDEdit also replaces NvrBoot. In previous versions of Windows, you could use NvrBoot to edit the EFI boot manager menu items.

BCD Stores

Physically, a BCD store is a binary file in the registry hive format. A computer has a system BCD store that describes all installed Windows Vista and Windows 7 operating systems and installed Windows boot applications. A computer can optionally have many non-system BCD stores. Figure C-1 shows an example of how the BCD hierarchy is implemented in a typical BCD store.

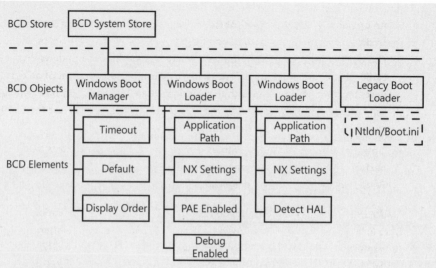

FIGURE C-1 The BCD hierarchy allows for multiple boot options.

A BCD store normally has at least two (and optionally, many) BCD objects:

- **A Windows Boot Manager object** This object contains BCD elements that pertain to the Windows Boot Manager, such as the entries to display in an operating system selection menu, boot tool selection menu, and time-out for the selection menus. The Windows Boot Manager object and its associated elements serve essentially the same purpose as the *[boot loader]* section of a Boot.ini file. A store can optionally have multiple instances of the Windows Boot Manager. However, only one of them can be represented by the Windows Boot Manager well-known globally unique identifier (GUID). You can use the GUID's alias, *{bootmgr}*, to manipulate a store with BCDEdit.

- **At least one and optionally several Windows Boot Loader objects** Stores contain one instance of this object for each version or configuration of Windows Vista, Windows Server 2008, or Windows 7 that is installed on the system. These objects contain BCD elements that are used when loading Windows or during Windows initialization such as no-execute (NX) page protection policy, physical address extension (PAE) policy, and kernel debugger settings. Each object and its associated elements serve essentially the same purpose as one of the lines in the *[operating systems]* section of Boot.ini. When a computer is booted into Windows, the alias *{current}* represents the associated boot loader object. When manipulating a store with BCDEdit, the default boot loader object has the alias *{default}*.

- **An optional Windows {ntldr} object**   The *{ntldr}* object describes the location of Ntldr, which you can execute to boot Windows XP or earlier versions of Windows. This object is required only if the system includes versions of Windows that are earlier than Windows Vista. It is possible to have multiple instances of objects that describe Ntldr. However, as with the Windows Boot Manager, only one instance can be represented by the *{ntldr}* well-known GUID alias. You can use the GUID's alias, *{ntldr}*, to manipulate a store with BCDEdit.

- **Optional boot applications**   Stores can optionally have BCD objects that perform other boot-related operations. One example is the Windows Memory Tester, which runs memory diagnostics.

MORE INFO   For detailed information about BCD, see "Boot Configuration Data in Windows Vista" at *http://www.microsoft.com/whdc/system/platform/ firmware/bcd.mspx*, and read "Boot Configuration Data Editor Frequently Asked Questions" at *http://technet.microsoft.com/en-us/library/cc721886.aspx*.

System Recovery

Windows Vista and Windows 7 replace the Recovery Console troubleshooting tool with the new System Recovery tool (part of WinRE). Typically, you will start the tool by pressing F8 before starting Windows and then choosing Repair Your Computer from the Advanced Boot Options screen. If that choice is not available because the hard disk has failed, you can start the tool by starting from the Windows 7 DVD and then clicking Repair Your Computer (after configuring the language options). This loads a specialized version of Windows Preinstallation Environment (Windows PE) and then displays the System Recovery tool. For step-by-step instructions on how to load the System Recovery tools, see the section titled "How to Start the System Recovery Tools" later in this appendix.

The System Recovery tools provide access to the following tools:

- **Startup Repair**   The Startup Repair tool can solve many common startup problems automatically. Startup Repair performs an exhaustive analysis to diagnose your startup problems, including analyzing boot sectors, the Boot Manager, disk configuration, disk integrity, BCD registry file integrity, system file integrity, registry integrity, boot logs, and event logs. It will then attempt to solve the problem, which may involve repairing configuration files, solving simple disk problems, replacing missing system files, or running System Restore to return the computer to an earlier state. Because Startup Repair performs these tasks automatically, you can solve startup problems much faster than performing the analysis and repair manually.

- **System Restore**   Windows automatically captures system state before installing new applications or drivers. You can later use the System Restore tool to return to this system if you experience problems. Because System Restore is available from the

System Recovery tools, you can use System Restore to repair problems that prevent Windows Vista or Windows 7 from booting. Startup Repair can prompt you to initiate a System Restore, so you might never need to access this tool directly.

- **System Image Recovery**   You use this tool to initiate a complete restore of the system hard disk. However, because any files saved since the last backup will be lost, you should use this only as a last resort.

- **Windows Memory Diagnostic**   The Windows Memory Diagnostics tool performs an automated test of the reliability of your computer's memory. For more information, see Appendix D, "Troubleshooting Hardware, Driver, and Disk Issues."

- **Command Prompt**   From the Command Prompt tool, you have access to many standard command-line tools. Some tools will not work properly, however, because Windows Vista is not currently running. For example, because WinRE does not include networking capabilities, network tools will not function correctly. However, several tools in WinRE are useful:

  - BCDEdit.exe for making changes to the BCD registry file

  - Diskpart.exe for viewing and changing disk partitioning

  - Format.exe for formatting partitions

  - Chkdsk.exe for finding and resolving some disk problems (note that Chkdsk cannot add events to the event log when started from System Recovery tools)

  - Notepad.exe for viewing log files or editing configuration files

  - Bootsect.exe (available on the Windows 7 DVD in the \Boot\ folder) for updating the master boot code for hard disk partitions to switch between the Windows 7 Boot Manager and Ntldr, used by Windows XP and earlier versions of Windows

  - Bootrec.exe for manually repairing disk problems if Startup Repair cannot fix them

Windows Boot Performance Diagnostics

Sometimes, Windows might start correctly but might take an unusually long time to do so. Such a problem can be difficult to troubleshoot because there's no straightforward way to monitor processes while Windows is starting. To help administrators identify the source of startup performance problems and to automatically fix some problems, Windows 7 includes Windows Boot Performance Diagnostics.

You can use the Group Policy settings to manage Windows Boot Performance Diagnostics in an Active Directory Domain Services (AD DS) environment. In the Computer Configuration\Policies\Administrative Templates\System\Troubleshooting and Diagnostics\Windows Boot Performance Diagnostics node, edit the Configure Scenario Execution Level policy. When this policy is enabled, you can choose from the following two settings:

- **Detection And Troubleshooting Only**   Windows Boot Performance Diagnostics will identify startup performance problems and will add an event to the event log, allowing administrators to detect the problems and manually troubleshoot them. Windows Boot Performance Diagnostics will not attempt to fix the problems, however.

- **Detection, Troubleshooting, And Resolution** Windows Boot Performance Diagnostics will identify startup performance problems and automatically take steps to attempt to alleviate the problems.

If you disable the setting, Windows Boot Performance Diagnostics will neither identify nor attempt to resolve startup performance problems. For Windows Boot Performance Diagnostics to function, the Diagnostic Policy Service must be running.

Settings for Windows Shutdown Performance Diagnostics, which function similarly to the Windows Boot Performance Diagnostics, are located in the Computer Configuration\Policies\ Administrative Templates\System\Troubleshooting And Diagnostics\Windows Shutdown Performance Diagnostics node.

Understanding the Startup Process

To diagnose and correct a startup problem, you need to understand what occurs during startup. Figure C-2 provides a high-level overview of the different paths startup can take.

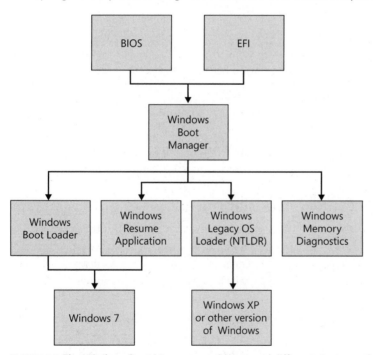

FIGURE C-2 The Windows Boot Manager provides several different startup paths.

The normal startup sequence for Windows 7 is:

1. Power-on self test (POST) phase.

2. Initial startup phase.

3. Windows Boot Manager phase.

4. Windows Boot Loader phase.

5. Kernel loading phase.

6. Logon phase.

This sequence will vary if the computer is resuming from hibernation or if a non–Windows 7 option is selected during the Windows Boot Manager phase. The following sections describe the phases of a normal startup process in more detail.

Power-on Self Test Phase

As soon as you turn on a computer, its processor begins to carry out the programming instructions contained in the BIOS or EFI. The BIOS and EFI, which are types of firmware, contain the processor-dependent code that starts the computer regardless of the operating system installed. The first set of startup instructions is the POST, which is responsible for the following system and diagnostic functions:

- Performs initial hardware checks, such as determining the amount of memory present
- Verifies that the devices needed to start an operating system, such as a hard disk, are present
- Retrieves system configuration settings from nonvolatile memory, which is located on the motherboard

The contents of the nonvolatile memory remain even after you shut down the computer. Examples of hardware settings stored in the nonvolatile memory include device boot order and Plug and Play (PnP) information.

After the motherboard POST completes, add-on adapters that have their own firmware (for example, video and hard drive controllers) carry out internal diagnostic tests.

If startup fails before or during POST, your computer is experiencing a hardware failure. Generally, the BIOS or EFI displays an error message that indicates the nature of the problem. If video is not functioning correctly, the BIOS or EFI usually indicates the nature of the failure with a series of beeps.

To access and change system and peripheral firmware settings, consult the system documentation provided by the manufacturer. For more information, refer to your computer's documentation and see the section titled "How to Diagnose Hardware Problems" later in this appendix.

Initial Startup Phase

After the POST, computers must find and load the Windows Boot Manager. Older BIOS computers and newer EFI computers do this slightly differently, as the following sections describe.

Initial Startup Phase for BIOS Computers

After the POST, the settings that are stored in the nonvolatile memory, such as boot order, determine the devices that the computer can use to start an operating system. In addition to floppy disks or hard disks attached to Advanced Technology Attachment (ATA), Serial ATA, and small computer system interface (SCSI) controllers, computers can typically start an operating system from other devices, such as the following:

- CDs or DVDs
- Network adapters
- Universal serial bus (USB) flash drives
- Removable disks
- Secondary storage devices installed in docking stations for portable computers

It is possible to specify a custom boot order, such as CDROM, Floppy, Hard Disk. When you specify CDROM, Floppy, Hard Disk as a boot order, the following events occur at startup:

1. The computer searches the CD-ROM for bootable media. If a bootable CD or DVD is present, the computer uses the media as the startup device. Otherwise, the computer searches the next device in the boot order. You cannot use a non-bootable CD or DVD to start your system. The presence of a non-bootable CD or DVD in the CD-ROM drive can add to the time the system requires to start. If you do not intend to start the computer from CD, remove all CDs from the CD-ROM drive before restarting.

2. The computer searches the floppy disk for bootable media. If a bootable floppy is present, the computer uses the floppy disk as the startup device and loads the first sector (sector 0, the floppy disk boot sector) into memory. Otherwise, the computer searches the next device in the boot order or displays an error message.

3. The computer uses the hard disk as the startup device. The computer typically uses the hard disk as the startup device only when the CD-ROM drive and the floppy disk drive are empty.

There are exceptions in which code on bootable media transfers control to the hard disk. For example, when you start your system by using the bootable Windows DVD, Windows Setup checks the hard disk for Windows installations. If one is found, you have the option of bypassing DVD startup by not responding to the Press Any Key To Boot From CD Or DVD prompt that appears. This prompt is actually displayed by the startup program located on the Windows DVD, not by your computer's hardware.

If startup fails during the initial startup phase, you are experiencing a problem with the BIOS configuration, the disk subsystem, or the file system. The following error message is common during this phase. It indicates that none of the configured bootable media types was available.

```
Non-system disk or disk error
Replace and press any key when ready
```

If you changed the disk configuration recently, verify that all cables are properly connected and jumpers are correctly configured. If booting from the hard disk, verify that all removable media have been removed. If booting from a CD or DVD, verify that the BIOS is configured to start from the CD or DVD and that the Windows medium is present. If the disk subsystem and BIOS are configured correctly, the problem may be related to the file system. For instructions on repairing the Master Boot Record (MBR) and the boot sector, see the section titled "How to Run Startup Repair" later in this appendix. For more information about configuring the boot order, consult your computer's documentation.

If you boot from the hard disk, the computer reads the boot code instructions located on the MBR. The MBR is the first sector of data on the startup hard disk. The MBR contains instructions (called *boot code*) and a table (called a *partition table*) that identify primary and extended partitions. The BIOS reads the MBR into memory and transfers control to the code in the MBR.

The computer then searches the partition table for the active partition, also known as a *bootable partition*. The first sector of the active partition contains boot code that enables the computer to do the following:

- Read the contents of the file system used.
- Locate and start a 16-bit stub program (Bootmgr) in the root directory of the boot volume. This stub program switches the processor into 32- or 64-bit Protected mode and loads the 32- or 64-bit Windows Boot Manager, which is stored in the same Bootmgr file. After the Windows Boot Manager loads, startup is identical for both BIOS and EFI computers.

> **NOTE** The stub program is necessary because 32-bit and 64-bit computers first start in Real mode. In Real mode, the processor disables certain features to allow compatibility with software designed to run on 8-bit and 16-bit processors. The Windows Boot Manager is 32-bit or 64-bit, however, so the stub program sets up the BIOS computer to run the 32-bit or 64-bit software properly.

If an active partition does not exist or if boot sector information is missing or corrupt, a message similar to any of the following might appear:

- Invalid partition table
- Error loading operating system
- Missing operating system

If an active partition is successfully located, the code in the boot sector locates and starts Windows Boot Loader (WinLoad) and the BIOS transfers execution to it.

Initial Startup Phase for EFI Computers

Startup for EFI computers initially differs from startup for BIOS computers. EFI computers have a built-in boot manager that enables the computer's hardware to choose from multiple operating systems based on user input. When you install Windows 7 on an EFI computer,

Windows adds a single entry to the EFI boot manager with the title Windows Boot Manager. This entry points to the \Efi\Microsoft\Boot\Bootmgfw.efi 32-bit or 64-bit EFI executable program—the Windows Boot Manager. This is the same Windows Boot Manager that is eventually loaded on BIOS-based computers. Windows configures the EFI boot manager to display the EFI startup menu for only 2 seconds and then load the Windows Boot Manager by default to minimize complexity and startup time.

If you install a different operating system or manually change the EFI boot manager settings, EFI might no longer load the Windows Boot Manager. To resolve this problem, use the Startup Repair tool, as described in the section titled "The Process of Troubleshooting Startup" later in this appendix. Alternatively, you might be able to update the EFI boot manager settings manually using your computer's built-in EFI tools. For more information about configuring EFI, consult your computer's documentation.

Windows Boot Manager Phase

The Windows Boot Manager is capable of natively reading supported file systems, and it uses that capability to parse the BCD registry file without fully loading the file system.

For computers that have a single operating system, Windows Boot Manager never displays a user interface. It does, however, wait for a few moments to allow the user to press a key to display the standard boot menu, as shown in Figure C-3, or to press F8 to choose Advanced Boot Options, as shown in Figure C-4. If the user does not press a key within a few seconds of POST completing, Windows Boot Manager starts the Windows Boot Loader, which in turn starts Windows 7.

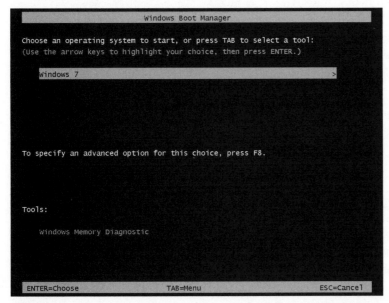

```
                          Windows Boot Manager

Choose an operating system to start, or press TAB to select a tool:
(Use the arrow keys to highlight your choice, then press ENTER.)

   Windows 7                                                      >




To specify an advanced option for this choice, press F8.




Tools:

     Windows Memory Diagnostic



ENTER=Choose                  TAB=Menu                ESC=Cancel
```

FIGURE C-3 Windows Boot Manager enables you to choose from multiple operating systems or start Windows Memory Diagnostics.

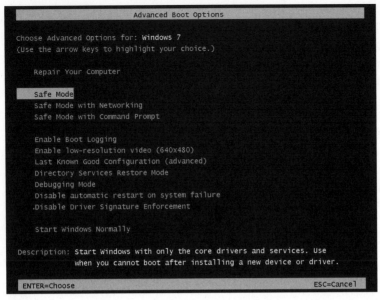

```
                    Advanced Boot Options

Choose Advanced Options for: Windows 7
(Use the arrow keys to highlight your choice.)

    Repair Your Computer

    Safe Mode
    Safe Mode with Networking
    Safe Mode with Command Prompt

    Enable Boot Logging
    Enable low-resolution video (640x480)
    Last Known Good Configuration (advanced)
    Directory Services Restore Mode
    Debugging Mode
    Disable automatic restart on system failure
   .Disable Driver Signature Enforcement

    Start Windows Normally

Description: Start Windows with only the core drivers and services. Use
            when you cannot boot after installing a new device or driver.


 ENTER=Choose                                    ESC=Cancel
```

FIGURE C-4 During startup, you can interrupt the default behavior of Windows Boot Manager to view the Advanced Boot Options.

For computers with multiple operating systems installed (such as both Windows 7 and Windows XP), Windows Boot Manager displays a menu of operating system choices at startup. Depending on what you choose, Windows Boot Manager will start a different process:

- If you choose Windows Vista or Windows 7, Windows Boot Manager starts the Windows Boot Loader to open Windows.

- If you choose Earlier Version Of Windows or another entry for Windows Server 2003, Windows XP Professional, Microsoft Windows 2000, or Microsoft Windows NT 4.0, Windows Boot Manager starts Ntldr, which then proceeds with the hardware detection phase.

- If you select another operating system, control is passed to the boot sector for the other operating system.

- If you choose Windows Memory Diagnostic by pressing the Tab key, Windows Boot Manager starts the diagnostic tool without first opening Windows.

Windows Boot Loader Phase

The Windows Boot Manager starts the Windows Boot Loader phase when the user chooses to load Windows Vista or Windows 7. The Windows Boot Loader does the following:

1. Loads the operating system kernel, Ntoskrnl.exe, but does not yet run it.

2. Loads the Hardware Abstraction Layer (HAL), Hal.dll. This will not be used until the kernel is run.

3. Loads the system registry hive (System32\Config\System) into memory.

4. Scans the HKEY_LOCAL_MACHINE\SYSTEM\Services key for device drivers and loads all drivers that are configured for the boot class into memory. The Windows Boot Loader does not, however, initiate the drivers. Drivers are not initiated until the kernel loading phase.

5. Enables paging.

6. Passes control to the operating system kernel, which starts the next phase.

Kernel Loading Phase

The Windows Boot Loader is responsible for loading the Windows kernel (Ntoskrnl.exe) and the HAL into memory. Together, the kernel and the HAL initialize a group of software features that are called the *Windows executive*. The Windows executive processes the configuration information stored in the registry in HKLM\SYSTEM\CurrentControlSet and starts services and drivers. The following sections provide more detail about the kernel loading phase.

Control Sets

The Windows Boot Loader reads control set information from the registry key HKEY_LOCAL_MACHINE\SYSTEM, which is stored in the file %SystemRoot%\System32\Config\System, so that the kernel can determine which device drivers need to be loaded during startup. Typically, several control sets exist, with the actual number depending on how often system configuration settings change.

The HKEY_LOCAL_MACHINE\SYSTEM subkeys used during startup are:

- \CurrentControlSet, a pointer to a ControlSet*xxx* subkey (where *xxx* represents a control set number, such as 001) designated in the \Select\Current value.

- \Select, which contains the following entries:

  - **Default** Points to the control set number (for example, 001=ControlSet001) that the system has specified for use at the next startup. If no error or manual invocation of the LastKnownGood startup option occurs, this control set number is designated as the value of the Default, Current, and LastKnownGood entries (assuming that a user is able to log on successfully).

  - **Current** Points to the last control set that was used to start the system.

  - **Failed** Points to a control set that did not start Windows Vista successfully. This value is updated when the LastKnownGood option is used to start the system.

  - **LastKnownGood** Points to the control set that was used during the last user session. When a user logs on, the LastKnownGood control set is updated with configuration information from the previous user session.

The Windows Boot Loader uses the control set identified by the \Select\Default value unless you choose the Last Known Good Configuration from the Advanced Boot Options menu.

The kernel creates the registry key HKEY_LOCAL_MACHINE\HARDWARE, which contains the hardware data collected at system startup. Windows supports an extensive set of devices, with additional drivers not on the Windows operating system DVD provided by hardware manufacturers. Drivers are kernel-mode features required by devices to function within an operating system. Services are features that support operating system and application functions and act as network servers. Services can run in a different context than user applications and typically do not offer many user-configurable options.

For example, the Print Spooler service does not require a user to be logged on to run and functions independently of the user who is logged on to the system. Drivers generally communicate directly with hardware devices, whereas services usually communicate with hardware through drivers. Driver and service files are typically stored in the %SystemRoot%\System32 and %SystemRoot%\System32\Drivers folders and use .exe, .sys, or .dll file name extensions.

Drivers are also services. Therefore, during kernel initialization, the Windows Boot Loader and Ntoskrnl use the information stored in the HKEY_LOCAL_MACHINE\SYSTEM\CurrentControlSet\Services*Servicename* registry subkeys to determine both the drivers and services to load. In the *Servicename* subkeys, the Start entry specifies when to start the service. For example, the Windows Boot Loader loads all drivers for which Start is 0, such as device drivers for hard disk controllers. After execution is transferred to the kernel, the kernel loads drivers and services for which Start is 1.

Table C-1 lists the values (in decimal) for the registry entry Start. Boot drivers (those for which Start is 0) and file system drivers are always loaded regardless of the value of Start because they are required to start Windows.

TABLE C-1 Values for the Start Registry Entry

VALUE	START TYPE	VALUE DESCRIPTIONS FOR START ENTRIES
0	Boot	Specifies a driver that is loaded (but not started) by the boot loader. If no errors occur, the driver is started during kernel initialization prior to any non-boot drivers being loaded.
1	System	Specifies a driver that loads and starts during kernel initialization after drivers with a Start value of 0 have been started.
2	Auto load	Specifies a driver or service that is initialized at system startup by Session Manager (Smss.exe) or the Services Controller (Services.exe).
3	Load on demand	Specifies a driver or service that the Service Control Manager (SCM) will start only on demand. These drivers have to be started manually by calling a Win32 SCM application programming interface (API), such as the Services snap-in.

VALUE	START TYPE	VALUE DESCRIPTIONS FOR START ENTRIES
4	Disabled	Specifies a disabled (not started) driver or service.
5	Delayed start	Specifies that less-critical services will start shortly after startup to allow the operating system to be responsive to the user sooner. This start type was first introduced in Windows Vista.

Table C-2 lists some of the values (in decimal) for the Type registry entry.

TABLE C-2 Type Registry Values

VALUE	VALUE DESCRIPTIONS FOR TYPE ENTRIES
1	Specifies a kernel device driver
2	Specifies a kernel-mode file system driver (also a kernel device driver)
4	Specifies arguments passed to an adapter
8	Specifies a file system driver, such as a file system recognizer driver
16	Specifies a service that obeys the service control protocol, runs within a process that hosts only one service, and can be started by the Services Controller
32	Specifies a service that runs in a process that hosts multiple services
256	Specifies a service that is allowed to display windows on the console and receive user input

Some drivers and services require that conditions, also known as *dependencies*, be met. You can find dependencies listed under the DependOnGroup and DependOnService entries in the HKEY_LOCAL_MACHINE\SYSTEM\CurrentControlSet\Services*Servicename* subkey for each service or driver. For more information about using dependencies to prevent or delay a driver or service from starting, see the section titled "How to Temporarily Disable a Service" later in this appendix. The Services subkey also contains information that affects how drivers and services are loaded. Table C-3 lists some of these other entries.

TABLE C-3 Other Registry Entries in the Servicename Subkeys

ENTRY	DESCRIPTION
DependOnGroup	At least one item from this group must start before this service is loaded.
DependOnService	Lists the specific services that must load before this service loads.
DisplayName	Describes the feature.

ENTRY	DESCRIPTION
ErrorControl	Controls whether a driver error requires the system to use the LastKnownGood control set or to display a Stop message.
	If the value is 0x0 (Ignore, No Error Is Reported), it does not display a warning and proceeds with startup.
	If the value is 0x1 (Normal, Error Reported), it records the event to the System Event Log and displays a warning message but proceeds with startup.
	If the value is 0x2 (Severe), it records the event to the System Event Log, uses the LastKnownGood settings, restarts the system, and proceeds with startup.
	If the value is 0x3 (Critical), it records the event to the System Event Log, uses the LastKnownGood settings, and restarts the system. If the LastKnownGood settings are already in use, it displays a Stop message.
Group	Designates the group that the driver or service belongs to. This allows related drivers or services to start together (for example, file system drivers). The registry entry List in the subkey HKEY_LOCAL_MACHINE\ SYSTEM \CurrentControlSet\Control\ServiceGroupOrder specifies the group startup order.
ImagePath	Identifies the path and file name of the driver or service if the ImagePath entry is present.
ObjectName	Specifies an object name. If the Type entry specifies a service, it represents the account name that the service uses to log on when it runs.
Tag	Designates the order in which a driver starts within a driver group.

Session Manager

After all entries that have Boot and Startup data types are processed, the kernel starts the Session Manager (Smss.exe), a user process that continues to run until the operating system is shut down. The Session Manager performs important initialization functions, such as:

- Creating system environment variables.
- Starting the kernel-mode portion of the Win32 subsystem (implemented by %SystemRoot%\System32\Win32k.sys), which causes Windows to switch from text mode (used to display the Windows Boot Manager menu) to graphics mode (used to display the Starting Windows logo). Windows-based applications run in the Windows subsystem. This environment allows applications to access operating system functions, such as displaying information to the screen.

- Starting the user-mode portion of the Win32 subsystem (implemented by %SystemRoot%\System32\Csrss.exe). The applications that use the Windows subsystem are user-mode processes; they do not have direct access to hardware or device drivers. Instead, they have to access Windows APIs to gain indirect access to hardware. This allows Windows to control direct hardware access, improving security and reliability. User-mode processes run at a lower priority than kernel-mode processes. When the operating system needs more memory, it can page to disk the memory used by user-mode processes.

- Starting the Logon Manager (%SystemRoot%\System32\Winlogon.exe).

- Creating additional virtual memory paging files.

- Performing delayed rename operations for files specified by the registry entry HKEY_LOCAL_MACHINE\SYSTEM\CurrentControlSet\Control\Session Manager\ PendingFileRenameOperations. For example, you might be prompted to restart the computer after installing a new driver or application so that Windows can replace files that are currently in use.

Session Manager searches the registry for service information contained in the following subkeys:

- HKEY_LOCAL_MACHINE\SYSTEM\CurrentControlSet\Control\Session Manager contains a list of commands to run before loading services. The Autochk.exe tool is specified by the value of the registry entry BootExecute and virtual memory (paging file) settings stored in the Memory Management subkey. Autochk, which is a version of the Chkdsk tool, runs at startup if the operating system detects a file system problem that requires repair before completing the startup process.

- HKEY_LOCAL_MACHINE\SYSTEM\CurrentControlSet\Control\Session Manager\ SubSystems stores a list of available subsystems. For example, Csrss.exe contains the user-mode portion of the Windows subsystem.

If startup fails during the kernel loading phase after another operating system was installed on the computer, the cause of the problem is likely an incompatible boot loader. Boot loaders installed by versions of Windows prior to Windows Vista cannot be used to start Windows Vista or Windows 7. Use System Recovery to replace startup files with Windows startup files.

Otherwise, if startup fails during the kernel loading phase, use boot logging to isolate the failing feature. Then use safe mode to disable problematic features (if possible) or use System Recovery to replace problematic files. For more information, see the section titled "Startup Troubleshooting Before the Starting Windows Logo Appears" later in this appendix. If you experience a Stop error during this phase, use the information provided by the Stop message to isolate the failing feature. For more information about troubleshooting Stop errors, see Appendix F, "Troubleshooting Stop Messages."

Logon Phase

The Windows subsystem starts Winlogon.exe, a system service that enables you to log on and log off. Winlogon.exe then does the following:

- Starts the Services subsystem (Services.exe), also known as the SCM. The SCM initializes services that the registry entry Start designates as Autoload in the registry subkey HKEY_LOCAL_MACHINE\SYSTEM\CurrentControlSet\Services*Servicename*.

- Starts the Local Security Authority (LSA) process (Lsass.exe).

- Parses the Ctrl+Alt+Delete key combination at the Begin Logon prompt (if the computer is part of an AD DS domain).

The logon user interface (LogonUI) feature and the credential provider (which can be the standard credential provider or a third-party credential provider) collect the user name and password (or other credentials) and pass this information securely to the LSA for authentication. If the user supplied valid credentials, access is granted by using either the default Kerberos V 5 authentication protocol or Windows NT LAN Manager (NTLM).

Winlogon initializes security and authentication features while PnP initializes auto-load services and drivers. After the user logs on, the control set referenced by the registry entry LastKnownGood (located in HKLM\SYSTEM\Select) is updated with the contents in the CurrentControlSet subkey. By default, Winlogon then starts Userinit.exe and the Windows Explorer shell. Userinit may then start other processes, including:

- **Group Policy settings take effect**   Group Policy settings that apply to the user and computer take effect.

- **Startup programs run**   When not overridden by Group Policy settings, Windows starts logon scripts, startup programs, and services referenced in the following registry subkeys and file system folders:

  - HKEY_LOCAL_MACHINE\SOFTWARE\Microsoft\Windows\CurrentVersion\Runonce
  - HKEY_LOCAL_MACHINE\SOFTWARE\Microsoft\Windows\CurrentVersion\Policies\Explorer\Run
  - HKEY_LOCAL_MACHINE\SOFTWARE\Microsoft\Windows\CurrentVersion\Run
  - HKEY_CURRENT_USER\Software\Microsoft\Windows NT\CurrentVersion\Windows\Run
  - HKEY_CURRENT_USER\Software\Microsoft\Windows\CurrentVersion\Run
  - HKEY_CURRENT_USER\Software\Microsoft\Windows\CurrentVersion\RunOnce
  - *SystemDrive*\Documents and Settings\All Users\Start Menu\Programs\Startup
  - *SystemDrive*\Documents and Settings*username*\Start Menu\Programs\Startup

Several applications might be configured to start by default after you install Windows, including Windows Defender. Computer manufacturers or IT departments might configure other startup applications.

Windows startup is not complete until a user successfully logs on to the computer. If startup fails during the logon phase, you have a problem with a service or application configured to start automatically. For troubleshooting information, see the section titled "How to Temporarily Disable Startup Applications and Processes" later in this appendix. If you experience a Stop error during this phase, use the information provided by the Stop message to isolate the failing feature. For more information about troubleshooting Stop errors, see Appendix F.

Important Startup Files

For Windows to start, the system and boot partitions must contain the files listed in Table C-4.

TABLE C-4 Windows Startup Files

FILE NAME	DISK LOCATION	DESCRIPTION
BootMgr	Root of the system partition	The Windows Boot Manager.
WinLoad	%SystemRoot%\System32	The Windows Boot Loader.
BCD	\Boot	A file that specifies the paths to operating system installations and other information required for Windows to start.
Ntoskrnl.exe	%SystemRoot%\System32	The core (also called the *kernel*) of the Windows operating system. Code that runs as part of the kernel does so in privileged processor mode and has direct access to system data and hardware.
Hal.dll	%SystemRoot%\System32	The HAL dynamic-link library (DLL) file. The HAL abstracts low-level hardware details from the operating system and provides a common programming interface to devices of the same type (such as video adapters).
Smss.exe	%SystemRoot%\System32	The Session Manager file. Session Manager is a user-mode process created by the kernel during startup. It handles critical startup tasks including creating page files and performing delayed file rename and delete operations.
Csrss.exe	%SystemRoot%\System32	The Win32 Subsystem file. The Win32 Subsystem is started by Session Manager and is required by Windows to function.
Winlogon.exe	%SystemRoot%\System32	The Logon Process file, which handles user logon requests and intercepts the Ctrl+Alt+Delete logon key sequence. The Logon Process is started by Session Manager. This is a required feature.

FILE NAME	DISK LOCATION	DESCRIPTION
Services.exe	%SystemRoot%\System32	The Service Control Manager is responsible for starting and stopping services and is a required feature of Windows.
Lsass.exe	%SystemRoot%\System32	The Local Security Authentication Server process is called by the Logon Process when authenticating users and is a required feature.
System registry file	%SystemRoot%\System32\Config\System	The file that contains data used to create the registry key HKEY_LOCAL_MACHINE\SYSTEM. This key contains information that the operating system requires to start devices and system services.
Device drivers	%SystemRoot%\System32\Drivers	Driver files in this folder are for hardware devices, such as keyboard, mouse, and video.

In Table C-4, the term *%SystemRoot%* is one of many *environment variables* used to associate string values, such as folder or file paths, to variables that Windows applications and services use. For example, by using environment variables, scripts can run without modification on computers that have different configurations. To obtain a list of environment variables that you can use for troubleshooting, type **set** at the Windows command prompt.

How to Configure Startup Settings

Windows Vista and Windows 7 enable administrators to configure startup settings using many of the same graphical tools that Windows XP provides. Command-line tools for configuring startup tools have been replaced with new tools, however, and you can no longer directly edit the startup configuration file (formerly the Boot.ini file). The following sections describe several techniques for configuring startup settings.

How to Use the Startup And Recovery Dialog Box

The simplest way to edit the BCD registry file is to use the Startup And Recovery dialog box. To use the Startup And Recovery dialog box to change the default operating system, follow these steps:

1. Click Start, right-click Computer, and then click Properties.
2. Click Advanced System Settings.
3. In Startup And Recovery, click Settings.

4. Click the Default Operating System list and then click the operating system that you
   want to boot by default.

   5. Click OK twice.

   The default operating system will automatically load the next time you start the computer.

How to Use the System Configuration Tool

The System Configuration tool offers more advanced control over startup settings,
including some ability to configure the BCD registry file. This tool is specifically designed
for troubleshooting, and you can use it to easily undo changes that you have made to the
computer's configuration (even after restarting the computer). If you make changes with
the System Configuration tool, it will remind users logging on that settings have been
temporarily changed—thus reducing the likelihood that settings will not be reset after the
troubleshooting process has been completed.

   Some common tasks for the System Configuration tool include:

- Temporarily disabling startup applications to isolate the cause of a post-logon
  problem.

- Temporarily disabling automatic services to isolate the cause of a pre-logon or
  post-logon problem.

- Permanently or temporarily configuring the BCD registry file.

- Configuring a normal, diagnostic, or selective startup for Windows Vista.

   To use the System Configuration tool, click Start, type **Msconfig**, and then press Enter. The
System Configuration tool provides five tabs:

- **General**   Use this tab to change the next startup mode. Normal Startup loads all
  device drivers and services. Diagnostic Startup is useful for troubleshooting startup
  problems, and it loads only basic devices and services. Use Selective Startup to specify
  whether you want to load system services or startup items.

- **Boot**   Use this tab to configure the BCD registry file and startup settings. You can
  remove startup operating system options, set the default operating system, configure
  advanced settings for an operating system (including number of processors, maximum
  memory, and debug settings), and configure Windows for Safe Boot or to boot without
  a graphical interface.

- **Services**   Use this tab to change the startup settings for a service temporarily. This
  is an excellent way to determine whether an automatic service is causing startup
  problems. After you disable a service, restart your computer and determine whether
  the problem still exists. If it does, you have eliminated one potential cause of the
  problem. You can then use this tab to re-enable the service, disable another service,
  and repeat the process. To disable services permanently, use the Services console.

- **Startup** Lists applications that are configured to start automatically. This is the best way to disable applications temporarily during troubleshooting because you can easily re-enable them later using the same tool. You should not use the System Configuration tool to permanently remove startup applications, however, because the System Configuration tool is designed to enable you to easily undo changes. Instead, you should manually remove the application.

- **Tools** Provides links to other tools that you can start.

NOTE The Win.ini, System.ini, and Boot.ini tabs do not appear in the System Configuration tool because those files have not been used since Windows XP.

Because the System Configuration tool is a graphical tool, it is primarily useful when Windows is booting successfully.

How to Use BCDEdit

The BCDEdit command-line tool provides you with almost unlimited control over the BCD registry file and configuration settings.

NOTE If you have a computer with both Windows XP and Windows 7 installed and you want to modify the BCD registry file from Windows XP, you can run BCDEdit from Windows XP by starting it directly from the Windows\System32 folder of your Windows 7 installation. Although this might be useful in some multiboot configurations, typically, you should run BCDEdit from the System Recovery command prompt if you cannot load Windows 7.

You must use administrative credentials to run BCDEdit from within Windows 7. To do this, follow these steps:

1. Click Start, click All Programs, and then click Accessories.
2. Right-click Command Prompt and then click Run As Administrator.

To view detailed information about using BCDEdit, run **BCDEdit /?** from a command prompt. The following sections describe how to perform specific tasks with BCDEdit.

How to Interpret BCDEdit Output

You can view settings currently defined in your BCD registry file by using the *bcdedit /enum* command. Optionally, you can follow the command with one of the following parameters to change which entries are displayed:

- **Active** The default setting that is displayed if you run *bcdedit /enum* without any additional parameters. Displays all entries in the Boot Manager display order.
- **Firmware** Displays all firmware applications.
- **Bootapp** Displays all boot environment applications.

- **Osloader**   Displays all operating system entries.
- **Resume**   Displays all resume from hibernation entries.
- **Inherit**   Displays all inherit entries.
- **All**   Displays all entries.

For example, to view the startup entry used to resume from hibernation, run the following command at an administrative command prompt.

```
bcdedit /enum resume
```

Similarly, to view all startup entries, use the following command.

```
bcdedit /enum all
```

How to Back Up and Restore Settings

Making changes to your BCD registry file can render your computer unbootable. Therefore, before making changes to your BCD registry file, you should make a backup copy, have a bootable Windows DVD available, and be prepared to restore the original BCD registry file.

To make a backup of your current BCD registry, call the *BCDEdit /export* command, as shown here.

```
bcdedit /export backupbcd.bcd
```

Later, you can restore your original BCD registry file by calling the *BCDEdit /import* command, as shown here.

```
bcdedit /import backupbcd.bcd
```

NOTE   The file name and extension you use are not significant.

If Windows is unbootable, follow the instructions in the section titled "The Process of Troubleshooting Startup" later in this appendix.

How to Change the Default Operating System Entry

To view the current default operating system entry, run the following command and look for the *default* line.

```
bcdedit /enum {bootmgr}
```

```
Windows Boot Manager
--------------------
identifier              {bootmgr}
device                  partition=\Device\HarddiskVolume1
description             Windows Boot Manager
locale                  en-US
inherit                 {globalsettings}
```

default	{current}
resumeobject	{24a500f3-12ea-11db-a536-b7db70c06ac2}
displayorder	{current}
toolsdisplayorder	{memdiag}
timeout	30

To change the default operating system entry, first run the following command to view the existing entries and make note of the identifier for the entry that you want to be the default.

```
bcdedit /enum
```

Then run the following command to set a new default (where *<id>* is the identifier for the new entry).

```
bcdedit /default <id>
```

For example, to configure the Windows Boot Manager to start the previous installation of Windows XP by default (which is identified as *{ntldr}*), run the following command.

```
bcdedit /default {ntldr}
```

To configure the currently running instance of Windows 7 as the default, run the following command.

```
bcdedit /default {current}
```

How to Change the Boot Menu Time-Out

The boot menu, by default, is displayed for 30 seconds if you have more than one boot menu entry. If you have only one boot menu entry, the menu is not displayed at all (although the Boot Manager does wait several seconds so that you can press a key to view the menu).

To change the time-out for the boot menu, use the *bcdedit /timeout seconds* command, as shown here.

```
bcdedit /timeout 15
```

How to Change the Order of Boot Manager Menu Items

To change the order of Boot Manager menu items, use the *bcdedit /display* command, and then list the menu item identifiers in the desired sequence, as shown in the following example.

```
bcdedit /display {current} {ntldr} {cbd971bf-b7b8-4885-951a-fa0344f5d71}
```

How to Create an Entry for Another Operating System

You can use BCDEdit to create an entry for an operating system other than Windows 7. You may need to add boot entries to the BCD registry file if you want to be able to load different operating systems on a single computer. Although Windows automatically creates boot entries for existing operating systems when installed, you might need to add a boot entry manually if you install another operating system after Windows 7 or if you want to load an operating system from a newly attached hard disk.

By default, the BCD registry file contains an entry called *{ntldr}* that is configured to start an older version of Windows from your C:\ partition. If you have only one older operating system and Earlier Version Of Windows does not currently appear on the computer's boot menu, you can use this existing entry to start the older operating system. To do this, call *BCDEdit /set* to configure the boot volume. Then add the entry to the Windows Boot Manager operating system menu by calling the *BCDEdit /displayorder* command. The following code demonstrates how to do this.

```
REM Modify the following line to identify the other OS' partition
REM The following line could also be, "bcdedit /set {ntldr} device boot"
bcdedit /set {ntldr} device partition=C:

REM The following line makes the entry bootable by adding it to the menu
bcdedit /displayorder {ntldr} /addlast
```

You can verify that the new entry will appear on the boot menu by running the command *bcdedit /enum ACTIVE* and looking for the Windows Legacy OS Loader entry.

If you need to be able to choose from multiple older Windows operating systems, you should choose the *{ntldr}* entry from the boot menu. The Windows Boot Manager will then pass control to Ntldr, which will display a menu based on the Boot.ini file that you can use to choose from all Windows operating systems.

If you want to create an entry for a non-Microsoft operating system, you can either create an entry using the *bcdedit /create* command, or you can copy the existing *{ntldr}* entry and update it for the operating system. To base a new entry on *{ntldr}*, copy the entry, update the boot loader path, and then add it to the boot menu by running these commands.

```
bcdedit /copy {ntldr} /d "Other operating system (or other description)"

REM The previous command will display a new GUID that identifies the copy.
REM Use the GUID in the following command, and modify the partition identifier as
    needed.
bcdedit /set {NEW-GUID} device partition=C:
```

NOTE Don't retype the GUID by hand—you're likely to make a mistake. Instead, copy it to the Clipboard as follows: Click the command menu in the upper-left corner of the command prompt window, click Edit, and then click Mark. Select the GUID text (including the brackets) and then press Enter on your keyboard. To paste the GUID to the command prompt, click the command menu, click Edit, and then click Paste.

Now run the following command to identify the operating system's boot loader.

```
REM Replace the last parameter with the boot loader filename
bcdedit /set {NEW-GUID} path \boot-loader
```

If *{ntldr}* was not part of the boot menu when you copied it, you also need to run the following command to add the copied entry to the boot menu.

```
bcdedit /displayorder {NEW-GUID} /addlast
```

Additionally, you might need to configure the operating system's own boot loader.

How to Remove a Boot Entry

Typically, you do not need to remove entries from the BCD registry file. Instead, you should simply remove entries from the Windows Boot Manager menu. To remove an entry from the menu, first run *bcdedit /enum* and note the boot entry's identifier. Then run the following command, substituting the identifier.

```
bcdedit /displayorder {GUID} /remove
```

For example, to remove the entry to load the previous version of Windows from the boot menu, you would run this command.

```
bcdedit /displayorder {ntldr} /remove
```

You can later re-add the entry to the boot menu by calling the following command.

```
bcdedit /displayorder {GUID} /addlast
```

To permanently remove an entry from the BCD registry, run the following command.

```
bcdedit /delete {GUID} /remove
```

You should permanently remove an entry only if you have removed the operating system files from the computer.

How to View and Update Global Debugger Settings

To view debugger settings for startup entries, run the following command.

```
bcdedit /enum
```

For more information about viewing entries, see the section titled "How to Interpret BCDEdit Output" earlier in this appendix. To change debugger settings for a startup entry, run the following command.

```
bcdedit /dbgsettings DebugType [debugport:Port] [baudrate:Baud]
[channel:Channel] [targetname:TargetName]
```

Replace the parameters with your custom settings, as described in the following list:

- **DebugType**   Specifies the type of debugger. DebugType can be SERIAL, 1394, or USB. The remaining options depend on the debugger type selected.
- **Port**   For SERIAL debugging, specifies the serial port to use as the debugging port.
- **Baud**   For SERIAL debugging, specifies the baud rate to be used for debugging.

- **Channel**   For 1394 debugging, specifies the 1394 channel to be used for debugging.
- **Target Name**   For USB debugging, specifies the USB target name to be used for debugging.

For example, the following command sets the global debugger settings to SERIAL debugging over com1 at 115,200 baud.

```
bcdedit /dbgsettings serial debugport:1 baudrate:115200
```

The following command sets the global debugger settings to 1394 debugging using channel 23.

```
bcdedit /dbgsettings 1394 CHANNEL:32
```

The following command sets the global debugger settings to USB debugging using target name *debugging*.

```
bcdedit /dbgsettings USB targetname:debugging
```

How to Remove the Windows 7 Boot Loader

If you want to remove Windows 7 from a dual-boot environment that includes Windows XP or an earlier version of Windows, follow these steps:

1. Use Bootsect.exe to restore the Ntldr.exe program. To do this, type the following command, where *D:* is the drive containing the Windows installation media.

   ```
   D:\Boot\Bootsect.exe –NT52 All
   ```

   After the computer restarts, it does not load the Windows Boot Manager program. Instead, Ntldr.exe loads and processes the Boot.ini file to start an earlier version of Windows.

2. If Windows 7 is not installed on the active partition, you can now delete or remove the partition where Windows 7 is installed.

> **NOTE**   You can follow these steps in any version of Windows. If you follow these steps in Windows Vista or Windows 7, run the commands from a command prompt that has elevated user rights. To do this, click Start, click Accessories, right-click the command prompt shortcut, and then click Run As Administrator.

How to Configure a User Account to Automatically Log On

Requiring users to enter credentials when their computers start is an important part of Windows security. If a user account automatically logs on, anyone who has physical access to the computer can restart it and access the user's files. Nonetheless, in scenarios in which a computer is physically secure, automatic logon might be preferred. To configure a workgroup computer (you cannot perform these steps on a domain member) to automatically log on, follow these steps:

1. Click Start, type **netplwiz**, and then press Enter.

2. In the User Accounts dialog box, click the account you want to automatically log on to. If it is available, clear the Users Must Enter A User Name And Password To Use This Computer check box.

3. Click OK.

4. In the Automatically Log On dialog box, enter the user's password twice. Click OK.

The next time you restart the computer, it will automatically log on with the local user account you selected. Configuring automatic logon stores the user's password in the registry unencrypted, where someone might be able to retrieve it.

How to Disable the Windows Startup Sound

By default, Windows plays a sound as part of the startup process. This sound can be useful for troubleshooting startup problems because it indicates whether you have reached a specific startup phase. If you prefer, you can disable the startup sound by following these steps:

1. Click Start and then click Control Panel.

2. In Control Panel, click Hardware And Sound.

3. Click Change System Sounds.

4. On the Sounds tab, clear the Play Windows Startup Sound check box. Click OK.

How to Speed Up the Startup Process

Although startup is a complex process and the time required varies from computer to computer, you can often reduce the startup time. To optimize settings that might improve startup time, follow these steps:

1. In the computer's BIOS settings, set the computer to boot first from the Windows boot drive. If you need to boot from removable media in the future, you will first need to change this setting.

2. In the computer's BIOS settings, enable Fast Boot, if available, to disable time-consuming and often unnecessary hardware checks.

3. If you have more than one boot menu item, reduce the boot menu time-out value using the Boot tab of the Msconfig tool. Alternatively, you can use BCDEdit to reduce the time-out value, as described in the section titled "How to Change the Boot Menu Time-Out" earlier in this appendix.

4. Clear disk space if free disk space is below 15 percent and then defragment the hard disk. Although defragmentation happens automatically by default, defragmentation is less effective if free disk space is low.

5. Disable unnecessary hardware using Windows Device Manager.

6. Use Windows ReadyBoost to cache some files used in the startup process to a USB flash drive.

7. Remove unnecessary startup applications.

8. For services (other than those included with Windows) that need to start automatically but do not need to start immediately, use the Services console to change the startup type to Automatic (Delayed Start). If services are set to start automatically but are not required, change the startup type to Manual.

For detailed startup performance troubleshooting, examine the Applications And Services Logs\Microsoft\Windows\Diagnostics-Performance\Operational Event Log. Events with IDs from 100 to 199 provide startup performance detail in the event of long startup times. In particular, event ID 100 indicates the startup time in milliseconds. Other events identify applications or services that are causing a startup performance degradation.

The Process of Troubleshooting Startup

Startup problems can be divided into three distinct categories:

- **Problems that occur before the Starting Windows logo appears**   These problems are typically caused by missing startup files (often as a result of installing a different operating system over Windows 7), corrupted files, or hardware problems. For information about troubleshooting problems that occur after logon, read the next section, "Startup Troubleshooting Before the Starting Windows Logo Appears."

- **Problems that occur after the Starting Windows logo appears but before the logon prompt is displayed**   These problems are typically caused by faulty or misconfigured drivers and services. Hardware problems can also cause failure during this phase of startup. For information about troubleshooting problems that occur after the Starting Windows logo appears but before logon, read the section titled "Startup Troubleshooting After the Starting Windows Logo Appears" later in this appendix.

- **Problems that occur after logon**   These problems are typically caused by startup applications. For information about troubleshooting problems that occur after logon, read the section titled "Troubleshooting Startup Problems After Logon" later in this appendix.

Startup Troubleshooting Before the Starting Windows Logo Appears

Troubleshooting startup problems is more challenging than troubleshooting problems that occur while Windows is running, because you cannot access the full suite of troubleshooting tools included with Windows. However, Windows does provide several tools that you can use to identify the cause and resolve the problem if you cannot start the operating system. Most important, you can start WinRE by booting from the Windows Vista DVD or directly from the computer's hard disk. WinRE can start automatically if Windows cannot start correctly. The WinRE tools include the Startup Repair tool, which can automatically fix many common startup problems.

Follow the process illustrated in Figure C-5 to troubleshoot startup problems that occur before the Starting Windows logo appears. After each troubleshooting step, you should attempt to start the computer. If the computer starts successfully or if startup progresses far enough to display the Starting Windows logo, you can stop troubleshooting.

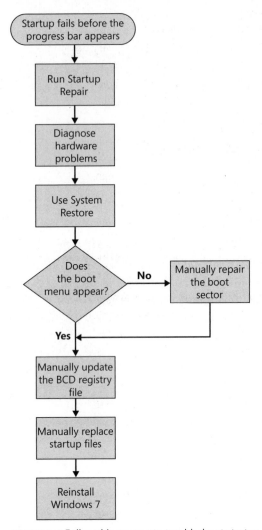

FIGURE C-5 Follow this process to troubleshoot startup problems before logon.

The following sections describe each of these troubleshooting steps in more detail.

NOTE After you enable Windows BitLocker, a lost encryption key can result in an unbootable computer.

How to Run Startup Repair

To run Startup Repair, open the System Recovery tools and then start Startup Repair, as described in the following sections.

HOW TO START THE SYSTEM RECOVERY TOOLS

Windows 7 automatically installs the System Recovery tools, which are capable of fixing almost any startup problem related to boot sectors, MBRs, or the BCD registry file. The Startup Repair tool can fix most startup problems automatically, without requiring you to understand the details of how an operating system loads. The tool is so straightforward that you could easily talk end users through the troubleshooting process remotely.

To start the System Recovery tools, follow these steps:

1. Restart the computer. If the System Recovery tools do not automatically start, restart the computer again, press F8 before the Starting Windows logo appears, and then choose Repair Your Computer from the Advanced Boot Options screen.

2. Select your language and keyboard input method and then click Next.

3. Select your user name and type your password. Then, click OK.

> **NOTE** Most Windows 7 computers have the System Recovery tools preinstalled by the computer manufacturer. On these computers, you can start the System Recovery tools faster by pressing F8 before the Starting Windows logo appears and then choosing Repair Your Computer from the Advanced Boot Options screen. These computers can also automatically detect startup failure (by noticing that the last startup failed) and start Startup Repair.

If you cannot start the System Recovery tools from the hard drive, insert the Windows DVD and configure the computer to start from the DVD. Then, follow these steps:

1. Insert the Windows DVD in your computer

2. Restart your computer. When prompted to boot from the DVD, press any key. If you are not prompted to boot from the DVD, you may have to configure your computer's startup sequence. For more information, see the section titled "Initial Startup Phase" earlier in this appendix.

3. Wait while Windows 7 setup loads.

4. When prompted, select your regional preferences and keyboard layout and then click Next.

5. Click Repair Your Computer to start RecEnv.exe.

6. When the System Recovery tools start, System Recovery scans your hard disks for Windows installations.

7. If the standard Windows drivers do not detect a hard disk because it requires drivers that were not included with Windows 7, click Load Drivers to load the driver and then select an operating system to repair. Click Next.

From this point, the steps are the same whether you loaded the System Recovery tools from the hard disk or the Windows DVD. If Windows failed to start during its last attempt, the Startup Repair tool will be started automatically. Otherwise, the Choose A Recovery Tool page appears, as shown in Figure C-6.

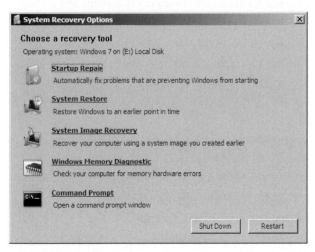

FIGURE C-6 System Recovery provides a variety of different troubleshooting tools.

HOW TO RUN STARTUP REPAIR

The simplest way to solve startup problems is to load the System Recovery tools, as described in the previous section, and then click Startup Repair and follow the prompts that appear. To run Startup Repair, follow these steps:

1. Click Startup Repair and then follow the prompts that appear. The prompts may vary depending on the problem that Startup Repair identifies. You might be prompted to restore your computer using System Restore or to restart your computer and continue troubleshooting.

2. After the Startup Repair tool has completed diagnosis and repair, click Click Here For Diagnostic And Repair Details. At the bottom of the report, Startup Repair lists a root cause, if found, and any steps taken to repair the problem. Log files are stored at %WinDir%\System32\LogFiles\SRT\SRTTrail.txt.

3. Restart the computer and allow Windows to start normally.

How to Use BootRec.exe

Startup Repair can automatically recover from most BCD problems. If you prefer to manually analyze and repair problems, you can use the command-line tool BootRec.exe by starting the System Recovery tools and then clicking Command Prompt in the System Recovery Options dialog box.

BootRec.exe supports the following command-line parameters:

- **/FIXMBR**   The /FIXMBR switch writes an MBR to the system partition.
- **/FIXBOOT**   The /FIXBOOT switch writes a new boot sector onto the system partition.
- **/SCANOS**   The /SCANOS switch scans all disks for Windows installations and displays entries currently not in the BCD store.
- **/REBUILDBCD**   The /REBUILDBCD switch scans all disks for Windows installations and provides a choice of which entries to add to the BCD store.

Windows XP Recovery Console Equivalents

Parveen Patel, Developer; Windows Reliability

The recovery console has been deprecated in Windows Vista and Windows 7, so what happened to all those wonderful commands that were available in recovery console? Well, we were hoping that you wouldn't need them anymore. But if you do, you'll be glad to know that most of them are available via the command line in WinRE. The recovery console commands listed in the following table are different or unavailable in WinRE.

RECOVERY CONSOLE COMMAND	WINRE EQUIVALENT(S)
BootCfg	BOOTREC /SCANOS
	BOOTREC /REBUILDBCD
	bcdedit
FIXBOOT	BOOTREC /FIXBOOT
FIXMBR	BOOTREC /FIXMBR
Map	DiskPart
Logon	Not needed
LISTSVC	Not available
ENABLE	Not available
DISABLE	Not available
SYSTEMROOT	Not available

All the remaining commands have the same name in WinRE. You can work around the unavailable services-related commands (LISTSVC, ENABLE, AND DISABLE) by using regedit to manually load the registry hive.

How to Diagnose Hardware Problems

If Startup Repair cannot solve the problem or if you cannot start Windows Setup, you might have a hardware problem. Although most hardware-related problems will not stop Windows Vista from successfully starting, hardware-related problems may appear early in the startup process; symptoms include warning messages, startup failures, and Stop messages. The causes are typically improper device configuration, incorrect driver settings, or hardware malfunction and failure. For detailed information about troubleshooting hardware problems, read Appendix D.

How to Use System Restore

Windows automatically captures system state before installing new applications or drivers. You can later use the System Restore tool to return to this system if you experience problems.

To start System Restore from within Windows (including safe mode), click Start, click All Programs, click Accessories, click System Tools, and then click System Restore.

To start System Restore when you cannot open Windows, follow these steps:

1. Start System Recovery tools, as described in the section titled "How to Start the System Recovery Tools" earlier in this appendix.

2. Click System Restore.

The System Restore Wizard appears. Follow these steps to restore Windows to an earlier state:

1. On the Restore System Files And Settings page of the System Restore Wizard, click Next.

2. On the Choose A Restore Point page, click a restore point. Typically, you should choose the most recent restore point when the computer functioned correctly. If the computer has not functioned correctly for more than five days, select the Show More Restore Points check box (as shown in Figure C-7) and then select a restore point. Click Next.

3. On the Confirm Disks To Restore page, click Next.

4. On the Confirm Your Restore Point page, click Finish.

5. Click Yes to confirm the system restore. System Restore modifies system files and settings to return Windows to the state it was in at the time the restore point was captured.

6. When System Restore is done, click Restart. You should now attempt to start the computer and identify whether the problem was resolved.

7. When the computer restarts, Windows will display a System Restore notification. Click Close.

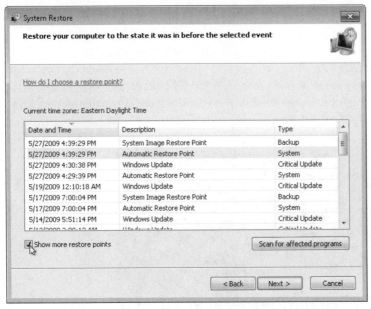

FIGURE C-7 You can solve some startup problems by using System Restore.

How to Manually Repair the Boot Sector

Startup Repair is by far the quickest and easiest way to solve most startup problems. However, if you are familiar with troubleshooting startup problems and simply need to fix a boot sector problem after installing another operating system, you can run the following command from a command prompt (including the Command Prompt tool in the System Recovery tools).

```
bootsect /NT60 ALL
```

Bootsect.exe is available from the \Boot\ folder of the Windows DVD and can be run from within WinRE or Windows 7.

After running Bootsect, you should be able to load Windows, but you may not be able to load earlier versions of Windows that are installed on the same computer. To load other operating systems, add entries to the BCD registry file, as described in the section titled "How to Create an Entry for Another Operating System" earlier in this appendix.

How to Manually Update the BCD Registry File

The simplest way to solve problems related to the BCD registry file is to run Startup Repair, as described earlier in this appendix. However, you can also use the System Recovery tools to update the BCD registry file manually by following these steps:

1. Load the System Recovery tools, as described in the previous section.

2. Click Command Prompt.

3. Use BCDEdit to update the BCD registry file.

For detailed information, read the section titled "How to Use BCDEdit" earlier in this appendix.

How to Manually Replace Files

If startup files are missing or become corrupted, Windows may not be able to boot successfully. Often, Windows will display an error message that shows the name of the missing file, as shown in Figure C-8.

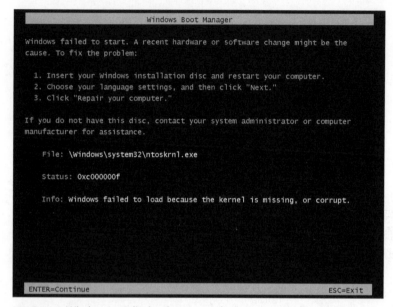

```
                    Windows Boot Manager

Windows failed to start. A recent hardware or software change might be the
cause. To fix the problem:

    1. Insert your Windows installation disc and restart your computer.
    2. Choose your language settings, and then click "Next."
    3. Click "Repair your computer."

If you do not have this disc, contact your system administrator or computer
manufacturer for assistance.

    File: \Windows\system32\ntoskrnl.exe

    Status: 0xc000000f

    Info: Windows failed to load because the kernel is missing, or corrupt.



 ENTER=Continue                                              ESC=Exit
```

FIGURE C-8 Windows can display the names of missing startup files, which you can then manually replace.

Startup Repair can automatically replace missing system files, but it may not detect corrupted files. However, you can manually replace files using the System Recovery command-line tool.

To replace files, follow these steps:

1. From another computer, copy the new files to removable media such as a CD-ROM or a USB flash drive. You cannot access Windows system files from the Windows DVD because they are stored within a Windows Imaging (WIM) file that is not accessible from within System Recovery.

2. Start System Recovery tools, as described in the section titled "How to Start the System Recovery Tools" earlier in this appendix.

3. After the System Recovery tools start, click Command Prompt.

4. Your removable media will have a drive letter, just like a hard disk. System Recovery tools assign hard disk letters starting with C and then assign letters to removable media. To identify the drive letter of your removable media, run the following commands.

```
C:\>diskpart
DISKPART> list volume

  Volume ###   Ltr   Label         Fs      Type          Size    Status      Info
  ----------   ---   -----------   -----   ----------    -------  ---------   --------
  Volume 0     C     Win7          NTFS    Partition      63 GB   Healthy
  Volume 1     E     Windows XP    NTFS    Partition      91 GB   Healthy
  Volume 2     D                   NTFS    Partition      69 GB   Healthy
  Volume 3     I                           Removable       0 B    No Media
  Volume 4     H                           Removable       0 B    No Media
  Volume 5     F     LR1CFRE_EN_   UDF     Partition    2584 MB   Healthy
  Volume 6     G     USBDRIVE      FAT32   Partition     991 MB   Healthy
```

  5. Use the *Copy* command to transfer files from your removable media to the computer's hard disk.

How to Reinstall Windows

Infrequently, startup files and critical areas on the hard disk can become corrupted. If you are mainly concerned with salvaging readable data files and using the Backup And Restore Center to copy them to backup media or a network location, you can perform a parallel installation of Windows. Although this may provide access to the file system, it will permanently damage your existing operating system and applications.

If you cannot start Windows after following the troubleshooting steps in this guide, you can reinstall Windows for the purpose of data recovery by following these steps:

  1. Insert the Windows DVD in your computer.

  2. Restart your computer. When prompted to boot from the CD/DVD, press any key.

  3. Windows Setup loads. When prompted, select your regional preferences and then click Next.

  4. Click Install Now.

  5. When prompted, enter your product key.

  6. Select the I Accept The License Terms check box and then click Next.

  7. Click Custom.

  8. On the Where Do You Want to Install Windows? page, select the partition containing your Windows installation and then click Next.

  9. When prompted, click OK.

Setup will install a new instance of Windows and will move all files from your previous installation into the \Windows.Old folder (including the \Program Files, \Windows, and \Users folders). You now have two choices for returning the computer to its original state:

  ■ **Reformat the system partition** If you have an automated deployment solution in place (as described in Part II of this book, "Deployment"), the quickest solution is to back up important files and redeploy Windows. If you need to manually reinstall Windows, you can follow this process:

1. Back up all important files by writing them to removable media, copying them to an external hard disk, or copying them to a shared folder on the network.

2. Reinstall Windows. This time, choose to reformat the system partition.

3. Reinstall all applications and reconfigure all custom settings.

4. Restore important files.

■ **Continue working with the current system partition**   You can move important files to the proper locations within the new instance of Windows. Then, reinstall all applications and reconfigure any custom settings. Finally, you can delete the original Windows instance by removing the \Windows.Old folder using Disk Cleanup.

Startup Troubleshooting After the Starting Windows Logo Appears

If your computer displays the graphical Starting Windows logo before failing, as shown in Figure C-9, the Windows kernel was successfully loaded. Most likely, the startup failure is caused by a faulty driver or service.

FIGURE C-9 Displaying the Starting Windows logo indicates that Windows 7 has successfully loaded the kernel.

Use the process illustrated in Figure C-10 to identify and disable the failing software feature to allow Windows to start successfully. After Windows starts, you can perform further troubleshooting to resolve the problem with the feature if necessary. If the startup problem occurs immediately after updating or installing a startup application, try troubleshooting the startup application. For information about troubleshooting startup applications, see the section titled "How to Temporarily Disable Startup Applications and Processes" later in this appendix.

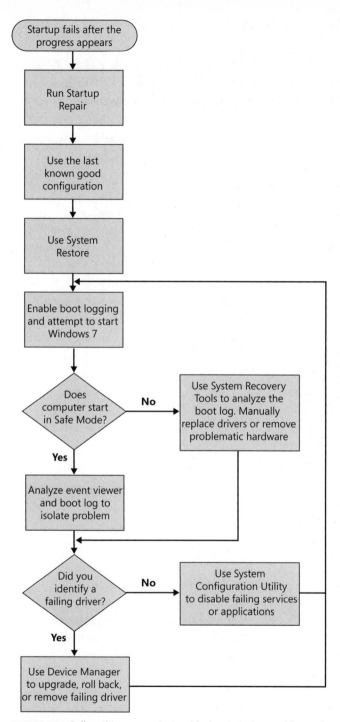

FIGURE C-10 Follow this process to troubleshoot startup problems after the Starting Windows logo appears but before logon.

The sections that follow describe each of these steps in more detail.

How to Run Startup Repair

Startup Repair can automatically fix many common startup problems, even if the problem occurs after the Starting Windows logo is displayed. Because Startup Repair is easy to use and has a very low likelihood of causing additional problems, it should be your first troubleshooting step. For detailed instructions, refer to the section titled "How to Run Startup Repair" earlier in this appendix.

After running Startup Repair, attempt to start your computer normally and continue with the troubleshooting process only if Windows fails to start.

How to Restore the Last Known Good Configuration

Last Known Good Configuration is usually used to enable the operating system to start if it fails after the Starting Windows logo is displayed. Using Last Known Good Configuration helps to correct instability or startup problems by reversing the most recent system, driver, and registry changes within a hardware profile. When you use this feature, you lose all configuration changes that were made since you last successfully started your computer.

Using the Last Known Good Configuration restores previous drivers and also restores registry settings for the subkey HKEY_LOCAL_MACHINE\SYSTEM\CurrentControlSet. Windows Vista does not update the LastKnownGood control set until you successfully start the operating system in normal mode and log on.

When you are troubleshooting, it is recommended that you use Last Known Good Configuration before you try other startup options, such as safe mode. However, if you decide to use safe mode first, logging on to the computer in safe mode does not update the LastKnownGood control set. Therefore, Last Known Good Configuration remains an option if you cannot resolve your problem by using safe mode.

To access the Last Known Good Configuration startup option, follow these steps:

1. Remove all floppy disks, CDs, DVDs, and other bootable media from your computer and then restart your computer.

2. Press F8 at the operating system menu. If the operating system menu does not appear, press F8 repeatedly after the firmware POST process completes but before the Starting Windows logo appears. The Advanced Boot Options menu appears.

3. On the Advanced Boot Options menu, select Last Known Good Configuration (Advanced), as shown in Figure C-11.

When Windows starts, it reads status information from the file %WinDir%\Bootstat.dat. If Windows detects that the last startup attempt was unsuccessful, it automatically displays the startup recovery menu, which provides startup options similar to the Advanced Boot Options menu, without requiring you to press F8.

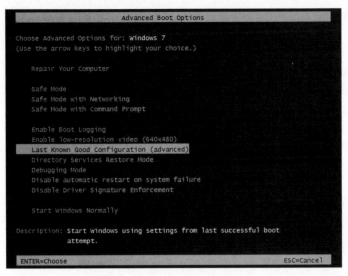

FIGURE C-11 Use Last Known Good Configuration to restore some settings to their state during the last time a user successfully logged on.

> **NOTE** If you suspect that changes made since you last successfully restarted the computer are causing problems, do not start Windows and log on normally—logging on overwrites the LastKnownGood control set. Instead, restart the computer and use the Last Known Good Configuration. You can also log on in safe mode without overwriting the Last Known Good Configuration. For more information about control sets, see the section titled "Kernel Loading Phase" earlier in this appendix.

How to Use System Restore

If Last Known Good Configuration fails to resolve the problem, you can manually perform a system restore if Startup Repair did not initiate it. However, Startup Repair would typically have taken this step already if it might have solved the problem. For information on how to use System Restore, see the section titled "How to Use System Restore" earlier in this appendix.

How to Enable Boot Logging

Boot logging is useful for isolating the cause of a startup problem that occurs after the operating system menu appears. You can enable boot logging by following these steps:

1. Remove all floppy disks, CDs, DVDs, and other bootable media from your computer and then restart your computer.

2. Press F8 at the operating system menu. If the operating system menu does not appear, press F8 repeatedly after the firmware POST process completes but before the Starting Windows logo appears. The Advanced Boot Options menu appears.

3. On the Advanced Boot Options menu, select Enable Boot Logging, as shown in Figure C-12.

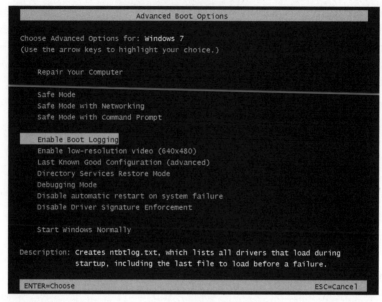

```
                    Advanced Boot Options

Choose Advanced Options for: Windows 7
(Use the arrow keys to highlight your choice.)

    Repair Your Computer

    Safe Mode
    Safe Mode with Networking
    Safe Mode with Command Prompt

    Enable Boot Logging
    Enable low-resolution video (640x480)
    Last Known Good Configuration (advanced)
    Directory Services Restore Mode
    Debugging Mode
    Disable automatic restart on system failure
    Disable Driver Signature Enforcement

    Start Windows Normally

Description: Creates ntbtlog.txt, which lists all drivers that load during
            startup, including the last file to load before a failure.

ENTER=Choose                                           ESC=Cancel
```

FIGURE C-12 Enabling boot logging can help you identify the cause of startup problems.

Windows starts and creates a log file at %WinDir%\Ntbtlog.txt. The log file starts with the time and version information and then lists every file that is successfully loaded, as shown here.

```
Microsoft (R) Windows (R) Version 6.1 (Build 7100)
 5 27 2009 17:57:37.500
Loaded driver \SystemRoot\system32\ntoskrnl.exe
Loaded driver \SystemRoot\system32\hal.dll
Loaded driver \SystemRoot\system32\kdcom.dll
Loaded driver \SystemRoot\system32\mcupdate_GenuineIntel.dll
Loaded driver \SystemRoot\system32\PSHED.dll
Loaded driver \SystemRoot\system32\BOOTVID.dll
Loaded driver \SystemRoot\system32\CLFS.SYS
Loaded driver \SystemRoot\system32\CI.dll
Loaded driver \SystemRoot\system32\drivers\wdf0100.sys
Loaded driver \SystemRoot\system32\drivers\WDFLDR.SYS
Did not load driver \SystemRoot\system32\drivers\serial.sys
Loaded driver \SystemRoot\system32\drivers\acpi.sys
```

The following sections will provide additional information about viewing and analyzing the boot log file.

How to Start in Safe Mode

Safe mode is a diagnostic environment that runs only a subset of the drivers and services that are configured to start in normal mode. Safe mode is useful when you install software or a device driver that causes instability or problems with starting in normal mode. Often, Windows can start in safe mode even if hardware failure prevents it from starting in normal mode. In most cases, safe mode allows you to start Windows and then troubleshoot problems that prevent startup.

Logging on to the computer in safe mode does not update the LastKnownGood control set. Therefore, if you log on to your computer in safe mode and then decide you want to try Last Known Good Configuration, this option is still available to you.

In safe mode, Windows uses the minimum set required to start the GUI. The following registry subkeys list the drivers and services that start in safe mode:

- Safe mode:
  HKEY_LOCAL_MACHINE\SYSTEM\CurrentControlSet\Control\SafeBoot\Minimal

- Safe mode with networking:
  HKEY_LOCAL_MACHINE\SYSTEM\CurrentControlSet\Control\SafeBoot\Network

To access safe mode, follow these steps:

1. Remove all floppy disks and CDs from your computer and then restart your computer.

2. Press F8 at the operating system menu. If the operating system menu does not appear, press F8 repeatedly after the firmware POST process completes but before the Starting Windows logo appears. The Advanced Boot Options menu appears.

3. On the Advanced Boot Options menu, select Safe Mode, Safe Mode With Networking, or Safe Mode With Command Prompt. Select Safe Mode if you do not require networking support. Select Safe Mode With Networking if you require access to the network for your troubleshooting—for example, if you must download an updated driver. Select Safe Mode With Command Prompt if you want to work at a command prompt.

When Windows starts, it reads status information from the file %SystemRoot%\Bootstat .dat. If Windows detects that the last startup attempt was unsuccessful, it automatically displays the startup recovery menu, which provides startup options similar to the Advanced Boot Options menu, without requiring you to press F8.

How to Identify Failing Drivers and Services

When you are troubleshooting, the method for determining which services and processes to temporarily disable varies from one computer to the next. The most reliable way to determine what you can disable is to gather more information about the services and processes enabled on your computer.

The following Windows tools and features generate a variety of logs that can provide you with valuable troubleshooting information:

- Event Viewer
- Sc.exe
- System Information
- Error reporting service
- Boot logs

Of these tools, only the boot logs are available when using System Recovery tools. All tools are available when using safe mode, however.

HOW TO ANALYZE STARTUP PROBLEMS IN SAFE MODE

Safe mode gives you access to all standard graphical troubleshooting tools, including those described in the following sections.

Event Viewer (Eventvwr.msc)

You can use Event Viewer (Eventvwr.msc) to view logs that can help you to identify system problems when you are able to start the system in safe or normal mode. When you are troubleshooting, use these logs to isolate problems by application, driver, or service and to identify frequently occurring issues. You can save these logs to a file and specify filtering criteria.

Event Viewer provides a minimum of three logs, as follows:

- **Application logs**   The Application log contains events logged by applications or programs. For example, a database program might record read or write errors here.
- **Security logs**   The security log holds security event records, such as logon attempts and actions related to creating, opening, or deleting files. An administrator can specify what events to record in the security log.
- **System logs**   The system log contains information about system features. Event Viewer logs an entry when a driver or other system feature does not load during startup. Therefore, you can use Event Viewer to search for information about drivers or services that did not load.

To use Event Viewer to obtain driver and service error information from the system log, follow these steps:

1. Click Start, right-click Computer, and then click Manage.
2. Under System Tools, expand Event Viewer, expand Windows Logs, and then click System.
3. Click the Action menu and then click Filter Current Log.
4. Under Event Level, select the Critical and Error check boxes.
5. In the Event source list, click Service Control Manager and then click OK.
6. Double-click an event entry to view details.

Not all startup problems result in an entry being added to the event log. Therefore, you might not find any related information.

System Information

If a startup problem occurs inconsistently and if you can start Windows in safe or normal mode, you can use System Information to view driver and service name, status, and startup information.

Using System Information, you can create lists of drivers that were processed during safe and normal mode startups. By comparing the differences between the two lists, you can determine which features are not required to start Windows. For diagnostic purposes, you can use this list of differences to help you determine which services to disable. In safe mode, disable a service and then try to restart the operating system in normal mode. Repeat this process for each service until you are able to start in normal mode.

To view service or driver information, follow these steps:

1. Click Start, type **msinfo32**, and then press Enter.

2. Depending on the information you want, do one or more of the following:

   - To view service information, expand Software Environment and then click Services.

   - To view the state of a driver, expand Software Environment and then click System Drivers. Information for each driver is in the right pane.

   - To view driver information arranged by category, expand Components and then select a category, such as Display.

   - To view problem devices, expand Components and then click Problem Devices. Examine the Error Code column for information relating to the source of the problem.

   - To view shared and conflicting resources (which do not always indicate a critical problem), expand Hardware Resources and then click Conflicts/Sharing. Examine the Resource and Device columns for devices that are incorrectly assigned overlapping resources. Remove or disable one of the devices or use Device Manager to change the resources assigned to the devices.

Error Reporting Service

The Windows error reporting service monitors your computer for problems that affect services and applications. When a problem occurs, you can send a problem report to Microsoft and receive an automated response with more information, such as news about an update for an application or device driver.

HOW TO USE DEVICE MANAGER TO VIEW OR CHANGE RESOURCES

Installing new hardware or updating drivers can create conflicts, causing devices to become inaccessible. You can use Device Manager to review resources used by these devices to identify conflicts manually.

To use Device Manager (Devmgmt.msc) to view or change system resource usage information, follow these steps:

1. Click Start, right-click Computer, and then click Manage.
2. Click Device Manager and then double-click a device.
3. Click the Resources tab to view the resources used by that device.
4. Clear the Use Automatic Settings check box.
5. Click Change Setting and specify the resources assigned to the device.

HOW TO ANALYZE BOOT LOGS

Boot logging lists the files that successfully and unsuccessfully processed during startup. You use boot logging to log the Windows features that are processed when you start your computer in safe mode and also in normal mode. By comparing the differences between the two logs, you can determine which features are not required to start.

Windows records the name and path of each file that runs during startup in a log, %WinDir%\Ntbtlog.txt. The log marks each file as successful ("Loaded Driver …") or unsuccessful ("Did Not Load Driver …"). Boot logging appends entries to Ntbtlog.txt when you start Windows in safe mode. Comparing normal mode and safe mode entries enables you to determine which services run in normal mode only—one of which must be the cause of the startup problem if Windows is able to start in safe mode successfully. The following lines are sample Ntbtlog.txt entries.

```
Loaded driver \SystemRoot\System32\DRIVERS\flpydisk.sys
Did not load driver \SystemRoot\System32\DRIVERS\sflpydisk.SYS
```

Note that not every "Did Not Load Driver" message necessarily indicates an error that would prevent Windows from booting, because many drivers are not required for Windows to start. To repair problems caused by problematic drivers when you can start safe mode, follow these steps:

1. Restart the computer and enable boot logging.
2. Restart the computer after it fails and then start safe mode.
3. Click Start and then type **%WinDir%\ntbtlog.txt**. The boot log file opens in Notepad.
4. Compare the list of drivers loaded in normal mode to the list of drivers loaded in safe mode. The driver that is causing the system to fail is one of the drivers listed with "Loaded Driver …" in the normal mode boot log, but listed with "Did Not Load Driver …" in the safe mode boot log.
5. In safe mode, use Device Manager to replace or roll back potentially problematic drivers, as described in the next section, "How to Roll Back Drivers." Start by replacing drivers that have been recently installed or updated. After replacing a driver, repeat this process until the system starts successfully in normal mode.

For the services that run only in normal mode, disable those services one at a time, trying to restart your computer in normal mode after you disable each service. Continue to disable services individually until your computer starts in normal mode.

To repair problems caused by problematic drivers when the computer does not start in safe mode, follow these steps:

1. Restart the computer and then load System Recovery tools.

2. Click Command Prompt. At the command prompt, type **Notepad %WinDir%\ntbtlog.txt**. Notepad opens and displays the boot log.

3. Compare the boot log created when the system failed to start in safe mode to a boot log created when the system started successfully in safe mode. If you do not have a boot log that was created when the system started successfully in safe mode, create a boot log on a similarly configured computer by starting it in safe mode. The driver that is causing safe mode to fail is one of the drivers that is not listed in the boot log that was created when the system failed but is listed with "Loaded Driver …" in the boot log created when safe mode started successfully.

4. Replace the driver file with a working version, using the Copy command at the command prompt. Start by replacing or deleting drivers that have been recently installed or updated. After replacing a driver, repeat this process until the system starts successfully in normal mode.

How to Roll Back Drivers

When you update a device driver, your computer might have problems that it did not have with the previous version. For example, installing an unsigned device driver might cause the device to malfunction or cause resource conflicts with other installed hardware. Installing faulty drivers might cause Stop errors that prevent the operating system from starting in normal mode. Typically, the Stop message text displays the file name of the driver that causes the error.

Windows provides a feature called Device Driver Roll Back that might help you restore system stability by rolling back a driver update.

NOTE You can use System Information or the Sigverif tool to determine whether a driver on your computer is signed and to obtain other information about the driver, such as version, date, time, and manufacturer. This data, combined with information from the manufacturer's Web site, can help you decide whether to roll back or update a device driver.

To roll back a driver, follow these steps:

1. Click Start, right-click Computer, and then click Manage.

2. Under System Tools, click Device Manager.

3. Expand a category (Network Adapters, for example) and then double-click a device.

4. Click the Driver tab and then click Roll Back Driver. You are prompted to confirm that you want to overwrite the current driver. Click Yes to roll back the driver. The rollback process proceeds, or else you are notified that an older driver is not available.

How to Temporarily Disable a Service

Many services automatically run at startup, but others are started only by users or by another process. When you troubleshoot startup issues that are related to system services, a useful technique is to simplify your computer configuration so that you can reduce system complexity and isolate operating system services. To decrease the number of variables, temporarily disable startup applications or services and re-enable them one at a time until you reproduce the problem. Always disable applications first before attempting to disable system services.

The System Configuration utility allows you to disable system services individually or several at a time. To disable a service by using the System Configuration utility, follow these steps:

1. Click Start, type **msconfig**, and then press Enter.

2. Do one of the following:

   - To disable all services, on the General tab, click Selective Startup and then clear the Load System Services check box.

   - To disable specific services, on the Services tab, click to clear the check boxes that correspond to the items you want to disable. You can also click Disable All to disable all items.

If you change any startup setting by using the System Configuration utility, Windows prompts you to return to normal operations the next time you log on. The System Configuration Utility prompt will appear each time you log on until you restore the original startup settings by clicking Normal Startup under Startup Selection on the General tab. To change a startup setting permanently, use the Services console, change a Group Policy setting, or uninstall the software that added the service.

Troubleshooting Startup Problems After Logon

If your computer fails immediately after a user logs on, use the process illustrated in Figure C-13 to identify and disable the failing startup application to allow the user to log on successfully. If the problem occurs immediately after updating or installing an application, try uninstalling that application.

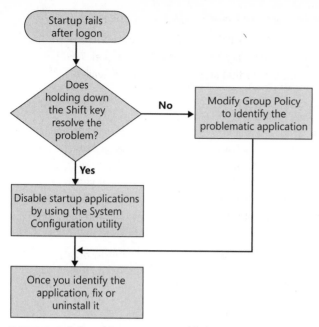

FIGURE C-13 Follow this process to troubleshoot startup problems that occur after logon.

How to Temporarily Disable Startup Applications and Processes

If a problem occurs after installing new software, you can temporarily disable or uninstall the application to verify that the application is the source of the problem.

Problems with applications that run at startup can cause logon delays or even prevent you from completing Windows startup in normal mode. The following subsections provide techniques for temporarily disabling startup applications.

HOW TO DISABLE STARTUP APPLICATIONS USING THE SHIFT KEY

One way you can simplify your configuration is to disable startup applications. By holding down the Shift key during the logon process, you can prevent the operating system from running startup programs or shortcuts in the following folders:

- %SystemDrive%\Users*username*\AppData\Roaming\Microsoft\Windows\Start Menu\ Programs\Startup

- %SystemDrive%\ProgramData\Microsoft\Windows\Start Menu\Programs\Startup

To disable the applications or shortcuts in the preceding folders, you must hold down the Shift key until the desktop icons appear. Holding down the Shift key is a better alternative than temporarily deleting or moving programs and shortcuts, because this procedure affects only the current user session.

To use the Shift key to disable applications and shortcuts in startup folders, log off the computer and then log on again. Immediately press and hold down the Shift key. Continue to hold down the Shift key until the desktop icons appear. If you can log on successfully, you have isolated the cause of the problem to your startup applications. Next, you should use the System Configuration utility to temporarily disable applications one by one until you identify the cause of the problem. With the cause of the problem identified, you can fix the application or permanently remove it from your startup programs.

HOW TO DISABLE STARTUP PROGRAMS USING THE SYSTEM CONFIGURATION UTILITY

The System Configuration utility allows you to disable startup applications individually or several at a time. To disable a startup program by using the System Configuration utility, follow these steps:

1. Click Start, type **msconfig**, and then press Enter.

2. You can disable all or selective startup applications:

   - To disable all startup applications, click the General tab, click Selective Startup, and then clear the Load Startup Items check box.

   - To disable specific startup items, click the Startup tab and then clear the check boxes that correspond to the items you want to disable temporarily. You can also click Disable All on the Startup tab to disable all items.

To change a startup setting permanently, you must move or delete startup shortcuts, change a Group Policy setting, or uninstall the application that added the startup application.

HOW TO DISABLE STARTUP APPLICATIONS CONFIGURED USING GROUP POLICY OR LOGON SCRIPTS

You can use the Group Policy snap-in to disable applications that run at startup. Local Group Policy can be applied to computers, in which case you need to edit the Group Policy settings on the computer that you are troubleshooting. Group Policy objects (GPOs) are frequently applied within AD DS domains, in which case you need to connect to the domain to edit the appropriate policy. Before modifying domain Group Policy settings, you should follow the steps described later in this section to disconnect the computer you are troubleshooting from the network to determine whether the problem is related to domain Group Policy settings.

To disable startup applications by using the Group Policy Management Editor snap-in, follow these steps:

1. Click Start, type **gpedit.msc**, and then click OK.

2. Within either Computer Configuration (for computer-wide startup applications) or User Configuration (for user-specific startup applications), expand Policies, expand Administrative Templates, expand System, and then click Logon.

3. Double-click Run These Programs At User Logon, which is a Group Policy setting. Next, do one of the following:

   - To disable all startup applications configured by that policy, click Disabled.

   - To selectively disable individual programs that are listed in the computer-specific or user-specific policy, click Show. In the Show Contents dialog box, select a program to disable and then click Remove.

You can change additional Group Policy settings that might help you simplify your computer configuration when you are troubleshooting startup problems by enabling the Do Not Process The Run Once List policy. If you enable this Group Policy setting, the computer ignores the programs listed in the following RunOnce subkeys the next time a user logs on to the computer:

- HKEY_LOCAL_MACHINE\SOFTWARE\Microsoft\Windows\CurrentVersion\RunOnce
- HKEY_CURRENT_USER\Software\Microsoft\Windows\CurrentVersion\RunOnce

Additionally, you can enable the Group Policy setting Do Not Process The Legacy Run List to disable the HKEY_LOCAL_MACHINE\SOFTWARE\Microsoft\Windows\CurrentVersion\Run subkey that startup applications might use. The programs listed in this subkey are a customized list of programs that were configured by using the System Policy Editor for Windows NT 4.0 or earlier versions. If you enable this Group Policy setting, Windows ignores the programs listed in this subkey when you start your computer. If you disable or do not configure this Group Policy setting, Windows processes the customized run list that is contained in this registry subkey when you start the computer.

Group Policy changes do not always take effect immediately. You can use the Gpupdate (Gpupdate.exe) tool to refresh local Group Policy changes to computer and user policies. After you refresh the policy, you can use the Group Policy Result (Gpresult.exe) tool to verify that the updated settings are in effect.

Group Policy settings can be applied locally or to an entire domain. To determine how settings are applied to a specific computer, use the Resultant Set Of Policy (Rsop.msc) tool. Then, edit those Group Policy objects to apply a change. For the purpose of isolating the source of the problem, you can prevent Group Policy, logon scripts, roaming user profiles, scheduled tasks, and network-related issues from affecting your troubleshooting by temporarily disabling the network adapter and then logging on by using a local computer account.

If local and domain Group Policy settings do not reveal the source of the startup problem, the application may be started by a logon script. Logon scripts are configured in the local or domain user properties. To view the logon script, open Computer Management and then view the user's properties. Then click the Profile tab. Make note of the path to the logon script and edit it in a tool such as Notepad to determine whether any startup applications are configured.

How to Permanently Disable Startup Applications and Processes

You can permanently disable a startup application in several ways, explained in the following sections.

UNINSTALL THE APPLICATION

If you find that recently installed software causes system instability or if error messages consistently point to a specific application, you can use Uninstall A Program under Programs in Control Panel to uninstall the software. If the application is required, you can install it in a lab environment and perform additional testing before reinstalling it on production computers.

MANUALLY REMOVE THE ENTRY

You can manually delete shortcuts from the Startup folder, remove startup entries from the registry, remove entries from Group Policy or logon scripts, or disable a service. For a list of registry subkeys that contain entries for service and startup programs, see the section titled "Logon Phase" earlier in this appendix.

Summary

Windows 7 automatically installs WinRE and improves startup, shutdown, and sleep recovery times. Although the startup improvements over Windows Vista are minimal, Windows Vista introduced many improvements over Windows XP that Windows 7 continues to support. These features include:

- Windows Boot Manager
- Windows Boot Loader
- The BCD registry file and the BCDEdit command-line tool
- System Recovery tools
- Startup Repair

If you are familiar with earlier versions of Windows, you will be comfortable troubleshooting most problems that occur in the kernel loading phase of startup or later. Fortunately, you (or any user) can resolve many common startup problems simply by running the Startup Repair tool from the Windows DVD.

Troubleshooting Hardware, Driver, and Disk Issues

> **NOTE** This material was originally published in a slightly different form in *Windows 7 Resource Kit* by Mitch Tulloch, Tony Northrup, Jerry Honeycutt, Ed Wilson, and the Windows 7 Team at Microsoft (Microsoft Press, 2010).

This appendix describes how to use the Windows 7 operating system to troubleshoot common hardware problems. This appendix is not intended to be a comprehensive guide to troubleshooting hardware; instead, it focuses on using Windows diagnostic and troubleshooting tools to solve hardware problems. First, this appendix describes improvements to Windows 7 that simplify the process of troubleshooting hardware problems. Then the appendix describes the process of using Windows tools for troubleshooting hardware problems.

For hardware problems that prevent Windows from starting, see Appendix C, "Configuring Startup and Troubleshooting Startup Issues." For network problems, see Appendix E, "Troubleshooting Network Issues." For problems that result in Stop errors (also known as *blue screens*), see Appendix F, "Troubleshooting Stop Messages."

Windows 7 Improvements for Hardware and Driver Troubleshooting

Windows 7 includes Reliability Monitor and Resource Monitor to simplify how you isolate the source of hardware problems, allowing you to reduce client computer downtime. Additionally, Windows 7 includes several troubleshooting features first introduced with Windows Vista. The following sections describe these improvements.

Windows Troubleshooting Platform

The Windows Troubleshooting Platform, new to Windows 7, is an extensible infrastructure for automated diagnosis of software and hardware problems. If you used Windows Network Diagnostics in Windows Vista, you're familiar with how Windows Troubleshooting Platform works.

To the user performing the troubleshooting, the Windows Troubleshooting Platform is a wizard that attempts to identify the source of the problem and might provide instructions to the user for solving the problem or might solve the problem directly. Users can launch a troubleshooting pack from several different locations. For example, if Windows Internet Explorer cannot open a Web site, the user can click the Diagnose Connection Problems button to launch Windows Network Diagnostics (implemented using the Windows Troubleshooting Platform). Users can also launch troubleshooting packs from Control Panel (located at Control Panel\All Control Panel Items\Troubleshooting) or Help And Support.

Built-in Troubleshooting Packs

Windows 7 includes built-in troubleshooting packs to correlate to the top 10 categories of Microsoft support calls, including power efficiency, application compatibility, networking, and sound. Table D-1 describes the troubleshooting packs that are built into Windows 7 or are currently available using the Windows Online Troubleshooting Service (WOTS). WOTS is a free online service that Windows 7 can use to download new or updated troubleshooting packs.

TABLE D-1 Windows 7 Troubleshooting Packs

TROUBLESHOOTING PACK	DESCRIPTION
Aero	Troubleshoot problems that prevent your computer from displaying Aero animations and effects
Playing Audio	Troubleshoot problems that prevent your computer from playing sound
Recording Audio	Troubleshoot problems that prevent your computer from recording sound
Printer	Troubleshoot problems that prevent you from using a printer
Performance	Adjust settings in Windows that can help improve overall speed and performance
System Maintenance	Clean up unused files and shortcuts and perform other maintenance tasks
Power	Adjust power settings to improve battery life and reduce power consumption
HomeGroup	Troubleshoot problems that prevent you from viewing computer or shared files in a HomeGroup
Hardware And Devices	Troubleshoot problems with hardware and devices
Internet Explorer Performance	Troubleshoot problems that prevent you from browsing the Web with Internet Explorer
Internet Explorer Safety	Adjust settings to improve browser safety in Internet Explorer

TROUBLESHOOTING PACK	DESCRIPTION
Windows Media Player Library	Troubleshoot problems that prevent music and movies from being shown in the Windows Media Player Library
Windows Media Player Settings	Reset Windows Media Player back to default settings
Windows Media Player DVD	Troubleshoot problems that prevent playing a DVD in Windows Media Player
Connection to a Workplace Using DirectAccess	Connect to your workplace network over the Internet
Shared Folders	Access shared files and folders on other computers
Incoming Connections	Allow other computers to connect to your computer
Network Adapter	Troubleshoot Ethernet, wireless, or other network adapters
Internet Connections	Connect to the Internet or to a particular Web site
Program Compatibility	Troubleshoot a program that doesn't work in this version of Windows
Search And Indexing	Troubleshoot problems finding items with Windows Search
Windows Update	Troubleshoot problems preventing Windows Update from working correctly

Running Troubleshooting Packs Remotely

You can run a troubleshooting pack across the network on a remote computer, which can allow you to diagnose common problems quickly and possibly solve them without walking the user through the troubleshooting process. The following Windows PowerShell commands, when run on a Windows 7 computer (either locally or remotely using Invoke-Command or the *-PSession cmdlets), will run the built-in Windows Aero troubleshooting pack, automatically attempt to resolve any problems, and store the results to the C:\DiagResult folder.

```
Import-Module TroubleshootingPack
$aero = Get-TroubleshootingPack $env:SystemRoot\Diagnostics\System\Aero
Invoke-TroubleshootingPack -Pack $aero -Result C:\DiagResult -unattend
```

You could also use this technique in a script to run a troubleshooting pack on multiple computers across the network; in combination with a custom troubleshooting pack, you could quickly determine which computers suffered from a specific problem or misconfiguration. Because troubleshooting packs can make configuration changes to solve problems, you could use this approach to detect and resolve a common problem without contacting users or manually connecting to computers.

Resource Monitor

IT professionals need deep insight into a computer's inner workings to efficiently troubleshoot problems. The more complex the problem is, the more detailed the information must be. For example, although Task Manager is sufficient to identify the process that is using the most processor time, IT professionals need a more powerful tool to identify which process is generating the most disk or network input/output (I/O).

To give IT professionals detailed information about resource utilization on a process-by-process basis, Windows 7 includes an improved version of Resource Monitor. As shown in Figure D-1, Resource Monitor displays this data in a format that provides rapid access to a great deal of information that you can use to easily explore process-specific details.

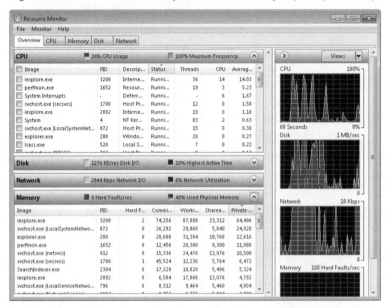

FIGURE D-1 Resource Monitor shows detailed, real-time performance data

Within seconds, you can use Resource Monitor to view:

- Which processes are using the most processor time and memory.

- Which processes are reading and writing the most data to the disk.

- How much network data each process is sending and receiving.

- How much memory each process is using.

- Why a process is nonresponsive.

- Which services are hosted within a SvcHost.exe process.

- Which handles, including devices, registry keys, and files, a process is accessing.

- Which modules, including dynamic-link libraries (DLLs) and other libraries, a process is accessing.

- Which processes are listening for incoming network connections or have network connections open.

Additionally, you can end processes and search online for information about a process. With Resource Monitor, IT professionals can quickly identify the source of performance and resource utilization problems, reducing the time required to troubleshoot complex issues.

Windows Memory Diagnostics

Application failures, operating system faults, and Stop errors are often caused by failing memory. Failing memory chips return different data than the operating system originally stored. Failing memory can be difficult to identify: Problems can be intermittent and might occur only under very rare circumstances. For example, a memory chip might function perfectly when tested in a controlled environment but begin to fail when the internal temperature of the computer becomes too high. Failing memory can also cause secondary problems, such as corrupted files. Often, administrators take drastic steps to repair the problem, such as reinstalling applications or the operating system, only to have the failures persist.

Windows includes Windows Memory Diagnostics to help administrators track down problems with unreliable memory. If Windows Error Reporting (WER) or Microsoft Online Crash Analysis (MOCA) determines that failing memory might be the cause of an error, the software can prompt the user to perform memory diagnostics without requiring an additional download or separate boot disk. Additionally, you can run Windows Memory Diagnostics by choosing a special boot menu option or by loading the Windows Recovery Environment.

If memory diagnostics identify a memory problem, Windows can avoid using the affected portion of physical memory so that the operating system can start successfully and avoid application crashes. Upon startup, Windows provides an easy-to-understand report detailing the problem and instructing the user on how to replace the memory. For detailed information, see the section titled "How to Use Windows Memory Diagnostics" later in this appendix.

Disk Failure Diagnostics

Disk reliability problems can vary in severity. Minor problems can cause seemingly random application failures. For example, if a user connects a new camera and the operating system fails to load the driver, disk corruption may be causing the problem. More severe problems can result in the total loss of data stored on the hard disk.

Windows can eliminate much of the impact of a disk failure by detecting disk problems proactively, before total failure occurs. Hard disks often show warning signs before failure, but earlier Windows operating systems did not record the warning signs. Windows now checks for evidence that a hard disk is beginning to fail and warns the user or the Support Center of the problem. The IT department can then back up the data and replace the hard disk before the problem becomes an emergency. For administrators, Windows acts as a guide through the process of backing up their data so that they can replace the drive without data loss.

Most new hard disks include Self-Monitoring Analysis and Reporting Technology (SMART) and Disk Self Tests (DSTs). SMART monitors the health of the disk using a set of degradable attributes, such as head-flying height and bad block reallocation count. DSTs actively check for failures by performing read, write, and servo tests.

Windows queries for SMART status on an hourly basis and regularly schedules DSTs. If Windows detects impending disk failure, Windows can start disk diagnostics to guide the user or IT professionals through the process of backing up the data and replacing the disk before total failure occurs. Windows can also detect problems related to a dirty or scratched CD or DVD and instruct the user to clean the media.

You can configure disk diagnostics using two Group Policy settings. Both are located in Computer Configuration\Policies\Administrative Templates\System\Troubleshooting And Diagnostics\Disk Diagnostic.

- **Disk Diagnostic: Configure Execution Level**   Use this policy to enable or disable disk diagnostic warnings. Disabling this policy does not disable disk diagnostics; it simply blocks disk diagnostics from displaying a message to the user and taking any corrective action. If you have configured a monitoring infrastructure to collect disk diagnostic events recorded to the event log and prefer to manually respond to events, you can disable this policy.

- **Disk Diagnostic: Configure Custom Alert Text**   Enable this property to define custom alert text (up to 512 characters) in the disk diagnostic message that appears when a disk reports a SMART fault.

For disk diagnostics to work, the Diagnostic Policy Service must be running. Note that disk diagnostics cannot detect all impending failures. Additionally, because SMART attribute definitions are vendor specific, different vendor implementations can vary. SMART will not function if hard disks are attached to a hardware redundant array of independent disks (RAID) controller.

NOTE   Many hardware vendors use SMART failures as a warranty replacement indicator.

Self-Healing NTFS

Windows Vista and Windows 7 include self-healing NTFS File System (NTFS), which can detect and repair file system corruption while the operating system is running. In most cases, Windows will repair file corruption without disrupting the user. Essentially, self-healing NTFS functions similarly to ChkDsk (described in the section titled "How to Use ChkDsk" later in this appendix), but it works in the background, without locking an entire volume. Specifically, if Windows detects corrupted metadata on the file system, it invokes the self-healing capabilities of NTFS to rebuild the metadata. Some data may still be lost, but Windows can limit the damage and repair the problem without taking the entire system offline for a lengthy check-and-repair cycle.

Self-healing NTFS is enabled by default and requires no management. Instead, it will serve to reduce the number of disk-related problems that require administrative intervention. If self-healing fails, the volume will be marked "dirty," and Windows will run ChkDsk on the next startup.

Improved Driver Reliability

Drivers should be more reliable in Windows Vista and Windows 7 than they are in previous versions of Windows. Improved I/O cancellation support is built into Windows Vista and Windows 7 to enable drivers that might become blocked when attempting to perform I/O to gracefully recover. Windows Vista and Windows 7 also have new application programming interfaces (APIs) to allow applications to cancel I/O operations, such as opening a file.

To help developers create more stable drivers, Microsoft provides the Driver Verifier. Developers can use the Driver Verifier to verify that their drivers remain responsive and to ensure that they correctly support I/O cancellation. Because driver response failures can affect multiple applications or the entire operating system, these improvements will have a significant impact on Windows stability. This improvement requires no effort from administrators; you will simply benefit from a more reliable operating system.

Improved Error Reporting

Windows 7 offers improved application reliability, and the new error reporting capabilities allow applications to continue to become more reliable over time. In earlier versions of Windows, application response failures were very hard for developers to troubleshoot, because error reporting provided limited or no information about them. Windows Vista and Windows 7 improve error reporting to give developers the information they need to permanently resolve the root cause of the problems, thus providing continuous improvements in reliability.

The Process of Troubleshooting Hardware Issues

Hardware problems can take several different forms:

- Hardware problems that prevent Windows from starting
- A newly installed hardware accessory that does not work as expected
- A hardware accessory that did work correctly, but now fails
- Unpredictable symptoms, such as failing applications and services, Stop errors, system resets, and accessories that behave unreliably

You should use a different process to troubleshoot each of these broad problem categories. The following sections discuss each of these suggested processes.

How to Troubleshoot Problems That Prevent Windows from Starting

Some hardware problems—especially those related to hard disks or core features such as the motherboard or processor—can prevent Windows from starting. For information about troubleshooting startup problems, see Appendix C.

How to Troubleshoot Problems Installing New Hardware

Often, you might have difficulty installing a new hardware feature, or an existing hardware feature might suddenly fail. If you are having trouble installing a new hardware feature, follow these steps:

1. If Windows will not start, see Appendix C.

2. Install any updates available from Windows Update.

3. Download and install updated software and drivers for your hardware. Hardware manufacturers often release updated software for hardware features after they release the hardware. You can typically download software updates from the manufacturer's Web site.

4. Remove and reinstall any newly installed hardware by strictly following the manufacturer's instructions. You often need to install the software before connecting the hardware. For more information, see the sections titled "How to Diagnose Hardware Problems" and "How to Troubleshoot Driver Problems" later in this appendix. For detailed information about troubleshooting universal serial bus (USB) devices, see the section titled "How to Troubleshoot USB Problems" later in this appendix. For information about troubleshooting devices that connect using Bluetooth, see the section titled "How to Troubleshoot Bluetooth Problems" later in this appendix.

5. Use Event Viewer to find any related events that might provide useful information for diagnosing the problem. Typically, drivers will add events to the System Event Log. However, drivers could add events to any log.

6. Install updated drivers for other hardware features, including basic input/output system (BIOS) and firmware updates for all hardware accessories and your computer. Updated drivers for other hardware features can sometimes solve incompatibility problems with new hardware.

7. If possible, move hardware to different connectors on your computer. For example, move internal cards to different slots, or connect USB devices to different USB ports. If this solves the problem, the original connector on your computer has failed or the device was not connected correctly.

8. Replace any cables used to connect the new hardware to your computer. If this solves the problem, the cable was faulty.

9. Connect the new hardware to a different computer. If the hardware fails on multiple computers, you might have faulty hardware.

10. Contact the failed hardware manufacturer for support. You might have a hardware or software failure; the hardware manufacturer can assist with additional troubleshooting.

How to Troubleshoot Problems with Existing Hardware

If a hardware feature that previously worked suddenly fails, follow these troubleshooting steps:

1. If Windows will not start, see Appendix C.

2. Use Reliability Monitor to determine how long the problem has been occurring and what related symptoms might be occurring. For more information, see the section titled "How to Use Reliability Monitor" later in this appendix. Then use Event Viewer to find any related events that might provide useful information for diagnosing the problem.

3. Install any updates available from Windows Update.

4. Roll back any recently updated drivers, even if they are for other devices. Driver problems might cause incompatibilities with different devices.

5. Download and install updated software and drivers for your hardware. Hardware manufacturers often release updated software for hardware features after they release the hardware. You can typically download software updates from the manufacturer's Web site.

6. Remove and reinstall any newly installed hardware. For more information, see the sections titled "How to Diagnose Hardware Problems" and "How to Troubleshoot Driver Problems" later in this appendix. For detailed information about troubleshooting USB devices, see the section titled "How to Troubleshoot USB Problems" later in this appendix.

7. Install updated drivers for other hardware features, including BIOS and firmware updates for all hardware accessories and your computer. Updated drivers for other hardware features can sometimes solve incompatibility problems with hardware.

8. Troubleshoot disk problems by using ChkDsk to identify and possibly fix disk-related problems. Disk problem can corrupt drivers, which might cause hardware to stop functioning. For more information, see the section titled "How to Troubleshoot Disk Problems" later in this appendix.

9. If possible, move hardware to different connectors on your computer. For example, move internal cards to different slots and connect USB devices to different USB ports. If this solves the problem, the original connector on your computer has failed or the device was not connected correctly.

10. Replace any cables used to connect the new hardware to your computer. If this solves the problem, the cable was faulty.

11. Connect problematic hardware to a different computer. If the hardware fails on multiple computers, you might have a hardware malfunction. Contact the hardware manufacturer for technical support.

12. Perform a system restore to attempt to return the computer to the latest state when it was functioning correctly. To use System Restore, see the section titled "How to Use System Restore" later in this appendix.

13. Contact the hardware manufacturer for support. You might have a hardware or software failure, and the hardware manufacturer can assist with additional troubleshooting.

How to Troubleshoot Unpredictable Symptoms

Hardware, driver, and disk problems can cause unpredictable symptoms when Windows is running, including:

- Failing applications and services
- Stop errors
- System resets
- Accessories that behave unreliably

Many different types of problems can cause these symptoms. To identify the source of these problems and possibly fix the issue, follow these steps. After each step, determine whether the problem continues.

1. If Windows will not start, see Appendix C.

2. Use Reliability Monitor to determine how long the problem has been occurring and what other related symptoms might be occurring. For more information, read the section titled "How to Use Reliability Monitor" later in this appendix. Then use Event Viewer to find any related events that might provide useful information for diagnosing the problem. Typically, drivers will add events to the System Event Log. However, drivers could add events to any log.

3. Install any updates available from Windows Update.

4. Install updated drivers available directly from the hardware manufacturer, including BIOS and firmware updates for all hardware accessories and your computer.

5. Roll back any recently updated drivers.

6. Troubleshoot disk problems by using ChkDsk to identify and possibly fix disk-related problems. To resolve problems related to low free disk space, run the Disk Cleanup Wizard. For more information, see the section titled "How to Troubleshoot Disk Problems" later in this appendix.

7. Test your memory for problems by using Windows Memory Diagnostics. For more information, see the section titled "How to Use Windows Memory Diagnostics" later in this appendix.

8. Remove unnecessary hardware features one by one. If the problem disappears after removing a hardware feature, that feature likely is causing the problem. Continue

troubleshooting that specific feature by following the steps listed in the section titled "How to Troubleshoot Problems with Existing Hardware" earlier in this appendix.

9. Perform a system restore to attempt to return the computer to the latest state when it was functioning correctly. To use System Restore, see the section titled "How to Use System Restore" later in this appendix.

10. Contact your computer manufacturer for support. You might have a hardware or software failure, and your computer manufacturer can assist with additional troubleshooting.

How to Diagnose Hardware Problems

Always remember to check basic issues before attempting to remove and replace parts. Before installing new peripherals, refer to your motherboard and device manuals for helpful information, including safety precautions, firmware configuration, and expansion slot or memory slot locations. Some peripheral manufacturers recommend that you use a bus-mastering PCI slot and advise that installing their adapter in a secondary slot might cause it to function improperly.

How to Use Device Manager to Identify Failed Devices

Windows 7 can detect hardware that is not working properly. View failed hardware by following these steps to use Windows Device Manager:

1. Click Start, right-click Computer, and then select Manage.

2. Under System Tools, click Device Manager.

3. Device Manager displays all devices. Problem devices (including any devices with which Windows 7 is unable to successfully communicate) are displayed with a warning sign. If no categories are expanded and no devices are visible, Windows did not detect a problem with any device.

How to Check the Physical Setup of Your Computer

If you have recently opened the computer case or the computer has been moved or shipped, connectors may have loosened. You should perform the following tasks to verify that connections are solid:

- **Confirm that the power cords for all devices are firmly plugged in and that the computer power supply meets hardware specifications**   Computer power supplies are available in different sizes and are typically rated between 200 and 400 watts. Installing too many devices into a computer with an inadequate amount of power can cause reliability problems or even damage the power supply. See the manufacturer's power specifications when installing new devices and verify that your computer can handle the increased electrical load.

- **Disconnect external accessories**   External accessories—such as those that connect using USB or IEEE 1394, PC cards, and ExpressCards—can malfunction and interfere with the startup process. You can identify the cause of the problem either by disconnecting devices one by one and attempting to start the computer after disconnecting each device or by disconnecting all the devices, restarting the computer, and then reconnecting the devices one by one.

- **Verify that you correctly installed and firmly seated all internal adapters**   Peripherals such as keyboards and video cards often must be installed and functioning to complete the initial startup phase without generating error messages. Adapters might become loose if the computer is moved or bumped or if the computer vibrates from moving parts such as hard disks.

- **Verify that you correctly attached cables**   Check that you have firmly seated all cable connectors by disconnecting and reconnecting cables. Search for damaged or worn cables and replace them as required. To ensure that contacts are solid, use a pencil eraser to clean dirty connectors.

- **Check the system temperature**   High temperatures inside a computer can cause unpredictable failures. Many computers will display internal temperatures for the processor, hard disk, graphics card, or other features if you start the Firmware menu. Graphical third-party tools also run within Windows for displaying temperature diagnostic information. If the temperature is high, verify that all fans are working properly and the vents are not blocked. Verify that the computer's case is completely assembled. Leaving panels open might seem like it would improve airflow, but it can actually misdirect air that should be cooling hot features. Verify that air can flow freely around the outside of the computer. Particularly with mobile PCs, verify that the computer is not resting on a soft surface that can prevent heat dissipation, such as a couch or carpet. Finally, reset processor and memory speeds to their default settings to verify that the computer has not been overclocked.

How to Check the Configuration of Your Hardware

If you have recently changed the hardware configuration of your computer, or you are configuring a new computer, you should check the configuration to identify the cause of a startup problem.

- **Verify that you correctly configured any jumpers or dual in-line package (DIP) switches**   Jumpers and DIP switches close or open electric contacts on circuit boards. For hard disks, jumper settings are especially important, because they can adversely affect the startup process if not correctly set. For example, configuring two master Advanced Technology Attachment (ATA) disks that are installed on the same channel or assigning duplicate small computer system interface (SCSI) ID numbers to devices in the same SCSI chain might cause a Stop error or error messages about hard disk failure.

- **Configure boot configuration data (BCD) references correctly when a hard disk is added** Installing an additional hard disk or changing the disk configuration in a computer can prevent Windows from starting. In this case, use the Startup Repair tool within System Recovery tools to automatically resolve the problem. For more information, see Appendix C.

- **Verify SCSI configuration** If your computer uses or starts from SCSI devices and you suspect that these devices are causing startup problems, you need to check the items listed in Table D-2.

TABLE D-2 Checklist for Troubleshooting SCSI Devices

ITEM	DESCRIPTION
All devices are correctly terminated.	Verify that devices are correctly terminated. You must follow specific rules for termination to avoid problems with the computer not recognizing an SCSI device. Although these rules can vary slightly from one type of adapter to another, the basic principle is that you must terminate an SCSI chain at both ends.
All devices use unique SCSI ID numbers.	Verify that each device located on a particular SCSI chain has a unique identification number. Duplicate identification numbers can cause intermittent failures or even data corruption. For newer devices, you can use the SCSI Configured AutoMagically (SCAM) standard. The host adapter and all devices must support the SCAM standard. Otherwise you must set ID numbers manually.
The BIOS on the startup SCSI controller is enabled.	Verify that the SCSI BIOS is enabled for the primary SCSI controller and that the BIOS on secondary controllers is disabled. SCSI firmware contains programming instructions that allow the computer to communicate with SCSI disks before Windows 7 starts. Disabling this feature for all host adapters causes a startup failure. For information about disabling or enabling the BIOS, refer to the documentation provided with your SCSI controller.
You are using the correct cables.	Verify that the connecting cables are the correct type and length and are compliant with SCSI requirements. Different SCSI standards exist, each with specific cabling requirements. Consult the product documentation for more information.
The firmware settings for the host SCSI adapter match device capabilities.	Verify that host adapter BIOS settings for each SCSI device are set correctly. (The BIOS for the SCSI adapter is separate from the computer motherboard firmware.) For each SCSI device, you can specify settings—such as Sync Negotiation, Maximum Transfer Rate, and Send Start Command—that can affect performance and compatibility. Certain SCSI devices might not function correctly if settings are set beyond the capabilities of the hardware. Consult the documentation for your SCSI adapter and device before changing default settings.

ITEM	DESCRIPTION
SCSI adapters are installed in a master PCI slot.	Verify that you installed the host adapter in the correct mother-board slot. The documentation for some PCI SCSI adapters recommends using busmaster PCI slots to avoid problems on 32-bit computers. Refer to the manufacturer's documentation for your motherboard or computer to locate these busmaster PCI slots. If your SCSI adapter is installed in a non-busmaster PCI slot, move it to a master slot to see whether the change improves operation and stability.

WARNING As a precaution, always shut down the computer and remove the power connector before troubleshooting hardware. Never attempt to install or remove internal devices if you are unfamiliar with hardware.

MORE INFO For more information about SCSI termination, see Microsoft Knowledge Base article 92765, "Terminating a SCSI Device," at *http://support.microsoft.com/?kbid=92765* and Microsoft Knowledge Base article 154690, "How to Troubleshoot Event ID 9, Event ID 11, and Event ID 15 Error Messages," at *http://support.microsoft.com/?kbid=154690*.

How to Verify That System Firmware and Peripheral Firmware Are Up to Date

You can sometimes trace instability and compatibility problems to outdated firmware. Whenever possible, use the latest firmware version. If Setup does not respond when you are installing the operating system, the cause might be the firmware for your DVD drive. Try upgrading the DVD firmware to the latest version.

How to Test Your Hardware by Running Diagnostic Tools

If the problem occurs after the power-on self test (POST) routine finishes but before Windows fully loads, run any diagnostic software that the manufacturer of the hardware adapter provides. This software typically includes self-test programs that allow you to quickly verify proper operation of a device and might help you to obtain additional information about the device, such as model number, hardware, and device firmware version.

Additionally, you can use Windows to run a memory test on your computer. For detailed instructions, see the section titled "How to Use Windows Memory Diagnostics" later in this appendix.

How to Simplify Your Hardware Configuration

Hardware problems can occur when you have both newer and older devices installed on your computer. If you cannot resolve problems by using safe mode and other options such as rolling back drivers, temporarily disable or remove Microsoft Internet Security and Acceleration (ISA) devices that do not support Plug and Play. If you can start Windows with these older devices removed, these devices are causing resource conflicts, and you need to manually reconfigure the resources assigned to them.

While you are diagnosing startup problems related to hardware, it is recommended that you simplify your configuration. By simplifying your computer configuration, you might be able to start Windows. You can then gradually increase the computer's hardware configuration complexity until you reproduce the problem, which allows you to diagnose and resolve the problem.

Avoid troubleshooting when you have several adapters and external peripherals installed. Starting with external and ISA devices, disable or remove hardware devices one at a time until you are able to start your computer. Reinstall devices by following the manufacturer's instructions, verifying that each is functioning properly before checking the next device. For example, installing a PCI network adapter and a SCSI adapter at the same time can complicate troubleshooting, because either adapter might cause a problem.

ISA devices cause a large share of startup problems related to hardware because the PCI bus does not have a reliable method for determining ISA resource settings. Device conflicts might occur because of miscommunication between the two bus types. To avoid ISA and PCI conflicts, try temporarily removing ISA devices. After you install a new PCI device, you can use Device Manager to determine which system resources are available to ISA devices. Then reconfigure the ISA devices that do not support Plug and Play to eliminate any conflicts. If the problems continue after you reinstall ISA devices and you cannot resolve them with assistance from technical support, consider upgrading to newer hardware.

Simplifying your computer configuration also helps when problems prevent you from installing Windows. For more information about simplifying your hardware configuration to resolve setup problems, see Microsoft Knowledge Base article 224826, "Troubleshooting Text-Mode Setup Problems on ACPI Computers," at *http://support.microsoft.com/?kbid=224826*.

How to Diagnose Disk-Related Problems

Disk-related problems typically occur before Windows starts or shortly afterward. Refer to Table D-3 for a list of symptoms, possible causes, and sources of information about disk-related startup problems.

TABLE D-3 Diagnosing Disk-Related Startup Problems

SYMPTOM, MESSAGE, OR PROBLEM	POSSIBLE CAUSE	FOR MORE INFORMATION

The POST routine displays messages similar to the following.
 	
`Hard disk error.`
`Hard disk absent/failed.`
	The system self-test routines halt because of improperly installed devices.	Verify that hardware is connected properly, as described earlier in this section.

The system displays MBR-related or boot sector–related messages similar to the following.
 	
`Missing operating system.`
`Insert a system diskette and restart the system.`
	The Master Boot Record (MBR) or partition boot sector is corrupt because of problems with hardware or viruses.	Run Startup Repair, as described in Appendix C.

The system displays messages about the partition table similar to the following.
 	
`Invalid partition table.`
`A disk-read error occurred.`
	The partition table is invalid because of incorrect configuration of newly added disks.	Run Startup Repair, as described in Appendix C. If Windows still fails to start, use the System Recovery command prompt to configure your disks.

You cannot access Windows after installing another operating system.	The boot sector is overwritten by another operating system's setup program.	Run Startup Repair, as described in Appendix C.
System files are missing.	Required startup files are missing or damaged, or entries in the BCD registry file are pointing to the wrong partition.	Run Startup Repair, as described in Appendix C.

The EFI boot manager or Windows Boot Manager displays messages similar to the following.
 	
`Couldn't find loader.`
`Please insert another disk.`
	System files are missing.	Run Startup Repair, as described in Appendix C.

CMOS or NVRAM disk configuration settings are not retained.	The CMOS memory or NVRAM is faulty, data is corrupted, or the battery that retains these settings needs replacing.	Follow the manufacturer's instructions for replacing or recharging the system battery.

Infrequently, disk-related issues such as corrupted files, file system problems, or insufficient free space might cause Stop messages to appear.

How to Use Built-In Diagnostics

Windows 7 includes several different tools to assist you in diagnosing the source of hardware problems. The following sections describe the most important tools.

How to Use Reliability Monitor

To view Reliability Monitor, click Start, type **Reliability** and then click View Reliability History. The chart provides a day-by-day report of any problems or significant changes. To view events that occurred on a specific day, click the day in the chart and then view the reliability details for more information. You can also click the drop-down list in the upper-right corner and then click Select All to view a report that contains all events that Windows has recorded.

From Reliability Monitor, you can access capabilities that were part of Problem Reports And Solutions in Windows Vista. At the bottom of the page, click View All Problem Reports or Check For Solutions To All Problems.

How to Use Data Collector Sets

The Performance snap-in includes data collector sets and corresponding reports that perform detailed analysis of different aspects of a computer's configuration and performance.

To use data collector sets and reports, follow these steps:

1. Click Start, right-click Computer, and then select Manage.

2. Expand Performance, expand Data Collector Sets, and then click System.

3. In the middle pane, right-click the data collector set you want to analyze and then click Start. For example, to analyze the computer's hardware, right-click System Diagnostics and then click Start. Windows 7 will begin collecting data.

4. Right-click the data collector set and then click Latest Report. Windows shows the report status while data is being collected (this might take several minutes). After enough data has been collected, the report is displayed. Figure D-2 shows a System Diagnostics report.

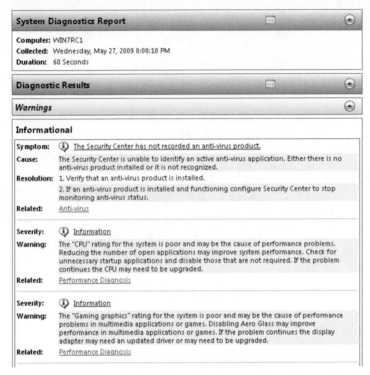

FIGURE D-2 The System Diagnostics report includes detailed information about the computer, including possible sources of hardware problems.

Examine the report to determine whether any of the causes might be related to the problem you are troubleshooting.

How to Use Windows Memory Diagnostics

Memory problems are one of the most common types of hardware problem. Memory problems can prevent Windows from starting and cause unpredictable Stop errors when Windows has started. Because memory-related problems can cause intermittent failures, they can be difficult to identify.

Fortunately, Windows includes Windows Memory Diagnostics, an offline diagnostic tool that automatically tests your computer's memory. Windows Memory Diagnostics tests your computer's memory by repeatedly writing values to memory and then reading those values from memory to verify that they have not changed. To identify the widest range of memory failures, Windows Memory Diagnostics includes three different testing levels:

- **Basic** Basic tests include:
  - MATS+
  - INVC
  - SCHCKR (which enables the cache)

- **Standard** All basic tests, plus:
  - LRAND
  - Stride6 (which enables the cache)
  - CHCKR3
  - WMATS+
  - WINVC
- **Extended** All standard tests, plus:
  - MATS+ (which disables the cache)
  - Stride38
  - WSCHCKR
  - WStride-6
  - CHKCKR4
  - WCHCKR3
  - ERAND
  - Stride6 (which disables the cache)
  - CHCKR8

Although the specifics of each of these tests are not important for administrators to understand, it is important to understand that memory testing is never perfect. Failures are often intermittent and may occur only once every several days or weeks in regular usage. Automated tests such as those done by Windows Memory Diagnostics increase the likelihood that a failure can be detected; however, you can still have faulty memory while Windows Memory Diagnostics indicates that no problems were detected. To minimize this risk, run the Extended tests and increase the number of repetitions. The more tests you run, the more confident you can be in the result. If you have even a single failure, it indicates faulty memory.

After Windows Memory Diagnostics completes testing, the computer will automatically restart. Windows will display a notification bubble with the test results, as shown in Figure D-3, and you can view events in the System Event Log with the source MemoryDiagnosticsResults (Event ID 1201).

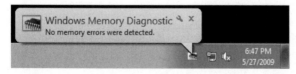

FIGURE D-3 Windows Memory Diagnostics displays a notification bubble after logon.

If you do identify a memory failure, it is typically not worthwhile to attempt to repair the memory. Instead, you should replace unreliable memory. If the computer has multiple memory cards and you are unsure which card is causing the problem, replace each card and then rerun Windows Memory Diagnostics until the computer is reliable.

If problems persist even after replacing the memory, the problem is caused by an outside source. For example, high temperatures (often found in mobile PCs) can cause memory to be unreliable. Although computer manufacturers typically choose memory specifically designed to withstand high temperatures, adding third-party memory that does not meet the same specifications can cause failure. Besides heat, other devices inside the computer can cause electrical interference. Finally, motherboard or processor problems may occasionally cause memory communication errors that resemble failing memory.

How Windows Automatically Detects Memory Problems

When Windows analyzes problem reports, it can determine that memory problems might be a source of the problem. If this happens, the Action Center prompts the user to run Windows Memory Diagnostics. Users can click a link to either restart Windows and test for memory errors immediately or wait until the next time the computer is restarted.

How to Schedule Windows Memory Diagnostics

If Windows is running, you can schedule Windows Memory Diagnostics for the next startup by following these steps:

1. Click Start, type **mdsched.exe**, and then press Enter.

2. Choose to restart the computer and run the tool immediately or schedule the tool to run at the next restart, as shown in Figure D-4.

   Windows Memory Diagnostics runs automatically after the computer restarts.

FIGURE D-4 You can schedule Windows Memory Diagnostics to run when you next restart your computer.

How to Start Windows Memory Diagnostics When Windows Is Installed

If Windows is already installed, you can start Windows Memory Diagnostics from the Windows Boot Manager menu. To do this, follow these steps:

1. Remove all floppy disks and CDs from your computer and then restart your computer.

2. If the Windows Boot Manager menu does not normally appear, press the spacebar repeatedly as the computer starts. If you are successful, the Windows Boot Manager menu will appear. If the progress bar appears, restart your computer and try again to interrupt the startup process by pressing the spacebar.

3. On the Windows Boot Manager menu, press the Tab button on your keyboard to select Windows Memory Diagnostics, as shown in Figure D-5, and then press Enter.

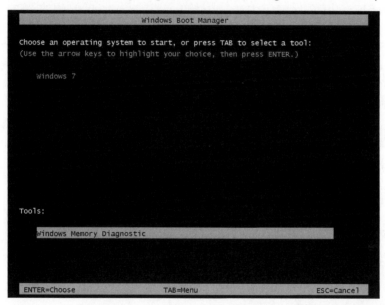

```
                        Windows Boot Manager

Choose an operating system to start, or press TAB to select a tool:
(Use the arrow keys to highlight your choice, then press ENTER.)


     Windows 7











Tools:
     Windows Memory Diagnostic




ENTER=Choose                TAB=Menu                ESC=Cancel
```

FIGURE D-5 You can start Windows Memory Diagnostics from the Windows Boot Manager menu.

Windows Memory Diagnostics will start and automatically begin testing your computer's memory. For information on how to configure the automated tests, see the section titled "How to Configure Windows Memory Diagnostics" later in this appendix.

How to Start Windows Memory Diagnostics from the Windows DVD

If Windows is not installed, you can run Windows Memory Diagnostics from the Windows DVD by following these steps:

NOTE If Windows 7 is installed but will not start, you can start System Recovery tools faster by pressing F8 before the Starting Windows logo appears and then choosing Repair Your Computer from the Advanced Boot Options screen.

1. Insert the Windows DVD into your computer.

2. Restart your computer. When prompted to boot from the DVD, press any key. If you are not prompted to boot from the DVD, you may have to configure your computer's startup sequence. For more information, see the section titled "Initial Startup Phase" in Appendix C.

3. Windows Setup loads. When prompted, select your regional preferences and then click Next.

4. Click Repair Your Computer.

5. Select your keyboard layout and then click Next.

6. System Recovery scans your hard disks for Windows installations. If the standard drivers do not detect a hard disk because the drivers were not included with Windows, click the Load Drivers button to load the driver. Select an operating system to repair and then click Next.

7. The Choose A Recovery Tool page appears. Click Windows Memory Diagnostic Tool.

Windows Memory Diagnostics will start and automatically begin testing your computer's memory. For information on how to configure the automated tests, read the next section. For more information about System Recovery tools, see Appendix C.

How to Configure Windows Memory Diagnostics

As shown in Figure D-6, you can configure different options for Windows Memory Diagnostics. You can use these options to configure more thorough (and more time-consuming) diagnostics.

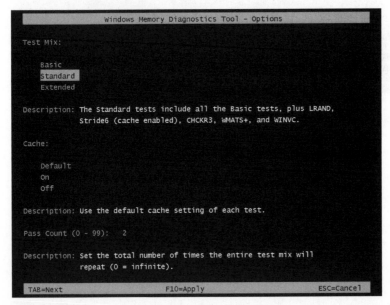

FIGURE D-6 You can configure Windows Memory Diagnostics to use more thorough testing procedures.

To view Windows Memory Diagnostics options, start Windows Memory Diagnostics and then press F1. You can configure three different settings, which you select by pressing the Tab key:

- **Test Mix**   The default set of tests, Standard, provides efficient testing while catching most common types of memory failures. To reduce testing time (and the types of failures that might be caught), choose Basic. To increase the types of failures that might be caught (as well as testing time), choose Extended.

- **Cache**   Some tests use the cache, while others disable the cache. Tests are specifically designed to use or disable the cache to identify problems with different memory features. Therefore, you should typically leave this as the default setting.

- **Pass Count**   This defines the number of iterations. Increase this number to provide more thorough testing and to increase the likelihood that you will identify any existing problems. The higher the Pass Count, the more likely you are to find problems.

After you have configured settings, press F10 to apply your changes. Windows Memory Diagnostics will then restart the tests.

How to Troubleshoot Disk Problems

Disk problems can cause unpredictable behavior in Windows. First, disk problems can lead to corrupted files because important system files and drivers are stored on your hard disk. Second, disk problems can lead to corruption in the page file or temporary files. Third, low disk space can lead to failed attempts to allocate disk space for temporary files. Any of these types of problems can cause unpredictable behavior. As a result, one step in troubleshooting hardware problems should be to check for disk problems and free up available disk space. Additionally, if you have a hard disk with nonvolatile caching, you can disable nonvolatile caching to determine whether the cache is causing problems.

The following sections provide information about troubleshooting disk-related problems.

How to Prepare for Disk Failures

You can take several steps to prepare yourself—and your computers—for troubleshooting disk problems before the problems occur. First, familiarize yourself with recovery and troubleshooting tools. Use of disk redundancy lessens the impact of hardware failures. Backups ensure minimized data loss when failures occur. Protect yourself from malicious attacks by using antivirus software. Finally, perform regular maintenance on your storage devices.

You should familiarize yourself with the System Recovery tools and have a Windows DVD available to start the tools if the hard disks are not available. For more information, see Appendix C.

Run ChkDsk /f /r regularly to fix file system problems that may appear because of faulty hardware, power failures, or software errors. Schedule downtime to reboot the computer and allow Autochk to resolve problems on boot and system volumes. Regularly review the ChkDsk output and the event log to identify problems that ChkDsk cannot fix.

For desktop computers that store critical, constantly updated data, use hardware disk redundancy (also known as RAID) to allow computers to continue to function if a hard disk fails. Keep replacement disks on hand.

At a minimum, back up critical files nightly. Redundancy does not eliminate the need for backups. Even redundant file systems can fail, and disk redundancy cannot protect against files that are corrupted by an application. You must restore corrupted files from an archival backup created before the corruption occurred.

Viruses, spyware, and other types of malware are a significant source of disk and file system problems. Follow these guidelines to avoid infecting computers with viruses:

- Install a virus detection program. Configure the virus detection program to automatically retrieve updated virus signatures.
- Use Windows Update to ensure that operating system files stay up to date.
- Keep applications up to date, especially Web browsers, which malware often abuses to install unwanted software. Windows Update distributes updates for Internet Explorer.
- Never run untrusted scripts or applications.
- Use Windows AppLocker to prevent users from running nonapproved software.

Although fragmentation will not cause a hard disk to fail, it will cause performance problems. To avoid performance problems, schedule the Defrag command-line tool to run regularly during off-peak hours. Store the output of the Defrag tool to a text file and review that text file regularly to ensure that defragmentation is performing as expected. To further minimize problems caused by fragmentation, ensure that all volumes have at least 15 percent free space available.

How to Use ChkDsk

ChkDsk (ChkDsk.exe) is a command-line tool that checks disk volumes for problems and attempts to repair any that it finds. For example, ChkDsk can repair problems related to bad sectors, lost clusters, cross-linked files, and directory errors. Disk errors are a common source of difficult-to-track problems, and ChkDsk should be one of the first tools you use when troubleshooting problems that do not appear to be the result of a recent system change. You must be logged on as an administrator or a member of the Administrators group to use ChkDsk.

Before running ChkDsk, be aware of the following:

- ChkDsk requires exclusive access to a volume while it is running. ChkDsk might display a prompt asking whether you want to check the disk the next time you restart your computer.
- ChkDsk might take a long time to run, depending on the number of files and folders, the size of the volume, disk performance, and available system resources (such as processor and memory).
- ChkDsk might not accurately report information in read-only mode.

ChkDsk Examples

To correct disk errors from a command line, open an administrative command prompt and type

`Chkdsk DriveLetter: /f /r`

For example, to check drive C for errors, type

`Chkdsk C: /f /r`

If you need to run ChkDsk on a large D volume and you want ChkDsk to complete as quickly as possible, type

`Chkdsk D: /f /c /i`

ChkDsk Syntax

The command-line syntax for ChkDsk is

`Chkdsk [volume[[path] filename]] [/f] [/v] [/r] [/x] [/i] [/c] [/b] [/l[:size]]`

Table D-4 lists all ChkDsk command-line parameters. Unless otherwise noted, parameters apply to any file system type.

TABLE D-4 ChkDsk Parameters

PARAMETER	DESCRIPTION

volume	Specifies the volume that you want ChkDsk to check. You can specify the volume by using any of the formats in the following examples:
	
	To run ChkDsk on the C volume, specify
	
	`c:`
	
	To run ChkDsk on a mounted volume called data that is mounted on the C volume, specify
	
	`c:\data`
	
	To run ChkDsk on a volume, you can specify the symbolic link name for a volume, such as
	
	`\\?\Volume{109d05a2-6914-11d7-a037-806e6f6e6963}\`
	
	You can determine a symbolic link name for a volume by using the *mountvol* command.

path	FAT/FAT32 only. Specifies the location of a file or set of files within the folder structure of the volume.
filename	FAT/FAT32 only. Specifies the file or set of files to check for `<a ID="wPopUp" HREF="HELP=glossary.hlp TOPIC=gls_fragmentation">fragmentation </a>`. Wildcard characters (* and ?) are allowed.
/f	Fixes errors on the disk. The volume must be locked. If ChkDsk cannot lock the volume, ChkDsk offers to check it the next time the computer restarts.

PARAMETER	DESCRIPTION
/v	On FAT/FAT32: Displays the full path and name of every file on the disk. On NTFS: Displays additional information or cleanup messages, if any.
/r	Locates <a ID="wPopUp" HREF="HELP=glossary.hlp TOPIC=glos_glo_cigj"> bad sectors </a> and recovers readable information (implies /f). If ChkDsk cannot lock the volume, it offers to check it the next time the computer starts.
	Because NTFS also identifies and remaps bad sectors during the course of normal operations, it is usually not necessary to use the /r parameter unless you suspect that a disk has bad sectors.
/x	Forces the volume to dismount first, if necessary. All opened handles to the volume are then invalid (implies /f). This parameter does not work on the boot volume. You must restart the computer to dismount the boot volume.
/i	NTFS only. Performs a less-detailed check of index entries, reducing the amount of time needed to run ChkDsk.
/c	NTFS only. Skips the checking of cycles within the folder structure, reducing the amount of time needed to run ChkDsk.
/l:size	NTFS only. Changes the size of the log file to the specified number of kilobytes. Displays the current size if you do not enter a new size.
	If the system loses power, stops responding, or is restarted unexpectedly, NTFS runs a recovery procedure when Windows restarts. This procedure accesses information stored in this log file. The size of the log file depends on the size of the volume. In most conditions, you do not need to change the size of the log file. However, if the number of changes to the volume is so great that NTFS fills the log before all metadata is written to disk, then NTFS must force the metadata to disk and free the log space. When this condition occurs, you might notice that Windows stops responding for 5 seconds or longer. You can eliminate the performance impact of forcing the metadata to disk by increasing the size of the log file.
/b	NTFS only. Re-evaluates bad clusters on the volume. This is typically not necessary, but it might allow you to reclaim some lost disk space on a hard disk with a large number of bad clusters. However, these clusters might experience problems in the future, decreasing reliability.
/?	Displays information about using ChkDsk.

How to Use the Graphical ChkDsk Interface

In addition to using the command-line version of ChkDsk, you can run ChkDsk from My Computer or Windows Explorer by following these steps:

1. Click Start and then click Computer.

2. Right-click the volume you want to check and then click Properties.

3. Click the Tools tab and then click Check Now.

4. Do one of the following:

   - To run ChkDsk in read-only mode, clear all check boxes and then click Start.

   - To repair errors without scanning the volume for bad sectors, select the Automatically Fix File System Errors check box and then click Start.

   - To repair errors, locate bad sectors, and recover readable information, select both the Automatically Fix File System Errors and Scan For And Attempt Recovery Of Bad Sectors check boxes and then click Start.

ChkDsk will run immediately if the volume is not in use and then display the results in a dialog box. If the volume is in use, ChkDsk will request that you schedule a disk check for the next time the computer is restarted.

How to Determine Whether ChkDsk Is Scheduled to Run

Windows might also configure ChkDsk to run automatically at startup if it detects problems with a volume. Volumes that Windows determines need to be checked are considered dirty. To determine whether a volume is considered dirty, run the following command at a command prompt.

```
Chkntfs volume:
```

For example, to determine whether drive C is considered dirty, run the following.

```
Chkntfs C:
```

You can also use the Chkntfs tool to prevent a dirty volume from being checked at startup, which is useful if you want to avoid the time-consuming ChkDsk process and will not be at the computer during startup to bypass ChkDsk. For more information, run the following at a command prompt.

```
Chkntfs /?
```

ChkDsk Process on NTFS Volumes

When you run ChkDsk on NTFS volumes, the ChkDsk process consists of three major stages and two optional stages. ChkDsk displays its progress for each stage with the following messages.

```
Windows is verifying files (stage 1 of 5)...
File verification completed.
CHKDSK is verifying indexes (stage 2 of 5)...
Index verification completed.
CHKDSK is verifying security descriptors (stage 3 of 5)...
Security descriptor verification completed.
CHKDSK is verifying file data (stage 4 of 5)...
File data verification completed.
CHKDSK is verifying free space (stage 5 of 5)...
Free space verification completed.
```

The following list describes each of the ChkDsk stages.

- **Stage 1: ChkDsk verifies each file record segment in the Master File Table**   During stage 1, ChkDsk examines each file record segment in the volume's Master File Table (MFT). A specific file record segment in the MFT uniquely identifies every file and directory on an NTFS volume. The percentage complete that ChkDsk displays during this phase is the percentage of the MFT that has been verified.

   The percentage complete indicator advances relatively smoothly throughout this phase, although some unevenness might occur. For example, file record segments that are not in use require less time to process than do those that are in use, and larger security descriptors take more time to process than do smaller ones. Overall, the percentage complete indicator is a fairly accurate representation of the actual time required for that phase.

- **Stage 2: ChkDsk checks the directories in the volume**   During stage 2, ChkDsk examines each of the indexes (directories) on the volume for internal consistency and verifies that every file and directory represented by a file record segment in the MFT is referenced by at least one directory. ChkDsk also confirms that every file or subdirectory referenced in each directory actually exists as a valid file record segment in the MFT and checks for circular directory references. ChkDsk then confirms that the timestamps and the file size information associated with files are up to date in the directory listings for those files.

   The percentage complete that ChkDsk displays during this phase is the percentage of the total number of files on the volume that are checked. For volumes with many thousands of files and folders, the time required to complete this stage can be significant.

   The duration of stage 2 varies because the amount of time required to process a directory is closely tied to the number of files or subdirectories listed in that directory. Because of this dependency, the percentage complete indicator might not advance smoothly during stage 2, though the indicator continues to advance even for large directories. Therefore, do not use the percentage complete indicator as a reliable representation of the actual time remaining for this phase.

- **Stage 3: ChkDsk verifies the security descriptors for each volume**   During stage 3, ChkDsk examines each of the security descriptors associated with each file and directory on the volume by verifying that each security descriptor structure is well formed and internally consistent. The percentage complete that ChkDsk displays during this phase is the percentage of the number of files and directories on the volume that are checked.

   The percentage complete indicator advances relatively smoothly throughout this phase, although some unevenness might occur.

- **Stage 4: ChkDsk verifies file data**   During stage 4 (which is optional), ChkDsk verifies all clusters in use. ChkDsk performs stages 4 and 5 if you specify the /r parameter when you run ChkDsk. The /r parameter confirms that the sectors in each cluster are usable. Specifying the /r parameter is usually not necessary, because NTFS identifies and remaps bad sectors during the course of normal operations, but you can use the /r parameter if you suspect the disk has bad sectors.

The percentage complete that ChkDsk displays during stage 4 is based on the percentage of used clusters that are checked. Used clusters typically take longer to check than unused clusters, so stage 4 lasts longer than stage 5 on a volume with equal numbers of used and unused clusters. For a volume with mostly unused clusters, stage 5 takes longer than stage 4.

- **Stage 5: ChkDsk verifies free space** During stage 5 (which is optional), ChkDsk verifies unused clusters. ChkDsk performs stage 5 only if you specify the */r* parameter when you run ChkDsk. The percentage complete that ChkDsk displays during stage 5 is the percentage of unused clusters that are checked.

How to Use the Disk Cleanup Wizard

With Disk Cleanup (Cleanmgr.exe), you can delete unneeded files and compress infrequently accessed files. This tool is primarily useful for resolving problems that might be related to a shortage of disk space. Insufficient free disk space can cause many problems, ranging from Stop errors to file corruption. To increase free space, you can do the following:

- Move files to another volume or archive them to backup media.
- Compress files or disks to reduce the space required to store data.
- Delete unneeded files.

To run Disk Cleanup, follow these steps:

1. Click Start and then click Computer.
2. Right-click the drive you want to clean and then select Properties. On the General tab of the Properties dialog box, click Disk Cleanup.
3. If prompted, click either My Files Only or Files From All Users On This Computer.
4. On the Disk Cleanup tab, select the files to delete and then click OK.

How to Disable Nonvolatile Caching

Windows Vista is the first Windows operating system to support caching hard disk data to a nonvolatile cache on hard disks with the required cache. Windows Vista and Windows 7 can use the cache to improve startup performance, improve the performance of frequently modified system data, and reduce utilization. In rare circumstances, the failing nonvolatile cache might cause problems. To eliminate the possibility that the nonvolatile cache is causing problems, you can disable different cache functionality using the following Group Policy settings (located in Computer Configuration\Administrative Templates\System\ Disk NV Cache):

- **Turn Off Boot And Resume Optimizations** Enable this policy to prevent Windows from using the nonvolatile cache to speed startup times.
- **Turn Off Cache Power Mode** Enable this policy to prevent Windows from putting disks into a nonvolatile cache power-saving mode, which enables the hard disk to spin down while continuing to use the nonvolatile cache.

- **Turn Off Non Volatile Cache Feature**   Enable this policy to completely disable all use of the nonvolatile cache.
- **Turn Off Solid State Mode**   Enable this policy to prevent frequently written files such as the system metadata and registry from being stored in the nonvolatile cache.

How to Troubleshoot Driver Problems

Drivers are software features that Windows uses to communicate with hardware accessories. Windows typically has dozens of drivers active at any given point, allowing it to communicate with your graphics card, hard disks, sound card, USB devices, and other hardware. Without a driver, hardware cannot function properly. Additionally, you might have problems with hardware if a driver is outdated or unreliable.

The following sections describe how to work with drivers to solve hardware problems.

How to Find Updated Drivers

Microsoft or hardware vendors occasionally release updated drivers to improve hardware performance and reliability. Many updates are available directly from Windows Update. To find and download any updates available for a computer, follow these steps:

1. Click Start, click All Programs, and then click Windows Update.
2. If available, click Check For Updates.
3. If Windows Update displays any optional updates, click View Available Updates.
4. Windows displays any driver updates if available. Select the update and then click Install.
5. Windows Update downloads any selected updates, creates a system restore point, and then installs the updates.

Additionally, hardware manufacturers might release updated drivers directly to users before they are available on Windows Update. Check manufacturer Web sites for updated drivers.

How to Use Driver Verifier

Windows 7 (and all versions of Windows since Microsoft Windows 2000) includes the Driver Verifier (Verifier.exe). You can run either graphical or command-line versions of the Driver Verifier. To run a command-line version, open a command prompt and then type **Verifier.exe**. To run the graphical version, click Start, type **Verifier.exe**, and then press Enter.

Driver Verifier is useful for isolating a problematic driver that is causing a computer running Windows to intermittently fail, because you can use the tool to configure Windows to actively test potentially problematic drivers. After driver verification has been configured for a driver,

Windows puts additional stress on the driver during normal operations by simulating conditions that include low memory and verification of I/O. Enabling driver verification for a problematic driver is highly likely to initiate a Stop error that identifies the driver.

To use Driver Verifier Manager to troubleshoot problems that might be related to a driver, enable driver verification for all drivers that might potentially be causing the problems. Restart the system and then wait. Driver verification happens in the background while the system performs normal tasks and might not yield immediate results. If a verified driver returns an inappropriate response, Driver Verifier will initiate a Stop error. If a Stop error has not occurred after several days, the verified drivers might not be the source of the problem you are troubleshooting. After you have completed the troubleshooting process, use Driver Verifier to delete the settings and disable driver verification.

> **NOTE** Use Driver Verifier only on nonproduction systems to identify a problematic driver. Using Driver Verifier greatly increases the likelihood of a Stop error occurring and decreases system performance.

To verify unsigned drivers, follow these steps:

1. Click Start, type **Verifier**, and then press Enter.
2. Click Create Standard Settings and then click Next.
3. Click Automatically Select Unsigned Drivers and then click Next.

   As shown in Figure D-7, Driver Verifier Manager finds unsigned drivers, enables verification of those drivers, and then displays the list of unsigned drivers.

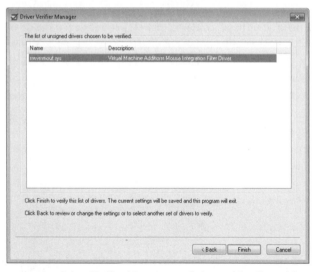

FIGURE D-7 Driver Verifier Manager can help you identify problematic drivers.

4. Click Finish.
5. Click OK and then restart the computer.

To verify all drivers, follow these steps:

1. Click Start, type **Verifier**, and then press Enter.

2. Click Create Standard Settings and then click Next.

3. Click Automatically Select All Drivers Installed On This Computer and then click Finish.

4. Click OK and then restart the computer.

To disable driver verification, follow these steps:

1. Click Start, type **Verifier**, and then press Enter.

2. Click Delete Existing Settings and then click Finish.

3. Click Yes.

4. Click OK and then restart the computer.

How to Use the File Signature Verification

File Signature Verification (Sigverif.exe) detects signed files and allows you to

- View the certificates of signed files to verify that the file has not been tampered with after being certified.

- Search for signed files.

- Search for unsigned files.

NOTE   Unsigned or altered drivers cannot be installed on x64-based versions of Windows.

Driver signing is a multistage process in which device drivers are verified. For a driver to earn this certification, it must pass a series of compatibility tests administered by the Windows Hardware Quality Labs (WHQL). Because of stringent WHQL standards, using signed drivers typically results in a more stable system. When troubleshooting a problem that might be caused by a driver, you might choose to remove unsigned drivers to eliminate the possibility that the unsigned driver is causing the problem. Although most unsigned drivers will not cause problems, they have not been verified by Microsoft and therefore have a higher risk of causing problems than signed drivers. Microsoft digitally signs drivers that pass the WHQL tests, and Windows performs signature detection for device categories such as:

- Keyboards

- Hard disk controllers

- Modems

- Mouse devices

- Multimedia devices

- Network adapters

- Printers

- SCSI adapters
- Smart card readers
- Video adapters

A Microsoft Corporation digital signature indicates that a driver file is an original, unaltered system file that Microsoft has approved for use with Windows. Windows can warn or prevent users from installing unsigned drivers. If a driver is not digitally signed, the user receives a message that requests confirmation to continue. Microsoft digitally signs all drivers included with Windows or distributed by Windows Update. When you download updated drivers from a manufacturer's Web page, always select drivers that are signed by Microsoft.

The following tools are useful for troubleshooting problems caused by unsigned files:

- File Signature Verification
- Device Manager
- Driver Verifier Manager

To identify unsigned drivers, follow these steps:

1. Click Start and then type **Sigverif**. Press Enter.

2. In the File Signature Verification window, click Start.

3. After several minutes, the Signature Verification Results page displays unsigned drivers. Unsigned drivers can be reliable, but they have not undergone the same testing that is required of signed drivers. If you are experiencing reliability problems, you should replace unsigned drivers with signed versions from Microsoft.

4. Click Close to return to the File Signature Verification window.

5. Click Close again.

How to Use Device Manager to View and Change Resource Usage

Installing new hardware or updating drivers can create conflicts, causing devices to become inaccessible. You can use Device Manager to review resources used by these devices to manually identify conflicts. Typically, however, you should let Windows automatically allocate resources. With modern hardware, there is almost never a valid reason to adjust resource usage manually, and you might cause more problems than you resolve.

To use Device Manager (Devmgmt.msc) to view or change system resource usage information, follow these steps:

1. Click Start, right-click Computer, and then click Manage.

2. Click Device Manager and then double-click a device.

3. Click the Resources tab to view the resources used by that device.

4. Click a resource and then clear the Use Automatic Settings check box.

5. Click Change Setting and then specify the resources assigned to the device.

How to Use System Restore

System Restore regularly captures system settings so that you can restore them later if you experience a problem. Using System Restore to return your computer to an earlier state should be one of your last troubleshooting steps, however, because it might cause problems with recently installed applications and hardware.

You can run System Restore from within either the System Recovery tools or from within Windows. To use System Restore from System Recovery tools (which is necessary only if Windows will not start), see Appendix C. To use System Restore from within Windows, follow these steps:

1. Click Start, click All Programs, click Accessories, click System Tools, and then click System Restore. The System Restore Wizard appears.

2. If this is the first time you are running the System Restore Wizard, click Next to accept the default restore point. Then, skip to step 4.

3. If you have run System Restore previously and it did not solve the problem, click Choose A Different Restore Point and then click Next.

4. On the Restore Your Computer To The State It Was In Before The Selected Event page, select the most recent restore point when the computer was functioning correctly. Click Next.

5. On the Confirm Your Restore Point page, click Finish. When prompted, click Yes.

6. System Restore restarts your computer. When the restart has completed, System Restore displays a dialog box to confirm that the restoration was successful. Click Close.

If System Restore does not solve your problem, you can do one of two things:

- **Undo the system restore**   The problem might not be the result of changes to your computer at all, but rather a hardware failure. Therefore, using System Restore might not solve your problem. Because restoring the computer to an earlier state might remove important changes to your system configuration, you should undo any restorations that do not solve your problem. To undo a system restore, simply rerun System Restore using the steps in this section and choose the default settings.

- **Restore an earlier restore point**   Your problem may be caused by recent changes to your computer, but the negative changes occurred before the most recent system restore. Therefore, restoring an earlier restore point might solve your problem. Repeat the steps in this section to restore to an earlier restore point.

How to Troubleshoot USB Problems

The most common way to connect external devices to a computer is USB. USB provides expandability without the complexity of connecting internal devices such as PCI cards. Connecting USB devices is so simple that most users can connect and configure USB devices without help from the Support Center (provided that they have sufficient privileges).

However, users do occasionally experience problems with USB devices. The following sections provide guidance for troubleshooting USB problems.

How to Solve USB Driver and Hardware Problems

If you do experience problems, following these steps might solve them:

1. Restart the computer. Some software might require the computer to be restarted before functioning properly. Additionally, restarting the computer forces Windows to detect the USB hardware again.

2. Install updated driver software, if available. Check Windows Update and the hardware manufacturer's Web site for updates.

3. Uninstall the device's driver and software, disconnect the USB device, restart the computer, and then follow the manufacturer's instructions to reinstall the software. Many USB devices require a driver. Typically, the driver should be installed before connecting the USB device. If you are experiencing problems with a USB device, the most likely cause is a driver problem. For information on how to troubleshoot the driver problem, see the section titled "How to Troubleshoot Driver Problems" earlier in this appendix. External storage devices such as USB flash drives and external hard drives typically do not require a driver, because the required software is built into Windows.

4. Disconnect the USB device and reconnect it to a different USB port. This can cause Windows to detect the device as new and reinstall required drivers. Additionally, this will solve problems related to a specific USB port, such as a failed port or power limitations.

5. Replace the USB cable with a new cable or a different cable that you know works properly.

Understanding USB Limitations

If you installed the USB device's software correctly and you are using the most up-to-date version of the driver, you still might have problems because of USB's physical limitations. Limitations that can cause problems include:

- **Insufficient power** Many USB devices receive power from the USB port. Connecting too many unpowered devices to a USB hub can result in a power shortage, which can cause a USB device to not respond properly. This is particularly common when using an unpowered external USB hub. To quickly determine whether a problem is power related, disconnect other USB devices and connect each USB device directly to the computer one by one. If devices work when connected separately but fail when connected simultaneously, the problem is probably power related. Decrease the number of devices or add a powered USB hub.

- **Excessive length** USB devices can be no more than 5 meters (16 feet) away from the USB hub to which they are connected. Although USB devices will never ship with cables longer than 5 meters (16 feet), some users connect USB extenders to allow longer distances. Depending on the quality of the cable and possible sources of interference, you might experience problems with shorter distances. To determine whether length is the source of problems, remove any USB extenders and connect the USB device directly to the computer.

- **Too many devices**   USB can support up to a maximum of 127 devices connected to a single USB host controller, which is more than enough for the vast majority of client computer scenarios. You can have a maximum of seven layers of USB hubs connected to the computer's USB host controller, and no more than five external hubs.

- **Insufficient bandwidth**   Most USB devices are designed to work within USB bandwidth limitations. However, video cameras in particular might need more bandwidth than USB is capable of providing. If you receive a "Bandwidth Exceeded" message, first try disconnecting other USB devices. If the message continues to appear, attempt to reduce the bandwidth used by the device by lowering the resolution of the camera. For best results with a video camera, connect it to an IEEE 1394 (also known as Firewire or iLink) port.

NOTE   If you see the message, "Hi-speed USB device is plugged into non-hi-speed USB hub," the USB device is USB 2.0, but the USB port is an earlier version. The device will probably work, but it will work slowly. You can improve performance by adding a USB 2.0 port to the computer.

How to Identify USB Problems Using Performance Monitor

If you are concerned that you may have a USB bandwidth or performance problem, you can identify the problem by using the Performance snap-in:

1. If the problem you need to identify occurs when you are actively using a USB device, connect the USB device that you want to troubleshoot and turn it on. If the problem occurs when you first connect the USB device, do not connect the device until after you have begun logging.

2. Click Start, right-click Computer, and then select Manage.

3. Expand System Tools, Performance, Monitoring Tools, and then click Performance Monitor.

4. On the Performance Monitor toolbar, click the green Add button.

5. In the Add Counters dialog box, in the Available Counters group, expand USB. If you are troubleshooting the failure of a USB device, add the following counters for the <All Instances> instance:

   - Iso Packet Errors/Sec

   - Transfer Errors/Sec

   If you are troubleshooting a USB performance problem, add the following counters for the <All Instances> instance:

   - Bulk Bytes/Sec

   - Avg. Bytes/Transfer

6. Click OK to add the counters to Performance Monitor.

Performance Monitor begins collecting data about your USB devices and connections. Attempt to reproduce the problem (for example, by copying a file to a USB hard disk or connecting a video camera). If you are troubleshooting performance problems, right-click the Performance Monitor display and click Clear immediately after you begin using the device to ensure the counters include only data created during your test. The longer you allow the test to run, the more accurate it will be. You should stop Performance Monitor before your test ends.

After reproducing the problem, pause Performance Monitor by clicking the Freeze Display button on the toolbar or by pressing Ctrl+F. Because you added performance counters for all instances, you probably have a large number of counters. To browse individual counters to identify the specific source of your problems, press Ctrl+H to enable highlighting.

Click the first counter in the list. After you select a counter, the graph related to that counter will be shown in bold. Examine the values for that particular counter. If the counter shows an error, make note of the USB controller and device causing the problem. Press the down arrow on your keyboard to select the next counter and continue analyzing USB performance values.

USB errors should not occur under normal circumstances; however, Windows can automatically recover from many USB errors without affecting the user. After you identify the source of the USB problems, follow the steps in the section titled "How to Solve USB Driver and Hardware Problems" earlier in this appendix.

If you are troubleshooting USB performance problems, examine the Bulk Bytes/Sec counter to identify the instance that relates to the device you are using. Then select the counter and make note of the Average value. Theoretically, USB 2.0 can transfer a maximum of 60,000,000 bytes/sec. However, this theoretical maximum will never be realized. More realistically, you might be able to achieve half that value. USB storage devices are often much slower, and performance will vary depending on the performance of the device itself. USB hard disks typically average less than 10,000,000 bytes/sec but can peak over 20,000,000 bytes/sec. Performance of hard disks will also vary depending on the portion of the disk being written to or read from, the size of the files being accessed, and the disk fragmentation.

How to Examine USB Hubs

Connecting a USB device to a computer can include several different layers:

- **A USB host controller, which is connected directly to your computer**   USB host controllers are often built into the computer's motherboard, but you can add them by using an internal adapter or a PC card. If the name of the controller includes the word "Enhanced," the controller supports USB 2.0.

- **A USB root hub, which is connected directly to the USB host controller**   Typically, USB root hubs are built into the same device that contains the USB host controller— your computer's motherboard or an adapter card.

- **Optionally, additional USB hubs that connect to the USB root hub to create additional USB ports**   USB hubs can be external devices that you add, they can be an internal device within a computer, or they can be built into a docking station.

You can use Device Manager to examine the USB controllers and hubs in a computer, determine their power capabilities, and examine the power requirements of the connected devices. This can help you to identify the source of a USB problem. To examine USB devices, follow these steps:

1. Click Start, right-click Computer, and then select Manage.

2. In the Computer Management console, click Device Manager (under System Tools).

3. In the right pane, expand Universal Serial Bus Controllers.

4. Right-click an instance of USB Root Hub (there might be several) and then click Properties.

5. Click the Power tab, as shown in Figure D-8. This tab displays the power capabilities of the hub and the power requirements of every connected device. To determine the requirements of any specific device, disconnect the devices and connect them again one by one.

FIGURE D-8 View USB root hub properties to determine power capabilities and requirements.

How to Troubleshoot Bluetooth Problems

Bluetooth is a wireless protocol for connecting accessories to computers. Bluetooth is commonly used to connect keyboards, mice, handheld devices, mobile phones, and global positioning system (GPS) receivers.

Bluetooth is simple enough to configure that most users can connect Bluetooth devices without help from the Support Center. However, users may occasionally have problems initiating a Bluetooth connection. Other times, a connection that previously worked may stop working for no apparent reason.

If you cannot successfully connect a Bluetooth device, try these troubleshooting steps:

1. Verify that the device is turned on and that the batteries are charged.

2. Place the device within a few feet of your computer (but not too close to your Bluetooth adapter). Additionally, verify that the device is not near other devices that use radio frequencies, such as microwave ovens, cordless phones, remote controls, or 802.11 wireless networks.

3. Verify that the device has Bluetooth enabled and that it is configured as discoverable. For security reasons, many devices are not discoverable by default. For more information, refer to the instructions that came with the device.

4. Install any updates available from Windows Update.

5. Download and install updated software and drivers for your hardware. Hardware manufacturers often release updated software for hardware features after they release the hardware. You can typically download software updates from the manufacturer's Web site.

6. Verify that Windows is configured to accept incoming Bluetooth connections.

7. Verify that security is configured correctly. You might have configured a nondefault passkey for your device. By default, many devices use 0000 or 0001 as a passkey.

8. Remove and reinstall the Bluetooth device.

Troubleshooting Tools

The sections that follow describe free Microsoft tools that can be useful for advanced troubleshooting.

DiskView

DiskView shows how files are physically laid out on your disk and allows you to view where specific files are stored. To run DiskView, save the file to a folder that is allowed to run executable files, such as C:\Program Files\. Specifically, you cannot save it to a Temporary Files folder. Then, right-click DiskView.exe and click Run As Administrator. Click the Volume list and select the volume you want to analyze. Then, click Refresh. DiskView will spend several minutes examining the contents of the disk.

As shown in Figure D-9, the main window displays how files are laid out on a section of your disk. Below the main window is a map that shows your entire disk. The black overlay shows which portion of the disk is displayed in the main window.

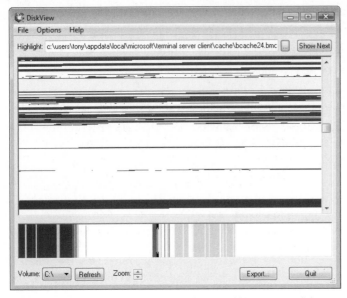

FIGURE D-9 DiskView shows the physical layout of files on your disk.

Click any file in the main window to display the name of the file in the Highlight box. To view a specific file, click the "..." button and select the file. You can download DiskView from *http://technet.microsoft.com/sysinternals/bb896650.aspx*.

Handle

Handle allows you to determine which process has a file or folder open. Handle is useful any time you need to update or delete a file or folder, but access is denied because the object is in use.

To run Handle, save the file to a folder that is allowed to run executable files, such as C:\Program Files\. Specifically, you cannot save it to a Temporary Files folder. Then, open an administrative command prompt and select the folder containing the Handle executable.

To view all open handles, run Handle without any parameters. To view which process has a particular file or folder open, run Handle with a portion of the file's name. For example, if the sample music file Amanda.wma is locked, you can identify which process has it open by running the following command.

Handle amanda

The following output demonstrates that Windows Media Player (Wmplayer.exe) has the file locked.

```
Handle v3.3
Copyright (C) 1997-2007 Mark Russinovich
Sysinternals - www.sysinternals.com

wmplayer.exe        pid: 3236     2C0: C:\Users\Public\Music\Sample Music\Amanda.wma
```

Because the output lists the process name and Process Identifier (PID), you can use Task Manager to kill the process, allowing you to access the locked file. You can download Handle from *http://technet.microsoft.com/en-us/sysinternals/bb896655.aspx*.

Process Monitor

Process Monitor is an extremely powerful troubleshooting tool that monitors file and registry accesses by an application. With Process Monitor, you can see exactly what an application is doing, allowing you to isolate the resources to which an application requires access. If an application fails because a resource is unavailable or access is denied, Process Monitor can allow you to identify the resource. Often, you can use that information to resolve the problem.

To run Process Monitor, save the file to a folder that is allowed to run executable files, such as C:\Program Files\. Specifically, you cannot save it to a Temporary Files folder. Then, right-click ProcMon.exe and click Run As Administrator.

When run, Process Monitor immediately begins capturing events. To stop or restart capturing events, press Ctrl+E or click Capture Events from the File menu.

To use Process Monitor, enable event capturing and then run the application that you want to monitor. After you perform the task that you need to analyze, stop event capturing.

Process Monitor displays all disk and file accesses that occurred while capturing was enabled, as shown in Figure D-10. To view events for just a specific process, right-click any event generated by the process and then click Include. Process Monitor will filter the displayed event so that only events generated by the selected process are visible. You can create more complex filters using the Filter menu.

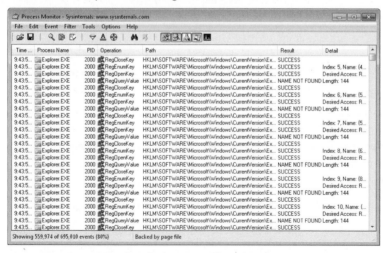

FIGURE D-10 Process Monitor displays every file and registry access by an application.

When examining the captured events, pay close attention to events with a result other than Success. Although non-Success events are common and normal, they are more likely to indicate the cause of an error.

You can download Process Monitor from *http://technet.microsoft.com/en-ca/sysinternals/bb896645.aspx*. For an example of how Process Monitor can be used, read "The Case of the Failed File Copy" at *http://blogs.technet.com/markrussinovich/archive/2007/10/01/2087460.aspx* and "The Case of the Missing AutoPlay" at *http://blogs.technet.com/markrussinovich/archive/2008/01/02/2696753.aspx*.

Summary

Problems can arise when connecting hardware to a computer. Fortunately, Windows 7 provides many different tools for diagnosing the source of the problem. In many cases, Windows 7 also provides the tools required to resolve the problem by updating software or reconfiguring the hardware. If the cause of the problem is failed hardware, the device will need to be repaired or replaced before it can be used with Windows 7.

Troubleshooting Network Issues

> **NOTE** This material was originally published in a slightly different form in *Windows 7 Resource Kit* by Mitch Tulloch, Tony Northrup, Jerry Honeycutt, Ed Wilson, and the Windows 7 Team at Microsoft (Microsoft Press, 2010).

Users often rely on network connectivity to do their jobs, and network failures can dramatically affect an organization's productivity. When failures occur, you need to quickly diagnose the problem. You will often need to escalate the troubleshooting to a network specialist. However, you can diagnose and resolve many common networking problems from a computer running the Windows 7 operating system.

This appendix describes how to use important network troubleshooting tools and provides step-by-step instructions for troubleshooting common network problems.

Tools for Troubleshooting

The following common network problems are listed with the tools most likely to be useful in isolating, diagnosing, and resolving them. These tools are described in the appropriate sections in this appendix unless otherwise noted.

- **Some clients cannot connect to a server** Arp, IPConfig, Nbtstat, Netstat, Network Monitor, Nslookup, PathPing, PortQry, Telnet Client, Windows Network Diagnostics
- **No clients can connect to a server** IPConfig, Network Monitor, PortQry, Telnet Client, Windows Network Diagnostics
- **Clients cannot connect to shared resources** IPConfig, Nbtstat, Net, Nslookup, Network Monitor, PortQry, Telnet Client, Windows Network Diagnostics
- **Clients cannot connect to the network** IPConfig, Windows Network Diagnostics
- **Network performance is poor or unpredictable** Network Monitor, Performance Monitor, PathPing, Resource Monitor, Task Manager

Many factors affect network performance and reliability, including remote connections, hardware configuration (network adapters or the physical network connection), and device drivers. Quite often, network difficulties are related to protocol configuration errors. For example, using incorrect settings in networks based on Transmission Control Protocol/Internet Protocol (TCP/IP) can affect IP addressing, routing, and IP security.

Windows 7 provides a collection of useful troubleshooting tools with which you can monitor and test network performance. Table E-1 lists the most important tools for troubleshooting network problems.

TABLE E-1 Network Troubleshooting Tools

TOOL	PURPOSE	MEMBERSHIP REQUIRED	DESCRIPTION
Arp	Displays and clears the Address Resolution Protocol (ARP) cache, which affects communications with hosts on the local network.	Users or Administrators, depending on the commands used	Operating system, command line
IPConfig	Displays network configuration information about the local computer, requests new dynamically assigned IP addresses, manages the Domain Name System (DNS) client resolver cache, and registers new DNS records.	Users or Administrators, depending on the commands used	Operating system, command line
Nblookup	Tests Windows Internet Naming Service (WINS) name resolution.	Users	Free download, command line
Nbtstat	Displays and clears network basic input/output system (NetBIOS) names.	Users	Operating system, command line
Net	Displays information about shared resources and connects to shared resources.	Users	Operating system, command line
Netsh	Views and modifies network configuration settings.	Users or Administrators, depending on the commands used	Operating system, command line
Netstat	Displays detailed information about open connections.	Users	Operating system, command line
Network Monitor	Captures and displays network traffic sent to and from the local computer.	Administrators	Free download, graphical user interface (GUI)

TOOL	PURPOSE	MEMBERSHIP REQUIRED	DESCRIPTION
Nslookup	Diagnoses DNS name resolution problems.	Users	Operating system, command line
PathPing	Diagnoses network connectivity, routing, and performance problems.	Users	Operating system, command line
Performance Monitor	Displays detailed information about hundreds of network performance counters.	Administrators	Operating system, GUI
PortQry	Identifies the availability of network services from a client that has the tool installed.	Users	Free download, command line
Resource Monitor	Displays information about network utilization.	Administrators	Operating system, GUI
Route	Displays and modifies the local computer's IP routing tables, which is primarily useful when multiple gateways are on the local network.	Users or Administrators, depending on the commands used	Operating system, command line
Task Manager	Quickly determines current network utilization, identifies processes that are using the network, and identifies processes that are consuming processor time.	Users or Administrators, depending on the commands used	Operating system, GUI
Telnet Client	Identifies the availability of network services from a client that does not have PortQry installed. This tool is an optional feature and is not installed by default.	Users	Operating system, command line
Test TCP	Tests TCP connectivity between two computers.	Users	Operating system, command line
Windows Network Diagnostics	Automatically diagnoses some network problems and provides a user-friendly interface for resolving them.	Users	Operating system, GUI

Arp

Arp (Arp.exe) is a useful command-line tool for diagnosing problems in connecting to systems on a LAN where communications between computers do not travel through a router. Arp is also useful for diagnosing problems related to the client communicating with the default gateway. When a client contacts a server on the same subnet, it must address the frame with both the media access control (MAC) address and the IPv4 address. The MAC address is a 48-bit number that uniquely identifies a network adapter.

Arp is the name of a tool; it is also the acronym for the Address Resolution Protocol (ARP), which is used to find the MAC address corresponding to an IPv4 address. When a client communicates with a system on the same LAN, ARP broadcasts a message to all systems on the LAN asking for a response from the system that has the requested IPv4 address. That system responds to the broadcast by sending its MAC address, and ARP stores the MAC address in the ARP cache.

Problems with ARP occur only occasionally. For example, if a system changes its network adapter, clients might store the incorrect MAC address in the ARP cache. You can also manually place MAC addresses into the ARP cache, but if a manually added MAC address is incorrect, communications sent to that IPv4 address will not succeed.

How to Identify a Problem with the ARP Cache

To identify an incorrect entry in the ARP cache, first determine the MAC addresses and IPv4 addresses of hosts or gateways on the LAN with which the computer cannot communicate (as shown in the *ipconfig /all* example in this section). View the ARP cache on the computer that is experiencing the problem. Compare the output with the correct IPv4 address and MAC address combinations. If an entry is incorrect, clear the ARP cache to resolve the problem.

To determine the MAC address of a computer, open a command prompt and run the following command. Then find the Physical Address line in the output for your network adapter (which appears in bold in the code shown here).

```
ipconfig /all
```

```
Ethernet adapter Local Area Connection:

   Connection-specific DNS Suffix  . : contoso.com
   Description . . . . . . . . . . : NVIDIA nForce Networking Controller
   Physical Address. . . . . . . . : 00-13-D3-3B-50-8F
   DHCP Enabled. . . . . . . . . . : Yes
```

After you use IPConfig to determine the correct MAC address, you can view the ARP cache on the problematic computer to determine whether the cached address is incorrect. To view the ARP cache, open a command prompt and run the following command.

arp –a

```
Interface: 192.168.1.132 --- 0xa
  Internet Address      Physical Address      Type
  192.168.1.1           00-11-95-bb-e2-c7     dynamic
  192.168.1.210         00-03-ff-cf-38-2f     dynamic
  192.168.1.241         00-13-02-1e-e6-59     dynamic
  192.168.1.255         ff-ff-ff-ff-ff-ff     static
  224.0.0.22            01-00-5e-00-00-16     static
```

How to Clear the ARP Cache

If you determine that one of the entries in the ARP cache is incorrect, resolve the problem by clearing the ARP cache. Clearing the ARP cache isn't harmful, even if all entries appear correct. Therefore, it's a safe step to take during troubleshooting.

To clear the ARP cache, open a command prompt and run the following command.

arp –d

Alternatively, you can clear the ARP cache by disabling and re-enabling a network adapter or by choosing the automated Repair option. For more information about the Arp tool, run **Arp -?** at a command prompt.

Event Viewer

The Windows Troubleshooting Platform records extremely detailed information in the System Event Log, both when problems occur and when network connections are successful. Additionally, administrators can use Wireless Diagnostics tracing to capture and analyze diagnostic information by using graphical tools.

You can find network diagnostic information in two places in Event Viewer:

- **Windows Logs\System** Look for events with a Source of Diagnostics-Networking. These events detail troubleshooting options that were presented to the user (Event ID 4000), the results of the user's choice (Event ID 5000), and detailed information gathered during the diagnosis process (Event ID 6100). When troubleshooting wireless networks, events also include the name of the wireless network adapter and whether it is a native Windows 7 driver or an older driver; a list of visible wireless networks with the signal strength, channel, and protocol (such as 802.11b or 802.11g) for each; and the list of preferred wireless networks and each network's configuration settings. Event descriptions resemble the following.

```
The Network Diagnostics Framework has completed the repair phase of operation.
The following repair option or work-around was executed:
Helper Class Name: AddressAcquisition
Repair option: Reset the network adapter "Local Area Connection"
Resetting the adapter can sometimes resolve an intermittent problem.
RepairGuid: {07D37F7B-FA5E-4443-BDA7-AB107B29AFB9}
The repair option appears to have successfully fixed the diagnosed problem.
```

- **Applications and Services Logs\Microsoft\Windows\Diagnostics-Networking\ Operational**   This event log details the inner workings of the Windows Troubleshooting Platform and will be useful primarily when escalating problems to Microsoft support.

IPConfig

IPConfig (Ipconfig.exe) is a useful command-line tool for troubleshooting problems with automatic configuration such as Dynamic Host Configuration Protocol (DHCP). You can use IPConfig to display the current IP configuration, identify whether DHCP or Automatic Private IP Addressing (APIPA) is being used, and release and renew an automatic IP configuration.

To view detailed IP configuration information, open a command prompt and run the following command.

```
ipconfig /all
```

This command displays the current IP configuration and produces output similar to the following.

```
Windows IP Configuration

        Host Name . . . . . . . . . . . . : Win7
        Primary Dns Suffix  . . . . . . . : hq.contoso.com
        Node Type . . . . . . . . . . . . : Hybrid
        IP Routing Enabled. . . . . . . . : No
        WINS Proxy Enabled. . . . . . . . : No
        DNS Suffix Search List. . . . . . : hq.contoso.com
                                            contoso.com

Ethernet adapter Local Area Connection:

        Connection-specific DNS Suffix  . : contoso.com
        Description . . . . . . . . . . . : NVIDIA nForce Networking Controller
        Physical Address. . . . . . . . . : 00-13-D3-3B-50-8F
        DHCP Enabled. . . . . . . . . . . : Yes
```

```
   Autoconfiguration Enabled . . . . : Yes
   Link-local IPv6 Address . . . . . : fe80::a54b:d9d7:1a10:c1eb%10(Preferred)
   IPv4 Address. . . . . . . . . . . : 192.168.1.132(Preferred)
   Subnet Mask . . . . . . . . . . . : 255.255.255.0
   Lease Obtained. . . . . . . . . . : Wednesday, September 27, 2009 2:08:58 PM
   Lease Expires . . . . . . . . . . : Friday, September 29, 2009 2:08:56 PM
   Default Gateway . . . . . . . . . : 192.168.1.1
   DHCP Server . . . . . . . . . . . : 192.168.1.1
   DHCPv6 IAID . . . . . . . . . . . : 234886099
   DNS Servers . . . . . . . . . . . : 192.168.1.210
   NetBIOS over Tcpip. . . . . . . . : Enabled
```

To determine whether DHCP addressing was successful, open a command prompt and run the following command.

ipconfig

This command produces output similar to the following.

```
Windows IP Configuration

Ethernet adapter Local Area Connection:

   Connection-specific DNS Suffix  . :
   Autoconfiguration IP Address. . . : 169.254.187.237
   Subnet Mask . . . . . . . . . . . : 255.255.0.0
   Default Gateway . . . . . . . . . :
```

If the IP address shown is in the range from 169.254.0.0 through 169.254.255.255, Windows used APIPA because the operating system was unable to retrieve an IP configuration from a DHCP server upon startup, and there was no alternate configuration. To confirm this, examine the IPConfig output for the DHCP Enabled setting without a DHCP server address.

To release and renew a DHCP-assigned IPv4 address, open a command prompt with administrative credentials and run the following commands.

ipconfig /release
ipconfig /renew

Windows will stop using the current IPv4 address and attempt to contact a DHCP server for a new IPv4 address. If a DHCP server is not available, Windows will either use the alternate configuration or automatically assign an APIPA address in the range of 169.254.0.0 through 169.254.255.255.

To release and renew an automatically assigned IPv6 address, open a command prompt and run the following commands.

ipconfig /release6
ipconfig /renew6

Nblookup

Windows Internet Naming Service (WINS) is a NetBIOS name resolution protocol. WINS performs a function for NetBIOS names similar to the function that DNS performs for host names. For many years, WINS name resolution was the most common way for computers running Windows to identify each other on networks. However, in Active Directory Domain Services (AD DS) domain environments, DNS is used by default, and WINS is primarily used to support older clients and applications.

For environments that still rely on WINS servers, Nblookup is a valuable tool for diagnosing WINS name resolution problems. Nblookup is not included with Windows but is available as a free download from *http://support.microsoft.com/kb/830578*. After saving Nblookup.exe to a computer, you can double-click the file to run it in interactive mode within a command prompt. Alternatively, command-line mode allows you to run it from any command prompt. The following examples demonstrate the use of command-line mode.

To look up a NetBIOS name using the computer's configured WINS server, run the following command.

```
nblookup computer_name
```

To look up a NetBIOS name using a specific WINS server, add the */s server_ip* parameter, as the following example demonstrates.

```
nblookup /s server_ip computer_name
```

For example, to look up the name COMPUTER1 using the WINS server located at 192.168.1.222, you would run the following command.

```
nblookup /s 192.168.1.222 COMPUTER1
```

NetBIOS names actually identify services, not computers. If you want to attempt to resolve a NetBIOS name for a specific service, use the */x* parameter and specify the service's NetBIOS suffix. For example, the following command would look up domain controllers (which use a NetBIOS suffix of 1C) in a domain named DOMAIN.

```
nblookup /x 1C DOMAIN
```

Because WINS is not typically relied on for name resolution by Windows 7 in AD DS environments, troubleshooting WINS name resolution is not discussed further in this appendix. For more information, refer to Chapter 8 of *Windows Server 2008 Networking and Network Access Protection* by Joseph Davies and Tony Northrup (Microsoft Press, 2008).

Nbtstat

Nbtstat (Nbtstat.exe) is a command-line tool for troubleshooting NetBIOS name resolution problems. NetBIOS is a session-layer protocol that formed the foundation of Microsoft network applications for several years. NetBIOS applications identify services on the network by using 16-character NetBIOS names. Each computer on a network might have several different NetBIOS names to identify NetBIOS services on that system.

Today, NetBIOS is implemented on TCP/IP networks by using NetBIOS over TCP/IP (NetBT). NetBT includes its own form of name resolution to resolve NetBIOS names to IP addresses. Names might be resolved by broadcast queries to the local network segment or by queries to a WINS server.

Unfortunately, NetBIOS name resolution is a common source of problems. You can use Nbtstat to reveal the NetBIOS names available on the local computer or remote computers. In troubleshooting scenarios, this helps you to verify that a NetBIOS service is available and its name is being correctly resolved.

To view the NetBIOS name cache, open a command prompt and run the following command.

```
nbtstat -c
```

This command produces output similar to the following.

```
Local Area Connection:
Node IpAddress: [192.168.1.132] Scope Id: []

                NetBIOS Remote Cache Name Table

        Name             Type      Host Address    Life [sec]
    ---------------------------------------------------------------
        WIN71        <00>  UNIQUE        192.168.1.196      602
        WIN72        <00>  UNIQUE        192.168.1.200      585
```

To view the local NetBIOS service names, open a command prompt and run the following command.

```
nbtstat -n
```

This command produces output similar to the following.

```
Local Area Connection:
Node IpAddress: [192.168.1.132] Scope Id: []

                NetBIOS Local Name Table

        Name             Type      Status
    ---------------------------------------------------
        WIN71        <00>  UNIQUE     Registered
        HQ           <00>  GROUP      Registered
        HQ           <1E>  GROUP      Registered
        HQ           <1D>  UNIQUE     Registered
        .._MSBROWSE__.<01>  GROUP      Registered
```

To view the NetBIOS names on a remote system by using the computer name, open a command prompt and run the following command.

`nbtstat –a computername`

For example:

`nbtstat –a win71`

This command produces output similar to the following.

```
Local Area Connection:
Node IpAddress: [192.168.1.132] Scope Id: []

        NetBIOS Remote Machine Name Table

    Name               Type         Status
    ---------------------------------------------
    WIN71        <00>  UNIQUE    Registered
    WIN71        <20>  UNIQUE    Registered
    MSHOME       <00>  GROUP     Registered
    MSHOME       <1E>  GROUP     Registered

  MAC Address = 00-15-C5-08-82-F3
```

Notice that the output is similar to the output when running *nbtstat –n* locally. However, this output also displays the remote computer's MAC address. To view the NetBIOS names on a remote system by using the IP address, open a command prompt and run the following command.

`nbtstat –A IP_Address`

Windows 7 (and all recent versions of Windows) prefers to use DNS host names instead of NetBIOS names. Therefore, if you have an AD DS domain with a DNS server configured, you will rarely need to troubleshoot NetBIOS names. However, Windows might still use NetBIOS names to communicate with computers on the local network and will use NetBIOS names if a host name cannot be resolved with DNS and you have configured a WINS server. To troubleshoot NetBIOS name resolution with WINS servers, use Nblookup, described earlier in this appendix.

Net

Net (Net.exe) is a command-line tool that is useful for changing network configuration settings, starting and stopping services, and viewing shared resources. Although other tools provide friendlier interfaces for much of the functionality provided by Net, Net is very useful for quickly determining the available shared resources on local or remote computers. When you are troubleshooting connections to resources, this tool is useful for verifying that shared resources are available and for verifying the names of those shared resources.

How to View Shared Folders on the Local Computer

Use the *net share* command to view shared resources located on the local computer. If the Server service is started, Net will return a list of shared resources names and locations. To view shared resources, open a command prompt and run the following command.

`net share`

This command produces output similar to the following.

```
Share name      Resource                            Remark

------------------------------------------------------------------------------
C$              C:\                                 Default share
D$              D:\                                 Default share
E$              E:\                                 Default share
print$          C:\Windows\system32\spool\drivers
                                                    Printer Drivers
IPC$                                                Remote IPC
ADMIN$          C:\Windows                          Remote Admin
MyShare         C:\PortQryUI
HP DeskJet 930C932C935C
                LPT1:               Spooled  HP DeskJet 930C/932C/935C
The command completed successfully.
```

How to View Shared Folders on Another Computer

Use the *net view* command to view shared resources located on another computer. To view shared folders on another computer, open a command prompt and run the following command.

`net view` *computer*

For example:

`net view` **d820**

This command produces output similar to the following.

```
Shared resources at d820

Share name    Type   Used as  Comment
------------------------------------------------------------------------------
In Progress   Disk
Printer       Print           Microsoft Office Document Image Writer
publish       Disk
SharedDocs    Disk
Software      Disk
The command completed successfully.
```

You can identify *Computer* by using the computer name, host name, or IP address. If you receive an "Access is denied" error message when attempting to view shares on a remote computer, establish a NetBIOS connection to the remote computer. For example, you could use *Net use* to establish a connection and then use *Net view,* as the following example demonstrates.

```
net use \\win7 /user:username
net view \\win7
```

Netstat

For a network service to receive incoming communications, it must listen for communications on a specific TCP or UDP port. When troubleshooting network problems, you might want to view the ports on which your computer listens for incoming connections to verify that a service is properly configured and that the port number has not changed from the default.

Netstat (Netstat.exe) is a useful command-line tool for identifying network services and the ports they listen on. Listing the ports a computer listens on is useful for verifying that a network service is using the expected port. It is common practice to change the port numbers that services listen on, and Netstat can quickly identify nonstandard listening ports.

To view open ports and active incoming connections, open a command prompt and run the following command.

```
netstat -a -n -o
```

Netstat will display a list of listening ports as well as outgoing connections and the Process Identifiers (PIDs) associated with each listener or connection. The following edited output from Netstat shows the listening ports on a computer running Windows that has Remote Desktop enabled.

```
Active Connections

   Proto  Local Address                       Foreign Address        State         PID
   TCP    0.0.0.0:135                         0.0.0.0:0              LISTENING     884
   TCP    0.0.0.0:3389                        0.0.0.0:0              LISTENING     1512
   TCP    0.0.0.0:49152                       0.0.0.0:0              LISTENING     592
   TCP    192.168.1.132:139                   0.0.0.0:0              LISTENING     4
   TCP    192.168.1.132:3389                  192.168.1.196:1732     ESTABLISHED   1512
   TCP    [::]:135                            [::]:0                 LISTENING     884
   TCP    [::]:445                            [::]:0                 LISTENING     4
   TCP    [::]:2869                           [::]:0                 LISTENING     4
   TCP    [::]:3389                           [::]:0                 LISTENING     1512
   UDP    [fe80::28db:d21:3f57:fe7b%11]:1900    *:*                                1360
   UDP    [fe80::28db:d21:3f57:fe7b%11]:49643   *:*                                1360
   UDP    [fe80::a54b:d9d7:1a10:c1eb%10]:1900   *:*                                1360
   UDP    [fe80::a54b:d9d7:1a10:c1eb%10]:49641  *:*                                1360
```

Notice that the line in bold is listening for incoming connections on TCP port 3389, which Remote Desktop uses. Because the Foreign Address column shows an IPv4 address, you can tell that a user is connected to the computer using Remote Desktop from a computer with the IP address of 192.168.1.196. If you notice that a computer is listening for incoming connections on unexpected ports, you can use the value in the PID column to identify the process. Tools such as the Processes tab in Task Manager can reveal which process is associated with a PID.

> **NOTE** To identify processes by PID in Task Manager, select the Processes tab. On the View menu, click Select Columns. Select the PID (Process Identifier) check box and then click OK.

Alternatively, if you can open a command prompt with elevated privileges, you can use the *–b* parameter to resolve applications associated with active connections. The following example demonstrates that using the *–b* parameter shows the associated process in brackets before each connection.

```
netstat –a –n –o –b
```

```
Active Connections

  Proto  Local Address           Foreign Address         State         PID
  TCP    0.0.0.0:135             0.0.0.0:0               LISTENING     828
  RpcSs
  [svchost.exe]
  TCP    0.0.0.0:3389            0.0.0.0:0               LISTENING     1444
  Dnscache
  [svchost.exe]
  TCP    0.0.0.0:49152           0.0.0.0:0               LISTENING     508
  [wininit.exe]
  TCP    0.0.0.0:49153           0.0.0.0:0               LISTENING     972
  Eventlog
  [svchost.exe]
  TCP    0.0.0.0:49154           0.0.0.0:0               LISTENING     1236
  nsi
  [svchost.exe]
  TCP    0.0.0.0:49155           0.0.0.0:0               LISTENING     1076
  Schedule
  [svchost.exe]
  TCP    0.0.0.0:49156           0.0.0.0:0               LISTENING     564
  [lsass.exe]
  TCP    0.0.0.0:49157           0.0.0.0:0               LISTENING     552
  [services.exe]
  TCP    169.254.166.248:139     0.0.0.0:0               LISTENING     4
```

TCPView, a free download from Microsoft, provides similar functionality with a graphical interface. TCPView is described later in this appendix.

Network Monitor

Network Monitor 3.3, a free download from *http://www.microsoft.com/downloads/*, is the most capable—and complicated—tool for analyzing network communications. Network Monitor is a protocol analyzer (commonly known as a *sniffer*) capable of capturing every byte transferred to and from a computer running Windows 7. An experienced system administrator can use Network Monitor to troubleshoot a wide variety of problems, including:

- Network performance problems.
- TCP connection problems.
- IP protocol stack configuration problems.
- Problems caused by network filtering.
- Application-layer problems with text-based protocols, including Hypertext Transfer Protocol (HTTP), Post Office Protocol (POP), and Simple Mail Transfer Protocol (SMTP).

Network Monitor performs a significant amount of interpretation of captured information by separating the different protocols involved in network communications. Network Monitor can even interpret most common application-layer protocols. For example, when analyzing HTTP traffic, Network Monitor automatically identifies the packet containing the HTTP request and lists the request method, Uniform Resource Locator (URL), referrer, user agent, and other parameters included in the request. This information is extremely useful when troubleshooting compatibility problems with a specific browser.

To analyze network traffic by using Network Monitor, follow these steps:

1. Download and install Network Monitor and then restart the computer to enable the Network Monitor driver for your network adapters.
2. Click Start, click All Programs, click Microsoft Network Monitor 3.3, and then click Microsoft Network Monitor 3.3.
3. Click New Capture.
4. With the New Capture tab selected, click the Select Networks tab and select one or more network adapters.
5. Click Start to begin capturing communications.
6. Switch to the application from which you want to capture the network traffic and then perform the steps to generate the traffic. For example, if you want to capture a request to a Web server, switch to Windows Internet Explorer and enter the Web address. After you have generated the traffic that you want to capture, return to Network Monitor.
7. On the Capture menu in Network Monitor, click Stop.
8. On the Network Conversations page, click the application you want to monitor.
9. In the Frame Summary pane, browse the captured frames. Click a frame to view its contents.

Figure E-1 shows a capture of a TCP connection and an HTTP request created by visiting a Web site with a browser. Because Iexplore.exe is selected in the Network Conversations pane, only frames sent to or from Internet Explorer are displayed. The Frame Summary pane lists the captured packets. The first three frames show the three-way TCP handshake. As you can see from the Frame Details pane, the selected frame shows Internet Explorer requesting / from the Web server. The following frame is the response, which is an HTTP 302 redirection to a different page. Frame 35 is Internet Explorer requesting the page to which it was directed, */en/us/default.aspx*.

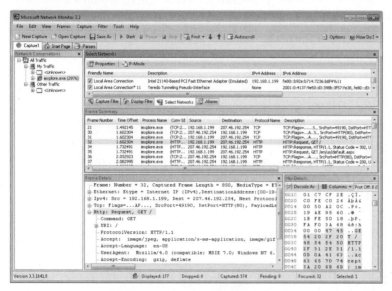

FIGURE E-1 Use Network Monitor to capture and analyze traffic.

MORE INFO For additional information about Network Monitor and to keep up with the latest improvements, read the Network Monitor Team blog at *http://blogs.technet.com /netmon/*.

Nslookup

Nslookup (Nslookup.exe) is the primary tool for isolating DNS name resolution problems when connected to the client experiencing the problems. Nslookup is a command-line tool capable of performing DNS lookups and reporting on the results. Other tools, such as PathPing, are capable of resolving host names to IP addresses and displaying the results, but only Nslookup displays the DNS server used to resolve the request. Additionally, Nslookup displays all the results returned by the DNS server and allows you to choose a specific DNS server rather than using the server automatically chosen by Windows.

Nslookup is the correct tool to use when troubleshooting the following types of problems:

- Clients take several seconds to establish an initial connection.
- Some clients can establish a connection to a server, but other clients experience problems.
- The DNS server is configured correctly, but clients are resolving host names incorrectly.

> **NOTE** The Hosts file, located in the %WinDir%\System32\Drivers\Etc folder, might contain static entries that override DNS lookups for most applications. Nslookup ignores this file, however. If applications resolve a host name differently than Nslookup, verify that the Hosts file does not contain an entry for the host name.

Verifying that the Default DNS Server Resolves Correctly

To verify that a client is able to resolve a host name to the correct IP address, open a command prompt and type the command **nslookup** *hostname.* Nslookup reports the server used to resolve the request and the response from the DNS server. If the client has been configured to use multiple DNS servers, this action might reveal that the client is not issuing requests to the primary DNS server.

To resolve a DNS host name to an IP address, open a command prompt and run the following command.

```
nslookup hostname
```

To resolve an IP address to a DNS host name by performing a reverse DNS lookup, open a command prompt and run the following command.

```
nslookup ipaddress
```

If the DNS server returns multiple IP addresses, Nslookup displays all addresses. Generally, applications use the first IP address returned by the DNS server. Some applications, including Internet Explorer, try each IP address returned by the DNS server until a response is received.

Verifying that a Specific DNS Server Resolves Correctly

One of the most common sources of DNS resolution problems is the caching of an outdated DNS address. Particularly on the Internet, DNS servers might continue to return an outdated IP address several hours after a change has been made to the DNS server containing the record. If some clients are unable to correctly resolve an IP address but other systems resolve it correctly, one or more DNS servers have probably cached the incorrect address. To identify the problematic DNS servers, use Nslookup to manually query each server.

To verify that a specific DNS server is able to resolve a host name to the correct IP address, open a command prompt and run the following command.

```
nslookup hostname server_name_or_address
```

Nslookup will query the specified server only, regardless of the DNS servers configured on the client. If a specific server returns an incorrect IP address, that server is the source of the problem. Generally, this problem will resolve itself after the incorrect entry expires in the DNS server's cache. However, you can also resolve the problem by manually clearing the DNS server's cache.

Verifying Specific Types of Addresses

You can also use Nslookup to verify specific types of addresses, including Mail eXchange (MX) addresses used to identify the mail servers for a domain.

To identify the mail server for a domain, open a command prompt and run the following command.

```
nslookup "-set type=mx" domainname
```

For example, to use Nslookup to view all MX servers listed for the domain microsoft.com using the client's default DNS servers, type the following command.

```
nslookup "-set type=mx" microsoft.com
```

Additionally, you can query a specific DNS server by listing the server name or IP address after the domain name in the following form.

```
nslookup "-set type=type" hostname server_name_or_address
```

The following command uses TCP to query the DNS server.

```
nslookup "-set vc" microsoft.com
```

The "–set vc" parameter configures Nslookup to use a virtual circuit. This test can be especially useful when you are expecting a large number of DNS records in response to a query.

PathPing

Perhaps the most useful tool for isolating connectivity problems from the client, PathPing (PathPing.exe) can help diagnose problems with name resolution, network connectivity, routing, and network performance. For this reason, PathPing should be one of the first tools you use to troubleshoot network problems. PathPing is a command-line tool whose syntax is similar to that of the Tracert and Ping tools.

NOTE Ping's usefulness has become very limited in recent years, and it is no longer an effective tool for determining the state of network services. Ping often reports that it cannot reach an available server because a firewall, such as Windows Firewall, is configured to drop Internet Control Message Protocol (ICMP) requests. If a host is still capable of responding to ICMP requests, Ping might report that the remote host is available even if critical services on the remote host have failed. To determine whether a remote host is responding, use the PortQry support tool instead of Ping.

To test connectivity to an endpoint, open a command prompt and run the following command.

`pathping destination`

The destination can be a host name, a computer name, or an IP address.

PathPing Output

PathPing displays its output in two sections. The first section is immediately displayed and shows a numbered list of all devices that responded between the source and the destination. The first device, numbered 0, is the host on which PathPing is running. PathPing will attempt to look up the name of each device, as shown here.

```
Tracing route to support.go.microsoft.contoso.com [10.46.196.103]over a maximum of
30 hops:  0  contoso-test [192.168.1.207]   1   10.211.240.1   2   10.128.191.245
3   10.128.191.73   4   10.125.39.213   5   gbr1-p70.cb1ma.ip.contoso.com [10.123.40.98]
6   tbr2-p013501.cb1ma.ip.contoso.com [10.122.11.201]
7   tbr2-p012101.cgcil.ip.contoso.com [10.122.10.106]
8   gbr4-p50.st6wa.ip.contoso.com [10.122.2.54]
9   gar1-p370.stwwa.ip.contoso.com [10.123.203.177]
10   10.127.70.6   11   10.46.33.225   12   10.46.36.210
13   10.46.155.17   14   10.46.129.51   15   10.46.196.103
```

To speed up the display of PathPing, use the *-d* command option to keep PathPing from attempting to resolve the name of each intermediate router address.

The second section of the PathPing output begins with the message "Computing statistics for *xxx* seconds." The amount of time for which PathPing computes statistics will vary from a few seconds to a few minutes, depending on the number of devices that PathPing found. During this time, PathPing is querying each of the devices and calculating performance statistics based on whether—and how quickly—each device responds. This section will resemble the following.

```
Computing statistics for 375 seconds...              Source to Here
This Node/LinkHop RTT     Lost/Sent = Pct  Lost/Sent = Pct  Address  0
                                           contoso-test [192.168.1.207]
                          0/ 100 =  0%  |  1   50ms
  1/ 100 =  1%    1/ 100 =  1%  10.211.24.1
                          0/ 100 =  0%  |  2   50ms
  0/ 100 =  0%    0/ 100 =  0%  10.128.19.245
                          0/ 100 =  0%  |  3   50ms
  2/ 100 =  2%    2/ 100 =  2%  10.128.19.73
                          0/ 100 =  0%  |  4   44ms
  0/ 100 =  0%    0/ 100 =  0%  10.12.39.213
                          0/ 100 =  0%  |  5   46ms
  0/ 100 =  0%    0/ 100 =  0%  gbr1-p70.cb1ma.ip.contoso.com [10.12.40.98]
                          0/ 100 =  0%  |  6   40ms
  2/ 100 =  2%    2/ 100 =  2%  tbr2-p013501.cb1ma.ip.contoso.com [10.12.11.201]
                          0/ 100 =  0%  |  7   62ms
  1/ 100 =  1%    1/ 100 =  1%  tbr2-p012101.cgcil.ip.contoso.com [10.12.10.106]
                          0/ 100 =  0%  |  8   107ms
  2/ 100 =  2%    2/ 100 =  2%  gbr4-p50.st6wa.ip.contoso.com [10.12.2.54]
                          0/ 100 =  0%  |  9   111ms
  0/ 100 =  0%    0/ 100 =  0%  gar1-p370.stwwa.ip.contoso.com [10.12.203.177]
                          0/ 100 =  0%  |  10  118ms
  0/ 100 =  0%    0/ 100 =  0%  10.12.70.6
                          0/ 100 =  0%  |  11  ---
100/ 100 =100%  100/ 100 =100%  10.46.33.225
                          0/ 100 =  0%  |  12  ---
100/ 100 =100%  100/ 100 =100%  10.46.36.210
                          0/ 100 =  0%  |  13  123ms
  0/ 100 =  0%    0/ 100 =  0%  10.46.155.17
                          0/ 100 =  0%  |  14  127ms
  0/ 100 =  0%    0/ 100 =  0%  10.46.129.51
                          1/ 100 =  1%  |  15  125ms
  1/ 100 =  1%    0/ 100 =  0%  10.46.196.103 Trace complete.
```

Based on PathPing's output, you can often quickly identify the source of your connectivity problems as a name resolution problem, a routing problem, a performance problem, or a possible connectivity issue. By using PathPing, you can also rule out active connectivity issues at the network layer or below.

Routing Loops

You can use PathPing to detect routing loops. Routing loops—a situation in which traffic is forwarded back to a router that has already forwarded a particular packet—are evident because the output from PathPing will show a set of routers repeated multiple times. For example, the following output indicates a routing loop between the routers at 10.128.191.245, 10.128.191.73, and 10.125.39.213.

```
Tracing route to support.go.microsoft.contoso.com [10.46.196.103]over a maximum of 30
hops:  0  contoso-test [192.168.1.207]    1  10.211.240.1    2  10.128.191.245
3  10.128.191.73    4  10.125.39.213    5  10.128.191.245
6  10.128.191.73    7  10.125.39.213    8  10.128.191.245    9  10.128.191.73
10  10.125.39.213 (...continued...)
```

Routing loops are generally caused by router or routing protocol misconfiguration, and further troubleshooting must be performed on the network routing equipment.

Performance Problems

The RTT column of the Performance section of the PathPing output might identify a performance problem. This column shows round-trip time (RTT) in milliseconds, which is the two-way latency of communications with that particular device. Although all networks will show gradually increasing latency as the hop count increases, a large latency increase from one hop to the next identifies performance problems.

Performance problems might also be evident from a high percentage shown in the Lost/Sent = Pct column. This column measures packet loss. Although packet loss in the single digits generally does not indicate a problem that would cause performance or connectivity problems, packet loss of greater than 30 percent generally indicates that the network node is experiencing problems.

> **NOTE** If a network device shows packet loss of 100 percent but packets are processed at later hops, the network device has been configured to not answer PathPing queries, which does not necessarily indicate a problem.

Possible Connectivity Issues

If the last item shown in the first section of PathPing output resembles the following example, PathPing was unable to communicate directly to the destination.

```
14      *         *         *
```

This might or might not indicate a possible connectivity problem, however. Although the device might be offline or unreachable, it is also likely that the destination—or a network node in the path to the destination—has been configured to drop the ICMP packets that PathPing uses to query devices. ICMP is disabled by default in many modern operating systems. Additionally, administrators often manually disable ICMP on other operating systems as a security measure to make it more difficult for malicious attackers to identify nodes on the network and to reduce the effects of some denial-of-service attacks.

If PathPing is unable to reach the destination, you should attempt to communicate directly with the application by using Telnet, as described in the section titled "Telnet Client" later in this appendix.

No Connectivity Issues

If the PathPing output indicates that PathPing was able to communicate successfully with the destination and the RTT time shown for the destination is less than 1,000 milliseconds, there are probably no name resolution or IP connectivity problems between the source and destination. However, PathPing will not show problems with a specific service or application. For example, PathPing might successfully communicate with a Web server even if the Web server services are stopped. For more information about troubleshooting application issues, see the section titled "How to Troubleshoot Application Connectivity Problems" later in this appendix.

Performance Monitor

You can use Performance Monitor, shown in Figure E-2, to view thousands of real-time counters containing information about your computer or a remote computer. When troubleshooting network performance problems, you can use Performance Monitor to view current bandwidth utilization in a more detailed way than provided by Task Manager or Resource Monitor. Additionally, Performance Monitor provides access to counters measuring retries, errors, and much more.

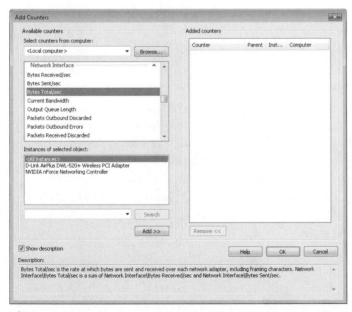

FIGURE E-2 Performance Monitor provides real-time, detailed network statistics.

Performance Monitor provides access to the following categories, which contain counters that might be useful for troubleshooting network problems:

- **.NET CLR Networking**   Examines network statistics for specific Microsoft .NET Framework applications. Use these counters if you are experiencing application-specific networking problems and the application is based on the .NET Framework.

- **BITS Net Utilization**   Provides statistics related to Background Intelligent Transfer Service (BITS), which is used to transfer files in the background. Windows Update, among other applications, uses BITS to transfer files. Use these counters if you think a network performance problem might be related to BITS transfers or if BITS transfers do not perform as expected.

- **Browser**   Provides statistics related to the Computer Browser service, which is used to browse network resources. Use these counters only if you are troubleshooting problems with browsing local networks, specifically for resources such as Windows XP or earlier versions of Windows.

- **ICMP and ICMPv6**   Provide ICMP statistics. ICMP is used by tools such as Ping, Tracert, and PathPing. Use these counters only if you are actively using ICMP to test network connectivity.

- **IPsec AuthIPv4, IPsec AuthIPv6, IPsec Driver, IPsec IKEv4, and IPsec IKEv6**   Provide Internet Protocol security (IPsec) statistics. Use these counters if you are experiencing networking problems and IPsec is enabled in your environment.

- **IPv4 and IPv6**   These categories provide Layer 3 networking information, such as fragmentation statistics. If you need to monitor total network utilization, you should use the Network Interface counters instead.

- **NBT Connection**   Provides information about bytes sent and received for NetBIOS networking, such as file and printer sharing.

- **Network Interface**   The most useful category for troubleshooting, this provides counters for all network traffic sent to and from a single network adapter. These counters are the most reliable way to measure total network utilization. Network Interface counters also provide information about errors.

- **Redirector**   Provides statistics gathered from the Windows redirector, which helps direct traffic to and from different networking features. Interpreting most of these counters requires a detailed understanding of the Windows network stack. However, the Network Errors/sec counter can be useful for diagnosing network problems.

- **Server**   Provides statistics related to sharing files and printers, including bandwidth used and the number of errors. Use these counters when troubleshooting file and printer sharing from the server.

- **TCPv4 and TCPv6**   Provide information about TCP connections. Of particular interest for troubleshooting are the Connection Failures, Connections Active, and Connections Established counters.

- **UDPv4 and UDPv6**   Provide information about UDP communications. Use these counters to determine whether a computer is sending or receiving UDP data, such as DNS requests. Monitor the Datagrams No Port/sec and Datagrams Received Errors counters to determine whether a computer is receiving unwanted UDP traffic.

To access Performance Monitor, follow these steps:

1. Click Start, right-click Computer, and then click Manage.

2. Expand System Tools, expand Performance, and then expand Monitoring Tools. Click Performance Monitor.

3. Add counters to the real-time graph by clicking the green plus sign on the toolbar.

Data Collector Sets

While you can use Performance Monitor to gather a custom set of information, it's generally quicker to start one of the built-in data collector sets. Both the System Diagnostics and System Performance data collector sets gather network performance counters that might reveal the cause of network problems.

To use a data collector set, follow these steps:

1. Click Start, right-click Computer, and then click Manage.

2. Expand Performance, Data Collector Sets, and System.

3. Under System, right-click System Diagnostics, and then click Start.

4. Starting diagnostics tracing causes Windows to collect detailed information about network adapters and overall operating system performance.

5. Now that you have started tracing, you should reproduce the networking problem. The data collector set will gather data for 60 seconds.

6. Windows takes a few seconds to generate a report after you stop tracing. Then, you can view the collected information in a report, as shown in Figure E-3. To view the report, under Performance, expand Reports. Then, expand System Diagnostics and click the latest report.

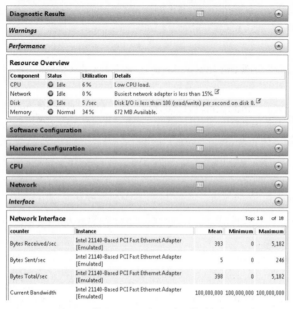

FIGURE E-3 Data collector sets show detailed information.

Depending on the type of report, it can include the following information:

- Computer make and model
- Operating system version
- A list of all services, their current states, and their PIDs
- Network adapter driver information and networking system files and versions
- Processor, disk, network, and memory utilization
- Total bandwidth of each network adapter
- Packets sent and received
- Active TCPv4 and TCPv6 connections

Resource Monitor

Windows 7 provides Resource Monitor so that you can view processor, disk, network, and memory utilization. Open Resource Monitor in one of two primary ways:

- Click Start, All Programs, Accessories, System Tools, and Resource Monitor.
- Open Task Manager, click the Performance tab, and then click Resource Monitor.

In the context of troubleshooting network issues, the Network section is the most interesting section of the Resource Monitor. The Network section displays bytes per minute that each process on your computer is using. With this information, you can identify a process that is transmitting large amounts of data and stop it if it should not be communicating on the network. To identify and terminate a process that is using the network, follow these steps:

1. Open Resource Monitor.

2. Expand the Network section. Click the Total column heading to sort the process list by bandwidth utilization.

3. The topmost process is sending and receiving the most data. Make note of the process name (in the Image column), the PID, and the remote computer (in the Address column). If this is enough information to identify the process, you can close the application now.

4. If the process is SvcHost.exe, you might not be able to identify the specific application generating the network traffic, because it is a Windows feature (or it is using a feature for communications). If it is a different process, open Task Manager.

5. In Task Manager, click the Processes tab, click the View menu, and then click Select Columns.

6. In the Select Process Page Columns dialog box, select the PID check box. Click OK.

7. Click the PID column to sort by process ID. Click the process that corresponds to the PID you identified as generating the network traffic using the Resource Monitor. If the PID does not appear, click Show Processes From All Users.

8. To identify the service, right-click the service and then click Go To Service. To stop the process, click End Process.

In most cases, an application that is sending or transmitting a large amount of data has a legitimate need for that data, and you should not terminate it. However, in some cases, the process may be associated with malware. Verify that the computer has Windows Defender enabled and that Windows Defender is up to date.

Ping

Ping is of limited usefulness today because most new computers drop Ping requests (which use ICMP). Therefore, you might ping a computer that is connected to the network but not receive any response. Additionally, a computer might respond to Ping requests even if a firewall is dropping all other traffic—misleading you into thinking that you had connectivity.

However, Ping is still the best tool to easily monitor network connectivity on an ongoing basis. After using PathPing to identify network hosts that respond to ICMP requests, you can use Ping to constantly submit Ping requests and thereby easily determine whether you currently have connectivity to the host. If you are experiencing intermittent connectivity problems, a Ping loop will indicate whether your connection is active at any given time.

To start a Ping loop, run the following command.

```
ping -t hostname
```

Replies indicate that the packet was sent successfully, while Request Timed Out messages indicate that the computer did not receive a response from the remote host. The following example indicates how to monitor the connection to a host at the IP address 192.168.1.1.

```
ping -t 192.168.1.1
```

```
Pinging 192.168.1.1 with 32 bytes of data:

Reply from 192.168.1.1: bytes=32 time=1ms TTL=64
Reply from 192.168.1.1: bytes=32 time<1ms TTL=64
Reply from 192.168.1.1: bytes=32 time<1ms TTL=64
Reply from 192.168.1.1: bytes=32 time<1ms TTL=64
Request timed out.
Request timed out.
Request timed out.
Request timed out.
Request timed out.
Reply from 192.168.1.1: bytes=32 time<1ms TTL=64
Request timed out.
Request timed out.
Reply from 192.168.1.1: bytes=32 time<1ms TTL=64
```

Note that Ping loops provide only an approximate estimation of connectivity. Ping packets will occasionally be dropped even if connectivity is constant. Additionally, because Ping sends requests sooner if a reply is received than if the reply times out, you cannot use the ratio of replies to time-out errors as a useful indication of network uptime.

Finding Blackhole Routers

Tim Rains, Program Manager; Windows Networking

Ping can be useful in determining whether upstream routers are black hole routers, which drop datagrams larger than a specific size. For more information, see *http://support.microsoft.com/kb/314825*.

If you want to use Ping from a Windows PowerShell script, use the Test-Connection cmdlet. The functionality is almost identical to Ping, with the added benefit of being able to specify the *–Source* parameter to initiate the ICMP requests from a remote computer.

PortQry

Directly query critical services on the remote host to determine whether it is available and accessible. You can use two troubleshooting tools to query services on a remote host: PortQry (Portqry.exe) and Telnet Client. PortQry is more flexible and simpler to use than Telnet Client; however, because it is not included with Windows (but can be downloaded from the Microsoft Web site), it might not be installed on all systems. Use Telnet Client to query remote services only when PortQry is not available.

PortQry version 1.22 is a TCP/IP connectivity testing utility that is included with the Windows Server 2003 Support Tools. For information on how to download these tools, see *http://support.microsoft.com/kb/892777*. PortqryV2.exe is a new version of PortQry that includes all the features and functionality of the earlier version and has new features and functionality. For information concerning PortqryV2.exe and how to download it, see *http://support.microsoft.com/kb/832919*. The following examples can be performed using either version.

> **NOTE** Information concerning PortQryUI, a user Interface for the original Portqry.exe command-line port scanner, can be found at *http://support.microsoft.com/kb/310099*, which includes a link for downloading this tool.

Identifying the TCP Port for a Service

A single computer can host many network services. These services distinguish their traffic from each other by using port numbers. When testing connectivity to an application by using Telnet, you must provide Telnet with the port number that the destination application is using.

> **NOTE** Most services allow the administrator to specify a port number other than the default. If the service does not respond to the default port number, verify that the service has not been configured to use a different port number. You can run Netstat on the server to list listening ports. For more information, see the section titled "Netstat" earlier in this appendix.

For a list of common port numbers, see the section titled "How to Troubleshoot Network Connectivity Problems" later in this appendix.

Testing Service Connectivity

After you have identified the port number for the service, you can use PortQry to test connectivity to that service. To test connectivity to a service, open a command prompt and run the following command.

```
portqry -n destination -e portnumber
```

For example, to test HTTP connectivity to *www.microsoft.com*, type the following command at the command line.

```
portqry -n www.microsoft.com -e 80
```

This command produces output similar to the following.

```
Querying target system called:
www.microsoft.com
Attempting to resolve name to IP address...
Name resolved to 10.209.68.190
TCP port 80 (http service): LISTENING
```

The destination might be a host name, computer name, or IP address. If the response includes LISTENING, the host responded on the specified port number. If the response includes NOT LISTENING or FILTERED, the service you are testing is not available.

> **NOTE** Netcat is a great non-Microsoft tool for testing connectivity to specific ports or determining on which ports a computer is listening for connections. Netcat is an open-source tool freely available from *http://netcat.sourceforge.net/*.

Determining Available Remote Management Protocols

When troubleshooting a computer remotely, you might need to determine which remote management protocols are available. PortQry can test the default port numbers for common remote management protocols and identify which protocols are available.

To determine which management protocols are available on a remote host, open a command prompt and run the following command.

```
portqry -n destination -o 32,139,445,3389
```

This command queries the remote host to determine whether Telnet Server, NetBIOS, Common Internet File System (CIFS), and the Remote Desktop are available.

Specifying the Source Port

Tim Rains, Program Manager; Windows Networking

The Portqry *-sp* option allows you to specify which source port you want to use for the connectivity test. Use this parameter to specify the initial source port to use when you connect to the specified TCP and UDP ports on the destination computer. This functionality is useful to help you test firewall or router rules that filter ports based on their source ports.

The following PortQry output indicates that the remote system will respond to NetBIOS, CIFS, and Remote Desktop requests, but not to Telnet requests.

```
Querying target system called:
192.168.1.200
Attempting to resolve IP address to a name...
IP address resolved to CONTOSO-SERVER
TCP port 32 (unknown service): NOT LISTENING
TCP port 139 (netbios-ssn service): LISTENING
TCP port 445 (microsoft-ds service): LISTENING
TCP port 3389 (unknown service): LISTENING
```

Route

All IP-based networked devices, including computers, have *routing tables*. Routing tables describe the local network, remote networks, and gateways that you can use to forward traffic between networks. In networks with a single gateway, the routing table is very simple and indicates that local traffic should be sent directly to the local network, whereas traffic for any network other than the LAN should be sent through the gateway.

However, some networks have multiple gateways. For example, you might have two gateways on a LAN: one that leads to the Internet and another that leads to a private network. In that case, the local computer's routing table must describe that specific networks are available through the internal gateway and all other networks are available through the Internet gateway.

NOTE A client computer is most often configured with multiple routes in remote access scenarios. Specifically, if a client is using a virtual private network (VPN) connection, there might be separate routes for the networks accessible through the VPN connection, and all other traffic will be sent directly to the Internet.

Typically, computers running Windows will be automatically configured with the correct routing table. For example, network administrators will configure the DHCP server to assign a default gateway. When making a VPN connection, the VPN server will provide routing information that Windows will use to update the routing tables. Therefore, you rarely need to use the Route command to view or update the routing table.

However, if you are having connectivity problems and you are connected to a remote network or if your local network has multiple gateways, you can use Route to diagnose routing problems and even test different routing configurations. To view the local computer's IPv4 and IPv6 routing tables, open a command prompt and run the following command.

```
C:\>route print
```

This command produces output similar to the following.

```
===========================================================================
Interface List
 11 ...00 80 c8 ac 0d 9e ...... D-Link AirPlus DWL-520+ Wireless PCI Adapter
  8 ...00 13 d3 3b 50 8f ...... NVIDIA nForce Networking Controller
  1 ......................... Software Loopback Interface 1
  9 ...02 00 54 55 4e 01 ...... Teredo Tunneling Pseudo-Interface
 12 ...00 00 00 00 00 00 00 e0  isatap.{B1A1A1DE-A1E5-4ED6-B597-7667C85F8999}
 13 ...00 00 00 00 00 00 00 e0  isatap.hsd1.nh.comcast.net.
===========================================================================

IPv4 Route Table
===========================================================================
Active Routes:
```

Network Destination	Netmask	Gateway	Interface	Metric
0.0.0.0	0.0.0.0	192.168.1.1	192.168.1.132	20
127.0.0.0	255.0.0.0	On-link	127.0.0.1	306
127.0.0.1	255.255.255.255	On-link	127.0.0.1	306
127.255.255.255	255.255.255.255	On-link	127.0.0.1	306
169.254.0.0	255.255.0.0	On-link	169.254.166.248	286
169.254.166.248	255.255.255.255	On-link	169.254.166.248	286
169.254.255.255	255.255.255.255	On-link	169.254.166.248	286
192.168.1.0	255.255.255.0	On-link	192.168.1.132	276
192.168.1.132	255.255.255.255	On-link	192.168.1.132	276
192.168.1.255	255.255.255.255	On-link	192.168.1.132	276
224.0.0.0	240.0.0.0	On-link	127.0.0.1	306
224.0.0.0	240.0.0.0	On-link	192.168.1.132	276
224.0.0.0	240.0.0.0	On-link	169.254.166.248	286
255.255.255.255	255.255.255.255	On-link	127.0.0.1	306
255.255.255.255	255.255.255.255	On-link	192.168.1.132	276
255.255.255.255	255.255.255.255	On-link	169.254.166.248	286

```
===========================================================================
Persistent Routes:
  None

IPv6 Route Table
===========================================================================
Active Routes:
```

If	Metric	Network Destination	Gateway
9	18	::/0	On-link
1	306	::1/128	On-link
9	18	2001::/32	On-link
9	266	2001:0:4136:e37a:14fc:39dc:3f57:fe7b/128	
			On-link
8	276	fe80::/64	On-link

```
 11    286 fe80::/64                    On-link
  9    266 fe80::/64                    On-link
 12    296 fe80::5efe:169.254.166.248/128
                                        On-link
 13    281 fe80::5efe:192.168.1.132/128
                                        On-link
  9    266 fe80::14fc:39dc:3f57:fe7b/128
                                        On-link
  8    276 fe80::41e9:c80b:416d:717c/128
                                        On-link
 11    286 fe80::c038:ad1f:3cc6:a6f8/128
                                        On-link
  1    306 ff00::/8                     On-link
  9    266 ff00::/8                     On-link
  8    276 ff00::/8                     On-link
 11    286 ff00::/8                     On-link
===========================================================================
Persistent Routes:
  None
```

Fully interpreting the routing configuration requires a detailed understanding of IP networking; however, you can quickly identify default routes for traffic being sent to your default gateway by locating the Active Route with a Network Destination and Network Mask of 0.0.0.0 for IPv4 routes and an Active Route with the prefix *::/0* for IPv6 routes. Other Active Routes with a Gateway assigned cause traffic for the specific Network Destination and Network Mask to be sent through that gateway, with a preference for the route with the lowest metric.

If you must manually update the IPv4 routing table (you should typically make changes to the network infrastructure that assigned the routes to the client), you can use the *route add, route change,* and *route delete* commands. For more information, type **route –?** at a command prompt.

To update the IPv6 routing table, you must use the *netsh interface ipv6 add|set|delete route* commands.

Task Manager

Task Manager (Taskmgr.exe) is a GUI tool that you can use to view or end a process or an unresponsive application. You can also use Task Manager to gather other information, such as CPU statistics. To start Task Manager, click Start, type **Taskmgr**, and then press Enter. Alternatively, you can right-click the taskbar and then click Task Manager.

The Windows Task Manager window contains six tabs: Applications, Processes, Services, Performance, Networking, and Users.

- The Applications and Processes tabs provide a list of applications or processes that are currently active on your system. These lists are valuable because active tasks do not always display a user interface, which can make it difficult to detect activity. Task Manager displays active processes and lets you end most items by clicking End Process. You cannot end some processes immediately; you might need to use the Services snap-in or Taskkill to end them. You can also customize Task Manager to increase or decrease the level of detail shown on the Processes tab.

- The Services tab displays running services and their PID. If you determine that a specific PID is using network resources and you find the PID on this tab, you know that a service is causing the network utilization. To stop a service, right-click it and then click Stop Service, as shown in Figure E-4.

FIGURE E-4 Use the Services tab to identify services by PID and stop them.

- The Performance tab graphically displays process and memory utilization. Viewing this tab quickly reveals the total utilization of all programs and services on the computer. The Performance tab also shows key performance counters including the number of processes, the number of threads, and the total physical memory installed in the system.

- The Networking tab shows the utilization of all network interfaces.

- With the Users tab, you can disconnect and log off active users.

To view detailed information about processes, follow these steps:

1. Start Task Manager and then click the Processes tab.

2. Optionally, click Show Processes From All Users.

3. On the View menu, click Select Columns.

4. Select or clear the columns that you want to add to, or remove from, the Processes tab.

5. Click OK to return to Task Manager.

To identify the cause of high processor utilization, follow these steps:

1. Start Task Manager and then click the Performance tab.

2. Click the View menu and then select Show Kernel Times (if it is not already selected).

3. Examine the CPU Usage History graph. If the graph shows values close to 100 percent, one process or multiple processes are consuming the bulk of the computer's processing capability. The red line shows the percentage of the processor consumed by the kernel, which includes drivers. If the bulk of the processing time is consumed by the kernel, verify that you are using signed drivers and have the latest version of all drivers installed. If the kernel is not responsible for the majority of the processor usage, continue following these steps to identify the process.

4. Click the Processes tab.

5. Click the CPU column heading twice to sort the processes by processor utilization with the highest utilization at the top of the list.

The process or processes consuming the processor will show high CPU utilization values. When the processor is not being used heavily, the System Idle Process shows high CPU utilization.

To find the PID of an application, follow these steps:

1. Start Task Manager and verify that the Process ID (PID) column is displayed on the Processes tab. If it is not displayed, open the View menu, click Select Columns, and then select PID. Click OK.

2. Click the Applications tab.

3. Right-click the application and then click Go To Process.

Task Manager will display the Processes tab. The process associated with the application will be highlighted. The PID is shown in the PID column.

To stop a process, follow these steps:

1. Start Task Manager and then click the Processes tab.

2. Right-click the process you want to stop and then click End Process.

Task Manager will attempt to end the process. If Task Manager fails, use Taskkill.

To identify the network utilization, start Task Manager and then click the Networking tab. Task Manager shows the utilization of each network adapter. The percentage of utilization is measured in relation to the reported Link Speed of the adapter. In most cases, network adapters are not capable of 100 percent utilization; peak utilization is approximately 60 percent to 70 percent.

TCPView

TCPView, shown in Figure E-5, monitors both incoming and outgoing connections, as well as listening applications, in real time. You can use TCPView to identify exactly which servers a client connects to, including the port numbers, or identify the clients connecting to a server.

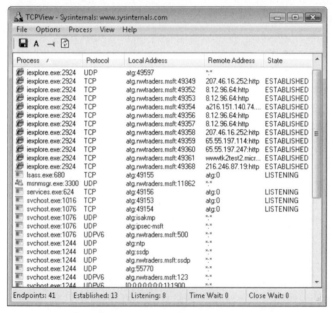

FIGURE E-5 TCPView allows you to monitor network connections in real time.

To download TCPView, visit *http://technet.microsoft.com/en-us/sysinternals/bb897437.aspx*. You do not need to install TCPView; simply copy the executable file to a folder that allows applications to be run (such as C:\Program Files\) and then double-click Tcpview.exe. TCPView also includes Tcpvcon.exe, a command-line tool that provides similar functionality.

Telnet Client

Although it is not primarily a troubleshooting tool, Telnet Client is extremely useful for determining whether TCP-based network services are reachable from a client. Most commonly used network services are TCP based, including Web services, mail services, and file transfer services. Telnet Client is not useful for troubleshooting UDP-based network services such as DNS and many streaming media communications.

Telnet Client is not installed by default in Windows 7. To install it, run the following command from a command prompt with administrative privileges.

```
start /w pkgmgr /iu:"TelnetClient"
```

Alternatively, you can install it by following these steps:

1. Click Start and then click Control Panel.
2. Click Programs.
3. Click Turn Windows Features On Or Off.
4. In the Windows Features dialog box, select the Telnet Client check box. Click OK.

Telnet Client is useful only for determining whether a service is reachable, and it will not provide information that you can use for troubleshooting name resolution, network performance, or network connectivity problems. Use Telnet Client only after you have used Ping to eliminate the possibility of name resolution problems. For more information about Ping, see the section titled "Ping" earlier in this appendix.

Testing Service Connectivity

After you have identified the port number for the service, you can use Telnet Client to test connectivity to that service. To test connectivity to a service, open a command prompt and run the following command.

```
telnet destination portnumber
```

For example, to test HTTP connectivity to *www.microsoft.com*, type the following command at the command line.

```
telnet www.microsoft.com 80
```

The destination might be a host name, computer name, or IP address. The response you receive will indicate whether a connection was established. If you receive the message "Could not open connection to the host," the host did not respond to the request for a connection on the port number you specified, and the service you are testing is unreachable.

If you receive any other response, including all text disappearing from the command window, the connection was successfully established. This eliminates the possibility that the problem you are troubleshooting is caused by a connectivity issue between the client and the server. Depending on the service you are testing, Telnet Client can be automatically disconnected, or the session might remain open. Either circumstance indicates a successful connection. If the Telnet Client session remains open, you should disconnect Telnet Client to close the connection.

To disconnect Telnet Client, follow these steps:

1. Press Ctrl+].
2. When the Microsoft Telnet> prompt appears, type **quit**.

Test TCP

With Test TCP, you can both initiate TCP connections and listen for TCP connections. You can also use the Test TCP tool for UDP traffic. With Test TCP, you can configure a computer to listen on a specific TCP or UDP port without having to install the application or service on the computer. This allows you to test network connectivity for specific traffic before the services are in place.

Test TCP (Ttcp.exe) is a tool that you can use to listen for and send TCP segment data or UDP messages between two nodes. Ttcp.exe is provided with Windows Server 2003 in the Valueadd\Msft\Net\Tools folder of the Windows Server 2003 or Windows XP Service Pack 2 (SP2) product CD-ROM.

Test TCP differs from Port Query in the following ways:

- With Test TCP, you can configure a computer to listen on a specific TCP or UDP port without having to install the application or service on the computer. This allows you to test network connectivity for specific traffic before the services are in place. For example, you could use Test TCP to test for domain replication traffic to a computer before you make the computer a domain controller.

- Test TCP also supports IPv6 traffic.

When you are using a TCP port, the following code shows the basic syntax for Ttcp.exe on the listening node (the receiver):

```
ttcp -r -pPort
```

When using a UDP port, use the following syntax.

```
ttcp -r -pPort -u
```

After starting Test TCP in receive mode, the tool will wait indefinitely for a transmission before returning you to the command prompt. The first time you use Test TCP to listen from a computer running Windows 7, you might be prompted to create a Windows Firewall exception. You must create the exception for Test TCP to work. If you choose to unblock the application, Windows Firewall will allow all traffic for that computer on the specified port in the future. Therefore, you will not need to create a new exception for that network type, even if you listen on a different port. In Windows Firewall, the exception is named Protocol Independent Perf Test Command.

When you are using a TCP port, the following code shows the basic syntax for Ttcp.exe on the sending node (the transmitter):

```
ttcp -t -pPort hostname
```

When using a UDP port, use the following syntax.

```
ttcp -t -pPort -u hostname
```

If the two computers are able to communicate, the transmitting computer will display output such as the following.

```
ttcp-t: Win7 -> 192.168.1.132
ttcp-t: local 192.168.1.196 -> remote 192.168.1.132
ttcp-t: buflen=8192, nbuf=2048, align=16384/+0, port=81  tcp  -> Win7
ttcp-t: done sending, nbuf = -1
ttcp-t: 16777216 bytes in 1423 real milliseconds = 11513 KB/sec
ttcp-t: 2048 I/O calls, msec/call = 0, calls/sec = 1439, bytes/call = 8192
```

Meanwhile, the receiving computer will display output similar to the following.

```
ttcp-r: local 192.168.1.132 <- remote 192.168.1.196
ttcp-r: buflen=8192, nbuf=2048, align=16384/+0, port=81  tcp
ttcp-r: 16777216 bytes in 1416 real milliseconds = 11570 KB/sec
ttcp-r: 3492 I/O calls, msec/call = 0, calls/sec = 2466, bytes/call = 4804
```

You can use Test TCP to connect to any computer listening for incoming TCP connections, even if that computer is not running Test TCP. However, to accurately test UDP connectivity, Test TCP must be running on both the receiver and transmitter. For example, to attempt a connection to *www.microsoft.com* on TCP port 80, you would run the following command.

ttcp -t -p80 www.microsoft.com

```
ttcp-t: local 192.168.1.196 -> remote 10.46.20.60
ttcp-t: buflen=8192, nbuf=2048, align=16384/+0, port=80  tcp  -> www.microsoft.com
send(to) failed: 10053
ttcp-t: done sending, nbuf = 2037
ttcp-t: 81920 bytes in 16488 real milliseconds = 4 KB/sec
ttcp-t: 11 I/O calls, msec/call = 1498, calls/sec = 0, bytes/call = 7447
```

In this example, the TCP connection was successful, even though the output includes the line "send(to) failed." If the connection was unsuccessful, the output would have included the phrase "connection refused." Alternatively, some servers will simply not respond to invalid communications, which will cause the Test TCP transmitter to pause indefinitely while it awaits a response from the server. To cancel Test TCP, press Ctrl+C.

Each instance of Test TCP can listen on or send to only a single port. However, you can run it in multiple command prompts to listen or send on multiple ports. For additional command-line options, type **Ttcp** at the command prompt.

Windows Network Diagnostics

Troubleshooting network problems is complicated, especially for users. Many users discover network problems when they attempt to visit a Web page with Internet Explorer. If the Web page is not available, Internet Explorer returns the message "Internet Explorer cannot display the webpage." The problem could be any one of the following, however:

- The user mistyped the address of the Web page.
- The Web server is not available.
- The user's Internet connection is not available.
- The user's LAN is not available.
- The user's network adapter is misconfigured.
- The user's network adapter has failed.

The cause of the problem is important for the user to understand. For example, if the Web server is not available, the user does not need to take any action—the user should simply wait for the Web server to become available. If the Internet connection has failed, the user might need to call her Internet service provider (ISP) to troubleshoot the problem. If the user's network adapter has failed, she should attempt to reset it and contact her computer manufacturer's technical support for additional assistance.

Windows Network Diagnostics and the underlying Windows Troubleshooting Platform assist users in diagnosing and, when possible, resolving network connectivity issues. When Windows 7 detects network problems, it will prompt the user to diagnose them. For example, Internet Explorer displays a link to start Windows Network Diagnostics if a Web server is unavailable, and the Network And Sharing Center will display a diagnostic link if a network is unavailable.

Applications might prompt users to open Windows Network Diagnostics in response to connectivity problems. To start Windows Network Diagnostics manually, open Network And Sharing Center, click Troubleshoot Problems, and follow the prompts that appear. Unlike many of the tools described in this appendix, Windows Network Diagnostics is designed to be useful without a deep understanding of network technologies.

The Process of Troubleshooting Network Problems

To most users, the term *connectivity problems* describes a wide range of problems, including a failed network connection, an application that cannot connect because of firewall filtering, and serious performance problems. Therefore, the first step in troubleshooting connectivity problems is to identify the scope of the connectivity problem.

To identify the source of a connectivity problem, follow these steps and answer the questions until you are directed to a different section:

1. Open the Network And Sharing Center by clicking the network icon in the system tray and then clicking Open Network And Sharing Center. At the bottom of the page, click Troubleshoot Problems and follow the prompts that appear. If Windows

Network Diagnostics does not identify or resolve the problem, please choose to send the information to Microsoft to help improve Windows Network Diagnostics. Then, continue following these steps.

2. Are you attempting to connect to a wireless network, but your connection attempt is rejected? If so, see the section titled "How to Troubleshoot Wireless Networks" later in this appendix.

3. Are you attempting to connect to a remote network using a VPN connection, but your connection attempt is rejected? If so, read "Troubleshooting Common VPN Related Errors" at *http://blogs.technet.com/rrasblog/archive/2009/08/12/troubleshooting-common-vpn-related-errors.aspx.*

4. Can you occasionally access the network resource, but it is unreliable or slow? If so, see the section titled "How to Troubleshoot Performance Problems and Intermittent Connectivity Issues" later in this appendix.

5. Can you access other network resources using different applications, such as e-mail or different Web sites? If not, you have a network connectivity problem or a name resolution problem. If you can contact servers using the IP address instead of the host name, see the section titled "How to Troubleshoot Name Resolution Problems" later in this appendix. If servers are not accessible when you specify an IP address or if you do not know an IP address, see the next section, "How to Troubleshoot Network Connectivity Problems."

6. Are you trying to join a domain or log on to your computer using a domain account but are receiving an error message that the domain controller is unavailable? If so, see the section titled "How to Troubleshoot Joining or Logging on to a Domain" later in this appendix.

7. Open a command prompt and run the command **Nslookup *servername.*** If Nslookup does not display an answer similar to the following, you have a name resolution problem. See the section titled "How to Troubleshoot Name Resolution Problems" later in this appendix for information on solving these problems.

```
C:\>nslookup contoso.com

Non-authoritative answer:
Name:    contoso.com
Addresses:  10.46.232.182, 10.46.130.117
```

8. Are you trying to connect to a shared folder? If so, see the section titled "How to Troubleshoot File and Printer Sharing" later in this appendix.

9. If other network applications work and name resolution succeeds, you might have a firewall problem. See the section titled "How to Troubleshoot Application Connectivity Problems" later in this appendix.

How to Troubleshoot Network Connectivity Problems

If you have a network connectivity problem, you will be unable to reach any network resource that can normally be accessed using the failed network. For example, if your Internet connection has failed, you will be unable to access Internet resources, but you might still be able to access resources on your LAN. If your LAN fails, however, nothing will be accessible. Most network connectivity problems result from one of the following issues:

- Failed network adapter
- Failed network hardware
- Failed network connection
- Faulty network cables
- Misconfigured network hardware
- Misconfigured network adapter

NOTE Often, people jump to the conclusion that the network has failed when only a single network resource has failed. For example, a failed DNS server will stop your computer from resolving host names, which would prevent the computer from finding resources on the network by name. Similarly, if the only network resource a user accesses is her e-mail server and that server has failed, the failure might appear to that user to be a total loss of connectivity. To avoid spending time troubleshooting the wrong problem, the processes in this appendix always start by isolating the cause of the problem.

After you isolate the failed feature, you can work to resolve that specific problem or you can escalate the problem to the correct support team. For example, if you determine that the network adapter has failed, you will need to contact the hardware manufacturer for a replacement part. If you determine that the Internet connection has failed, you will need to contact your ISP. To isolate the cause of a network connectivity problem, follow these steps:

1. Open the Network And Sharing Center by clicking the network icon in the system tray and then clicking Open Network And Sharing Center. At the bottom of the page, click Troubleshoot Problems and follow the prompts that appear. If Windows Network Diagnostics does not identify or resolve the problem, continue following these steps.

2. Open a command prompt on the computer experiencing the problems. Run the command *ipconfig /all*. Examine the output as follows:

   - If no network adapters are listed, the computer either lacks a network adapter or (more likely) it does not have a valid driver installed. Refer to Appendix D, "Troubleshooting Hardware, Driver, and Disk Issues," for more information.

   - If all network adapters show a Media State of Media Disconnected, the computer is not physically connected to a network. If you are using a wireless network, see the section titled "How to Troubleshoot Wireless Networks" later in this appendix. If you are using a wired network, disconnect and reconnect both ends of the network cable. If the problem continues, replace the network cable. Attempt to connect a different computer to the same network cable; if the new computer can connect successfully, the original computer has a failed network adapter. If neither computer can connect successfully, the problem is with the network wiring, the network switch, or the network hub. Replace the network hardware as necessary.

- If the network adapter has an IPv4 address in the range of 169.254.0.1 through 169.254.255.254, the computer has an APIPA address. This indicates that the computer is configured to use a DHCP server, but no DHCP server is available. With administrative credentials, run the following commands at a command prompt.

```
ipconfig /release
ipconfig /renew
ipconfig /all
```

If the network adapter still has an APIPA address, the DHCP server is offline. Bring a DHCP server online and restart the computer. If the network does not use a DHCP server, configure a static or alternate IPv4 address provided by your network administration team or your ISP. For more information about IPConfig, read the section titled "IPConfig" earlier in this appendix.

- If all network adapters show DHCP Enabled: No in the display of the *ipconfig /all* command, the network adapter might be misconfigured. If DHCP is disabled, the computer has a static IPv4 address, which is an unusual configuration for client computers. Update the network adapter IPv4 configuration to Obtain An IP Address Automatically and Obtain DNS Server Address Automatically, as shown in Figure E-6. Then configure the Alternate Configuration tab of the IP Properties dialog box with your current, static IP configuration.

FIGURE E-6 Enable DCHP for most client computers.

For most networks, set client configuration to Obtain An IP Address Automatically.

3. Having arrived at this step, you know that your computer has a valid, DHCP-assigned IPv4 address and can communicate on the LAN. Therefore, any connectivity problems are caused by failed or misconfigured network hardware. Although you cannot solve the problem from a client running Windows, you can still diagnose the problem. View the output from the *ipconfig* command and identify the IPv4 address of your default gateway. Verify that the IPv4 address of the default gateway is on the same subnet as the network adapter's IP address. If they are not on the same subnet, the default gateway address is incorrect—the default gateway must be on the same subnet as the client computer's IPv4 address.

> **NOTE** To determine whether an IPv4 address is on the same subnet as your computer's IPv4 address, first look at your subnet mask. If your subnet mask is 255.255.255.0, compare the first three sets of numbers (called octets) in the IPv4 addresses (for example, 192.168.1 or 10.25.2). If they match exactly, the two IPv4 addresses are on the same subnet. If your subnet mask is 255.255.0.0, compare the first two octets. If your subnet mask is 255.0.0.0, compare only the first octet (the first grouping of numbers before the period in the IP address). If any of the numbers in the subnet mask are between 0 and 255, you will need to use binary math and the AND operation to determine whether they are on the same subnet.

4. Attempt to ping the default gateway using the following command.

   `ping default_gateway_ip_address`

   For example, given the following IPConfig output:

   ```
   Ethernet adapter Local Area Connection:

       Connection-specific DNS Suffix  . : hsd1.nh.contoso.com.
       Link-local IPv6 Address . . . . . : fe80::1ccc:d0f4:3959:7d74%10
       IPv4 Address. . . . . . . . . . . : 192.168.1.132
       Subnet Mask . . . . . . . . . . . : 255.255.255.0
       Default Gateway . . . . . . . . . : 192.168.1.1
   ```

   you would run the following command.

   `ping 192.168.1.1`

   If the Ping results show "Request timed out," your computer has the incorrect IP address configured for your default gateway, your default gateway is offline, or your default gateway is blocking ICMP requests. If the Ping results show "Reply from ...," your default gateway is correctly configured, and the problem is occurring elsewhere on the network.

NOTE Ping is not a reliable tool for determining whether computers or network equipment are available on the network. Today, to reduce security risks, many administrators configure devices not to respond to Ping requests. However, Ping is still the most reliable tool for testing routers, and most administrators configure routers to respond to Ping requests from the local network. It's a good idea to ping your network equipment when everything is working properly just to determine whether it responds under normal conditions.

5. Use the *Tracert* command to test whether you can communicate with devices outside your LAN. You can reference any server on a remote network; however, this example uses the host *www.microsoft.com*.

```
C:\>tracert www.microsoft.com
```

```
Tracing route to www.microsoft.com [10.46.19.30]
over a maximum of 30 hops:
  0  win7.hsd1.nh.contoso.com. [192.168.1.132]
  1  192.168.1.1
  2  c-3-0-ubr01.winchendon.ma.boston.contoso.com [10.165.8.1]
  3  ge-3-37-ur01.winchendon.ma.boston.contoso.com [10.87.148.129]
  4  ge-1-1-ur01.gardner.ma.boston.contoso.com [10.87.144.225]
  5  10g-9-1-ur01.sterling.ma.boston.contoso.com [10.87.144.217]
```

The 0 line is your client computer. The 1 line is the default gateway. Lines 2 and above are routers outside your local area network.

- If you see the message "Unable to resolve target system name," your DNS server is unreachable because the DNS server is offline, your client computer is misconfigured, or the network has failed. If your DNS server is on your LAN (as displayed by the *ipconfig /all* command) and you can still ping your router, the DNS server has failed or is misconfigured; see the section titled "How to Troubleshoot Name Resolution Problems" later in this appendix for more information on these issues. If your DNS server is on a different network, the problem could be either a network infrastructure problem or a name resolution problem. Repeat this step, but use Ping to contact your DNS server IP address (as displayed by the *ipconfig /all* command). Then, follow the steps outlined in the section titled "How to Troubleshoot Name Resolution Problems" later in this appendix to further isolate the issue.

- If nothing responds after line 1, your default gateway cannot communicate with external networks. Try restarting the default gateway. If the default gateway is connected directly to the Internet, the Internet connection or the device that connects you to the Internet (such as a cable or DSL modem) might have failed. Contact your ISP for additional troubleshooting.

- If the same gateway appears multiple times in the Tracert route, the network is experiencing a routing loop. Routing loops can cause performance problems or cause communications to fail entirely. Networks typically fix routing loops automatically; however, you should contact your network support team to make sure they are aware of the problem. The following Tracert output demonstrates a routing loop, because nodes 5, 6, and 7 repeat.

```
C:\>tracert www.contoso.com

Tracing route to www.contoso.com [10.73.186.238]
over a maximum of 30 hops:
  0  d820.hsd1.nh.contoso.com. [192.168.1.196]
  1  192.168.1.1
  2  c-3-0-ubr01.winchendon.ma.boston.contoso.com [10.165.8.1]
  3  ge-3-37-ur01.winchendon.ma.boston.contoso.com [10.87.148.129]
  4  ge-1-1-ur01.gardner.ma.boston.contoso.com [10.87.144.225]
  5  10g-9-1-ur01.sterling.ma.boston.contoso.com [10.87.144.217]
  6  te-9-2-ur01.marlboro.ma.boston.contoso.com [10.87.144.77]
  7  10g-8-1-ur01.natick.ma.boston.contoso.com [10.87.144.197]
  8  10g-9-1-ur01.sterling.ma.boston.contoso.com [10.87.144.217]
  9  te-9-2-ur01.marlboro.ma.boston.contoso.com [10.87.144.77]
 10  10g-8-1-ur01.natick.ma.boston.contoso.com [10.87.144.197]
 11  10g-9-1-ur01.sterling.ma.boston.contoso.com [10.87.144.217]
 12  te-9-2-ur01.marlboro.ma.boston.contoso.com [10.87.144.77]
 13  10g-8-1-ur01.natick.ma.boston.contoso.com [10.87.144.197]
```

- If any routers on line 2 or above respond (it doesn't matter if the final host responds), the client computer and the default gateway are configured correctly. The problem exists with the network infrastructure, or your Internet connection may have failed. Follow the troubleshooting steps described in the next section, "How to Troubleshoot Application Connectivity Problems," or contact network support to troubleshoot the problem.

To double-check your results, repeat these steps from another client computer on the same network. If the second client computer exhibits the same symptoms, you can be confident that part of the network infrastructure has failed. If the second client can successfully communicate on the network, compare the IPConfig /all output from the two computers. If the Default Gateway or DNS Server addresses differ, try configuring the problematic computer with the other computer's settings. If this does not resolve the problem, the problem is unique to the problematic computer and may indicate a hardware or driver problem (see Appendix D).

How to Troubleshoot Application Connectivity Problems

Sometimes, you might be able to access the network with some applications but not others. For example, you might be able to download your e-mail but not access Web servers. Or, you might be able to view pages on a remote Web server but not connect to the computer with Remote Desktop.

Several issues might cause these symptoms (in rough order of likelihood):

- The remote service is not running. For example, Remote Desktop might not be enabled on the remote computer.

- The remote server has a firewall configured that is blocking that application's communications from your client computer.

- A firewall between the client and server computer is blocking that application's communications.

- Windows Firewall on the local computer might be configured to block the application's traffic.

- The remote service has been configured to use a non-default port number. For example, Web servers typically use TCP port 80, but some administrators might configure TCP port 81 or a different port.

To troubleshoot an application connectivity problem, follow these steps:

1. Before you begin troubleshooting application connectivity, first verify that you do not have a name resolution problem. To do this, open a command prompt and run the command **Nslookup *servername***. If Nslookup does not display an answer similar to the following example, you have a name resolution problem. See the section titled "How to Troubleshoot Name Resolution Problems" later in this appendix.

```
C:\>nslookup contoso.com
```

```
Non-authoritative answer:
Name:    contoso.com
Addresses:  10.46.232.182, 10.46.130.117
```

2. Identify the port number used by the application. Table E-2 lists port numbers for common applications. If you are not sure which port numbers your application uses, consult the application's manual or contact the technical support team. Alternatively, you can use a protocol analyzer, such as Network Monitor, to examine network traffic to determine the port numbers used.

TABLE E-2 Default Port Assignments for Common Services and Tasks

SERVICE NAME OR TASK	UDP	TCP
Web servers, HTTP, and Internet Information Services (IIS)		80
HTTP- Secure Sockets Layer (SSL)		443
DNS client-to-server lookup (varies)	53	53
DHCP client		67
File and printer sharing	137	139, 445
FTP-control		21
FTP-data		20

SERVICE NAME OR TASK	UDP	TCP
Internet Relay Chat (IRC)		6667
Microsoft Office Outlook (see POP3, IMAP, and SMTP for ports)		
Internet Mail Access Protocol (IMAP)		143
IMAP (SSL)		993
LDAP		389
LDAP (SSL)		636
Message Transfer Agent (MTA) – X.400 over TCP/IP		102
POP3		110
POP3 (SSL)		995
RPC endpoint mapper		135
SMTP		25
Network News Transfer Protocol (NNTP)		119
NNTP (SSL)		563
POP3		110
POP3 (SSL)		995
SNMP	161	
SNMP Trap	162	
SQL Server		1433
Telnet		23
Terminal Server and Remote Desktop		3389
Point-to-Point Tunneling Protocol (PPTP)		1723
Joining an AD DS domain		
(See the section titled "How to Troubleshoot Joining or Logging on to a Domain" later in this appendix for more information.)		

After identifying the port number, the first step in troubleshooting the application connectivity problem is to determine whether communications are successful using that port. If it is a TCP port, you can use PortQry, Test TCP, or Telnet. Of those three tools, Telnet is the least flexible, but it is the only tool included with Windows (but note that it is not installed by default). For more information about Telnet, including how to install it, see the section titled "Telnet Client" earlier in this appendix.

To test a TCP port with Telnet, run the following command.

`Telnet **hostname_or_address TCP_port**`

For example, to determine whether you can connect to the Web server at *www.microsoft* *.com* (which uses port 80), you would run the following command.

`Telnet www.microsoft.com 80`

If the command prompt clears or if you receive text from the remote service, you have successfully established a connection. Close the command prompt to cancel Telnet. This indicates that you can connect to the server; therefore, the server application is listening for incoming connections and no firewall is blocking your traffic. Instead of troubleshooting the problem as a connectivity issue, you should consider application-level issues, including:

- **Authentication issues**   View the server's Security Event Log or the application's log to determine whether it is rejecting your client connections because of invalid credentials.
- **Failed service**   Restart the server. Test whether other client computers can connect to the server.
- **Invalid client software**   Verify that the client software running on your computer is the correct version and is configured properly.

If Telnet displays "Could not open connection to the host," this indicates an application connectivity issue, such as a misconfigured firewall. Follow these steps to continue troubleshooting the problem:

1. If possible, verify that the server is online. If the server is online, attempt to connect to a different service running on the same server. For example, if you are attempting to connect to a Web server and you know that the server has file sharing enabled, attempt to connect to a shared folder. If you can connect to a different service, the problem is almost certainly a firewall configuration problem on the server.

2. Attempt to connect from different client computers on the same and different subnets. If you can connect from a client computer on the same subnet, you might have an application configuration problem on the client computer. If you can connect from a client computer on a different subnet but not from the same subnet, a firewall on the network or on the server might be filtering traffic from your client network.

3. If possible, connect a client computer to the same subnet as the server. If you can connect from the same subnet but not from different subnets, a router-based firewall is blocking traffic. If you cannot connect from the same subnet, the server has a firewall that is blocking traffic. Alternatively, the server application might not be running or might be configured to use a different port.

4. Log on to the server and use Telnet to attempt to connect to the server application port. If you can connect to the server from the server but not from other computers, the server definitely has firewall software configured. Add an exception for the application to the firewall software. If you cannot connect to the server application

from the server, the application is not listening for connections or is configured to listen for incoming connections on a different port. Refer to the application documentation for information on how to start and configure the application. If the server is running Windows, you can use Netstat to identify on which ports the server is listening for incoming connections. For more information, read the section titled "Netstat" earlier in this appendix.

How to Troubleshoot Name Resolution Problems

Computers use numeric IP addresses (such as 192.168.10.233 or 2001:db8::1) to identify each other on networks. However, IP addresses are difficult for people to remember, so we use more friendly host names (such as *www.contoso.com*). *Name resolution* is the process of converting a host name to an IP address, and DNS is by far the most common name resolution technique.

Many apparent connectivity problems are actually name resolution problems. If any of the following problems occur, the client will be unable to contact a server using its host name:

- DNS servers have failed.
- The network connecting the client to the DNS server has failed.
- A host name is missing from the DNS database.
- A host name is associated with an incorrect IP address. Often, this happens because a host has recently changed IP addresses and the DNS database has not been updated.
- The client does not have DNS servers configured or is configured with the incorrect DNS server IP addresses.

To diagnose a name resolution problem, follow these steps:

1. Open the Network And Sharing Center by clicking Start, clicking Network, and then clicking Network And Sharing Center. If a red X is displayed over a network link, click the link to start Windows Network Diagnostics and follow the prompts that appear. Windows Network Diagnostics can solve many common configuration problems. If Windows Network Diagnostics does not identify or resolve the problem, continue following these steps.

2. Verify that you can connect to other computers using IP addresses. If you cannot connect to servers by using their IP address, the source of your problem is network connectivity rather than name resolution. See the section titled "How to Troubleshoot Network Connectivity Problems" earlier in this appendix. If you can connect to servers by using their IP address but not by using their host names, continue following these steps.

> **NOTE** When your network is working properly, look up the IP addresses of several different computers, including computers on your subnet, other subnets on your intranet, and computers on the Internet. Test the IP addresses to verify that they respond to Ping requests. Keep this list available so that you can use the IP addresses to test for network connectivity without relying on name resolution.

3. Open a command prompt and use Nslookup to look up the host name you are attempting to contact, as the following example shows.

```
Nslookup www.microsoft.com
```

Examine the output.

- If Nslookup displays addresses or aliases for the host name, name resolution was successful. Most likely, the server you are trying to reach is offline, you have a connectivity problem preventing you from reaching the server, the application you are using is misconfigured, or the DNS server database is incorrect. See the sections titled "How to Troubleshoot Network Connectivity Problems" and "How to Troubleshoot Application Connectivity Problems" earlier in this appendix. If you believe the DNS server database is incorrect, contact your DNS server administrator.

- If Nslookup displays only "DNS request timed out," the DNS server is not responding. First, repeat the test several times to determine whether it is an intermittent problem. Then, use the *ipconfig* command to verify that the client computer has the correct DNS servers configured. If necessary, update the client computer's DNS server configuration. If the DNS server's IP addresses are correct, the DNS servers or the network to which they are connected are offline. Contact the server or network administrator for additional assistance.

- If Nslookup displays the message "Default servers are not available," the computer does not have a DNS server configured. Update the client network configuration with DNS server IP addresses or configure the computer to acquire an address automatically.

4. If you can connect to the server from a different client computer, run **ipconfig /all** from a command prompt to determine which DNS servers the client computer is configured to use. If the IP addresses are different, consider changing the problematic client computer to use those IP addresses.

How to Verify Connectivity to a DNS Server

Although DNS traffic can use either TCP port 53 or UDP port 53, UDP is almost always used because it is more efficient for short communications. Because Telnet always uses TCP, it is not useful for testing UDP DNS connectivity. Instead, you can install and use the PortQry tool, as described earlier in this appendix.

To test for connectivity to DNS traffic, install PortQry, and then run the following command.

```
portqry -n DNS_server_name_or_IP_address -p UDP -e 53
```

If PortQry can connect to the specified DNS server, it will respond with "LISTENING." If PortQry cannot connect, it will respond with "LISTENING OR FILTERED." After displaying "LISTENING OR FILTERED," PortQry will attempt to issue a DNS request to the remote computer and then will display whether the server responded to the request.

If you prefer graphical tools, you can use the PortQueryUI tool to query for UDP port 53, as shown in Figure E-7.

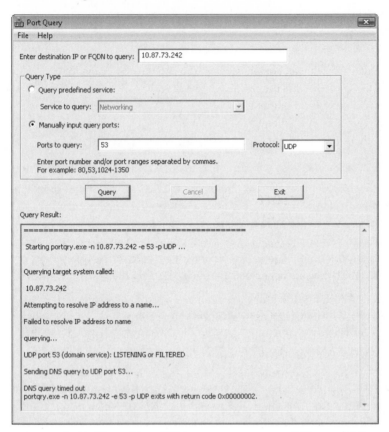

FIGURE E-7 PortqryUI provides a GUI that you can use to test DNS connectivity.

How to Use the Hosts File

You can use the Hosts file as another name resolution method. You might do this if you know that your DNS server is unavailable or the database is out of date, you need to access a server, and you know the server's IP address. It's also useful when you've recently installed a new server and you want to contact it using a host name before the DNS database is updated. Although you can typically contact servers using their IP addresses, Web sites often need to be reached using the correct host name, and IP addresses might not work.

Your Hosts file is located at %WinDir%\System32\Drivers\Etc\Hosts. It is a text file, and you can edit it using Notepad. To open the Hosts file, run Notepad using administrative permissions. Then, open the Notepad %WinDir%\System32\Drivers\Etc\Hosts file (it does not have a file extension). To add an entry to the Hosts file to enable name resolution without using DNS, add lines to the bottom of the Hosts file, as demonstrated here for IPv4 and IPv6 addresses.

```
192.168.1.10 www.microsoft.com
10.15.33.25 www.contoso.com
2001:db8::1   www.microsoft.com
```

After updating the Hosts file, you can contact servers by using the host name. When an entry is in the Hosts file, Windows will use the associated IP address without contacting a DNS server. In fact, the only application that bypasses the Hosts file is Nslookup, which always contacts DNS servers directly. Remember to remove entries from the Hosts file after you finish using them; otherwise, you might have name resolution problems later if the server's IP address changes.

How to Troubleshoot Performance Problems and Intermittent Connectivity Issues

Often, network problems don't result in total loss of connectivity. Network problems also can be file transfers that take longer than they should for your network bandwidth, jumpy streaming audio and video, or extremely unresponsive network applications.

To troubleshoot network performance problems, you must first identify the source of the problem. Several different components can cause performance problems:

- **The local computer**   Your local computer might have an application that is using all of the processor's time, thus slowing down everything on your computer, including networking. Alternatively, failing hardware or problematic drivers can cause performance problems or intermittent failures. To solve these problems, you can stop or reduce the impact of problematic applications, replace hardware, or upgrade drivers.

- **The network infrastructure**   Overutilized routers cause increased latency and dropped packets, both of which can cause performance problems and intermittent failures. Routing problems, such as routing loops, can cause traffic to be routed through an unnecessarily long path, increasing network latency. Sometimes, such as when you are using a satellite link, latency and the performance problems caused by latency are unavoidable. Although solving network infrastructure problems is outside the scope of this book, you can identify the source of the problem so that you can escalate the problem to the correct support team.

- **The server**   If the server is overutilized, all network communication to that server will suffer performance problems. Solving server performance problems is outside the scope of this book. However, when you have identified the source of the problem, you can escalate it to the correct support team.

To identify the source of a network performance problem, follow these steps. After each step, test your network performance to determine whether the problem still exists.

1. Start Task Manager by right-clicking the taskbar, clicking Task Manager, and then clicking the Performance tab. If processor utilization is near 100 percent, that might cause the perceived network performance problem. Click the Processes tab, find the process that is using the processor time, and close it.

2. In Task Manager, click the Networking tab. This tab shows a chart for each network adapter installed in the computer. If network utilization is near the practical capacity of the network link, that is the cause of your performance problem. For wired Ethernet networks (such as 10 megabits-per-second [Mbps], 100-Mbps, or 1,000-Mbps links), utilization cannot typically exceed about 60 to 70 percent of the link speed. For wireless networks, utilization cannot exceed about 50 percent of the link speed. However, wireless utilization often peaks at much lower than 50 percent of the link speed, so even 15 or 20 percent utilization may indicate that your performance problems are caused by insufficient bandwidth on the wireless network. To identify the source of the bandwidth, click the Performance tab in Task Manager and then click Resource Monitor. In Resource Monitor, expand the Network section, as shown in Figure E-8. Identify the process that is creating the most bandwidth, the PID, and the destination server. You can then return to Task Manager to identify the specific process creating the network bandwidth. Stop the process to determine whether it is the cause of your performance problems.

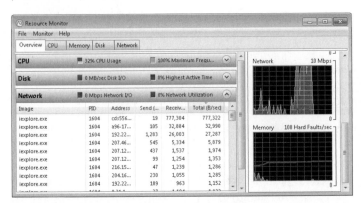

FIGURE E-8 Use Resource Monitor to help identify the source of network bandwidth.

NOTE The network utilization displayed in Task Manager and Resource Monitor only accounts for traffic sent to or from your computer. If another computer on your network is using bandwidth, that bandwidth won't be available to you—but neither Task Manager nor Resource Monitor can show you bandwidth used by other hosts.

3. If possible, use the same application to connect to a different server. If the performance problem occurs when connecting to different servers, the problem is probably local host or network related. Performing the following steps will help you

further isolate the problem. If the problem occurs only when connecting to a single server, the problem might be related to the server's performance or performance problems with the network to which the server is attached. Contact the server administrator for assistance.

4. If possible, run the same application from a different computer on the same network. If both computers experience the same problem, the problem is probably related to network performance. The following steps will help you further isolate that problem. If other computers on the same network do not experience the same problem, it is probably related to your local computer. First, apply any updates and restart the computer. Then, install any network adapter driver updates. If problems persist, replace network cables and replace the network adapter. For more information, see Appendix D.

At this point in the troubleshooting process, you have identified the network infrastructure as the most likely source of your problem. Open a command prompt and then run the PathPing tool, using your server's host name. PathPing will identify the route between your computer and the server and then spend several minutes calculating the latency of each router and network link in the path.

Ideally, each network link will add only a few milliseconds of latency (displayed in the RTT column) onto the time measured for the prior link. If latency increases more than 100 milliseconds for a single link and stays at that level for following links, that link may be the cause of your performance problems. If the link is a satellite or intercontinental link, that latency is to be expected and probably cannot be improved.

If, however, the link is your Internet connection or another network that is part of your intranet, your performance problems may be caused by overutilized network infrastructure. For example, if several computers are backing up their disk content to a folder on the network, a link can become overutilized, which can cause performance problems. Similarly, if several users are transferring large files across your Internet connection, other applications (especially real-time video or audio streaming, such as Voice over IP [VoIP]), may suffer. Contact network support for assistance. You might also be able to use Quality of Service (QoS) to prioritize time-sensitive traffic over file transfers.

> **NOTE** If you are an administrator on a Small Office/Home Office (SOHO) network, you can quickly determine whether other computers on the network are causing Internet performance problems by connecting your computer directly to your Internet connection and disconnecting all other computers. If the problems disappear, another computer on your network is causing the problem.

If the same gateway appears multiple times in the PathPing route, the network is experiencing a routing loop. Routing loops can cause performance problems or cause communications to fail entirely. Networks that use routing protocols typically fix routing loops automatically; however, you should contact your network support team to make sure they are aware of the problem. The following PathPing output demonstrates a routing loop, because nodes 5, 6, and 7 repeat.

```
C:\>pathping www.contoso.com
```

```
Tracing route to www.contoso.com [10.73.186.238]
over a maximum of 30 hops:
  0  d820.hsd1.nh.contoso.com. [192.168.1.196]
  1  192.168.1.1
  2  c-3-0-ubr01.winchendon.ma.boston.contoso.com [10.165.8.1]
  3  ge-3-37-ur01.winchendon.ma.boston.contoso.com [10.87.148.129]
  4  ge-1-1-ur01.gardner.ma.boston.contoso.com [10.87.144.225]
  5  10g-9-1-ur01.sterling.ma.boston.contoso.com [10.87.144.217]
  6  te-9-2-ur01.marlboro.ma.boston.contoso.com [10.87.144.77]
  7  10g-8-1-ur01.natick.ma.boston.contoso.com [10.87.144.197]
  8  10g-9-1-ur01.sterling.ma.boston.contoso.com [10.87.144.217]
  9  te-9-2-ur01.marlboro.ma.boston.contoso.com [10.87.144.77]
 10  10g-8-1-ur01.natick.ma.boston.contoso.com [10.87.144.197]
 11  10g-9-1-ur01.sterling.ma.boston.contoso.com [10.87.144.217]
 12  te-9-2-ur01.marlboro.ma.boston.contoso.com [10.87.144.77]
 13  10g-8-1-ur01.natick.ma.boston.contoso.com [10.87.144.197]
```

How to Troubleshoot Joining or Logging on to a Domain

Administrators often encounter problems when joining a computer running Windows to an AD DS domain. Additionally, users might receive error messages about domain controllers being unavailable when trying to log on to their computer with a domain account.

The first step in troubleshooting domain join problems is to click Details in the Computer Name/Domain Changes dialog box to view the error information. For example, the error shown in Figure E-9 indicates that the DNS server does not have a DNS entry for the domain controller. If you want to view this error information after closing the Computer Name/ Domain Changes dialog box, open the %WinDir%\Debug\Dcdiag.txt log file.

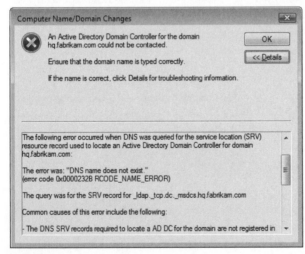

FIGURE E-9 In most cases, Windows will reveal the source of the problem in the detailed error message.

How to Analyze the NetSetup.Log file

If the Computer Name/Domain Changes dialog box does not reveal the source of the problem, view the %WinDir%\Debug\Netsetup.log file. This log details the process of joining a domain as well as the details of any problems encountered. For best results, compare a log file generated on a computer that successfully joined your domain to a computer that failed to join the domain. For example, the following entry indicates that the computer successfully located the *hq.contoso.com* domain controller (note the return value of 0x0).

```
----------------------------------------------------------------
NetpValidateName: checking to see if 'HQ.CONTOSO.COM' is valid as type 3 name
NetpCheckDomainNameIsValid [ Exists ] for 'HQ.CONTOSO.COM' returned 0x0
NetpValidateName: name 'HQ.CONTOSO.COM' is valid for type 3
----------------------------------------------------------------
```

The following entry indicates that the computer failed to locate the *hq.fabrikam.com* domain controller (note the return value of 0x54b).

```
----------------------------------------------------------------
NetpValidateName: checking to see if 'hq.fabrikam.com' is valid as type 3 name
NetpCheckDomainNameIsValid for hq.fabrikam.com returned 0x54b, last error is 0x3e5
NetpCheckDomainNameIsValid [ Exists ] for 'hq.fabrikam.com' returned 0x54b
----------------------------------------------------------------
```

If you see this type of name resolution failure during an unattended setup but you are able to manually join a domain, verify that clients are receiving a valid DHCP configuration. Specifically, verify that the DNS server addresses are correct and that the identified DNS servers contain service location (SRV) resource records for your domain controllers in the format _ldap._tcp.dc._msdcs.*DNSDomainName.*

If you see an error resembling the following, it indicates that the computer was previously joined to a domain using the same computer name but a different account. Joining the domain might fail because the administrative user account does not have permission to modify the existing account. To work around the problem, change the computer name, have the computer account deleted from the domain, or use the original user account to join the computer to the domain.

```
NetpManageMachineAccountWithSid: NetUserAdd on '\\hq.contoso.com' for
'43L2251A2-55$' failed: 0x8b0
04/06 06:36:20 SamOpenUser on 3386585 failed with 0xc0000022
```

If you see an error resembling the following, it indicates that the client could not establish a Server Message Block (SMB) session to the domain controller to manage the client computer account. One possible cause of this issue is missing WINS registrations for a domain controller.

```
NetUseAdd to \\ntdev-dc-02.ntdev.corp.microsoft.com\IPC$ returned 53
```

To reproduce this problem (and test whether you have fixed it), open a command prompt and run the following command.

```
net use \\<server from above>\ipc$ /u:<account used for join> <password>
```

To determine whether the edition of Windows supports joining a domain, search for the keyword *NetpDomainJoinLicensingCheck* (most recent entries are at the bottom of the log file). If the *ulLicenseValue* is anything other than 1, it indicates that the edition of Windows cannot join a domain. To join a domain, a computer must be running the Windows 7 Professional, Windows 7 Enterprise, or Windows 7 Ultimate operating systems. The following shows a log file entry for a computer running a supported version of Windows (as indicated by *ulLicenseValue=1*).

```
NetpDomainJoinLicensingCheck: ulLicenseValue=1, Status: 0x0
```

How to Verify Requirements for Joining a Domain

To join or log on to a domain successfully, you must meet several different requirements. When troubleshooting a problem joining a domain, verify each of these requirements:

- **The client computer must be able to resolve the IP address for a domain controller**   In most enterprise networks, client computers receive an IP address assignment from a DHCP server, and the DHCP server provides addresses for AD DS–enabled DNS servers that can resolve the domain controller IP address. If another DNS server is configured, you should update the client computer's IP configuration to use an AD DS–enabled DNS server. If this is not possible, you can add two records to your existing DNS server that resolve to a domain controller's IP address:

  - The _ldap._tcp.dc._msdcs.*DNSDomainName* SRV resource record, which identifies the name of the domain controller that hosts the AD DS domain. *DNSDomainName* is the DNS name of the AD DS domain the computer is attempting to join.

  - A corresponding address (A) resource record that identifies the IP address for the domain controller listed in the _ldap._tcp.dc._msdcs.*DNSDomainName* SRV resource record.

- **The client computer must be able to exchange traffic with the domain controller on several different TCP and UDP ports**   These ports include:

  - TCP port 135 for RPC traffic

  - TCP port 389 and UDP port 389 for LDAP traffic

  - TCP port 636 for LDAP over SSL traffic

  - TCP port 3268 for LDAP Global Catalog (GC) traffic

  - TCP port 3269 for LDAP GC SSL traffic

  - TCP port 53 and UDP port 53 for DNS traffic

  - TCP port 88 and UDP port 88 for Kerberos traffic

  - TCP port 445 for SMB (also known as CIFS) traffic

- **The administrator must have privileges to add a computer to a domain** Administrators who add a computer to a domain must have the Add Workstations To Domain user right.
- **The computer must be running Windows 7 Professional, Windows 7 Enterprise, or Windows 7 Ultimate** Windows 7 Starter, Windows 7 Home Basic, and Windows 7 Home Premium operating systems cannot join a domain.

How to Troubleshoot Network Discovery

With Network Discovery, users can browse shared network resources from the Network window. On private networks, this is convenient because users can connect to resources without knowing the names of other computers on the network. On public networks, however, Network Discovery is a security concern because it will announce the presence of the computer on the public network and users might use it to connect to a potentially malicious computer.

For these reasons, Network Discovery is enabled on private networks but disabled on public networks by default. When connected to an AD DS domain, Network Discovery is controlled by Group Policy settings but is disabled by default. Therefore, if the Network window does not display shared resources on the local network, it is almost certainly because Network Discovery is disabled. To remedy this, follow these steps (all of which require administrator privileges and can increase your computer's exposure to security attacks):

1. Verify that the Function Discovery Provider Host service is running.
2. Verify that Windows Firewall has exceptions enabled for Network Discovery.
3. Change the type of network from public to private. Alternatively, you can manually enable Network Discovery by opening the Network And Sharing Center window and enabling Network Discovery.

How to Troubleshoot File and Printer Sharing

Several different factors can cause problems with connecting to shared files and printers (which use the same communications protocols):

- Windows Firewall or another software firewall is blocking traffic at the client or server.
- A network firewall between the client and server is blocking traffic.
- The client is providing invalid credentials, and the server is rejecting the client's connection attempt.
- Name resolution problems prevent the client from obtaining the server's IP address.

First, start troubleshooting from the client computer. If the server is a computer running Windows 7 and you have administrator access to it, you can also troubleshoot from the server. The two sections that follow assume that the client and server belong to a domain.

How to Troubleshoot File and Printer Sharing from the Client

Follow these steps to troubleshoot problems connecting to shared files and printers:

1. If you can connect to the shared folder but receive an Access Is Denied message when attempting to open the folder, your user account has permission to access the share but lacks NTFS File System (NTFS) permissions for the folder. Contact the server administrator to grant the necessary NTFS file permissions. If the server is a computer running Windows 7, see the section titled "How to Troubleshoot File and Printer Sharing from the Server" later in this appendix.

2. Verify that you can resolve the server's name correctly. At a command prompt, type **ping *hostname***. If Ping displays an IP address, as shown here, you can resolve the server's name correctly. It does not matter whether the server replies to the pings. If this step fails, it indicates a name resolution problem. Contact your AD DS or DNS administrator.

   ```
   ping server
   ```

   ```
   Pinging server [10.1.42.22] with 32 bytes of data:
   ```

3. Attempt to connect using the server's IP address, as identified in the previous step, rather than the server's host name. For example, instead of connecting to *server*\printer, you might connect to \\10.1.42.22\printer.

4. From a command prompt, attempt to establish a connection to a server using the *net use* \\ip_address command. If it succeeds, you have sufficient network connectivity, but your user account lacks privileges to connect to the folder or printer share. Have the server administrator grant your account the necessary share permissions. Share permissions are separate from NTFS file permissions.

5. Use Telnet or PortQry to test whether your computer can connect to TCP port 445 of the remote computer. If you cannot connect using TCP port 445, test TCP port 139. For instructions on how to test for connectivity using a specific port, see the section titled "How to Troubleshoot Application Connectivity Problems" earlier in this appendix. If you cannot connect using either TCP port 139 or TCP port 445, verify that File And Printer Sharing is enabled on the server. Then, verify that the server has a firewall exception for TCP ports 139 and 445 or that an exception in Windows Firewall is enabled for File And Printer Sharing.

6. Attempt to connect to the server using an account with administrative credentials on the server. If you can connect with a different account, your normal account lacks sufficient credentials. Have the server administrator grant your account the necessary

privileges. Depending on the server configuration, you might be able to identify authentication problems by viewing the Security Event Log. However, logon failure auditing must be enabled on the server for the events to be available.

If you are still unable to connect, continue troubleshooting from the server. If you do not have access to the server, contact the server administrator for assistance.

How to Troubleshoot File and Printer Sharing from the Server

To troubleshoot file and printer sharing from a server running Windows 7 that is sharing the folder or printer, follow these steps:

1. Verify that the folder or printer is shared. Right-click the object and then click Sharing. If it does not indicate that the object is already shared, share the object and then attempt to connect from the client.

2. If you are sharing a folder and it is not already shared, right-click the folder and click Share. In the File Sharing Wizard, click Change Sharing Permissions. If the File Sharing Wizard does not appear, the Server service is not running. Continue with the next step. Otherwise, verify that the user account attempting to connect to the share appears on the list or that the user account is a member of a group that appears on the list. If the account is not on the list, add it to the list. Click Share and then click Done.

3. Verify that the Server service is running. The Server service should be started and set to start automatically for file and printer sharing to work.

4. Verify that users have the necessary permission to access the resources. Right-click the object and then click Properties. In the Properties dialog box, click the Security tab. Verify that the user account attempting to connect to the share appears on the list, or that the user account is a member of a group that appears on the list. If the account is not on the list, add it to the list.

5. Check the Windows Firewall exceptions to verify that it is configured properly by following these steps:

   a. Click Start and then click Control Panel.

   b. Click Security and then click Windows Firewall.

   c. In the Windows Firewall dialog box, note the Network Location. Click Change Settings.

   d. In the Windows Firewall Settings dialog box, click the Exceptions tab. Verify that the File And Printer Sharing check box is selected.

   e. If the File And Printer Sharing exception is enabled, it applies only for the current network profile. For example, if Windows Firewall indicated your Network Location was Domain Network, you might not have the File And Printer Sharing exception enabled when connected to private or public networks. Additionally, Windows Firewall will, by default, allow file and printer sharing traffic from the local network only when connected to a private or public network.

How to Troubleshoot Wireless Networks

Wireless networks are now very common. However, users often have problems connecting to wireless networks, because these networks are more complex than wired networks. To troubleshoot problems connecting to a wireless network, follow these steps.

1. Verify that the wireless network adapter is installed and has an active driver. From Network And Sharing Center, click Change Adapter Settings. If your wireless network connection does not appear as shown in Figure E-10, your network adapter or driver is not installed. See Appendix F, "Troubleshooting Stop Messages," for more information.

FIGURE E-10 Network Connections will display the adapter if your wireless network adapter and driver are properly installed.

2. If a wireless network adapter is installed, right-click it in Network Connections and then click Diagnose. Follow the prompts that appear. Windows might be able to diagnose the problem.

Network Diagnostics

Tim Rains, Program Manager; Windows Networking

Network Diagnostics is capable of diagnosing more than 180 different issues related to wireless networking. To get the most from network diagnostics for wireless networks, ensure that you are using native WiFi drivers instead of legacy WiFi drivers. To determine which type of driver(s) is installed on a system, run the following command at a command prompt.

```
netsh wlan show drivers
```

In the resulting output, look for the line labeled "Type." It should be either legacy WiFi Driver or Native Wi-Fi Driver. If a legacy WiFi driver is installed, contact the manufacturer of the wireless network adapter to see whether a native WiFi driver for the adapter is available.

3. Open Event Viewer and view the System Event Log. Filter events to view only those events with a Source of Diagnostics-Networking. Examine recent events and analyze the information provided by the Windows Troubleshooting Platform for the possible source of the problem.

4. Verify that wireless networking is enabled on your computer. To save power, most portable computers have the ability to disable the wireless network radio. Often, this is controlled by a physical switch on the computer. Other times, you must press a special, computer-specific key combination (such as Fn+F2) to enable or disable the radio. If the wireless radio is disabled, the network adapter will appear in Network Connections but it will not be able to view any wireless networks.

5. If the wireless network adapter shows Not Connected, attempt to connect to a wireless network. Within Network Connections, right-click the Network Adapter and then click Connect. In the Connect To A Network dialog box, click a wireless network and then click Connect.

6. If the wireless network is security enabled and you are prompted for the passcode but cannot connect (or the wireless adapter indefinitely shows a status of Identifying or Connected With Limited Access), verify that you typed the passcode correctly. Disconnect from the network and reconnect using the correct passcode.

7. If you are still unable to connect to a wireless network, perform a wireless network trace and examine the details of the report for a possible cause of the problem, as described in the section titled "How to Troubleshoot Performance Problems and Intermittent Connectivity Issues" earlier in this appendix.

If the wireless network adapter shows the name of a wireless network (rather than Not Connected), you are currently connected to a wireless network. This does not, however, necessarily assign you an IP address configuration, grant you access to other computers on the network, or grant you access to the Internet. First, disable and re-enable the network adapter by right-clicking it, clicking Disable, right-clicking it again, and then clicking Enable. Then, reconnect to your wireless network. If problems persist, move the computer closer to the wireless access point to determine whether the problem is related to signal strength. Wireless networks have limited range, and different computers can have different types of antennas and therefore different ranges. If the problem is not related to the wireless connection itself, read the section titled "How to Troubleshoot Network Connectivity Problems" earlier in this appendix.

> **NOTE** This section focuses only on configuring a wireless client running Windows 7; it does not discuss how to configure a wireless network infrastructure. For more information, refer to Chapter 10 of *Windows Server 2008 Networking and Network Access Protection* by Joseph Davies and Tony Northrup (Microsoft Press, 2008).

How to Troubleshoot Firewall Problems

Many attacks are initiated across network connections. To reduce the impact of those attacks, Windows Firewall by default blocks unrequested, unapproved incoming traffic and unapproved outgoing traffic. Although Windows Firewall will not typically cause application problems, it has the potential to block legitimate traffic if not properly configured. When troubleshooting application connectivity issues, you will often need to examine and possibly modify the client's or server's Windows Firewall configuration.

Misconfiguring Windows Firewall can cause several different types of connectivity problems. On a computer running Windows 7 that is acting as the client, Windows Firewall might block outgoing communications for the application (though blocking outgoing communications is not enabled by default). On a computer running Windows 7 that is acting as the server (for example, a computer that is sharing a folder), Windows Firewall misconfiguration might cause any of the following problems:

- Windows Firewall blocks all incoming traffic for the application.
- Windows Firewall allows incoming traffic for the LAN but blocks incoming traffic for other networks.
- Windows Firewall allows incoming traffic when connected to a domain network but blocks incoming traffic when connected to a public or private network.

The symptoms of client- or server-side firewall misconfiguration are the same: application communication fails. To make troubleshooting more complex, network firewalls can cause the same symptoms. Answer the following questions to help identify the source of the problem:

1. Can you connect to the server from other clients on the same network? If the answer is yes, you have a server-side firewall configuration problem that is probably related to the configured scope of a firewall exception. If adjusting the scope of the firewall exception does not solve the problem, it is probably caused by a network firewall, and you should contact your network administrators for further assistance.

2. Can you connect to the server when the client is connected to one type of network location (such as a home network or a domain network), but not when it is connected to a different type of network location? If the answer is yes, you have a client-side firewall configuration problem that is probably caused by having an exception configured for only one network location type.

3. Can other clients on the same network connect to the server using the same application? If the answer is yes, you have a client-side firewall configuration problem that is probably caused by having a rule that blocks outgoing traffic for the application.

4. Can the client connect to other servers using the same application? If the answer is yes, you have a server-side firewall configuration problem, and the server needs a firewall exception added. If adding an exception does not solve the problem, it is probably caused by a network firewall, and you should contact your network administrators for further assistance.

Summary

Windows 7 can automatically diagnose many common network problems. Other problems are more complicated and require you as an administrator to perform additional troubleshooting to isolate the source of the problem. When you have isolated the source of the problem, you may be able to fix the problem yourself. If the problem is related to a failed network circuit or another factor outside of your control, isolating the problem allows you to escalate the issue to the correct support team and allow the support team to resolve the problem as quickly as possible.

Troubleshooting Stop Messages

NOTE This material was originally published in a slightly different form in *Windows 7 Resource Kit* by Mitch Tulloch, Tony Northrup, Jerry Honeycutt, Ed Wilson, and the Windows 7 Team at Microsoft (Microsoft Press, 2010).

When Windows detects an unexpected problem from which it cannot recover, a Stop error occurs. A Stop error serves to protect the integrity of the system by immediately stopping all processing. Although it is theoretically possible for Windows to continue functioning when it detects that a core feature has experienced a serious problem, the integrity of the system would be questionable, which could lead to security violations, system corruption, and invalid transaction processing.

When a Stop error occurs, Windows displays a *Stop message*, sometimes referred to as a *blue screen*, which is a text-mode error message that reports information about the condition. A basic understanding of Stop errors and their underlying causes improves your ability to locate and understand technical information or perform diagnostic procedures requested of you by technical support personnel.

Stop Message Overview

Stop errors occur only when a problem cannot be handled by using the higher-level error-handling mechanisms in Windows. Normally, when an error occurs in an application, the application interprets the error message and provides detailed information to the system administrator. However, Stop errors are handled by the kernel, and Windows is only able to display basic information about the error, write the contents of memory to the disk (if memory dumps are enabled), and halt the system. This basic information is described in more detail in the section titled "Stop Messages" later in this appendix.

As a result of the minimal information provided in a Stop message and the fact that the operating system stops all processing, Stop errors can be difficult to troubleshoot. Fortunately, they tend to occur very rarely. When they do occur, they are almost always caused by driver problems, hardware problems, or file inconsistencies.

Identifying the Stop Error

Many different types of Stop errors occur. Each has its own possible causes and requires a unique troubleshooting process. Therefore, the first step in troubleshooting a Stop error is to identify the Stop error. You need the following information about the Stop error to begin troubleshooting:

- **Stop error number**   This number uniquely identifies the Stop error.
- **Stop error parameters**   These parameters provide additional information about the Stop error. Their meaning is specific to the Stop error number.
- **Driver information**   When available, the driver information identifies the most likely source of the problem. Not all Stop errors are caused by drivers, however.

This information is often displayed as part of the Stop message. If possible, write it down to use as a reference during the troubleshooting process. If the operating system restarts before you can write down the information, you can often retrieve the information from the System Event Log in Event Viewer.

If you are unable to gather the Stop error number from the Stop message and the System Log, you can retrieve it from a memory dump file. By default, Windows is configured to create a memory dump whenever a Stop error occurs. If no memory dump file was created, configure the system to create a memory dump file. Then, if the Stop error reoccurs, you will be able to extract the necessary information from the memory dump file.

Finding Troubleshooting Information

Each Stop error requires a different troubleshooting technique. Therefore, after you identify the Stop error and gather the associated information, use the following sources for troubleshooting information specific to that Stop error:

- **Microsoft Debugging Tools For Windows Help**   Install Microsoft Debugging Tools For Windows and consult Help for that tool. This Help contains the definitive list of Stop messages, including many not covered in this appendix, and explains how to troubleshoot a wide variety of Stop errors. To install Debugging Tools For Windows, visit *http://www.microsoft.com/whdc/devtools/debugging/*.
- **Microsoft Knowledge Base**   The Knowledge Base includes timely articles about a limited subset of Stop errors. Stop error information in the Knowledge Base is often specific to a particular driver or hardware feature and generally includes step-by-step instructions for resolving the problem.
- **Microsoft Help and Support**   For related information, see Microsoft Help and Support at *http://support.microsoft.com*.
- **Microsoft Product Support Services**   If you cannot isolate the cause of the Stop error, obtain assistance from trained Microsoft Product Support Services personnel. You might need to furnish specific information and perform certain procedures to help technical support investigate your problem. For more information about Microsoft product support, visit *http://www.microsoft.com/services/microsoftservices/srv_enterprise.mspx*.

Stop Messages

Stop messages report information about Stop errors. The intention of the Stop message is to assist the system administrator in isolating and eventually resolving the problem that caused the Stop error. Stop messages provide a great deal of useful information to administrators who understand how to interpret the information in the Stop message. In addition to other information, the Stop message includes the Stop error number, or bugcheck code, that you can use to find or reference troubleshooting information about the specific Stop error at *http://technet.microsoft.com*.

When examining a Stop message, you need to have a basic understanding of the problem so that you can plan a course of action. Always review the Stop message and record as much information about the problem as possible before searching through technical sources. Stop messages use a full-screen character mode format, as shown in Figure F-1.

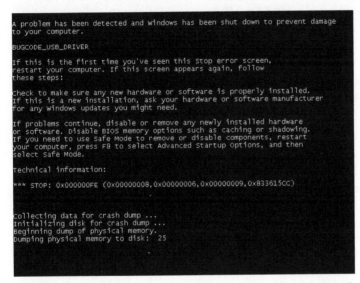

FIGURE F-1 Stop messages display information to help you troubleshoot the Stop error.

As shown in Figure F-1, a Stop message screen has several major sections, which display the following information:

- Bugcheck Information
- Recommended User Action
- Technical Information
- Driver Information (if available)
- Debug Port and Dump Status Information

Bugcheck Information

The Bugcheck Information section lists the Stop error descriptive name. Descriptive names are directly related to the Stop error number listed in the Technical Information section.

Recommended User Action

The Recommended User Action section informs the user that a problem has occurred and that Windows was shut down. It also provides the symbolic name of the Stop error. In Figure F-1, the symbolic name is BUGCODE_USB_DRIVER. It also attempts to describe the problem and lists suggestions for recovery. In some cases, restarting the computer might be sufficient because the problem is not likely to recur. But if the Stop error persists after you restart the operating system, you must determine the root cause to return the operating system to an operable state. This process might involve undoing recent changes, replacing hardware, or updating drivers to eliminate the source of the problem.

Technical Information

The Technical Information section lists the Stop error number, also known as the bugcheck code, followed by up to four Stop error–specific codes (displayed as hexadecimal numbers enclosed in parentheses), which identify related parameters. Stop error codes contain a *0x* prefix, which indicates that the number is in hexadecimal format. For example, in Figure F-1, the Stop error hexadecimal code is 0x000000FE (often written as 0xFE).

Driver Information

The Driver Information section identifies the driver associated with the Stop error. If a file is specified by name, you can use safe mode to verify that the driver is signed or has a date stamp that coincides with other drivers. If necessary, you can replace the file manually (in Startup Repair or in safe mode) or use Roll Back Driver to revert to a previous version. For more information about Startup Repair and safe mode, see Appendix C, "Configuring Startup and Troubleshooting Startup Issues." For more information about troubleshooting drivers, see Appendix D, "Troubleshooting Hardware, Driver, and Disk Issues." Figure F-1 does not display a driver name.

Debug Port and Dump Status Information

The Debug Port and Dump Status Information section lists Component Object Model (COM) port parameters that a kernel debugger uses, if enabled. If you have enabled memory dump file saves, this section also indicates whether one was successfully written. As a dump file is being written to the disk, the percentage shown after *Dumping physical memory to disk* is incremented to 100. A value of 100 indicates that the memory dump was successfully saved.

For more information about installing and using kernel debuggers, see the section titled "Using Symbol Files and Debuggers" later in this appendix.

Types of Stop Errors

A hardware or software problem can cause a Stop error, which causes a Stop message to appear. Stop messages typically fit into one of the following categories:

- **Stop errors caused by faulty software**   A Stop error can occur when a driver, service, or system feature running in Kernel mode introduces an exception. For example, a driver attempts to perform an operation above its assigned interrupt request level (IRQL) or tries to write to an invalid memory address. A Stop message might seem to appear randomly, but through careful observation, you might be able to associate the problem with a specific activity. Verify that all installed software (especially drivers) in question is fully Windows 7–compatible and that you are running the latest versions. Windows 7 compatibility is especially important for applications that might install drivers.

- **Stop errors caused by hardware issues**   This problem occurs as an unplanned event resulting from defective, malfunctioning, or incorrectly configured hardware. If you suspect a Stop error is caused by hardware, first install the latest drivers for that hardware. Failing hardware can cause Stop errors regardless of the stability of the driver, however. For more information about how to troubleshoot hardware issues, see Appendix D.

- **Executive initialization Stop errors**   Executive initialization Stop errors occur only during the relatively short Windows executive initialization sequence. Typically, these Stop errors are caused by corrupted system files or faulty hardware. To resolve them, run Startup Repair as described in Appendix C. If problems persist, verify that all hardware features have the latest firmware and then continue troubleshooting as described in Appendix D.

- **Installation Stop errors that occur during setup**   For new installations, installation Stop errors typically occur because of incompatible hardware, defective hardware, or outdated firmware. During an operating system upgrade, Stop errors can occur when incompatible applications and drivers exist on the system. Update the computer's firmware to the version recommended by the computer manufacturer before installing Windows. Consult your system documentation for information about checking and upgrading your computer's firmware.

Memory Dump Files

When a Stop error occurs, Windows displays information that can help you analyze the root cause of the problem. Windows writes the information to the paging file (Pagefile.sys) on the %SystemDrive% root by default. When you restart the computer in normal or safe mode after a Stop error occurs, Windows uses the paging file information to create a memory dump file in the %SystemRoot% folder. Analyzing dump files can provide more information about the root cause of a problem and lets you perform offline analysis by running analysis tools on another computer.

You can configure your system to generate three types of dump file:

- **Small memory dump files**   Sometimes referred to as *minidump files,* these dump files contain the least amount of information but are very small. Small memory dump files can be written to disk quickly, which minimizes downtime by allowing the operating system to restart sooner. Windows stores small memory dump files (unlike kernel and complete memory dump files) in the %SystemRoot%\Minidump folder, instead of using the %SystemRoot%\Memory.dmp file name.

- **Kernel memory dump files**   These dump files record the contents of kernel memory. Kernel memory dump files require a larger paging file on the boot device than small memory dump files and take longer to create when a failure has occurred. However, they record significantly more information and are more useful when you need to perform in-depth analysis. When you choose to create a kernel memory dump file, Windows also creates a small memory dump file.

- **Complete memory dump files**   These dump files record the entire contents of physical memory when the Stop error occurred. A complete memory dump file's size will be slightly larger than the amount of physical memory installed at the time of the error. When you choose to create a complete memory dump file, Windows also creates a small memory dump file.

By default, Windows is configured to create kernel memory dump files. By default, small memory dump files are saved in the %SystemRoot%\Minidump folder, and kernel and complete memory dump files are saved to a file named %SystemRoot%\Memory.dmp. To change the type of dump file Windows creates or to change their location, follow these steps:

1. Click Start, right-click Computer, and then select Properties.
2. Click Advanced System Settings.
3. In the System Properties dialog box, click the Advanced tab. Under Startup And Recovery, click Settings.
4. Use the drop-down Write Debugging Information list and then select the debugging type.
5. If desired, change the path shown in the Dump File box. Figure F-2 shows the Startup And Recovery dialog box.

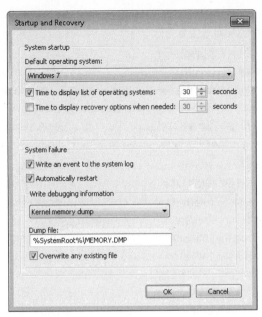

FIGURE F-2 Use the Startup And Recovery dialog box to change dump types and locations.

6. Click OK twice and then restart the operating system if prompted.

The sections that follow describe the different types of dump files in more detail.

Configuring Small Memory Dump Files

Small memory dump files contain the least amount of information, but they also consume the least amount of disk space. By default, Windows stores small memory dump files in the %SystemRoot%\Minidump folder.

Windows always creates a small memory dump file when a Stop error occurs, even when you choose the kernel dump file or complete memory dump file options. Small memory dump files can be used by both Windows Error Reporting (WER) and debuggers. These tools read the contents of a small memory dump file to help diagnose problems that cause Stop errors. For more information, see the sections titled "Using Memory Dump Files to Analyze Stop Errors" and "Using Windows Error Reporting" later in this appendix.

A small memory dump file records the smallest set of information that might identify the cause of the system stopping unexpectedly. For example, the small memory dump includes the following information:

- **Stop error information** Includes the error number and additional parameters that describe the Stop error.
- **A list of drivers running on the system** Identifies the modules in memory when the Stop error occurred. This device driver information includes the file name, date, version, size, and manufacturer.

- **Processor context information for the process that stopped** Includes the processor and hardware state, performance counters, multiprocessor packet information, deferred procedure call information, and interrupts.

- **Kernel context information for the process that stopped** Includes offset of the directory table and the page frame number database, which describes the state of every physical page in memory.

- **Kernel context information for the thread that stopped** Identifies registers and IRQLs and includes pointers to operating system data structures.

- **Kernel-mode call stack information for the thread that stopped** Consists of a series of memory locations and includes a pointer to the initial location. Developers might be able to use this information to track the source of the error. If this information is greater than 16 kilobytes (KB), only the topmost 16 KB is included.

A small memory dump file requires a paging file of at least 2 megabytes (MB) on the boot volume. The operating system saves each dump file with a unique file name every time a Stop error occurs. The file name includes the date the Stop error occurred. For example, Mini011007-02.dmp is the second small memory dump generated on January 10, 2007.

Small memory dump files are useful when space is limited or when you are using a slow connection to send information to technical support personnel. Because of the limited amount of information that can be included, these dump files do not include errors that were not directly caused by the thread that was running when the problem occurred.

Configuring Kernel Memory Dump Files

By default, Windows systems create kernel memory dump files. The kernel memory dump file is an intermediate-size dump file that records only kernel memory and can occupy several megabytes of disk space. A kernel memory dump file takes longer to create than a small dump file and thus increases the downtime associated with a system failure. On most systems, the increase in downtime is minimal.

Kernel memory dumps contain additional information that might assist troubleshooting. When a Stop error occurs, Windows saves a kernel memory dump file to a file named %SystemRoot%\Memory.dmp and creates a small memory dump file in the %SystemRoot%\Minidump folder.

A kernel memory dump file records only kernel memory information, which expedites the dump file creation process. The kernel memory dump file does not include unallocated memory or any memory allocated to user-mode programs. It includes only memory allocated to the Executive, kernel, Hardware Abstraction Layer (HAL), and file system cache, in addition to nonpaged pool memory allocated to kernel-mode drivers and other kernel-mode routines.

The size of the kernel memory dump file will vary, but it is always less than the size of the system memory. When Windows creates the dump file, it first writes the information to the paging file. Therefore, the paging file might grow to the size of the physical memory. Later, the dump file information is extracted from the paging file to the actual memory dump file. To ensure that you have sufficient free space, verify that the system drive would have free space greater than the size of physical memory if the paging file were extended to the size of physical memory. Although you cannot exactly predict the size of a kernel memory dump file, a good rule of thumb is that roughly 50 MB to 800 MB, or one-third the size of physical memory, must be available on the boot volume for the paging file.

For most purposes, a kernel memory dump file is sufficient for troubleshooting Stop errors. It contains more information than a small memory dump file and is smaller than a complete memory dump file. It omits those portions of memory that are unlikely to have been involved in the problem. However, some problems do require a complete memory dump file for troubleshooting.

> **NOTE** By default, a new kernel memory dump file overwrites an existing one. To change the default setting, clear the Overwrite Any Existing File check box. You can also rename or move an existing dump file prior to troubleshooting.

Configuring Complete Memory Dump Files

A complete memory dump file, sometimes referred to as a *full dump file,* contains everything that was in physical memory when the Stop error occurred. This includes all the information included in a kernel memory dump file, plus user-mode memory. Therefore, you can examine complete memory dump files to find the contents of memory contained within applications, although this is rarely necessary or feasible when troubleshooting application problems.

If you choose to use complete memory dump files, you must have available space on the *systemdrive* partition large enough to hold the contents of the physical RAM. Additionally, you must have a paging file equal to the size of your physical RAM.

When a Stop error occurs, the operating system saves a complete memory dump file to a file named %SystemRoot%\Memory.dmp and creates a small memory dump file in the %SystemRoot%\Minidump folder. A Microsoft technical support engineer might ask you to change this setting to facilitate data uploads over slow connections. Depending on the speed of your Internet connection, uploading the data might not be practical, and you might be asked to provide the memory dump file on removable media.

> **NOTE** By default, new complete memory dump files overwrite existing files. To change this, clear the Overwrite Any Existing File check box. You can also choose to archive or move a dump file prior to troubleshooting.

How to Manually Initiate a Stop Error and Create a Dump File

To be absolutely certain that a dump file will be created when a Stop error occurs, you can manually initiate a Stop error by creating a registry value and pressing a special sequence of characters. After Windows restarts, you can verify that the dump file was correctly created.

To initiate a crash dump manually, follow these steps:

1. Click Start and type **Regedit**. On the Start menu, right-click Regedit and click Run As Administrator. Respond to the User Account Control (UAC) prompt that appears.

2. In the Registry Editor, navigate to HKEY_LOCAL_MACHINE\SYSTEM\CurrentControlSet\Services\i8042prt\Parameters.

3. On the Edit menu, click New, DWORD (32-bit) Value, and then add the following registry value:

   - Value Name: CrashOnCtrlScroll
   - Value: 1

4. Close the Registry Editor and then restart the computer.

5. Log on to Windows. While holding down the right Ctrl key, press the Scroll Lock key twice to initiate a Stop error.

You cannot manually initiate a Stop error on a virtual machine that has virtual machine extensions installed.

Using Memory Dump Files to Analyze Stop Errors

Memory dump files record detailed information about the state of your operating system when the Stop error occurred. You can analyze memory dump files manually by using debugging tools or by using automated processes provided by Microsoft. The information you obtain can help you understand more about the root cause of the problem.

You can use WER to upload your memory dump file information to Microsoft. You can also use the following debugging tools to analyze your memory dump files manually:

- Microsoft Kernel Debugger (Kd.exe)
- Microsoft WinDbg Debugger (WinDbg.exe)

You can view information about the Stop error in the System Log after a Stop error occurs. For example, the following information event (with a source of Bugcheck and an Event ID of 1001) indicates that a 0xFE Stop error occurred.

```
The computer has rebooted from a bugcheck.  The bugcheck was: 0x000000fe (0x00000008,
0x00000006, 0x00000001, 0x87b1e000). A dump was saved in: C:\Windows\MEMORY.DMP.
```

Using Windows Error Reporting

When enabled, the WER service monitors your operating system for faults related to operating system features and applications. By using the WER service, you can obtain more information about the problem or condition that caused the Stop error.

When a Stop error occurs, Windows displays a Stop message and writes diagnostic information to the memory dump file. For reporting purposes, the operating system also saves a small memory dump file. The next time you start your system and log on to Windows as Administrator, WER gathers information about the problem and performs the following actions:

1. Windows displays the Windows Has Recovered From An Unexpected Shutdown dialog box, as shown in Figure F-3. To view the Stop error code, operating system information, and dump file locations, click View Problem Details. Click Check For Solution to submit the minidump file information and possibly several other temporary files to Microsoft.

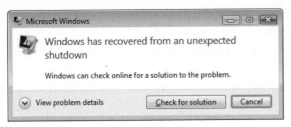

FIGURE F-3 Windows prompts you to check for a solution after recovering from a Stop error.

2. You might be prompted to collect additional information for future errors. If prompted, click Enable Collection, as shown in Figure F-4.

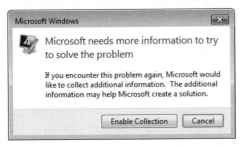

FIGURE F-4 Windows might prompt you to collect additional information for future error reports.

3. You might also be prompted to enable diagnostics. If prompted, click Turn On Diagnostics, as shown in Figure F-5.

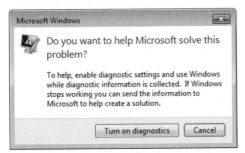

FIGURE F-5 Windows might prompt you to enable diagnostics to gather more troubleshooting information.

4. If prompted to send additional details, click View Details to review the additional information being sent. Then, click Send Information.

5. If prompted to automatically send more information about future problems, choose Yes or No.

6. When a possible solution is available, Action Center displays an icon in the system tray with a notification message.

7. Open Action Center to view the solution. Alternatively, you can search for View All Problem Reports in Control Panel.

If WER does not identify the source of an error, you might be able to determine that a specific driver caused the error by using a debugger, as described in the next section.

Using Symbol Files and Debuggers

You can also analyze memory dump files by using a kernel debugger. Kernel debuggers are primarily intended to be used by developers for in-depth analysis of application behavior. However, kernel debuggers are also useful tools for administrators troubleshooting Stop errors. In particular, kernel debuggers can be used to analyze memory dump files after a Stop error has occurred.

A *debugger* is a program that users with the Debug Programs user right (by default, only the Administrators group) can use to step through software instructions, examine data, and check for certain conditions. The following two examples of kernel debuggers are installed by installing Debugging Tools For Windows:

- **Kernel Debugger**   Kernel Debugger (Kd.exe) is a command-line debugging tool that you can use to analyze a memory dump file written to disk when a Stop message occurs. Kernel Debugger requires that you install symbol files on your system.

- **WinDbg Debugger**   WinDbg Debugger (WinDbg.exe) provides functionality similar to Kernel Debugger, but it uses a graphical user interface (GUI).

Both tools allow users with the Debug Programs user right to analyze the contents of a memory dump file and debug kernel-mode and user-mode programs and drivers. Kernel Debugger and WinDbg Debugger are just a few of the many tools included in the Debugging Tools For Windows installation. For more information about these and other debugging tools included with Debugging Tools For Windows, see Help in Debugging Tools For Windows.

To use WinDbg to analyze a crash dump, first install the debugging tools available at *http://www.microsoft.com/whdc/devtools/debugging/*.

To gather the most information from a memory dump file, provide the debugger access to symbol files. The debugger uses symbol files to match memory addresses to human-friendly module and function names. The simplest way to provide the debugger access to symbol files is to configure the debugger to access the Microsoft Internet-connected symbol server.

To configure the debugger to use the Microsoft symbol server, follow these steps:

1. Click Start, point to All Programs, point to Debugging Tools For Windows, right-click WinDbg, and then click Run As Administrator.

2. Select Symbol File Path from the File menu.

3. In the Symbol Path box, type

   SRV*_localpath_*http://msdl.microsoft.com/download/symbols

   where *localpath* is a path on the hard disk that the debugger will use to store the downloaded symbol files. The debugger will automatically create *localpath* when you analyze a dump file.

   For example, to store the symbol files in C:\Websymbols, set the symbol file path to **"SRV*c:\websymbols*http://msdl.microsoft.com/download/symbols"**.

4. Click OK.

Debuggers do not require access to symbol files to extract the Stop error number and parameters from a memory dump file. Often, the debugger can also identify the source of the Stop error without access to symbols.

> **NOTE** You can also download symbol files for offline use from *http://www.microsoft.com/whdc/devtools/debugging/.*

To analyze a memory dump file, follow these steps:

1. Click Start, point to All Programs, point to Debugging Tools For Windows, right-click WinDbg, and then click Run As Administrator.

2. Select Open Crash Dump from the File menu.

3. Type the location of the memory dump file and then click Open. By default, this location is %SystemRoot%\Memory.dmp.

4. In the Save Workspace Information dialog box, click No.

5. Select the Command window.

As shown in Figure F-6, the Bugcheck line tells you the Stop error number. The Probably Caused By line indicates the file that was being processed at the time of the Stop error.

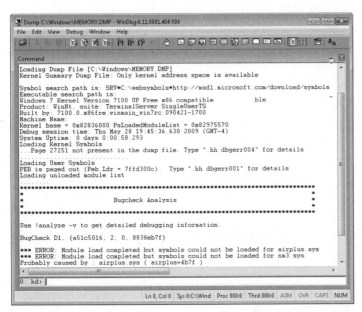

FIGURE F-6 WinDbg displays the Stop error code and the driver that caused the Stop error.

The Command window displays feedback from the debugger and allows you to issue additional commands. When a crash dump is opened, the Command window automatically displays the output of the *!analyze* command. In many cases, this default information is sufficient to isolate the cause of the Stop error.

If the default analysis does not provide all the information you need for troubleshooting, run the following command in the Command window.

```
!analyze -v
```

This command will display the *stack*, which contains a list of method calls preceding the Stop error. This might give clues to the source of a Stop error. For example, the following stack trace output, created by calling *!analyze –v*, correctly indicates that the Stop error was related to the removal of a universal serial bus (USB) device, as shown by the bold text.

```
STACK_TEXT:
WARNING: Frame IP not in any known module. Following frames may be wrong.
ba4ffb2c ba26c6ff 89467df0 68627375 70646f52 0x8924ed33
ba4ffb5c ba273661 88ffade8 8924eae0 89394e48 usbhub!USBH_PdoRemoveDevice+0x41
ba4ffb7c ba26c952 88ffaea0 89394e48 00000002 usbhub!USBH_PdoPnP+0x5b
ba4ffba0 ba26a1d8 01ffaea0 89394e48 ba4ffbd4 usbhub!USBH_PdoDispatch+0x5a
ba4ffbb0 804eef95 88ffade8 89394e48 88eac2e0 usbhub!USBH_HubDispatch+0x48
ba4ffbc0 ba3f2db4 88eac228 88eac2e0 00000000 nt!IopfCallDriver+0x31
ba4ffbd4 ba3f4980 88eac228 89394e48 89394e48 USBSTOR!USBSTOR_FdoRemoveDevice+0xac
ba4ffbec b9eed58c 88eac228 89394e48 89394f48 USBSTOR!USBSTOR_Pnp+0x4e
```

Being Prepared for Stop Errors

Some useful software- and hardware-related techniques can help you prepare for Stop errors when they occur. Stop messages do not always pinpoint the root of the problem, but they do provide important clues that you or a trained support technician can use to identify and troubleshoot the cause.

Prevent System Restarts After a Stop Error

When a Stop error occurs, Windows displays a Stop message related to the problem. By default, Windows automatically restarts after a Stop error occurs unless the system becomes unresponsive. If Windows restarts your system immediately after a Stop error occurs, you might not have enough time to record Stop message information that can help you analyze the cause of a problem. Additionally, you might miss the opportunity to change startup options or start the operating system in safe mode.

Disabling the default restart behavior allows you to record Stop message text, information that can help you analyze the root cause of a problem if memory dump files are not accessible. To disable the Automatically Restart option, follow these steps:

1. Click Start, right-click Computer, and then select Properties.
2. Click Advanced System Settings.
3. In the System Properties dialog box, click the Advanced tab. Then, under Startup And Recovery, click Settings.
4. In the System Failure box, clear the Automatically Restart check box.

If you cannot start your computer in normal mode, you can perform the preceding steps in safe mode.

Record and Save Stop Message Information

With the automatic restart behavior disabled, you must restart your computer manually after a Stop message appears. Stop messages provide diagnostic information, such as Stop error numbers and driver names, which you can use to resolve the problem. However, this information disappears from the screen when you restart your computer. Generally, you can retrieve this information after the system is restarted by examining the memory dump file, as described in the section titled "Using Memory Dump Files to Analyze Stop Errors" earlier in this appendix. In some situations, Stop error information is not successfully logged; therefore, it is important to record the information displayed in the Stop message for future reference. Before restarting the system, take the following actions to ensure that you have saved important information, which you can refer to when using the resources listed in this appendix.

To record and save Stop message information, follow these steps:

1. Record data that is displayed in the Technical Information and Driver Information sections of the Stop message for later reference. These sections are described in the section titled "Stop Messages" earlier in this appendix.

2. Record and evaluate suggestions in the Recommended User Action section. Stop messages typically provide troubleshooting tips relevant to the error.

3. Check the Debug Port and Dump File Status sections to verify that Windows successfully created a memory dump file.

4. If a memory dump file does exist, copy the file to removable media, another disk volume, or a network location for safekeeping. You can use Startup Repair to copy the dump file if you are not able to start Windows in normal mode or safe mode.

Analyzing memory dump files can assist you with identifying root causes by providing you with detailed information about the system state when the Stop error occurred. By following the preceding steps, you can save important information that you can refer to when using the resources listed in the section titled "Stop Messages" earlier in this appendix. For more information about creating and analyzing memory dump files, see the section titled "Memory Dump Files" earlier in this appendix.

Check Software Disk Space Requirements

Verify that adequate free space exists on your disk volumes for virtual memory paging files and application data files. Insufficient free space might cause Stop errors and other symptoms, including disk corruption. To determine the amount allocated to paging files, see the section titled "Memory Dump Files" earlier in this appendix.

You can move, delete, or compress unused files manually or by using Disk Cleanup to increase free space on disk volumes.

To run Disk Cleanup, click Start, type **Cleanmgr**, and then press Enter. Follow the prompts to increase free disk space on your system drive. Note that Disk Cleanup provides you with the option to delete memory dump files.

Install a Kernel Debugger and Symbol Files

You can use a kernel debugger to gather more information about the problem. For more information about installing and using debugging tools, see the section titled "Using Memory Dump Files to Analyze Stop Errors" earlier in this appendix.

Hardware Malfunction Messages

Stop messages also take the form of hardware malfunction messages. Like all Stop messages, they are displayed in non-windowed text mode. These Stop messages occur after the processor detects a hardware malfunction; the first one or two lines of the message contain a description. The error description typically points to a hardware problem, as shown in this example.

```
Hardware malfunction.
Call your hardware vendor for support.
```

Prior to proceeding with the recommendation provided by the message, it is best to contact the manufacturer for technical support. Record the information displayed after the first two lines of the message, which might prove useful to the support technician.

Under certain circumstances, driver problems can generate Stop messages that appear to be related to a hardware malfunction. For example, if a driver writes to the wrong I/O port, the device at the destination port might respond by generating a hardware malfunction message. Errors of this kind, which are typically detected and debugged in advance of public release, underscore the need to periodically check for updated drivers.

Stop Message Checklist

Stop messages provide diagnostic information, such as Stop codes and driver names, that you can use to resolve the problem. However, this information disappears when you restart your computer. Therefore, for future reference, it is important to record the information displayed. When a Stop message appears, follow these steps before restarting the system:

1. Record any data found in the Bugcheck Information and Driver Information sections for future reference.

2. Record and evaluate suggestions found in the Recommended User Action section. Stop messages typically provide troubleshooting tips relevant to the error.

3. Check the Stop message Debug Port and Dump Status Information section to verify that Windows successfully dumped memory contents to the paging file. Then proceed with your troubleshooting efforts.

4. After you resolve the problem or can at least start the computer, you can copy the memory dump file to another location, such as removable media, for further evaluation. Analyzing memory dump files can assist you with identifying root causes by providing you with detailed information about the system state when the Stop message occurred. For more information about creating and analyzing memory dump files, see the section titled "Memory Dump Files" earlier in this appendix.

By following the preceding steps, you can save important information to which you can refer when using the resources listed in the section titled "Stop Message Overview" earlier in this appendix. Stop messages do not always point to the root of the problem, but they do provide important clues that you or a trained support technician can use to identify and troubleshoot a problem.

Check Your Software

The following are useful software-related techniques that you can use to recover from problems that cause Stop messages.

Check Software Disk Space Requirements

Verify that adequate free space exists on your disk volumes for virtual memory paging files and application data files. Insufficient free space might cause Stop messages and other symptoms, including disk corruption. Always check the minimum system requirements recommended by the software publisher before installing an application. To determine the amount allocated to paging files, see the section titled "Memory Dump Files" earlier in this appendix. You can move, delete, or compress unused files manually or by using Disk Cleanup (Cleanmgr.exe) to increase free space on disk volumes.

Use the Last Known Good Configuration

If a Stop message occurs immediately after you install new software or drivers, use the Last Known Good Configuration startup option to undo the registry and driver changes. To use this option, restart your computer and then press F8 when prompted to activate the Windows Advanced Options menu. Last Known Good Configuration is one of the available options. For more information about Windows startup and recovery options, see Appendix C.

Use Disaster Recovery Features

Disaster recovery features such as System Restore and Driver Rollback can undo recent changes. For more information about recovery options, see Appendix C.

Restart the System in Safe Mode

Safe mode is a diagnostic environment that loads a minimum set of drivers and system services, increasing your chances of successfully starting the operating system. After Windows has started, you can enable or disable drivers and make the necessary changes to restore stability. To enter safe mode, restart your computer and then press F8 when prompted to activate the Windows Advanced Options menu. Safe mode is one of the available options. For more information about startup and recovery options, see Appendix C.

Use Startup Repair

You can use Startup Repair to perform advanced operations, such as replacing corrupted files. You can also disable a service by renaming the file specified in a Stop message. For more information about using Startup Repair to recover from startup problems, see Appendix C.

Check Event Viewer Logs

Check the Event Viewer System and Application logs for warnings or error message patterns that point to an application or service. Record this information and refer to it when searching for more information or when contacting technical support.

Check Application and Driver Compatibility

Categories of software known to cause Stop messages if they are not fully compatible with Windows 7 (such as those meant for previous versions of Windows) include backup, remote control, multimedia, CD mastering, Internet firewall, and antivirus tools. If temporarily disabling a driver or uninstalling software resolves the problem, contact the manufacturer for information about an update or workaround. You need to disable a service that is causing Stop errors or other problems rather than stop or pause it. A stopped or paused service runs after you restart the computer. For more information about disabling services for diagnostic or troubleshooting purposes, see Appendix C.

Install Compatible Antivirus Tools

Virus infection can cause problems such as Stop errors (for example, Stop 0x7B) and data loss. Before running antivirus software, verify that you are using updated virus signature files. Signature files provide information that allows the antivirus scanning software to identify viruses. Using current signature files increases the chances of detecting the most recent viruses. Verify that your virus scanner product checks the Master Boot Record (MBR) and the boot sector. For more information about MBR and boot sector viruses, see Appendix D.

Check for and Install Service Pack Updates

Microsoft periodically releases service packs containing updated system files, security enhancements, and other improvements that can resolve problems. You can use Windows Update to check for and install the latest versions as they become available. To check the service pack revision installed on your system, click Start, right-click Computer, and then click Properties.

Report Your Errors

You can find out more information about the conditions that caused the Stop message by using WER. For more information about options for analyzing memory dump files, see the section titled "Using Memory Dump Files to Analyze Stop Errors" earlier in this appendix.

Install Operating System and Driver Updates

Occasionally, Microsoft and third parties release software updates to fix known problems.

Check Information Sources

You might find information about a workaround or solution to the problem. Information sources include the Knowledge Base and the manufacturer's technical support Web page.

Install and Use a Kernel Debugger

You can use a kernel debugger to gather more information about the problem. The Debugging Tools Help file contains instructions and examples that can help you find additional information about the Stop error affecting you. For more information about installing and using debugging tools, see the sections titled "Stop Message Overview" and "Using Memory Dump Files to Analyze Stop Errors" earlier in this appendix.

Check Your Hardware

You can use the following hardware-related techniques to recover from problems that cause Stop messages.

Restore a Previous Configuration

If a Stop message appears immediately after you add new hardware, see if removing or replacing the part and restoring a previous configuration resolves the problem. You can use recovery features such as Last Known Good Configuration, Driver Rollback, and System Restore to restore the system to the previous configuration or to remove a specific driver. For more information about startup and recovery options, see Appendix C.

Check for Nondefault Firmware Settings

Some computers have firmware that you can use to change hardware settings such as power management parameters, video configuration, memory timing, and memory shadowing. Do not alter these settings unless you have a specific requirement to do so. If you are experiencing hardware problems, verify that the firmware values are set to the default values. To restore the default firmware values, follow the instructions provided by the computer or motherboard manufacturer.

Check for Non-Default Hardware Clock Speeds

Verify that the hardware is running at the correct speed. Do not set clock speeds for features such as the processor, video adapter, or memory above the rated specification (overclocking). This can cause random errors that are difficult to diagnose. If you are experiencing problems with overclocked hardware, restore default clock speed and CPU voltage settings according to the instructions provided by the hardware manufacturer.

Check for Hardware-Related Updates

Check the manufacturer's Web site to see if updated firmware is available for your system or individual peripherals.

Check by Running Hardware Diagnostic Tools

Run hardware diagnostic software to verify that your hardware is not defective. These tools are typically built into or bundled with your hardware.

Check ATA Disk and Controller Settings

If your system uses ATA storage devices such as hard disks, determine whether the firmware setting Primary IDE Only is available. If the setting is available, enable it if the second ATA channel is unused. Verify that primary and secondary device jumper settings are set correctly. Storage devices (including CD and DVD-ROM drives) use their own firmware, so check the manufacturer's Web site periodically for updates. Verify that you are using a cable that is compatible with your device—certain ATA standards require that you use a different cable type.

Check for SCSI Disk and Controller Settings

If your system uses an SCSI adapter, check for updates to device drivers and adapter firmware. Try disabling advanced SCSI firmware options, such as sync negotiation for low-bandwidth devices (tape drives and CD-ROM drives). Verify that you are using cables that meet the SCSI adapter's requirements for termination and maximum cable length. Check SCSI ID settings and termination to ensure that they are correct for all devices. For more information, see Appendix D.

Check for Proper Hardware Installation and Connections

Verify that internal expansion boards and external devices are firmly seated and properly installed and that connecting cables are properly fastened. If necessary, clean adapter card electrical contacts using supplies available at electronics stores. For more information about troubleshooting hardware, see Appendix D.

Check Memory Compatibility

If a Stop message appears immediately after you add new memory, verify that the new part is compatible with your system. Do not rely solely on physical characteristics (such as chip count or module dimensions) when purchasing new or replacement memory. Always adhere to the manufacturer's specifications when purchasing memory modules. For example, you can fit a memory module rated for 66-megahertz (MHz) or 100-MHz operation (PC66 or PC100 RAM, respectively) into a system using a 132-Mhz memory bus speed, and it might initially appear to work. However, using the slower memory results in system instability. To test memory, use Windows Memory Diagnostics, as described in Appendix D.

Check by Temporarily Removing Devices

Installing a new device can sometimes cause resource conflicts with existing devices. You might recover from this problem by temporarily removing devices not needed to start the operating system. For example, temporarily removing a CD-ROM or audio adapter might allow you to start Windows. You can then examine the device and operating system settings separately to determine what changes you need to make. For more information about simplifying your hardware configuration for troubleshooting purposes, see Appendix C.

Check by Replacing a Device

If you are unable to obtain diagnostic software for the problem device, install a replacement to verify that this action resolves the problem. If the problem disappears, the original hardware might be defective or incorrectly configured.

Check Information Sources

You might be able to find information about a workaround or solution to the problem. Information sources include the Knowledge Base and the manufacturer's technical support Web page.

Contact Technical Support

As a last resort, Microsoft technical support can assist you with troubleshooting. For more information about Microsoft technical support options, see the Support link on the Microsoft Web site at *http://www.microsoft.com*.

Summary

Stop errors can be frustrating to troubleshoot. However, by following the procedures outlined in this appendix, you can identify the source of Stop errors and begin working to resolve them. Most of the time, Stop errors are caused by drivers or faulty hardware. If Stop errors are caused by drivers, you need to work with the hardware manufacturer to develop an improved driver. If a Stop error is caused by faulty hardware, you should repair or replace the hardware.

Answers

Chapter 1: Lesson Review Answers

Lesson 1

1. **Correct Answer: A**

    A. Correct: Chkdsk can reveal bad sectors on the disk. Bad sectors can cause system freezes.

    B. Incorrect: Disk Defragmenter reduces data fragmentation on hard disks. Fragmentation results in slower performance, but it is not likely to cause a system freeze.

    C. Incorrect: Startup Repair is used to fix startup problems with a computer, but it is not likely to fix system freezes.

    D. Incorrect: Device Manager is not most likely to reveal a problem on the system. On the one hand, Device Manager can reveal driver problems, which can indeed cause system freezes. However, in this particular scenario, there have been no software changes to the system other than critical Windows Updates. The problem reported is therefore more likely to be related to hardware damage.

2. **Correct Answer: D**

    A. Incorrect: Although Chkdsk can reveal hard disk errors that could cause the problem, Startup Repair checks for more types of errors and is more likely to fix the problem.

    B. Incorrect: Reliability Monitor is a tool that enables you to check the stability of a system in its recent history. Because you are not able to start the system, you cannot access Reliability Monitor. In addition, Reliability Monitor, unlike Startup Repair, does not fix problems automatically.

    C. Incorrect: Windows Memory Diagnostic does not help in this situation. The message indicates that the partition table is invalid. Therefore, the problem is related to the hard disk and not to memory.

    D. Correct: Startup Repair helps to fix systems that fail to start. It runs a number of different checks on the hard disks and attempts to diagnose why the computer does not start. It then automatically attempts to repair any problems found. Startup Repair is the best tool for this situation because it is designed to fix precisely this kind of error.

Lesson 2

1. **Correct Answer: D**

    A. **Incorrect:** Power plans in Control Panel enable you to choose when certain devices, such as the monitor, should sleep. Power plans do not affect the functionality of hot-swapping.

    B. **Incorrect:** Chkdsk checks for errors on disks and attempts to repair any that are found. Running Chkdsk will not affect the functionality of hot-swapping.

    C. **Incorrect:** You can use jumpers to set master or subordinate relationships on IDE drives. These jumpers would not affect the functionality of hot-swapping on an external SATA drive.

    D. **Correct:** Even if you have hardware that supports hot-swapping, you can only use this functionality if the BIOS supports it. For this reason, you need to upgrade to a BIOS that supports hot swapping, and then you need to verify that hot-swapping is enabled in the BIOS Setup program.

2. **Correct Answer: B**

    A. **Incorrect:** Chkdsk analyzes hard disks for errors such as bad clusters. These errors do not lead to sluggish performance; they lead to data corruption, screen freezes, and stop errors.

    B. **Correct:** Disk fragmentation leads to sluggish performance. Although Disk Defragmenter is scheduled to run at night once per week, one can change or disable this default setting. Analyzing disk fragmentation lets you know whether this is the cause of the performance trouble.

    C. **Incorrect:** Startup Repair does not help with sluggish performance. It fixes startup errors.

    D. **Incorrect:** Windows Memory Diagnostic checks for damage to physical memory. This kind of damage is very unlikely to generate sluggish performance. Windows Memory Diagnostic is used most often to diagnose stop errors.

Chapter 1: Case Scenario Answers

Case Scenario 1: Troubleshooting Stop Errors

1. Reliability Monitor.
2. Windows Memory Diagnostic.
3. Replace the faulty memory module.

Case Scenario 2: Troubleshooting System Crashes

1. The problem has occurred while the user is engaged in different software activities, so it is unlikely to be caused by particular software. Also, there is no stop error when the computer restarts.
2. You should verify that the CPU fan is working.

Chapter 2: Lesson Review Answers

Lesson 1

1. **Correct Answers: B and C**

   A. **Incorrect:** You could use Ping to determine if the mail server is connected to the network. However, Ping does not indicate whether the mail server is responding to incoming e-mail requests—it's possible that the mail server is online but the mail service itself has stopped.

   B. **Correct:** You can use Telnet to connect to the TCP port that you use to download incoming e-mail. If the mail server responds to the Telnet request, you know that the mail server is responding correctly and that no firewall is blocking the connection attempt.

   C. **Correct:** Like Telnet, you can use PortQry to determine whether the mail service is responding on the mail server. PortQry is not included with Windows 7, however.

   D. **Incorrect:** PathPing determines whether a host and every router between your computer and the remote host are responding. It has the same disadvantage as Ping, however it does not determine whether the mail service itself is responding.

2. **Correct Answer: D**

   A. **Incorrect:** This is a private IP address. However, APIPA, the technique that Windows uses to assign an IP address when no DHCP server is available, does not use this range.

   B. **Incorrect:** The special IP address 127.0.0.1 always refers to the local host, whether or not DHCP configuration was successful.

   C. **Incorrect:** This is a private IP address. However, APIPA, the technique that Windows uses to assign an IP address when no DHCP server is available, does not use this range.

   D. **Correct:** Any IP address starting with 169.254 is an APIPA address. Windows assigns an APIPA address when a DHCP server is not available.

3. **Correct Answers: B and D**

   A. **Incorrect:** Nslookup is useful for identifying name resolution problems. However, you cannot use it to test routers on your network.

   B. **Correct:** Tracert sends ICMP packets to every host between your computer and the destination, creating a simple network map. If one of the routers has failed, the list of routers between your client and the destination ends before the destination network. If the local router has failed, no routers are displayed at all.

   C. **Incorrect:** Ipconfig can be used to view your current IP configuration. However, you cannot use it to query remote routers.

   D. **Correct:** PathPing provides similar functionality to Tracert, but it provides more detailed performance information.

Lesson 2

1. **Correct Answer: A**

   A. **Correct:** Nslookup sends a query to a DNS server and reports whether the DNS server was available and whether the name could be resolved.

   B. **Incorrect:** Ipconfig reports the current IP configuration. Additionally, with the */release* and */renew* parameters, you can use it to retrieve a new IP address from the DHCP server. Although you could use it to determine the IP address of your DNS server, you would not be able to use it to test the DNS server.

   C. **Incorrect:** Ping tests connectivity to a remote host. Although you could try pinging your DNS server, that wouldn't tell you whether you were able to successfully resolve host names.

   D. **Incorrect:** Netstat shows current connections and cannot be used to identify name resolution problems.

2. **Correct Answers: A and C**

   A. **Correct:** If the DNS server is offline, name resolution always fails. However, network requests that do not require a DNS server still succeed. Therefore, if the DNS server is offline, you would be unable to access Web servers by host name, but you might be able to access them using their IP addresses.

   B. **Incorrect:** The HOSTS file stores manually configured host names and IP addresses. However, it is almost never used and is never relied upon as the primary name resolution method.

   C. **Correct:** If the client has the wrong IP address configured for the DNS server, the requests would go unanswered. To resolve this problem, change the client's network configuration so that it is configured with the correct IP address of the DNS server.

   D. **Incorrect:** If the client had an APIPA address, it would be unable to access any computer on an external network, including Internet Web servers.

3. **Correct Answer: C**

   A. **Incorrect:** Looking up the server's host name with Nslookup is a good idea—it would allow you to verify that the DNS record had been updated. However, other clients are able to connect to the new database server. Therefore, you already know that the record has been updated. To resolve the problem, clear the DNS cache.

   B. **Incorrect:** These commands retrieve a new IP configuration from the DHCP server. They would not flush the DNS cache.

   C. **Correct:** The DNS client running Windows 7 can cache host names when they are resolved. If a DNS record is updated, as it is in this example, the DNS client running Windows 7 might continue to use the now-incorrect IP address for the host name. To resolve this, you should flush the DNS cache.

   D. **Incorrect:** This command displays the current IP configuration. It would not flush the DNS cache.

Lesson 3

1. **Correct Answer: D**

   A. **Incorrect:** The Diagnostics-Networking log does contain useful information logged by Windows Network Diagnostics; however, the information is not as detailed as that contained in the WLAN-AutoConfig log.

   B. **Incorrect:** The System log does contain information from Windows Network Diagnostics; however, the information is not as detailed as that contained in the WLAN-AutoConfig log.

   C. **Incorrect:** The Wired-AutoConfig log contains information about connecting to wired networks, not wireless networks.

   D. **Correct:** The WLAN-AutoConfig log contains the details of all wireless connection attempts, whether successful or unsuccessful. That log allows you to determine which wireless network the user attempted to connect to and the reason for the failure.

2. **Correct Answers: B and C**

   A. **Incorrect:** If you didn't have a wireless adapter installed, Device Manager would not show it under Network Adapters.

   B. **Correct:** If the wireless radio is turned off, it is still visible in Device Manager. However, you are not able to view any wireless networks—which exactly matches your symptoms.

   C. **Correct:** If the wireless network does not broadcast an SSID, you need to create a wireless profile manually before you can connect to the network. Most wireless networks do broadcast an SSID, however, so although this is a valid option, the most likely cause is that the wireless radio has been turned off.

   D. **Incorrect:** Authentication failures occur only after you attempt to connect to the wireless network.

3. **Correct Answer: C**

   A. **Incorrect:** WEP uses a static key and thus does not require an additional infrastructure server.

   B. **Incorrect:** Like WEP, WPA-PSK uses a static key.

   C. **Correct:** WPA-EAP authenticates users to a RADIUS server, which provides the benefit of greater manageability but does require at least one infrastructure server.

   D. **Incorrect:** Like WEP and WPA-PSK, WPA2-PSK uses a static key.

Chapter 2: Case Scenario Answers

Case Scenario 1: Troubleshooting a Network Problem

1. First, have Gordon run Windows Network Diagnostics. That diagnoses the most common network problems and can fix some problems automatically.

2. To determine whether the problem is with the local network, have Gordon attempt to contact a network resource on his local network. For example, have Gordon attempt to ping his default gateway or use PathPing to test the connection to a resource on the WAN. If he can reach the default gateway but not resources on the WAN, the problem is related to the WAN.

3. Have Gordon attempt to contact a network resource using the IP address, rather than the host name. For example, if Gordon can browse *www.microsoft.com* using one of the Web site's IP addresses but cannot browse the Web site using the host name, the problem is definitely related to name resolution.

Case Scenario 2: Troubleshooting Problems Connecting to a Wireless Network

1. Parry probably has a weak wireless connection. To fix it, Parry should move closer to the wireless access point. If you managed the wireless network, you might be able to improve it by moving the wireless access point, adjusting the power of the transmitter, or replacing the antenna. However, at a public wireless access point, you do not have control over these factors.

2. Compatibility problems can also cause unreliable wireless connections. For example, if the wireless access point uses a poor or outdated implementation of the wireless standards, the wireless connection might experience those symptoms.

Chapter 3: Lesson Review Answers

Lesson 1

1. **Correct Answer: C**

   A. **Incorrect:** The Server service is required on the server, but not on the client.

   B. **Incorrect:** The Workstation service is required on the client, but not on the server.

   C. **Correct:** The File And Printer Sharing firewall exception is required on the server. If the exception is not enabled, or it is blocked by another firewall rule, the server is unable to accept incoming connections to the shared printer.

   D. **Incorrect:** By default, client computers can establish outgoing connections to any server. Therefore, the client computer does not need to have the File And Printer Sharing firewall exception enabled.

2. **Correct Answers: B and C**

   A. **Incorrect:** The Workstation service establishes file and print sharing connections from the client computer to the server. It is required only on the client computer.

   B. **Correct:** The Print Spooler service manages print jobs and is required on both the client and the server.

C. **Correct:** The Server service accepts incoming file and printer sharing connections from client computers. It is required only on the server.

D. **Incorrect:** The Peer Name Resolution Protocol service is required for some network applications, such as Remote Assistance, but it is not used for printer sharing.

3. **Correct Answer: D**

A. **Incorrect:** You can use the Services console to start and stop services, including the Workstation, Server, and Print Spooler services. However, you cannot use it to manage drivers.

B. **Incorrect:** You can use Device Manager to change drivers for most hardware. However, Device Manager does not support printers.

C. **Incorrect:** The Event Viewer console displays events logged by applications and different components of the operating system. However, you cannot use it to manage drivers.

D. **Correct:** The Advanced tab of the Printer Properties dialog box allows you to change the driver for a printer.

Chapter 3: Case Scenario Answers

Case Scenario 1: Troubleshooting Insufficient Privileges

1. His user account does not have permission to print to the printer.

2. You need to modify the permissions on the printer to grant the manager Print privileges.

Case Scenario 2: Troubleshooting a Printer Problem

1. You should ask the user questions to narrow down the cause of the problem so that you can optimize the process of diagnosing the issue. For example, to determine the likelihood that the problem is driver-related, you could ask the user if she has updated the driver, installed any updates, or installed any printer-related software. You might also ask the user when the last time she printed was, so that you can check Reliability Monitor to determine if any updates were installed since the printer last worked.

2. Because the printer is shared across the network, you should verify that you can connect to the printer. Stop the Offline Files service, and then issue the command *net view \\server*. If the connection succeeds, then you know that the client can connect to the server, and you should investigate driver-related issues, printer settings, and hardware problems. If the connection fails, then you know the issue is related to printer sharing, network connectivity, a firewall, or a service. If you determine that it is a network problem, you could use the Ping tool to verify that the client can resolve the server's host name and that the client and server have network connectivity. If the client can ping the server, you could use the PortQry tool to verify that a firewall is not blocking printer-sharing communications.

3. Many problems can cause a user to be unable to print, but fortunately you have already eliminated privilege and hardware issues. Other possible problems include a lack of network connectivity, a client or server service that is not started, a driver problem on the client, and printer settings on the client.

Chapter 4: Lesson Review Answers

Lesson 1

1. **Correct Answers: A, B, and D**

   A. Correct: You can authenticate to a shared folder using credentials from Credential Manager.

   B. Correct: You can authenticate to a shared printer using credentials from Credential Manager.

   C. Incorrect: Credential Manager cannot complete the user name and password fields in an HTML form.

   D. Correct: If the Web site uses HTTP authentication, which causes the Web browser to prompt the user for credentials rather than using an HTML form, Credential Manager can supply the user name and password automatically.

2. **Correct Answer: B**

   A. Incorrect: The Audit Logon Events audit policy logs local authentication attempts, as well as authentication attempts to the local computer from domain user accounts. However, enabling success auditing would log successful authentication attempts in which the user's credentials were correctly validated. It would not log unsuccessful attempts.

   B. Correct: The Audit Logon Events audit policy logs local authentication attempts, as well as authentication attempts to the local computer from domain user accounts. Selecting failure auditing adds an event when the user fails to authenticate for any reason, including providing invalid credentials.

   C. Incorrect: The Audit Account Logon Events audit policy audits only authentication requests received by domain controllers. Therefore, it would have no impact on a member computer running Windows 7.

   D. Incorrect: The Audit Account Logon Events audit policy audits only authentication requests received by domain controllers. Therefore, it would have no impact on a member computer running Windows 7.

3. **Correct Answers: A and D**

   A. Correct: Enabling auditing for logon attempts audits all authentication attempts to the local computer, including logging on locally.

   B. Incorrect: Enabling auditing for logon attempts audits all authentication attempts to the local computer, but not remote computers. However, the remote Web server might add an audit event to its own event log, if auditing is enabled.

C. **Incorrect:** Enabling auditing for logon attempts audits all authentication attempts to the local computer, but not remote computers. However, the remote file server might add an audit event to its own event log if auditing is enabled.

D. **Correct:** Enabling auditing for logon attempts audits all authentication attempts to the local computer, including authentication at a UAC prompt. This includes UAC prompts that simply require the administrator to click Continue.

Lesson 2

1. **Correct Answers: B and D**

A. **Incorrect:** An expired certificate would cause Internet Explorer to display a different message.

B. **Correct:** If an attacker redirected traffic to a malicious server with an SSL certificate, the malicious server's SSL certificate probably wouldn't be issued for the same name by a trusted CA. Therefore, Internet Explorer would alert the user that the common name listed in the certificate doesn't match the name in the shortcut.

C. **Incorrect:** An untrusted CA would cause Internet Explorer to display a different message.

D. **Correct:** The most likely cause of this error is that the user typed a valid host name for a legitimate server but the server's certificate does not include the host name as the common name, and the host name does not appear on the SAN list. Any name that does not appear as the common name or in the SAN list in the certificate causes Internet Explorer to display this error.

2. **Correct Answers: B and C**

A. **Incorrect:** Internet Explorer can render animated GIFs, or any images, without requiring a Protected Mode prompt.

B. **Correct:** Embedded audio requires a plug-in even if it uses Windows Media Player. Before the plug-in is activated, the user must click the Information Bar to enable the plug-in.

C. **Correct:** Embedded video requires a plug-in, even if it uses Windows Media Player. Before the plug-in is activated, the user must click the Information Bar to enable the plug-in.

D. **Incorrect:** Viewing the source code of a Web page requires Internet Explorer to open Notepad. In Internet Explorer 7.0, this required elevated privileges, which caused Internet Explorer to display a Protected Mode confirmation prompt. Windows Internet Explorer 8.0 no longer requires elevated privileges to view source code, however.

3. **Correct Answer: B**

A. **Incorrect:** The Protected Mode Compatibility Layer doesn't need to virtualize storing a cookie.

B. **Correct:** If an add-on attempts to store a file in the Documents folder, the Protected Mode Compatibility Layer will redirect the file to \%Userprofile%\AppData\Local\ Microsoft\Windows\Temporary Internet Files\Virtualized to protect the user's security.

    C. Incorrect: Web applications can prompt the user to upload a file without the request being redirected.

    D. Incorrect: Add-ons can store files in the Temporary Internet Files folder without the Protected Mode Compatibility Layer virtualizing the request.

4. **Correct Answers: B and C**

    A. Incorrect: To run an ActiveX control, the user must click the Information Bar. Right-clicking the Web page does not provide that as an option.

    B. Correct: The easiest way to enable an ActiveX control is to click the Information Bar.

    C. Correct: Sites on the Trusted Sites list automatically run most ActiveX controls.

    D. Incorrect: Disabling Protected Mode does not cause ActiveX controls to run automatically.

Lesson 3

1. **Correct Answer: C**

    A. Incorrect: BitLocker Drive Encryption is not related to EFS.

    B. Incorrect: The Computer Management console includes many snap-ins, but it does not include the Certificates snap-in.

    C. Correct: Use the Certificates console to back up and restore EFS certificates. This allows you to access EFS-encrypted files after moving them to a different computer.

    D. Incorrect: You can use the Services snap-in to manage services. However, you cannot use it to manage certificates.

2. **Correct Answer: A**

    A. Correct: EFS certificates are located in the Certificates – Current User\Personal\ Certificates node.

    B. Incorrect: EFS certificates are not stored in this node.

    C. Incorrect: EFS certificates are per-user, not per-computer.

    D. Incorrect: EFS certificates are per-user, not per-computer.

3. **Correct Answers: A, B, and D**

    A. Correct: If a computer has a TPM, you can enable BitLocker without requiring the user to enter a key or connect a USB flash drive.

    B. Correct: If a computer has a TPM, you can configure Windows to prompt the user for a PIN before loading the operating system.

    C. Incorrect: If a computer does not have a TPM, your only option is to have the user insert a USB flash drive at startup. You must have a TPM to use PIN security at startup.

    D. Correct: With or without a TPM, you can configure BitLocker to require the user to insert a USB key at every startup.

Chapter 4: Case Scenario Answers

Case Scenario 1: Recommend Data Protection Technologies

1. No. File permissions protect data only while the operating system is running. If an attacker has physical access to a computer, the attacker can easily load a different operating system that ignores NTFS file permissions.

2. Yes, encryption protects data even if an attacker has physical access to a computer. Windows 7 includes two types of data encryption: EFS and BitLocker. EFS encrypts individual files, whereas BitLocker encrypts the entire system partition.

3. Both EFS and BitLocker allow you to share files across a network. In fact, neither type of encryption provides any protection across the network.

Case Scenario 2: Unwanted Internet Explorer Add-On

1. You can remove it using the Manage Add-Ons dialog box. To open that dialog box, start Internet Explorer, click the Tools button on the toolbar, click Manage Add-Ons, and then click Enable Or Disable Add-Ons.

2. Yes. Internet Explorer does not install add-ons from most Web sites automatically. Instead, it displays an information bar, and users need to click the information bar to install the add-on. In addition, Protected Mode requires administrative privileges before some types of add-ons can be installed (but Protected Mode prompts the user only if the add-on requires elevated privileges).

3. You can use the Group Policy settings in User Configuration\Administrative Templates\ Windows Components\Internet Explorer\Security Features\Add-on Management to enable or disable specific add-ons throughout your organization. For example, you could use this to list all add-ons created by your internal development team in the Add-On List setting and then enable the Deny All Add-Ons Unless Specifically Allowed In The Add-On List setting to block other add-ons.

Chapter 5: Lesson Review Answers

Lesson 1

1. **Correct Answer: B**

   A. **Incorrect:** This is the correct policy setting, but you want to use Group Policy, not Local Security Policy. If you were to use Local Security Policy, you would have to make the configuration change on every computer in the domain.

   B. **Correct:** This policy setting enables UAC prompts for the built-in Administrator account. You want to use Group Policy so that the change is enforced throughout the domain.

C. **Incorrect:** This policy setting enables UAC prompts for all domain administrators except the built-in Administrator account. In addition, you want to use Group Policy so that the change is enforced throughout the domain.

   D. **Incorrect:** Although you want to use Group Policy, this is not the correct policy setting to change. This policy setting enables UAC prompts for all domain administrators except the built-in Administrator account.

2. **Correct Answer: C**

   A. **Incorrect:** You need to instruct users to adjust the automatic scan. This solution merely adds another scan and does not address the source of the problem.

   B. **Incorrect:** This solution could still cause an unnecessary depletion of battery power if the scan starts while the computer is idle for a few minutes and using the battery. You want the scan to run only during suitable times, such as at a time when the user knows the computer is using AC power.

   C. **Correct:** You need to let the users set the schedule for the automatic scan so that the scan can be performed at a time they know is suitable.

   D. **Incorrect:** Your goal is to avoid reducing battery power without reducing the protection provided by Windows Defender. If you disable automatic scanning, it reduces the protection by Windows Defender, so this solution does not meet your requirements.

Chapter 5: Case Scenario Answers

Case Scenario 1: Resolving Malware Infections

1. Open Task Manager and end any processes and services that seem suspicious. Then, disable the services in the Services console.

2. First, you can try to reinstall the anti-malware client software. Second, if the computer is running too slowly to install this software, you can perform an offline anti-malware scan from a bootable CD if you have such a CD available. Finally, you can start an anti-malware scan from over the network, such as from an online source or from a local server that hosts your anti-malware software.

Chapter 6: Lesson Review Answers

Lesson 1

1. **Correct Answer: D**

   A. **Incorrect:** Configuring the VPN client to establish an SSTP-type VPN will not solve the problem. SSTP-type VPNs do not allow users to preserve the VPN connection when they switch wireless access points. Only IKEv2 VPNs provide this feature.

   B. **Incorrect:** The encryption strength of a VPN connection does not affect whether the connection has mobility. Mobility is a feature of IKEv2 VPNs.

C. **Incorrect:** The authentication for the VPN does not affect whether the connection has mobility. This feature requires IKEv2 VPNs.

D. **Correct:** Mobility (also called VPN Reconnect) is a feature of IKEv2 VPNs. When they initiate a connection, VPN clients running Windows 7 are configured by default to request an IKEv2 VPN connection first from the VPN server. However, the VPN server running RRAS can answer this request for an IKEv2 VPN only if the server is running Windows Server 2008 R2.

2. **Correct Answer: B**

   A. **Incorrect:** Although the VPN server does need to obtain and install a server certificate, you do not need to install this certificate on the client. The server certificate is presented to the client when the client connects.

   B. **Correct:** For the client to be able to validate the server certificate presented by the VPN server, the client needs to trust the CA that has issued the certificate to the VPN server. To trust the CA, the root certificate of that CA needs to be installed in the Trusted Root Certification Authorities certificate store on the client.

   C. **Incorrect:** By default, the Type Of VPN setting is configured as Automatic. This configuration is sufficient and does not need to be changed. When the Type Of VPN setting is configured as Automatic, a VPN connection in Windows 7 attempts to connect first by means of IKEv2.

   D. **Incorrect:** IKEv2 VPNs do not require a computer certificate for the VPN client.

Lesson 2

1. **Correct Answer: B**

   A. **Incorrect:** DirectAccess clients can run Windows 7 Enterprise, Windows 7 Ultimate, and Windows Server 2008 R2.

   B. **Correct:** DirectAccess clients can run Windows 7 Enterprise, Windows 7 Ultimate, and Windows Server 2008 R2.

   C. **Incorrect:** DirectAccess clients can run Windows 7 Enterprise, Windows 7 Ultimate, and Windows Server 2008 R2.

   D. **Incorrect:** DirectAccess clients can run Windows 7 Enterprise, Windows 7 Ultimate, and Windows Server 2008 R2.

2. **Correct Answer: D**

   A. **Incorrect:** In DirectAccess, both the client and server need to authenticate each other with certificates.

   B. **Incorrect:** In DirectAccess, both the client and server need to authenticate each other with certificates.

   C. **Incorrect:** DirectAccess relies on IPv6. The DirectAccess client must obtain an IPv6 address from a native IPv6 router or from an IPv6 transition technology such as 6to4, Teredo, or IP-HTTPS.

D. Correct: DirectAccess requires IPv6, not IPv4. In the absence of an available IPv6 network, DirectAccess must establish IPv6 connectivity over IPv4 by using an IPv6 transition technology such as 6to4, Teredo, or IP-HTTPS.

Chapter 6: Case Scenario Answers

Case Scenario 1: Troubleshooting a Remote Access VPN

1. To resolve the issues with VPN performance, you need the VPN client to negotiate an IKEv2 type VPN successfully. This is the first type of VPN that a client running Windows 7 attempts when its Type Of VPN setting is set to Automatic. For this to happen, you need to obtain a server certificate for the VPN server from a CA, and you need to install this server certificate on the VPN server. You then need to ensure that the certificate of the root CA that has issued this certificate is installed in the Trusted Root Certification Authorities store on each VPN client.

2. To enable clients running Windows 7 to establish a VPN connection successfully from behind remote firewalls and NAT devices, you need to make sure that the VPN clients can negotiate an SSTP VPN successfully. The requirements for this type of VPN are the same as those for an IKEv2 VPN, so no additional steps need to be taken beyond those described in the answer to question 1. If the network infrastructure between the VPN client and server prevents a client running Windows 7 from establishing an IKEv2 VPN, clients running Windows 7 by default automatically attempt to negotiate an SSTP VPN.

Case Scenario 2: Troubleshooting DirectAccess

1. You should first try to configure the Teredo interface because the client is assigned a private IPv4 address. (Use the command *netsh interface teredo set state type=enterpriseclient servername=FirstPublicIPv4AddressOfDirectAccessServer.*)

2. You should first try to configure the 6to4 interface because the client is assigned a public IPv4 address. (Use the command *netsh interface 6to4 set relay name= FirstPublicIPv4AddressOfDirectAccessServer.*)

Chapter 7: Lesson Review Answers

Lesson 1

1. **Correct Answer: B**

   A. Incorrect: If you rely on employees to start Windows Update manually, they will inevitably forget. As a result, computer security suffers in the long term because important updates will not be installed.

   B. Correct: For small organizations, it typically is not worth the effort to configure a WSUS server. Therefore, the default configuration of downloading updates directly from Microsoft is sufficient.

C. Incorrect: For small organizations that do not have a requirement to approve updates, WSUS is unnecessary.

D. Incorrect: SMS is designed for enterprises with complex software management needs. It would be unnecessarily time-consuming to deploy SMS for a small organization.

2. **Correct Answer: C**

   A. Incorrect: If you rely on employees to start Windows Update manually, they will inevitably forget. As a result, computer security suffers in the long term because important updates will not be installed.

   B. Incorrect: Configuring Windows Update to retrieve updates directly from Microsoft would not give IT the opportunity to review and approve updates prior to deployment.

   C. Correct: WSUS will give the IT department the ability to approve updates before deployment.

   D. Incorrect: SMS is designed for enterprises with complex software management needs. It would be unnecessarily time-consuming to deploy SMS for most organizations with only 100 computers.

3. **Correct Answers: C and D**

   A. Incorrect: Earlier versions of Windows used the Update.exe tool to install updates. Windows 7 uses the built-in Wusa.exe tool instead.

   B. Incorrect: Use Msiexec.exe to install Windows Installer files with an .Msi extension. You cannot use Msiexec.exe to install Windows 7 updates from Microsoft, however.

   C. Correct: Although updates for earlier versions of Windows were published using .Exe files, updates for Windows 7 are not executable files.

   D. Correct: Windows 7 updates are distributed in .Msu files. Windows 7 includes the Wusa.exe command-line tool for installing updates from a batch file or at the command line.

Chapter 7: Case Scenario Answers

Case Scenario 1: Distribute Updates

1. Although it's not always required for offices this small, WSUS would provide the ability to test and approve updates before deployment. Configuration Manager 2007 could also provide this capability, but the infrastructure and cost aren't justifiable for a network this small.

2. Yes, WSUS must be installed on a server. In this case, you could install it on the computer running Windows Server 2008 R2.

3. Yes, WSUS works with clients running both Windows XP and Windows 7.

4. You could use AD DS Group Policy settings to configure the client computers.

Case Scenario 2: Audit Updates

1. You can use WSUS to identify computers that have not installed the update.

2. Yes, you can use the MBSA tool, a free download from Microsoft, to scan the network and identify computers that do not have the update installed.

3. From Control Panel, they can click Programs. Then, under Programs And Features, they can click View Installed Updates. They should look for the update by the KB number.

Chapter 8: Lesson Review Answers

Lesson 1

1. **Correct Answers: A, B, and D**

   A. **Correct:** The forwarding computer must have the Windows Remote Management service started in order to forward events.

   B. **Correct:** The collecting computer must have the Windows Remote Management service started in order to receive events.

   C. **Incorrect:** IIS is not required for Windows Remote Management Services, even though Windows Remote Management uses HTTP for communications by default.

   D. **Correct:** The forwarding computer must receive incoming Windows Remote Management connections. Therefore, a Windows Firewall exception must be enabled. The *winrm quickconfig* command does this automatically.

   E. **Incorrect:** Event forwarding is not enabled by default.

2. **Correct Answer: C**

   A. **Incorrect:** You can use the Event Viewer snap-in to create and manage subscriptions. However, Event Viewer does not enable you to set a custom interval. Instead, you must use the Wecutil command-line tool.

   B. **Incorrect:** The Windows Remote Management command-line tool (Winrm) is used to configure the Windows Remote Management service. You cannot use it to manage subscriptions.

   C. **Correct:** The Windows Event Collector command-line tool (Wecutil) is the correct tool for changing subscription settings that cannot be changed from the Event Viewer snap-in.

   D. **Incorrect:** Use the Windows Events Collector command-line utility (Wevutil) to manage events and event logs. You cannot use it to manage subscriptions

3. **Correct Answer: A**

   A. **Correct:** Choosing Minimize Latency sets the interval to 30 seconds. However, it might take longer for events to synchronize depending on factors such as waiting for the Windows Remote Management service to start.

   B. **Incorrect:** The default setting for subscriptions, Normal, has a timeout of 15 minutes.

C. Incorrect: Minimize Latency sets the interval to 30 seconds, not 30 minutes.

D. Incorrect: If you choose the Minimize Bandwidth subscription optimization, 6 hours is the default setting.

4. **Correct Answer: D**

   A. Incorrect: This command is required only in workgroup environments; you do not need to run this command in AD DS environments.

   B. Incorrect: This command is required only in workgroup environments. In addition, you need to run this command on the collecting computer, not the forwarding computer.

   C. Incorrect: In an AD DS environment you do not need to change group memberships on the collecting computer.

   D. Correct: To allow a subscription to work with the default authentication setting of Machine Account, you must add the collecting computer's machine account to the forwarding computer's Event Log Readers local group.

Lesson 2

1. **Correct Answer: A**

   A. Correct: If a computer is slow, the best way to start Task Manager is to press Ctrl+Alt+Del. You can end a process from either the Applications or Processes tab.

   B. Incorrect: You can use the System Configuration Utility to prevent programs or services from starting automatically. However, you cannot use it to stop programs that are already running.

   C. Incorrect: You cannot open Task Manager by pressing Alt+Tab. The Alt+Tab key combination is used to switch to an application that is already running. Instead, you should press Ctrl+Alt+Del.

   D. Incorrect: You cannot use the System Configuration Utility to stop programs that are already running.

2. **Correct Answer: C**

   A. Incorrect: Running on battery power does not affect disk fragmentation. In fact, it typically does not affect disk performance in any way.

   B. Incorrect: So long as there is sufficient free disk space, a large paging file does not affect disk fragmentation.

   C. Correct: When a disk is low on free space, Windows must write new data to any available location, even if the file being written is too big to fit in the location. Any remaining data must be written to a different location, causing fragmentation. Reading and writing fragmented files can take much longer than reading and writing contiguous files because the drive head must move between each file fragment.

   D. Incorrect: Flash drives can become fragmented exactly like traditional, magnetic hard disks. However, fragmentation does not affect the performance of flash drives.

3. **Correct Answers: C and D**

    A. **Incorrect:** The algorithms that Windows 7 use to access virtual memory do not change when a computer is on battery power.

    B. **Incorrect:** Memory access is the same whether a computer is plugged in or using battery power.

    C. **Correct:** Wireless interfaces often support a power-saving mode that can reduce wireless range and performance when the computer is on battery power. If the performance impact is too significant, you can adjust the power setting.

    D. **Correct:** By default, Windows 7 uses a power-saving mode when displaying video while the computer is on battery power. You can disable this power-saving feature from within the advanced power settings.

Chapter 8: Case Scenario Answers

Case Scenario 1: Monitoring Kiosk Computers

1. You could configure event forwarding from the kiosk computers to your computer and forward just the event that you want to know about.

2. You should use the Minimize Latency bandwidth optimization technique because it's important to receive notification of the new events as soon as possible, and the number of computers is small enough that bandwidth should not be a problem.

3. You could configure a scheduled task with a trigger for Event ID 4226. Then you could configure an action for the scheduled task that sends an e-mail to your computer or mobile phone.

Case Scenario 2: Troubleshooting a Performance Problem

1. The best tools for identifying the source of a performance problem are Task Manager and Performance Monitor. With either tool, you could determine which process was using the most processor time and memory. Then, you could examine the application and determine why it was consuming so many resources.

2. Often, performance problems that build up over time are caused by memory leaks. With a memory leak, an application consumes more and more resources the longer the application is run. In theory, memory leaks shouldn't occur because an application should free up resources as it finishes working with them. However, some applications, especially custom applications, do not follow programming best practices and as a result might have this type of flaw.

Chapter 9: Lesson Review Answers

Lesson 1

1. **Correct Answer: D**

   A. **Incorrect:** The warning message that users receive would occur whether they were local administrators or not. For the error not to appear, the publisher certificate needs to be deployed to the Trusted Publishers certificate store.

   B. **Incorrect:** The warning message that users receive would occur whether they were domain administrators or not. For the error not to appear, the publisher certificate needs to be deployed to the Trusted Publishers certificate store.

   C. **Incorrect:** You do not need to install the publisher certificate in the Trusted Publisher store. You need to install the root certificate for Contoso.com in the Trusted Root Certification Authorities store.

   D. **Correct:** The warning message appears because clients are not configured to trust certificates from Contoso.com. To prevent the message from appearing, the root certificate for the Contoso.com CA needs to be installed in the Trusted Root Certification Authorities store on all client computers. Using Group Policy is the best way to achieve this.

2. **Correct Answer: C**

   A. **Incorrect:** Because the file you want to block is an .Msi file, you need to create a Windows Installer rule.

   B. **Incorrect:** Because you want to block a set of versions of the same file, you need to specify the Publisher rule condition. A File Hash condition can apply only to one version of a file.

   C. **Correct:** You need to create a Windows Installer rule because you want to block an .Msi file. You need to specify and configure the Publisher rule condition because you want to block multiple versions of the same file.

   D. **Incorrect:** Because you want to block a set of versions of the same file, you need to specify the Publisher rule condition. A File Hash condition can apply only to one version of a file.

Lesson 2

1. **Correct Answer: A**

   A. **Correct:** This situation is suitable for System Restore. It undoes the update to Windows and makes no other changes to the system.

   B. **Incorrect:** Restoring old user files does not affect the functioning of the application. You need to undo the change that has caused the application to fail.

C. Incorrect: Event Forwarding is useful when you want to monitor many computers for a specific event or set of events. In this case, you need only undo a specific system change, not monitor for an event.

D. Incorrect: Reinstalling the application might or might not help. However, since the Windows Update was optional, it is best to simply remove it. Installing the optional update caused the application to fail.

2. **Correct Answer: A**

A. Correct: Detect Application Failures Caused By Deprecated Windows DLLs or COM Objects is the only policy that actually helps detect why a running application has failed.

B. Incorrect: Enabling the Notify Blocked Drivers policy lets a user be notified when drivers are blocked because of compatibility issues. The policy does not help diagnose why an application has failed.

C. Incorrect: The Detect Application Install Failures policy helps diagnose application installation failures. In this question, the application has already been installed successfully.

D. Incorrect: The Detect Application Installers That Need To Be Run As Administrator policy helps diagnose application installation failures. In this scenario, the application has already been installed successfully.

3. **Correct Answer: B**

A. Incorrect: A 16-bit application can run in the 32-bit version of Windows 7; however, it cannot run in the 64-bit version of Windows 7.

B. Correct: Because of the UAC feature of Windows 7, programs that require administrator privileges must be rewritten to handle the approval messages that appear when administrative tasks are performed.

C. Incorrect: Because of Windows Resource Protection in Windows 7, the operating system intercepts any application requests to write to protected areas of the registry and redirects the write to a safe area. Because Windows 7 has been designed to perform this sort of redirection, this type of application is not the most likely one to require updates to run properly in Windows 7.

D. Incorrect: Because of Windows Resource Protection in Windows 7, the operating system intercepts any application requests to write to protected areas of the registry and redirects the write to a safe area. Because Windows 7 has been designed to perform this sort of redirection, this type of application is not the most likely one to require updates to run properly in Windows 7.

Chapter 9: Case Scenario Answers

Case Scenario 1: Restricting Software with AppLocker

1. You should specify the Publisher condition.

2. No, they will not be able to run other Windows Installer programs. Once you create a rule in AppLocker, all programs associated with the rule type (here, Windows Installer programs) are blocked unless they are allowed specifically.

Case Scenario 2: Configuring Application Compatibility Settings

1. You should alter the application compatibility settings of the program to run it in Windows XP compatibility mode.

2. Enable the Detect Application Install Failures policy setting in Group Policy.

Glossary

A

Action Center A tool in Windows 7 that serves as a starting point for troubleshooting. Action Center notifies the user of any critical actions that the user should take to maintain the health and integrity of the system, and it provides easy links to other tools such as troubleshooters, Reliability Monitor, and System Restore.

ActiveX A technology that enables powerful applications with rich user interfaces to run within a Web browser.

Automatic Private IP Address (APIPA) An IP addressing technique that assigns an address in the range 169.254.0.0 through 169.254.255.255. APIPA allows computers that don't have IP address settings to communicate across a LAN.

B

basic input/output system (BIOS) The firmware in the computer that begins to execute as soon as a computer is turned on. A BIOS includes a Setup utility that specifies a boot order, which indicates the sequence of devices that the BIOS investigates for an operating system. The computer's BIOS is also responsible for providing certain hardware functionality to the operating system, functionality such as power management (ACPI), booting from a network or USB device, and hot-swapping.

BitLocker Drive Encryption A feature of Windows 7 that is capable of encrypting the entire system volume, thus protecting the computer in the event of attacks that bypass the operating system security.

C

Chkdsk A tool you can use to check and possibly repair disk errors such as bad sectors.

Collecting computer The computer that is configured to collect events in an event forwarding relationship.

critical update A small update that resolves a single problem with Windows or other Microsoft software.

D

Disk Defragmenter A tool that reduces data fragmentation and improves performance. In Windows 7, Disk Defragmenter is scheduled by default to run automatically on Wednesday morning at 1 AM.

E

Encrypting File System (EFS) A feature of Windows 7 that is capable of encrypting specific files and folders, thus protecting the data in the event of attacks that bypass the operating system security.

Event forwarding The process of sending specific events from a forwarding computer to a collecting computer, where an administrator can monitor them more easily.

Exception An incoming connection that is allowed through a firewall. A typical exception is associated with a port or network application. Also called an *allow rule*.

F

Folder Redirection A feature of Windows that can transparently redirect the target of some common user folders. For example, you can use Folder Redirection to redirect each user's local Documents folder to a personal folder on a network share.

Forwarding computer The computer that is generating events in an event forwarding relationship.

H

Hibernation A zero-power state that stores the computer's memory to disk but takes longer to recover.

hotspot A wireless network intended for public use. Most hotspots do not have any security. Some hotspots require users to pay before they can access the Internet.

L

latency In network communications, the time it takes for a packet to travel between hosts. High latency connections don't necessarily cause bandwidth or throughput to drop. However, latency causes problems with real-time communications such as Voice over IP (VoIP).

Listener A configuration setting that forwards specific incoming network communications to an application.

M

Malware A general term that refers to a variety of unwanted software such as viruses, worms, spyware, and Trojan horses.

Mandatory Integrity Control (MIC) A feature of Windows 7 that labels processes, folders, files, and registry keys using one of four integrity access levels: system, high, medium, and low.

Microsoft Systems Center Configuration Manager 2007 (Configuration Manager 2007) The preferred method for distributing software and updates in large enterprise networks, Configuration Manager 2007 provides highly customizable, centralized control over update deployment, with the ability to audit and inventory client systems.

multifactor authentication A type of authentication that requires two or more authentication techniques to validate a user's credentials. For example, users might be required to both insert a smart card and type a password.

N

name resolution The process of converting a host name to an Internet Protocol (IP) address. DNS is by far the most common name-resolution technique.

Network location One of four security categories (Home, Work, Public, or Domain) that is applied to every network connection.

O

Offline Files A feature of Windows that enables you to keep a local copy of files that are stored on a network share. When you disconnect from the network, you can then open and edit these local copies. The local copy is synchronized automatically with the source file on the network share when you later reconnect.

P

pilot group A small subset of the computers in an organization that receive an update before wider deployment. If an update causes an application compatibility problem, the pilot group is likely to discover the incompatibility before it affects more users.

Point And Print The ability to install printer drivers automatically.

Previous Versions A feature of Windows that enables you to restore easily previous versions of files or folders that have been saved by restore points or Windows backups.

print queue A first-in, first-out collection of documents waiting to be printed.

Protected Mode A feature of Internet Explorer 7.0 and Windows Internet Explorer 8.0 that causes the browser to run with very limited privileges. This provides protection even if malicious code on a Web site successfully exploits Internet Explorer.

Protected Mode Compatibility Layer A feature of Internet Explorer 7.0 and Windows Internet Explorer 8.0 when running on Windows Vista or Windows 7 that redirects requests for protected resources to safer locations. For example, any requests for the Documents folder are redirected automatically to \%Userprofile%\ AppData\Local\Microsoft\Windows\Temporary Internet Files\Virtualized.

Pull delivery mode In the context of event forwarding, the collecting computer initiates a connection to the forwarding computer to retrieve events.

Push delivery mode In the context of event forwarding, the forwarding computer initiates a connection to the collecting computer to send events.

Q

Quality Assurance (QA) A department within an organization that maintains test computers in a lab environment with standard configurations and applications. QA can help identify problems with updates prior to deployment.

R

Reliability Monitor A tool in Windows 7 that enables you to view the stability of the local system in recent history.

Restart Manager A feature of Windows Vista and Windows 7 that enables programs to coordinate with Windows to free up resources that need to be upgraded, with the goal of reducing the number of reboots required by updates.

Roaming user profile A personal user profile that is stored on a network share and that applies to the user regardless of which computer on the network he or she logs on to.

Rootkit A form of malware that runs at a lower level than the operating system. Rootkits can be very difficult, or completely impossible, to detect.

S

service pack A large update that resolves many problems with Windows or other Microsoft software. Service packs typically supersede dozens of critical updates and might add new features to the operating system.

Service Set Identifier (SSID) The name of the wireless network.

Spyware Software that is secretly installed on a computer and gathers information about user behavior, usually for the purposes of market research.

Standby A low-power state that allows the computer to recover in a few seconds.

Startup Repair A tool that you can use to fix automatically many common errors that prevent Windows 7 from starting. Available as one of the System Recovery Options.

System Recovery Options A set of recovery tools available in the Windows Recovery Environment.

T

troubleshooting pack A set of scripts that provide functionality for Windows troubleshooters through the Windows Troubleshooting Platform.

U

User profile The collection of data that comprises a user's individual environment—data including a user's individual files, application settings, and desktop configuration.

V

Virus A hidden, self-replicating, and self-installing program. Viruses carry a payload that typically damages or compromises a computer. Viruses need an external mechanism such as e-mail to be transported over networks.

W

Windows Boot Manager A menu that enables you to choose an operating system to start when more than one is available. When only one operating system is available, you can force Windows Boot Manager to appear by repeatedly pressing the spacebar as the system starts.

Windows Memory Diagnostic A tool that checks the integrity of physical memory in the system.

Windows Recovery Environment A Windows-like operating system that you can use to fix Windows problems offline. In Windows 7, Windows Recovery Environment is available through the Repair Your Computer option on the Advanced Boot Option menu. You can also start the Windows Recovery Environment by booting from the Windows 7 DVD.

Windows Resource Protection A feature of Windows Vista and Windows 7 in which requests by programs to write to protected areas of the operating system are intercepted and redirected to safe areas.

Windows Server Update Services (WSUS) A version of the Microsoft Update service that you can host on your private network. WSUS connects to the Windows Update site, downloads information about available updates, and adds them to a list of updates that require administrative approval.

Windows XP Mode In Windows 7, a downloadable enhancement to Virtual PC in which you can access and interact with programs transparently in a guest Windows XP virtual machine. Windows XP Mode requires a CPU with Intel-VT or AMD-V technology.

Wired Equivalent Protection (WEP) An early wireless security standard that is now easily cracked by a knowledgeable attacker.

Wi-Fi Protected Access (WPA) A wireless security standard that improves upon WPA by offering much better data protection. WPA is available as either Wi-Fi Protected Access; preshared key (WPA-PSK; also known as WPA-Personal), which uses a passphrase for authentication; or Protected Access-Wired Equivalent Protection (WPA-EAP; also known as WPA-Enterprise), which uses domain credentials or a certificate for authentication. WPA2 offers improved security over WPA with similar functionality.

Worm A hidden, self-replicating, self-installing, and self-propagating program. Worms can exploit weaknesses found in software to compromise a system.

Index

Symbols and Numbers

6to4, 253, 257
802.1X, 87
802.1X authentication, 142

A

Account expiration, 138
Account lockout, 136
Accounts
  untrusted, 143–44
Action Center
  alerts, 3–4
  definition, 2
  troubleshooting with, 2–3
ActiveX, 150
ActiveX add-ons, 150–52
ActiveX Installer Service, 152–54
ActiveX Opt-in configuration,
    150–51
AD DS browsing, 111
AD DS domain
    environments
  add-ons and, 149
AD DS domains, 299
  collecting computer, 301–02
  event subscription, 302–05
  forwarding computer, 299–301
  HTTPS, 305–06
AD DS environments
  Nblookup and, 540
  Nbtstat, 542
  Windows Boot Performance
    Diagnostics, 444

Add-On List, 149
Add-ons, 147
  ActiveX add-ons, 150–52
  ActiveX Installer Service, 152–54
  AD DS domain environments, 149
  enabling and disabling, 148
  starting without, 149
Admin Approval Mode, 203–04
Administrator privileges, 197
Administrator rights
  verification of, 340–41
Administrators
  UAC notifications for, 197–98
Adware, 196
Alerts
  enabling, 3–4
All Users profile (User Profile), 421
Allow Print Spooler To Accept Client
    Connections, 111
Allow rules, 373
Allowed programs
    (exceptions), 383–84
Alternate hosting, 311
Always-on connectivity
  DirectAccess, 252
Antivirus software
  misconceptions about, 194
  Windows Defender and, 211
Antivirus tools
  installation of, 614
AppData (User Profile), 422
Application compatibility, 308–10
  alternate hosting, 311
  Application Compatibility
    Diagnostics and Group Policy
    settings, 312–13
  Application Compatibility
    Toolkit (ACT), 311–12

operating system changes, 310
security enhancements, 310
Stop messages, 614
Windows 7 built-in compatibility
    tools, 310–11
Application Compatibility
    Diagnostics, 312–13
Application Compatibility
    Manager, 362
Application Compatibility Toolkit
    (ACT), 311–12
Application Compatibility Toolkit
    Data Collector, 363
Application connectivity problems,
    64–66, 576–80
Application constraints
  verification of, 344
Application dependencies
  verification of, 344
Application Identity Service, 350
Application install failures, 364
Application installers, 364
Application layer protocols, 264
Application Program Interfaces
    (APIs), 358
AppLocker, 299–302
Arp (Arp.exe), 533, 536–37
Arp cache, 537
ATA disk diagnostic tools, 616
Audit Account Logon Events, 139
Audit Logon Events, 139
Auditing
  authentication problems, 138–41
Authentication, 132, 229
  auditing, 138–41
  Credential Manager, 133–34
  definition, 132–33
  lesson review, 145–46

645

About the Authors

TONY NORTHRUP, MVP, MCSE, MCTS, and CISSP, is a Microsoft Windows consultant and author living in New London, Connecticut. Tony started programming before Microsoft Windows 1.0 was released, but he has focused on Windows administration and development for the last 15 years. He has written about 25 books covering Windows development, networking, and security. Among other titles, Tony is coauthor of *Windows 7 Resource Kit, Windows Vista Resource Kit,* and *Windows Server 2008 Networking and Network Access Protection (NAP).*

When he's not writing, Tony enjoys photography and travel. Tony lives with his girlfriend, Chelsea, her daughter, Madelyn, and three dogs. You can learn more about Tony by visiting his personal Web site at *http://www.northrup.org* and his technical blog at *http://www.vistaclues.com*.

J.C. MACKIN, MCITP, MCTS, MCSE, MCDST, and MCT, is a consultant, trainer, and writer who has been working with Microsoft networks since Microsoft Windows NT 4.0. He is author or coauthor of many Microsoft Press Self-Paced Training Kits (including those for exams 70-291, 70-642, and 70-643) and of the *Windows Essential Business Server 2008 Administrator's Companion.* When he's not working with computers, J.C. can be found with a camera wandering the streets of small medieval towns in Europe.

Get Certified—Windows® 7

Desktop support technicians and administrators—demonstrate your expertise with Windows 7 by earning a Microsoft® Certification focusing on core technical (MCTS) or professional (MCITP) skills. With our 2-in-1 *Self-Paced Training Kits*, you get a comprehensive, cost-effective way to prepare for the certification exams. Combining official exam-prep guides + practice tests, these kits are designed to maximize the impact of your study time.

What do you think of this book?

We want to hear from you!

To participate in a brief online survey, please visit:

microsoft.com/learning/booksurvey

Tell us how well this book meets your needs—what works effectively, and what we can do better. Your feedback will help us continually improve our books and learning resources for you.

Thank you in advance for your input!

Stay in touch!

To subscribe to the *Microsoft Press® Book Connection Newsletter*—for news on upcoming books, events, and special offers—please visit:

microsoft.com/learning/books/newsletter